SECOND EDITION

TECHNOLOGY NOLOGY in the CLASSROOM

FOR NOW AND IN THE FUTURE

Janice L. Nath
Professor Emeritus
University of Houston -
Downtown

Irene Chen
University of Houston -
Downtown

Kendall Hunt
p u b l i s h i n g   c o m p a n y

Kendall Hunt
publishing company

www.kendallhunt.com
Send all inquiries to:
4050 Westmark Drive
Dubuque, IA 52004-1840

Published in the United States of America

Contents

Introduction

When beginning a second edition of a book, most authors know that time will have produced new information which must be included. In a technology book such as this one, however, we find that information is flashing by at the speed of light. Many effective sites and information remain, but, indeed, so much more information that is exciting for teachers and learners is available.

As noted before, we envisioned that new classroom teachers would not only have the ability to use new technology tools but would also have the knowledge and skills to search out the best for their students and to weigh both the positive and negative ramifications of using all that technology has to offer. These are times when new generations of students are "native" technology users, and their teachers must be skilled, reflective, and creative to prepare them for even more amazing times ahead.

This vision drove our first edition and continues to spur us and our colleagues to carefully examine their content to construct or update chapters that would make a positive difference for both preservice and inservice teachers. These chapters continue to present classroom cases and ideas for integrating technology into EC-12 classrooms in various subjects and in other areas of teaching, such as reflection, multiculturalism, educational psychology, special education, and so forth. These chapters were written to provide the reader with concrete examples and, indeed, to serve as a spark for other creative classroom avenues or to set out the pathway for becoming excellent detectives to search out the most effective ideas and resources that become available.

In this volume, as in the first, we have touched upon many connections that go beyond simple computer literacy. Teachers in the twenty-first century must also consider issues of assistive technology and the American Disabilities Act, diverse learners, English language learners, the digital divide, laws and school policies regarding technology use, Internet security, learning theory, and social issues and needs—among many others. Digital tools open the doors for enhanced learning at every turn and make it possible to more fully fulfill teachers' capacities for the many roles and responsibilities that they shoulder in teaching with technology. In that respect, it is our hope that the reader comes away with a clearer picture of what it means to be an intentional, reflective teacher with technology, seeing all the connected aspects which can affect the learner.

Technology cannot only make work easier and faster, but it can create a true magic for both the teacher and the learner. We want our teachers to use that magic in their own classrooms.

Organization of the Text

This text, as written by those involved in teacher preparation, is designed to strengthen instructional technology, content areas, and other areas of teaching and learning coupled with technology.

The volume is divided into three parts: (1) Educational Technology Supporting the Content Areas, (2) Using Educational Technology for Best Practices in Schools and for Teacher Education, and (3) Technology Supporting Educational Psychology and Culturally Responsive Teaching. Section 1 focuses on the following content combined with technology: literacy, social studies, science, and mathematics. In addition, this section addresses technology with young children, special education, and English language learners. Teachers must also become competent with professional growth and development; therefore Section 2 discusses topics on technology in other areas of teaching and learning: generic models of teaching, technology standards, legal and ethical use, assessment, and portfolios. Chapters in this section also cover electronic help with certification testing, creating a reflective teaching practice, and technology governance. Section 3 includes a chapter on how educational psychology and technology should work together and one on how culturally responsive teachers integrate technology in teaching and learning. It also moves forward to the threats and opportunities that the digital citizens will bring to education.

Acknowledgments

Our thanks to the many people who have helped to create this volume: the chapter authors and those at Kendall Hunt, especially Beth Trowbridge who "made it happen." We also thank Kannan Poojali Vadivelu in production, who "worked the puzzle" of each page so well. We appreciate all of those whose special knowledge will contribute to new generations of learners.

About the Authors

Sergei Abraovich, Ph.D., has over 40 years of research and teaching experience in mathematics (e.g., differential equations, control theory) and mathematics education. His current scholarly interests are in the use of technology at all educational levels, including K-16. His most recent book is titled *Diversifying Mathematics Teaching: Advanced Educational Content and Methods for Prospective Elementary Teachers* (Singapore, World Scientific, 2017).

Beverly Alford is Assistant Professor of early childhood at the University of Houston-Downtown. Her educational focus is on children ages birth through age seven years. Dr. Alford explores how young children develop in authentic, nontraditional education settings as well as the effects of standardized learning outcomes on young children. Her background in early childhood is varied and extensive, having worked in both the public and private sectors. In addition to her background with early childhood education students, she has created and presented professional development services to administrators, teachers, and parents; designed both undergraduate and graduate-level early childhood programs; and served as a program evaluator while working as assistant director at a research center.

Franklin S. Allaire, Ph.D. (@misterallaire on Twitter), is an assistant professor in the Department of Urban Education at the University of Houston - Downtown where he brings 15 years of experience as a high school science teacher to his undergraduate and graduate courses in elementary and secondary science methods. His research interests focus on issues impacting the success of underrepresented minorities in STEM-related fields; the construction, intersection, and salience of professional identity; and the innovative use of technologies and pedagogies in the professional development of science teachers and teacher candidates.

Dr. EunJin Bahng is an associate professor in the School of Education at the College of Human Sciences, Iowa State University. She was a state coordinator for the nation-wide online mentoring program entitled e-Mentoring for Student Success and also led two mentoring programs for elementary science teachers in Iowa. Bahng's scholarship involves the development of online and hybrid-mentoring programs for newly hired science teachers. These are designed to foster effective changes in teaching practices and identities and concentrate on the teaching of science as inquiry. Since 2014, Bahng has been studying high school students and undergraduate students in STEM areas as well as working scientists in South Korea, Japan, Italy, and the United States. This line of research explores the complexities of culture, society, and science (e.g., women in science and stereotypic images of scientists). Bahng, with her colleagues, was the recipient of the Journal of Research in Science Teaching Best Paper Award in 2012 from the National Association for Research in Science Teaching. She coauthored a textbook, *Children Doing Physics*. Currently, she is the leader of the science team within the elementary education program and has been appointed as an affiliated science educator for the DREAM team scientists at CERN for five years (2015 to 2020). Finally, she is a mentor for ISU's Preparing Future Faculty Program as well as for the international student graduate learning community.

Christine Beaudry, Ed.D., is Assistant Professor of social studies education at Nevada State College. Her research focuses on critical, constructivist, and community-based approaches to social studies curriculum and education, multicultural and culturally responsive teaching, and teacher preparation and retention. Her current work examines the experiences of teacher candidates and novice teachers in classrooms with culturally and linguistically diverse students. She also has several years of teaching experience in public schools at both elementary and secondary levels. She can be reached at christine.beaudry@nsc.edu.

Dr. Ronald S. Beebe is Associate Professor of educational research and Chair of the Urban Education Department at the University of Houston - Downtown. He teaches courses on educational research, classroom-based research, assessment and evaluation, culture of the urban school, and statistics. His current research focuses on the impact of classroom-based research on teacher and student outcomes as well as issues of equity and social justice. He has been awarded grants for work in student success, minority teacher recruitment, faculty professional development, and program evaluation. Additionally, his collaborative research includes investigating vocational outcomes, psychological practice, and online learning and assessment, with publications addressing career and vocational outcomes, professional development school practice, social justice, and online assessment. His presentations include international and national conferences on teacher cultural competence, vocational assessment, teacher education practice, online pedagogy and assessment, program assessment and evaluation, and the impact of classroom-based research on inservice teachers, preservice teachers, and P-12 students.

Dr. Crystal Belle is the director of Teacher Education/assistant professor at Rutgers University-Newark. Her experiences are vast and include teaching in NYC public schools as a middle school and high school English teacher, working as a literacy coach/consultant in underserved schools in the Bronx, and teaching graduate courses in the English Education Department at Teachers College of Columbia University, where she earned her doctorate. Her work has been featured in several reputable journals, including *The Journal of Adolescent and Adult Literacy* and the *Journal of Black Studies*.

Katrina Borders (master of education in administration and supervision from the University of Houston - Main Campus) has over 18 years of teaching and instructional coaching experience in K–12 schools. She is committed to assisting educators create collaborative and supportive learning environments in which all students will thrive.

Christal Gooding Burnett, Ed.D., is an associate professor of bilingual education in the Department of Urban Education at the University of Houston - Downtown. She holds a doctorate of education in international educational development with an emphasis on bilingual/bicultural studies and family and community education from Teachers College, Columbia University. Dr. Burnett received her B.A. in Spanish from Carnegie Mellon and her M.A. in language learning from Stanford. She also has teaching experience as a bilingual elementary teacher. Her teaching and research interests include the education of emergent bilinguals, family involvement, and educational opportunities for underrepresented populations. Dr. Burnet currently serves as Interim Assistant Chair of the Department of Urban Education. She can be reached at burnettc@uhd.edu.

Irene Linlin Chen received her doctorate of education in instructional technology and is currently Professor in the Department of Urban Education at the University of Houston - Downtown. Dr. Chen has had diverse professional experiences. Previously, she has been an instructional technology specialist, a learning technology coordinator, and a computer programmer/analyst. She has taught numerous graduate and undergraduate courses in instructional technology and curriculum and instruction and has delivered many K–12 inservice training sessions and professional development activities for educators. Dr. Chen has made many state, national, and international conference presentations in instructional technology, including at Oxford, UK.

Kwang-lee Chu has a Ph.D. in measurement and statistics from the College of Education of Florida State University, a master's degree in school counseling from Clemson University, and a B.S. in home economic from Fu-Jen University in Taiwan. She has taught in various educational settings in Taiwan prior to studying in the United States. Her 20 plus years of working experience in the United States are in program evaluation and standardized large-scale state achievement tests. The goals of both types of work are first, to assist state agencies in developing, tracking, and reporting services or tests; and second, to plan and implement evidence collection methods to prove that the services or tests comply with federal funding requirements.

Myrna D. Cohen, Ed.D., is Professor of education at the University of Houston - Downtown. Her teaching experience includes grades 2 to 12, as well as undergraduate and graduate classes in higher education. She has held leadership positions in several national and state organizations and has received state awards for her organizational work. She is coeditor of a number of books on teacher education. She served for eight years as the chair of the Department of Urban Education and served for five years as Associate Dean of the College of Public Service.

Michael L. Connell, Ph.D. and Professor, has over 30 years of mathematics education experience at both graduate and undergraduate levels working with students in field-based teacher certification programs. His research interests lie at the intersection between educational technology, learning theory, and mathematics education. He has written, presented, and published extensively in these areas.

Colin Dalton, Ed.D., is an assistant professor of literacy education and TESOL. His teaching and research interests include literacy development and practice utilizing alternate text to develop lifelong readers.

C. Matthew Fugate is Assistant Professor of educational psychology at the University of Houston - Downtown. He received his doctorate in gifted, creative, and talented studies from Purdue University. Previously, Matthew worked as an elementary teacher, gifted coordinator, and magnet coordinator in the Houston Independent School District. His research interests include twice-exceptional students and students from underserved populations. Matthew has presented to audiences nationally and internationally on topics related to twice exceptionality, Total School Cluster Grouping, program development, and creativity. He is an active member of the National Association for Gifted Children and the Texas Association for Gifted and Talented. Matthew also serves as the associate editor of *Teaching for High Potential*.

Viola M. Garcia is Professor Emeritus in the Department of Urban Education at the University of Houston - Downtown where she served as chair of the department. She was the recipient of the UH-D Faculty Award for Service in 2006. Dr. Garcia joined the National School Boards Association board of directors in 2014. She is past president of the Texas Association of School Boards and a current member of the Aldine ISD school board where she has served since 1992. She is active in the National Association of Latino Elected and Appointed Officials Leadership Initiatives and, as past president of the Mexican American School Board Members Association, serves as an advocate on public school issues affecting Latino students. She received a doctor of education degree from the University of Houston in educational leadership and cultural studies in higher education administration, a master of education from the University of Houston in curriculum and instruction, and a bachelor of science in elementary education from Texas Woman's University.

José María Herrera is an assistant professor of elementary social studies methods at the University of Texas at El Paso and has taught courses in the fields of social studies education (K-8), critical pedagogy, and history. Dr. Herrera holds a B.S. in applied learning development from the University of Texas at Austin, an M.A. in history from the University of Texas at El Paso, and a Ph.D. from Purdue University in United States history. Dr. Herrera is certified in bilingual, Spanish, and secondary history education and has 10 years of experience teaching in the public schools. His research interests in education are focused primarily on two issues: (1) developing effective and practical social studies instructional techniques for teachers, particularly critical reasoning skills, and (2) the status of social studies as a major subject at the elementary level.

Amelia Hewitt holds an Ed.D. in early childhood education. She is currently an associate professor at the University of Houston-Downtown. Her primary area of interest is in addressing the needs of the whole child through developmentally appropriate teaching. Her current research as coinvestigator focuses on the emotional and cognitive effects of collaborative partnerships between university faculty and university students, children, and teachers. She can be reached at hewitta@uhd.edu.

John Kelly is an associate professor in the Urban Education Department at the University of Houston - Downtown. Dr. Kelly holds a Ph.D. in special education from the University of Texas, a master's degree in education from Prairie View A&M University, and a bachelor of commerce degree from Rice University.

Dr. Kelly teaches special education courses that provide preservice teachers with the conceptual knowledge they require in order to offer students with disabilities the opportunity to flourish in the classroom.

Dr. Hsin-Hui Grace Lin is a professor in the Department of Teacher Leadership and New Literacies at the University of Houston at Victoria. She has a Ph.D. in child and family studies from the School of Human Ecology at the University of Wisconsin–Madison, a master's degree in human development at Utah State University, and a B.S. in home economics from Fu-Jen Catholic University. She was a high school teacher in Taiwan. Dr. Lin started working as a principle investigator in the Center of Research and Policy on Basic Skills at Tennessee State University, after obtaining her Ph.D. degree. Before coming to Houston, she worked as a manager of Data Management and Analysis under the Division of Policy, Planning and Research in the Department of Children's Services of State of Tennessee and as an assistant professor in the Department of Family and Consumer Sciences at Tennessee State University. Dr. Lin teaches developmental psychology courses. Her research focuses on students' academic achievements. Dr. Lin serves as a columnist for the Preschool Education Monthly in Taiwan and provides parenting and educational talks for the Texas Chinese Radio Station.

Sue Mahoney is retired and was previously an associate professor at the University of Houston - Downtown in the Department of Urban Education. She received her masters and doctorate from Texas A&M University. She taught educational technology courses to undergraduate and graduate students. Dr. Mahoney also served in the administration of UHD's Urban Education department as an assistant chair for undergraduate programs and as program director for the department's graduate and alternative certification programs. Her research interests include student buy-in to online classes, mentoring in the online environment, and effective teaching practices for the online environment.

Diane M. Miller, Ph.D., is Assistant Professor of literacy at the University of Houston - Downtown in the Department of Urban Education, where she focuses on preparing preservice teachers to deliver reading and writing instruction to their students with authenticity, excellence, and engagement. To support her teaching, Dr. Miller's scholarly work is devoted to content area literacy and standards. Additionally, she serves as a board member of the West Houston Area Council of Teachers of English, the Local Arrangements Committee Co-Chair for the 2018 Conference of the National Council of English, and President of the Texas Council of Teachers of English Language Arts for 2018. Dr. Miller enjoys travel, either with her students or with her blended family of five, and she is a proud graduate of public schools—all in Texas: Atlanta High School, the University of Texas at Austin (B.A.), Texas A&M University-Texarkana (M.A.), and Texas A&M University at College Station (Ph.D.). She can be contacted at petersond@uhd.edu.

Laura A. Mitchell, Ed.D., is an associate professor at the University of Houston - Downtown. She teaches bilingual education, literacy, and culture in the Department of Urban Education. She completed her doctorate of education at Fielding Graduate University in 2009. Laura's love for teaching and learning has led her to the University of Houston - Downtown. With her experience working in elementary schools as a bilingual education teacher, campus coordinator, and an assistant principal for 26 years, she combines her enthusiasm for teaching multilingual students, leading teachers to discover their own teaching passions, with researching with scholarly writing.

Dr. Janice L. Nath is Professor Emeritus at the University of Houston - Downtown. She has coedited 14 previous books in teaching and teacher education and has served as editor of the *Texas Forum* of Teacher Education. Dr. Nath received the Howsam Award from the Texas Association of Colleges for Teacher Education and the Booker Award from the Texas Association of Teacher Educators in recognition of significant contributions to the teacher educator preparation process in Texas, and in addition, has received her university's Award for Excellence in Scholarly and Professional Activity. She has served as Associate Dean of the College of Public Service and has presented numerous times internationally, nationally, and at the state and local levels on various topics in teacher education, including at Oxford, UK on instructional technology.

Tina Nixon, Ed.D., is an adjunct professor at the University of Houston - Downtown. In addition to her work there, she has designed and revised a number of online courses in the area of teacher education and educational technology. Dr. Nixon has also served in various roles of education at the K-12 level. She is honored to serve as an assistant principal for K-5 students. Her work has been published in several sources, and she has co-presented at several local, state, national and international conferences. Dr. Nixon earned a doctorate in educational leadership and educational technology from the University of Phoenix. She continues to serve her community and others through a number of service projects. Her proudest service comes from her work as Chief Operations Officer for the Jha'Kyric Nixon Scholarship, which helps aspiring high school graduates pursue a higher education.

Kim Pinkerton, Ed.D., is Associate Professor of reading at Texas A&M University Commerce and a literacy educator with 20 years of experience teaching at the K–12 and college/university levels. She has experience as a literacy researcher and teacher educator, focusing on teachers as readers and writers, authentic literacy instruction, and phonological awareness development and practices. She can be contacted at kim.pinkerton@ tamuc.edu.

Bernard E. Pohl, Jr., Ed.D., is Assistant Professor of education at the University of Houston - Downtown. He currently teaches critical issues in social studies and social studies methods. Previously, he was a special education and social studies teacher at Cypress Fairbanks Independent School District in Northwest Houston for 10 years. He earned his doctorate in education from the University of Houston - Main. His research interests are on moral and ethical issues in social studies and special education.

Jacqueline J. Sack, Ed.D., is an associate professor at the University of Houston - Downtown and has almost 30 years of mathematics education experience, including K–12 teaching, instructional coaching, and undergraduate and graduate mathematics methods instruction. Her research interests focus on 2D and 3D visualization for all grade levels. She has presented and published in these areas nationally and internationally over the past 12 years.

Libi Shen has a Ph.D. from the University of Pittsburgh, PA. She began her college teaching career in 1989. She is a contributing author for the following books: (1) *Educational, Behavioral, Psychological Considerations in Niche Online Communities*; (2) *Cases on Critical and Qualitative Perspectives in Online Higher Education*; (3) *Online Tutor 2.0: Methodologies and Case Studies for Successful Learning*; (4) *Emerging Priorities and Trends in Distance Education: Communication, Pedagogy, and Technology*; (5) *Identification, Evaluation, and Perceptions of Distance Education Experts*; (6) *Cybersecurity Breaches and Issues Surrounding Online Threat Protection*; (7) *Handbook of Research on Human Factors in Contemporary Workforce Development*; and (8) *Psychological, Social, and Cultural Aspects of Internet Addiction*.

Dr. Jane Thielemann-Downs is retired and was previously Professor at the University of Houston - Downtown in the Department of Urban Education. During her career she has taught both graduate and undergraduate courses with specialties in reading/language arts and educational psychology. Her research has focused on resiliency theory, the implementation of technology in teaching, and higher education administration. She is a children's book author (*Frederic Remington, Artist of the West,* and *The Cursing Cure*) and has written numerous teacher preparation books and chapters for teacher certification exam preparation.

Dr. Ashwini Tiwari is an assistant professor in the Urban Education Department at the University of Houston - Downtown where he primarily teaches special education courses. Prior to joining UHD, Dr. Tiwari held a faculty position at the University of Texas Rio Grande Valley. He holds a Ph.D. in education from the Pennsylvania State University, a M.A. in special education from the University of Arizona, and a bachelor's degree in rehabilitation/special education from Osmania University, India. Dr. Tiwari's research is centered around examining issues of educational inequity with a focus on special education in comparative contexts.

Dr. Leigh Van Horn is Professor of language and literacy in the Department of Urban Education of the University of Houston - Downtown. She has received her university's faculty awards for both teaching and service. Her research interests include empathy in teaching and literacy experiences, literacy curriculum, and family literacy. She is currently serving as the Interim Dean for the College of Public Service.

Dr. Mei-Chih Wang, as a prior school teacher, children's choir director, certified CDA advisor, trainer of Federal Head Start Program teachers, and federal grant reviewer for U.S. Department of Education, always enjoys sharing her life story and diverse experiences with preservice and inservice teachers. She was the recipient of the Outstanding Faculty Advisor Award at the University of Louisiana at Lafayette in 2011 and Outstanding Service Award at Lone Star College-CyFair in 2016. Dr. Wang is currently an adjunct faculty appointed by the University of Houston - Downtown, Lone Star College-CyFair, and Springfield College Houston. Courses taught include the fields of early literacy, early childhood development, program design and instruction, assessment and evaluation, differentiated instruction, internship, TExES preparation, and learning framework for first-year experiences. She holds a doctorate of education degree in curriculum and instruction with an emphasis in early childhood from the University of Houston, a master of science in curriculum and instruction from the University of Houston - Clear Lake, and a bachelor of science in education from National Taiwan Normal University.

Carolyn Wade holds an Ed.D. in early childhood education. She earned her doctorate in early childhood curriculum and instruction from the University of Houston and served as an assistant professor at the University of Houston - Downtown. She currently teaches music to preschool children. Her primary area of interest is in addressing the needs of the whole child through a fully integrated curriculum using developmentally appropriate teaching. Her research focuses on using music and the arts to enhance developmentally appropriate teaching and assessment of young children. Her email address is carolynevewade@yahoo.com.

Dr. Stephen A. White has been in the field of education for over 40 years. He has been a classroom teacher for grades 2 to 12. While in the classroom, Dr. White taught Spanish/ESL/bilingual education. After leaving the classroom, Dr. White worked in the publishing business as a national consultant. As such, he presented at local, state, national, and international conferences. Presently, Dr. White is a lecturer at the University of Houston - Downtown.

Sissy S. Wong is an associate professor of science education in the College of Education at the University of Houston. She teaches elementary and secondary science methods courses that incorporate technology to support and enhance science learning. Her research focuses on highly effective science instruction that supports academic language development and inquiry-based science instruction with English language learners. She also explores methods to maximize elementary teacher candidates' development of pedagogical content knowledge, understanding of the nature of science, and aptitude to implement inquiry-based instruction in high needs settings. Wong, with her colleagues, was the recipient of the National Association for Research in Science Teaching's *Journal of Research in Science* Teaching award in 2012. A paper she coauthored also received recognition by the National Science Teachers Association for Research Worth Reading in 2014.

Part I
Educational Technology Supporting the Content Areas

Chapter 1

Using Technology to Develop Literacy

Kim Pinkerton, *Texas A&M University Commerce*

Amelia Hewitt, Diane M. Miller, Leigh Van Horn, and Colin Dalton
University of Houston - Downtown

Meet Mr. Jackson

Mr. Jackson has just finished reading *Catalina Magdalena Hoopensteiner Wallendiner Hogan Logan Bogan was Her Name* by Tedd Arnold (2004) to his first-grade class.

Mr. Jackson tells his class, "This story is special because of the character Catalina's name."

Sherry excitedly expresses, "Yeah, her name is funny. It has a rhythm."

Mr. Jackson explains the concept of rhyme in Catalina's name. He teaches the students about the rhyme in each part of her name (first, middle, last).

Mr. Jackson encourages his students to create their own names. He shares his first: Mike Bike Neil Beil

wavebreakmedia / shutterstock.com

Jackson Fackson Sackson. Each child then writes his or her name in rhyme and creates an audio file using hardware available in the classroom. Mr. Jackson then instructs students to write their own stories to accompany their names through digital programs like iMovie. Students illustrate their stories and narrate them using the digital program.

Sherry can't wait to share her creation. She volunteers to show her movie first to the class. She starts by saying, "This is the story of Sherry Berry Lynn Bynn Robinson Cobinson Tobinson."

Introduction

Technology is no longer a novel entity. Gray's 1925 claim, "Every teacher a teacher of reading" remains true today; however, the context of the twenty-first century necessitates that literacy skills and technology be integrated into all content areas, extending that old adage (Shanahan, 2015)–rather than acting as a side note. Technology is a *form* of communication, and it brings with it different forms of understanding.

The multimodal literacies of today encompass a wide range of different pathways to communicate; our shifting notions are constantly reflecting what it means to be a reader and writer. In this chapter, we focus on the most essential components of literacy instruction and how to enhance these with technology. From the most elemental components of phonemic awareness to the complex aspects of reading comprehension and written expression, literacy moves through these areas in a fluid and recursive way. We believe in an interactive approach to literacy instruction which provides students with both the skills and the strategies they need to be successful. Even though the chapter is organized around the most powerful ways to use technology, when integrating writing and technology with phonemic awareness, phonics, vocabulary, fluency, and reading comprehension, teachers should always begin at the place where the individual student is on his or her path to becoming a literate citizen.

Teachers should seriously consider how we are infusing technology formats, often called modes, into our reading and writing instruction. It is not simply using technology because it is there; it is knowing first what one wants to teach and then making the decision that technology is going to help to enhance the experience and create a level of understanding. The National Council of Teachers of English (NCTE, 2008, n.p.) advises against an "exclusive emphasis on digital literacies." Instead, the multiple modes of expression—digital and traditional— "ought to be integrated into the overall literacy goals of the curriculum." We need to consider matters such as what the students need, when they need it, and how best to help them develop a particular literacy skill or strategy.

In this chapter, we offer authentic technology experiences to use at different phases in the development of students' progress in literacy. We want you to know that, just as we developed the ideas for this chapter based on what we saw as needs for beginning teachers, every teacher can do the same for his/her students. As you read our suggestions for incorporating technology into the literacy classroom, please keep in mind your school district's regulations regarding Internet access, privacy, and safety for students. Ensure that acceptable use policies are applied when appropriate, and confirm parental/guardian consent for posting students' images and work in public spaces—both physical and electronic. Sites such as Edublogs.com enable you to safeguard your students' work and limit the users who have access to the items you post online. We hope that these ideas will be used as a framework and that this framework will help scaffold the processes needed to develop learning experiences for students who use technology in the most powerful ways. As teachers of all content areas, we must learn to "read" students and then respond to what we have learned to help in their achievement. We want to analyze them as we would study a character and try to predict what they individually need in literacy instruction.

Using Technology to Teach Phonological and Phonemic Awareness

Why Is Teaching Phonological Awareness Critical to Literacy Development?

Phonological awareness is one of the most basic, foundational components of literacy that promotes reading and spelling success (International Reading Association [IRA] & National Association for the Education of Young Children [NAEYC], 1998; National Institute of Child Health and Human Development [NICHHD], 2000; Yopp & Yopp, 2000, 2009]). This is an awareness of language that develops when parents, caregivers, and teachers expose children to talking, singing, and playing with language. The ability to discriminate sound and become aware of language sound patterns may even begin to develop before a child is born as mothers engage in talk with others and as they talk to, read to, and sing to their in utero infants (Gerhardt & Abrams, 2000). The further development of phonological awareness should occur naturally when young children are given many opportunities to hear and play with language, and all of this can occur before children know anything about letters and phonics. This awareness can also be further developed through systematic, developmentally appropriate sound awareness instruction (Yopp & Yopp, 2000, 2009).

Phonological awareness includes awareness that our language is made of large chunks of sound (sentences), that our sentences are made of smaller chunks of sound (words), and that our words are made of even smaller parts (syllables, onset and rime, or individual sounds). A more complicated level of phonological awareness, known as phonemic awareness, involves the manipulation of phonemes, which are the smallest units of sound in language (Yopp & Yopp, 2000, 2009). Children can learn to manipulate individual sounds by segmenting (taking apart), blending (putting together), isolating (identifying a sound), deleting (taking away a sound), and substituting (removing a sound and adding a new one in its place).

While the concept of phonological awareness is foundational to literacy learning, it is also one of the most complicated concepts for parents and teachers to understand. Many children enter formal education settings with gaps. While some levels of phonological awareness (like phonemic awareness) are harder to learn than others, phonological awareness instruction does not necessarily have to occur in a linear manner (Yopp & Yopp, 2009).

Developing phonological awareness is a natural part of the curriculum for most prekindergarten teachers who offer learning opportunities through activities such as read-alouds, word play, rhyming activities, and so forth. When planning activities for children, teachers need to consider the idea that some children may enter school with certain gaps in their phonological development. This is an area where technology can make a difference. Technology can assist teachers in closing phonological development gaps by enhancing classroom-based lessons with technology-infused phonological activities. Investigations of the effectiveness of computer-aided instruction to develop phonological awareness skills in young children have been conducted. Some increases in skill level were found, but there were also indications that a multisensory approach may be of importance (Mitchell & Fox, 2001). Combining teacher instruction and engagement with various forms of technology may provide the right balance of seeing, hearing, saying, and doing to increase levels of phonological development.

Using Technology to Construct Ideas About Sounds

When teachers expose children to phonological awareness, they approach it in a very authentic, natural manner. Teachers can help children understand the complexity of sound in our language by engaging in the simplest activities. Songs, play, and many similar strategically planned learning experiences can build a foundation for sound awareness. Technology offers a wonderful place to begin.

The use of song in classrooms has been a part of learning for decades; furthermore, parents have an awareness of the importance of song when they sing nursery rhymes with their children. For teachers who feel that they do not have extensive musical repertoires, technology allows access to music through digital media devices like iPads or smartphones with media sources like iTunes, Amazon MP3, or other streaming services like Spotify or Pandora. Popular music collections and artists who have graced early childhood classes for years can now be found through these digital media devices and sources. For example, Raffi (1998) has a fun collection called *Singable Songs for the Very Young.* "Down by the Bay," "Willoughby Wallaby Woo," and "Baa Baa Black Sheep" are just a few of the selections available through this album. Even author Sandra Boynton (2004, 2013) can be found on iTunes in Sandra Boynton's *Philadelphia Chickens* and *Frog Trouble.* "Dinosaur, Dinosaur" and "Busy, Busy, Busy" are very lively rhyming songs that are sure to get children in motion and playing with the sounds in the English language.

Monkey Business Images / Shutterstock.com

JPagetRFPhotos / Shutterstock.com

Technology also affords teachers the opportunity to find song lyrics at the click of a button. Songdrops.com and kids.niehs.nih.gov (National Institute of Environmental Health Sciences) offer such lyrics for free. "Do Your Ears Hang Low," "Daisy Bell (Bicycle Built for Two)," and "Ten Little Monkeys" are just a few of the lyric texts that teachers can access. Teachers can print these lyrics and practice singing the songs before introducing them to the students. Songdrops.com offers 60 free downloads for teachers and has music on iTunes for purchase, and the National Institute of Environmental Health Sciences now has some music for free as well. Other Internet Websites and apps offer opportunities for music downloads such as Allmusic.com, iHeart Radio, and iTunes Radio.

In addition, a variety of Internet Websites offer access to both song and visual media to accompany the tune. YouTube has a plethora of videos available for free. Kids TV-Nursery Rhymes and Children's Songs offers song videos like "Morning Song," "If You Are Happy and You Know It," and many more. Children Love to Sing, also on YouTube, offers song videos like "We're Going to the Zoo" and "Animal Song." These include many animal pictures and videos to accompany the lyrics. Teachers and children can sing and move to the music—all while receiving the added benefit of sound awareness and development.

Using Technology to Introduce/Teach Sound Awareness

Encouraging children to listen to and contemplate sounds they hear is one way for them to formulate phonological ideas. Constructing ideas about sounds can be simply practiced through poems and read-alouds. Teachers can offer children opportunities to engage in games individually, with a partner, or in a small-group setting. Through technology, teachers can provide students that extra practice necessary to help close phonological gaps.

Read-alouds should happen in classrooms daily. Read-alouds provide ample opportunity for discussion of language and sound and do not require large amounts of class time. Audio books from iTunes, Android, or other related vendors and online storytelling Websites allow the listener to enjoy the beauty of the story; teachers can also take time to teach students how to contemplate the sounds of our language, and children can hear the sound of language through audio books. Teachers can use Websites like Barnes and Noble's Online Storytime to expose students to authors like Audrey Penn reading *The Kissing Hand* (1993) and to see images from the text. Justbooksreadaloud.com provides read-alouds of popular books such as *Chrysanthemum* (1991) by Kevin Henkes. Using online tools for read-alouds offers children the opportunity to hear varied vocal inflections, which heightens sensitivity to sound differences.

Teachers can take this one step further and purposefully use sounds from the online books in lesson planning. For example, Mr. Phan, a kindergarten teacher, plays with the beginning sound in *Chrysanthemum* by creating a rhythmic poem that can be read aloud over and over. He then provides opportunities for students to engage in sound play with their own name. See Figure 1.1 for an example of how Mr. Phan develops sound play with a student named Kasandra.

What's in My Name?
Chrysanthemum Sound Learning
Poem Format

K/k/for Kasandra
First letter of first name   Sound of first letter   First Name

Catching, Kittens, Kangaroos
Word that starts with   Word that starts with   Word that starts with
the same sound   the same sound   the same sound

Kites, Cats, & Kaleidoscopes
Word that starts with   Word that starts with   Word that starts with
the same sound   the same sound   the same sound

K/k/for Kasandra
First letter of first name   Sound of first letter   First Name

Figure 1.1 A name chant based on sound play.

Using Technology to Apply/Practice Using Sounds

Developmentally appropriate use of technology requires children to apply what they have learned through the use of hands-on application. Using technology to practice phonological skills can render developmentally appropriate, high-impact sound encounters. In the development of these practical sound activities, teachers should consider cooperative learning through small-group experiences, such as in centers and through peer learning projects that are led by students.

Since rhyme matching is easier for young children to master (Paulson, 2004), teachers can begin with the iTune app Rhyming Words. This app provides users pictures that can be touched to hear the word associated with each picture. Then, pictures can be matched as rhymes. After students become proficient in rhyme matching, they can begin to create their own rhymes. Digital voice recorders allow students to capture their own phonological awareness understandings. Using voice memos to create rhyming, word approximation chants can help build upon even more advanced phonemic awareness skills. For example, a small group of students can record a three-word rhyme that may include word approximations (nonsense words). A group of students in Mrs. Gray's class record "Bibbidi, Bobbidi, Boo" ("The Magic Song," 1948) (Cambourne, 1995). Then, the next group listens to the created rhyme and records a new version by changing initial phonemes. They may choose "Zibbidi, Zobbidi, Zoo." After all small groups complete the recording, groups illustrate their rhyme; these can be transferred into a wordless digital book through software tools like PowerPoint or online tools like Storybird or Tikatok and read and reread many times as well as shared with parents and peers. For extension and challenge, each group can create a new rhyme pattern and start the process again.

The use of digital video allows students to practice phonological awareness in the most authentic method. Images, sound, and actions convey real-world use of sound and language. One possible use of video is the creation of a "Name Band" musical group. Initially, students practice with their own names by videoing themselves using musical instruments like tambourines and maracas to shake out the syllables in their first names. Students can be encouraged to create fun "Name Band" costumes to accompany their performances. Then, students form new "Name Bands" with their peers. Each group will create various musical rhythm patterns using the syllables in their names. For example, perhaps Amelia, Haley, Carolyn, Kendall, and Kim form a "Name Band." They create costumes, a musical pattern using their syllable rhythms, and their own instruments to accompany their sound rhythm. See the example below in Figure 1.2.

> A • mel • ia, A • mel • ia (shake tambourines)
> Kim (cymbals)
> Ha • ley, Ha • ley, Ha • ley (rhythm sticks)
> Kim (cymbals)
> Car • o • lyn, Car • o • lyn (blocks)
> Kim (cymbals)
> Ken • dall, Ken • dall, Ken • dall (triangle)
> Kim (cymbals)

Figure 1.2 Name band syllable play.

Pete Pahham / Shutterstock.com

Students can share their videos with peers and parents. These may also be included in the digital books mentioned above. As an extension, each "Name Band" member can rename herself, choosing unique names, and she can start the video process once more.

Conclusion

Clearly, technology can advance phonological awareness development. Multiple technology tools lend themselves to authentic practices that allow for many connections and create opportunities for real-world application of language learning and development. Because sound is an essential component of language learning, phonological awareness and technology naturally complement each other. Obviously, teachers need to make deliberate choices in teaching. Integrating technology into phonological awareness development is no different. In order for learning to be developmentally appropriate, technology needs to be chosen wisely to fit the needs of the students.

Invitation to *Consider This!*

- Listen to Betty White read *Harry the Dirty Dog* (Gene Zion, 1956) on the storylineonline.net Website.
  - What language play could a teacher use to engage students in using this story?
  - Encourage students to create their own story using language play.
- Give students a video recording device and challenge them to practice phonological awareness.
  - What kinds of things could they do?
  - What other devices could they use?
- Visit the additional Websites in the Recommended Resources list at the end of this chapter; which are the most effective ones for phonological awareness connections?
  - How could students use these Websites to deepen their phonological awareness knowledge?
  - How could teachers use these Websites to deepen their phonological awareness instruction?
  - Which other Websites or apps would you add to this list?

Using Technology to Teach Graphophonemic Awareness

Why Is Teaching Graphophonemic Awareness Critical to Literacy Development?

Graphophonemic awareness is the understanding of the smallest unit of written language (a letter) in combination with the smallest unit of spoken language (a sound). Graphophonemic awareness is commonly referred to as letter/sound correspondence, alphabetic principle, or phonics. This concept defines the idea that students, when they are learning language, move from sound-only awareness to an understanding that our language is made of symbols and that those symbols correspond directly to the particular sounds (Gillon, 2004; Yopp & Yopp, 2009). The ability to correspond to letters and sounds and read a text "requires that children develop both awareness of the phonemes in spoken language, and knowledge of letter and sound patterns" (Mitchell & Fox, 2001, p. 316). In fact, Yopp and Yopp (2000) point out that, without phonological awareness, the letter systems are "arbitrary" (p. 131). It is essential for children to make a connection between sounds and letters. Technology can aid in this letter/sound connection.

There are some basic concepts to consider when teaching graphophonemic awareness. First, teachers must be aware of the pureness of sounds in our language. In other words, teachers must be skilled in pronouncing the sounds appropriately and deliberately. For example, /p/ should involve a quick movement of the lips together and apart with an almost imperceptible breath sound that can be felt by holding one's hand in front of the lips. This is in opposition to pronouncing /p/ as /puh/.

Teachers should be purposeful in their development of graphophonemic activities. Children will enter early childhood classrooms with varying levels of graphophonemic knowledge. Some may not have any awareness of letter names and how those names correspond to the sounds that they know; others may know some of the letter names and sound correspondences, yet a few children may have knowledge of complex letter–sound relationships. Teachers should

assess students while they are engaged in meaningful activities to determine where each one is in the process of learning the alphabetic principle. Activities should be constructed based on the needs of each individual child.

Finally, graphophonemic instruction should be developmentally appropriate and meet students at their levels of schematic knowledge (prior understandings children have stored in their brain). For example, most young children have an awareness of the sounds that are in their names. Teachers can use this knowledge as a springboard for teaching letter-sound correspondence. The focus on names can be extended to family members, classmates, and, finally, to the names of familiar objects in their environment. As in most learning, graphophonemic awareness can be so much more meaningful for students when they see how it applies to their daily lives.

Technology is a useful tool to customize graphophonemic instruction. It offers a vast array of ideas for practice and can be integrated easily into lessons and activities for students. Technology can assist teachers in making connections for students between schematic knowledge of spoken sound and print awareness. It essentially enhances and extends the teacher's lessons and improves the relationship children have with graphophonemic learning.

Using Technology to Construct Ideas About Graphophonics

When teachers engage students in graphophonemic activities, these experiences can be simple, but they should always be practical in nature so that students see how useful the knowledge can be in terms of their literacy learning. Every new letter-sound relationship taught should empower children to be readers and writers. The purposeful planning of activities that allow for technology integration can ensure this outcome.

Early childhood educators can use songs and read-alouds in the classroom as natural ways to connect sounds and words to reading. Many sing-alongs found on the Internet display words on the screen to allow the singer to follow the lyrics and rhythm. On YouTube, LittleBabyBum® offers several videos of familiar tunes where each word is highlighted for students to practice one-to-one sound and word matching. Teachers can share songs like the "Itsy Bitsy Spider," "The Wheels on the Bus," and "Old MacDonald." iTunes has apps, such as Nursery Rhymes by Tinytapps, that display the lyrics for interactive nursery rhymes like "Yankee Doodle," "London Bridge," and "Jack and Jill." In addition, teachers can find read-aloud apps through Apple, Google, and Android sources. As an example, the Read Me Stories app shares creative original stories and folklore read-aloud while words are highlighted on the screen. The Website en.childrenslibrary.org offers free global literature from a variety of contributors. Other Websites like ReadingA-Z.com offer a selection of original digital stories for free download and purchase. Finally, digital books can be read to students through apps like iBooks.

Most importantly, students should hear the teacher reading and should watch and listen as the teacher points to the words on the screen. Teachers can show students how written language and sound work together by sharing these digital experiences. Although numerous videos are available for teachers to access showing pronunciations of words and sounds, a teacher should be watchful about utilizing these. A number of videos found on YouTube can, at times, be inadequate when it comes to pronunciation. Children should hear words and sounds pronounced correctly. A teacher can carefully select perfect examples, and he/she should also practice pronunciations before introducing words and sounds to students.

Using Technology to Introduce/Teach Graphophonics

Once teachers have cultivated students' unde ~~Question 2~~ h phonemic awareness instruction and exposed children to the written language ~~...~~ ead-alouds, a natural bridge to the more distinct elements of graphophonics is built. Developmentally appropriate practice through whole-group interactions related to natural alphabetic principle activities encourages students to inquire about individual letter-sound relationships, which gives children the ability to begin to read and write simple words. For example, teachers need to consider differentiated instruction and student interest when teaching phonics, as opposed to only teaching letters by the week and other isolated, linear instructional approaches.

Extending on sound play with children's names (see phonological awareness), teachers can have students create a name collage through simple computer programs like PowerPoint, Keynote, or Glogster.

In Mrs. Jimenez's first-grade classroom, each child uses a camera or searches the Internet to capture pictures that represent the initial sound in his/her name; these images are then uploaded to a computer to create the initial letter. As the child learns more sounds in his/her name, he/she uses the computer program to insert, crop, and arrange more images in the shape of each individual letter of his/her name.

As an extension, the student adds to his/her name collage by positioning the name in the center of the screen and then bordering the name collage with a draw tool that creates lines. Outside of this border, the student then adds more pictures of images from the sounds of his/her name and attempts spelling approximations for each image (Figure 1.3). Mrs. Jimenez then takes these striking name collages and combines them to create a digital class book of names for each student, serving as one of their first books for independent reading.

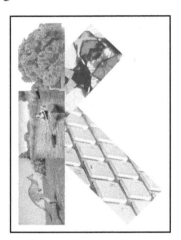

Figure 1.3   Using digital images to promote letter-sound correspondence for Kim.

Using Technology to Apply/Practice Using Graphophonics

Once students understand how sounds and words connect and can create and read their own simple books, technology can be used to engage students in small-group or peer-learning activities that promote meaningful connections. These experiences encourage higher-level analyses, which lead to more finite studies of letter-sound correspondence. Touch-screen digital technologies like iPads, new Windows programs, and Samsung Galaxy tablets afford opportunities for children to make practical applications by writing letters and words directly on a screen. Doodle Buddy and Drawing Desk apps are two that are easy to use. Children can easily create, edit, save, and reword these written images infinitely. This type of technology adds another dimension to sensory writing tools like shaving cream, sand, and rice. With the use of a stylus, tools such as these are much more developmentally appropriate in terms of learning to make the proper strokes for writing, rather than having them trace preprinted letters and words or write between the lines on paper.

Children as young as prekindergarten age can use digital dictation tools to record stories about their own drawings and illustrations. Students simply speak their story into the device, and the story is typed on the screen for students to read. Stories can then be downloaded, printed, and added to the illustrations. Dictation tools like Google Docs' speech recognition add-on and Notes on the iPad and/or iPhone provide these capabilities. For example, to use notes on the iPad and/or iPhone, go to notes, click on the microphone to the left of the space bar, then speak or say the story, and press done when finished. The student's dictation can be emailed directly to the teacher's email account, downloaded, and printed for the student to use. Other technology applications that are easily utilized by the students include SpeakText, which allows students to convert speech to text and share speech through social networks such as Facebook, Twitter, email, and SMS text messaging. Natural Readers allows students to type words, and these words are read back to them, helping them to check the spelling of newly acquired words.

In the "Name Band" activity mentioned in the phonological awareness section, students used video technology to record themselves performing a name chant. To broaden this idea, teachers can urge students to use a dictation tool to record the performed chant. Students print the lyrics of the chant, add a photograph, or draw a picture of the "Name Band" players, and then share it with other students, peers, or parents. This encourages students to "show off" their creativity while extending sound, letter, and word knowledge.

Monkey Business Images / Shutterstock.com

Technology undoubtedly is a tool that can empower children to become readers and writers in the classroom by offering opportunities to extend and increase graphophonemic awareness. It is essential for teachers to use technology in developmentally appropriate ways to integrate sound, letter, and word relationships in daily classroom activities. Assimilating technology requires that teachers contemplate best practices and tailor activities to meet the individual needs of the students. Teachers must offer meaningful, high-level exercises to prepare students for success as future readers and writers.

Invitation to *Consider This!*

- Use a Smartboard to have students practice with letters or word learning. Try this game for younger students www.bemboszoo.com and this game www.teacher.scholastic.com/writewit/poetry/poetry_engine.htm# to learn about poetry for older students.
  - What could a teacher do to extend the learning and/or increase the connections for students?
  - How can students be encouraged to create their own games to enhance their graphophonemic awareness?
- Have students extend digital dictation to Movie Maker or iMovie and challenge them to record their favorite stories. Once recorded, have students add illustrations for each page.
  - What kinds of stories do they develop?
  - What kinds of illustrations do they choose?
- Visit the Websites and apps in the Recommended Resources list insert and consider which are the most effective for graphophonemic awareness connections.
  - How could students use these Websites and/or apps to broaden their knowledge about letter, sound, and word connections?
  - How could teachers use these Websites and/or apps to enhance their instruction about letter, sound, and word connections?
  - What other Websites or apps would you add to this list?

Using Technology to Teach Vocabulary

Why Is Teaching Vocabulary Critical to Literacy Development?

The single sentence below comes from an award-winning young-adult trade book. In it, there are nine words that could stop a reader who does not have strong vocabulary knowledge.

> To move so large a body of troops, with all their necessary *appendages*, across a river a full mile wide with a *rapid current* in the face of a *victorious*, well-disciplined army nearly three times as *numerous* as his own, and a *fleet* capable of stopping the *navigation* so that not one boat could have passed over, seemed to present most *formidable obstacles*. (Meltzer, 1987, p. 98)

Readers must understand the words that make up the text in order to comprehend it. To have a strong knowledge of vocabulary is to have a deep understanding of large numbers of words; that is, students need to be able to read the words, write the words, think of the words, speak the words, view the words, and visually represent the words with confidence. Brabham, Buskist, Henderson, Paleologos, and Baugh (2012) note that "children who begin school with limited vocabularies tend not to catch up with and instead fall farther behind more knowledgeable peers" (also see Chall, Jacobs, & Baldwin, 1990; Graves, 1986). Vocabulary learning takes place more commonly in vocabulary-rich environments where children have (a) multiple, varied, and interactive exposures to large numbers of words; (b) opportunities to engage with vocabulary learning strategies; and (c) the motivation to apply and practice what they have learned. With this literacy-focused chapter, the following section on vocabulary will help teachers learn ways to incorporate technology to assist students in constructing ideas about words, to introduce and teach word-learning strategies to readers, and to show students how to apply and practice what they have learned. As information and communication technologies (ICTs) continue to expand, teachers should search for and develop ideas about powerful ways to engage students in vocabulary building.

Using Technology to Construct Ideas About Words

Teachers can use free word cloud tools such as Wordle or WordSift to: (a) identify key words in a passage, (b) determine what words might need to be pre-taught to students before they read, and (c) engage students in talking about word meanings.

To use WordSift, one opens the Website wordsift.org, chooses and copies a printed text, and inserts the text in the WordSift text box. The application will generate a word cloud of the fifty most frequent words in the text in alphabetical order. The words will be of varying size, depending upon their frequency in the text. A user may click on any word in the cloud to see Google images of the word, to see a word wall displaying definitions for the word, and to see the sentences in the text that contain the word. A user may also sort the words in the cloud from the rarest to the most common to help decide the words that should be pre-taught before reading. Users can also click on the word cloud to highlight words.

For a demonstration of WordSift from Martin Luther King's "I Have a Dream" speech, see the list of "sample texts" on the wordsift.org homepage. There are several other samples to see there as well.

Mr. Garza, a fourth-grade teacher, engages students in talking about word meaning by displaying a word cloud, choosing a word, and then examining the Google images together. Next, he reads the sentences from the text that contains the word and talks about the meaning of that particular word in the context of the writer's world. He then invites students to work with a partner and choose a word or two to examine and discuss. Partners share their investigations and discoveries in a whole class discussion. Students add these words to their own personal electronic dictionaries. These dictionaries could simply be compiled cumulatively using word processing software such as Microsoft Word. Mr. Garza could extend this word work by showing the relationship of multiple words related to a particular content of study, such as social studies or archeology (see Figure 1.4).

Web-based tools such as ABCYa (www.abcya.com/word_clouds.htm), Worditout (www.worditout.com/word-cloud/make-a-new-one) and Tagxedo (www.tagxedo.com) can be used to create word cloud images that show the relationship of key words and relevant content words.

Figure 1.4   Word cloud on "Archeology" (showing relationship between archeology and other content areas).

Using Technology to Introduce/Teach Word Learning

Readers can integrate their growing knowledge by organizing related words into sets or language gestalts (Pace & Nilsen, 2003). This idea builds upon theory-based research about the usefulness of semantic mapping and features analysis as vocabulary acquisition strategies. Young readers may begin learning and collecting related words using Montessori Crosswords, an inexpensive application that allows them to drag and drop letters onto a grid to form words that correspond to images. When readers touch the letter, they hear the phonetic sound of the letter. There are a number of levels, including simple words with one sound, three sounds, consonant blends, and words related to a theme (language gestalts). Themes can include *houses, animals, nature, food, clothes, colors, vehicles,* and others. After participating in the thematic experiences in Montessori Crosswords, young readers might work with the teacher to identify and map words related to a topic or concept found in a text or text set. For example, students might begin to organize words related to the zoo after a read-aloud and discussion of *Polar Bear, Polar Bear, What Do You Hear?* (Martin, 1991), *Inside a Zoo in the City* (Capucilli, 2002), and *The View at the Zoo* (Bostrom, 2015), which contain words and illustrations for many animals to be found in a zoo. Brabham et al. (2012, p. 527) include a table of text sets for teaching concepts and semantically related words for *sizes, feelings, night/day, noises, speeds,* and *actions.*

Word mapping and feature analysis may be especially relevant for English language learners who can be confused about hypernyms (the general topic or superordinate) and hyponyms (specific items included in the general classification or subordinate) (Carlo et al., 2004). For example, readers of *One of Each* (Hoberman, 1997) learn about the hypernym, *house,* and many of the hyponyms that might be included in the larger topic of *house,* those being *window, door, staircase, floor, closet, bedroom, kitchen, fireplace,* and so on. Within this text, there is also the hypernym *furniture* and the associated hyponyms, *clock, bookcase, cupboard, bed, table, chair, bureau,* and *footstool.* Readers may use electronic display boards to create visual representations of concept circles (Tompkins, 2001) that include the hypernym in the center of the circle with all the hyponyms surrounding it. Websites such as kidspiration.com and creately.com provide easy visual interpretations to show this type of thinking. Using online programs like bubbl.us, these concept circles can then be used to generate an electronic display of an interactive semantic feature analysis chart (Figure 1.5) that students can complete together while engaged in discussion.

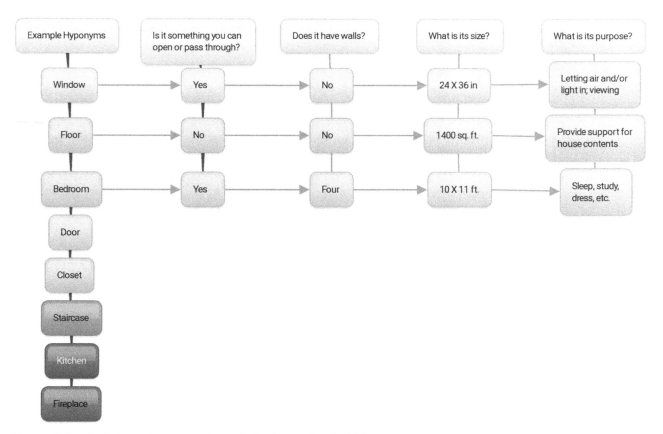

Figure 1.5 An interactive semantic analysis chart using bubbl.us.

Using Technology to Apply/Practice Word Learning

Readers can use media such as hyperlinked PowerPoint slides, wikis, or blogs to create multimedia glossaries that allow them to apply and practice their word learning. This strategy might be particularly helpful to readers who are learning content-area vocabulary. Dalton and Grisham (2011) suggest that readers might create a PowerPoint slide that includes an image, a caption, a definition, a personal connection, an audible representation of the word, and a reference. These individual student-created "pages" could be linked to one another so that readers are creating and sharing a multimedia glossary that represents their study of an aspect of the content area (see Figure 1.6).

Word SLaPPs is a customizable vocabulary application that can be used by teachers or students. Teachers can use the application to create learning experiences that are geared specifically to individual students or small groups. Students can use it to demonstrate their knowledge of content area vocabulary. Users can name categories, upload photographs from their personal libraries of images, record their voices asking questions, and/or provide information about the photographs.

A limitation of the app is that students can only ask viewers questions. Viewers then tap on the image that "answers" the question. To see a demonstration of this application, search for "Word SLaPPs demonstration video."

Research has shown us that "typically developing children learn 3,000 or more words each year, which breaks down to about 10 per day and 50 to 70 words per week" (Brabham et al., 2012). Many of these words are first encountered indirectly through wide reading (Nagy & Herman, 1985), and for this reason, teachers will want to encourage their students to read widely in both traditional books and e-books.

Reading electronic or e-books may be motivational to students because the experience is interactive and uses specific means to invite readers to stop and think or do as they read. Schugar, Smith, and Schugar (2013) note the need for research that examines the features of e-books and their relationship to comprehension.

Venomous Creatures

Venomous: Poisonous

Tetrodotoxin: The poison contained in the skin, blood, and organs of the puffer or blowfish.

I'll have the puffer fish!

The puffer, also known as a blowfish or a fugu, is the world's most dangerous food. Not all puffer fish are venomous, but most are. The fishes' skin, blood, and organs contain a poison called tetrodotoxin. An amount equal to what might be found on the head of a pin is enough to kill a human. There are chefs who are specially licensed to prepare puffer fish for restaurants. The poison in the puffer fish is also being tested for use as a non-addictive pain killer for patients with cancer. Each fish can provide six hundred doses of the puffer poison drug.

I have never eaten a blowfish and certainly do not think that I am brave enough to try one! I have seen dried blowfish hanging in a seafood restaurant for decoration. Some were even electrified and had little light bulbs inside of them. This is about as close as I want to get to the puffer fish, blowfish, or fugu!

Reference:

Singer, M. (2007). *Venom*. Plain City, OH: Darby Creek Publishing.

Cigdem Sean Cooper / Shutterstock.com

Image © Shutterstock.com

Figure 1.6   A multimedia glossary entry.

Students in Ms. Alamilla's third-grade class who are studying crocodilia, specifically the alligator and crocodile subgroups, use Word SLapPs to demonstrate their learning. Some choose images that show the heads of the reptiles and ask viewers, "Which is the crocodile?" "Which is the alligator?" Those who respond would find that the answer is that the crocodile's snout is more pointed, while the alligator's snout is wide and rounded. Students could be asked to expand this experience by creating another set containing images of a fish, a turtle, and an Egyptian plover (a bird). The question could then be "Which of these are not eaten by crocodiles?" The answer is the Egyptian plover, a bird that actually goes inside the crocodile's mouth and cleans its teeth (Simon, 1999).

Tyler Olson / Shutterstock.com

Further exploration would help us fully understand how e-books may contribute to helping readers make meaning or understand what they read. Schugar et al. explain further, adding that some of the interactions within e-books may be distracting to readers. Teachers who want to suggest e-books as a motivator to encourage wide reading and vocabulary development should examine and review the e-books to ensure that the interactions help readers make text-based inferences and/or develop understanding of difficult vocabulary. Fortunately, in many e-books, the illustrations and surrounding text help readers infer meaning, just as they would in a traditional book. Additional features of e-books often include the ability for the reader to click on an unknown word and hear the word spoken and/or to listen to a definition of the word. Readers may also be able to highlight words or phrases of interest and take notes. The next section of the chapter will cover how e-books and digital stories can be used to enhance fluency.

Readers of traditional texts can go to Websites such as Dictionary.com to hear words pronounced and defined. Figure 1.7 depicts this type of entry for the word *discombobulate*. They can also type unknown words into a search engine like Google and retrieve results such as a series of graphic, audio, and video definitions.

Ebner and Ehri (2013) conducted a study to determine the effectiveness of a structured think-aloud process that uses the Internet to learn vocabulary. Participants were asked to read a text and access online resources when they encountered a word they did not know. The experimental group was asked to remember that the goal was to learn the meaning of the listed terms and their relationship to the article being read. Next, they were read the text and engaged in a think-aloud to determine how an Internet search would help them. During and after the search, they

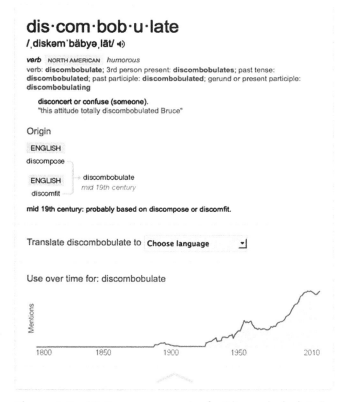

Figure 1.7   Dictionary.com entry for "discombobulate."

Readers begin with a reading of the picture book, *Miss Alaineus: A Vocabulary Disaster* (Frasier, 2000). Throughout the book, readers are treated to in-text definitions such as:

> Even my own mother laughed a little at the part about drawing for extra credit, but at least she stopped fast and said, "You know what I always say . . . There's gold in every mistake." **Gold?** *A bright yellow precious metal of great value?* **Mistake?** *Something done, said, or thought in the wrong way?* "Impossible," I told her. **Impossible:** *not capable of happening.*

> *(Note: As you read this excerpt from the book you may notice that the word "gold" is defined literally, rather than contextually as it might have been. If the word "gold" were defined contextually we would see a definition of "gold" as denoting something of value. That is part of the humor of this particular book.)*

> The in-text definition demonstrated in this picture book was the inspiration for an interactive Reader's Theater program. Following the reading, small groups of students in Ms. Allen's third-grade class chose picture books, text excerpts from novels, informational books, excerpts from content area textbooks, or other texts. As they read the text together, they selected words that they feel users would need to have defined. They then wrote or typed a "script" of the text and included definitions of these words as "asides" (an actor's comment intended only for the audience) or as hyperlinks. A user of the text would be able to read the screen and, simultaneously, hear the Reader's Theater script performed by the student writers. When the user encounters one of the linked words, he or she could click on the link and hear one of the writers reading the words.

were asked to verbalize their thoughts about how the online search was helping them reach their goal of learning the word. The researchers found that students using the structured think-aloud process had significantly greater vocabulary gains over students who were not asked to participate in the think-aloud.

Traditional texts might be used as the basis for an interactive audio recording that provides users with the opportunity to highlight or click on a word and hear it defined.

Invitation to *Consider This!*

- Conduct an Internet online search to identify potential sets of texts to address particular topics or concepts.
- Create your own multimedia presentation for a word or concept to share with students.
- Examine digital stories on your own and/or look at review sites such as *Digital Storytime (*www.digital-storytime.com) and *Smart Apps for Kids* (www.smartappsforkids.com) to see reviews and information about interactive e-books that could motivate wide reading and vocabulary building.
- Visit the Websites and apps in the Recommended Resources list at the end of this chapter and consider which ones are the most effective for vocabulary study.
  - How could students use these Websites to deepen their vocabulary knowledge?
  - How could teachers use these Websites to deepen their vocabulary instruction?
  - *What other Websites or apps would you add to this list?*

Using Technology to Teach Fluency

Why Is Teaching Fluency Critical to Literacy Development?

> His childhood, his friendships, his carefree sense of security—all of these things [seem] to be slipping away. With his new, heightened feelings, he was overwhelmed by sadness at the way the others had laughed and shouted, playing at war. But he knew that they could not understand why, without the memories. He felt such love for Asher and for Fiona. But they could not feel it back, without the memories. And he could not give them those. (Lowry, 1993, p. 135)

To adequately comprehend the stated and implied meaning of this passage from *The Giver* (Lowry, 1993), students must be able to read accurately at a pace that allows for the timely completion of each sentence. In order to accomplish this, readers must possess a vast sight word vocabulary that allows them to comprehend words without having to pause to decode them. Additionally, fluent readers are able to identify logical groups of more than one word and read them with a single fixation. While accomplishing these tasks, readers must recognize and replicate the author's intended expression. Finally, fluent readers connect content from the text to their existing background knowledge. As one can see, reading fluency is a multifaceted skill. It has three main components: automaticity (reading rate), accuracy, and prosody (tone, inflection, pacing, etc.). In addition, teachers are encouraged to teach the components of fluency together, using purposeful repeated reading experiences (Rasinski, 2006). Fluency must be mastered and applied at the subconscious level in order for readers to concentrate on comprehension—the main purpose in reading. Therefore, fluency is the bridge to comprehension (the topic of the final section of this chapter). In addition, fluent reading and fluent writing are synonymous. Fluent readers have the propensity to apply these skills to their own writing.

Using Technology to Introduce/ Teach Fluency

New teachers embarking on a career in education will witness children swapping their bulging backpacks full of textbooks for sleek messenger bags containing electronic devices that hold all their school-related reading material. These electronic devices will hold all the students' textbooks, novels, class notes, assignments, projects, and even tests.

Simply reading a novel on an e-reader like the Nook or Kindle requires similar fluency skills used while reading traditional paper books. However, readers can change the font size and orientation of the text and have immediate access to a dictionary or thesaurus to determine the meanings of unfamiliar words. Reading textbooks on a tablet or a laptop/desktop computer may also require students to view linked visual material (e.g., videos, maps, charts, tables, diagrams, and photos). Clicking back and forth from the main text of the textbook to these embedded links can disrupt traditional fluency skills (Schugar, Smith & Schugar, 2014). However, utilizing the font tools, orientation options, the dictionary, and text-to-speech options can support components of comprehension like fluency (Larson, 2010). Therefore, teachers must prepare students to read both types of texts with fluency. To show students how e-readers can be used to promote fluency, teachers must model digital text features and give students time to explore the e-reader tools. Teachers should show students how the text font can be enlarged and that the page can be turned and read vertically. Both features can be useful in enhancing automaticity and accuracy. In addition, teachers can model the use of the digital dictionary. This allows students to click on a word and immediately see a meaning reference, which could enhance prosody. These features can be compared to a printed text, and students can discuss how these enhanced features in the digital text could assist fluent reading. Students should be given time to explore other features that they feel would help them to read more fluently. Conversely, teachers must also allow students time to discover the features, like embedded videos and maps, that may reduce their capability to stay fluently engaged in the text. Some e-readers have text-to-speech capabilities, which allow students to hear the text being read with adjusted rates of reading and voice selections (male/female). Students can then listen to the text while following along and monitoring their own fluency. Additionally, if readers are using an e-reader app, like Kindle, on an iPad, it is possible for students to open the iPad's voice recorder and record his/her own reading of select portions of the text. The student can then listen to his/her reading and evaluate how well each of the three levels of fluency are addressed (automaticity, accuracy, and prosody). Students can then make individual plans for how to improve fluency during the next reading attempt. The plans can be typed directly into the annotations feature on the Kindle, affording the students with a record of fluency development throughout the text (Larson, n.d.).

Electronic versions of children's picture books allow teachers to project large images of the books onto screens and electronic whiteboards. These huge electronic images of children's picture books make big books appear tiny by comparison. Students can clearly see both the pictures and the text in electronic picture books. This provides teachers with an added dimension to the reading aloud of these illustrated books. Kindergarten and first-grade teachers use a pointer to demonstrate directionality on the large projected images of these books. Students at higher grade levels can use the illustrations to enhance comprehension and follow along with the text, as the teacher models fluent reading.

The International Children's Digital Library (www.en.childrenslibrary.org) provides teachers, parents, and children with free access to electronic versions of popular children's picture books from around the world. The books are displayed in their original format without animation, sound effects, or audio readings. The Tumble Book Library (www.tumblebooklibrary.com/Default.aspx?ReturnUrl=%2f) is an online library of e-book versions of children's books, graphic novels, and videos.

The e-books come with the option of playing a professionally produced audio recording of each text. Playing the audio accompaniments to the text allows readers to follow along and hear well-paced, expressive readings that are perfect for children regardless of whether they are at home, in the car, or in other locales. For students to become fluent readers themselves, they need to hear fluent readers (Stahl & Heubach, 2005).

School districts can purchase branches of the Tumble Book Library for prices beginning at $599 per year for a deluxe branch for K-3 and $799 per year for K-5 (based on 2017 pricing), which includes extension activities and lessons targeting the Common Core State Standards (Tumble Book Library, 2017). Notably, the company offers many discount structures; in addition, free, limited access to the Tumble Book Library is often available through the children's section of local public library Websites.

Utilizing digital readers during Sustained Silent Reading (SSR), a well-recognized fluency development activity in schools, allows children to select books independently. As an added benefit, they can easily change books at the click of a button without disturbing the rest of the class. Students disrupting SSR sessions with requests to go to the library and groans of "I don't like this book" will be greatly diminished when choice is right at their fingertips.

Technology to Apply/Practice Fluency

Literacy comes in many forms. Technology developments in the twenty-first century constantly serve to redefine what it means to be literate. Terms such as new literacies, media literacy, and multimodal literacies have all been created in an effort to portray what NCTE (2008) describes as "the interplay of meaning-making systems (alphabetic, oral, visual, etc.) that teachers and students should strive to study and produce" (para, 1). As we demonstrate throughout this chapter, teachers can easily utilize technology tools to enhance the well-established components of literacy instruction, such as fluency. These tools provide new modes of communication, challenging the notion that printed texts are the only means to encourage reading and writing development.

Patrick Foto / Shutterstock.com

Technological innovations ranging from video games to podcasts can facilitate students' growth as they become more fluent readers and writers. For example, teachers should encourage parents of gamers to purchase games that contain the reading of directions, setting and character descriptions, and lengthier passages that establish the plot as a major component of playing (Abrams & Gerber, 2014). In addition to reading the onscreen narratives throughout the games, many titles, especially those in the modern fantasy genre, are linked to children's novels. Game titles read like a who's who of popular young-adult literature, including series like Harry Potter (Rowling, 1997 to 2007), Hunger Games (Collins, 2008 to 2010), and Twilight (Meyer, 2005 to 2011). Simulation games like SimCity, SimEarth, and SimLife require vast amounts of reading and also build students' prior knowledge on a variety of social and political issues, resulting in more fluent future reading. Additionally, many games emphasize perspective and are described using literary terminology such as first-person and third-person points of view.

Reading subtitles while viewing foreign language films also allows students to develop reading fluency skills, including: (a) improving reading endurance (concentration); (b) developing a broader sight word vocabulary; (c) expanding fixations to logically grouped words; and (d) building formal, linguistic, and content schema (Dalton, 2012). Viewing and reading age-appropriate subtitled foreign films provides students with another genre of fun reading material for free, voluntary reading. Krashen (2004) contends that free, voluntary reading encourages students to read extensively, resulting in improved reading fluency, comprehension, writing style, vocabulary, spelling, control of grammar, and oral/aural language skills.

Vadym/Zaitsev / Shutterstock.com

Besides offering students an enjoyable experience, singing well-known song lyrics with musical accompaniment can develop crucial reading skills (Gupta, 2006), increasing sight word vocabulary, fluency, and pronunciation. Teachers can download music lyrics from the Internet and create a handout containing the lyrics for each student. During class, the teacher can play the song on YouTube with only the musical accompaniment playing as the students read the lyrics and sing along. The lyrics for The Beatles' song "Yellow Submarine," for example, contains numerous words that appear on common sight word lists of the most frequently used words in the English language. Frequent exposure to these sight words while performing the song enables students to read the same words with better fluency when they reencounter them in other reading formats.

Karafun, a karaoke platform available both online and as an app, provides a similar experience for older readers. The song lyrics appear on the screen, the text is highlighted at the appropriate time when it is supposed to be read, and the lyrics are softly playing in the background. This experience of following the song lyrics at the prescribed pace gives students a chance to train their eyes to quickly attend to the text, which could improve both accuracy and automaticity through the fun of singing. The tempo of the songs can even be adjusted for beginners. Tune into Reading, a song-based reading program, offers teachers even more control over the karaoke-style experience. Songs can be matched to students based on reading level, and the program offers feedback regarding the level of fluency with which the songs are read. Biggs, Homan, Dedrick, Minnick, and Rasinski (2008) have found evidence that using software that allows for repeated, purposeful readings of texts does lead to reading gains.

Utilizing digital cameras, audio recording devices, and digital production programs like Microsoft Movie Maker and Apple iMovie provides teachers with a multitude of fluency development activities. Students can develop digital stories, requiring them to create research questions, identify and evaluate information, interpret and use graphic sources, organize and record new information, and summarize and draw conclusions from multiple sources (National Governors Association Center for Best Practices & Council of Chief State School Officers, 2010). This multifaceted interaction with language develops reading fluency through the development of well-rounded literacy skills. Another popular activity to promote fluency development, Reader's Theater, can be enhanced with technology. Websites, like Aaron Shepard's RT Page (www.aaronshep.com/rt), provide professional and entertaining examples of scripts being read and performed fluently. In addition, teachers can find sample scripts and tips for teaching students how to write their own Reader's Theater scripts. Using professional judgment and staying mindful of the privacy mentioned at the beginning of this chapter, teachers can also record and post student performances of Reader's Theater, a commonly utilized reading fluency and comprehension development activity. Venues such as social media sites, podcasts, video blogs, and video-sharing sites like YouTube, TeacherTube, and Vimeo provide a far-reaching distribution of the students' work.

Invitation to *Consider This!*

- View YouTube postings of students participating in Reader's Theater (some examples are www.youtube .com/watch?v=0AMQDQS48qE and www.youtube.com/watch?v=HKhThfo6N5U).
- Watch a subtitled foreign film and monitor your own reading fluency and comprehension.
- View digital stories that are posted on TeacherTube.
- Sing several songs at the next karaoke night, paying attention to the reading skills involved.

- Play a simulation video game and recognize the reading skills involved and the schema development potential of the game's content.
- Read a novel on an e-reader, utilizing the font changing and reference features.
- Read a textbook online and recognize the different fluency and comprehension skills involved when you access the embedded materials.
- Visit the Websites and apps in the Recommended Resources list at the end of this chapter and consider which ones are the most effective for fluency practice.
  - How could students use these Websites to improve their fluency?
  - How could teachers use these Websites to vary their fluency instruction?
  - What other Websites or apps would you add to this list?

Using Technology to Teach Reading Comprehension
Why Is Teaching Comprehension Critical to Reading?

A seventh-grade student recalls his elementary school reading, "When we were supposed to be reading in class, I would just lean up against the wall in the reading corner and look at the book and think about something else. When the teacher would come by, I would make my eyes move and pretend I was reading" (L. Van Horn, personal communication, May 12, 1998).

This student was not reading for comprehension; he was simply looking at the words. What does it mean to comprehend? To comprehend is to ". . . grasp the nature, significance, or meaning of" something, be it an act, an entity, or a text (Comprehend, 2014). In the field of literacy, we generally use the phrase "to make meaning" when we refer to the act of comprehending a text. We define a text as both printed text and visual text. In other words, a painting, a photograph, an advertisement, or a Website could all be considered texts, just as a news article, short story, comic, novel, or informational piece would also be considered texts. Thanks to social media outlets like Snapchat, students are now "picting" or creating stories with just images. Yes, while "picting" is not a form of academic literacy, it does require basic literacy skills, including story sequencing. Theorist and educator, Louise Rosenblatt (2005) writes:

> A reader implies someone whose past experience enables him or her to make meaning in collaboration with a text. Even if the reader immediately rereads the same text, a new relationship exists, because the reader has changed, now bringing her memory of the first encounter with that text and perhaps new preoccupations. (p. x)

Rosenblatt believed, as do we, that it is critical for readers to *actively engage* with texts. The way that one engages in reading a text differs, depending upon the text and our purpose for reading. For example, we might read a short story and begin by calling up our prior knowledge and experiences. Then again, we might make personal connections to what we are reading. We might read the same short story at another time and focus on the author's use of the grammatical device of repetition. We teach reading comprehension in order to initiate readers into what Smith (1988) called "the literacy club" to define a place where we are ". . . participating in literate activities with people who know how and why to do these things" (p. 9), a place where people read and write with us.

Just as we are reaching to define text in a broader sense, we are also now defining literacy to include the digital world that encases us. Sanders (2012) connects Rosenblatt's theories of the literary experience with the current, more evanescent modes of text. Literacy is no longer about navigating the paper-based written word— nor is it even confined by just the written word. Multimodal literacy includes so much more, and, according to Abrams and Gerber (2014), it is very complex. They propose that our definition of literacy should include everything from "traditional print to social media posts to video games" (p. 19). Therefore, as we invite our students to join Smith's "club," and as we work to deepen their levels of comprehension, we must contemplate how to build a bridge across this vast chasm that is now literacy.

Advanced technology tools can help us engage our students in making meaning while reading and writing. Here, teachers will learn about ways to use these new definitions of literacy to help readers construct ideas about comprehension, ways to use technology to introduce and teach comprehension strategies to readers, and ways for readers to use technology to apply what they have learned about comprehension. ICTs will continue to expand, and it will be vital for teachers to continue to search and develop ideas about meaningful ways to engage their students in comprehension building with ever-evolving multimodal texts.

Using Technology to Construct Ideas about Comprehension

Reading comprehension instruction can begin with young children. Reading aloud and with emergent and early readers is essential for developing understandings of a text (Beck & McKeowan, 2001; Fisher, Flood, Flapp, & Frey, 2004; Hickman, Pollard-Durodola, & Vaugh, 2004). There are many picture books appropriate for the development of comprehension skills. For example, Chris Van Allsburg's and David Weisner's picture books provide opportunities for readers to question, predict, and infer meaning. In addition to traditional paper texts, there are technology tools that afford young readers opportunities to traverse the world of comprehension. Reading is Fundamental (www.rif.org/literacy-resources/apps/our-book/) offers apps for Google, Android, and Amazon that include simple stories that can be read and then provides students with the opportunity to draw and/or write the rest of the story, requiring that the students comprehend the written text and then add to that text in meaningful ways. As readers engage with text, they are making continuous discoveries. They compare what they read with what they already know, what they want to know, and what they have learned.

Creately.com is a Website containing K–12 graphic organizer templates. Students who are beginning to learn about the importance of activating prior knowledge before reading might use the interactive online KWL chart to document their thoughts before, during, and after reading. This can be done collaboratively or individually. Before reading, students will list what they know (K) that is related to the topic they are going to read about and what they want (W) to learn about as they read. After reading, students can list what they have learned (L). Because the act of reading and talking together about what we read often generates further questions, we suggest having students add a column documenting what they now (N) want to learn as a result of the initial reading, so the chart becomes a KWLN. Once students have a list of additional questions and wonderings, they can use a tool such as Wiki.org to begin their search. Wikis allow readers to enter a topic and link to Wikipedia research on the topic. This would be a starting point in the search for information since the nature of Wikipedia allows for multiple editors whose work is only validated by the general online community. When developmentally appropriate, students should further verify and corroborate their findings with additional, more reliable sources. Regardless of the depth of research, students engaging in these types of activities begin to construct ideas about how readers make meaning.

In addition to technology tools that help students activate schema before reading and organize information during reading, teachers can take an even bigger leap over the chasm and b[...]assroom (Sanders, 2012). For traditional teachers of literacy, it seems a bit improbab[...] *Question 4* [...] players to be literate in ways that extend beyond the written word and often involv[...]typically associated with school-based learning" (Abrams & Gerber, 2014, p. 18). These researchers tell us that online games encourage gamers to understand character and plot. These games require participants to pay attention to the details so that they can make inferences about where new paths will take them next. They must question motives of other characters; they must connect to previous gaming experiences. All of these are essential for understanding a text. What if teachers used online games to help students engage in metacognition about the reading comprehension processes? Could students learn how to better comprehend by analyzing the strategies they use for online games?

Using Technology to Introduce/Teach Comprehension

Digital book trailers have been shown to motivate students and expand their comprehension abilities. Working on digital book trailers provides students with the opportunity to read and talk with one another. Calkins (2001) notes that an important aspect of comprehension is the "social world of the classroom." She states, "When we teach comprehension, much of what we teach is a depth of listening, understanding, and response. Part of teaching comprehension, then, is making a place for astute and active listening" (p. 49). In addition, researchers have found that ". . . many [students] responded that they liked to read more and had learned to understand books better because the activity had helped them to better visualize the story" (Gunter & Kenny, 2012, p. 156). Research shows that students who lacked confidence in their writing abilities felt that they could express their understandings about the texts read by using digital book trailers. Students felt less hindered by a dependence on "first having to master vocabulary and sentence constructs—something they often struggle with" (p. 149).

Digital book trailers can promote practice with visualization and evidence-driven summarization. The premise behind this technology-based activity is that students can create advertisements for their books, similar to movie trailers. DigitalBooktalk.net is an excellent site that includes many examples of book trailers created by students, teachers, and others with an interest in literacy education. These can be shared as models of what a book trailer can be.

After reading a text, students can design their book trailers using a storyboard. StoryboardThat.com provides an online storyboard generation platform. As part of the process of building their storyboards, students have to reflect on their visualizations and revisit the text in order to bring their imagined characters, settings, and scenes to life (see Figure 1.8). In addition, they must make decisions about the most significant elements needed to convey the story without giving too much away. They want their viewers to know just enough

Figure 1.8 Teachers can use the illustrations of publilshed books to show students how to design book trailers.

about the book to want to read it—but not know so much that they *don't* have to read it. It is a delicate balance and requires close reading and honed summarization skills to create a perfect trailer that will hook viewers.

Once the storyboard has been created, student directors can begin transforming their ideas into digital movies. Programs such as Movie Maker for Windows or iMovie for Mac provide enough tools to include music, images, movie clips, voiceovers, and so on. Animoto, another online tool similar to these two software programs, provides another method for movie creation. If students feel that their creativity is stifled by these traditional movie-making programs, perhaps teachers can allow students to create their own anime (computer or hand-drawn animation) book trailer. Voki.com and GoAnimate4Schools.com both allow users to select anime characters, scenes, and narration, which can easily be transformed into a book trailer. The final product, whether traditional or anime, is a short advertisement that brings a book to life and highlights the best of the plot. The ultimate goal for the student would be to entice others to read the book.

In addition to digital retellings, such as book trailers, teachers can utilize movie companions to books being read by their students. Book-based movies can be used to both assist and enhance reading comprehension. For students who struggle with visualization while reading, a movie clip can be shown before reading. The clip provides a visual foundation for characters and settings. Students can be taught to develop those initial visuals by adding their own interpretations as they read. Gunter and Kenny (2012) found that some students in their study just needed to "'get a visual'" first (p. 156). Teachers can guide students in the advantages of both, noting that the book or story often gives the reader deeper insight into thoughts after the movie shows the action.

Teachers can also engage students in comparative analysis to further this process. After reading a text, students can then watch the movie. Evaluations of similarities and differences can be conducted. They can analyze why directors make decisions to alter characters, switch settings, and modify plots. Students can ultimately choose which they prefer—the book or the movie. The important component to this activity is that students must justify their examinations with evidence from their experiences with both.

Using Technology to Apply/Practice Comprehension

We began this subsection about reading comprehension with the idea of initiating readers into the literacy club. Readers who are in the "club" will want to apply what they are learning by sharing their ideas about current reading selections, planning future reading, joining a discussion group about a particular book or author, contacting an author, or even posting something they have written. Goodreads.com is a free Website that accommodates all of these needs. Otis Chandler (2014), the co-founder of Goodreads, writes that "Knowledge is power, and power is best shared among readers" (www.goodreads.com/about/us). Similarly, Coiro (2012) says that ". . . emerging learning standards demand that online readers be personally productive, be socially responsible, and be able to collaborate with other members of a networked global community" (p. 646). Users join Goodreads by entering a name and an email and creating a password. They may upload a photo and basic information and then begin posting. Users are provided with three shelves: read, currently reading, and to-read. Additional shelves can be created and labeled by the user to suit his or her personal interests. Readers can enter a book title and author, rate a book with stars, write a review for the book, and include information about the date the book was read. Books can be sorted by author, title, date read, and so on. A distinct feature of Goodreads is that readers can learn about the books their friends are reading. They can also create book discussion groups and talk about a book online. According to the Website (www.goodreads.com/about/us), "groups can be public, moderated, restricted by domain, or secret." Readers can have discussion groups with their classmates or even with people around the world! Key features of this particular aspect are the possibilities for co-constructed meaning making and transformation of thought. Readers talking with one another about their own understanding of a text may develop a greater depth of knowledge. Readers grappling with the ideas in a text may alter or further develop their thinking based on insights gained through collaboration with others. We close this section with a thought about the growing importance of facilitating reader interactions with multiple texts and platforms:

> . . . becoming a fully literate text navigator includes more than the ability to interpret and critically construct meanings. A navigator effectively uses and creates all types of texts. In a world that offers almost infinite sources of information (and misinformation) and bombards us with all kinds of manipulative advertising and varieties of entertainment that exclude, ignore, and silence entire groups of people, a navigator takes charge, makes informed choices, intrepidly explores the sometimes "treacherous waters" found in the texts of our world, and, most important, feels prepared to deal with the seas of texts not yet present in our world, (Campbell & Parr, 2013, pp. 138–139)

Invitation to *Consider This!*

- Log on to Creately and explore the various graphic organizer platforms available. Create a graphic organizer depicting what is available and how you might use it in your classroom.
- Create your own Goodreads site and begin tracking your reading and that of some members of your literacy club of professional peers.
- Think of your favorite book and create a storyboard using StoryboardThat. Then transform your ideas into a book trailer.
- Visit the Websites and apps in the Recommended Resources list at the end of this chapter and consider which ones are the most effective for developing comprehension skills.
  - How could students use these Websites to increase their comprehension?
  - How could teachers use these Websites to strengthen their comprehension instruction?
  - What other Websites or apps would you add to this list?

Conclusion

Writing this chapter together has helped us think about and explore many ways to infuse technology with literacy. We hope that you will use these ideas and your experiences in the Invitation to *Consider* This! activities as a beginning point for your own explorations during your internship and in your future classroom. Remember, technology today won't be the technology of tomorrow for literacy teachers, so it is important to "keep up" with all the exciting things that may come and currently cannot even be imagined. It is our hope that you will find a way to share your discoveries with us. In this rapidly changing environment, we continue to consider how to fully use the technology tools available to us to help our students become successful and fully literate citizens.

References

Abrams, S. S., & Gerber, H. R. (2014). Cross-literate digital connections: Contemporary frames for meaning making. *English Journal, 103*(4), 18–24.

Bear, D. R., Invernizzi, M., Templeton, S., & Johnston, F. (2012). *Words their way: Word study for phonics, vocabulary, and spelling instruction* (5th ed.). Upper Saddle River, N.J: Pearson Prentice Hall.

Beck, I. L., & McKeown, M. G. (2001). Text talk: Capturing the benefits of read-aloud experiences for young children. *The Reading Teacher, 55,* 10–20.

Biemiller, A. (2001). Teaching vocabulary: Early, direct, sequential. *American Educator, 25*(1), 24–28.

Biemiller, A. (2004). Teaching vocabulary in the primary grades: Vocabulary instruction needed. In J. F. Baumann & E. J. Kame'enui (Eds.), *Vocabulary instruction: Research to practice* (pp. 28–40). New York, NY: Guilford Press.

Biggs, M.C., Homan, S.P., Dedrick, R., Minick, V, & Rasinski, T. (2008). Using an interactive singing software program: A comparative study of struggling middle school readers. *Reading Psychology, 29*(3), 195–213.

Brabham, E., Buskist, C., Henderson, S. C., Paleologos, T., & Baugh, N. (2012). Flooding vocabulary gaps to accelerate word learning. *The Reading Teacher, 65*(8), 523–533.

Calkins, L. (2001). *The art of teaching reading.* New York, NY: Addison-Wesley Educational Publishers, Inc.

Cambourne, B. (1995). Toward an educationally relevant theory of literacy learning: Twenty years of inquiry. *The Reading Teacher, 49*(3), 182–190.

Campbell, T., & Parr, M. (2013). Mapping today's literacy landscapes: Navigational tools and practices for the journey. *Journal of Adolescent and Adult Literacy, 57*(2), 131–140.

Carlo, M., August, D., McLaughlin, B., Snow, C., Dressler, C., Lipman, D., Lively, T., & White, C. (2004). Closing the gap: Addressing the vocabulary needs of English-language learners in bilingual and mainstream classrooms. *Reading Research Quarterly, 39*(2), 188–215.

Chall, J. S., Jacobs, V. A., & Baldwin L. E. (1990). *The Reading Crisis: Why poor children fall behind.* Cambridge, MA: Harvard University Press.

Chandler, O. (2014). *About Goodreads: A message from our CEO and co-founder.* Retrieved from www.goodreads.com/about/us

Coiro, J. (2012). Digital literacies. *Journal of Adolescent and Adult Literacy, 55*(7), 645–648.

Comprehend. (2014). In *Merriam-Webster's online dictionary.* Retrieved from www.merriam-webster.com/dictionary/comprehend

Cunningham, A. E., & Stanovich, K. E. (2003). Reading matters: How reading engagement influences cognition. In J. Flood, D. Lapp, J. Squire, & J. Jenson (Eds.), *Handbook of research on teaching in the English language arts* (Vol. 2, pp. 857–867). Mahwah, NJ: Lawrence Erlbaum.

Dalton, B., & Grisham, D. L. (2011). eVoc strategies: 10 ways to use technology to build vocabulary. *The Reading Teacher, 64*(5), 306–317.

Dalton, C. (2012). Subtitled foreign films as reading texts: *The Twilight Samurai. English in Texas, 42*(1), 31–34.

Ebner, R. J., & Ehri, L. C. (2013). Vocabulary learning on the Internet: Using a structured think-aloud procedure. *Journal of Adolescent and Adult Literacy, 56*(6), 480–489.

Fisher, D., Flood, J., Lapp, D., & Frey, N. (2004). Interactive readalouds: Is there a common set of implementation practices? *The Reading Teacher, 58,* 8–17.

Gerhardt, K., & Abrams, R. (2000). Fetal exposures to sound and vibroacoustic stimulation. *Journal of Perinatology, 20*(8), S21.

Gillon, G. T. (2004). *Phonological awareness: From research to practice.* New York, NY: Guilford Press.

Graves, M. F. (1986). Vocabulary learning and instruction. In E. Z. Rothkopf (Ed.), *Review of Research in Education* (pp. 49–89). Washington, D.C: American Educational Research Association.

Gray, W. S. (1925). A modern program of reading instruction for the grades and high school. In G. M. Whipple (Ed.), *Report of the National Committee on Reading: 24th Yearbook of the National Society for the Study of Education, Part 1* (pp. 21–73). Bloomington, IL: Public School Publishing Company.

Gunter, G. A., & Kenny, R. F. (2012). UB the director: Utilizing digital book trailers to engage gifted and twice-exceptional students in reading. *Gifted Education International, 28,* 146. doi:10.1177/0261429412440378

Gupta, A. (2006). Karaoke: A tool for promoting reading. *Reading Matrix, 6*(2), 80–89.

Harvey, S., & Goudvis, A. (2007). *Strategies that work: Teaching comprehension for understanding and engagement.* Portland, ME: Stenhouse Publishers.

Hickman, P., Pollard-Durodola, S., & Vaughn, S. (2004). Storybook reading: Improving vocabulary and comprehension for English-language learners. *The Reading Teacher, 57,* 720–730.

International Reading Association (IRA) & National Association for the Education of Young Children (NAEYC). (1998). *Learning to read and write: Developmentally appropriate practices for young children.* Newark, DE: International Reading Association; Washington, DC.

Krashen, S. (2004). *The power of reading: Insights from the research.* Englewood, CO: Libraries Unlimited.

Larson, L. C. (2010). Digital readers: The next chapter in e-book reading and response. *The Reading Teacher, 64*(1), 15–22.

Larson, L. T. (n.d.). *Going digital: Using e-book readers to enhance the reading experience. ReadWriteThink.* Retrieved from www.readwritethink.org/classroom-resources/lesson-plans/going-digital-using-book-30623.html?tab=1#tabs

Mitchell, M. J., & Fox, B. J. (2001). The effects of computer software for developing phonological awareness in low-progress readers. *Reading Research and Instruction, 40*(4), 315–332. doi:10.1080/19388070109558353

Nagy, W., & Herman, P. A. (1985). Incidental vs. instructional approaches to increasing reading vocabulary. *Educational Perspectives, 23*(1), 16–21.

National Council of Teachers of English (NCTE). (2008). Multimodal literacies and technology. Retrieved from www .ncte.org/governance/multimodalliteracies

National Governors Association Center for Best Practices & Council of Chief State School Officers. (2010). *Common Core State Standards for English language arts and literacy in history/social studies, science, and technical subjects.* Washington, DC: Authors.

National Institute of Child Health and Human Development (NICHHD). (2000). *Report of the National Reading Panel: Teaching children to read.* Bethesda, MD: Author.

Pace, A., & Nilson, D. (2003). Vocabulary development: Teaching vs. testing. In R. Robinson (Ed.), *Readings in reading instruction* (pp. 196–204). New York, NY: Pearson.

Paulson, L. H. (2004). *The development of phonological awareness skills in preschool children: From syllables to phonemes* (Doctoral dissertation). Retrieved from www.scholarworks.umt.edu/etd/9522

Rasinski, T. (2006). Reading fluency instruction: Moving beyond accuracy, automaticity, and prosody. *The Reading Teacher, 59*(7), 704–706.

Rosenblatt, L. (2005). *Making meaning with texts: Selected essays.* Portsmouth, NH: Heinemann.

Sanders, A. (2012). Rosenblatt's presence in the new literacies research. *Talking Points, 24*(1), 1–6.

Schugar, H. R., Smith, C. A., & Schugar, J. T. (2013). Teaching with interactive picture e-books in grades K-6. *The Reading Teacher, 66*(8), 615–624.

Schugar, H., Smith, C., & Schugar, J. (2014). *Teaching with interactive picture e-books in grades K–6. Reading Rockets.* Retrieved from www.readingrockets.org/article/teaching-interactive-picture-e-books-grades-k-6

Shanahan, C. (2015). Disciplinary literacy strategies in content area classrooms. In H. Casey, S. Lenski, & C. Hryniuk-Adamov. *Literacy practices that adolescents deserve* (Special Series). doi:10.1598/e-ssentials.8069

Smith, F. (1988). *Joining the literacy club: Further essays into education.* Portsmouth, NH: Heinemann.

Stahl, S. A., & Heubach, K. M. (2005). Fluency-oriented reading instruction. *Journal of Literacy Research, 37,* 25–60.

Sweeney, A. (2004). *Teaching the essentials of reading with picture books.* New York, NY: Scholastic, Inc.

Tompkins, G. (2001). *Literacy for the 21st century. A balanced approach.* Upper Saddle River, NJ: Pearson.

Tumble Book Library. (2014). *Pricing.* Retrieved from www.tumblebooklibrary.com/Pricing.aspx

Yopp, H. K., & Yopp, R. H. (2000). Supporting phonemic awareness development in the classroom. *The Reading Teacher, 54*(2), 130–143.

Yopp, H. K., & Yopp, R. H. (2009). Phonological awareness is child's play. *Beyond the Journal: Young Children on the Web,* 1–9.

Recommended Resources

Literature

Bostrom, K. L. (2015). *The view at the zoo.* Nashville, TN: Ideals.

Capucilli, A. (2002). *Inside a zoo in the city.* New York, NY: Scholastic.

Collins, S. (2010). *The hunger games.* New York, NY: Scholastic.

Collins, S. (2013). *Catching fire.* New York, NY: Scholastic.

Collins, S. (2014). *Mockingjay.* New York, NY: Scholastic.

Frasier, D. (2000). *Miss Alaineus: A vocabulary disaster.* New York, NY: Harcourt.

Henkes, K. (2008). *Chrysanthemum.* New York, NY: HarperCollins.

Hoberman, M. A. (1997). *One of each.* New York, NY: Scholastic.

Lowry, L. (1993). *The giver.* Boston, MA: Houghton Mifflin.

Martin, B. Jr. (1991). *Polar bear, polar bear what do you hear?* New York, NY: Henry Holt and Company.

Meltzer, M. (1987). *The American revolutionaries: A history in their own words 1750—1800.* New York, NY: HarperTrophy.

Meyer, S. (2006). *Twilight.* New York, NY: Little Brown Books for Young Readers.

Meyer, S. (2008). *New moon.* New York, NY: Little Brown Books for Young Readers.

Meyer, S. (2009). *Eclipse.* New York, NY: Little Brown Books for Young Readers.

Meyer. S. (2010). *Breaking dawn.* New York, NY: Little Brown Books for Young Readers.

O'Connor, J. (2005). *Fancy Nancy.* New York, NY: HarperCollins.

Rowling, J. K. (1998). *Harry Potter and the sorcerer's stone.* New York, NY: Scholastic Press.

Rowling, J. K. (1999). *Harry Potter and the chamber of secrets.* New York, NY: Scholastic Press.

Rowling, J. K. (1999). *Harry Potter and the prisoner of Azkaban.* New York, NY: Scholastic Press.

Rowling, J. K. (2000). *Harry Potter and the goblet of fire.* New York, NY: Scholastic Press.

Rowling, J. K. (2003). *Harry Potter and the order of the phoenix.* New York, NY: Scholastic Press.

Rowling, J. K. (2005). *Harry Potter and the half-blood prince.* New York, NY: Scholastic Press.

Rowling, J. K. (2007). *Harry Potter and the deathly hallows.* New York, NY: Scholastic Press.

Simon, S. (1999). *Crocodiles and alligators.* New York, NY: HarperCollins.

Singer, M. (2007). *Venom.* Plain City, OH: Darby Creek Publishing.

Websites

Digital-storytime.com

Edublogs.org

Glogster.com

Google Doc.'s speech recognition add-on

Inspiration.com/Kidspiration

Storybird.com

Tikatok.com

Wordle.net

WordSift.org

Word SLaPs demonstration www.youtube.com/watch?v=19ag9oHgu1g

Songs to Raise *Phonological/Phonemic Awareness & Graphophonics*

Children Love to Sing example songs:

   "Animal Song" www.youtube.com/watch?v=KOwwaDh9W5E

   "We're Going to the Zoo" www.youtube.com/watch?v=6xAqZJNrF2s

Kids TV-Nursery Rhymes and Children's Songs example songs:

   "Morning Song," www.youtube.com/watch?v=ycJHbHvq35U&t=95s

   "If You are Happy and You Know It," www.youtube.com/watch?v=QpghmUkqLdU

LittleBabyBum® example songs:

   "Itsy Bitsy Spider" www.youtube.com/watch?v=p77hQrdjPVk

   "The Wheels on the Bus" www.youtube.com/watch?v=bRE3t0qvDTE

   "Old MacDonald" www.youtube.com/watch?v=120pv_pI1aI

National Institute for Environmental Health Sciences example songs:

   "Do Your Ears Hang Low" www.kids.niehs.nih.gov/games/songs/childrens/do-your-ears-hang-low/index.htm

   "Daisy Bell (Bicycle Built for Two)" www.kids.niehs.nih.gov/games/songs/childrens/daisy-bell/index.htm

   "Ten Little Monkeys" www.kids.niehs.nih.gov/games/songs/childrens/ten-little-monkeys/index.htm

   www.allmusic.com

   www.songdrops.com

Raffi (1998). Singable Songs for the Very Young examples:

   "Down By The Bay" www.youtube.com/watch?v=Yt1czlnCUCg

   "Willoughby Wallaby Woo" www.youtube.com/watch?v=H5MPTXPKNIw

   "Baa Baa Blacksheep"www.youtube.com/watch?v=wKJNrKxjcO0

Sandra Boynton (2004-2013). Philadelphia Chickens and Frog Trouble examples:

   "Dinosaur, Dinosaur" www.youtube.com/watch?v=uCyLnLoDscg

   "Busy, Busy, Busy" www.youtube.com/watch?v=AwQTjf0HTk8

Games to Raise Phonological/Phonemic Awareness & Graphophonics

www.bemboszoo.com

www.readinga-z.com/

teacher.scholastic.com/clifford1/flash/concentration/index.htm

teacher.scholastic.com/writewit/poetry/poetry_engine.htm#

www.abcfastphonics.com/index.html

www.bbc.co.uk/schools/wordsandpictures/index.shtml
www.letters-and-sounds.com/phase-2-initial-sound-game-1.html
www.professorgarfield.org/Phonemics/chickenCoop.html
www.professorgarfield.org/Phonemics/greenhouse/greenhouse.html
www.professorgarfield.org/Phonemics/hay_loft/hay_loft.html
www.professorgarfield.org/Phonemics/introCharacters.html
www.professorgarfield.org/Phonemics/pig_waller/pig_waller.html
www.professorgarfield.org/Phonemics/pumpkin_patch/pumpkin_patch.html
www.rif.org
www.starfall.com/n/level-k/letter-c/load.htm?f
www.teachyourmonstertoread.com/games/tm1/demo

Online Books to Raise Phonological/Phonemic Awareness & Graphophonics

Online Storytime example book:
   The Kissing Hand www.youtube.com/watch?v=0URlsHiPy10
Just Books Read Aloud example book:
   The Silly North Wind and the Clever Sun: An Aesopian Fable www.justbooksreadaloud.com/ReadToMe.php?vid=Sill
      yNorthWindAndSun&iP=IndexCategory.php&t=Short&p1=&p2=
Storyline Online example book:
   Harry the Dirty Dog (Gene Zion, 1956) www.storylineonline.net/books/harry-the-dirty-dog/

Vocabulary, Fluency, & Comprehension

animoto.com/education/classroom
www.aaronshep.com/rt/
bubbl.us
creately.com/Free-K12-Education-Templates
dictionary.com
www.digitalbooktalk.net
en.childrenslibrary.org
goanimate4schools.com/public_index
www.goodreads.com
www.karafun.com/
www.naturalreaders.com/download.htm
www.readinga-z.com/
www.smartappsforkids.com
www.storyboardthat.com
www.tuneintoreading.com/
www.teachertube.com
www.vimeo.com
www.tumblebooklibrary.com/Default.aspx?ReturnUrl=%2f
www.voki.com
www.wikimindmap.org
www.youtube.com/watch?v=0AMQDQS48qE
www.youtube.com/watch?v=HKhThfo6N5

Software/Applications (Apps)

Software

*i*Movie (Apple)
iTunes (Apple)
Movie Maker (Microsoft)
Keynote (Apple)
PowerPoint (Microsoft)
SimCity

SimEarth
SimLife
Spotify

Apps

Phonological and Graphophonemic Awareness Apps—Use these apps to practice sound awareness or letter–sound correspondence.
ABC Magic Phonics-Learning Sounds and Letters
ABC abc Phonics Letter Sounds & Writing + First Words
ABC Reading Magic Apps
Endless Alphabet
Nursery Rhymes by Tinytapps
Rhyming Words by Innovative Investments Limited
Comprehension Apps is an app for extension of text understanding
Our Book by Us by Reading is Fundamental

Other Apps Mentioned in the Text
Doodle Buddy
Drawing Desk
iBooks
iHeart Radio
iTunes Radio
Montessori Crosswords—Fun Phonics Games for Kids
Read Me Stories—Children's Books
SpeakText
Word SLapPs Vocabulary

Glossary

Fluency—the ability to read text quickly and accurately with comprehension and expression (Sweeney, 2004).

Graphophonemic Awareness/Alphabetic Principle/Graphophonics/Letter Sound—understanding of the smallest unit of written language (a letter) in combination with the smallest unit of spoken language (a sound). The alphabetic principle shows that students move from sound-only awareness of our language to understanding that our language is made of symbols and that those symbols correspond directly to the particular sounds.

Correspondence/Phonics—the ability to match letters and sounds; knowing the shapes of letters and names of letters; knowing about irregularities in letter/sound correspondence (Bear, Invernizzi, Templeton, & Johnston, 2012).

Phonemic Awareness—(a subset of phonological awareness) recognition of individual phonemes; phoneme (smallest unit of sound) (Yopp & Yopp, 2009).

Phonological Awareness—general awareness that our language is made of sound; concerned only with phonemes; sounds only; we are not looking at letters at all (Yopp & Yopp, 2009).

Reading Comprehension—understanding what is read. Reading without comprehension is simply word calling (Harvey & Goudvis, 2007).

Vocabulary—knowledge of word meaning. A well-developed vocabulary is an essential part of school success (Cunningham & Stanovich, 2003), and vocabulary instruction needs to be part of instruction for students at all ages (Biemiller, 2001, 2004).

Chapter 2

The Use of Technology and Social Studies

José María Herrera, *University of Texas at El Paso*

Bernardo Pohl, *University of Houston - Downtown*

Christine Beaudry, *Nevada State College*

Meet Mr. Cotera

Mr. Cotera was amazed at how much social studies education has changed since his days in elementary school. He fondly remembered the time when an ex-Peace Corps volunteer had been invited to his classroom to talk about his experiences serving in Botswana. He loved hearing about life in a different culture directly from a person who had lived, worked, and interacted with the people of that faraway land. That singular experience breathed life to the lessons that his sixth-grade teacher taught concerning Africa that year.

At the moment, Mr. Cotera's sixth graders were videoconferencing directly with Mr. Albert, a Peace Corps volunteer who was still in the field. Students were talking with Mr. Albert and his students in Ecuador, and they were enjoying a lively interchange about life, school, and other aspects of each other's culture (see Figure 2.1). Three more video conference calls were planned with other volunteers in Peru, Paraguay, and Colombia to allow students the opportunity to explore a wide variety of Latin American cultures. Mr. Cotera reflected on how technology not only increased the number of speakers he could bring into his classroom but how it turned a normally secondhand experience into a firsthand journey of discovery for his students. Indeed, technology had brought the world into Mr. Cotera's classroom.

Figure 2.1   An Ecuadorian middle school student explains the love of football/soccer to middle school students in the United States via videoconferencing.

Technological developments and the expansion of Web-based information sources over the last two decades have revolutionized the instruction of social studies. The continued development of computers and use of e-tablets in the classroom as well as the growing scope and cache of information available in the Internet have provided the modern-day social studies teacher with a plethora of options to develop and enrich effective instruction. For example, various presentation and multimedia editing tools, whether computer-based or Web-based software like TimeToast, Nearpod, and Animoto, allow teachers and students to construct more sophisticated presentations that take advantage of students' varied learning styles. The digitization of books, newspapers, photographs, letters, and other archival materials by academic and government institutions provides a wealth of *primary documents* ("originals" from those people who actually "lived" the event in some way) that have become available for use in the classroom that were not easily obtainable in the past. As an example, if one wanted an image of the original U.S. Constitution, various sites provide a projectable image. In addition, digitized archives can instantly provide letters from settlers, explorers, or those participating in various wars or other major events throughout much of history. Notably, advances in online communication allow classrooms located countries, states, cities, or schools apart to communicate, share ideas, and enrich our understanding of each other.

In this chapter, we discuss the common technology options available for the classroom teacher and provide examples of how to effectively integrate them into the instructional practices for social studies. First, we will review hardware and social studies software that is commonly available in schools. Afterward, we will examine Web resources and engage in discussions and strategies applicable to the four main strands in social studies (history, geography, government, and economics) with detailed activities and ideas.

Hardware

When considering the available hardware in the social studies classroom, a teacher must examine its use not only for themselves but also for their students. Many modern-day classrooms are equipped with an electronic white-board and a computer or even laptops. Document cameras have replaced overhead projectors, staples of the last century's classrooms. Many schools are equipped with digital projectors—either in the classroom or made available to check out from the school library or media centers. In addition, e-tablets and Internet-enabled cell phones have started to become widely available in classrooms, providing new platforms for group activities, rapid assessment opportunities, and new and fluid forms for delivering more personally interactive instruction to students.

Of all the pieces of hardware, certainly the most important tool available to social studies teachers is the computer. A computer, with an Internet connection and its abundance of useful software, is an invaluable tool to help an instructor plan and organize lessons, conduct research, and engage students in innovative approaches to learning. The computer presents numerous opportunities and possibilities for the constructivist-minded teacher. This is particularly true due to the abundance of primary material that is made available online by international, national, state, and local governmental agencies, universities, libraries, museums, and other archival sources, which can be accessed by teachers and students and used in multiple ways in the classroom. Items that would once have required special fieldtrips to the source of the material or official requests by the teacher can be accessed and employed instantaneously in the classroom. Coupled with a digital projector and a scanner, the computer can replace most of the image projection operations of older technologies.

The use of e-tablets can provide teachers with a tool that can help students work on material at their own pace and allows greater facility for easy collaboration. Unlike conventional computers, e-tablets do not take up classroom space and are easily portable, allowing students to share the device fluidly or take with them to other parts of the classroom as they work. E-tablets can also be linked using certain software like Nearpod so that *teachers can deliver content* to students directly and to use the platform for receiving student feedback and even assessing understanding. Especially at the high school level, many students today have access to or own a personal, Internet-enabled cell phone like Samsung's Galaxy series or Apple's iPhone. Like e-tablets, they are powerful portable computers and, when used judiciously, can help a teacher maximize available Internet-enabled hardware for research and other activities. These phones are also equipped with cameras that can take pictures and video and have the capacity to download apps which that can be useful for the social studies classroom in areas such as mapping and weather programs.

Some pieces of hardware evolve from past technologies, replacing older features and improving upon their function. For instance, the digital document camera is superior to the overhead projector. Unlike the overhead, teachers do not need to make transparencies beforehand of the objects they want to project. The digital document camera can focus upon any object, image, or text and project a perfect reproduction on a screen or whiteboard. Color projections like maps (once prohibitively expensive to reproduce for use on overheads) are no longer a factor limiting a teacher's planning—when there is a document camera available. A teacher can project objects as he/she sees fit without having to organize the images to make transparencies or be forced to limit the number of images because of potential costs. The ability to project 3-D images allows the teacher to place artifacts under the digital document camera so that students can examine them from their seats. Digital cameras and electronic whiteboards are not always found in every classroom, but they are usually available within a school for teachers' use. A scanner is another piece of hardware that is not available in every classroom but is very beneficial to teachers. The most important use of a scanner is that it allows one to acquire material that does not already exist digitally or cannot be accessed online. For example, if multiple copies are needed, one can easily scan information on a printer. One can also use a scanner to upload hard copies of materials to Websites and emails. Digital cameras can be equipped to take both still pictures and video. These can be saved onto computers and can be manipulated using a number of photo and video editing programs.

Software

The real value in computers lies in their ability to access material over the Internet along with the variety of software that is available to manipulate, organize, or employ the information a teacher can obtain online (see Figure 2.2). Programs like MS PowerPoint and Prezi allow teachers considerable flexibility in organizing seamless presentations. Both are user friendly and can also be easily manipulated by learners to create their own presentations. MS Movie Maker and other similar software programs create a platform for teachers and students to edit existing video recordings or to construct new ones from photo images. These programs provide for considerable manipulation of both video and audio effects. Adobe Photoshop, Animoto, and other animation software give users the ability to create their own images or manipulate existing images. Audio production and editing software, like Apple GarageBand, provide students opportunities to create and record music, dialogue, and sound effects. Edmodo, a social learning platform targeted for K–12 students, serves a function similar to a Blackboard page and allows teachers to set up discussions, post assignments, and deliver grades, and, in addition, the user can embed document, audio, and video files. These are only a sample of some of the most used software. Certainly, programs like Word, Excel, Publisher, and Visio have their own applications, and they will also be mentioned in the chapter.

Nearpod (www.nearpod.com), a Web-based tool designed specifically for use with e-tablets, lets the teacher create interactive media presentations that they can then share with their students. Using iPads or similar tablet devices, students can interact with the materials and are able to respond to questions, polls, or other activities that the teacher has embedded into the presentation. It allows teachers to easily monitor student participation and collect immediate data that can be incorporated into the lesson or used for assessing student performance. One of the most exciting features is using the product to take students on a virtual reality tour of a historical space. When using this feature, the student, instead of sitting stationery and clicking on a screen or using his or her finger to move an image, changes the position of the iPad, which, in turn, changes the view of a space, giving them the illusion that they are observing that space in real time (see a Nearpod tutorial at www.youtube .com/watch?v=uF9LKcATlAw).

A final piece of software to consider is the use of historically-based games. Elementary students from the 1990s remember learning about the pioneer's hardships moving west through the classic video game, Oregon Trail. The game provided students an understanding of the importance of planning, good decision-making, and even luck in achieving the goal of reaching the Willamette Valley. Today, there is a plethora of games available that are appropriate for different grade levels and subjects that can be employed by K–12 teachers. Most of these games employ resource management and strategic decision-making to achieve goals ranging from building civilizations to completing a journey. The Sid Meirer's *Civilization* series is particularly well suited for classroom instruction and is considered the pioneer of historical turn-based, strategy games. The original incarnation of the game has students creating a civilization from scratch, progressing from 4,000 B.C. until the present. The series has multiple updates and historically specific versions, including one (*Colonization*) focused solely on colonization of the Western Hemisphere. This version would make an excellent long-term project for students in an early American history class since the ultimate goal of the game is for the colony to eventually declare

Figure 2.2   Visual representation: Data can be colorfully organized and displayed using a variety of infographic tools.

independence. Many of the earlier titles are available as freeware, and the *Civilization* series has been updated as recently as 2016 with *Civilization VI* (www.commonsensemedia.org/lists/games-that-teach-historyw). *Historia*, another simulation game of history and strategy from the ancient world to modern times, is soon to be available at Histrionix.com. It is currently offered as an exciting non-technological version. To obtain a listing of games with historical settings, visit www.en.wikipedia.org/wiki/Category:Video_games_with_historical_settings.

The Web

As mentioned earlier, the most powerful instructional tool available to a teacher is a Web-connected computer. With an unrestricted Web connection, a teacher can obtain an abundance of information, primary documents, lesson plans, videos, and audio files as well as acquire easy access to rapid communication with people around the world. Students can also access the Internet to conduct a variety of research. As illustrated in the opening story, the teacher used a simple Skype connection and a projector to set up a "classroom visit" from a person in another country. In terms of available informational sources, the Web can provide substantial research, unique lesson ideas and instructional material to enrich teaching. Combined with existing computer software, teachers and students can manipulate these sources into a variety of project ideas like digital timelines, artifact studies, remote conferences,

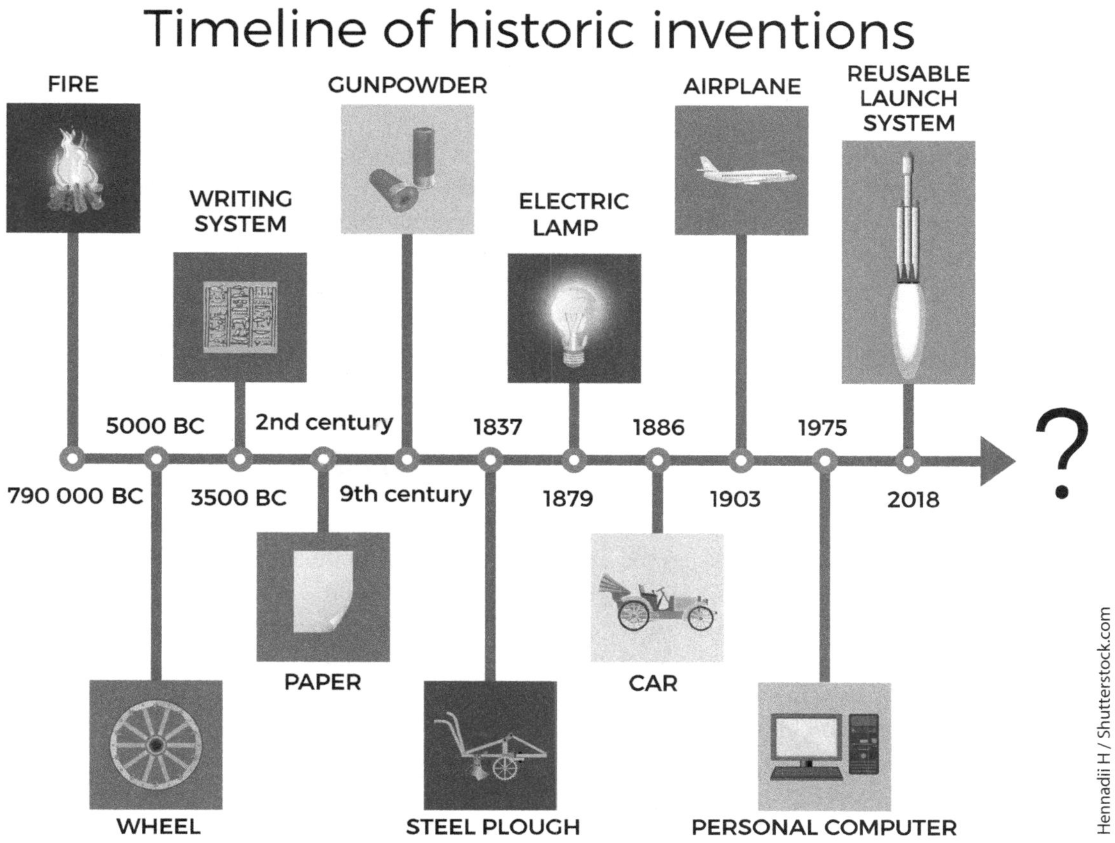

Timeline of historic inventions

Figure 2.3 Timeline: This image demonstrates the type of graphic possibilities in constructing a timeline.

blogs, and visual and audio productions (see Figure 2.3). For instance, using MS Visio, students can draft a perfect timeline and easily attach text and/or images garnered from the Internet to create a clean and legible product. Even more impressive is TimeToast (www.timetoast.com), a product designed specifically for making easy, interactive timelines. This free software makes it simple for students to add images and text and to keep them organized in a clean, chronological format. The software allows the user to add a large number of events (no more than 40–50 entrées are recommended, although it can support up to 150). A person examining one of these timelines is able to click on an event and have it enlarged on the page for easier reading. TimeToast allows a person to collaborate with others in creating the timeline and to publish or print the completed project. A teacher can also find multiple images of written and cultural artifacts and project them on the board for students to examine.

As mentioned at the opening of the chapter, a teacher can set up a remote conference with a variety of guest speakers, multiplying the amount of opportunities available to tap into valuable human resources. Now teachers can use programs such as Skype, host Google Hangouts, and use Apple FaceTime to bring authors into the classroom and/or collaborate with teachers and students from other countries and states.

Using digital cameras, a teacher can set up and film a performance. Using movie-editing software, teachers or students can then professionally edit the film both for image and sound quality. Mrs. Kenton's third-grade class was studying the community, so she assigned learning groups to shoot a variety of short film clips on a segment of their area. One group took community helpers, another took mapping the main municipal areas, and so forth. All were put together to create the "Our Town" class project.

The greatest concern for teachers in dealing with the Web is in determining the quality and legitimacy of accessible sources. School and district policies can also erect considerable barriers to the free usage of the Internet. For instance, while one can normally access useful freeware on the Web, existing school policies and the variable reliability of sites limit the type of downloads permitted. This is especially frustrating when some school district block all videos on sites like YouTube, which do contain a fair number of valuable videos for social studies, due to the fear that inappropriate sites will be accessed. Some school districts have rectified the issue by writing scripts that allow distinct levels of filters for teachers and students. For example, some teachers have access to YouTube to find teaching material, but students can only view a site if teachers organize and display it using a variety of software and paste the YouTube link into online programs available, including easily accessible ones such as SafeShare and TeacherTube.

In addition, some districts erect bandwidth barriers that can similarly restrict what can be downloaded. Such school and district policies have prompted some tech-savvy teachers into downloading appropriate materials at home on a flash drive for use in their classroom. However, a teacher must always be sure that any material brought into the class is in line with school or district policies and restrictions and that it enhances instruction.

The remainder of the chapter will be divided into four sections dedicated to strategies dealing with each of the major strands in social studies. Each section will examine the use of technology in four ways in the context of social studies education: (a) data collection, (b) sensory aids, (c) student production, and (d) research. In addition, detailed application examples will be included.

Teaching History with Technology

The instruction of history can benefit considerably from recent technological developments. At its most basic, computer resources and software can aid the instructor in presenting more effective information to his/her class. Document cameras can help a teacher seamlessly share an object such as a seventeenth-century map with his or her entire class, rather than passing an image around individually to each child. As another example, the opening scene of *Saving Private Ryan* provides a visceral experience of the D-Day landings unmatched by anything on the written page. An audio file of Dr. Martin Luther King's "I Have a Dream" speech can deliver the proper emotional tone of that moment in history. A copy of an authentic letter from a Union soldier can bring a personal touch to the daily reality of the Civil War. A historical "Fakebook" page can allow a student to assume the identity of a historical character, speak in his/her voice in conversation with others, and provide an alternative platform to the typical research report. In addition, some museums are digitizing their holdings and making them accessible online. In short, there are multiple ways in which teaching history can benefit from current technology tools to become more authentic for learners. Click to visit a number of historical "Fakebook" pages:

Napoleon Bonaparte
  www.classtools.net/fb/38/fBQMimf
Martin Luther King, Jr.
  www.classtools.net/fb/5/ZFj2dLB
Leonardo Da Vinci
  www.classtools.net/fb/11/M4Lcj8k

Data Collection/Research

In terms of data collection, current technology can be employed in a variety of means. In the broadest terms, Internet sources provide a multitude of sites that teachers and students can visit to enrich their understanding of a particular historical era. One useful site, especially for those teaching and studying about Texas history, is the *Handbook of Texas Online*, an online site published by the Texas historical society (www.tshaonline.org/handbook). Through this site, students and teachers can access a detailed encyclopedia of significant people and events in the history of Texas. The site also gives access to most of the back issues of the society's journal, the *Southwestern Historical Quarterly* (www.tshaonline.org/shqonline/digital-content). If a search for Lorenzo de Zavala is launched, for example, the webpage will provide a detailed account of his life and provide multiple links that connect to articles detailing events and people with whom he interacted. The *Portal of Texas History*, a site administered by the University of North Texas, contains digitized copies of important archival documents related to Texas (www.texashistory.unt.edu). Searchers can actually read and/or print copies of these documents, providing them an opportunity to examine notable events in the history of Texas at a firsthand level. In the continued search for Lorenzo de Zavala, one can, for example, find letters and other primary documents pertaining to his life (see Figure 2.4). Through his letters, students can obtain a more intimate portrait of the man who was the first Vice President of the Texas Republic and his concerns and interests pertaining to the Lone Star State. In terms of national or world history, a teacher can find many primary documents by typing in such searches as "Mayflower primary documents" (mayflowerhistory.com/primary-sources-and-books) or "Historical letters on the making of the Atomic Bomb" (www.nsarchive.gwu.edu/NSAEBB/NSAEBB162/). One can even view a letter from Christopher Columbus to King Ferdinand and Queen Isabel from 1493 or many other documents for world history.

Historical newspaper databases are excellent ways for students to examine the culture and concerns of people of different times in history. The biggest obstacle is that many of these databases, like ProQuest and Readex, are paid subscription sites, so if a school or teachers do not have an account, they are not accessible. A few important sites, though, are free. Chief among them is the site maintained by the National Archives (www.chroniclingamerica.loc.gov/) which contains newspapers from 1789 to 1924 (see Figure 2.5). The Chicago Tribune, one of America's leading newspapers, maintains access for a reasonable fee to their archives which are quite user friendly (www.archives.chicagotribune.com/). Another useful archive, the Hemeroteca Nacional Digital de Mexico (www.hndm.unam.mx/index.php/es/), contains a large cache of Latin American newspapers and can serve as a useful tool when working with Spanish language speakers.

In terms of hardware, the audio and recording capabilities of phones and electronic tablets have greatly facilitated the ability of students to engage in oral history projects or to collect images to create their own virtual field trips. The following project demonstrates the ways various technological sources can be used.

Figure 2.4 Unlike archives of the past, some modern archives are equipped with computers for working with electronic catalogs.

Figure 2.5 Archives of the U.S. Building in Washington DC.

Mr. Wells had his high school students engage in an oral history project interviewing local Vietnam veterans. In order to help students craft good interview questions, he first had them access the Chicago Tribune digital archive to read newspapers from the mid to late 1960s to help them understand the mood of the country as well as to get a taste for daily life in America in that era. He then asked students to collaborate and discuss what they learned about America in the 1960s, writing down details concerning such elements as politics, culture, and the economy. After the discussion, students drafted common well-informed questions which they would employ in their interviews. Students used their own phone cameras to record their interviews on video, which they then downloaded on computers and spliced together into a multimedia Prezi presentation. The students were able to project their completed presentations on a smartboard so that they could easily interact with the material as they presented it to an audience.

Visual Aids

Programs like Prezi, Keynote, or Google Slides can help teachers to seamlessly deliver visuals during a history lesson. The availability of online archival images and documents provides the teacher with the basic materials to enhance his or her oral instruction. This is also a place where family archives can also be a possible addition. Figure 2.6 is a *photograph taken by a family* member at a major event. A teacher can collect a series of images, including primary documents, photos, and maps and organize them into an electronic presentation that will coordinate with the lecture and enrich students' experiences (see Figure 2.7). Text can be included with the images or in separate slides. Video and photo clips can be imbedded into slides to further deepen the quality of the instruction. Most electronic presentation tools also include a variety of extras to enhance the visual appeal of the slides. The ability to jump slides and return to a point of origin allows the presenter to avoid being forced into a linear presentation. Teachers can also upload their presentations into their Google Drive to make the slides available to students. Teachers can choose to share a link for students to view the material or let students serve as collaborators by inserting additional videos, images, or materials that they may be asked to gather. Unlike MS PowerPoint, Google Slides allows teachers to cite resources, such as Websites and images directly within the slide, using the "research tool" feature. This is especially helpful for both teachers and students. The student interest and level of engagement that can be created for social studies in exciting presentations should definitely replace the "reading of the chapter and answering the question in the back" of yesteryear.

The following discussion is intended to outline how Mr. Cotera used online archival resources and a Nearpod slideshow to construct an effective historical presentation. Nearpod (www.nearpod.com) is a cloud-based electronic presentation platform, with all products saved on the Nearpod server.

Photo © Jose E. Herrera

Figure 2.6   Mexican President Gustavo Diaz Ordaz greeting José Herrera Arango, leader of the Pharmaceutical Laboratory Workers Union.

Since the world was commemorating the 100th anniversary of World War I, Mr. Cotera wanted to craft a project that took advantage of the increased interest that the event generated. He started by visiting a Website maintained by the British Library containing the leading articles dealing with this war (www.bl.uk/world-war-one). He then proceeded to the Website for the National World War I Museum and Memorial (www.theworldwar.org/explore/online-collections-database) to obtain more information concerning America's role in the war. The Website contains images of pictures, letters, and other documents, which not only provide visual contexts for students but also provided a way for Mr. Cotera to construct an effective narrative for his classes.

A good lecture generally follows a "story pattern", and, using Nearpod, Mr. Cotera organized the images effectively to tell the story in a way that coordinated with his talk. To make teaching more student centered, each image was arranged in his presentation in such a way as to stimulate conversation with the students and help them explore the pertinent themes in a specific order. To help provide students with a sense of the national mood when the United States declared war, Mr. Cotera did a search for newspaper headlines of the era and found a large sample of images that could be copied and pasted onto the presentation. Students accessed these images and were provided examples of different newspapers to read. He asked students to consider: Do all the news reports cover the event in a similar tone? Are there variations between the ways the news is reported in different newspapers? What do some of the letters from American soldiers tell us about how they quantified their experiences?

Bureau of Medicine and Surgery / National Archives

A Yank equips a horse with a gas mask for mustard gas in WWI.

Furthermore, as he continued into the year and further into modern history, the National Archives contained a series of pages that include documents, audio files, and images that pertain to World War II and Pearl Harbor and could be downloaded by teachers to imbed into their presentation, including an audio clip of President Roosevelt delivering the "Day - of - Infamy" speech (www.archives.gov/education/lessons/day-of-infamy). In addition, these sites include lesson ideas and tips for more effective use of the primary documents that they provide. He also accessed film footage of the attack for students. Finally, as a point of comparison, Mr. Cotera played audio recordings of other American presidents articulating their reasons for engaging in a war.

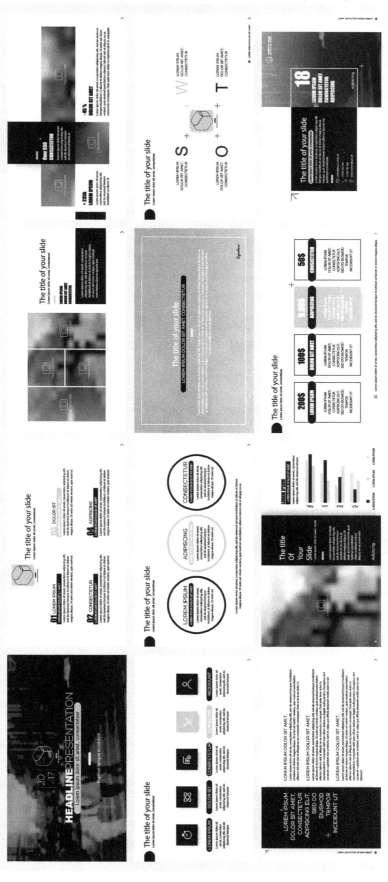

Figure 2.7 Tools can be used for infographics. Presentation templates, such as flyers and leaflets, corporate reports, marketing, advertising, annual reports, and banners, can be used for social studies reports.

Another way to employ visual aids is through artifact studies. With today's technology, a teacher or student can collect a large variety of artifact images that can be projected on screen and will allow learners to examine and explore the material culture of people in the past (see Figure 2.8). For example, a teacher can make a search of the artifacts found upon the body of Otzi, the nearly intact cadaver of a prehistoric man found in the Alps. The search will return a considerable number of detailed images that will allow students to examine and deduce information about the life and technological achievements of prehistoric people in Europe. An excellent Website for obtaining images of actual archeological digs and artifacts is the Archeology Data Services site (www.archaeologydataservice.ac.uk/learning.xhtml).

Figure 2.8 Monte Alban: A Pre-Columbian city located in Oaxaca, Mexico.

Although not designed with younger children in mind, the Archeology Image Bank section of the site provides a great number of images that can be downloaded and examined for older students after logging in. Another useful site is *Archeology for Kids* (www.archaeology.mrdonn.org/) with links for teaching learners how to conduct and organize their own archeological dig.

In addition, certain sites have experimented with providing virtual reality tours of their spaces. One of the most impressive was created by the Mount Vernon Ladies Organization, who own and preserve George Washington's home (www.mountvernon.org/site/virtual-tour). They created a virtual tour of the first president's home, providing 360-degree views of the interior spaces (including out buildings), allowing students to examine in detail the daily life of the former president. The online Website for the U.S. Holocaust Memorial Museum (www.ushmm.org/information/exhibitions/online-exhibitions) is one of the best examples of a complete and fully interactive virtual experience. The site contains 16 online exhibits that deal with various aspects of the Holocaust. Each exhibit contains a combination of hyperlinked text, timelines, video and audio clips that merit detailed examination by any teacher endeavoring to instruct students upon the Holocaust. For those who teach world history, the following site has a nice step-by-step walk through an Imperial Era Roman villa that can provide students a template for creating their own virtual field trip (www.villa-rustica.de/intro/indexe.html).

Technology and Student Products

Naturally, every piece of technology that has been discussed so far can also be placed in the hands of the students to make their own products. At a time where there is great concern for authentic assessment of student learning, technology projects provide one of the best platforms to accurately gauge student performance and encourage them to take ownership of their education. One of the more exciting technological combinations is the pairing of moviemaking software with the availability of affordable digital cameras. These two technology tools, coupled with downloadable digital audio/visual files (as well as a scanner), can bring to life the old school report! The documentary report is one of the best ways to motivate students to spur their best effort on the venerable book report. This type of technology report combines multiple literacy elements with social studies objectives and provides students an authentic platform upon which they can demonstrate such skills as understanding the main ideas, logical sequencing, summarization, and oral skills. In addition, the various elements that go into producing a documentary benefit different learning styles, making this approach perfect for group projects.

A teacher can start by downloading a documentary film from the PBS series *The American Experience* (www.pbs.org/wgbh/americanexperience). These are some of the best examples of the art of documentary filmmaking and will provide students a quality visual example for their own project. The teacher should be sure to explain salient features of the art form—from the selection of images to the way in which narration, sound effects, and music affect the tone of the story. Teachers can have students select a subject relevant to what the class is currently studying. Teachers like Ms. Bhatiya, for example, in her integrated writing unit talked to students about how the director of the movie *Pompeii* took his fascination with ancient Roman history into making meticulous digital images that meshed with his story line. There were many artifacts that were easily accessed online to recreate the images true to the science of the volcanic explosion of Mount Vesuvius along with the actual ash-covered city from those times. Some of his inspiration for characters came from the excavated body casts of those who had actually been killed in the explosion and from the beautifully preserved mosaics which are also available on the Web.

Let us assume that a student-centered instructor engages his class upon the topic of the American Civil War by generating a multitude of suitable documentary subjects from battles, campaigns, individual personalities, political issues, and events that form the basis of a documentary. The teacher then provides a list of these potential topics. A teacher should be sure to generate a robust list so that no student feels like he or she had to settle on an unwanted subject because of being the last to make a selection. After students have selected a topic, they are tasked with researching their subject and planning a documentary (or, in the case of Ms. Bhatiya, a historically correct drama/story). A teacher must be sure to adjust the expected length of time of the documentaries based on the age of the students. The younger the students are, the more likely they will require direct help from the teacher to complete the project. Teachers can create a Symbaloo, which is a start page with multiple links that will reduce the time students use searching the Internet and allow them to focus more on the actual documentary. At the elementary level, the documentaries should probably be no more than 5 minutes in length. Students first develop the script for their presentation using available primary and secondary sources, and they time them (see Figure 2.9 through Figure 2.14). They download images, video, and music that they plan to incorporate into their documentaries, following copyright guidelines.

The following are a sampling of the available Websites that provide either primary material or links that students could, for example, use for a Civil War project:

The Civil War Trusts Primary Sources page:

www.civilwar.org/education/history/primarysources

Library of Congress Primary Documents Website

www.loc.gov/rr/program/bib/ourdocs/CivilWarRecon.html

Cornell University Library Civil War Documents
ebooks.library.cornell.edu/m/moawar/waro.html

National Archives: Teaching with Documents

www.archives.gov/education/lessons/civil-war-docs

Providing students with a large piece of butcher paper allows a backdrop so that they can construct a storyboard (which resembles comic book panels with notes matching dialogue, music, and images) to plan

Figure 2.9 Students can use an array of primary sources, such as photos, postcards, and letters.

Figure 2.10 Maps and diaries are also good examples of primary sources.

Figure 2.11 Historical newspapers are also considered primary sources when they are part of a historical event, such as a newspaper printed during WWI.

Figure 2.12 Historical newspapers are also considered primary sources when they are reporting part of a historical event, such as a newspaper on 9/11.

Figure 2.13 Encyclopedias, textbooks, and digital archives are considered secondary sources.

Figure 2.14 Interviewing people such as war veterans is an example of a primary source.

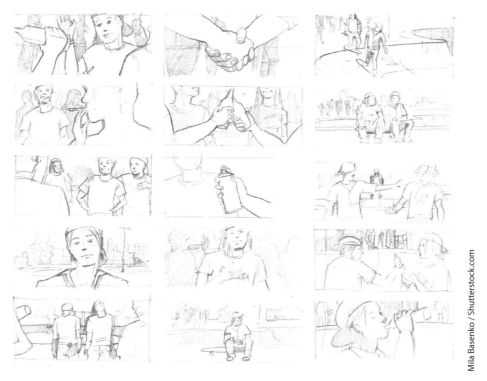

Mila Basenko / Shutterstock.com

Figure 2.15 A pencil storyboard.

and construct their final product (see Figure 2.15). Once this has been completed, teachers have the option to ensure that time should be apportioned at the school's computer lab or a schedule for the classroom computers made to facilitate the process of editing the movies. If a campus uses mobile devices, this can be done seamlessly by taking pictures using the device and uploading them into moviemaking programs. For example, pictures can be taken with the camera on a smartphone or pad and uploaded using the same device into the iMovie application. Movie-editing software lets students manipulate the individual panels, thus permitting placement and edited video and images to exact time frames. The software contains functions that allow the user to implement special effects like color tone and transitional breaks. Once the visual elements are in place, students are able to overlay the audio elements at their discretion. When completed, students can then burn the completed product on a video CD or other media formats. Students also have the option of uploading the video into Vimeo and then embedding them on the teacher's Website or within a learning management system such as Moodle. As mentioned, this can also be an opportunity to teach copyrighting as an important responsibility in social studies.

Teaching Geography with Technology

Students today are encouraged to become information producers rather than passive information takers. They are expected to synthesize, analyze, and conceptualize information that is important and crucial. Technology and the Internet have increased the availability of tools that enhance students' learning experience related to geography. As a result, geography teachers have ample availability of technology tools for the classroom for data collection, visual aids, student production, and research enrichment (Al-Bataineh, Anderson, Toledo, Wellinski, 2008; Dawson, 2008; Harris, Mishra, & Koehler, 2009; Wright & Wilson, 2009).

Data Collection: Geographic Information System

At the forefront of geography and technology, there is the geographic information system (GIS). GIS has taken the geography world by storm, and it would be very hard to overlook its present value as a teaching tool (Benaivis, 2008; Demicri, 2011; Fitchett & Good, 2012; Henry & Semple, 2012; Kerski, Demicri, & Milson, 2013). GIS is an information system that stores, analyzes, manipulates, and presents geographic data for analysis and interpretation. When addressing and utilizing data, the uses for GIS are infinite. For example, a class can analyze the historical tectonic movement of a country, visualize the shopping habits of a particular neighborhood or zip code, or track the monthly rainfall or snowfall amount of a state or province. This information could also be used for city planning, natural disaster rescues, and many more practical purposes.

Each day the use of data in the world increases, and more people are using economic, political, social, cultural, and geographic statistics to understand their world and daily lives. Benaivis (2008) points out that one area where he sees this increase is in the use of geospatial data, which is information about regions and places. The pressing need to efficiently use and present such data has encouraged the creation of powerful and sophisticated hardware and software such as GIS to access and interpret this information through maps, charts, and tables (see Figure 2.16). In one example of its use, Andersen (2011) explains how in the state of Utah, teachers, students, and community leaders are utilizing GIS in communities and neighborhoods to understand the local use of water reservoirs, using this information for the conservation of lakes, creeks, and rivers. Furthermore, GIS has extensively been used in several cities in the "Mapping Our City" project. In this project, students in Boston, for instance, used GIS to understand the historic physical changes of the Boston Harbor (Sanders, Kajs, & Crawford, 2001). The Yale Genocide Studies Program (www.gsp.yale.edu) and the U.S. National Holocaust Memorial Museum Mapping Initiative (www.ushmm.org/maps) are using GIS and digital mapping to explore historic and contemporary genocide activities around the world (Fitchett & Good, 2012). In the past, GIS has been used to understand areas of the world more susceptible to imperialism and colonization, patterns of regional and global economic development, and the concentration of children population in high- and low-income urban areas (Lloyd, 2001).

As a tool, GIS is widely available as a stand-alone software or Web-based interface format, and it can be obtained commercially or as Open Source (see Figure 2.17). Commercially, GIS is available through ESRI, Autodesk's MapGuide, Bentley Systems, ERDAS, InteGraph, and MapInfo, among others. As open source software, GIS is available through GRASS, QGIS, OSGeo, SAGA, ILWIS, and IDRISI.

www.esri.com

www.top20sites.com/gis

In the classroom, GIS is becoming a very popular tool to use for understanding patterns of migration and urban sprawl (see Figure 2.18). For example, GIS for History (www.gisforhistory.org), a project by the University of Illinois and The National Endowment for Humanities, uses statistical census data to provide ready-to-use lessons, maps, and statistical information regarding early immigration in this country. Teachers can use different lessons from this Website to help students explore geographic factors in such topics as the Great Migration of African Americans in the 1920s or Latino immigration patterns.

www.ammig.gisforhistory.org/module/4.html

www.ammig.gisforhistory.org/module/1.html

Figure 2.16   GIS can be used during emergency evacuation.

Figure 2.17   GIS is a geographic information system to gather Earth data.

Figure 2.18   GIS is used to gather data about historical migration patterns.

Besides the full lessons, each section in this Website provides full interactive GIS maps.

Mrs. Blakely uses the GIS maps in her Great Migration lessons (www.ammig.gisforhistory.org/module/4.html) to research African American urban migration patterns of minorities in industrial centers in the early 1900s. First, she introduces the subject to the class by identifying basic migration vocabulary, including the concepts of push and pull factors (what causes people to move away from or move to a particular location). Then, she uses primary sources, such as letters, diary entries, and city records, to help the students understand migration motives for leaving a place and the life of the immigrants once they had arrived and became settled in a new city. Using visual primary sources such as photographs, Mrs. Blakely adds a human context to the understanding of migration. By using photographs, students can visually explore the life of an immigrant. The following two Websites contain images and other documents pertaining to the migration of Southerners. The first site looks at overall Southern migration, while the other three specifically address the migration of Southern African Americans into the northern cities. The last Website in particular has a large selection of visual images.

www.faculty.washington.edu/gregoryj/diaspora/photos.htm

www.blackpast.org/aah/great-migration-1915-1960

In addition to photos, Mrs. Blakely can add an extra element to her assignment with the students with the introduction of videos. As we know, if used properly, videos can be a powerful addition to a lesson. In the case of the Great Migration, the Internet and YouTube have some valuable resources for the student.

History Brief: The Great Migration

www.youtube.com/watch?v=Ak1Uk8-3EE8

The Great Migration Explained: US History Review

www.youtube.com/watch?v=DcEPxlGGn-Y

Once students have explored the online primary documents and videos, they access the Website GIS for history and use the "Great Migration" data map and access more pictures (see Figure 2.19).

Mrs. Blakely divides the class into groups, and each group explores urban migration pockets during different decades. Using the maps, students discover the areas the immigrants preferred to settle and the type of transportation used. Using primary sources, students identify the reasons for leaving. They also explore the preferred cities and neighborhoods. Using GIS, students can investigate the population change of a particular neighborhood in a particular city as well as map migration patterns there. Mrs. Knight, the grade-level language arts teacher, follows this lesson by having students write an essay about where each student might like to live when he or she grows up and why (using some of the information they have gained in Mrs. Blakely's social studies class). A positive point about these Websites and the information available is that they are free of charge, and teachers such as Mrs. Blakely and Mrs. Knight can create lessons such as the one mentioned at a very low cost.

Figure 2.19 GIS is a valuable tool to explore early 1900 migration.

Visual Aids: Google Earth®

Educators would be hard pressed to find a geography class in recent years where Google Earth (GE) has not been employed. GE has become a regular staple for geography teachers due to the benefits of using its geospatial visual aids to promote a rich learning environment in schools; as such, GE has become the tool of choice in many social studies classrooms. GE is not precisely a true GIS but a virtual map, globe, and GIS. However, teachers have been using it as a substitute for GIS due to the geospatial qualities of the program and the ease of data manipulation.

Figure 2.20   The bird's eye view of a city.

As a geospatial visual tool, GE has many appealing features (see Figure 2.20). It is a free Web-based tool that is easy to use with an easy interface, making it an attractive alternative to commercially available GISs (Demicri, Karaburun, & Kilar, 2013). The evolution of GE through the years is another reason why it is a favorite geographic tool of teachers. The days when GE was a simple tool that only provided a zoomed view of a street or a 3-D model of a major U.S. or Canadian city have passed. The latest versions of GE provide the most recent NASA satellites pictures, weather maps that are updated within the hour, up-to-the-minute oceanic and

Mr. Nguyen, for example, started his lesson by analyzing NASA's night satellite pictures of the world. The one below shows the United States. By doing this, the students began to explore the areas of the world with highest and lowest economic activity by identifying the areas with the greatest and least energy consumption. Then, Mr. Nguyen divided his class into different groups, assigning each group a different city, country, or region of the world. Using other tools, students added captions, videos, and sounds to create a multimedia presentation. Students further enhanced this experience by comparing current Google street-level pictures of an area with older pictures to analyze the economic changes throughout the area's history (see Figure 2.21).

Figure 2.21   A Google Maps car mapping the city.

volcanic information, and instant traffic reports, among many other features. The possibilities for using GE in the classroom range from mapping current regional conflicts (Weidmann & Kuse, 2009) or exploring geologic evolution (Parker, 2011) to creating e-portfolios about the historical movement of music or virtual tours of Paris (Guertin, Stubbs, Millet, Lee, & Bodek, 2012).

The popularity of GE is unquestionable. With it also comes the abundant resources that are available for teachers and students on the Internet. GE is also an exceptional tool for virtual applications. For instance, students can use GE to understand the economic development of a country or region. Today, teachers and students will be able to find many resources on the Web with excellent resources.

www.google.com/earth

www.lessonplanet.com

www.gelessons.com/lessons

www.google.com/earth/educators

erc.carleton.edu/sp/library/google_earth/index.html

Student Production: Social Network/Digital Media/Blogosphere

Today, a teacher would most likely be surprised to find students who are not connected to Twitter®, Facebook®, Skype®, Snapchat®, or Instagram® (see Figure 2.22). Wikipedia, for example, lists well over 150 Websites for social networking, including 18 Websites that have more than 100 million registered users. We have even seen the interesting phenomenon of politicians, including the President of the United States, using Twitter or other social media to communicate their ideas. Virtual communities are here to stay—and, increasingly, they are part of daily life. Educators can no longer ignore the fact that their students are digital natives who socialize, take virtual/online classes, and conduct a great portion of their life in the virtual communities of the Internet.

Figure 2.22   Social networks promote greater connectivity.

For quite some time, educators have heard calls to incorporate social studies as a matter of course into the social network community (Green, 2001). As recent literature continues to highlight the benefits and need for constructivist student-centered learning (Beck, 2003; Britzman, 2003; Craig, 2005; Goldstein, 1995; Kincheloe, 1997; Sanacore, 2005), many scholars see social and virtual networks as the perfect pedagogical model for geography students (Dawson, 2008; Wang, Hsu, & Green, 2013; Zip, Parker, & Wyly, 2013). For the most part, social studies and geography teachers have used Websites that are available to the general education community (e.g., Edmodo, Sophia, Teacher 2.0, Edutopia, iTeach, edWeb), adapting these Websites to their needs and to what they want to accomplish in the classroom. However, we are witnessing the appearance of some noteworthy social networks, which are specifically tailored for the geography teacher. Several of these areas are discussed below.

National Geographic (www.nationalgeographic.com) has, in reality, become the "one-stop shop" for almost everything related to geography, even offering a blog and social network section (see Figure 2.23). Another major geographic Website is the World Factbook, which is generated by the CIA (Central Intelligence Agency), providing opportunities for students and teachers to set up a virtual classroom, sign up for blogs and global collaborative activities, and join chats in the geographic community.

Geography Blog (www.geographyblog.eu/wp) is another social network specific for geography lovers. Created as a class project by Churchill Community School, the Website has become very successful in promoting geography in the virtual community in the form of traditional blogs. The Website is run by students, so, unfortunately, activity slows down when schools are not in session. However, it does contain many current events' news such as the current wildfires and other issues. Other good geography blog Websites are GeoLounge (www.geolounge.com), Diversity Amid Globalization (www.gad4blog.wordpress.com/author/ lesrowntree), and Political Geography Now (www .polgeonow.com).

Geography Blog and My Wonderful World currently seem to be the most popular geography Websites, capturing the attention of teachers and students. However, there are other noteworthy geography Websites for social networking. If one wants to combine social activism and geography, then New

Figure 2.23 National Geographic has been the geographic authority for many decades.

Geography (www.newgeography.com) is available. This Website offers news and reports about the latest policies, economic trends, and urban demographic issues. New Geography is specifically tailored for those living in urban areas, offering readers the chance to subscribe, submit written pieces, and join virtual conversations. If a teacher wants his/her class to explore how government policies affect the urban landscape, this is an excellent Website. Another Website worth visiting is Geography Blogs (www.geographyblogs.com). The Website contains current events and articles related to geography, providing bloggers a vivid space where to discuss the latest trends in geography.

Blogging is an excellent way to engage students. Teachers can utilize blogs, for example, to encourage students to share their work. For instance, in the GIS immigration project discussed earlier, students can use blogs to share ideas, new tools, Websites, and relevant information for the project. Teachers can require the students to

An example of this can also be seen in Mrs. Mitchell's class. Mrs. Mitchell, who had lived in Japan, was excited to teach a unit on Kyoto. She wanted her students to explore the country and its customs, so she first showed her young students some of her own pictures coupled with more professional images in a presentation. During center time, she allowed students to use the street views to visit some of the more famous sites along with neighborhoods (during cherry blossom time) and to use the *Hear Japanese Survival Phrases*. As children had a cup of green tea and experimented with chopsticks for their snack, they watched a slide show of Japanese castles with a photo gallery of samurai artifacts and traditional Japanese clothing.

Mrs. Mitchell brought in her own futon quilt that she had used to sleep on while living there, showed pictures of an inn where she had stayed with pictures of traditional sleeping arrangements (on the floor), and gave each student his/her name in Japanese to copy during art (www.japanesetranslator .co.uk/dictionaries/your-name-in-japanese). She pulled up TripAdvisor for Kyoto ryokans (traditional inns) during math time and showed students how to look at the pictures and decide in which one they wanted to "virtually" stay, including the cost and its location on the map of Kyoto. The class elected to "stay" at the Momijiya Annex. Mrs. Mitchell then pulled up some McDonald's, Burger King, and KFC menus from Japan to compare prices and types of food offered. Children noted that some different items included the Teriyaki Mac Burger and a Shrimp Filet-o. There was also a cup of Ramen noodles with chopsticks on the menu. Students converted the yen to the dollar for several items using a converter on Mrs. Mitchell's phone app. Finally, children listened to traditional Japanese music from YouTube (e.g., www.youtube.com/watch?v=pPFabRaQI-0) and compared it with the Top Japanese song of the year on YouTube as well. The combination of real and virtual experiences made this lesson a powerful cultural introduction to another country.

post preliminary work so that their students can provide each other with feedback and suggestions for the final product. Furthermore, blogs can be used to showcase final presentations. In the case of geography, blogs can be used to explore different regions, summer travels, imaginary trips, and much more. In Mr. Dewey's class, learners pick a city such as Rome to explore. Using GE street view, each day the entire class explores a different famous street of the chosen city, each of which covers a specific time period in history. Then, using a blog, each student narrates how, as a tourist, he or she would spend a day in that part of the city.

Research Enrichment: Websites

Research has always been a key component of learning, and the Internet is increasingly becoming our main research tool. As such, when it comes to geography, research, and the Internet, the amount of resources and Websites available to teachers and students is enormous, and it would be a titanic effort to enumerate all of them. With that said, it is worth mentioning some of the prominent names when it comes to geography research tools available on the Internet and to always advise teachers to use their search engines to find others that may be new.

As mentioned, National Geographic is at the top of the list of resources for both teachers and students. Students can learn how to use historical maps, start conservation projects, and set up virtual classrooms. National Geographic offers one of the largest collections of digital maps that students and teachers can access via the Internet.

The National Aeronautics and Space Administration (NASA; www.nasa.gov) Website offers a unique perspective for those who like to explore our planet from a different perspective (see Figure 2.24). From

Figure 2.24 Agencies such as the NASA provide very useful and informative Websites.

watching a spacewalk in the International Space Station to the latest satellite images exploring cyclone patterns in the Pacific, exciting information can be found at the NASA homepage. The Website does require a certain amount of maneuvering, and it is not quite as user friendly as other more popular government Websites. However, the Website does offer resources that geography lovers, teachers, and students should consider. For example, in their Digital Learning Network, a list of events shows the earth from space, the history of women in space, mapping the moon, and other topics that the social studies teacher might employ. In addition, NASA offers gaming through Moonbase Alpha, as one "steps into the role of an explorer in a futuristic lunar settlement." Other gaming opportunities exist in social studies in all areas, including community issues (SimCity; Civilization IV), history (The Oregon Trail; Roman Town), battle and economic strategies, and others.

The National Oceanic and Atmospheric Administration (NOAA; www.noaa.gov) Website is a helpful resource for those whose interests lie in meteorology, the environment, and geography (see Figure 2.25). The agency is responsible for the National Hurricane Center, National Oceanographic Data Center, National Weather Service, and National Marine Fisheries Services, among other agencies. Moreover, each of these subagencies has its own Website, offering a wealth of information and data to those who want to learn more about the environment. Studying wind patterns in the desert, analyzing the movement of the

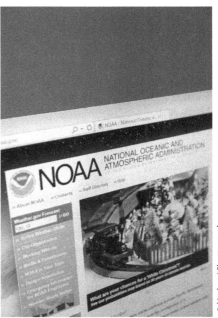

Figure 2.25 Websites such as NOAA provide excellent information about weather.

polar caps in the Artic, or observing the migration of mammals in the Pacific Ocean is only a mouse click away at the NOAA homepage.

Other notable government agencies with excellent geographic information on their Websites are the CIA with its World Factbook (www.cia.gov/library/publications/the-world-factbook), U.S. Geological Survey (www .usgs.gov), Library of Congress (www.loc.gov), and the Smithsonian Institution (www.si.edu).

As noted, it would be impossible to list every Website available to geography teachers on the Internet. However, in terms of data collection, the government Websites often appear to offer the best resources. Other suitable places that geography teachers can visit in the Internet are: the Perry-Castañeda Map Collection at the University of Texas (www.lib.utexas.edu/maps), Maps of India (www.mapsofindia.com), the British Weather Service (www.metoffice.gov.uk), European Space Agency (www.esa.int/ESA), Yale University Genocide Project (www.gsp.yale.edu), United Nation's Food and Agriculture Organization (www.fao.org), and World Wildlife Fund (www.worldwildlife.org). All of these Websites are easily accessible.

Teaching Economics with Technology

Current technology offers multiple options for hands-on learning in economics that will breathe life into what many students may consider a dry subject. When most students think about economics, they usually focus on the quantitative side (the numbers/statistics) of the discipline but ignore the equally important qualitative element (attempts to see reasons behind the numbers, using interviews, shadowing, etc.). The following lesson ideas provide multiple options for addressing both elements, giving students the tools to apply knowledge, collect data, and synthesize solutions to practical economic issues.

Data Collection/Research

Data collection is an integral part of economic education. Both the qualitative and quantitative elements depend on accurate data to formulate strategies and make wise economic decisions. Both students and teachers can use Excel to program spreadsheets and to organize information from surveys and studies. Easier to employ, in terms of both data collection and evaluation, are sites like SurveyMonkey, which allows the user to make and launch surveys of 10 questions or less for free. The site will also categorize responses and provide visuals that can be customized and downloaded for presentations. Even elementary-aged students can design and launch simple surveys, allowing them to engage in "market research activities" that will help guide decision-making.

At higher levels, individual students can engage in their own market research projects using SurveyMonkey and employ the results for a variety of projects (see Figure 2.26). One potential project would involve students creating a piece of print advertising to sell a particular product. Students could set up a survey that asks responders to identify certain preferences like color, text styles, graphics, and other elements and use the data to guide design decisions. When students present their finished product, they use the data to explain their design choices.

Students can also use programs such as Google Forms to create surveys and disaggregate data. Google Forms is a free Google app that allows an increased number of questions. Students and teachers can use tools similar to SurveyMonkey within Google Sheets to break down data and create visuals.

Besides SurveyMonkey and Google Forms, students and teachers have an array of other platforms at their disposal for creating surveys. For example, the free version of Typeform offers unlimited questions and answers. Zoho Survey offers a free version with unlimited surveys. Survey Gizmo also offers a free version with unlimited surveys and questions but limits the surveys to 50 respondents. Other free platforms include Lime Survey and Survey Planet. Additionally, applications such as Poll Everywhere (www .polleverywhere.com) offer opportunities to integrate a variety of interactive live survey formats into classroom activities.

Bloomicon / Shutterstock.com

Figure 2.26 Mobile devices are becoming increasingly popular for the use of quick response surveys.

The following project taken on by Mr. Avalos provides a practical example in his third-grade classroom that collects both quantitative and qualitative data and helps students plan their perfect end-of-school party. He has a brainstorming lesson with students. The class must decide (among other items) what food, decorations, and activities should be part of the celebration. Mr. Avalos sets up a simple survey that provides a variety of categories for each element on which students must decide. On the survey, students must not only select their preferred food, decorations, and activities (quantitative data), but they must also explain their choices (qualitative data). When all the students have taken the survey, Mr. Avalos demonstrates the final quantitative (numbers) results to the students. The qualitative data are then analyzed by the class so that students can understand the personal reasoning for each student's selection. Mr. Avalos is also able to have students view their comments through a word cloud. In this manner, students can understand that in the world of economics, not everyone gets what they want, but there is a rational way to address and meet the needs and/or preferences of the majority of the members of a selected group.

Visual Aids

There are a variety of electronic visual aids available for economics lessons. The aforementioned SurveyMonkey allows the user the option of turning data into a variety of charts that can be organized into a presentation tool and projected onto a projector screen or whiteboard. Similarly, live Poll Everywhere surveys and archived results can be accessed directly online through its site or embedded into presentations. Sites like TargetMap (www.targetmap.com) provide existing maps with a variety of economic themes (from the practical such as world unemployment rates to the whimsical like the consumption rates of a particular company's products) that can be used in the classroom. Another good site to use for creating maps and editing is Scribble Maps (www.scribblemaps.com), which allows users to import existing maps in a variety of formats: PDF, JPG, or KML. With the help of the site's user-friendly editor, users can add any information into existing maps with easy. Through the Internet, users can also find videos that can help them use these sites:

Scribble Maps Basic Tutorials:

www.youtube.com/watch?v=Hy_Gfk6d K8g&list=PL6FAA42D3D309C1A9

TargetMap Basic Steps:

www.youtube.com/watch?v=cJgtAZ0mIIU

Sites like TargetMap and Scribble Maps allow the user to input data to create their own economic themed maps that can be shared in the classroom (see Figure 2.27). In addition, sites like Vintage Ad Browser (www.vintageadbrowser.com) contain accessible databases full of different product ads

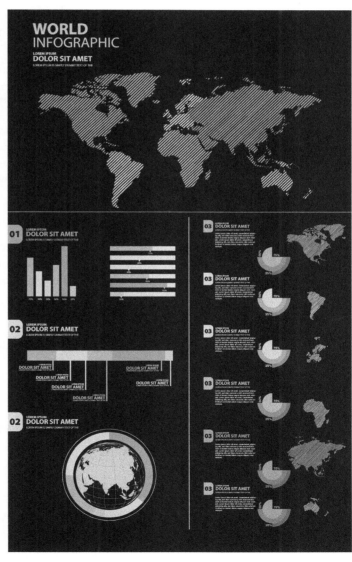

Figure 2.27 Theme maps and infographics can be of great use with economics.

kowition / Shutterstock.com

Mrs. Krueger's lesson provides an example of how to use the Vintage Ad Browser site for charting the development of food advertising in America (see Figure 2.28). She goes to the Vintage Ad Browser site to select and download samples of food ads throughout the decades (and if possible, find ads that sell a similar type of product). She downloads copies of the Poster Document Analysis Worksheet located in the National Archives Website (www.archives.gov/education/lessons/worksheets) to help students analyze each advertisement. Her students then compare and chart the evolution of advertising trends. There are a variety of conclusions and economic lessons that can be derived from this exercise. For example, some questions might include: What do these observations say about people's consumption habits at different times in America's history? How have advertisers changed the way they present such products to the public? Do the ads target specific groups of people based on such elements as gender, race, or other demographic factors? Another teacher, Mr. Keithly, provides his students with menus from a restaurant from the last 3 years and asks groups of students to compare them. Students find that items have gone up

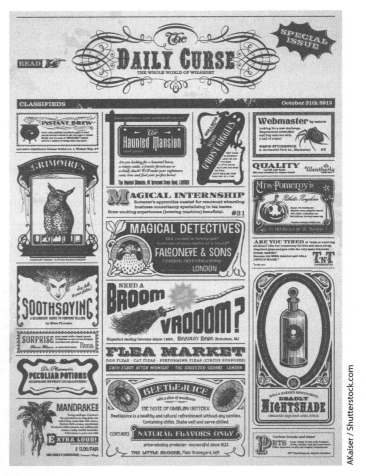

AKaiser / Shutterstock.com

Figure 2.28   Vintage ads are valuable sources to study historical economic patterns.

considerably in price, but there is not a big change in items. He presents students with a generated list of prices from the grocery store needed to make some of the items, the wages that the restaurant pays, the rent, and the electric bill. Each group then creates its own food business with these issues in mind.

(from the 1830s to the present day) that can be employed to compare consumer habits and interests as well as to chart the evolution of marketing trends for selected products.

Developing Student Products

The best way to learn about economic principles is through constant testing and application. The mysteries of the market are not so opaque if one considers the role of information in promoting clarity. Certainly, the Web has revolutionized the speed and availability of information that is available for application in economics-based projects. The real trick is in helping students discover how a certain piece of information can affect economic issues.

Mr. Lang is conducting a class concerning commodities. Among the most essential information the teacher must convey is to identify the location of those commodities. A dedicated search can provide students with information concerning the most important or potentially most valuable world commodities. One news story from 2012 suggests that 14 commodities (oil, natural gas, aluminum, copper, nickel, zinc, gold, silver, platinum, cotton, sugarcane, corn, wheat, and soybeans) presented the greatest potential for investment. Mr. Lang's students can then use this information to chart the most valuable sources for those commodities. Various sites provide information identifying the top soybean-producing countries, for example. A quick look would indicate to students that more than 80% of soybean production is dominated by just three countries—the United States, Brazil, and Argentina. Students can input the production statistics on an Excel spreadsheet and then use TargetMap or Scribble Map to produce a visual representation of the major soybean producers (and duplicate similar maps for other important commodities).

Using newspapers and other news sources, students can identify issues that can affect the production of these commodities (i.e., conflicts, weather events, political instability, new production opportunities, pest infestation, laws about land use, new technological developments, etc.) and, by extension, affect their price in the marketplace. Mr. Lang can then help students chart changes in commodities' prices to gauge how these types of events affect the value of commodities. For instance, he may help students to see what would happen to the price of soybeans if Argentina suffered a drought or if China (the fourth largest producer) tripled their cultivation of the crop. A drop-in production of soybeans would affect the cost of animal feed (soybeans are the most common and cheapest source of protein), thus affecting the price of animal products like meat and dairy. Soybeans are also used to make resins and other byproducts that can be used to make everything from crayons and makeup to plastics. In addition, soybeans are a major source of biodiesel fuel. In other words, this one simple crop and its various applications are thoroughly interconnected into the world economy. The long-term goal is for students to develop the ability to predict the general trend in commodities' prices and to understand how prices are affected by global events. From a student standpoint, when groceries and other necessities are high, there is less family money for entertainment.

While such a project could have certainly been done in the age before the Internet, the amount and speed of research as well as the accuracy and timeliness of the information obtained would have made it an impractical classroom project. Learning these economic principles will help students learn how to be wiser consumers, an invaluable skill in our market-based economy.

Simulation applications like Lemonade Stand (www.omsi.edu/exhibitions/moneyville/activities/lemonade/lemonadestand.htm), accessible for free online from the Oregon Museum of Science and Industry, provide additional interactive approaches to exploring these concepts, particularly for younger learners, who may be developing initial understandings of basic economic concepts, such as supply and demand, profit and loss, and market conditions. This simulation, in which students manage a virtual lemonade stand, offers three difficulty settings that include progressively more factors that influence the cost of production and consumer demand for lemonade. Based on factors, including the cost of producing a single pitcher of lemonade and daily weather conditions, players must decide how many pitchers of lemonade to produce and how much to charge for each cup of lemonade (see Figure 2.29 and Figure 2.30). They then watch as a single in-game day elapses and concludes with a visual depiction, including a bar graph, of their profit or loss for the day. Comments from customers regarding the demand and price for lemonade guide players' decisions for the next day. After one in-game week elapses, the game

Figure 2.29   Projects such as the neighborhood lemonade stand are excellent exercises that can teach the students consumer economics.

Figure 2.30   School fundraisings, such as bake sales and car washes, are great economic activities for students.

concludes with a summary of the cumulative profits from each day of play. Another free online simulation, also named Lemonade Stand (www.coolmath-games.com/0-lemonade-stand), available from the site Cool Math Games [the free version contains ads]), operates from a similar premise but incorporates additional variables related to cost and production that must be managed, including the quantity of cups, lemons, sugar, and ice cubes purchased as well as the lemonade recipe itself. Simulations such as these enable students to immerse themselves in interactive learning environments in which they can continually develop and apply their evolving understandings of foundational economic concepts.

Finally, several additional useful Websites deserve mention. The first is Numbeo (www.numbeo.com/common) which provides timely worldwide demographic information from cost of living to quality of life indices. The second Website is the historical cost of living calculator sponsored by the American Institute for Economic Research (www.aier.org/cost-living-calculator), which will calculate the relative value of money from different American historical eras. Additionally, Dollar Street (www.gapminder.org/dollar-street/matrix), created by the Swedish organization Gapminder, provides images from the daily lives of families living at different income levels in countries across the world. All of these sites can easily be used and incorporated into a variety of economics-based projects and lessons. Both provide excellent opportunities for instructing students on the relative value of money and costs in various contexts.

Students in Ms. Olsen's room use Numbeo and Dollar Street to engage in a project that allows them to compare the cost of living between two countries. Students create a slide show demonstrating contrasting images, taken from Dollar Street, of such items as housing, food, entertainment, and daily life while linking them with the information they obtained on such items from Numbeo. Students then visually and statistically compare the relative meaning of cost of living. The historical cost of living calculator provides an easy tool for teaching young children relative value.

Ms. Fiaritto obtains supermarket circulars to have her elementary-age students plan "a dinner party." Using the information, learners determine a total cost for the party and then, using the cost of living calculator, they determine what they would actually spend to obtain the same items in a different era (see Figure 2.31). For instance, a party that would cost $150.00 in 2013 would have only cost $5.72 in 1913. Using another site titled MeasuringWorth.com (www.measuringworth.com/datasets/uswage/result.php), students are able to compare the yearly salaries of unskilled workers in 1913 ($179.00) to those of 2013 ($17,827.44). By dividing the cost by the salary, the students would be able to determine that a worker in 1913 would be spending 3.2% of their salary to throw such a dinner party in comparison to a worker in 2013 who would only be expending 0.8% or clearly one fourth of what his ancestor paid one hundred years earlier. Students could thus appreciate that the relative cost and value of items are a vital component for understanding the historical cost of living and the difficulties people faced in the past.

Figure 2.31   Elementary-age students can plan "a dinner party" by supermarket circulars.

Using similar types of activities, they can begin to see economic trends in times of depression, inflation, and many others. Having an economically savvy population bodes well for individuals, their families, and the country.

Teaching Government with Technology

The traditional government class continues to focus its attention in equipping students with the basic knowledge of government structure, voting participation, and citizen rights. However, new curriculums demand that students do more than absorb knowledge; they must become active knowledge producers as well. While other areas of social studies have flourished in the use of technology, its use generally continues to be absent from the government classroom, aside from the common blog. Although the technological tools presented in the following lessons are more commonly used in other social studies subjects (such as geography), these tools can also enhance the civic experience of students.

Data Collection

Although we discussed GIS in the context of geography education, it is equally as valuable for teaching government. Because GIS is an information system that stores, analyzes, manipulates, and presents geographic data, the same data can be explored for understanding potential political issues. For example, various forms of demographic data can be analyzed, such as the shopping habits of a particular neighborhood or zip code or the religious/ethnic concentrations found in certain geographic areas, to deduce certain commonalities or points of

Mrs. Hernandez employed GIS to help students understand voting patterns during critical election years. First, she introduced the subject with the class in identifying basic voting vocabulary, including the concepts of political participation, suffrage, and turnout. Then, she used primary sources (e.g., letters, campaign Websites, and city records) to help the class understand both political motives and the crucial issues that were dominating local, state, and national elections. The Website for the Gallup Company provides a great deal of current and historical statistical data concerning politics, the economy, and social issues that can be used to study trends (www.gallup.com). Visual aids, such as flyers, videos, and advertisements, add a visual context to the understanding of the political process. The frequencies with which certain issues are addressed provide students with an understanding of what issues are dominating the current conversation. Powerful questions emerge when students were asked to verbalize what they saw and how they saw it. Mrs. Hernandez then had her students use readily available voter data from databases such as the Census Bureau (www.census .gov) and other data sources (see Figure 2.32 and Figure 2.33). The class was divided into different groups, and, using the data, each group explored a congressional district.

Using the data obtained, the students interpreted and analyzed the data with user-friendly software, such as ArcGIS for Windows or Canvas for Macintosh. With this information, there are multiple possibilities; for example, students can predict election outcomes, future trends, possible places where traditional election patterns can be reversed, and much more.

Figure 2.32 U.S. Census Bureau homepage.

Figure 2.33 An electronic voting machine.

interests for a community. For instance, the amount of time people spend in attending religious services would give a person a reasonable idea of how influential religious concerns would be to a certain community. Thus, in a government class, GIS can be easily used to understand and predict voting patterns throughout specific districts.

In the elementary grades, using electronic surveys to collect classroom data begins to show students how recording their answers or preferences works statistically. SMS Poll (www.smspoll.net) records votes and charts results and infographics through digital devices.

Visual Aids: Google Earth®

In the government class, GE can be a prime tool for virtual applications.

In Mrs. Ahmad's government class, students use GE to further explore a candidate (see Figure 2.34). She often starts her lesson by analyzing a candidate's road schedule during presidential or state elections. Then, she divides the class into different groups, assigning each group a different candidate. Using GE, the student selects a certain number of stops their candidate makes. Using GE Placemark, the students can add captions, videos, and sounds to create a multimedia presentation of their assigned candidate. In this way, students can create a GE Tour of a political candidate. Information that can be gathered digitally from online editions of local newspapers can help students chart the issues that the candidates are addressing at each stop. In this way, students can discern whether each candidate is consistent with the selection of issues that they address, and they can also see if a candidate changes his or her message based on the community they are addressing. In doing so, students can also deduce what issues candidates perceive as being of importance to each of the communities they visit and/or if they are staying consistent in their overall messages.

Figure 2.34   US Presidential Election result on an iPad.

Furthermore, by visiting Websites such as C-SPAN (www.c-span.org/) or the White House (www.whitehouse .gov), students can keep themselves up to date with congressional hearings and government events, becoming more familiar with the candidate's position on certain issues. Students can visit an incumbent candidate's congressional Website (www.house.gov) or the senate's Website (www.senate.gov) and explore the candidate's past congressional attendance and voting record (see Figure 2.35 and Figure 2.36).

Figure 2.35   U. S. House of Representatives Homepage.
Source: www.house.gov

Figure 2.36   U. S. Senate Homepage.
Source: www.senate.gov

Student Production: The Blogosphere

Virtual communities are here to stay; more and more, they are becoming a part of our daily lives. The result is that social networks are no longer exclusive novelties for the computer gurus. As noted, teachers cannot ignore the fact that individuals socialize, take virtual/online classes, and conduct a great portion of their life in the virtual communities of the Internet for entertainment, for making connections, and for many other social issues (see Figure 2.37). For example, during the tragic loss of Malaysia Flight 370 in 2014, social communities were used to ask hundreds of international volunteers to help in the search of the downed plane.

Figure 2.37   Blogging has become a very popular activity for government classes.

As recent literature continues to highlight the benefits and need for constructivist student-centered learning (Beck, 2003; Britzman, 2003; Craig, 2005; Goldstein, 1995; Kincheloe, 1997; Sanacore, 2005), many scholars see social and virtual networks as the perfect pedagogical model for students (Dawson, 2008; Wang et al., 2013; Zip et al., 2013).

For the most part, social studies classes have used Websites that are available to the general education community (e.g., Edmodo, Blackboard Learn, Sophia, Teacher 2.0, Edutopia, iTeach, edWeb), adapting these Websites to their needs and to what they want to accomplish in the classroom. However, numerous blogs sites are available for the government teacher and student.

Blogs are incredibly rich resources and places to share ideas and be engaged in meaningful discussions. Teachers can use the US Government Teachers Blog (www.usgovteducatorsblog.blogspot.com) to share their latest ideas and discussions about government in the high school classroom. Other similar sites are:

Teaching American Government (www.blog.teachingamericanhistory.org)

Abay's Government Class Blog (www.abay-gov.blogspot.com)

Blogging is an exciting way to have one's class become highly engaged. Teachers can utilize blogs (or wikis), for example, to encourage the students to share their work. For instance, in returning to Mrs. Ahmad's Google Earth Candidate Tour government lesson, students can use blogs to share ideas, new tools, Websites, and relevant information for the project. Another social studies teacher, Mr. Long, requires his students to post preliminary work so that they can provide each other with feedback and suggestions for a final product. In the blog, students can post the links to their candidate's latest speech or tour stop. Furthermore, blogs can be used to showcase a final presentation. In the case of government classes, blogs can be used to tap into the electoral pulse of different regions. Using GE street view, each day an entire class can explore the geographic feature of a candidate's new stop, analyzing the economic, ethnic, and cultural background of that region.

There is another opportunity to help students explore the dissemination of political ideas and opinions in addition to blogging—political cartoons. The United States has a fine tradition of political cartoonists—from Thomas Nast to Herb Block. Political cartoons are an innovative way to highlight complex political ideas or critiques and present them in a more accessible medium. Examining cartoons and producing them can help students distill the root of political issues. A teacher may start by visiting a selection of Websites dedicated to prominent political cartoonists. One example is the Herb Block Foundation Website, which contains a sizable selection of the influential cartoonist's best work (www.herbblockfoundation.org). Block's career spanned almost 70 years from the Great Depression to the election of George W. Bush, so that students can see the evolution of the cartoonist's work as well as to understand his political points of view. One can also select to view multiple cartoons written by different artists concerning a specific issue. If students were to conduct a Google images search like "Gun Control Political Cartoons," the search should return a large selection of cartoons. A cartoon analysis worksheet from the National Archives can be downloaded to help structure the activity (www.archives .gov/education/lessons/worksheets/cartoon_analysis_worksheet.pdf). Students can examine the cartoons and compare them to each other. By discussing how the cartoonist uses certain images and short text to get across a certain idea, Mrs. Avalos, a fifth-grade teacher, then provides students with an important political issue and asks them to produce a political cartoon of their own that illustrates their stance and views. There are three Websites that can be easily used for students to construct their own political cartoons:

> Makebeliefscomix—allows the user to make a simple three-panel comic that can be sent to oneself: (www.makebeliefscomix.com/Comix)
>
> Pixton—provides the user with considerable flexibility when it comes to making cartoons, like multiple panel designs and layering (www.pixton.com)
>
> Toondo—the most flexible in terms of graphic manipulation, and the company does offer reasonable pricing for teachers to use their product; however, students can benefit by using the free features (www.toondoo.com/ createToon.do)

The first two sites are free to use and are often sufficient to calm the concerns of less artistic students. The third site has reasonable bimonthly rates for educators, which is charged per student—about a dollar a student on average. The site is extremely flexible in design selections, allowing a great number of options for making comic strips to comic books (see Figure 2.38).

Figure 2.38 Political cartoons are one of the most common projects in government classes and are enhanced by technology.

Research Enrichment: Websites

Research has always been a critical component of learning about the government and political issues, and the Internet is increasingly becoming the main research tool. As such, when it comes to government, research, and the Internet, a wealth of connections exists. With the amount of resources and Websites available to teachers and students, it would be an overwhelming effort to enumerate all of them. With that said, it is worth mentioning a few of the more popular names for social studies research tools available on the Internet.

The U.S. government Website (www.usa.gov) is at the top of the list, offering innumerable resources for education. The Website offers a link to every government agency Website made available to the public.

In this Website, students can find out how to contact their congressional representative, explore the White House, learn voting regulations, explore different laws, and even become involved in different blogs. For those looking for original pictures, audio, and other primary sources, the Library of Congress (www.loc.gov) or the National Archives (www.archives.gov) are excellent sources. In these Websites, researchers can find unedited audios of early presidential speeches, unique pictures of the Great Depression, or drawings of a slave cabin.

Elementary teachers will be delighted to use Kids.gov (www.kids.usa.gov). This is the official U.S. government Website specifically for children. It is full of interactive games, lessons, quizzes, videos, tutorials, and much more. Universities, foundations, agencies, such as the Library of Congress, Smithsonian Museums, the Census Bureau, FBI, CIA, NASA, NOAA, the United Nations, and other countries' governments, offer Websites full of information, including sections for teachers and students. This site provides these resources free of charge as a public service.

The information gathered on these Websites can be useful for the projects mentioned in these sections. For example, in her government classroom, Mrs. Barrera can have students use GIS to investigate the political process in the United States. The students can gather the information available in these Websites and then use GIS software such as ArcView or Google Map Maker to create their own maps. Blogs can be used to share the information gathered and/or to present the students' multimedia presentations. In the end, the limitless possibilities of technology use will depend on the creativity that teachers use to design motivating and meaningful lessons. As mentioned earlier, there is no rationale for students to find their social studies lessons as simply "read the pages and do the questions at the end of the chapter." There is plenty of technology available that will allow the events and facts of the past and present to come vibrantly alive.

Conclusion: The Twenty-First-Century Social Studies Classroom

Technology has, without doubt, enormous potential in the teaching of social studies. Throughout this chapter, tools, applications, and uses, as well as some of the innovative ways for teaching and learning, have been presented. Technology, with its new advances, global interconnection, and networks, has changed and revolutionized the social studies classroom, much as the printing press, the light bulb, or the television did decades ago. In the Information Age, we are just beginning to grasp the possibilities of the twenty-first-century social studies classroom.

Notably, technology has allowed the modern teacher to have a plethora of informational sources available at the touch of a fingertip. It allows the creation of projects that help students apply the lessons of the classroom in new and innovative ways. Finally, it is a valuable tool for helping students form bridges between different regions and cultures. In an increasingly global society, ignorance of other people, other places, and other customs hampers our ability to construct a better nation and world. With the technological tools that are now available to teachers, we can increasingly prepare our students to become more knowledgeable and better informed citizens of the nation and the world.

References

Al-Bataineh, A., Anderson, S., Toledo, C., & Wellinski, S. (2008). A study of technology integration in the classroom. *International Journal of Instructional Media, 35*(4), 381–387.

Andersen, D. (2011). Community mapping: Putting the pieces together. *The Geography Teacher, 8*(1), 4–9.

Beck, U. (2003). Toward a new critical theory with a cosmopolitan intent. *Constellations, 10*(4), 453–468.

Benaivis, L. (2008). Applying the GIS in school education: The experience of Japanese geography teachers. *Geografija, 44*(2), 36–40.

Britzman, D. P. (2003). *Practice makes practice: A critical study of learning to teach.* Albany, NY: SUNY Press.

Craig, C. J. (2005). The epistemic role of novel metaphors in teachers' knowledge constructions of school reform. *Teachers and Teaching, 11*(2), 195–208.

Dawson, S. (2008). A study of the relationship between student social networks and sense of community. *Educational Technology & Society, 11*(3), 224–238.

Demicri, A. (2011). Using Geographic Information Systems (GIS) at schools without a computer laboratory. *Journal of Geography, 110*, 49–59.

Demicri, A., Karaburun, A., & Kilar, H. (2013). Using Google Earth as an educational tool in secondary school geography lessons. *International Research in Geographical & Environmental Education, 22*(4), 277–290.

Fitchett, P. G., & Good, A. J. (2012). Teaching genocide through GIS: A transformative approach. *The Clearing House: A Journal of Educational Strategies, Issues and Ideas, 85*(3), 87–92.

Goldstein, B. S. (1995). Critical pedagogy in a bilingual special education classroom. *Journal of Learning Disabilities, 28*(8), 463–475.

Green, T. (2001). Tech talk for social studies teachers: Virtual expeditions: Taking your students around the world without leaving the classroom. *Social Studies, 92*(4), 177–179.

Guertin, L., Stubbs, C., Millet, C., Lee, T. K., & Bodek, M. (2012). Enhancing geographic and digital literacy with a student-generated course portfolio in Google Earth. *Journal of College Science Teaching, 42*(2), 32–37.

Harris, J., Mishra, P., & Koehler, M. J. (2009). Teachers' technological pedagogical content knowledge and learning activity types: Curriculum-based technology integration reframed. *Journal of Research on Technology in Education, 41*(4), 393–416.

Henry, P., & Semple, H. (2012). Integrating online GIS into the K–12 curricula: Lessons from the development of a collaborative GIS in Michigan. *Journal of Geography, 111*(1), 3–14.

Kerski, J. J., Demirci, A., & Milson, A. J. (2013). The global landscape of GIS in secondary education. *Journal of Geography, 112*(6), 232–247.

Kincheloe, J. L. (1997). Fiction formulas: Critical constructivism and the representation of reality. In W. G. Tierney & Y. S. Lincoln (Eds.), *Representation and text: Reframing the narrative voice* (pp. 57–80). Albany, NY: State University of New York.

Lloyd, W. (2001). Integrating GIS into the undergraduate learning environment. *Journal of Geography, 100*, 158–161.

Parker, J. D. (2011). Using Google Earth to teach the magnitude of deep time. *Journal of College Science Teaching, 40*(5), 23–27.

Sanacore, J. (2005). Increasing student participation in the language arts. *Intervention in School and Clinic, 41*(2), 99–104.

Sanders Jr., R. L., Kajs, L. T., & Crawford, C. M. (2001). Electronic mapping in education: The use of geographic information systems [Electronic version]. *Journal of Research on Technology, 34*(2), 121.

Wang, S.-K., Hsu, H.-Y., & Green, S. (2013). Using social networking sites to facilitate teaching and learning in the science classroom. *Science Scope, 36*(7), 74–80.

Weidmann, N. B., & Kuse, D. (2009). WarViews: Visualizing and animating geographic data on civil war. *International Studies Perspectives, 10*(1), 36–48.

Wright, V. H., & Wilson, E. K. (2009). Using technology in the social studies classroom: The journey of two teachers. *Journal of Social Studies Research, 33*(2), 133–154.

Zip, L., Parker, R., & Wyly, E. (2013). Facebook as a way of life: Louis Wirth in the social network. *Geographical Bulletin, 54*(2), 77–99.

Chapter 3

Teaching Science with Technology

Sissy S. Wong, *University of Houston Main Campus*

EunJin Bahng, *Iowa State University*

Franklin S. Allaire, *University of Houston - Downtown*

Meet Mrs. Calander

Mrs. Calander, an elementary teacher, is preparing a science unit on life cycles of plants and animals. During the unit, students will be growing plants from seeds and raising mealworms (*Tenobrio molitor*) for the class project. She wants to integrate technology in the projects to increase her students' technology literacy. As she looks online, she is overwhelmed by the options of Websites, lesson ideas, and tools she can use. Mrs. Calander starts to wonder how she can purposefully select what to integrate into her science class and what she should consider when integrating technology into her classroom.

Tyler Olson / Shutterstock.com

How Can Technology Support Science Learning?

Incorporating technology into science instruction increases creativity, motivation, participation, and collaboration in the classroom because it engages students in real-world learning and promotes problem-solving skills (Lombardi, 2007). Teaching inquiry-based science using technology provides many authentic experiences, which are experiences that reflect real-world situations and their solutions. According to Lombardi, students who engage in authentic learning experiences are able to:

- *determine* reliable from unreliable information;
- exhibit *patience* during sustained learning experiences;
- *synthesize* patterns and trends in various settings;
- be *flexible* in considering different disciplines and cultural components in formulating problems and solutions.

Although these skills are important for learning in all content areas, they specifically align with those required to develop scientific literacy.

Science teachers have integrated technology in instruction for decades (see Figure 3.1). For example, laboratory exercises have often included technology, like digital scales, microscopes, and graphing calculators. In fact, science teachers were the first to include handheld devices like probes and microcomputers to collect data in the 1980s (Wallace, 2002). Science teachers recognize that including technology is not only beneficial because it supports student learning of content, development of critical science skills, and increases engagement in science, but it also provides authentic learning experiences since real scientists utilize technology with similar problems and tools.

Teaching science with technology also acculturates students into the field of science and represents how "science is done" in our constantly changing world. Using technology supports the teaching of science content that students should learn and incorporates the nature of science, or how science happens, and how scientific knowledge develops (Lederman, 2007). Scientists are often the first to integrate technologies in their work, and scientific accomplishments are often supported by cutting-edge applications of technology. A comprehensive science education experience therefore involves "a commitment to the inclusion of technology–both as a tool for learning science content and processes and as a topic of instruction in itself" (American Association for the Advancement of Science [AAAS], 1993: National Research Council [NRC], 1996, as cited by Flick & Bell, 2000, p. 39). The Next Generation Science Standards (NGSS Lead States, 2013) also advocate for meaningful integration of technology by stating that the nature of science, science content understanding, and meaningful inclusion of engineering and technology is necessary for students to develop scientific literacy.

Integrating technology effectively is complex. To integrate technology effectively takes understanding of content, pedagogy, and the technologies themselves. The benefits, however, are important to student learning of content, mastery of skills, and engagement in science. Teachers recognize the importance of integrating technology in the science classroom and know that when used purposefully, technology mediates authentic science learning experience by providing access to data, scientific tools, and other resources. Due to the advantages of integrating technology in teaching and the prevalence of technology in science and our society today, it has become a major expectation for teachers to be proficient in incorporating educational technology into their instruction (Lyublinskaya & Zhou, 2008).

Figure 3.1   Children begin with hands-on experimentation and then move to incorporating technology for recording and comparing results.

Considering Students When Incorporating Technology into the Science Classroom

When implementing technology as a meaningful tool in the science classroom, science teachers need to consider students' knowledge of and experiences with technology. While some students are technologically savvy, others may be novices. For example, the Digital Divide may be prevalent in low-income areas with students from less affluent homes (and even those from other countries in which technology is not well advanced), which may create learners who are not "digital natives"—even in the upper grade levels. However, many students will have had various experiences and knowledge of scientific tools such as microscopes as well as more common forms of technology like digital cameras, MS Office applications, using an Internet search engine, and so forth. It is important to be prepared to assist students so that all can access the benefits of using technology in science learning.

Even the National Association for the Education of Young Children (NAEYC, n. d.) provides considerable resources for science, technology, engineering, and mathematics (STEM) at www.naeyc.org/STEM for beginning science and technology in the early childhood years (see Figure 3.2). The association notes:

> From their earliest years, children engage with the world in ways that can promote learning related to science, technology, engineering and mathematics (STEM). They balance blocks to build a wall; bat at a mobile to make it spin; and push and pull magnets together and apart. Research shows that the earlier we guide and support children's wonder about the world—and thereby identify opportunities for children to acquire foundational STEM skills—the more successful they are in all areas of learning later on. (para. 1)

Figure 3.2   A science teacher helps younger children to see science in action.

It is also important for science teachers to pay attention to students' learning styles. Teachers tend to implement technology tools that are aligned with their own learning styles—not necessarily with those of their students. Science teachers should be aware of the full spectrum of students' learning styles and provide alternative technology tools and electronic activities that are better aligned with their students' individual learning styles. Motivation may also be a factor with science and technology. Teachers may feel that *any* technology task may be motivating for today's science student. That may not necessarily be the case. Students must be well prepared for using the electronic science tools involved. Those students who have extensive technological experience will feel motivated to use them, but those who are not as comfortable may feel apprehensive of activities where technology is at the forefront. Using learning groups is one excellent way of supporting learners who are less able with technology.

In addition, science teachers also need to be sensitive to culture, gender, and special needs of their students when implementing technology tools for teaching science (see Figure 3.3). For instance, traditionally, males are often stereotyped as the scientists, while female students are known to have poorer self-concepts about science and can tend to avoid science tasks that are not familiar to them (Baker & Piburn, 2007). Therefore, science teachers need to make special efforts to provide technology tools that will alleviate traditional self-concepts regarding gender.

Figure 3.3   Microscopes have become more advanced, even for younger "scientists."

Educational Technology as a Way to Mediate Access to Content

There are many ways to integrate technology for richer learning in science, and one common approach is to utilize the Internet as a way to access content information. With a wireless or wired connection, science students can access the Internet with desktop computers, laptop computers, tablet computers, smartphones, and other devices. Through the Internet, there are multiple avenues to access information, including webpages, videos, podcasts, and games. One very common avenue to access information is through application software, or apps. There are numerous science-related apps that are specifically designed to provide access to portable science libraries and/or research stations. Apps with information about the Periodic Table of Elements (www.itunes .apple.com/gb/app/k12-periodic-table-of-the-elements/id480742053?mt=8) and planets in the solar system are designed to give users quick access to complicated information. For example, the app *Molecules (www .sunsetlakesoftware.com/molecules)* goes beyond quick access to information by providing three-dimensional (3-D) images of molecules that can be manipulated with the pinch or flick of the user's fingers. There are also apps that are best used in conjunction with a smartphone. For example, *Science Journal* (www.play.google.com/ store/apps/details?id=com.google.android.apps.forscience.whistlepunk&hl=en) uses a smartphone's sensors to record data on light levels, sounds levels, and movement.

The Internet helps to ensure that students (and teachers) receive the latest information on a topic throughout rapid changes in science knowledge. The following are examples of some formats outlined by Martin (2012) for teachers to consider when planning inquiry-based science lessons incorporating the Internet (see Table 3.1).

Table 3.1 Examples of Internet Formats and Resources

Type	Use	Examples
Application software (Apps)	Apps are forms of software that can run on computers, smartphones, tablets, or other electronic devices. They provide access to specific information, tools, and games. Carefully selected apps can provide teaching resources to teachers as well as learning opportunities for students.	The Elements, K–12 Periodic Table of Elements, Video Science, Science Glossary, Skeletal Systems
Blogs	Websites that contain text, audio, and videos on a topic. Students can use blogs to present a topic, review a topic, increase engagement in a topic, and initiate questions. Students can also initiate a blog as a means to communicate and collaborate with others about science topics.	National Geographic Blogs, NASA Earth Observatory Blogs
Communications software	Free or paid versions of software that mediate audio and video communication via the Internet. This software may be useful to foster collaboration in real time between students and peers around the world and to experts in the science fields.	Skype, Google Hangouts FaceTime
Globs	Virtual posters that can include text, audio, photos, and music. Posters can be shared with others over time to show changes or process in science.	Canva, Glogster, Pic-Collage, PosterMyWall
Podcasts and vodcasts	Podcasts are digital audio files distributed over the Internet (i.e., Vodcasts are digital videos distributed over the Internet). Both are one-way and can be accessed to introduce, teach, or review topics in science.	NOVA science NOW, EdTech Talk, DiscoveryNews, NOVA Vodcast
Presentation Tools	These are various tools that allow for integration of text, audio, and images in a single product. Students can create interactive slide shows or digital stories as products of their science learning.	MS Office applications, Prezi, Brainshark
Science games	Scientific games can help students in learning about science. Carefully selected games can introduce, reinforce, or elaborate on concepts as well as promote problem-solving and critical thinking skills. Games can also be used to connect science with other subjects, such as mathematics, technology, and engineering.	EcoKids, Immune Attack, CSI Web Adventure, Animal Jam, Discovery Kids, Amusement Park Physics
Web applications	Websites that provide a place for teachers and students to ask questions to experts in the field.	Ask-A-Scientist, Ask-A-Biologist

Type	Use	Examples
WebQuests	An inquiry-based activity that challenges students to complete a basic task that supports learning of science content. Typically, the process and guidance are provided by the teacher for the suggested Websites.	WebQuest.org
Wikis	Websites that can be edited and involve a collaborative effort to construct and update. Teachers and students can include thoughts, observations, ideas, and questions for feedback from other people.	PBworks, Wikipedia, Wikispaces

Online resources can support learning, but the amount of information can also be overwhelming to both teachers and students. Without careful planning by the teacher, students can become unfocused and frustrated during online searches. To keep students focused on the topic under study, teachers must make sound decisions on how to evaluate Websites to ensure they are appropriate for students and decide how to make them accessible to students. According to Martin (2012), teachers should ask the following when evaluating Websites for student use:

- Is the science content accurate and up to date?
- What are the qualifications of the author or organization that created the Website?
- Is the site age appropriate and user friendly?
- Does it provide links to other quality Websites that are on the same topic or closely related to the same topic?
- Does it suggest accommodations for diverse learners, such as English Language Learners and students with disabilities?

Once teachers have explored and bookmarked the many Internet options to support science content learning, it may be advisable to create Websites for their students to begin their exploration. On these Websites, teachers can include content, assignments, and other resources. Some teachers may also digitally record and upload lessons that occurred in the class so that students can review them.

Educational Technology as a Way to Maximize Students' Science Learning

The Flipped (or inverted) classroom is a concept where lessons or materials are uploaded to the Internet prior to the class. By having students review material online before class as an introduction, or after class for review, class time can be used for activities or discussions. This strategy can be a particularly beneficial option for science teachers to consider since it would provide maximum laboratory time during school hours.

The methods used to "flip" classrooms include the use of videos on YouTube, Google Docs, Google Hangouts and Dropbox. Research into flipped classrooms tells us that when used effectively, flipped classrooms can address all four of the general types of knowledge—procedural, factual, conceptual, and metacognitive—described in Bloom's revised taxonomy (Milman, 2012). Research into flipped classrooms has also found that when properly structured, flipped classrooms can positively impact cooperation between students, innovation, in-class student/ teacher interactions, and higher-order thinking (Kim, Kim, Khera, & Getman, 2014; Strayer, 2012).

Science teachers who are interested in flipping their classrooms have the option of creating their own videos to use with their students. The sophistication and user-friendliness of video editing software has made it easier for teachers and students to create their own videos for flipped classroom use. Additionally, Websites, such as YouTube (www.youtube.com) and TeacherTube (www.teachertube.com), have made it easy to share teacher- and student-generated videos. However, there are videos already available online through both YouTube and TeacherTube. Teacher and flipped classroom advocate Paul Anderson (www.bozemanscience.com) has over 600 videos posted on YouTube covering science topics in chemistry, physics, environmental science, and biology. CrashCourse (www.youtube.com/channel/UCX6b17PVsYBQ0ip5gyeme-Q) is another YouTube Channel with over 700 videos covering the sciences as well as the language arts, civics, and philosophy. The Khan Academy (www.khanacademy.org) has over 6,000 videos on both their Website and YouTube.

Mr. Salinas, a secondary school teacher uses videos from Flocabulary.com to support his flipped classroom. In this case, he assigns his students to watch a video on the animal classification of the Six Kingdoms as an introduction to the topic. Students watch this video before class as many times as they want or need. To support his students as they watch the video, the teacher provides them with a graphic organizer or a series of questions to answer about the contents of the video. Additionally, students apply the knowledge they gained from the video by playing a classification game on Interactive Sites for Education (science) (www .interactivesites.weebly.com/science.html). Instead of lecturing about the Six Kingdoms with students taking notes, class time becomes more active with the teacher putting students into six expert groups. Each group shares the main points they learned about a specific kingdom and creates a presentation to share with the rest of the class about that particular kingdom.

Burlingham / Shutterstock.com

Kim et al. (2014) recommend nine design principles to help in running a flipped classroom effectively (p. 29):

- Provide an opportunity for students to gain first exposure to content prior to class
- Provide an incentive for students to prepare for class (i.e., online discussions or having students provide questions via YouTube comments)
- Provide a mechanism to assess student understanding
- Provide clear connections between in-class and out-of-class activities
- Provide clearly defined and well-structured guidance
- Provide enough time for students to carry out assignments
- Provide facilitation for building a learning community
- Provide prompt/adaptive feedback on individual or group works
- Provide technologies familiar and easy to access

Things to Consider . . .

Due to safety and privacy concerns, some schools and districts are creating policies governing the creation and distribution of self-made educational videos. Consultation with school and/or district administrators before creating and distributing content-related videos for one's flipped classroom is highly recommended. Teachers who post self-made (or downloaded) videos must make sure the content of the resources reinforces the ideas and practices essential to doing science safely in school settings. According to the National Science Teachers Association ([NSTA], 2005), teachers must be aware of the following when creating videos for public viewing:

- Follow the school and district policies for safety standards, handling of hazardous materials, and disposal of chemical and biological waste.
- Reinforce safety procedures such as wearing eye protection, aprons, and protective clothing.
- Practice safety procedures when handling chemicals, fire, and biohazards.
- Include safety concerns and rules with demonstrations in the video.

It is also pertinent to note that Internet safety should be a priority in and out of the classroom. Teachers need to be explicit in their instructions on Internet safety. School firewalls and filters are helpful in preventing access to inappropriate Websites, but other measures should be taken to ensure a safe and meaningful experience on the Internet. When preparing students to access the Internet, teachers should arrange all monitors so that they are visible during the activity (Martin, 2012). According to Craig (1999), students should be taught Internet etiquette, or netiquette in the classroom, which includes:

- Obtain permission for the topic before using the Internet.
- Focus on only the topic that was approved.
- Check for spelling to ensure searches are focused on topic.
- Read the description of Websites before selecting, and never opening a Website that is flagged as possibly harmful.
- Take notes, if appropriate, and keeping track of addresses (URLs) of useful Websites.
- Never give out personal information (even to those who are in the scientific community).
- Report cyberbullying to a trusted adult immediately.

"Netiquette" and technology guidelines that are specific for the science classroom include:

- Be aware of science ideas of experiments that may be dangerous. Never replicate experiments (especially from Websites) without proper approval, supervision, and guidance.
- Follow laboratory safety guidelines that gives clear instructions for how to handle and care for laboratory technology (have students sign a laboratory safety contract to reinforce the importance of safety when working with laboratory and expensive, and perhaps fragile, technology equipment).
- Ensure technology is age appropriate for the students to maximize science learning.
- Provide time and opportunity to learn about technology so that it can be used safely and effectively.
- Make sure students are aware of cords and other technology hazards that may obstruct walking paths, and ensure that they move about the classroom with caution.
- Be sure that students are accessing resources and Websites that are equitable to all students.

Although these tips are important, they are not all inclusive. (Please refer to other chapters in this book for additional information on Internet safety for students.) As technology evolves and teachers see ways that Internet utilization advances, it is vital to be updated on methods and aspects of Internet safety and to practice them in and out of the classroom.

Technology as a Way to Access and Collect Data

It is essential for students to learn how to collect electronic data with technology in the science classroom. Using technology to collect data supports the development of basic science skills such as measurement as well as the "integrated process skills of interpreting data and formulating models" (Park, 2008, p. 33). One common tool that can be useful in science learning is the smartphone. Smartphones have become increasingly widespread among secondary and college/university students due to their continuously increasing computer power, faster and more powerful processors, larger amounts of hard drive space, increased photo, video, and graphic capabilities, and an ever-expanding library of software. Additionally, cell phones have become increasingly accessible to school-aged children. A 2016 Nielson report on Mobile Media showed that adults 18 years and older spent an average of 25 hours on media every week (Casey, 2017). There is also research showing that smartphones have become ubiquitous among middle and high school students in urban school districts and, therefore, have the potential to reach and attract students from underrepresented minority groups to STEM-related fields (Annetta, Burton, Frazier, Cheng, & Chmiel, 2012; Libman & Huang, 2013; Lucking, Christmann, & Wighting, 2010).

In the context of the science classroom, cell phones can also be extremely useful tools to support the learning process. Today's smart cellular phones can include built-in calculators, high-resolution cameras, video recording and editing options, dictionaries, global positioning systems, a variety of internal sensors, access to thousands of science-related apps, and Internet capability. These features, along with students' familiarity with their own devices, make them ideal for use in science classrooms and labs (Lucking et al., 2010). Specifically, smartphone and tablet features can be useful to students within subject areas. In physics, students can use the internal accelerometer to devise experiments exploring forces and motion (Vieyra, Vieyra, Jeanjacquot, Marti, & Monteiro, 2015). These smart devices' slow-motion video feature can be used to record and analyze data that might otherwise happen too quickly to see with the naked eye, such as analyzing falling/bouncing objects and certain types of chemical reactions. Additionally, biology teachers can encourage students to take "cellfies" by carefully holding smartphone cameras against the eyepiece of a microscope. For example, videos released by Instructables.com and PBS Digital Studios show how to construct microscopes specifically for smartphones using items that can be found in any hardware store.

Smart devices that can capture a digital image can be used when upper elementary students learn about the "big idea" of the interdependent relationships among ecosystems.

Mrs. Wan has students organized in collaborative learning groups to design a milkweed bug or mealworm habitat that consists of four essential elements—food, water, shelter, and space. Each team comes up with their own focus questions (or teachers and students can establish a focus question for the class such as, "How are milkweed bugs or mealworms related within food chains?" or "What are milkweed bugs' or mealworms' main food sources?").

After the class makes a decision about their focus questions, each team then proceeds with pre-experimentation activities in order to explore and share their prior knowledge related to food webs by using a visual workspace such as Kidspiration or KidPix software to create associated words and symbols and to build concept maps related to their focus questions. It is also important at this stage for a teacher to engage students in building foundational skills needed to understand and properly use the targeted technology being used in each lesson.

Once each team has built their habitats, they become involved in collecting data by taking still pictures and video clips of their milkweed bugs or mealworms throughout the project (see Figure 3.4). As a long-term project, each group keeps a digital science journal by creating a Pinterest-style rolling-board at a social networking site that is safe for kids (e.g., Yoursphere). This enables students to post and

Figure 3.4   A student learns how to collect data in a life science project.

share daily or weekly digital imagery of changes in their milkweed bugs or mealworms. Later, students engage in data analysis of their collection of images and address feedback made by the classmates posted on the social networking site they are using. After engaging in data analysis and creating knowledge statements related to their initial focus questions, families and friends may be invited to an open house day (or even a "digital open house") in which the students showcase their multimedia slide shows or digital stories.

The example of Mrs. Wan's life science investigation is just one of the many types of data collection activities and projects that students can do with technology. Keep in mind that students do not have to collect original data to engage in inquiry-based investigations. Students can use accurate data from a number of Internet sources to engage in analysis. One example is from the U.S. Geological Survey (USGS; www.usgs.gov/products/data-and-tools/gis-data) that provides current data on various geologic topics.

Selected Examples of Probes/Sensors

Subject Area	Probe/Sensor
Biology	• Hand-Grip Heart Rate Monitor • Temperature Sensor • CO2 Gas Sensor • O2 Gas Sensor • SpectroVis Plus Spectrophotometer
Chemistry	• Gas Pressure Sensor • pH Sensor • Temperature Sensor • Conductivity Probe • SpectroVis Plus Spectrophotometer
Physical Science/Physics	• Dual-range Force Sensor • Gas Pressure Sensor • Motion Detector • Temperature Sensor • Accelerometers

Figure 3.5 List of Vernier probeware.

Another form of technology that is often associated with science learning is probeware and sensors. These are devices used to make scientific measurements and typically consist of probes and software that are used in conjunction with microprocessors such as computers and calculators (Park, 2008). Probeware/sensors allow for collection of data in real time and measurement of different variables. There are many types of probeware/sensors, and the information they can collect and analyze is diverse. For example, Vernier produces over 70 types of probeware/sensors, software, and microprocessors for K–12 science education.

The company Vernier (www.vernier.com) is also developing smartphone technology along with their patented probes and software programs to increase student access to technology in science (see Figure 3.5). With the help of a Go Wireless Link from Vernier, students can record temperature, pH, or exercise/resting heart rate using digital probes and have that data sent directly to their smartphone wirelessly.

Figure 3.6 Child using voltmeter to do experiments on electricity.

Research supports the use of probeware for the simultaneous display of data collected in real time (see Figure 3.6). According to Thornton (2008), incorporating probeware to collect data in real time resulted in the following benefits:

• Students were able to connect concrete measurements of physical phenomenon with "simultaneous production of the symbolic representation" (p. 6), which helps students learn abstract concepts.
• Real-time data collection fosters critical thinking skills by focusing on data analysis and conclusion formation over data collection and management.
• Real-time data collection promotes collaboration and learning between peers.

- When used purposefully, probeware use can increase students' spatial visualizations, which is essential in the field of physics.
- Probeware is accessible to novice students as well as technologically sophisticated students.

Probeware/sensors can also help students understand mathematical relationships between measured variables and build models of phenomenon (Park, 2008). Students who regularly used probeware/sensors during science activities scored significantly higher on assessments than those who did not use probeware/sensors (National Center for Education Statistics, 2002) (see Figure 3.7).

Considerations for integrating technology to collect electronic data:

Figure 3.7 Students using an oscilloscope to measure voltage over time.

- Ensure that lessons and activities are inquiry-based. Technology can be used in teacher-centered and student-centered ways. Consider how to integrate technology in ways that support student-driven learning opportunities.
- Consider the best tool available for what it is that students need to measure. To understand what the best tool available may be, recognize what tools are capable of doing and how they might be modified to collect data about related topics.
- Learning how to use technology can be time consuming. If the tool will only be used for a limited number of lessons or to teach a limited number of objectives, consider whether the time required to teach how to use the tool is justified.
- Although there are many benefits to incorporating probeware/sensors in science teaching, they should be used purposefully. For example, a thermometer may be more efficient and easier to use when measuring temperature for a single occurrence. Probeware/sensors would be appropriate when measuring temperature over time because of the devices' capacity to create representations of the changes during the data collection period.

Technology as a Means to Access and Analyze Data

Technology in the science education classroom includes Web-based (online) sources that can increase access to resources and information. Educational researchers have concluded that authentic activities take place in real-life locations, and experiences can also occur through thorough Web-based learning opportunities (Herrington, Oliver, & Reeves, 2003). In fact, Web-based learning situations provide access to many of the same resources that scientists use in their work (Lombardi, 2007).

Inquiry-based learning using online data can increase students' interest in science, their use of inquiry skills, and their content knowledge (Trundle, 2008). With the immense amount of information available online, students should be able to explore and find a topic in which they find interest. This interest can make the topic more relevant and inspire student-driven questions and inquiry investigations (Windschitl, 1998). The personal investment in the topic and engagement in inquiry-based activities provide opportunities to apply inquiry skills to investigate and learn about the topic.

There are various Websites that can provide access to scientific data. For example, the USGS provides data on topics such as water quality, climate, and land use, as well as natural hazards such as volcanic and earthquake activity (see Figure 3.8). On the USGS Website, there are data sets that can be utilized to create tables and graphs to develop data representations. The data can be compared and analyzed to understand patterns and trends of the changes on Earth. USGS also has resources for teachers and students in the teaching and learning of geological sciences (www.education.usgs.gov).

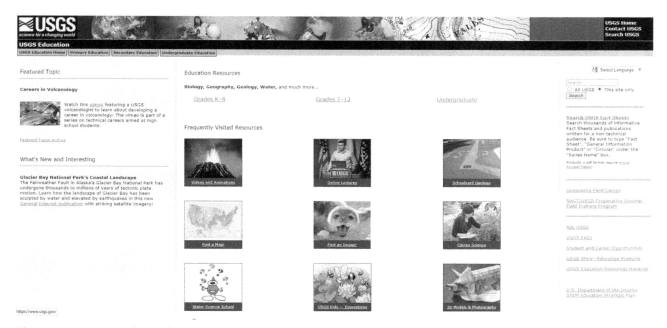

Figure 3.8 U.S. Geological Survey "Education Resources" webpage.
Source: USGS

Table 3.2 Example KWHL Chart on Animal Observations

K	W	H	L
What I know	**What I Want to Know**	**How will I find information?**	**What I learned**
Animals live in the zoo and in the wild. Animals eat food. There are many types of animals. Many animals have fur. Many animals sleep a lot.	How long do pandas live? What does the panda eat? Why are pandas endangered? Where are pandas from?	Use the Internet. Read books. Observe pandas via the webcam. Ask the teacher. Ask a scientist.	The panda eats bamboo. They are endangered because the bamboo forests are being cut down. Pandas are from China. Pandas live by themselves in the wild.

Another example is from the San Diego Zoo (www.zoo.sandiegozoo.org/content/video-more). Students may select animals to observe through San Diego Zoo's various animal cams. Possible animals they can observe include tigers, apes, koalas, pandas, polar bears, condors, and elephants. Student can be encouraged to ask questions like:

- What kind of animal is it?
- What are they doing, and why is it important to their species?
- What kinds of foods do they eat?
- How do they play?
- What do their habitats look like in the zoo versus in the wild?
- In what ways has the zoo matched this (or not)?

Students can use a graphic organizer, like a KWHL chart, to record their observations (see Table 3.2). A teacher can also use a KWHL chart to assess students' learning of scientific knowledge over time.

Students may also complete a digital animal journal to keep a record of observations. This will provide an opportunity for students to use inductive reasoning skills and analyze the data they collected over the period of time to answer questions they developed during the project.

Analyzing and representing data is an important skill for science education. Graph literacy, which includes the ability to compose and interpret graphs, is critical for students to understand and communicate findings. Students can compose graphs by hand, but software such as MS Excel is a common tool that students can use to record their collected data and data transformations. In MS Excel, students can create various graphs, including column, line, pie, and bar graphs. For instance, a group of students who have been engaged in learning about the life cycle of mealworms can create a table using MS Excel to represent the rate of metamorphosis of their mealworms (see Figure 3.9). This clustered column graph can be used to discuss the life cycle of mealworms.

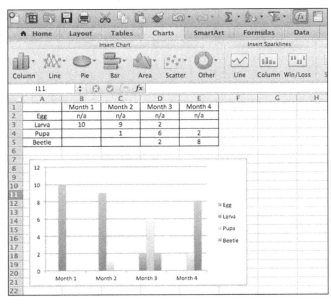

Figure 3.9 Screen capture of MS Excel Spreadsheet and Bar Graph of Mealworm Data.
Source: author

This method can also be applied to the life cycles of plants. For instance, students who have been engaged in observing the growth of sweet pea flowers can measure the changes inroots and stems over time and then transform their data table to a line graph. This line graph can be used to discuss the primary and secondary growth of plants. Students can also learn to use common functions and formulas in Excel, such as finding the sum, average, frequencies, and count of numbers.

Through Websites such as those from the USGS and the San Diego Zoo, students can investigate questions about our natural world. Like scientists, students will get to create their own conclusions from data as well as consider incomplete and uncertain information, examine complex patterns, and encounter the complexity of real-life science. With technological tools, students have opportunities to use actual scientific data and engage in authentic science exploration and learning while analyzing and representing data using graphical representations.

Table 3.3 includes additional examples of Websites with scientific data that students can access and analyze.

Table 3.3 Example of Websites with Scientific Data

Organization	Website	Suggestions
The United States Naval Observatory (USNO)	aa.usno.navy.mil/data/docs/RS_OneDay.php	Students can retrieve complete sun and moon data for one day.
National Oceanic and Atmospheric Administration (NOAA)	www.noaa.gov	Students can collect weather-related data.
The Cornell Lab of Ornithology	cams.allaboutbirds.org/all-cams	This is all about birds—students have recorded their live birds' cams.
Annenberg Learner Interactives	www.learner.org/interactives/parkphysics/index.html	Students can design a roller coaster.
Your Weight on other worlds	www.exploratorium.edu/ronh/weight	Students can collect data about their weights on different planets (i.e., Mercury, Venus, and others).

Things to Consider . . .

Although online sources can provide opportunities for data collection and analysis, there are aspects to consider for the science classroom (Trundle, 2008):

- Maintain focus on the topic by suggesting certain webpages for students to explore. There is so much information available online that students may become overwhelmed or drift off-task if they begin their exploration without guidance. Rubrics can often provide timelines and structure for completion as well as guidelines for quality.
- Consider what data are appropriate for the topic and grade level of students. There are many excellent Websites with data, but teachers must consider what is cognitively appropriate for the age of the students in relation to the objectives and goals of the science lesson.
- Think about how to make relevant data accessible. Since schools and districts may have firewalls, there may be limits on what can be accessed. Being prepared with accessible sources of data for a lesson will help ensure that it goes forth smoothly.

Technology as a Means for Videos, Animations, Imagery, Models, and Simulations

Technology can provide access to scientific phenomena via videos, models, simulations, images, and haptics (to be discussed later). These resources can help students learn abstract ideas and access visuals that may assist in the learning of scientific concepts.

Videos and Animations

As noted earlier, there are many Internet resources that provide videos and animations of scientific phenomena (e.g., YouTube). When used before a lesson, videos and animations can help introduce a topic or initiate discussion that reveals prior knowledge on a topic. When used after students explore a topic, videos and photos can help with concept development by providing greater explanations or elaboration on a topic. Video clips and animations can easily help illustrate abstract ideas. For example, teachers can use Web-based video clips to support the ideas behind the processes of digestion (e.g., www.kidshealth.org) or how the Earth's land masses have changed as viewed from space (www.landsat.gsfc.nasa.gov).

Teachers must ensure the video model's safety procedures are sound and age appropriate when selecting online media and videos for viewing (NSTA, 2005). One example can be found at www.youtube.com/watch?v=xJG0ir9nDtc. As a reminder, this includes making sure those in the video are wearing appropriate clothing and protective gear and that they are practicing safe handling of chemicals, fire, and biohazards. Videos should also be explicit in the safety concerns that are related to their content.

Students can also create videos, digital stories, and animations to explain their understanding, or elaborate on a topic. Software that students can use to create voiceover presentations, videos, or digital stories includes Windows Movie Maker, iMovie, or Brainshark. Animation tools such as AniMaker (www.animaker.com), GoAnimate (www.goanimate.com), OpenToonz (www.opentoonz.github.io/e), Plotagon (www.plotagon.com), or xtranormal (www.xtranormal.com) are available for students to use either for free or for a monthly fee. Creating videos or animations not only helps teachers assess student understanding of a concept but supports student-centered instruction that encourages creativity, collaboration, and application of knowledge to new situations.

Models and Simulations.

Teachers can use models and simulations for numerous science concepts (e.g., to explore how various forms of precipitation may impact erosion of a landscape). 3-D printing technology, if integrated with specific learning goals and pedagogical strategies, can lead to efficient and meaningful science learning and teaching experiences. Specifically, this emerging technology of made-to-order objects on a desktop affords students the opportunity to engage in building objects, prototypes, and models within free online virtual reality platforms (see Figure 3.10) such as Sketchup (www.sketchup.com/) or Tinkercad (www.tinkercad.com.) Subsequently, these computer-assisted digital designs are printed as 3-D objects at a low cost (see Figure 3.11). Reports from the NSTA (2013) indicate that these types of inexpensive fabrication technologies can help students see how STEM fields are connected. Other benefits include students being able to understand the relationship between scientific concepts and real-world contexts.

For integrating 3-D printing technology, teachers are encouraged to use a project-based learning strategy and provide real-world scenarios for students to solve real-world problems (e.g., renovating an old farm to modernize crop transport, building an emergency rescue boat for lifeguards) (Morales, Bang, & Andre, 2012). Also, it is important to provide students with multiple chances to modify, discuss, and then refine their digital designs as well as their 3-D printed models (NSTA, 2013).

Figure 3.10 Student experiences virtual reality.

Another example of building models can be done via Internet sources. One is the Atom Builder (www.pbs.org/wgbh/aso/tryit/atom). On this Website, students are challenged to manipulate parts of an elemental atom to design a neutral atom. Students can build models of atoms and molecules to understand the interaction between charged particles and what occurs when bonds form or break between atoms.

Yet another Web-based simulator is the University of Colorado Boulder's Physics Education Technology Project (PhET). PhET provides multiple simulators on various mathematics and science topics (see Figure 3.12) such as genetic adaptation, energy transformation, plate tectonics, and molecular structures (www.phet.colorado.edu/en/simulations/category/new). In PhET's Build-A-Molecule simulator (www.phet.colorado.edu/en/simulation/build-a-molecule), for example, students can explore simulated molecules and practice creating molecules from atoms (see Figure 3.13). This hands-on approach reinforces the meaning of subscripts and coefficients in molecular formulas. The simulators also help students connect molecular names with multiple visual representations of different molecules. In the States-Of-Matter-Basics simulator (www.phet.colorado.edu/en/simulation/states-of-matter-basics), users can explore the differences between solids, liquids, and gases, and the impact of volume, temperature, and pressure on each state (see Figure 3.14). This helps students to see the movement of molecules through changes in states of matter and explore the relationships between each state and volume, temperature, and pressure.

Figure 3.11 3-D printing technology examples.

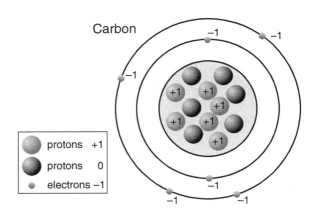

Figure 3.12 Screen capture from Atom Builder.

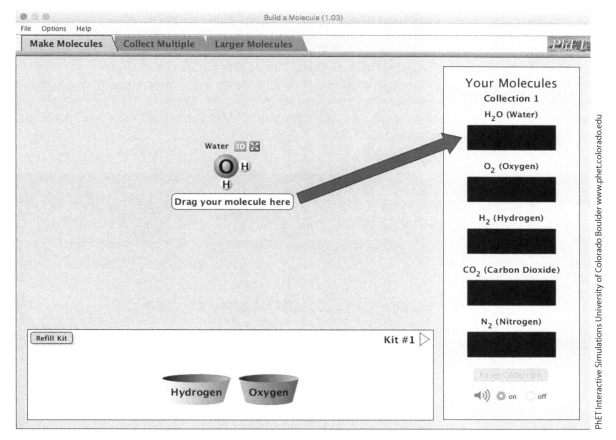

Figure 3.13 Screenshot of PhET's Build-A-Molecule simulator.

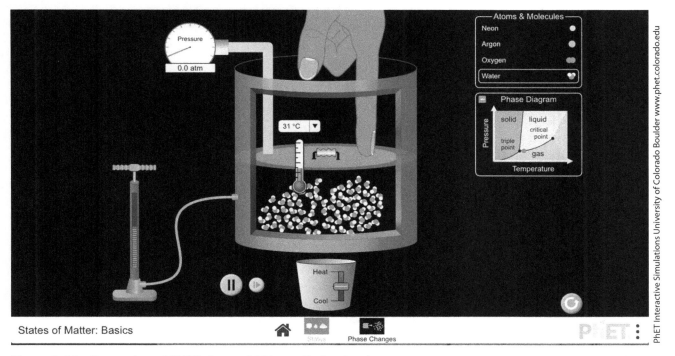

Figure 3.14 Screenshot of PhET's States-Of-Matter-Basics simulator.

Imagery and simulation technology can even help students "travel in space." The National Aeronautics Space Administration (NASA) Website (www.nasa.gov) is a great resource for images and simulations. Specifically, collaboration between NASA and the Jet Propulsion Laboratory has resulted in online simulation and modeling programs that students can access to learn and explore our solar system (e.g., www.space.jpl.nasa.gov). Through this online simulator, students can change their location in the solar system to show what they are viewing from that perspective (see Figure 3.15). For example, students can simulate viewing the different moons of Jupiter from the planet Jupiter or "view" our sun from Mars by modifying the settings provided on the Website.

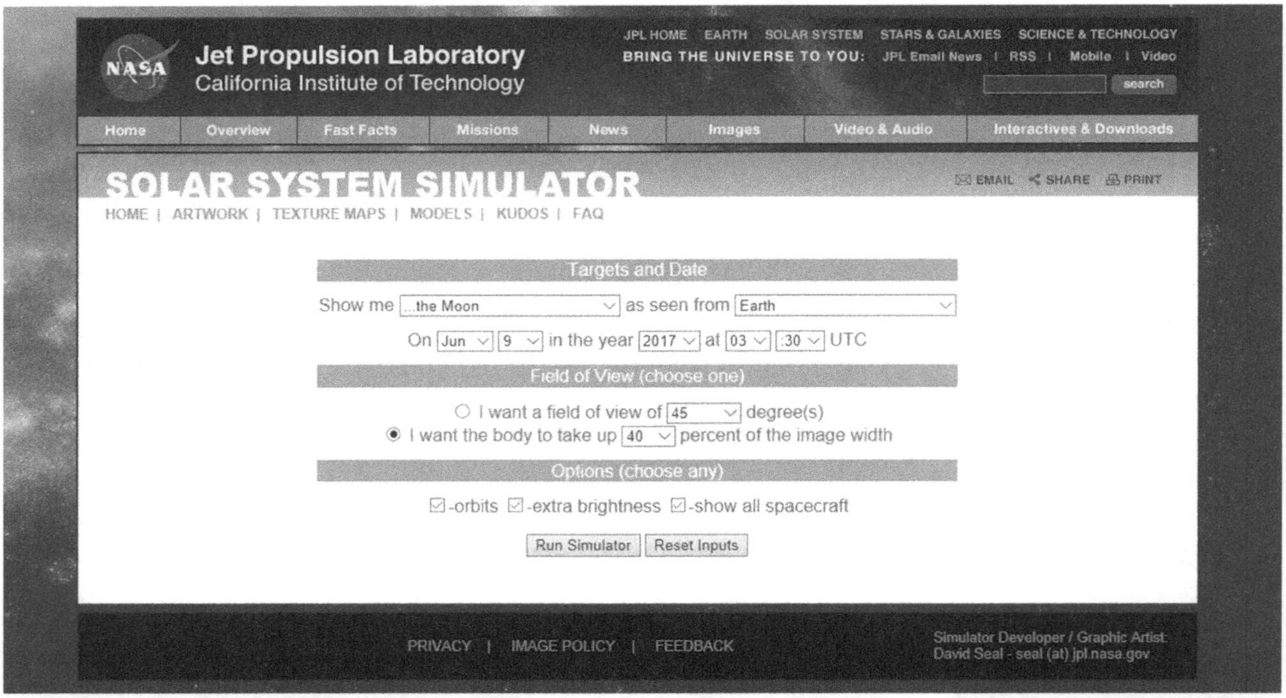

Figure 3.15 NASA Jet Propulsion Laboratory Home Page (www.space.jpl.nasagov).
Source: NASA

Students can also modify the date and time of the simulations to view changes over time. For example, an inquiry activity on phases of the moon may include opportunities for students to explore images of the moon over a period of one month (see Figure 3.16). Students may be asked to observe the moon and note anything interesting. By comparing images of the moon over time, students may construct patterns and understanding of the phases of the moon and how they change over time.

Figure 3.16 Simulation using settings from Figure 3.15.
Source: NASA

Haptic Technology

Technology can even help students feel and experience force, pressure, and temperature via haptic devices which are physical devices that students can hold or touch and are programmed to provide realistic reactions for choices or motions completed by the user. The physical movement involved in this type of technology may support learning of content (Paul, 2014) as well as increase engagement in the content. For example, haptic devices have been developed to allow students to control space shuttles in a simulation of exploration of our solar system. As the student maneuvers the virtual spaceship with a handheld device, he or she can feel an increase in temperature as the "ship" veers closer to the sun. When the student maneuvers the spaceship to land on a planet, the device will resist the user's hand, simulating the pull of gravitational force. Common haptic devices that students may already interact with include video gaming controls. For example, in car racing games, Nintendo's Wii handheld controls may vibrate when one car collides with another. There is an expectation that more of these types of devices will enter the science classroom in years to come. One can certainly see their potential for fostering student learning of science concepts.

Table 3.4 includes examples of Internet resources for images and visualizations:

Table 3.4 Example of Internet Resources for Images and Visualizations

Organization	Website	Suggestions
Mars student imaging project	www.mars.nasa.gov/msip	Students can take a picture of Mars using a camera on the NASA's Mars Odyssey orbiter.
Try Science	www.tryscience.org/fieldtrips/fieldtrip_home.html	Virtual field trips to science centers, experiments, etc.
Edheads	www.edheads.org	Students can engage in virtual activities that meet state and national standards (e.g., simple machines, virtual knee surgery, stem cell heart repair, etc.) Students can engage in interactive Web platforms designed for children.
InnerBody	www.innerbody.com	Students can learn about human body systems using a virtual human anatomy system.
Virtual Lab	www.mhhe.com/biosci/genbio/virtual_labs/BL_16/BL_16.html	Students can become virtually involved in frog dissections.
U.S. Environmental Protection Agency (EPA)	www.epa.gov/kidshometour	Students can learn about chemicals (including their basic uses and interactions) around their households.

Things to Consider . . .

Suggestions on how to meaningfully integrate images and visualizations include:

- Purposefully choosing images and videos that target the specific content and instructional goals to provide a view of what students may not normally see.
- Using images and visualizations to provide clarification or stimulate questions and interest.
- Including meaningful images or simulations that stimulate questioning and student inquiry. Ask questions such as:
  - What do you see?
  - What do you think the different colors represent?
  - What do you see when you compare these different images?
- The focus should be on student-driven observations and conclusions and not on the teacher pointing out what should be noticed (Bell & Park, 2008).

- Simulations should supplement instruction and not replace it (Bell & Smetana, 2008). Consider what the simulation can do that another strategy cannot, the time it will take to implement the simulation, and how the simulation can be integrated in a student-centered way. Technology can be a less expensive and less time-consuming way to provide an experience, but if the "real" experience is available and ethical for students, it must be considered first.
- Determine how the simulation can be incorporated so that the focus remains on the content. Technology may become distracting due to the time required to learn how to use the tools. It can also become distracting because the interactive nature of some technology, and its application can be *overly* engaging for students. One way to help students maintain focus is to help students work through the initial setup or manipulations so that they can utilize the simulation as intended.

Technology as a Means to Inquiry and Collaborate with the Scientific Community

Technology is important for authentic science learning experiences, but these experiences must also include collaboration and community participation (Lombardi, 2007) within the school or with others outside of the school setting. Collaboration is essential for students to share and construct knowledge through social interaction (Brooks & Brooks, 1999). Social networking tools can connect students with other students at a different location or experts in the field to share questions and ideas.

Students can use technology to synchronously (together in real time) or asynchronously (at various times) to share information and products within a group or across groups with blogs, e-portfolios, video-capture tools, and online platforms (Lombardi, 2007).

Connecting students with scientists can provide an engaging and authentic learning experience. Communications software (e.g., Skype or Google Hangouts) may be used to connect students with scientists from around the world. This could be an opportunity for scientists to share their work and current findings with students to support and enrich the ideas under study. For example, NASA's Johnson Space Center provides opportunities for elementary and secondary schools to connect with astronauts aboard the International Space Station via a live downlink (www.nasa.gov/offices/education/centers/johnson/downlinks). Schools can also contact local colleges and universities to set up opportunities for scientists and researchers to visit schools and students.

Prior to any student/scientist interaction, students should prepare questions to ask the scientist to gain insight into the topic as well as the science profession. The opportunity to see scientists in authentic contexts may also remind students that science is a diverse field. Scientists themselves are diverse—as well as their areas of study. Scientists can be of any gender, any ethnicity, various ages, and in various environments. Misconceptions about science can be confronted when students see that science does not always happen in a laboratory and that scientists can be of any race or gender. Connecting students with a diverse array of scientists in various fields can help to reinforce that there are many areas in science that they can pursue.

Collaboration allows students to compare their own science processes and knowledge with others. Students also develop greater understanding of the nature of science when students compare how scientists in different cultures or settings address and explore scientific phenomena. Science is socially and culturally embedded. With technology, students can develop a more complex and authentic image of what science is and how scientists "do" science.

Citizen Science

The need for public understanding of the processes and goals in scientific research has never been greater—so much so that science organizations and professionals often include an educational component in their research design (Bonney et al., 2009; Dickinson et al., 2012; Jordan, Gray, Howe, Brooks, & Ehrenfeld, 2011). "Citizen Science" enables the public to assist in genuine scientific research through the collection and analysis of large amounts of data (see Figure 3.17). Individual teachers and schools have encouraged students to participate in Citizen Science-type projects for many years; however, access to the Internet both at school and home now allow the public to participate in scientific data collection and analysis all over the world and beyond. Table 3.5 provides examples of online resources for Citizen Science.

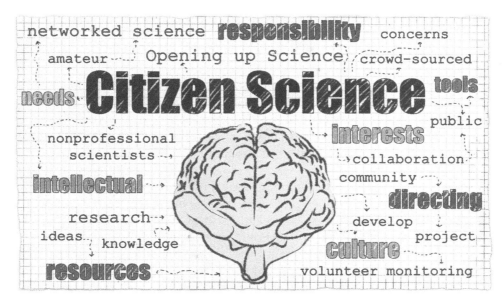

Figure 3.17 Citizen Science enables the public to assist in genuine scientific research through the collection and analysis of large amount of data.

Table 3.5 Citizen Science Websites

Website	Use
www.scientificamerican.com/citizen-science/	Database of Citizen Science research projects listed on the Scientific American Website.
www.zooniverse.org/projects?discipline=language&page=1&status=live	The world's largest platform for science volunteers around the world. Enables research between volunteers and professional scientists and boasts numerous publications as a result of research conducted through their platform.
www.projectnoah.org	Designed out of New York University's Interactive Telecommunications Program in early 2010, Project Noah is a platform which enables people to use their mobile devices to reconnect with the natural world and appreciate local wildlife.
www.planethunters.org	Utilized data from NASA's *Kepler* spacecraft to analyze light patterns in stars for the detection of exoplanets.

Although not all scientific fields are represented by Citizen Science research, volunteers can actively participate and contribute to research in ornithology, astronomy, atmospheric sciences, botany, herpetology, and molecular biology. As interest in involving the public in scientific research has increased, so have available avenues to participate in Citizen Science.

Project Noah (www.projectnoah.org) encourages users to explore the natural world that is in their backyards by taking photos of plants and animals (spottings) with their smartphone, uploading them to the online database, and identifying them. *Project Noah* also combines aspects of social media by allowing members to comment on each other's spottings and make suggestions regarding species identification. *Planet Hunters* (www.planethunters.org), another example, allows individuals to analyze data from NASA's Kepler spacecraft to search for exoplanets (planets outside of our solar system) via a characteristic drop in light as they pass in front of their parent star. This platform, with hundreds of thousands of volunteers, has led to significant scientific discoveries and publications. *Bold Systems* (www.boldsystems.org) takes cataloging life on planet Earth to the molecular level through the acquisition, storage, analysis, and publication of DNA barcode records

(Ratnasingham & Hebert, 2007). Websites such as Zooniverse (www.zooniverse.org) and www.citizenscience.org are clearinghouses of both large and small Citizen Science research projects. These projects can be incorporated into science classrooms and enable students and teachers to actively participate in scientific research and discovery.

In addition to scientific research and discoveries, data collected by Citizen Scientists can be used to save lives and improve the environment. For instance, six months after Hurricane Harvey hit the Texas Gulf Coast, causing historical flooding, the Texas state climatologist office called for the assistance of citizens, seeking observations of the distribution of rainfall amounts made during Hurricane Harvey to help determine the effects of the storm. In addition to any observations, they are also interested in the sites where the data were collected and the gauges used.

Specifically, the state climatologist office made requests through Houston local news channels for citizens to complete a brief online survey. The survey prompt read, "By participating in this survey, you will help in figuring out the amount of rain that fell during Hurricane Harvey. Other scientists will use the data provided to consider the effects of rain on residents and the environment in the Houston area. We will also use data from different gauges to see how well they measured the storm's rain." The state government will use the contributed data to build a better model for the future to help avoid the drastic damage by flooding which occurred during this storm (www.abc13.com/weather/heres-how-you-can-help-with-hurricane-harvey-research-/3069822 and www.climatexas.tamu.edu/harvey/survey/index.html).

The full potential of Citizen Science is just beginning to be understood, but researchers such as Dickinson et al. (2012) note that Citizen Science research projects have had profound positive impacts on the level of civic engagement in science by allowing "the public to participate in authentic research experiences at various stages in the scientific process and using modern communications tools to recruit and retain participants" (p. 291).

Next Generation Educational Technology

Educators are constantly thinking of ways to integrate next generation technology in the science classroom. Although many tools are not necessarily generated for educational purposes, many have applications that can help students be more engaged and creative during the learning process (Luckerson, 2014). For example, 3-D imaging software, such as Maya or Blender, allows students to add details such as texture and shading to animations, models, and simulations. The following are examples of additional next generation technology that can be used to foster science learning:

- While used primarily for commercial and entertainment purposes, augmented reality (AR) holds great promise as a learning tool for science education. AR has the potential for inquiry-based approaches to science learning, as it: presents content and phenomena in 3-D perspectives; enables situated learning; supports a learner's sense of presence, immediacy, and immersion; visualizes the invisible; and bridges formal and informal learning (Brandt, Nielsen, Georgsen, & Swensen, 2015; Wu, Lee, Chang, & Liang, 2013).
- 3-D printers are becoming increasingly affordable and accessible. For example, MakerBot is a 3-D printer that can be found in over 5,000 schools in the United States. Students can use these printers to create models for educational purposes. Students can create cars to learn about physics or frogs to learn about anatomy. Students have also used 3-D printers to create functional artificial limbs when tasked to address a current need in society.
- Next generation textbooks such as the SmartBook by McGraw-Hill (www.mheducation.com/highered/platforms/smartbook.html) will highlight important concepts and assess students at the end of chapters through quizzes. Teachers can also access student data from the SmartBook to gauge student progress.
- Chalkboards of tomorrow will be connected with student computers. For example, Hewlett-Packard is developing a touchscreen chalkboard that will allow students to duplicate notes and access multimedia through a wireless connection from the chalkboard to the students' individual computers.

- Classroom desks of tomorrow will be designed to be more adaptable to changing needs during lessons. Currently, there are mobile desks that convert from individual desks to a larger work surface to foster small group activities.
- Forward thinking toys are being developed to teach important topics, such as compassion and empathy. For instance, the Empathy Toy (empathytoy.com), which was funded by Kickstarter, is a toy found in classrooms around the world that engages students in creating a building block structure while blindfolded. Having empathy for others is critical when working in collaborative groups during science activities and investigations, and, indeed, much of scientific research involves decisions for real people in critical situations.

A Framework for Integrating Technology into the Science Classroom (TPACK)

The Technological Pedagogical Content Knowledge (TPACK) framework (Koehler & Mishra, 2009) can help explain the essential areas of knowledge needed to effectively integrate technology in schools (see Figure 3.18). According to the TPACK framework, learning-to-teach science with technology includes three essential knowledge fields: content knowledge (CK), pedagogical knowledge (PK), and technology knowledge (TK). When the three knowledge fields of CK, PK, and TK are merged together, four new intersecting areas of knowledge emerge in the framework: pedagogical content knowledge (PCK), technological content knowledge (TCK), and technological pedagogical knowledge (TPK). Ultimately, the intersection between CK, PK, and TK results in TPACK. The following figure brings each of these areas forth so that the teacher can see the "big picture" and the details of what he or she should know when approaching a science/technology lesson.

The TPACK framework should be used as a thinking tool to consider important kinds of knowledge for effective teaching with technology. In this framework, the role of content, pedagogy, and technology is equally important as the combination of the three forms of knowledge. According to Koehler and Mishra

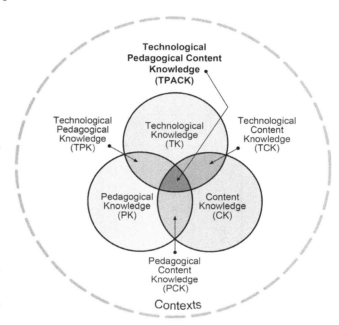

Figure 3.18 The Technological Pedagogical Content Knowledge (TPACK) Framework for learning-to-teach science with technology.
Source: Reproduced by permission of the publisher, © 2012 by tpack.org

(2009), the individual and interrelated nature of content, pedagogy, and technology in the TPACK framework is complex. Teachers need to be flexible when negotiating each of these areas, and they should also know that each one also affects all of the others in various ways. Please refer to Table 3.6 for examples of how the TPACK framework can apply in the context of science teaching.

Understanding the different forms of technology and the insight that thinking deeply about one's teaching brings through the TPACK framework may help teachers integrate technology in effective and purposeful ways. It also illuminates the highly complex field that is science teaching. Often, each component of TPACK is studied on an individual basis. The power of the TPACK framework is to consider how these domains interact to reveal the complex nature of knowledge and practice. Technology is a powerful tool that can enhance or hinder science teaching and learning. It should not be oversimplified or used without purpose.

Table 3.6 Components of the TPACK Framework

Knowledge Field	Description	Examples in the context of science teaching	Examples of self-generated questions	Examples of what I currently know
Content knowledge (CK)	Knowledge about the subject or content that is to be taught. Not only is the CK in science different than other subject areas like history or language arts, the CK is also different by age of the students and grade levels.	• Knowledge of science concepts and the nature of science Scientific inquiry. • Scientific facts, theories, methods, and evidence-based reasoning.	Q) What are the content objectives of my lesson? Q) What are the major ideas I want to ensure my students understand about food chains and food webs?	• Food chains are linear sequences that show the energy transformation from one living organism to another via food. • Food webs show the interconnected pathways between different food chains in an ecosystem.
Pedagogical knowledge (PK)	Knowledge about the general techniques, methods, and instructional practices of the act of teaching and teaching for understanding. PK includes educational goals and rationales as well as understanding "how students learn, general classroom management skills, lesson planning, and student assessment" (Koehler & Mishra, 2009, p. 64).	• General strategies for teaching, learning, and assessment. • Cooperative learning strategies. • Knowledge of students and their lived experiences. • Understanding how students construct knowledge and learn skills. • Knowledge of "cognitive, social, and developmental theories of learning and how they apply to students in the classroom" (Koehler & Mishra, 2009, p. 64).	Q) What would be the most effective teaching and learning methods for my upcoming lesson (e.g., classroom management, collaborative learning roles, teacher roles, and diagnostic, formative and summative assessments)?	• Student-centered, inquiry-based science learning and teaching • The 5E Model of Instruction (Engage-Explore-Explain-Elaborate-Evaluate)
Techno-logical knowledge (TK)	Knowledge that is necessary to think about and work with technology and how to apply technology in and out of the classroom setting. TK includes the notion that technology can help or hinder objectives and being able to recognize changes in technology and adapt to the changes.	• How to use a microscope, digital scale, graphing calculator, etc.	Q) In what ways may I apply available technology tools and resources that will work best to achieve the goals of my upcoming lesson?	• Websites • Databasesa • Simulations • Tools for collaboration

Knowledge Field	Description	Examples in the context of science teaching	Examples of self-generated questions	Examples of what I currently know
Pedagogical content knowledge (PCK)	Knowledge of what pedagogy is appropriate and necessary to teach certain content and how to translate content for teaching. "PCK covers the core business of teaching, learning, curriculum, assessment and reporting, such as the conditions that promote learning and the links among curriculum, assessment, and pedagogy" (Koehler & Mishra, 2009, p. 64).	• How to teach science content, such as food chains and food webs? • How to teach science content to students of specific grade levels, such as fourth grade, seventh grade, or eleventh grade?	Q) In what ways may I interpret the targeting of big ideas, scientific practices, and crosscutting concepts? Q) In what ways can I find ways to represent these three dimensions? Q) In what ways can I tailor the instructional materials to students' prior knowledge?	• Alignment among objectives, activities, and assessments. • The best strategies to teach the content to the diverse student population.
Technological content knowledge (TCK)	Knowledge of how content and technology interact, including benefits and constraints. Teachers need to recognize that content can be influenced by specific technology, and they should be able to purposefully select technology that will support content learning.	• How to select technology to teach the science content? • How to use technology to teach the science content? • Consider the time investment of teaching students to use the technology in comparison to the frequency of using the tool. • What is the best tool to teach the concept?	Q) What do I know about the ways in which certain types of technology tools and resources either facilitate or hinder the learning of scientific concepts? Q) Based on these initial assessments, what are my choices of technologies for the scientific concepts?	• Class Websites and blogs. • Handheld digital devices (e.g., tablet computers and probeware/sensors). • Interactive media. • Laptops. • Mobile devices (M-learning) (e.g., PIAZZA). • Online media (e.g., YouTube). • Data sets from Internet sources. • Simulation and modeling programs.

(Continued)

Table 3.6 Components of the TPACK Framework (*Continued*)

Knowledge Field	Description	Examples in the context of science teaching	Examples of self-generated questions	Examples of what I currently know
Technological pedagogical knowledge (TPK)	Knowledge of how technology can impact teaching and learning. TPK is important since most technologies were not created for educational purposes. TPK allows teachers to be creative and open-minded in recognizing the limits and possibilities of technology and adapting the technology to support teaching and learning.	• Instead of having the whiteboard at the front of the room mainly for teacher use, consider how to make it accessible by all students to promote brainstorming and collaboration. • Software like Microsoft Office Suite was designed for business settings. Consider other options like Google docs to support collaboration between students, teachers, and others outside of the classroom.	Q) What do I know about how certain types of technology tools and resources either facilitate or hinder teaching and learning? Q) Based on these initial assessments, what are the choices of technologies for my teaching and learning? Q) In what ways can these technologies be cross-examined in terms of how students learn and inquiry-based, student-centered learning?	• Class Websites and blogs. • Handheld digital devices (e.g., tablet computers and probeware/sensors). • Interactive media. Laptops. • Mobile devices (M-learning) (e.g., PIAZZA). • Online media (e.g., YouTube). • Data sets from Internet sources. • Simulation and modeling programs.
Technological pedagogical content knowledge (TPACK)	Knowledge of effective instruction integrating technology, pedagogy, and content. Teachers need to recognize that different circumstances and contexts impact how CK, PK, and TK is considered. Teachers must be flexible in how to negotiate the three forms of knowledge and highlight the complexities of each.	• The combination of knowing the science content, how to teach the science content, and what technology is the most appropriate to teach the science content. • What are the strategies and technologies most appropriate for teaching various content (e.g., food chains and food webs).	Q) What are the elements of effective learning-to-teach science with technology?	• Incorporating simulation software in an inquiry-based lesson to teacher—food webs and food chains.

Note: Koehler, M. J., & Mishra, P. (2009). What is technological pedagogical content knowledge? *Contemporary Issues in Technology and Teacher Education, 9*(1), 60–70.

Summary

Teachers must carefully consider the complexity of teaching science with technology. Technology can help students to access content, collect data, and analyze data. Technology can also provide images and simulations as well as connect students with the scientific community. The TPACK framework can also help to unpack the components of the complex task of science teaching. Although technology offers many benefits, teaching science with technology requires purposeful planning and meaningful integration of technology. It is not simply asking students to create a slideshow or assigning students to use the Internet to research a topic. Technology must be incorporated purposefully, intentionally, and equitably in the science classroom.

Mrs. Calander continues to think about the complexity of teaching science with technology. There are many resources to consider. Remembering the TPACK framework helped her to bring together all of the components of the complex task of teaching science. Mrs. Calander realizes that teaching science with technology is not simply showing students a video clip, asking small groups to use a digital tool to collect data without purpose, or having students go on to the Internet. Incorporating technology in the science classroom requires a detailed plan with multiple goals, rationales, and thoughtful integration of the many tools available. She begins to think through the process of what students must know combined with what technology tools would best support them. The lesson begins to take shape and the TPACK framework reminds her of the many details that go into having students learn and be excited about science.

References

Annetta, L., Burton, E. P., Frazier, W., Cheng, R., & Chmiel, M. (2012). Augmented reality games: Using technology on a budget. *Science Scope, 36*(3), 54–60.

Baker, D. R., & Piburn, M. D. (2007). *Constructing science in middle and secondary school classrooms*. Needham Height, MA: Allyn and Bacon.

Bell, L., & Park, J. C. (2008). Digital images and video for teaching science. In R. L. Bell, J. Gess-Newsome, & J. Luft (Eds.), *Technology in the secondary science classroom* (pp. 9–22). Arlington, VA: NSTA press.

Bell, R. L., & Smetana, L. K. (2008). Using computer simulations to enhance science teaching and learning. In R. L. Bell, J. Gess-Newsome, & J. Luft (Eds.), *Technology in the secondary science classroom* (pp. 23–32). Arlington, VA: NSTA press.

Bonney, R., Cooper, C. B., Dickinson, J., Kelling, S., Phillips, T., Rosenberg, K. V., & Shirk, J. (2009). Citizen Science: A developing tool for expanding science knowledge and scientific literacy. *BioScience, 59*(11), 977–984.

Brandt, H., Nielsen, B. L., Georgsen, M., & Swensen, H. (2015). Augmented reality for science education. Lecture Notes in Computer Science. In *EC-TEL 2015*. Retrieved from www.ucviden.dk/ws/files/32050386/Augmented_Reality_for_Science_Education.pdf

Brooks, J., & Brooks, M. (1999). Chapteer 9: Becoming a constructivist teacher. In J. Brooks & M. Brooks (Eds.), *In search of understanding: The case of constructivist classrooms* (pp. 101–118). Alexandria, VA: ASCD.

Casey, S. (2017). 2016 Nielsen Social Media Report. Retrieved from www.nielsen.com/us/en/insights/reports/2017/2016-nielsen-social-media-report.html

Craig, D. V. (1999). Science and technology: A great combination. *Science and Children, 36*(4), 28–32.

Dickinson, J., Shirk, J., Bonter, D., Bonney, R., Crain, R. L., Martin, J., Phillips, T., & Purcell, K. (2012). The current state of citizen science as a tool for ecological research and public engagement. *Frontiers in Ecology and the Environment, 10*(6), 291–297.

Flick, L., & Bell, R. (2000). Preparing tomorrow's science teachers to use technology: Guidelines for science educators. *Contemporary Issues in Technology and Teacher Education, 1*(1), 39–60.

Herrington, J., Oliver R., & Reeves, T. C. (2003). Patterns of engagement in authentic online learning environments. *Australian Journal of Educational Technology, 19*(1), 59–71. Retrieved from www.ascilite.org.au/ajet/ajet19/herrington.html

Jordan, R. C., Gray, S. A., Howe, D. V., Brooks, W. R., & Ehrenfeld, J. G. (2011). Knowledge gain and behavioral change in citizen-science programs. *Conservation Biology, 25*(6), 1148–1154.

Kim, M. K., Kim, S. M., Khera, O., & Getman, J. (2014). The experience of three flipped classrooms in an urban university: An exploration of design principles. *The Internet and Higher Education, 22*, 37–50.

Koehler, M. J., & Mishra, P. (2009). What is technological pedagogical content knowledge? *Contemporary Issues in Technology and Teacher Education, 9*(1), 60–70.

Lederman, N. G. (2007). Nature of science: Past, present, and future. In S. K. Abell & N. G. Lederman (Eds.), *Handbook of research on science education* (pp. 831–880). Mahwah, NJ: Lawrence Erlbaum Associates.

Libman, D., & Huang, L. (2013). Chemistry on the go: Review of chemistry apps on smartphones. Journal of Chemical Education, *90*(3), 320–325.

Lombardi, M. (2007). *Authentic learning for the 21st century: An overview.* Educause Learning Initiative, ELI Paper 1/:2007. Retrieved from www.alicechristie.org/classes/530/EduCause.pdf

Luckerson, V. (2014, September 22). Too cool for school: Disruptive tech is changing how kids learn. *Time, 184*, 16.

Lucking, R. A., Christmann, E. P., & Wighting, M. J. (2010, January). Cell phones for science. *Science Scope, 33*, 58–61.

Lyublinskaya, I., & Zhou, G. (2008). Integrating graphing calculators and probeware into science methods courses: Impacts on preservice elementary teachers' confidence and perspectives on technology for learning and teaching. *Journal of Computers in Mathematics & Science Teaching, 27*(2), 163–182.

Martin, D. J. (2012). *Elementary science methods: A constructivist approach.* Independence, KY: Wadsworth.

Milman, N. B. (2012). The flipped classroom strategy: What is it and how can it best be used? *Distance Learning, 9*(13), 85–87.

Morales, T., Bang, E., & Andre, T. (2012). A one-year case study: Understanding the rich potential of project-based learning in a virtual reality class for high school students. *Journal of Science Education and Technology, 22*(5), 791–806.

National Association for the Education of the Young Child (NAEYC). (n. d.). Science, technology, engineering and math resources for early childhood. Retrieved from www.naeyc.org/STE

National Center for Education Statistics. (2002). *Science highlights: The nation's report card 2000.* U.S. Department of Education Office of Educational Research and Improvement. NCES 2002–452. Retrieved from www.nces.ed.gov/nationsreportcard/pubs/main2000/2002452.asp

National Science Teachers Association (NSTA). (2005). *Safety in the science classroom.* (Safety Issue Papers by NSTA's Safety Advisory Board). Washington, DC: Author.

NGSS Lead States. (2013). *Next generation science standards: For states, by states.* Washington, DC: The National Academies Press.

NSTA Reports. (2013, September). Teaching STEM in 3D. National Science Teachers Association. Retrieved from www.static.nsta.org/pdfs/2013SeptemberReports.pdf

Park, J. C. (2008). Probeware tools for science investigations. In R. L. Bell, J. Gess-Newsome, & J. Luft (Eds.), *Technology in the secondary science classroom* (pp. 33–42). Arlington, VA: NSTA press.

Paul, A. M. (2014, July 9). Is the body the next breakthrough in education tech? *The Hechinger Report.* Retrieved from www.hechingerreport.org/content/body-next-breakthrough-education-tech_16629/

Ratnasingham, S., & Hebert, P. D. N. (2007). BOLD: The barcode of life data system (www.barcodinglife.org). *Molecular Ecology Notes, 7*, 355–364. doi:10.1111/j.1471-8286.2006.01678.x

Strayer, J. F. (2012). How learning in an inverted classroom influences cooperation, innovation and task orientation. *Learning Environments Research, 15*(2), 171–193.

Thornton, R. K. (2008). Effective learning environments for computer supported instruction in the physics classroom and laboratory. In M. Vicentini & E. Sassi (Eds.), *Connecting research in physics education with teacher education.* International Commission on Physics Education. Retrieved from www.web.phys.ksu.edu/icpe/Publications/teach2/Thornton.pdf

Trundle, K C. (2008). Acquiring online data for scientific analysis. In R. L. Bell, J. Gess-Newsome, & J. Luft (Eds.), *Technology in the secondary science classroom* (pp. 53–62). Arlington, VA: NSTA press.

Vieyra, R., Vieyra, C., Jeanjacquot, P., Marti, A., & Monteiro, M. (2015, December). Turn your smartphone into a science laboratory. *The Science Teacher, 82*, 32–40.

Wallace, R. M. (2002, May). *Technology and science teaching: A new kind of knowledge.* Paper presented at the Technology and its Integration in Mathematics Education (TIME) conference, Battle Creek, MI. Retrieved from www.msu.edu/course/cep/953/readings/WallaceTimeFinal.pdf

Windschitl, M. (1998). Independent student inquiry: Unlocking the resources of the World Wide Web. *NASSP Bulletin, 82*, 93–98.

Wu, H. K., Lee, S. W. Y., Chang, H. Y., & Liang, J. C. (2013). Current status, opportunities and challenges of augmented reality in education. *Computers & Education, 62*, 41–49.

Chapter 4

Teaching and Learning Mathematics in Technologically Intensive Classrooms

Michael L. Connell and Jacqueline Sack, *University of Houston - Downtown*

Sergei Abramovich, *State University of New York at Potsdam*

Meet Ms. Josephson

Ms. Josephson, the lead mathematics teacher at River View Middle School, is concerned by her students' declining problem-solving scores. She is perplexed because these same students' **computation** scores have been going up. After sharing this concern with her principal, she has been asked to provide suggestions to update the software used in the school's computer lab. As she investigates further, she is amazed at the resources available to reinforce computation, but, unfortunately, that is not the problem her students are facing. There are also many resources to address problem-solving; however, the problems do not relate to the curriculum she is responsible for teaching. How can she bridge between the skills her students have and the problems they need to solve?

Michaeljung / shutterstock.com

Where Are We Now?

Mathematics instruction is currently undergoing significant shifts concerning the nature of content as well as the manner in which foundational understandings are to be developed. For example, the National Council of Teachers of Mathematics (NCTM), through their ongoing efforts to implement their Principles and Standards for School Mathematics (2000), has been changing the face of what constitutes mathematics and how we think about its teaching and learning. Of particular note for this chapter is that this focus includes an increased emphasis upon the dual nature of mathematics itself, which must be understood if technology is to be used

---

effectively. Basically, when viewed as a content area, mathematics has a "bit of a split personality." To use an example from language art, there are parts of mathematics that function very much like a noun (the concepts of mathematics), while others function much more like a verb (procedures, which many think of as "actually 'doing' math").

Such a language-based analogy has a long history in mathematics education. Max Beberman (1925 to 1971), often regarded as one of the pioneers in modern mathematics education reform, felt that without a proper language in which to ask and answer questions, mathematics can degenerate into training students to give rote answers to trivial exam questions (www.web.math.rochester.edu/people/faculty/rarm/beberman.html). Many teacher candidates can attest to the accuracy of this observation.

As one develops such a proper language, Davis (1992) hinted at a noun/verb distinction within which children learn many parts of mathematics as "operations," and only later, as a result of reflecting upon their actions, do they come to see that each process can be seen as a thing in itself. Sfard (1991) went further and illustrated that abstract notions such as number and function can be thought of in two fundamentally different ways—as objects acting in a noun-like fashion, or operationally, as verbs acting as procedures. To have an overall comprehensible picture of mathematics, a learner *and* a teacher must have a clear understanding of how mathematics works in both ways.

To expand on this notion, when a teacher uses the word *sphere*, most students will picture a rounded ball-like shape in their mind. This memory is very "noun-like" in that it may be described, and its properties can be expanded. For example, a student could initially have thought about a baseball. This evokes a different set of properties than if they had thought of a tennis ball, a golf ball, or a table tennis ball. If we think of a "baseball" as being a noun, then "seamed" is an adjective which may be used to describe it. Therefore, we see that a baseball has raised seams, a tennis ball is fuzzy, a golf ball is dimpled, and a table tennis ball is smooth. They also have different sizes, bounce differently, have different colors, and so on.

Despite these additional properties, there is a "sphere-like" property common to each. As a more formal concept of "sphere" is developed, this core mathematical idea plays a noun-like role. The properties which a sphere can have, such as radius and location, play the role of adjectives. A sphere can have a radius of 5 cm in the same sense that a baseball can have seams. The seams are a property of the baseball (Figure 4.1), and the radius is a property of the sphere. Clearly, there are many "noun-like" portions of mathematics which play an important role in developing new ideas. This type of mathematical understanding gives us things to think *about* and forms the basis for later, more formalized *concepts*.

Now, let us consider an alternate type of mathematical structure—a *procedure*, or set of actions. If a student had earlier pictured a baseball when asked to visualize a *sphere,*

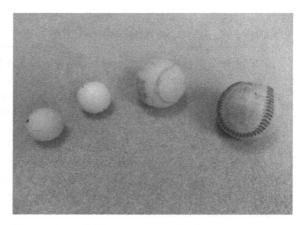

Figure 4.1   Different types of spheres.
Source: Michael L. Connell

it might be perfectly natural to have also pictured themselves or others throwing the ball. This is an action which can be performed **on** the ball. Other reasonable actions, or *verbs*, might include catching the ball, hitting the ball, and scoring the winning home run!

In a very similar way, there are mathematical *procedures*, or sets of actions that we can naturally perform *on* the sphere. For example, we can increase or decrease its radius (Figure 4.2), rotate it around an axis (Figure 4.3), or move it from one spatial location to another (Figure 4.4).

These actions are just as natural to perform on a sphere as throwing would be to a baseball. Like the actions performed on a baseball, they are "verb-like" in nature and describe what can be done with (or to) the "nouns." Such ideas form the basis for later, more formalized *procedures*. The role technology can play in visualizing these ideas for learners should not be overlooked. The graph in Figure 4.5, for example, was created using a computer-based spreadsheet but could just as easily have been done using a smartphone app, an online graphics program, or a handheld calculator.

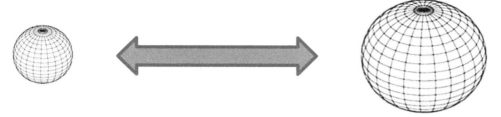

Figure 4.2 Changing a sphere's radius.
Source: Michael L. Connell

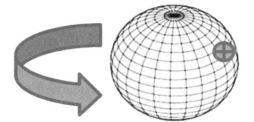

Figure 4.3 Rotating a sphere.
Source: Michael L. Connell

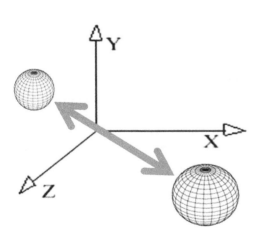

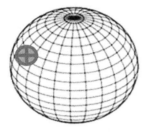

X	Y
-5	-7
-4	-5
-3	-3
-2	-1
-1	1
0	3
1	5
2	7
3	9
4	11
5	13

Figure 4.4 Moving a sphere through space.
Source: Michael L. Connell

Figure 4.5 Graph of Y = 2X + 3.
Source: Michael L. Connell

Things become a little more complicated, however, when the mathematics described has both noun and verb-like features (i.e., requiring understanding of both ***content*** and ***process*** components). For example, the number "2" can be a noun describing a position in a sequence or how many of something one might have. In this case, we are clearly using the noun-like features. In a different context, however, "2" can describe: (a) how many times something appears (as in the case of filling a bowl of cereal "2" times); (b) a base used by computers to represent other numbers (this is also called binary); (c) or the power to which a quantity is raised as shown in $X^2 + 3$.

Most students are familiar with situations like this in their daily lives. A baseball can be sitting on a table or undergoing motion in a game. It can even be placed atop a trophy to symbolize a major victory following that homerun mentioned earlier! Unfortunately, most students (and a few teachers) are less familiar with the dual nature of mathematics.

For students to develop meaningful mathematical understandings, they should have many rich experiences in mathematics from these two markedly different perspectives. Therefore, as we select appropriate technology, we need to allow learners to experience mathematical structures containing both concepts to think *about*—the "noun-like" content features and processes to think with—the "verb-like" procedural features. Once a teacher can see this "dualism" about mathematics, it has major impacts on potential roles of technology in the mathematics classroom.

This can be shown very clearly when considering multiplication strategies.[1] Multiplication is used to compute area, and area can be used to illustrate multiplication—so both the concept and procedure can be illustrated at once. The Algebra Tiles application from the National Library of Virtual Manipulatives (found at www.nlvm .usu.edu/en/nav/frames_asid_189_g_3_t_2.html?open=activities&from=category_g_3_t_2.html) was used in Figure 4.6 to model this example: $(X + 1)(Y + 2)$.

In this figure, we see a rectangle being formed from placing representative tiles along two dimensions—$X + 1$ in the vertical direction and $Y + 2$ in the horizontal direction. The resulting algebraic product is shown by the area itself. To fill this rectangle, the student needs to use an XY piece, two X pieces, one Y piece, and two single squares of the Virtual Manipulatives. When this is written out in standard form, it shows that $(X + 1)$ $(Y + 2) = XY + 2X + Y + 2$. In order to get to this point, however, students need to be able to utilize both the conceptual and procedural aspects of the representation created through interaction with this application. The rectangle is the noun, and "how it got there" is the verb.

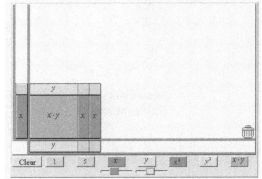

Figure 4.6 $(X + 1)(Y + 2)$.
Source: Michael L. Connell

As this example shows, thanks to technology, it is now possible for learners to experience both the conceptual (noun-like) and procedural (verb-like) aspects of mathematics using the same types of data and use of similar tools to those of practicing mathematicians.

It does not stop here! As technological tools in the classroom have become more sophisticated, the user interface has become much more amenable to direct student manipulation. For example, the National Library of Virtual Manipulatives mentioned above provides an extensive collection of applets (www.nlvm.usu.edu/en/ nav/vlibrary.html), making it possible to use virtual manipulatives directly paralleling those traditionally used in mathematics classrooms (e.g., fraction bars, money, color chips, base blocks, tangrams, and many more). This site allows students to directly experience both the noun- and verb-like features of mathematics. If the students have had earlier experience with the more traditional physical manipulatives upon which the virtual is based—base ten blocks, for example—these can be highly effective tools and enable an entirely new set of student interactions with mathematics (Abramovich, 2012).

Starting with this type of technologically enabled tools that are capable of embodying both concept and process, there is tremendous expansion of mathematical reasoning that may be brought into the classroom. For example, the computer can serve as a tool to record the information that has been generated by the students' activities, capture the essence of the activity by allowing the students to organize their work in powerful structures, and create formal records of action that may be shared or used in later problem-solving endeavors and shared globally via the Internet.

---

1. Another application from this resource will be used later as an example of a high-level interaction with technology.

Object-Based Tools/Data in Mathematics Teaching and Learning

Today, object-based tools can create multiple representations which, when implemented properly, can be a significant asset in developing mathematical power, flexibility, and applications. What is often missing, however, is meaningful data for these tools to work with. Technology comes to the rescue here as well. There are many sites containing real-world data for use in the classroom. Figure 4.7 shows some of these found at www.csss-science.org/classroom.shtml.

An important distinction should be made at this point. Effective technology use does not involve simply visiting a Web page that presents information or a step-by-step demonstration of a process. Such information is important on occasion, but this does not constitute a particularly powerful understanding and does not take full benefit of the potential interactions between the student and technology. As the examples in this chapter should serve to illustrate, such a use of technology is analogous to using a valuable painting to kill grass. While it is true that grass *can* be killed by blocking sunlight from reaching it for a long enough time and a painting could certainly be used in this fashion, this would certainly be a poor use for such a valuable resource!

In the same way, when used together with a student-centered and a meaning-driven approach to teaching, technology can do so much more than the mental equivalent of killing grass! It can lead to new levels of mathematics understanding and representations of concepts far more powerful than that generally experienced in today's classrooms. As with all other content areas and teaching skill, we want to move learners from lower levels of thinking to higher levels. Perhaps in no other content area is it so important to see learning technology as a "means to an end".

An effective tool to think with in learning mathematics, as we have noted, should encompass both the ***noun*** and the ***verb*** (i.e., both the ***conceptual*** and the ***procedural*** aspects of mathematics). Let's see if this perspective can be shown more clearly by expanding upon the multiplication example shown earlier.

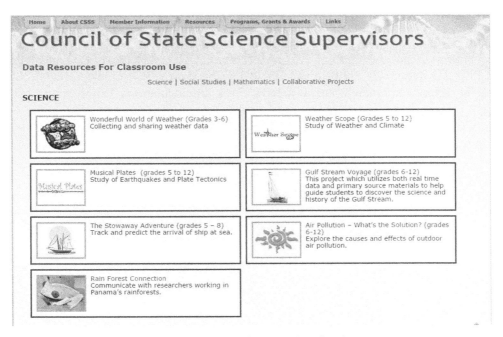

Figure 4.7   An example of a repository of online data for classroom use.
Source: www.csss-science.org/classroom.shtml

Multiplication Table

x	0	1	2	3	4	5	6	7	8	9	10	11	12
0	0	0	0	0	0	0	0	0	0	0	0	0	0
1	0	1	2	3	4	5	6	7	8	9	10	11	12
2	0	2	4	6	8	10	12	14	16	18	20	22	24
3	0	3	6	9	12	15	18	21	24	27	30	33	36
4	0	4	8	12	16	20	24	28	32	36	40	44	48
5	0	5	10	15	20	25	30	35	40	45	50	55	60
6	0	6	12	18	24	30	36	42	48	54	60	66	72
7	0	7	14	21	28	35	42	49	56	63	70	77	84
8	0	8	16	24	32	40	48	56	64	72	80	88	96
9	0	9	18	27	36	45	54	63	72	81	90	99	108
10	0	10	20	30	40	50	60	70	80	90	100	110	120
11	0	11	22	33	44	55	66	77	88	99	110	121	132
12	0	12	24	36	48	60	72	84	96	108	120	132	144

Figure 4.8   The Multiplication Table: An example of a
Low-Level Interaction.
Source: www.math2.org/math/general/multiplytable.htm

A common task in mathematics education is that of developing an understanding of basic multiplication. This task can be approached using three levels of technology-enabled objects. First, look at a very simple case where a technologically enabled *object* simply presents static information to a student—often in the form of facts to be memorized. An example of such a **Low-Level Interaction** may be found at www.math2.org/math/general/ multiplytable.htm and should be intimately familiar to most readers—the multiplication table (see Figure 4.8).

In this example, technology simply presents this object as information—as a Web page. Although it is excellent to have this as an informational chart, the level of interaction is low, and the resulting understanding is primarily of promoting student awareness of existing information. It is much like having the multiplication chart taped to a student's desk, but this is mobile on handheld devices. It provides a quick and easy tool for those who have not learned or cannot learn their tables well and a check for calculations. However, this example does not take advantage of the true power of technology, and, aside from saving paper and ink, really does not have any advantage over a simple printed page. Despite this, however, it is surprising how often students encounter this type of model in technology use. In such cases, students are presented with a static text or information display which is presented in a static form which cannot be directly interacted with. Killing grass, anyone?

There is at least one time, however, when such a static representation works very well. When the students themselves create it! For example, a very common task in elementary school is developing a personal meaning for geometric concepts and definitions. PowerPoint is a natural tool to share the results of a geometry scavenger hunt, for example, and allows the students to practice taking, editing, and selecting digital photographs representing these ideas.

In finding examples, it is a good idea to encourage students to find two examples—one naturally occurring and one man-made—for each item from a list drawn from the grade level curriculum. Students then create a PowerPoint where each item comprises a single slide. Depending on their grade level, for each item they might: (1) give their definition, (2) describe their find, (3) provide a photograph(s), (4) identify why their example(s) should be considered accurate, and (5) show what a "textbook" example would look like. An example of such a slide for the term "Parallel Lines" is shown in Figure 4.9.

The ability to quickly share, comment, and edit their finds allows their ideas to be expanded. In this case, although the final product is a static representation, the process leading to its creation is a highly interactive and meaningful activity.

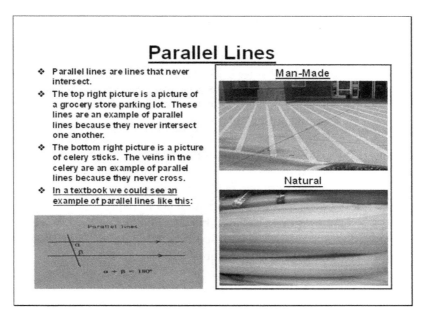

Figure 4.9   Geometry scavenger hunt.
Source: Michael L. Connell

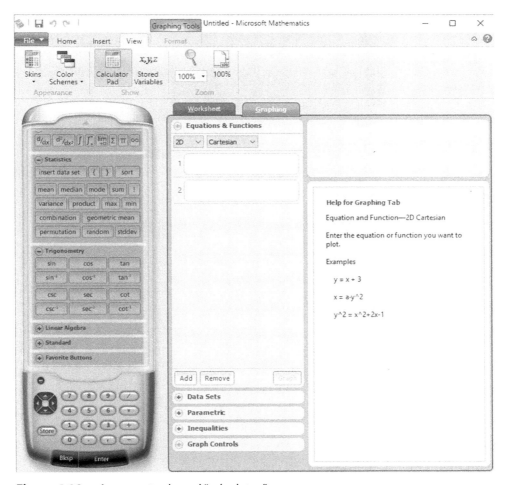

Figure 4.10   A computer-based "calculator."
Source: Michael L. Connell

In a more powerful **Medium-Level Interaction**, the student can act directly upon the technological object itself. In this case, the understandings which emerge are created by the student who acts upon the technologically enabled object (whose properties were both programmed and presented in a form allowing for easy manipulation by the student). At its most simple form, the student chooses to press certain keys to try for a particular result, and the device reacts. When a student uses a calculator, for example, this is typically the level of interaction they experience. This is true whether using a traditional calculator or a computer-emulated calculator such as that shown in Figure 4.10.

Along this line, a very rich set of useful calculators can be found online at *Calculator Soup*. Their very impressive listing of potential tools may be accessed at: www.calculatorsoup.com/calculators. Among other tools, they include calculators for loan, mortgage, time value of money, math, algebra, trigonometry, fractions, physics, statistics, time and date, and conversions. Since many of the pages show work and/or equations, they can be quite helpful to the student trying to understand their calculations.

Such tools can be extremely powerful in allowing students to explore and apply number to parts of the universe that would otherwise be unavailable to them. For example, using the interactive tool at www.htwins .net/scale, it is possible to explore the relative sizes of objects in the universe ranging from the smallest units of space time to the largest cosmic structures (see Figure 4.11).

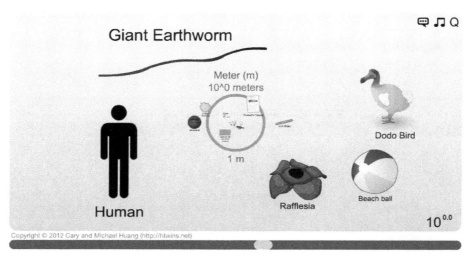

Figure 4.11   The scale of the universe.
Source: www.htwins.net/scale

X	1	2	3	4	5	6	7	8	9	10	11	12
1	1	2	3	4	5	6	7	8	9	10	11	12
2	2	4	6	8	10	12	14	16	18	20	22	24
3	3	6	9	12	15	18	21	24	27	30	33	36
4	4	8	12	16	20	24	28	32	36	40	44	48
5	5	10	15	20	25	30	35	40	45	50	55	60
6	6	12	18	24	30	36	42	48	54	60	66	72
7	7	14	21	28	35	42	49	56	63	70	77	84
8	8	16	24	32	40	48	56	64	72	80	88	96
9	9	18	27	36	45	54	63	72	81	90	99	108
10	10	20	30	40	50	60	70	80	90	100	110	120
11	11	22	33	44	55	66	77	88	99	110	121	132
12	12	24	36	48	60	72	84	96	108	120	132	144

Figure 4.12   A computer-generated Multiplication Table: An example of a **Medium-Level Interaction**.
Source: Keith Bell/Shutterstock.com

A multiplication-based example of this **Medium-Level Interaction** may be found at: www.mathsisfun .com/tables.html. This Web site provides an alternative view of our old friend, the multiplication table.

In this more powerful example, the object does more than just provide an answer. In addition to a correct numerical answer, the object created an alternate representation which then was presented to the student. This ability of objects to interact with the student and with other objects provides for a tremendous leverage in their utility and power. In the second multiplication table example shown in Figure 4.12, the second level of object creation was fairly transparent to the student. This served primarily to provide an alternate representation that would hopefully be familiar to the student—in this case, modeling multiplication using an area model. Although relatively simple, in many ways this latter example exhibits some of the characteristics of a **High-Level Interaction**.

In a truly **High-Level Interaction**, the direction of the interaction still originates with an action being performed by a student, generally in response to a problem situation or problem-solving goal. As was the case with **Medium-Level Interactions**, the student performs actions of their choice directly upon the object. The object may, depending upon the supporting programming or context, link to other conceptually related objects for additional processing or representational purposes. In other cases, the student may interact with intermediary objects to create specific representations and tools of their own design and choice.

An example of such a **High-Level Interaction** is shown in Figure 4.13, which was created using the applet at www.nlvm.usu.edu/en/nav/frames_asid_192_g_1_t_1.html?from= category_g_1_t_1.html.

This pair of screenshots shows a student's interaction with yet another multiplication object to model the multiplication problem 23 × 11. In this case, the object allows the student the ability to change a number of important aspects of the model. For example, it is possible to change from the *Lattice* representation shown in these diagrams, which should be familiar to Montessori teachers, to *Grouping* and *Common* models used in typical textbooks. Once a representation is chosen, the associated records of activity and problem setting automatically change. This allows the student to explore not just one but many different ways of representing

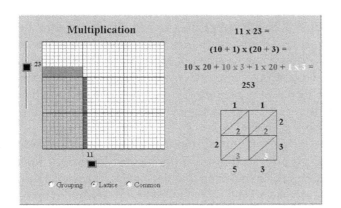 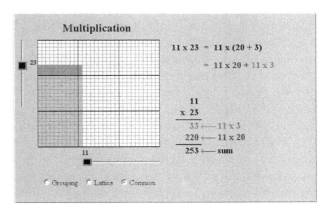

Figure 4.13   The Multiplication Table: An example of a **High-Level Interaction**.
Source: www.nlvm.usu.edu/en/nav/frames_asid_192_g_1_t_1.html?from=category_g_1_t_1.html

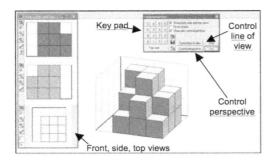 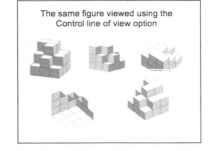

Figure 4.14   The Geocadabra Construction Box.
Source: Jacqueline Sack

the problem. As a tool offering **High-Level Interaction**, it is important to spend some time actually interacting with it! Try modeling a few multiplication problems on your own prior to continuing.

Another outstanding and freely available example of a **High-Level Interaction** is *Geocadabra* (Lecluse, 2005), which through its Construction Box module allows learners of all grade levels to construct, view, and manipulate complex, multi-cube structures as 2-D, conventional representations or as top, side, and front views or numeric top-view grid codings (see Figure 4.14). By clicking successively on a grid position on the keypad shown in Figure 4.14, a corresponding stack of cubes appears. By right-clicking, the stack may be reduced in height or removed. As the figure is constructed, the front, side, and top views dynamically change. The show (or hide) views, keypad or 2-D figure options can be preselected according to instructional goals. The Control-line-of-view option allows the user to move the figure dynamically using the mouse or by clicking on the arrows at the ends of the space's triaxial system that appears on the Construction Box control window. The size of the top-view rectangular grid can be adjusted from 2 to 8 units in width and depth according to user preference.

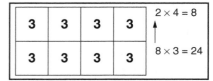

Of note, researchers (e.g., Outhred, Mitchelmore, McPhail, & Gould, 2003; Battista, 1999) have observed the difficulty that many students have with making sense of the abstract volume formula and of being able to represent 3-D figures such as rectangular prisms on paper. Using the Construction Box to build such figures and representing them using the Top-View numeric grid (see example in Figure 4.15) takes care of the conceptualization and the drawing.

Figure 4.15 A 24-cube prism represented via a top view (numeric grid).
Source: Jacqueline Sack

Problems in Teaching and Learning in the Mathematics Classroom

Many of these instructional issues are also present in traditional mathematics classrooms—even in the absence of technology. In many mathematics classrooms, instruction typically emphasizes procedures, memorizing algorithms, and finding the "one right answer" at the fastest speed possible. Unfortunately, in such environments, reasoning, problem-solving, and sensibility are rarely addressed—if at all. Mathematics, as it is often presented in these settings, is not a subject open for discussion, debate, or creative thinking—nor are students encouraged to find alternative ways to solve a problem or different procedures for carrying out an operation (Abramovich & Connell, 2014). When this happens students often become adept memorizers of procedures—but, they are typically unable to interpret their results or apply their findings.

To draw upon our earlier language example, students become verb-strong, but they do not understand the nouns they are acting upon! Procedural and computational expertise can result from this, but little else. Such students are able to follow the algorithms necessary to solve a problem but cannot understand why or how those algorithms answer the question at hand. Given this, it is hardly surprising that many students became imbued with rigid mental representations of mathematical problems and lack any ability to apply metacognitive strategies. The consequences of this often escape the typical classroom teacher. This is not said to fault teachers but to draw attention to this problem.

Consider this story problem as an example, "Harry ate a hamburger and drank a glass of milk which totaled 495 calories. The milk contained half as many calories as the sandwich. How many calories were in the sandwich and how many in the milk?" You may want to try to solve this problem yourself before proceeding! This type of problem is good for students to address with the focus on healthier eating in today's world.

As Campione, Brown, and Connell (1988) showed, this version of the problem is generally solved nicely by students. However, once one changes the supporting text slightly to include pricing information for the sandwich and milk, to update the calorie information, and to change the name of the store where Harry purchased the hamburger and milk, things go off the rails quickly--especially if the name of the store happens to be Seven-Eleven!

In a follow-up study, students were given their choice of representations, computational processing, and checking. In nearly half of the students' work, the answers did not match with any of the previously used solution methods or answers from the earlier study (If you really must know . . . the milk had 165 calories, if you want to check your earlier work).

However, the answers did make an odd sort of sense—once the initial disbelief passed. Answers from this new set of students included 77, 18, 7, 11, 1 4/7, and so on. The students obviously had taken the two smallest numbers they saw in the problem and then simply applied operations—with no regard to meaning or reasonableness. The presence of extraneous information triggered a series of nearly automatic calculations which took the place of careful problem-solving and reasoning. It should be noted that the students' calculations were done perfectly.

When the participating teachers looked at the results, they were understandably shocked. These were average students who had scored well on every test (of computation) they had taken in their class the year they had encountered *Harry and the Hamburger*. Their lack of ability to flexibly transfer their computational abilities (the procedural **verb**) to any meaningful problem situation (the underlying **noun**) brought a previously hidden problem into the open.

Using Technology for Solving *Harry and the Hamburger* Problem

When students understand the relationships presented in the problem setting, however, it is easy to use an appropriate technology, a spreadsheet for example, in solving the *Harry and the Hamburger* problem. Furthermore, once it is created, the same spreadsheet can be used for posing a multitude of similar problems with different data but sharing the same deep structure. The use of a spreadsheet in this case is particularly powerful, as it enables the distribution of calories between milk and the hamburger to be shown both numerically and geometrically. The latter case is shown in the bottom part of Figure 4.16, when calories in milk are shown to be one-third of the total calories. If you look carefully at Figure 4.16, you can see a slider attached to the cell representing calories in milk. This is a tool which can be used by the students to alter the number of calories until their total number is equal to 495.

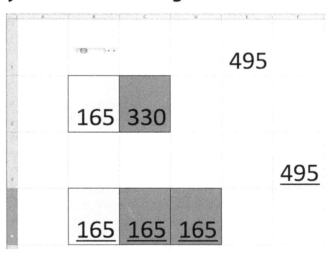

Figure 4.16   A spreadsheet for *Harry and the Hamburger* Spreadsheet.
Source: Michael L. Connell

Technology's Potential Contribution to Mathematics Classroom

Problems such as those shown in the *Harry and the Hamburger* scenario are all the more unfortunate since flexibility appears to be a characteristic valued in many domains. Researchers from many fields associate the flexible application of rules and strategies with expertise and higher levels of cognitive operations. Indeed, one key to evaluating successful learning in this newer approach to mathematics instruction would be student flexibility in choosing and using mental representations.

Technology in its myriad forms, which today includes object-oriented interfaces and tools geared specifically to enable students to perform specific actions upon specific objects (remember the verbs and nouns!), lends itself perfectly to action upon object models of learning and instruction underlying the examples from this introduction. Some of these include Step-by-Step Development of Mental Activities (Leontiev, 1979), Action Reification (Tall, Thomas, Davis, Gray, & Simpson, 2000; Sfard, 1991), and Action on Objects (Connell, 2001) to name a few. This linkage between suggestions from educational learning theory and the object classes created by technology is far too powerful to allow going to waste.

As these introductory examples show, computer-generated visualizations and representations can be used to help the student create a new way of thinking, discussing, and building understanding in an inquiry-oriented environment. Finally, however, mathematical meaning is best made by students' performance with actual actions upon actual objects (real-world **nouns** and **verbs**, please!). In order for this to occur, the eventual objects created by the technology must become real in the minds of the students. It must become understandable and real to a learner, and it must possess well-defined attributes in the mind of the student such that the eventual symbol generated by the experience has well-defined properties. To increase further understanding, there is a wealth of videos on the Web where students can search for and access experts explaining mathematics in various ways, and teachers can easily find problems and examples that focus upon the exact concepts they are teaching.

Grade Level Examples

Bear in mind that these examples are not intended to be a cookbook or recipe. Instead, these examples should be considered as illustrations, showing how the principles described thus far might be used to guide technology. As you do so, you will see that there are some common instructional strategies present across all grade levels.

Remember an important lesson from *Harry and the Hamburger*! Technology should **never** be used to shortcut careful reasoning and planning. If students do not know what they are doing **without** technology, they will not know what they are doing **with** technology. The only difference being is that students will be able to hide their lack of knowledge behind the "correct answers" that they achieved by manipulations of numbers (without meaning) using tools whose computational accuracy is far beyond their own numerical literacy.

Pre-K to Grade 5

To encourage students to explore the world around them with mathematics, it is necessary to develop a classroom climate where problems can be viewed as having more than a single, correct, easily computable answer. In algebra, we learn that even simple problems can have one solution, no solution, or infinitely many solutions.

It is important that the experiences leading to these cases be developed early in children's mathematical experiences. In doing so it is sometimes necessary to simplify problems to allow the students' emerging understandings to be utilized in exploring the situation at hand. Students, in this example, will explore a situation where there is more than a single answer. Their work will be supported by initial hands-on activity which is then followed with appropriate supporting technology. This approach—hands-on first, then technology for exploration second—is a very powerful model in developing this desirable classroom climate.

The children in this example, a classroom of second graders, were originally presented with a fairly open-ended problem requiring much more than the calculation of a single correct answer.

> *The average temperature for the week increased by 1°, and the temperature on Monday, Tuesday, and Wednesday did not change; then what temperature changes occurred on Thursday and Friday? Find and list all the possible combinations of temperature changes on Thursday and Friday.*

This problem has a "low floor and a high ceiling" in the words of Jo Boaler (2014).[2] As such, this means that the problem is relatively easy to get started on and then allows for significant mathematics development. This "low floor, high ceiling" property will be seen in each of the chapter examples.

Originally, the students, when asked this question (even in a spreadsheet environment that allowed for manually changing temperature through scroll bars and interactively observing the change in average temperature), were not able to handle the multiplicity of answers.[3] The maximum number of possible combinations of temperature changes found by one of the students was two:

> *"You have to change Friday 5 up. You move Thursday up 3 and you move Friday up 2."*

---

2. For a discussion of this phrase, together with a parent-friendly video on the importance of change in mathematics teaching see www.youtube.com/watch?v=pOOW0hQgVPQ

3. A full discussion of this example may be found in Abramovich, Easton, and Hayes (2012).

Initially, children's concrete thinking proved to be a barrier for exploring the multiplicity of answers. It was found, however, that concrete activity was effective in overcoming the deficiency of concrete thinking finding multiple answers. The second graders were given the following task: *How many ways can one put five rings on two fingers?* Experimentally, without using mathematics, the children found all six ways of putting five rings on two fingers and recorded their findings as shown in Figure 4.17.

After this experience, a second grader was able to answer the earlier question asked about temperature as follows:

> *Fri increased by two and thurs increased by three. Fri increased by four and thurs increased by one. Fri increased by five and thurs increased by zero. Fri increased by three and thurs increased by two. Fri increased by one and thurs increased by four. Fri increased by zero and thurs increased by five. THAT WAS FUN!!!!!!!!!!!!!!!!!!!*

Figure 4.17   Concrete activity as a means of understanding multiple answers.
Source: Abramovich, Easton, & Hayes, 2012

Seeing problem posing and problem-solving as two sides of the same coin enables a child to attempt to answer self-posed questions either individually or with the help of a teacher. In this example, the posing and solving of problems was supported by a spreadsheet. The students had been given a weather forecast for the next five days: Monday 6°, Tuesday 22°, Wednesday 24°, Thursday 18°, and Friday 20°. They were provided with a spreadsheet as shown earlier in Figure 4.16, and with this support, a student was able to explore the following self-posed problem:

"What would happen to the average temperature if Friday's temperature dropped 20 degrees?"

It should be noted that these, and the comments which follow, were students' actual words and reflect the spelling that was used.

As one can see in Figure 4.18, the environment used by these students resembles a Nintendo DS. This is what Abramovich, Easton, and Hayes (2014) call an integrated spreadsheet. Such a spreadsheet is created by combining a traditional spreadsheet with images of technology—such as a Nintendo DS, a PlayStation Portable, or an iPhone—already familiar to young children. This is easily done by pasting a picture on the background of a spreadsheet. Such familiar images helped in reducing anxiety often felt by novice users of computers. It also allows for a familiar interface for young children in presenting and processing information. In this example, the problems that children were exploring displayed on the colored "screen" of the Nintendo DS and the space for them to enter an answer is always in the transparent box.

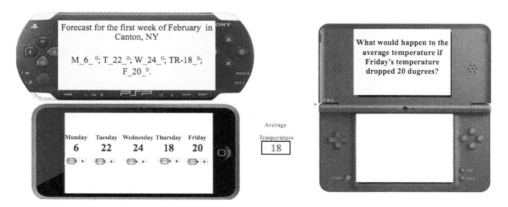

Figure 4.18   Posing a question (the top-right textbox).

Grade 6 to Grade 8

Francesca and the Factory. This activity illustrates how the appropriate use of technology can support extensive mathematical investigation, including making mathematical connections. As such, the "low floor, high ceiling" concept is directly utilized. The mathematics which underpins this activity is easily accessible and, with the support of technology, potentially quite rich. Indeed, this problem setting allows for multiple competencies (both on the part of the teacher and that of the student) to be addressed.

Without the use of supporting technology, it typically takes several days of tedious calculations for sufficient data to be generated to get to the richer underlying mathematics. Thanks to the modern spreadsheet, the explorations of Francesca's factory allow more time to be spent on building connections between deeper levels of mathematical content than was previously possible—including a powerful link forward from pre-algebra into limits and pre-calculus. As is recommended that for all activities in this chapter, the initial problem setting and procedure choices are all done prior to the introduction of the spreadsheet technology.

Francesca and the Factory

Unexpectedly, Francesca received an inheritance from her aunt—a 10 dkm⁴ × 10 dkm factory space in one of the most sought-after locations in the manufacturing district. Unfortunately, with that inheritance came some debts that her aunt owed that Francesca must also pay off. Fortunately, she has a plan to both maximize her use of factory space and honor her aunt's debts. At the end of one year, she will reduce the width of the floor space she is utilizing by 1 dkm and increase the length 1 dkm with the monies from the difference in space going to the debts, so, starting in the second year she will have a 11 dkm × 9 dkm floor space for her 3-D printers. This will be done each year until there is nothing left (i.e., 20 dkm × 0 dkm). Francesca will definitely have to be strategic in her planning but will work hard to make the most of this opportunity.

Help Francesca explore what to expect over the next 10 years. As a start, for each year find:

1. How much floor space will Francesca lose from the preceding year?
2. How much floor space will Francesca lose from the first year?
3. How will the shape of available factory flooring change over time?

After reading through the problem situation, see if you can predict the various changes in factory floor space after the first **three** years have been computed. By the time you are done, you will generally be able to identify some of the connections in the problem. Typically, students by this time will recognize that they will be computing areas and comparing one year to another.

A good teacher question to ask at this point is: "Is there a way to predict what happens in the 5th year? The 6th?" With the addition of spreadsheet, an excellent bridging question is, "How can we organize our work to make prediction easier?" This last question quite commonly leads to a row and column layout which can be directly translated into a spreadsheet later.

In exploring the *Francesca and the Factory* problem, even prior to the introduction of the spreadsheet, some fascinating mathematics can be shown. If a student draws out what the factory floor space would look like each year on a single figure, he or she will be able create graphic representations similar to those shown in Figures 4.19 to 4.21.

From here, the possibilities for exploration open up. For example, to show the floor space lost for any given year relative to the beginning year (the fourth year is shown), take the rectangle gained for that year (A), rotate it (B and C), and place it inside the original figure to show the total amount lost (D).

---

4. A *decameter*—abbreviated as *dkm*, although rarely used, is part of the standard metric system and is equal to 10 meters. The benefit of the use in this problem is than an even more obscure metric unit—the *Are* —is equal to the area of a 10 meter × 10 meter square. Thus, the initial area of the inherited factory space is equal to 100 Ares, or 1 Hectare, so each following calculation is easily expressed in terms of a percentage of the starting Hectare. Therefore, this problem can be used to reinforce the metric system together with its naming conventions as well as the immediate mathematics.

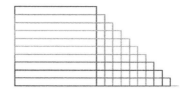

Figure 4.19   Changes in the available floor space.

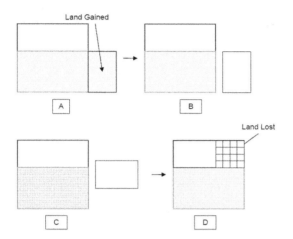

Figure 4.20   Where the space is going from Year One.

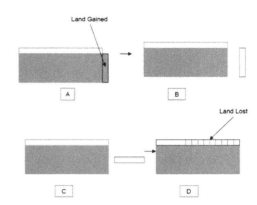

Figure 4.21   Where the floor is going from the preceding year.

It can quickly be shown that the space lost for each year that this is done will be a perfect square—which certainly hints at some interesting patterns to come!

To show the floor space lost for any given year relative to the preceding year (the difference between the fourth year and fifth year is shown), take the rectangle representing the floor space gained for that year (A), rotate it (B and C), and place it inside the preceding figure to show the total amount lost (D).

The sequence of odd numbers this generates likewise hints at areas for investigation as shown in Figure 4.22.

Elapsed Year	Length	Width	Area	Floor space loss from preceding year	Floor space lost from first year	Perimeter (Caution tape required)	Perimeter loss from preceding year	Perimeter loss from first year
0	10	10	100					
1	11	9	99	1	1	40		
2	12	8	96	3	4	40	0	0
3	13	7	91	5	9	40	0	0
4	14	6	84	7	16	40	0	0
5	15	5	75	9	25	40	0	0
6	16	4	64	11	36	40	0	0
7	17	3	51	13	49	40	0	0
8	18	2	36	15	64	40	0	0
9	19	1	19	17	81	40	0	0
10	20	0	0	19	100	40	0	0

Figure 4.22   Data and calculations confirmed using a spreadsheet.
Source: Michael L. Connell

These examples draw heavily upon the dual process-concept nature of multiplication developed in the earlier chapter examples. As such, these sketches both represent specific processes **and** the solution to problems. This preliminary exploration provides a context for the following spreadsheet explorations as well as providing important clues for exploration. The following screenshot from **Francesca and the Factory.xls** shows one possible way of representing the problem situation.[5]

When relationships between cells are observed and can be generalized, the formula bar, shown in Figure 4.23, can be used to create many of the cells; for example, cell B12 was defined as being:

Figure 4.23 The Formula (Function) bar.

This makes it easy to copy cell B12, together with its attributes, and easily copy these—filling out the respective columns. This ability to copy relationships between cells, including functional relationships, helps in the students' understanding and exploration of the mathematical situation.

In a like fashion, each of the following cells can be defined using the formula bar as shown in Figure 4.24 as being:

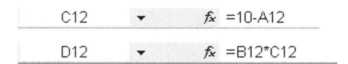

Figure 4.24 Using the Formula (Function) bar.

As shown in Figure 4.25, the increments in year can be defined in cell A13 as being:

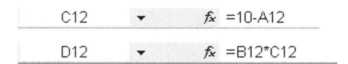

Figure 4.25 Last steps in creating the spreadsheet.

Once relationships are recognized and their underlying functions identified, it becomes easy to create meaningful function tables of values. In this example, we can see this by copying cell A13 into cells A14 through A22. In a like fashion, it is possible to copy cells B12, C12, and D12 into cells B13 through B22, C13 through C22, and D13 through D22. This is a bit different than the typical use of data tables serving as the basis for function identification. In this case, the function is created first and used to create a table of data for exploration.

An examination of the formula bar for Column B (fx = 10 + A12), Column C (fx = 10 − A12), and Column D (fx = B12*C12) provides a possible avenue to explore the concept of difference of squares (i.e., the length (10 + A12) and width (10 − A12)) being used in the area calculation. In this case, Column D's function is equivalent to B12*C12 which in turn is equivalent to (10 + A2)*(10 − A12).

Depending upon the classroom, this may not be followed up, but it does provide an important clue which could be utilized in further exploration into the mathematics underlying the *Francesca and the Factory* problem. By making explicit the relationships between cells, the formula bar can often be used in this fashion to gain hints as to potential mathematical underpinnings. The mathematics which may be found "beneath the rules" can then be made available for student explorations.

---

5. All screenshots were created using Microsoft Excel.

The remaining columns look at some of the other interesting interactions immediately springing from the problem situation. Each cell in Column E, E13, for example, was computed using instructions shown in Figure 4.26.

$$E13 \qquad \blacktriangledown \qquad f_x = D12\text{-}D13$$

Figure 4.26   Differences from the preceding year.

When this is done, the sequence of odd numbers is generated, leading to questions concerning where this shows up in the graphical and functional representations generated in the group activity.

Figure 4.27 shows how the function action in Column F was generated.

$$F13 \qquad \blacktriangledown \qquad f_x = \$D\$12\text{-}D13$$

Figure 4.27   Differences from the first year.

The $ sign preceding the D and the 12 indicates that this location will be locked in and used as the reference for each of the cells generated by copying it. This ensures that each subsequent year's difference will be computed taking the first year as the comparison.

Now a sequence of squares is generated, once again leading to questions concerning where this shows up in the graphical and functional representations generated.

Figure 4.28 shows the graphs which were generated by these actions:

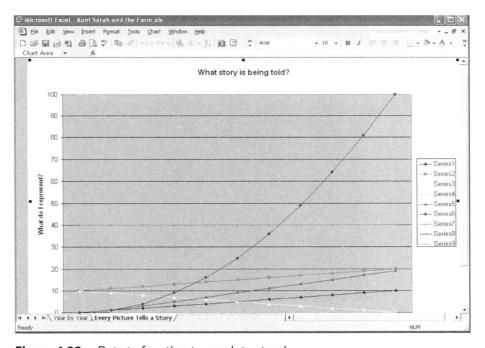

Figure 4.28   Data to function to graph to story!

It is now up to the students to describe which series gives rise to each graph and why. They should also be able to link their graphic representation created prior to the use of the spreadsheet (typically, done using graph paper) to these graphs.

An important conclusion that one can draw from this investigation is that given the perimeter of a rectangle, no smallest area exists, whereas the square (i.e., rectangle with congruent adjacent sides) has the largest area. However, as noted by Kline (1985), "A farmer who seeks the rectangle of maximum area with given perimeter might, after finding the answer to his question, turn to gardening, but a mathematician who obtains such a neat result would not stop there" (p. 133). This note motivates extending *Francesca and the Factory* problem using the computational power of a spreadsheet.

Technology-Enabled Extensions

Of course, technically, in order for a line graph to be properly used, a case must be made that there will not be any changes in the line as the difference between sampling times becomes infinitely small. This provides an easy link to the calculus which may be made via the spreadsheet.

This can be shown by first changing the spreadsheet so that the "change point" occurs every month instead of every year. This action effectively changes the difference between points on the line graphs by 1/12. This is easily done as shown in Figure 4.29 by changing cell A13 to be:

Figure 4.29   Links to advanced math.

Now we can reconstruct the full table (all 120 rows of it!) with a simple set of copy instructions. Figure 4.30 shows the results of this action:

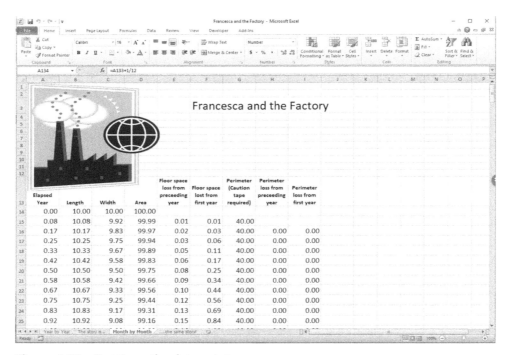

Figure 4.30   Ten times the data points.
Source: Michael L. Connell

We can now reconstruct the earlier graphs using this more finely tuned set of measurements. The result of this action is shown in Figure 4.31.

This is the identical shapes as shown in the earlier set of graphs. *The underlying equivalency can be better shown by changing the chart type to not plot the locations of the individual data points.* In a like fashion, we can narrow the limit to the day, the hour, the minute—to any degree we might choose . . . in each case since the underlying functions are the same, the graphs will maintain the same shape! Technology has enabled us to develop in a very intuitive fashion the notions of limit which underpin differential calculus. Without technology, this amazing development is not possible.

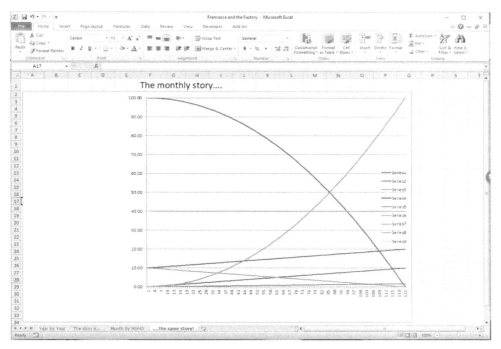

Figure 4.31   Identical curves from identical functions.

High School (Secondary)

One of the major tasks in the high school environment lies in developing the ability to work with abstract concepts. With its ability to provide an interface between functions and graphs, technology can be an invaluable tool in this effort. The figures shown in this section were created with the *Graphing* Calculator (version 4.0) produced by Pacific Tech (Avitzur, 2011). However, any of a number of Web-based apps, programs, or handheld devices could have done just as well. It is a tribute to the power of technology that once the mathematics is understood, there are a variety of tools which might be used. The opposite is also true, however. If the mathematics is not understood, it does not matter how many tools you have access to.

Consider the question of constructing the graphs of the functions $y = x$ and $y = x^2$ in a single drawing. This construction is shown in Figure 4.28 and leads to the question of constructing just the parabolic segment as shown in Figure 4.32.

In order to construct the parabolic segment, one has to describe the points inside the parabolic segment in the form of inequalities. First, an x-coordinate of any point (x, y) that belongs to the parabolic segment satisfies the inequalities $0 < x < 1$, where $x = 0$ and $x = 1$ are the points of intersection of the graphs $y = x$ and $y = x^2$. Second, its y-coordinate satisfies the inequalities $f(x) < y < g(x)$ where $f(x) = x^2$ and $g(x) = x$.

These properties of the points that belong to the parabolic segment can be expressed in the form of simultaneous inequalities:

$$x - y > 0, \quad y - x^2 > 0, \quad x > 0, \quad x < 1$$

In addition, the reflection of the parabolic segment in the line $x = 1$ can be expressed through another set of inequalities by substituting $2 - x$ for x:

$$(2 - x) - y > 0, \quad y - (2 - x)^2 > 0, \quad (2 - x) > 0,_2 (2 - x) < 1$$

To clarify, note that if X_1 and X_2, $X_2 > X_1$, are symmetrical about $X = 1$, then $\frac{X_1 + X_2}{2} = 1$, whence $X_2 = 2 - X_1$.

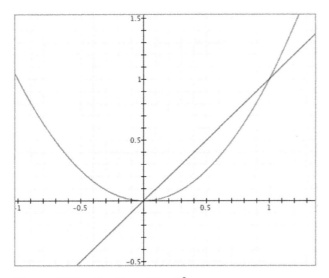

Figure 4.32   Y = X and Y = X².

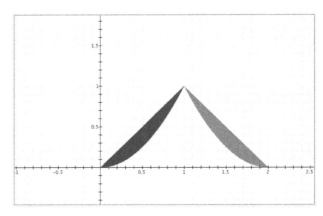

Figure 4.33   A parabolic segment and its reflection in the line $x = 1$.

Likewise, the set of points that belong to the border of the parabolic segment can be described through inequalities. First, the graph of the upper border (a part of the line $y = x$) can be described as a set of points (x, y) for which the values of the coordinates x and y are ε—close to each other; that is, $|y - x| < \varepsilon$. Second, the graph of the lower border (a part of the parabola $y = x^2$) can be described as a set of points (x, y) for which the values of y are ε—close to the values of x^2. Finally, once again, the inequalities $0 < x < 1$ characterize the points that belong to the border. In the context of the *Graphing Calculator*, these properties of the points that belong to the border of the parabolic segment can be expressed in the form of the union of simultaneous inequalities.

$$|y - x| < \varepsilon, \quad x > 0, \quad x < 1;$$

$$|y - x^2| < \varepsilon, \quad x > 0, \quad x < 1;$$

Adding another union of simultaneous inequalities

$$|y - (2 - x)| < \varepsilon, \quad 2 - x > 0, \quad 2 - x < 1;$$

$$|y - (2 - x)^2| < \varepsilon, \quad 2 - x > 0, \quad 2 - x < 1;$$

yields the right-hand side of the digital fabrication shown in Figure 4.34. In Figure 4.34 $\varepsilon = 0.02$.

Using technology to enable students to construct graphs of areas in the plane and their borders by using two-variable inequalities illustrates "the way in which software can embody a mathematical definition" (Conference Board of the Mathematical Sciences, 2001, p. 132).

Finally, since students in the secondary environment are capable of a higher level of abstract reasoning and independent work, they can directly benefit from many of the public domain "textbooks" that are available online. For example, the National Science Foundation supported the development of one such "text" for Statistics—*Online Statistics: An Interactive Multimedia Course of Study* (www.onlinestatbook.com).

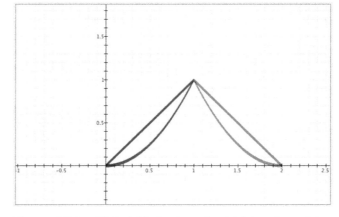

Figure 4.34   Digital fabrication of ε-thick borders of the parabolic segment and its reflection.

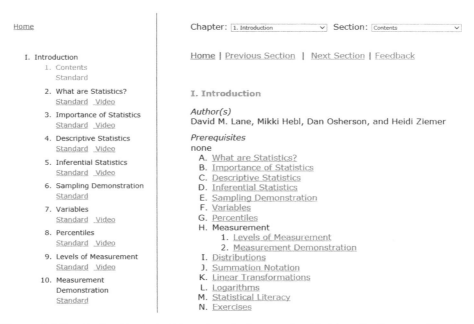

Figure 4.35 Online Statistic Education: An Interactive Multimedia Course of Study.

As shown in Figure 4.35, this resource for teaching and learning introductory statistical analysis contains a complete textbook, a free PDF version, video vignettes, work templates, interactive demonstrations, specially formatted versions for mobile devices, and so on. For instructors wanting to use these materials, a free instructor's manual, PowerPoint Slides, and question sets are available.

Suggestions for Classroom Technology Use

From the examples presented in this chapter, we would like to offer the following suggestions for classroom technology use:

1. Begin by developing basic numeracy. Students cannot effectively act upon numbers, regardless of technology, without a rich understanding of number concepts. Be sure that students recognize that number can serve as both a **noun** and a **verb** and are able to provide examples of both situations.
2. Once numeracy, a deep understanding of the foundations of number and its uses, are in place, be certain that the basic operations are also thoroughly understood in both their **noun** and **verb** settings. It is far too easy for the correct answers provided by technology to hide student misconceptions and lack of foundational understandings. *Remember the hamburger!*
3. Whenever possible, use technology to confirm your thinking, not replace it. Perform a few sample calculations to test your ideas, use technology to check your calculations and confirm you are on the correct path, and then use the tools of technology to explore emerging ideas more efficiently.
4. Remember the examples of the embedded spreadsheets. Pick your technology to match the developmental needs and experiences of your students.
5. [Look for "beneath the rules"] moments. Often technology can provide important clues as to [what mathematics may] be built in the emerging mathematics. In *Francesca's Factory* for example, [there are multiple concepts] which could serve as the basis of future explorations.
6. Remember to use technology to pose problems, not just as a means to increase the speed of solutions. The ability to pose questions, even when their immediate methods of solution are not readily apparent, is a major goal in mathematics education.
7. If one truly understands the questions that one is asking, it becomes possible to select an appropriate technology to help explore possible answers. If the questions being asked are not understood, then **NO**

technology will be able to assist. Numerical answers can be generated, but these numbers might not even relate to the questions being asked.

8. Do use the massive amount of teacher resources the Internet has to offer with ideas for teaching with technology for all types of mathematics and various grade levels, for many types of technology usage, and many types of software and tools (i.e., Wii, blogs, tutorials, electronic whiteboard suggestions, YouTube videos, mathematical memory songs, making electronic games, digital cameras use, WebQuests, apps, and many more). Resources often include those to help teachers offer interesting problems (with or without technology). For example, type in "real world math problems" to a browser for a great number including many which are technology and STEM (Science, Technology, Engineering, and Mathematics). Electronic resources for students include a great many tutorials for all grade levels, including those for upper level mathematics.

Question 5

9. Do take into account the time needed to teach the use of the technology tools so that students can use them quickly, easily, and without frustration.

10. Remember that classroom technology is a moving target. By focusing upon the mathematics that is to be taught, teachers should be able to adapt when a newer program, instructional package, or textbook is to be adopted. Teachers should not allow themselves to become so centered on *how* to enter the correct keystrokes that they forget *why* they are doing so!

Summary

If we take the student-centered and meaning-driven approach to mathematics education advocated in this chapter, the questions become what tools and abilities are necessary for success, and how can educational technology be used as a tool in acquiring these?

These are crucial questions, as the nature of the "tools" which are provided to students to "think with" comes to significantly shape their performance and cognitive styles. For example, two-digit division may constitute a legitimate problem when paper and pencil are the only tools available for the student to use but are no longer a problem when calculators are available. When technology is available for students' use, the situation shifts again. A legitimate problem with technology might involve the identification and selection of what data to include in the problem, identification of the problem goals, and selection of appropriate procedures and control statements to obtain and verify the desired results.

Let us be careful not to transfer a misplaced belief that mathematics education is solely about developing speed of process over to our thinking about technology uses. Modern technology is capable of blinding speeds of process—so this cannot be viewed as our end goal. If students are to internalize and construct meanings from experiences, there must be time to reflect upon the nature of the experiences and how they connect with the students' existing mathematical knowledge. Great care must be taken to allow students to construct their own knowledge and representations and then establish the linkages with other (also student-constructed) tools, representations, and concepts—many of which are technology dependent.

Recommended Resources Council of State Science Supervisors

Data resources for classroom use. www.csss-science.org/classroom.shtml

MathIsFun: Learn Your Multiplication Tables. www.mathsisfun.com/tables.html

National Library of Virtual Manipulatives. Rectangle Multiplication. www.nlvm.usu.edu/en/nav/frames_asid_192_g_1_t_1.html?from=category_g_1_t_1.html (2014, June 16).

References

Abramovich, S. (2012). Counting and reasoning with manipulative materials: A North American perspective. In N. Petrovic (Ed.), *The interfaces of subjects taught in the primary schools and possible models of integrating them* (pp. 9–20). Sombor, Serbia: The University of Novi Sad Faculty of Education Press.

Abramovich, S., & Connell, M. (2014). Using technology in elementary teacher education: A sociocultural perspective. *ISRN (International Scholarly Research Network) Education,* Article ID 245146, 9 pages, doi: 10.1155/2014/345146.

Abramovich, S., Easton, J., & Hayes, V. O. (2012). Parallel structures of computer-assisted signature pedagogy: The case of integrated spreadsheets. *Computers in the Schools (special issue on Signature Pedagogy)*, 29(1–2), 174–190.

Abramovich, S., Easton, J., & Hayes, V. O. (2014). Integrated spreadsheets as learning environments for young children. *Spreadsheets in Education*, 7(2), Article 3.

Avitzur, R. (2011). *Graphing calculator* (Version 4.0). Berkeley, CA: Pacific Tech.

Battista, M. (1999). Fifth graders enumeration of cubes in 3D arrays: Conceptual progress in an inquiry-based classroom. *Journal for Research in Mathematics Education, 30*, 417–448.

Campione, J. C., Brown, A. L., & Connell, M. L. (1988). Metacognition: On the importance of understanding what you are doing. In R. I. Charles & E. Silver (Eds.), *Teaching and assessing mathematical problem solving.* Volume 3 (pp. 93–114). Reston, VA: National Council of Teachers of Mathematics.

Chapter 1: Max. (n.d.). Retrieved from www.web.math.rochester.edu/people/faculty/rarm/beberman.html Max Beberman - New Math Pioneer

Conference Board of the Mathematical Sciences. (2001). *The mathematical education of teachers.* Washington, DC: The Mathematical Association of America.

Connell, M. L. (2001). Actions upon objects: A metaphor for technology enhanced mathematics instruction. In D. Tooke & N. Henderson (Eds.), *Using information technology in mathematics* (pp. 143–171). Binghamton, NY: Haworth Press.

Davis, R. B. (1990). *Learning mathematics: The cognitive science approach to mathematics education.* Norwood, NJ: Ablex.

Kline, M. (1985). *Mathematics for the non-mathematician.* New York, NY: Dover.

Lecluse, A. (2005). *Geocadabra (Computer software).* Retrieved from www.home.casema.nl/alecluse/setupeng.exe

Leontiev, A.N. (1979). The problem of activity in psychology. In J. V. Wertsch (Ed.), *The concept of activity in Soviet psychology* (pp. 37–72). Armonk, NY: Sharpe.

National Council of Teachers of Mathematics. (2000). *Principles and standards for school mathematics.* Reston, VA: Author.

Outhred, L., Mitchelmore, M., McPhail, D., & Gould, P. (2003). Count me into measurement: A program for the early elementary school. In D. Clements & G. Bright (Eds.), *Learning and teaching measurement: 2003 NCTM yearbook* (pp. 81–99). Reston, VA: National Council of Teachers of Mathematics.

Sfard, A. (1991). On the dual nature of mathematical conceptions: Reflections on processes and objects as different sides of the same coin. *Educational Studies in Mathematics*, 22(1), 1–36.

Tall, D., Thomas, M., Davis, G., Gray, E. M., & Simpson, A. (2000). What is the object of the encapsulation of a process? *Journal of Mathematical Behavior, 18*(2), 223–241. ISSN 0732-3123.

Chapter 5

Technology and Developmentally Appropriate Practice for Young Children

Amelia Hewitt, *University of Houston - Downtown*

Carolyn Wade, *Houston, Texas*

Hsin-Hui Grace Lin, *University of Houston - Victoria*

Beverly Alford, *University of Houston - Downtown*

Meet Ben and Maya and their teacher

Ben and Maya, two pre-kindergarteners, are chattering excitedly as they take turns playing with an iPad. "It's B, Ben. Choose B," squeals Maya.

Ben says, "I know, Maya, B **IS** the letter. It's **MY** letter for Ben." Ben chooses B, and the two children giggle when they see they chose correctly.

Maya says, "Okay, now me! My turn!" Several letters appear on the screen, and the two children watch for a moment. Both seem unsure, and Ben begins touching the letters.

"No, Ben! It's my turn! I'll do it," Maya yells. Maya begins frantically touching each letter to hear the sound the letter makes.

The excitement alerts the teacher, who is nearby. The teacher approaches the children, but she watches them before saying anything.

Lordn / Shutterstock.com

Ermolaev Alexander / shutterstock.com

Ben says, "Maya, it's **THAT** one!" Ben points to the letter C. "C is for cat and cake. It's C, Maya! Pick C!"

Maya ignores Ben and continues touching each letter to hear the sounds. Maya laughs and says, "Look at that one! Look at the D. It's dancing." She presses D over and over and erupts into laughter.

Ben looks frustrated and looks up at the teacher for help. "She won't choose C! It's C! I told her!"

The teacher says, "I know, Ben. I heard you tell her that. I'm proud of you for knowing the correct answer, but right now, it's Maya's turn. Remember what we discussed about touching each letter first and repeating the sounds you hear before choosing a letter? Maya is trying all of the letters."

"But . . . she keeps doing it," Ben says.

"That's okay," says the teacher. "The D is silly!" The teacher then wiggles like the D, and the children laugh. The teacher stays near the children and watches for a few moments until she is sure the two have settled back into play. Maya eventually takes Ben's advice and chooses C. Both delight in the joy of the correct answer, and Maya hands the iPad to Ben. Ben begins the next round by touching each letter to hear the sound, and both children repeat the sounds the letters make.

The above scenario depicts play and interaction with technology in the prekindergarten classroom. This kind of play is optimal for learning centers in classrooms where children are involved in small group work and in content-related play (as guided by state and national standards). These two children chose the technology play center where the iPad is one of many options available to the children. What is clear from the scenario is that the teacher's rules for play with the iPad and the particular application the children were enjoying were made clear to the children before the two ever sat down to play.

Tania Kolinko / Shutterstock.com

The teacher's role in this scenario is vital to the success of technology in the classroom because she sets the learning objectives, rules, and guidelines for play and interaction as well as guides the children as they play with the technologies. Further, this teacher expanded the possibilities for the use of technology in her classroom to what is a more real-world situation outside the classroom. Should she have one isolated child learning basic tablet skills silently with an application or two children interactively learning letters and letter sounds while negotiating the bumpy road of sharing and respectful socialization in the scenario? The teacher thoughtfully planned and created an environment for the children where they are learning how to navigate the iPad, how to identify letters and sounds, and how to take turns—all while following the classroom rules. This is an example of how, when implemented appropriately using planning and developmentally appropriate practice (DAP), technology can be an asset to the early childhood classroom.

Pedagogy, by definition, is the method and practice of teaching. Early childhood education naturally envelops the method of practice and teaching. Understanding pedagogy leads to early childhood teachers who interact and support children as they work—while also informing others of and advocating for the importance of developmentally appropriate teaching with peers, administrators, parents, and others. Understanding pedagogy assists early childhood teachers in recognizing the importance of appropriate teaching methods in helping children understand their environment and in learning new concepts and skills. Understanding pedagogy allows early childhood teachers to value the practice of teaching that encourages authentic, high impact experiences in order to make connections with the real world.

The most common pedagogical belief in early childhood is that play is at the center of learning. Play is a natural context whereby young children explore to grow, develop, and learn.

"When you asked me what I did in school today and I say, 'I just played.' Please don't misunderstand me. For you see, I am learning as I play. I am learning to enjoy and be successful in my work. Today I am a child and my work is play." (Anita Wadley, 1974)

Through play, young children learn to make sense of the world around them while engaging in activities that promote higher-level thinking. Play is generally initiated by children and controlled by children. It allows children to collaborate with others while solving problems and practicing decision-making skills. Play offers children an opportunity to learn at their own pace and discover their own interests.

While "allowing children to play" sounds like a natural and simple directive, from a pedagogical perspective, there are many items to weigh and consider. An astute teacher knows that simply allowing children time to play is not enough to ensure appropriate and memorable learning opportunities for children. There are many pieces to the puzzle of the young child's classroom learning experience that include: (a) choosing the correct materials with which the children will engage, (b) planning the instruction about the materials and their use, and (c) assessing children's learning. Each of those items is an integral part of the learning process and environment of the early childhood classroom, and these elements do not stop with the introduction of technology. Teachers who set up the correct environment will direct many of the outcomes that they desire.

There are also additional considerations when specific curricular standards are addressed. State and national standards may be mandated by schools, which further compound the teacher's role in the child's learning environment. Teachers must integrate the required standards (including technology standards), while carefully balancing the growth of the child's social-emotional, physical, and cognitive development. This extensive list of items with which teachers must grapple seems daunting. These issues can, however, be addressed, knowing that such matters are interrelated and can be encapsulated under the umbrella of an early childhood teacher's most important pedagogical approach noted earlier as *developmentally appropriate practice*, commonly referred to as DAP. We clearly saw this demonstrated in the scenario earlier.

When turning to the place of technology in the world today, we find that it has been improved significantly within the past few decades. New technology, including that for young children, has changed most people's lives in many different ways. Although benefits from the advances in new technologies have aided many facets of people's work and play, we should not ignore the pitfalls from using technology as well. When educators have a deep understanding of the impact of technology on young children's learning, they will be able to provide better learning environments that incorporate authentic technology activities.

In this chapter, we discuss the importance of learning through play, DAP, and technology in the early childhood classroom. We also discuss the advantages

and pitfalls of technology and offer guidance for the many technological choices available for the early childhood classroom. Finally, we will look to the future possibilities of technology in classrooms for young children where the teacher's ongoing role as the facilitator encourages the young child's explorations and discoveries.

Developmentally Appropriate Practice

Technology is an integral part of the world today and should be included in the early childhood classroom; however, all teachers of young children, birth through age 8, must employ the tenets of DAP before any teaching activities, new curriculum, or instructional devices are deemed acceptable for use in the early childhood classroom. DAP is the lens through which early childhood education and best practices for children are viewed. The National Association for the Education of Young Children (NAEYC, 2009) is widely recognized as the prevailing authority on DAP guidelines and recommendations for young children. This association offers a set of DAP guidelines that teachers of young children follow, centering on a child's: (a) age, (b) individuality, (c) culture, and (d) developmental cognitive, social, emotional, and physical levels. DAP supports a hands-on, active classroom where children use their existing knowledge to gain new knowledge through exploration and play. DAP classrooms are child-centered with the teacher taking the role of classroom facilitator.

Age is the first determining factor of DAP, both chronologically and developmentally. A child's chronological age does not always match a child's developmental age. It is important to consider both in the child-centered classroom. Teachers should observe and note children's performance in all areas of development (cognitive, physical, emotional and social). As children grow, develop, and master the world around them, they move through the areas of development and achieve milestones. It is imperative for the early childhood teacher to recognize that each child grows and develops individually and reaches milestones in his or her own time. When a child has not yet mastered every milestone for his or her age, DAP teachers take note but do not panic. The child's development is a work in progress. Simply put, the child may still be working toward that milestone.

The teacher must take the child's development into account and understand that development (or lack thereof) in one area may affect a child's development in another area. For instance, a teacher who notices a child's language development is delayed may also notice that the child's social development has been affected by the language delay. A teacher who carefully considers the many facets of age indicators understands that, while a child may not have reached a milestone, he or she is developing and may need extra time, encouragement, and instruction to reach these developmental milestones. As teachers recognize individual differences in student learning, they differentiate instruction in today's classroom. This can be a key area for technology as young children fine-tune motor skills with mouse manipulation or appropriate touch screens that, in turn, aid in cognitive thinking (such as seriation or sorting) and social skills (such as problem solving in groups).

Individuality is the second identifying factor of DAP. Because providing the extra time and attention children need to develop is part of the teacher's job, the teacher must create opportunities for children to play and develop according to their individual needs. This second component of the definition of DAP, individual appropriateness, is imperative to a child's progress in the classroom. Teachers have classrooms with many children, and each individual child comes to school with his or her own knowledge, development, likes, dislikes, learning preferences, and experiences. When planning for the classroom, teachers should evaluate the needs of individual children and make decisions for the classroom based upon each child's needs.

The third identifying factor of DAP, cultural appropriateness, is also an integral piece of the DAP puzzle, and it works hand in hand with the child's age and individuality. Because children are unique and come from a variety of backgrounds and traditions, a teacher should make every effort to learn about each child's culture and create a classroom that nurtures respect, sensitivity, and understanding for all. This is especially important with technology, as children may come from a culture that values technology with parents who have the means to provide it from an early age, or, on the other hand, children may come from a culture and/ or economic status that has not allowed them past (or current) technological access. Children can thrive and grow in classrooms that foster cultural awareness and appreciation for others, and those efforts help to nurture self-respect and self-acceptance within each child.

Along with considering a child's age, individuality, and culture, a teacher also needs to plan the method by which children will learn in the classroom. The fourth identifying factor of DAP is developing the whole child (cognitive, social, emotional, physical). As noted, DAP supports the fact that children learn best through play. High-impact, real life experiences where children can explore and have fun through play is a fundamental part of the young child's learning process. Children's learning should be experiential and hands-on as opposed to traditional classrooms that employ worksheets, silence, and all teacher-directed activities. When children's interest levels are high, as they are during play, learning and development are a natural outgrowth of the play process. With careful planning, a teacher can implement play as the primary method by which children are learning in the early childhood classroom. When considering technology with young children, play must be at the forefront of consideration in planning activities to ensure cognitive, social, emotional, and physical development.

Developmentally Appropriate Practice, Technology, and Development

The saturation of technology and digital media into the homes, schools, and the lives of young children for both entertainment and educational purposes is inescapable. Television and video remain the most frequently and widely used types of screen media, but access to mobile devices by children as young as 2 years of age is increasing (Rideout, 2014). While some fear that greater exposure to technology and digital media will impair areas of children's brain development and lead to poorer executive functions and self-regulation (Courage & Troseth, 2016; Greenfield, 2015), some scientists and child developmentalists take a more measured approach, striving to comprehend the beneficial factors and effects of digital media and recognizing that new technologies are here to stay.

The National Institute for Early Education Research (NIEER, 2011) has stated that, notwithstanding the ever-increasing technological toys available for children, parents and early childhood professionals should provide ample time for children to "explore their own creativity through imaginative, child-directed play for future innovations in technology and beyond." Hirsh-Pasek et al. (2015) reviewed the literature on the science of learning from the fields of neuroscience, education, psychology, cognitive science, and linguistics to propose four pillars for evaluating the educational potential of technology and mobile device applications (apps) for children over the age of 2 years. They suggested that: (a) learning occurs when the learner is active rather than passive; (b) learning occurs when the learner is engaged (not distracted); (c) learning occurs when the content is meaningful; and (d) learning is maximized by social interaction (Hirsh-Pasek et al., 2015). Their findings suggested that parents, educators, and other stakeholders ought to carefully evaluate technology and apps, avoiding those that do not promote engagement and socially interactive experiences.

The American Academy of Pediatrics (AAP) (2016) has detailed its position regarding screen time and how to strike a healthy balance between the use of digital media and children's development. For children younger than 18 months, the AAP discourages the use of screen media. For children 18 to 24 months, the AAP advises against children using media by themselves; rather, the organization advises parents to introduce digital, high-quality programming/apps and to use them with their children. Regarding children older than 2 years, the AAP states that media limits are ve___ ___ ___ e of high-quality programming should occur for no more than 1 hour or less per ___ ___ (2016, October) suggests that parents co-view or co-play with their children, finding other activities in which to engage together that are healthy for the body and mind.

The NAEYC and the Fred Rogers Center also adopted and published a joint position statement on *Technology and Young Children*, advising educators and families to consider the latest, ongoing public health recommendations when placing appropriate limits on technology and media use for children from birth to age 8 (NAEYC, 2012). Their joint statement highlighted the following six ideas:

- When used intentionally and appropriately, technology and interactive media are effective tools to support learning and development.
- Intentional use requires early childhood teachers and administrators to have information and resources regarding the nature of these tools and the implications of their use with children.

- Limitations on the use of technology and media are important.
- Special considerations must be given to the use of technology with infants and toddlers.
- Attention to digital citizenship and equitable access is essential.
- Ongoing research and professional development are needed.

One of the key points in NAEYC's statement is that teachers should select, use, integrate, and evaluate digital media in intentional and developmentally appropriate ways, paying careful attention to the appropriateness and the quality of the content, the child's experience, and the opportunities for co-engagement. Likewise, a review of the literature on the potential harms and benefits of digital media abstracted the same general message across all studies: the potential of technology to support young children's learning is determined by the quality of the media and the way in which it is implemented (Rvachew, 2016). Teachers of all ages of children are encouraged to monitor studies that are continuing to emerge on technology use by the young.

A significant consideration concerning the quality of technology and young children involves the rise of technology in children's everyday lives and questions parents and educators may have about the appropriate length of time spent in front of screens. This is of particular importance as it relates to young children and teachers' use of technology in the classroom (NAEYC, 2012). The United States Department of Education (2016) recently published a policy statement concerning technology use in the classrooms for children ages 2 to 8. The recommendation states that technology and screen time in the classroom should not take the place of active learning, unstructured play, and creative play. Active, hands-on participation and play should remain the primary teaching methods during the school day. While the recommendation does not offer specific time guidelines for teachers, it does suggest that each classroom teacher should assess the direct usefulness of the technology and how it relates to lesson planning in a specific classroom.

The American Academy of Pediatrics (AAP) (2016) recommendation differs from the U.S. Department of Education regarding a time limit on use of technology with young children under the age of 6. The AAP's recommendation is that: children under 18 months do not use screen media other than for video phone calls; 18- to 24-month-olds can view high-quality children's programming with parents; age 2- to 5-year-olds should have screen time limited to 1 hour per day; and 6-year-old children should limit the time spent in front of screens. The 6-year-old age group recommendation mirrors the Department of Education's guidelines in its suggestion that screen time should not take the place of activity and interaction with family and peers. The AAP further suggests that time designated without media, such as family meals and bedtime, are important.

With careful consideration of recommendations by NAEYC, the United States Department of Education, and the AAP, teachers who employ DAP in their classrooms and who monitor technology usage for length of time and for technology's direct contribution to learning can open their classrooms to enhanced learning opportunities for young children.

Technology Usage

When all of the elements of DAP, play, and assessment are considered, screening of possible technologies for the early childhood classroom can begin. As mentioned earlier, NAEYC and the Fred Rogers Center for Early Learning and Children's Media at Saint Vincent College, in 2012, released a joint research-based position statement, *Technology and Interactive Media as Tools in Early Childhood Programs Serving Children Birth through Age 8.* This specifically states that, "Technology should not be used for activities that are not educationally sound, not developmentally appropriate, or not effective (electronic worksheets for preschoolers, for example)" (p. 4). However, technology usage has grown dramatically during the past half century and impacts children daily, making technology an integral part of children's lives. The list of popular technology products includes televisions, phones,

Monkey Business Images / Shutterstock.com

computers, cell phones, cameras, electronic tablets, and video players as well as software and applications. (Rideout, Foehr, & Roberts, 2010).

Technology usage may vary according to income levels which can add to the difficulty of choosing appropriate technology applications. Among all the technology products, television was found the most popular media for families (Gutnick, Robb, Takeuchi, & Kotler, 2011). TV is especially popular among younger children. However, the influence of the Internet is growing fast. In 2017, nearly all children age 8 and under lived in an American household with some type of mobile device. In 2017, 95 percent of families had a mobile device, yet in 2011, less than 10 percent of families had a tablet; that has grown to nearly 80 percent having a tablet in 2017. Children's use of media has also changed. In 2017, children 8 and under spent an average of about two-and-a-quarter hours a day with screen media. The average amount of time spent with mobile devices each day has tripled since 2011, going from 5 minutes a day in 2011 to 15 minutes a day in 2013 to 48 minutes a day in 2017 (Robb, 2017)–not to mention the time children spendt on video games, music, and other gadgets. Technology is clearly present in most, if not all, children's lives. It is definitely influencing the way children grow and learn, making it imperative for teachers to take this into consideration when planning learning activities that best meet the needs of the early childhood learner.

Advantages of Using Technology

Modern technology has changed people's ways of thinking, entertaining, and connecting with the rest of the world. There are many ways that a person can find the information that he or she needs. including watching TV, listening to the radio, or searching information online. Smartphones, laptops, electronic tablets, and computers allow people to network and communicate with others through the Internet. Popular social media such as Facebook, Twitter, and emails provide venues for people to keep in touch with one another. We can expect that children will need and want to have skills to use these tools.

Some technology products are designed for learning in addition to fun. These products can be wonderful learning tools for enriching children's learning experiences and allowing them to learn at their own pace. For example, Penuel et al. (2009) examined technology usage in a classroom and students' learning outcome. This study included 398 preschool children whose teachers adopted a technology-enhanced curriculum by intentionally presenting curriculum content in videos, teacher-led activities, and computer games. Students watched the videos and participated in related large group activities. This meant that in the classrooms, their teachers co-viewed the videos and provided coherent activities. Students in this study showed improvement in their literacy skills, such as naming letters, knowing the sounds of letters, knowing concepts of story and print, and recognizing letters in a child's own name.

Maria Uspenskaya / Shutterstock.com

Technology can improve teaching and learning for young children if teachers plan with intention. It is important for teachers to encourage young children to explore varied technology products/applications and find ones that best meet the needs of the children. Moreover, teachers must remember that for children to reap the most benefit from technology use, it must be based upon developmental guidelines.

Pitfalls of Using Technology

Although technology can bring many positive effects on people's lives, some negative outcomes with using technology have been found—particularly with young people. Children who spent many hours using technology products were predisposed to having several problems. First, this kind of activity had a negative impact on the children's health, resulting in lack of sleep time or development of irregular sleep patterns (Zimmerman, 2008). Second, some of these children were found to be incapable of paying attention and had difficulties following instructions (Hastings et al., 2009). Their attention spans were too short, which prevented them from learning effectively. Third, school-aged children were found to have lower grade performances and often had more learning problems as compared to their classmates. Furthermore, poor language development was also found to be associated with children who spent considerable time using technology (Hastings et al., 2009).

Additional research findings show that children who spent many hours using technology products tended to have poor social skills. These children often spent their time playing games and did not interact with others. Violent videos and technology games have become more accessible to young children. Due to their inability to distinguish between the virtual and real worlds, young children who spent more time watching violent videos or playing violent games were found to exhibit more behavior problems (Anderson, Gentile, & Buckley, 2007; Dubow, Huesmann, & Greenwood, 2007).

Technology can still provide positive learning opportunities for young children despite the pitfalls. Technology devices can be used in a manner that can support children's development and encourage children's curiosity and exploration. First, teachers must always double-check that the software and applications do not contain any sexual or violent content. Secondly, teachers should consider their students' ages, and the activities they select should match with the children's physical, cognitive, and social-emotional developmental levels. Lastly, teachers should ask themselves, "What benefits can children obtain from incorporating technology into teaching?" By using DAP to guide the implementation of technology teaching and learning in the classroom are enhanced.

Technology in the Classroom

Most children come to school already equipped with a basic knowledge in technology. From the time they are born, children are now immersed in a world that is made up of technological advances. Teachers must ensure that all children in the classroom are provided ample opportunities and time with technology (Copple & Bredekamp, 2009). As teachers, we should make the most of the inherent knowledge shared by children and encourage technology in ways that benefit learning. Children need time to develop skills and learn to use technology in ways that benefit learning. Technology is a tool for young children to use that can assist in solving problems, locating information, and learning at their own pace. Teachers, however, must be cognizant of how young children grow, develop, and learn before introducing technology into the classroom. It is imperative for teachers to remember that children learn by doing, and, in a DAP environment, technology should be utilized as a way to engage children to explore, discuss, and document learning. As children become proficient with the use of technology as a tool in the classroom, teachers can and should take advantage of the great resources available.

Approaches to Developmentally Appropriate Technology

With a plethora of information at one's fingertips, it is often daunting and sometimes difficult to choose and provide the most appropriate approaches to technology. Teachers must stay abreast of current technological trends and be knowledgeable about which trends offer the best opportunities for young students to learn. Teachers must also be cognizant of when and how to utilize technology for the best developmental experiences. They must make informed decisions about using technology based on the activity(ies) occurring. Each approach offers its own solution to learning. Teachers should carefully consider these approaches as they use them in the classroom.

Information presented in the next section gives insight into technology approaches that offer a developmentally appropriate guide to authentic learning. Teachers can build confidence about what technology to use, how to use it, and when to assess its effectiveness in the classroom. In essence, teachers become technology connectors using *"technivity"* to enhance and expand knowledge.

Developmentally Appropriate Devices Used in Technology

Kindle Fire or Other E-readers

The Kindle Fire digital device is designed mainly for reading eBooks. The device allows the user to read newspapers, magazines, and other text. This particular device can also be used by children to highlight, copy, and save information to be downloaded at their convenience. View the following video to learn how to use the Kindle Fire in one's classroom.

Kindle Fire in the Classroom
www.youtube.com/watch?v=yp1fgfMuG0w

Technivity with the Kindle

1st Grade

Mrs. Clayborn's first-grade class reads the Kindle book *The Farm Yard* by Abby Sage (2014). As they read, the children highlight high frequency words that they know. Once the story is complete, children list of all the words they found in their personal Word Journal. Using words from their personal Word Journal, children write their own story about animals.

iPad/iPhone/iPod/Windows Surface Tablets

Smart devices are designed for the user to perform various tasks and encourage interaction with technology. Children utilize smart devices in the classroom by playing games, which is effective for practicing skills in various subject areas as well as interacting with music and art. Smart devices can be used to create videos of projects and/or take pictures to document the progress of assignments. Children can create virtual presentations, write stories, and illustrate stories with applications that allow them to draw and even "paint" their own art work virtually. Some smart surface tablet technology to consider includes Fable Tablet by Isabella Products, offering children a 7" screen to view. Collections that are "kid-friendly" can be downloaded from vizitme.com. Another smart technology surface

tablet is Samsung Kids Galaxy Tab E Lite. It offers a 7-inch screen as well and is compatible with most apps. These tablets cost between $85 and $100. They are easy to carry and manipulate with small hands.

All these devices make use of *apps* or software applications that are designed in the form of games and can be used for educational as well as entertainment purposes. Many of today's children grow up with knowledge about computer apps and are savvy about utilizing applications before entering the classroom. Teachers can facilitate that accumulated knowledge by preparing activities that take advantage of all that technology has to offer. In the classroom, applications offer hands-on experiences to children that connect skills to real life. For example, when children read about frogs on the iPad and then watch a video about the life cycle of the frog and the frog in its environment, they make connections about how the animal grows and lives. They make comparisons to themselves when they see how the animal moves, eats, and interacts as well as with the life cycle of other animals. Following developmentally appropriate guidelines, teachers have the power to teach children how to use technology to its fullest potential and not just use it as a "time filler." Please visit www.ipads4teaching.net for updated apps to utilize in teaching. Storytelling, collaboration, and creativity are just a few to find at this site.

Technivity with the iPad

PK/K

Ms. Gomez reads the iPad book *Gossie* by Olivier Dunrea (2002) aloud in a small group using a pointer to track the words read. Once the story is complete, children create props and become characters or items from the book as they act out the story. The teacher records their play to share with parents and/or to keep for various assessment purposes.

Digital Cameras

Digital cameras use a lens to capture images and video that can be stored for later use. In the classroom, teachers can use digital cameras to record videos and take photographs that document and help to better assess learning. Teachers can assess children's progress by studying images that have been archived throughout the school year. Children can easily upload videos and photographs recorded during activities or projects to files on the classroom computer (see Figure 5.1). They can use digital photographs to create stories, journals, and interest inventories to share ideas or document steps or progress on a project. Children can take their pictures one step further to create their own books out of the digital pictures taken. They can "read" their books in class and share them with their peers and family. Although these examples of graphic literacy may not replace the picture on the refrigerator door, they will be precious to most parents, when shared.

Figure 5.1   A young girl enjoys using a smartphone to take pictures.

Technivity with the Digital Camera

2nd Grade

Mr. Wong groups children in the classroom into partner pairs. Children work with their partner to take photos of items and rooms around the school. Children create a collage of their photos and prepare a written paragraph description of *Our School in Pictures* using descriptive words. This type of experience can also be important in having children understand categories, so Mr. Wong also assigns them in groups or as individuals to take pictures of "real life" rectangles they see in their school for one of his mathematics activities. There are a number of sites and apps that help to make electronic collages, including Canva (www.canva.com/create/photo-collages) where one's own pictures can be loaded or stock items can be used.

Voice Recorders

Voice recorders are small devices that are easily used to record verbal memos for later playback. These usually come with an output option (normally a *USB* port) so that recordings can be easily downloaded onto a computer. Children can use voice recorders in the classroom for all types of projects. For example, children can record narratives, interviews, sounds needed for particular projects, music, and performances. They can create their own unique rhymes and songs that assist with literacy and mathematics skills as well as share their recordings with others to make meaningful connections to literacy and mathematics skills being presented. Often when children share their work with other children, they come to understand the concept better and are able to see that concept presented in different ways. These experiences ensure that children learn new information in ways that are appropriate for their individual needs.

Technivity with the Voice Recorder
Prek/K—2nd Grade

Ms. Nguyen allows children to work individually or in partner pairs as a band. They plan a song, chant, or rhyme. Then, they create a tune for their song, chant, or rhyme. The children can create musical instruments or use ones from the classroom. They name their song, chant, or rhyme and record it using the voice recorder. Ms. Nguyen downloads the recordings to the computer, and children type lyrics and create a music video to accompany the recording.

Garnet Photo / Shutterstock.com

Interactive boards can now be found in many classrooms across the country. These boards project displays from the computer. They usually attach to a portable stand that can be moved around the classroom. However, they can also be attached directly to the wall. View the following video to learn how to use whiteboards in the classroom at www.youtube.com/watch?v=ftej0udAasQ. Children can use interactive boards to participate in activities that the teacher has approved or created to practice skills that they are learning in the classroom. They can also access Websites and play games that the teacher has approved to assist in the transfer of information. Children can practice skills and interact with games while exploring concepts on the interactive board. They can work individually or in small groups as they interact with technology up close and personal.

Examples of such interactive Websites are:

- Math Playground
  www.mathplayground.com
- FunBrain.com
  www.funbrain.com
- Cool Math 4 Kids
  www.coolmath4kids.com
- Kids Math Games
  www.kidsmathgamesonline.com

Technivity with the Interactive Board
K—5th Grade

Mr. Garcia practices mathematic skills by using the Website *Mr. Wolfe's Math (www.sites .google.com/a/norman.k12.ok.us/mr-wolfe-s-math-interactive-whiteboard/home)*. Children in the classroom practice various math skills while interacting with the program.

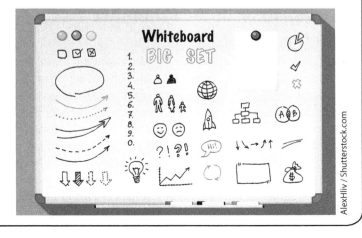

AlexHliv / Shutterstock.com

- Math Games—PBS Kids
  www.pbskids.org/games/math
- Alphabet Soup—PBS Kids
  www.pbskids.org/sesame/games/alphabet-soup/20
- Interactive Whiteboard Resources for Teachers
  www.whiteboardblog.co.uk/2009/07/20-interactive-whiteboard-resources-for-teachers

Teachers who plan well will use interactive boards to watch live Web lectures and have children participate in webinars. This device has the capability to engage and connect children from all over the world through live streams.

Developmentally Appropriate Tools and the Computer

Live Conference Apps (Skype/Oovoo/Zoom)

Live conference apps like Skype/Oovoo/Zoom are basically video phone calls that allow the user to see with whom they are speaking through the camera on the computer. The basic services of these video cams are usually free to users. Basic Skype services allow users to communicate at one time. Basic Oovoo services allow for up to six users to communicate at one time. Zoom services offer video conferencing and collaboration through video or phone conferencing. These apps assist teachers in bringing the outside world into the classroom. Teachers can partner with other teachers across the world to have live chats as well as teaching sessions that bring learning from around the world directly to the children they are teaching. Teachers can also bring in people from the community to help children understand concepts or gain information about topics being studied. For example, children would enjoy learning about the birth of a new giraffe at the local zoo. Invite the zoo keeper to communicate with the class via Skype and open the children up to a whole new meaning of "trip to the zoo." By using these "video telephones", so to speak, teachers bring children from faraway places or from the classroom next door closer, and they actually see other children in real time learning from the natural environment. By utilizing Websites like The Complete Educator's Guide To Using Skype Effectively in the Classroom (www.theedublogger.com/2011/04/03/the-complete-educators-guide-to-using-skype-effectively-in-the-classroom) or Zoom in the Classroom (www.youtube.com/watch?v=bjO7Zzm5MfY), teachers can master the art of the video call.

Evgeniya Uvarova / Shutterstock.com

Technivity with the Computer

Any Grade Level

Mrs. Johnson sets up a video call to another grade level or partnering class in the same grade level. Children brainstorm, share ideas, and/or partner on projects by interacting and chatting live with the other students. Mrs. Johnson makes the first video call as a class. Children choose partners or small groups and then communication begins on an as needed basis. Mrs. Johnson collaborates with the teacher/s from the other class and shares lessons and/or reads stories during video calls as well. She was able to also make some contacts from The Teacher's Corner (www.theteacherscorner.net/penpals). Read about an American teacher who arranged videoconferencing with a classroom in Peru. They set up name games between the children, teaching a simple song to each other, counting, and so forth (www.langwitches.org/blog/2008/11/16/videoconferencing-with-elementary-school-students).

Graphic Organizers/PowerPoint/Draw

Graphic organizers and programs like PowerPoint/Draw are organizers to put information into visual formats. These programs help the user to record information in an organized manner. Using the multitude of readily available graphic organizers for downloading, children can create charts and graphs to record information for better understanding. They can then present information to others to show what they have learned. Teachers can utilize these programs for helping their lessons become more visual. They can organize facts and pictures into graphics to help connect information.

Technivity with a Graphic Organizer

2nd Grade

Mr. Lopez partners children during a themed study of the rainforest. Partner pairs create a graphic organizer to show what they are interested in researching about the rainforest. Graphics must include a topic, three questions children want to learn about the topic, and a project idea that will present the information learned upon completion of the research.

Topic _____

Name _____   KWL

What I know	What I wonder	What I learned

Source: authors

Windows Movie Maker

Windows Movie Maker is a program that allows the user to create movies and stories. Children can create movies and/or stories that represent content learned. Teachers can assist younger children by inserting illustrations into the program and having the students narrate their specific media clips.

Technivity . . . Try It!

1st Grade

Ms. Dunn has her first-grade class work individually or in partner pairs to create a story. Children complete the story with illustrations using a draw tool or using paint or pencil paper methods. Ms. Dunn then inserts the illustrations into the Movie Maker program. Children narrate each slide of the story. They share with other classes or parents. Older students in the elementary movie making club create their own stories and film them. An example of this is *The Ghost of Bethke* created by fourth- and fifth-grade students using an iPad. (www.youtube.com/watch?v=g9UQYqOaFnc).

dotshock / Shutterstock.com

Approaches to using technology in the classroom encourage engagement and foster meaningful connections with information. They drive creative thinking and active participation. These approaches, however, are only as good as the teacher who plans them. Teachers should think about technology as an intentional part of the classroom that can assist in helping students make connections to understand what they are learning.

"Technology does not drive purposeful learning; teachers' intentional instructional planning does" (Meaningful Technology Integration in Early Learning, 2008, p. 3). As teachers plan activities and information to present to children, they must include technology that enhances and informs curriculum.

Assessment Approaches to Technology

Teachers who utilize approaches to technology intentionally support developmentally appropriate real-world learning while facilitating purposeful activity. They encourage children to grow and learn to the fullest potential. As children interact and make advances technologically, it is essential for teachers to assess student outcomes. Technology can also help to create a very clear picture of the child and his/her abilities, which, in turn, drives instruction for the future.

Assessment in the early childhood classroom is ongoing. It begins the very first day of school and is repeated each day until the very last day of school. Teachers of young children use observational assessment methods, such as checklists, rubrics, rating scales, anecdotal records, and portfolios, to record students' physical, cognitive, social, and emotional progress throughout the year. Assessments (that are highly aided by technology) provide valuable information about individual students as well as the general growth and development of all students in an early childhood classroom (NAEYC, 2009).

Teachers of young children assess learning for their own knowledge about how children are developing in the classroom and to help parents keep abreast of their child's growth and development. Through assessment teachers can easily inform parents of strengths and weaknesses in a child's development as well as provide suggestions on developmental technologies that can assist that child's learning. It is important to note that teachers must be aware of each child's physical capabilities to manipulate certain technology rather than the actual knowledge he or she has about a particular content. Authentic assessment allows for teachers to focus on what children can do instead of what they can't. It aligns naturally with developmentally appropriate approaches to teaching with technology.

Teachers utilizing authentic assessment must ensure that they are meeting standards and are teaching what is expected developmentally for the age, individuality, and culture of each child. According to Hewitt and Jenkins (2012), authentic assessment allows teachers to understand what is happening in the classroom while analyzing their own teaching styles and approaches to learning. Teachers become participants in the process of assessing and collecting important information that guides their teaching. The results obtained through authentic assessment can assist in "planning curriculum, making thematic unit decisions, selecting instructional strategies, partnering, or grouping students for projects or centers" (p. 13). One prime use of technology for teachers would be in creating individual portfolios. Digital portfolios for each child can be stored for quick accessibility and can include both student work and videos to help show growth or difficulties throughout the year. One example of ideas for fine motor skills shows still shots, but these could easily include video examples as well (www.prekinders.com/finemotor-portfolios).

Many states have standards and competencies set for various age groups of children. In the state of Texas, for example, the Texas Essential Knowledge and Skills (2013) require that teachers address children's technologically skills. It is suggested that children ages 5 to 8: understand basic knowledge and skills; engage in communication and collaboration; begin research and information fluency; foster critical thinking, problem-solving, and decision-making for digital citizenship; and learn technology operations and concepts. Because the NAEYC (2012) sets guidelines for technology that are rooted in DAP, their position statement on technology reflects the importance of intentional teaching to benefit young children's development through the use of technology. A spiral curriculum, where technology information is introduced at an early age and repeats in difficulty as the child grows and learns, ensures that teachers begin instruction at the correct level and that the knowledge and skills increase appropriately in difficulty with age and/or development each year. Copple and Bredekamp (2009) state that for children who are in preschool through the primary grades, teachers should "make thoughtful use of computers and other te~~c~~ _Question 2_ ~~~~ ." (pp. 174, 242, 315). See Chapter 9 in this book for further information on inte~~~~ s for teachers.

Observational, Authentic Assessments

Observational, authentic assessments are performance-based assessments that occur in natural settings and focus on what children know about the skills and activities being assessed. They allow the teacher to measure student performance and outcomes using developmentally appropriate methods. There are several observational, authentic assessments that are useful and support intentional outcomes when assessing the use of technology to enhance student performance.

There are apps available to assist teachers in assessing students. However, this area still has much room to grow. One such app is Confer. It is an app that can help the teacher create groups of students and take notes about them directly on an iPhone or iPad. Another app that has note-taking capabilities is Teacher Pal. It facilitates taking roll, can take notes on behaviors, and can add notes about students. It is available for the iPhone or iPad in addition to the Android platform.

Anecdotal Record

For an example, see Anecdotal Notes (www.youtube.com/watch?v=gt-HIcZPzyI). Anecdotal records are notes or anecdotes taken of actual activities and/or events that are taking place in the classroom. The content of anecdotal records can be about individual students or a small group of students and tell a story about the students involved. Anecdotal records should reflect facts about the activity being observed. An anecdotal record may be taken on an event that lasts a short time or up to several minutes (see Figure 5.2). The following Websites also give information on creating anecdotal records:

www.slideshare.net/mbuurstra/observing-children-and-writing-anecdotal-records

www.prekinders.com/anecdotal-records

When writing an anecdotal record, a teacher should follow these simple steps:

- Describe the setting and time.
- Tell the names of the students being observed.
- Write exactly what is being observed; use quotes when possible. Avoid judgments when writing the observation. Save these thoughts for the "comments" section.
- Comment or give conclusions about what was observed.

Checklists

Create a Checklist in Microsoft Word. A checklist is a simple list of skills or items that the teacher creates to ensure children have accomplished particular skills. Teachers can observe children involved in technology use

---

Anecdotal Recording Form

Observer:

Children/Observed Time:

Description of Observation:

Notes/Comments:

Figure 5.2   Anecdotal recording form.
Source: authors

Checklist of Technology Skills

	KEY
	/ = skill visible; needs more practice
	* = accomplished skill first time
	∧ = skill not visible

Child			
Skill Assessed	3	2	1
Child			
Skill Assessed	3	2	1
Child			
Skill Assessed	3	2	1
Child			
Skill Assessed	3	2	1

Figure 5.3   Checklist of technology skills.
Source: authors

and simply check off the skills they have accomplished. A comment section can be added to the checklist for teachers to write particular information observed (see Figure 5.3). To create a checklist, go to the following site: Checklist in Microsoft Word (www.youtube.com/watch?v=PvxlzzNFlEA). The following Websites also give information on creating checklists:

www.teachthought.com/pedagogy/simple-checklist-can-improve-learning

pblchecklist.4teachers.org/index.shtml

When creating a checklist follow these simple steps:

- Determine the skill(s) to assess.
- Create a chart with child(ren)'s names.
- Create columns with dates/comment space for using checklist several times.
- Create a key for tracking assessment results.

The teac   Question 3   or any skill that he or she wants to note with this type of technology.

Scored Authentic Assessment

Analytic Rubric

An analytic rubric is a set of guidelines with specific criteria that allows the teacher to assign grades to projects or activities. It works well in grade levels where performance is rated through a grading system. It can be given to children prior to beginning an activity or project so that they will also know the expectation(s) for scoring and can better match their efforts to those as they are working. Analytic rubrics contain specific descriptors that define what to look for at each level of performance. Indicators are given to let the child and the assessor know what to look for in the work (see Figure 5.4 based on third-grade Texas essential element objectives).

Rubric for Technology Application

Skill Assessed	3	2	1	Total:
Publishes product using different media collaboratively	Uses at least 3 different media in product	Uses at least 2 different media in product	Uses at least 1 media in product	
Selects and uses font attributes, colors, white space, graphics for multiple communication media	Uses all characteristics of multiple communication media in product	Uses at least 2 characteristics for multiple communication media in product	Uses at least 1 characteristic for multiple communication media in product	
Collaborates with partner/s through personal learning communities	Collaborates with partner through personal learning community/ies 3 or more times	Collaborates with partner through personal learning community/ies 2 times	Collaborates with partner through personal learning community/ies at least 1 time	
			Total Score:	

Figure 5.4 Rubric for Technology Application.
Source: authors

When creating an analytic rubric follow these simple steps:

- Determine the skill(s) to assess.
- Determine how much the assignment is worth in points. This varies by assignment. The figure above shows a rubric with points ranging from 1 to 3. The total score for this rubric is 9 points.
- Create criteria to meet each point value chosen. Let 3 be the greatest and 1 be the least. Figure 5.4 shows 3 is the greatest value and 1 is the least.
- Create a grid/chart with the points and criteria that describe each point value.

When used appropriately, observational, authentic assessment takes into account all developmental levels and considers the needs of each individual child in the classroom. Assessing students should focus on information that allows teachers to make informed decisions about future curriculum while following developmentally appropriate guidelines. As children learn new technologies, they will progress at different paces; however, all children should make progress. Teachers must be well equipped with appropriate knowledge about how children grow and learn cognitively, physically, and socially. They must understand new technological advances and be cognizant of the fact that each child will assimilate new information at different rates and in different w... Most importantly, teachers must be well versed in state mandates and new advances in technology; in es... ...vvy.

Question 4

Be a Tech-Savvy Teacher

A "tech-savvy teacher" always follows three Ps when teaching: Prepare, Practice, and Perform.

Prepare *in order to stay current and informed* as a tech-savvy teacher. It is imperative to be cognizant of new advances in technology and try out new things in the classroom. Children are often well informed when it comes to the latest and most exciting new technology. Teachers should encourage children to share with others and "teach the teacher." What better way to promote *"technivity"* than to have the child as the teacher!

Other important information to keep in mind:

- Choose open-ended technology that offers children a chance to interact not only with the programs but with each other.
- Don't be afraid of technological advances.

Remember, the more teachers stay current in technological advances, the better prepared they are to assist children in their learning.

Practice *new technology often* to encourage children to interact and collaborate on building knowledge through interactions. Setting up activities and projects that promote collaboration among groups of children/partners or collaborative groups of four to six students will be of great benefit to children to keep working and to the teacher as children assist each other for "how to . . ." rather than calling on the teacher to help every time. Children working in these small collaborative partnerships groups often generate new ideas and work well above their developmental levels as they discuss and problem solve to inform their peers.

Teachers must practice new technology as much as possible. Even though it is sometimes intimidating to try new things, they must not let their own inhibitions limit what they can do in the classroom. By practicing what they don't know, it will help them to learn it and improve their skills. Practicing with children will help to perfect it, always keeping in mind that all technology choices should have the child at the forefront.

Perform *well with technology*. Once teachers are comfortable with new technology, they can bring about intended learning outcomes in the classroom by using various approaches to technology. Moreover, teachers can connect technology experiences with state-mandated guidelines to ensure well-rounded exploration.

As mentioned, states establish guidelines for children to experience in technology. The NAEYC (2012) is working to ensure that those states involved in the new Common Core national standards adhere to the tenets of DAP, but they suggest that teachers may need additional training and appropriate tools. They also suggest that ongoing learning opportunities be made available to teachers in addition to appropriate curriculum materials. All of these will aid in teachers in performing their best with technology and optimize the knowledge and skills of young learners. Teachers are responsible for providing experiences that enhance children's growth and development with technology on a daily basis and can easily integrate concepts into lessons that allow children to practice skills through hands-on applications. For example, when teaching a lesson about animal habitats to young children, it is easy for teachers to use videos, stories, and natural zoological sites to enhance information presented to children during the lesson. In addition, children can utilize the smartboard, tablets, or computer to further their own knowledge by researching particular animals in their habitats. Teachers should make a point to perform with technology in some way daily. Even simple tasks such as email, note-taking, or reading stories for fun can generate learning authentically. Regardless of the technological task, teachers should perform it well and often.

Technology for Optimum Learning

Classroom teachers meet the needs of all learners by making sure to utilize various teaching styles with technology. They must think about what's best for children and plan accordingly. Grouping children encourages use of varied learning styles. For example, teachers pair visual learners with auditory and kinesthetic learners. When children in groups begin to discuss, clarify ideas, and evaluate others' ideas, they use higher-level thinking skills (Clifford, 2012). Gardner (1983) suggests that children have many diverse abilities that focus on multiple ways of learning. By focusing on relevant technological activities, teachers can ensure that children will make use of these diverse abilities and connect learning to the real world. Children who are provided technology that supports their individual styles of learning and levels of knowledge and skills will make progress in all areas of development (Gardner, 1999).

As an early childhood classroom teacher, assigning projects and activities for students to complete on their own should encourage challenges for children and incorporate technology naturally while offering challenges that encourage children to develop problem-solving skills. Teachers should be able and willing to facilitate new technology for children as well as be comfortable and well versed with the technology chosen.

Teachers should strive to create high impact experiences while integrating technology to facilitate appropriate activities and make intentional decisions about developmentally (and individually) appropriate approaches for children. They also consider the proper environment and equipment to support the growth and learning of new skills that foster higher-level thinking and a positive foundation for the years ahead of technology use that children will need in today's world.

Helpful Sites for Tech-Savvy Teachers

Early Childhood Teacher:
www.earlychildhoodteacher.org/blog/ece-technology-10-trending-tools-for-teachers

Using Technology in the Early Childhood Classroom:
www.teacher.scholastic.com/professional/bruceperry/using_technology.htm

PBS Kids:
www.pbskids.org

Early Childhood:
www.earlychildhood.com

Gayles's Preschool Rainbow:
www.preschoolrainbow.org

The Activity Idea Place:
www.123child.com/

For Teachers and Classroom Staff:
www.headstartinclusion.org/teachers

13 Activities for Kids Using Technology in an Off-Screen:
www.handsonaswegrow.com/kids-using-technology-activities/125

Learning Sites for Kids (and Teachers):
www.edtechideas.com/125-sites-for-kids

References

American Academy of Pediatrics. (2016). *Where we stand: Screen time.* Retrieved from www.healthychildren.org/English/family-life/Media/pages/Where-We-Stand-TV-Viewing-Time.aspx

American Academy of Pediatrics. (2016, October). *American Academy of Pediatrics announces new recommendations for children's media use.* Retrieved from www.aap.org/en-us/about-the-aap/aap-press-room/pages/american-academy-of-pediatrics-announces-new-recommendations-for-childrens-media-use.aspx

Anderson, C. A., Gentile, D. A., & Buckley, K. E. (2007). *Violent video game effects on children and adolescents: Theory, research, and public policy.* New York, NY: Oxford Press.

Clifford, M. (2012). *Facilitating collaborative learning: 20 things you need to know from the pros.* Retrieved from www.opencolleges.edu.au/informed/features/facilitating-collaborative-learning-20-things-you-need-to-know-from-the-pros

Common Sense Media, & Rideout, V. (2011). *Zero to eight: Children's media use in America.* Retrieved from Common Sense Media www.commonsensemedia.org/research/zero-to-eight-childrens-media-use-in-america

Copple, C., & Bredekamp, S. (Eds.). (2009). *Developmentally appropriate practice in early childhood programs serving children from birth through age 8* (3rd ed.). Washington, DC: NAEYC.

Courage, M. L., & Troseth, G. L. (2016). *Infants, toddlers and learning from screen media.* In R. E. Tremblay, M. Boivin, & R. D. Peters (Eds.), *Encyclopedia on early childhood development.* Retrieved from www.child-encyclopedia .com/technology-early-childhood-education/according-experts/infants-toddlers-and-learning-screen-media

Dubow, E. F., Huesmann, L. R., & Greenwood, D. (2007). Media and youth socialization. In J. E. Grusec & P. D. Hastings (Eds.), *Handbook of socialization* (pp. 404–430). New York, NY: Guilford Press.

Dunrea, O. (2002). *Gossie.* Boston, MA: Houghton Mifflin.

Gardner, H. (1983). *Frames of mind: The theory of multiple intelligences.* New York, NY: Basic Books.

Gardner, H. (1999). *The disciplined mind: Beyond facts and standardized tests, The K-12 education that every child deserves.* New York, NY: Simon and Schuster.

Greenfield, S. (2015). *Mind change: How digital technologies are leaving their mark on our brains.* New York, NY: Random House.

Gutnick, A., Robb, M. B., Takeuchi, L., & Kotler, J. (2011). *Always connected: The new digital media habits of young children.* New York, NY: The Joan Ganz Cooney Center at Sesame Workshop.i

Hastings, E. C., Karas, T. L., Winsler, A. Way, E., Madigan, A., & Tyler, S. (2009). Young children's video/computer game use: Relations with school performance and behavior. *Issues in Mental Health Nursing, 30*(10), 638–649.

Hewitt, A., & Jenkins, K. (2012). Assessment 101: Attitudes and approaches for effective and authentic assessment. *Early Years, 33*(2), 10–14.

Hirsh-Pasek, K., Zosh, J. M., Golinkoff, R. M., Gray, J. H., Robb, M. B., & Kaufman, J. (2015). Putting education in "educational" apps: Lessons from the science of learning. *Psychological Science in the Public Interest, 16*(1), 3–34.

Meaningful Technology Integration in Early Learning. (2008). *Beyond the journal. Young children on the web.* Retrieved from assistedtechnology.weebly.com/uploads/3/4/1/9/3419723/onourminds.pdf

National Association for the Education of Young Children (2009). *DAP Position Statement.* Retrieved from www .naeyc.org/files/naeyc/file/positions/PSDAP.pdf

National Association for the Education of Young Children and the Fred Rogers Center for Early Learning and Children's Media at Saint Vincent College. (2012). *Technology and interactive media as tools in early childhood programs serving children from birth through age 8.* Retrieved from www.naeyc.org/sites/default/files/globally-shared/downloads/PDFs/resources/topics/PS_technology_WEB.pdf

National Association for the Education of Young Children. (2012). *The Common Core State Standards: Caution and opportunity for early childhood education.* Retrieved from www.naeyc.org/files/naeyc/11_CommonCore1_2A_rv2.pdf

National Institute for Early Education Research. (2011). *Child's play: Should preschoolers engage with technology or good-old fashioned fun?* Retrieved from www.nieer.org/2011/06/30/childs-play-should-preschoolers-engage-with-technology-or-good-old-fashioned-fun

Penuel, W. R., Pasnik, S., Bates, L., Townsend, E., Gallagher, L. P., Llorente, C., & Hupert, N. (2009). *Preschool teachers can use a media-rich curriculum to prepare low-income children for school success: Results of a randomized controlled trial.* New York and Menlo Park, CA: Education Development Center, Inc., and SRI International.

Rideout, V. J. (2014). *Learning at home: Families' educational media use in America. A report of the Families and Media Project.* New York, NY: The Joan Ganz Cooney Center at Sesame Street Workshop.

Rideout, V., Foehr, U. G., & Roberts, D. (2010). *Generation M2 Media in the lives of 8-18-year-olds: A Kaiser Family Foundation Study.* Retrieved from www.kaiserfamilyfoundation.files.wordpress.com/2013/04/8010.pdf

Robb, M. (2017). *Kids' screen time shifts dramatically toward phones and tablets.* Retrieved from www.commonsense-media.org/blog/kids-screen-time-shifts-dramatically-toward-phones-and-tablets

Rvachew, S. (2016). *Technology in early childhood education: overall commentary. Encyclopedia on Early Childhood Development.* Retrieved from www.child-encyclopedia.com/technology-early-childhood-education/according-experts/technology-early-childhood-education-overall

Sage, A. (2014). *The farm yard.* Kindle.

Texas Essential Knowledge and Skills (TEKS). (2013). *Texas Education Agency.* Retrieved from www.tea.state.tx.us

U.S. Department of Education, Office of Educational Technology, Office of Early Learning, U.S. Department of Health and Human Services. (2016). *Early learning and educational technology policy brief.* Retrieved from www.tech .ed.gov/files/2016/10/Early-Learning-Tech-Policy-Brief.pdf

Wadley, A. (1974). *Just playing. A narrative poem.* First published in advertisement/enrollment brochure for Children's World Inc. Retrieved from www.anitawadley.com/Site/Welcome.html

Zimmerman, F. J. (2008). *Children's media use and sleep problems: Issues and unanswered questions.* Henry J. Kaiser Family Foundation. Retrieved from www.kff.org/other/issue-brief/childrens-media-use-and-sleep-problems-issues

Additional Videos and Resources

Kindle book
   The Farm Yard by Abby Sage (2014)

iPad book
   Gossie by Olivier Dunrea (2002)

How Do Preschoolers Use Technology Video
   www.youtube.com/watch?v=7fKRhgnio2g

Introducing Technology to Young Children
   www.youtube.com/watch?v=29ylsrxof48

Kindle Fire in the Classroom
   www.youtube.com/watch?v=yp1fgfMuG0w

Electronic Image
   www.canva.com/create/photo-collages

Pen Pal Teachers: The Teacher's Corner
   www.theteacherscorner.net/penpals

Videoconferencing with Elementary School Students
   langwitches.org/blog/2008/11/16/videoconferencing-with-elementary-school-students

The Ghost of Bethke created by fourth- and fifth-grade students using an iPad
   www.youtube.com/watch?v=g9UQYqOaFnc

Portfolio
   www.prekinders.com/finemotor-portfolios

Anecdotal Record
   www.youtube.com/watch?v=gt-HIcZPzyI
   www.slideshare.net/mbuurstra/observing-children-and-writing-anecdotal-records
   www.prekinders.com/anecdotal-records

Checklists
   www.youtube.com/watch?v=PvxlzzNFlEA
   www.teachthought.com/pedagogy/simple-checklist-can-improve-learningpblchecklist.4teachers.org/index.shtml

Examples of Interactive Whiteboard Websites

Whiteboards in the Classroom
   www.youtube.com/watch?v=ftej0udAasQ

Math Playground
   www.mathplayground.com

FunBrain.com
   www.funbrain.com

Cool Math 4 Kids
   www.coolmath4kids.com

Ms. Wolf's Math
Interactive Whiteboard Games
www.sites.google.com/a/norman.k12.ok.us/mr-wolfe-s-math-interactive-whiteboard/home

Kids Math Games
www.kidsmathgamesonline.com

Math Games—PBS Kids
pbskids.org/games/math

Alphabet Soup—PBS Kids
pbskids.org/sesame/games/alphabet-soup

Whiteboards in the Classroom
www.youtube.com/watch?v=ftej0udAasQ

Interactive Whiteboard Resources for Teachers
www.whiteboardblog.co.uk/2009/07/20-interactive-whiteboard-resources-for-teachers

Chapter 6

Technology and Special Education

Bernardo Pohl, Ashwini Tiwari, John Kelly, and Katrina Borders
University of Houston - Downtown

Meet Stephen

Mrs. Wang is amazed at how much academic progress Stephen is achieving now in her class. He is not only making passing grades for her, but he is excelling and passing all of his classes with excellent marks. For the first time, he is being considered for honor classes for next year, and this year, he had even made the honor roll twice. This is a considerable difference from 2 years ago, when Stephen was failing every class and was considering dropping out of school for home-schooling and private tutoring—that is, until he arrived at Oak Park Senior High School.

Stephen, a tenth grader, was born with mild cerebral palsy affecting his motor skills. His disability affects his writing, as he writes very slowly, and this makes it difficult for him to keep up with the fast pace of the classroom. He has also been diagnosed with a learning disability in writing and reading comprehension, particularly with speech recognition and word prediction. The introduction of technology as part of his accommodations helps him tremendously. He uses a laptop with word processing, text-to-speech software, and electronic textbooks, which help him to stay on the same level as the rest of the class. The introduction of technology in Stephen's accommodations has made a huge difference in his life. Today, he uses the word processor to take notes in the class, allowing him to keep pace with the teacher's lecture and concentrate on the content rather than his handwriting. The text-to-speech software helps him tremendously in his reading and oral testing. The word processor also aids his writing skills, since he continues to struggle with spelling and grammar usage.

Lisa F. Young / Shutterstock.com

Technology has made a world of difference in Stephen's life and in his education. Technology also has made a difference for his teachers. They no longer have to find the time for orally reading the materials to him or for testing him orally. They can more easily grade his work without having to decipher his writing or mark numerous grammar errors. Technology has made the educational process a "win/win" situation for all.

Introduction

The education of students with special needs is wide-ranging, and includes students with a variety of physical and mental disabilities **and** those with special gifts and talents (Valentine, 2007). This chapter addresses the primary technology tools used to enhance the education for this population of students. Because this area is so extensive, it is beyond the scope of this chapter to address each need. Teachers are always encouraged to search out new technological resources for each student who is differently abled in his or her classroom—as each learner will be an individual with his or her own specific label and needs.

In assisting those with special needs, teachers should understand the difference among *impairment, disability,* and *handicapped.* In the past, as stated by Roblyer and Doering (2016), these words have been used synonymously; however, a clear distinction needs to be made so that professionals who provide special services have a clear understanding when they are implementing and using technology with their students with special needs.

According to Roblyer and Doering (2016), **impairment** is an abnormality, which results in the absence of a physical or psychological function. This can occur at birth (congenital) or acquired later in life (accident or disease). A **disability** is a limitation caused by an impairment, which limits a human activity in a normal environment (e.g., learning, moving, communicating, hearing, manipulating) (Wise, 2012). A **handicap** is when a person encounters difficulties in functioning and interacting with the environment (Gargiulo, 2014) due to an impairment or disability (Elbro, 2014). Garigulo (2014) states that depending on the contexts and circumstances, a disability might not be a handicap as long as the barriers that impede the person's functions/interactions are eliminated. An example would be a student in wheelchair who could fully access the school campus. It is important for those individuals and professionals who provide special needs services to not make preliminary assumptions about individuals with impairments, disabilities, and handicaps. Individuals with special needs do not necessarily have limitations in performing a task and/or a lack of quality of life (Abberley, 1987; Baglieri & Knopf, 2004; Friend & Bursuck, 2015). Moreover, it is imperative to understand that a handicap is not what defines a human being (Pohl, 2013). Teachers must, however, see one of their roles as that of a "matchmaker" with the right technology to increase a student's chances of reaching his/her full potential in school and in his or her future.

In the United States, federal laws ("PL 94-142: Education for All Handicapped Children Act," 1975) and Section 504 of the Rehabilitation Act recognize several types of disabilities. These laws also entitle those who are affected by one or more of the listed disabilities to special services in a number of ways, including technology. Almost everyone is likely to know somebody whose life has been altered by one of these disabilities in some form: autism, visual/hearing impairment, emotionally disturbed, developmental delay, intellectually disability, orthopedic impairment, other health impairments (OHI), speech/language impairment, traumatic brain injury, and/or multiple disabilities. To begin to address these types of needs, the teacher first needs to understand the range of the most common categories of disabilities in the classroom: (1) physical (with use of mobility equipment or dealing with muscular dystrophy, Lou Gehrig's disease, sclerosis, or others); (2) sensory (visual or hearing); (3) cognitive (many levels of intelligence, memory, self-expression, information processing, and others); (4) psychiatric (social phobias, bipolar or other personality disorders); (5) health-related (chronic conditions such as diabetes, epilepsy, cancer, and others).

In recent years, the ongoing developments in technology have revolutionized the field of special education. The development of "touchscreen" computers and recent advancements in software and adaptive technology and, more recently, several "apps" have provided the special education and regular classroom teacher with a plethora of options in assisting students. Some AT help students circumvent the actual physical task of writing, while others facilitate spelling, punctuation, grammar, word usage, and organization. For example, even a portable recorder and basic software such as MS Word and Ginger Page (www.gingersoftware.com)

allow teachers and students (such as Stephen) to deal with the difficulty of taking notes and writing in class, thus allowing students to concentrate on the content of the class rather than on the barriers to academics. The digitization of books and other written materials has made it considerably easier for students to tackle the difficulty of reading and understanding text. For example, a student with mild vision impairment who has a reading assignment in his/her textbook will find that all major publishing houses provide audio versions of textbooks with extra digital material. In the age of tablets, laptops, and smartphones, "text-to-speech" software is readily available and free of charge (or for minimal costs) for the student with special needs to use. There are several smart phone applications both for iOS and android that help students access the materials presented in the class. Proloquo2Go is one such application that provides voice for students with speech impediments. Notably, advances in communication and technology allow teachers and students to move away from the impediments of the disability to learning. These are just a few of the modern-day tools for students in special needs situations. Every teacher and student should expect continuous developments to be on the horizon, so the commitment to stay "on the cutting edge" of adapting technology for students like Stephen must be made by teachers who are, in turn, assisted by their school's and/or district's special education team and technology specialists.

IDEA (The Individual with Disabilities Education Act), which was enacted in 1990 and was reauthorized in 2004 by Congress, defines assistive technology (AT) as any device that helps the individual access an environment independently (Roblyer & Doering, 2016), restores loss capacities (Turnbull, Turnbull, Whemeyer, & Shogren, 2016), and/or maintains or improves functional capabilities (Friend & Bursuck, 2015). The proper distribution and availability of AT is secured by the TECH ACT of 1988 (the Technology Related Assistance Amendment to IDEA) (Turnbull et al., 2016), which ensures the proper allocation of funds. This guarantees that the access of AT to special needs students is free of charge. In this chapter, we discuss the hardware and software that is more commonly available to students with special needs to access their curriculum, examine applications, and see lesson samples and other curricular ideas.

The Least Restrictive Environment

Teachers in all grade levels will have students with special needs at some point in their careers, so they will need to be familiar with the applicable terms and options for their students. The least restrictive environment (LRE) ruling requires that a student with special needs be placed in a regular classroom (rather than a separate/self-contained special education room) to the most extent possible. Placement is determined by an Admissions, Review, and Dismissal (ARD) (or IEP) Committee and the student's individualized educational program (IEP) (Heward, 2013). This committee ensures the proper placement and services that the student with special needs will receive. The committee also determines what type of technology will best benefit each individual student, which must then be provided by the district at no cost to the parents. The regular classroom teacher will be a part of this committee, so it is his or her job *and* moral commitment to have knowledge of technology tools (as guided by the special education team) and, if selected for the student, to use them with the student in his/her classroom once available. It is essential that all teachers, general or special education, are very knowledgeable about the procedures of special education (Friend & Bursuck, 2015; Turnbull et al., 2016). It is also vital that they know the basic terminology used in special education.

Terminology
- **Admission, Review, and Dismissal Committee (ARD):** The team responsible for: admitting a student to special education services; generating educational decisions, including technology (in an IEP); and reviewing the child's progress (at least once yearly). They may also terminate services (dismiss).
- **Individual with Disability Education Act (IDEA) (October 30, 1990):** A federal law which regulates how states and public agencies provide special education and related services to children with disabilities. It addresses the educational needs of children with disability from age 3 to 18/21 in cases that involve any of the 14 identified disabilities.
- **Section 504:** A federal law that requires public schools to provide free and appropriate education to those students who have a disability other than 14 disabilities listed in IDEA.

- **Assistive technology (AT):** Any type of equipment or device, commercialized or freely acquired, which helps to improve access and functionality of individuals with disabilities.
- **Free and Appropriate Public Education (FAPE):** This part of Public Law 94-142 law guarantees those who are identified as disabled (from ages 3 to 22) access to a public education paid for by the district by requiring proper and accessible services, education that takes place with nondisabled students to the maximum extent possible, the right to nondiscriminatory evaluation, and the establishment of due process.
- **Least Restrictive Environment (LRE):** The right of a student with a disability to access the regular curriculum and attend classes with nondisabled students to the maximum extent possible.
- **Individualized Education Plan (IEP):** A document created by the ARD/IEP Committee/Team that describes the educational goals, objectives, and services for an identified student for the academic year determined by relevant professionals (including the regular classroom teacher), translators (if needed), parents or other caregivers, and even the child (if appropriate).
- **No-Tech Solution:** Procedures and services that do not require the need for equipment.
- **Low-Tech equipment:** Inexpensive and non-sophisticated devices and equipment such as hard copies of notes, pencil grips, Velcro fasteners, and so forth.
- **Mid-tech equipment:** Sophisticated mechanical devices such as hydraulic lifts and wheelchairs.
- **High-tech equipment:** Devices or support that require specialized and sophisticated equipment such as a computer, electronic equipment, and software. Often, this equipment may require specialized training and support.
- **Response to Intervention (RTI):** A current approach to struggling students that emphasizes helping them early prior and after their identification as having a learning disability and supporting them with up to three tiers of quality, monitored interventions.
- **Differentiated Instruction:** Instructional approaches used to reach students with different learning styles, abilities to absorb information, and ways to express learned information.

Determining the Needs

It is highly unlikely that Mrs. Wang was able to help Stephen with his academic success without any assistance and planning. Preparation by Stephen's ARD (or IEP) team and regular classroom teacher was required in order to determine what worked best for him inside the classroom. It is clear that Stephen's success required Mrs. Wang to develop a plan of action, which she could do in phases:

1. Phase 1: Assess the student's need(s).
2. Phase 2: Survey the environment and the student's physical mobility.
3. Phase 3: Assess AT available.
4. Phase 4: Determine learning outcome and objectives.
5. Phase 5: Prepare instructional setting.
6. Phase 6: Develop a response to intervention plan/instructional plan.

Stephen's accommodations were not selected at random; the process required a team to assess his needs and the expectations for each change in his IEP that has finally led to success. Mrs. Wang started her assessment of Stephen's need by surveying his physical needs (see Table 6.1): vision,

Table 6.1 Technology Checklist

Environmental survey related to physical needs identified in the student's IEP. **Directions:** Check proposed devices/tools that will enhance the student's learning outcomes.		Grading Cycle:_____ Student Name:_____ Student ID:_____ Subject:_____ HR Teacher:_____	
Vision	√	**Seating and Positioning**	√
Functions independently with standard classroom tools and layout		Functions independently with standard classroom tools and layout	
May benefit from the use of assistive technology in this area:		*May benefit from the use of assistive technology in this area:*	
Magnifier (handheld)/digital camera		Nonslip surface on chair	
Large print books		Bolster, cushion, foot blocks	
Antiglare filters		Adjustable tables, desks, equipment mounts, etc.	
CCTV (closed circuit television)		Supports, restraints	
Screen magnifier		Adapted/alternate chair	
Screen magnification software		Custom-fitted wheelchair	
Screen color contrast		Side layer	
Screen reader/text reader		Stander	
Braille materials/translation		Pressure monitors	
Enlarged or Braille/tactile labels for keyboard		Other: Ball chair Therapy ball Wiggle seat T-stool HowdaHug seats Bean bag	
Alternate and assisted keyboard/enlarged keys			
Braille keyboard and/or note taker			
Monitor mounts (placement height for wheelchairs, etc.)			
Motion sensors/electronic orientation devices			
Other: Print to speech scanner software (e.g., Kurzweil 1000) Braille note/Voice note			

(Continued)

Hearing	√	Mobility	√
Functions independently with standard classroom tools and layout		Functions independently with standard classroom tools and layout	
May benefit from the use of assistive technology in this area:		*May benefit from the use of assistive technology in this area:*	
Pen and paper, email, or tweet reminders		Walker	
Computer/portable word processor or tablet		Grab bars and rails	
Signaling device		Manual wheelchair, tray, parts	
Closed captioning		Powered wheelchair	
Real-time captioning		Powered scooter	
Computer-aided note-taking		Powered mobility toy	
Flash alert signal on computer		Moisture guards	
Personal amplification system/hearing aid		Adjustable wands, head pointers	
FM or loop system*		Floor-mounted grab bars in restroom with alert button	
Infrared system			
Other: Communication Access Real-time Translation (CART) system Sound field system		Other: Switches mounted on wheelchair Ramps Automatic page turner Enlarged grip Automatic door opener Moth sticks	

*Frequency/system used in public settings to reduce background noise by delivering sound straight from the source to the participant's ear/headset.

hearing, and motor skills. By doing this, not only did she know what was needed, but she was also able to discover what her classroom had and what the room was missing: Does she need a desk for wheelchairs? Does her classroom have motion-sensitive switches? Is there a computer in the classroom with the proper software? These types of questions can be answered by completing a survey such as this one.

AT not only helps students with special needs to access the curriculum, it also helps the individual access the environment (Friend & Bursuck, 2015; Haq & Elhoweris, 2013). We have noted that Stephen, for example, has mild cerebral palsy, and he does have some difficulty accessing the environment. Teachers do have an array of technology available that will help students move better within an environment. From motion sensors for lighting to magnetic keys, individual free access to the environment in schools could be (but, too often, has not been) updated to help students take advantage of all that is available to help them in their classroom and school (see Figure 6.1). Table 6.2 shows some of the assistive and smart technology used for free access.

Constantine Pankin / Shutterstock.com

Figure 6.1 Magnetic security lock for doors with two indicators and magnetic card key.

Table 6.2 Assistive and Smart Tools for Operating Within the Environment

Assistive Customized Technology
• Loop induction amplifiers • Audible reminder devices • Keyless doors with magnetic cards or fob keys • Video/voiced recognize entry system • Power-assisted doors • Infrared sensors for sinks, soap dispensers, towels, and toilets in washrooms; roll under sinks; bars • Motion sensor light switches
Smart Technology
• Automatic switches (and those students can use by other means than touch [puffing, squeezing, etc.]) • Automatic alerts systems for students who leave the classroom without permission • Turn off automatic switches • Open door alarms • Electronic pointers based on eye movement/brainwaves • Joysticks • Trackballs (movable ball on top)

Students need to be able to freely access an environment; however, it is equally important for them to have equal access to the curriculum. There is ample hardware and software that helps to ensure that students can properly perform in the classroom. From computers to scanners to spell-checkers to digital worksheets, equipment can aid a student's productivity in the classroom. It is undeniable that Stephen's success was ensured by the proper access to the proper technology. However, careful planning and consideration went into the proper selection of the resources he needed to function in the classroom, and this will remain a continuous process of assessing and updating throughout his schooling to find the best matches. The availability of these products is extensive. In the following sections, we will discuss the most commonly available technology (hardware and software).

Hardware and Software

Today, the special education teacher and/or regular classroom teacher with mainstreamed students must consider the incredible availability of hardware for the classroom. The time has passed when students with special needs and their teachers fail to overcome many of the physical barriers imposed by a disability. Hugh Herr, an MIT professor who has designed and wears two "bionic legs" (due to a mountain climbing incident, yet remains a climber) believes that there is no such thing as a disability but feels, instead, that technology has just not caught up for everyone yet (Strickland, 2014). For photographs and more information on Hugh Herr, go to: www.en.wikipedia.org/wiki/Hugh_Herr. As teachers of students with special needs, keeping up with the latest technology can provide that "mountain climbing experience" academically when they provide students with better tools. For example, modern classrooms are equipped with electronic whiteboards, sound systems, digital projectors, headphones, laptops, and much more, allowing the student who is differently abled to eliminate many of the challenges created by a disability and focus on their content and lessons. From the simple acts of printing up hard copies of notes to using headphones and speech-to-text software to read books, technology has revolutionized today's classroom for students with special needs.

Of all tools available, the computer is the most fundamental and instrumental piece of technology in the classroom, perhaps making it the most valuable piece of hardware available to teachers of students with special needs. Teachers benefit from this technology in many ways. The computer serves as a resource for lesson planning, research, and delivery of instruction for special needs. Lessons that have required extensive planning, materials, and team coordination can be completed with the click of a mouse because many options and ideas can be easily accessed from the Internet. The hardware works together with software such as Microsoft PowerPoint to, for example, allow teachers to digitize notes, store them in a Website, and then have students access them from virtually anywhere. Paired with specialized keyboards, there are touchscreen monitors, tablets, and other specialized equipment that give students many options. With some of the combinations above, the need for always providing a printed-out copy or having the student struggle with taking notes is eliminated. The teacher and the student can concentrate on the actual instruction. From delivering videos, connecting to the Internet, providing notes, drawing/painting, calculating, and creating music, the computer is often the key that opens new doors to students with special challenges. Today, for example, a high school student with special challenges can utilize CAD (computer-aided design) to create floor plans in a drafting class with the guidance of a laser pointer. Young students no longer need the help of an assistant to solve a 500-piece puzzle. Communications can be enhanced for autistic students (www.youtube.com/watch?v=oIGrxzPMVtw&t=168). All of these and more can be done with a touchscreen monitor or with a mouse. Students with short-term memory can be reminded of assignments with a tweet or a text message. Coupled with the right software and hardware, such as MS Office and microphones, the computer can help the teacher deliver instruction in a far more efficient manner. Search YouTube for "children using adaptive technology" in your search engine to see many other videos of children with special needs using adaptive technology.

It is hard to ignore what technology and hardware can do today for the student with reading comprehension, hearing/visual impairment, or communication problems. Microphones, headphones, speakers, and computers make an excellent team when paired with text-to-speech or speech-to-text software. Cassette tapes and analog recording have been replaced with digital recording, saving time and resources for teachers and students. As noted, districts and schools no longer have to spend countless hours recording a textbook. Teachers and students can use scanners and software to scan and digitally read a desired section of the book. A student with mild vision impairment can take a picture of the page in the book and have the page read to him or her through a smartphone, and a student needing oral testing administration can have a test be read at his or her own pace with the help of a tablet or laptop. Students with reading comprehension or visual impairment can use text-to-speech software such as JAWS®Screen Reader or optical character recognition (OCR) software to help them read and understand the text. Almost everyone is familiar with the famous scientist Stephen Hawking who cannot speak but still gives lectures. His computer generates his words orally via an infrared sensor, and a blink-switch on his glasses interfaces with his computer to use a voice synthesizer (text-to-speech/TTS). This technology also allows him to access other computer tools, such as emails and the Internet. These types of communication tools may become more applicable for students with aphasia or autism in the future.

Table 6.3 shows some examples of helpful hardware available for teachers to use with different disabilities:

Table 6.3   Helpful AT for Accessing Content and Curriculum

Visual Disability	Auditory Disability
Screen magnifier Screen reader Speech recognition Speech synthesizer Large print Refreshable one-line Braille	Telecommunication Devices for the Deaf (TDD) Closed captioning The Ease of Access feature within Windows Control Panel Computer sound light signalers
Cognitive Disability	**Motor Disability**
Reading tools Speaking text Word scanners Screen readers Grammar/spell-checkers Automatic reminders	Pointing devices SIP devices Trackballs On-screen keyboards Keyboard enhancers/delayers Automatic key text

Software

The real value for teachers in AT lies in the endless availability of software, which, coupled with the power of the Internet, allows students and teachers to explore possibilities never imagined before. For example, MS Office, with its major components like Word, Excel, and PowerPoint, has become an indispensable tool for instruction and classroom work. MS PowerPoint gives teachers the seamless possibility of organizing instruction and delivering materials in ways that are particularly helpful to students with special needs. For instance, teachers using PowerPoint can "voice over" slides so that students can listen to presentations multiple times. Motivation for students is greater and attention is better during presentations with pictures, recordings, and embedded film clips. Research does show that students who have access to technology are more engaged in the classroom (Offen, 2013).

Technology is always changing and improving. Fortunately, for all of us, technology has also become more accessible than ever before, significantly enhancing the quality of life of the disabled. For example, the portability of tablets and laptops along with word processing software allows the student with handwriting difficulties to comfortably take notes and keep pace with the rest of the class so that the student can concentrate on the lesson instead of the actual and (often torturous) physical act of writing. Programs such as these allow considerable manipulation of content, freeing teachers and students from the worries of dealing with the physical limitation(s) of a disability.

Software and other AT are changing the classroom, and they should not go unnoticed by those who are educating students with special needs as alternative forms of assessment. Students can edit a movie or create a picture collage documentary or digital painting; these software programs can definitely help the student with challenges achieve many of his or her goals. Furthermore, as the principle dictum for IDEA is the LRE, teachers can use learning management systems (LMS), such as Edmodo and Blackboard, to create chat rooms and blogs, allowing students to be fully integrated in the social aspect of the classroom. The major benefit of using a LMS is that teachers can maintain a controlled and safe environment (Scott, 2012). As social and independent skills are essential components of the IEP, social virtual spaces will become essential tools for the teacher.

It is undeniable that software has enhanced the learning experience of students because of its many classroom advantages. However, a teacher must weigh carefully the students' needs with what type of software he or she will use. Different software have different functions. Word processors are not simply tools used for writing. For example, a word processor's editing capabilities can help with organizational skills.

Word prediction programs in the market let users select a desired word from an on-screen window. These types of programs predict words from the first few typed letters. The word can then be selected from the list and inserted into the text by entering a number, clicking the mouse, or other means. Word prediction programs help support literacy, increase written productivity and accuracy, and increase vocabulary skills through word prompting. SoothSayer Word Prediction (www.ahf-net.com/soothsayer/) manufactured by Applied Human Factors is an example of a keyboard filter that helps with word prediction.

If a school budget does not permit expensive systems, the keyboard filters of MS Word also include several typing aids such as word prediction and add-on spelling checkers. Some of these commonly and lesser known features can be used to reduce the number of keystrokes and make writing easier for special populations. As an example, imagine one must type the uppercase letter "V." Keyboard filters enable users to quickly access the letters they need and to avoid inadvertently selecting the wrong key. Software that assists with word prediction and visual organization can assist with reading comprehension, and scanning software can help a student spell and edit his or her work. Table 6.4 shows how some software can assist the student with some basic skills.

A special type of software is operating systems (OS), which is an essential component of the system software in a computer system. Application programs such as MS Office usually require an OS to function. OS manages computer hardware and software resources and provides common services for computer programs. In education, Microsoft Windows and Apple MAC OS are commonly known, followed by Google Chrome OS.

The Windows Control Panel is a part of the Windows OS graphical user interface which allows users to change accessibility options and control user accounts. Users can visit the "Ease of Access Center" to change and test keyboard settings, including the cursor blink rate and key repeat rate, change mouse settings, start on-screen keyboards, set up alternatives for sounds, and other functions. Once the setup is confirmed through the "Ease of Access Center" on the OS, all software applications take the instructions and function consistently.

Table 6.4   Software that Can Be Used as AT

Software	Spelling	Writing	Editing	Reading Comprehension	Organizational Skills
Word Processing	X	X	X		X
Talking Text	X	X	X		X
Word Prediction	X	X	X	X	X
Scanning Software	X		X	X	X
ORC Software	X		X	X	
Visual Organizer		X	X		X
Spell-checker	X	X	X	X	
Electronic Highlighters		X	X	X	X

Table 6.5   Helpful Web Resources for AT

Website	Disability	Description
Google Accessibility (www.google.com/accessibility)	Vision	Helps the visually impaired use Google's popular software such as Chrome, Android, e-books, and Gmail
Blind Get Educated Blogspot (www.blindgeteducated.blogspot.com)	Vision	Provides an array of information for the visually impaired such as helping them to use the iPad or word processors
National Center for Learning Disability (www.ncld.org)	Learning disability	A rich Website with a variety of information for the learning disabled; assists students with AT for dyslexia and dysgraphia
Apps for Children with Special Needs (www.a4cwsn.com)	Learning disability	1000 recommended apps for children with special needs
Various Low Low-Tech Assistive Technology (www.pinterest.com/utahatprogram/low-tech-assistive-technology/?lp=true)	Multiple disabilities	Assists in adapting low-tech AT

The Mac OS does have a control panel; however, most general system configuration can be done through the System Preferences within the Apple menu on the left corner of the screen.

Data inputs are usually accomplished through computer keyboards. The accessibility resources of most OS explain ways to make keyboards quick and convenient for using keyboard shortcuts. Another way to customize users' experience is through keyboard settings. For students who frequently mistype due to paralysis or have difficulty releasing a key once it is depressed, Filter Keys can be turned on so that Windows ignores when students press the same key rapidly or when they press keys for several seconds unintentionally. For students who have difficulty pressing complicated key combinations at the same time, such as Ctrl+Alt+Del keys, Sticky Keys can be turned on so that students can press keys one at a time, and students who have a touch PC can type without an external keyboard.

Some software companies and Websites are committed to building accessibility into products and to providing accessibility resources for educators and students alike (see Table 6.5). For instance, Microsoft Corporation's Accessibility Guide for Educators page (www.education.microsoft.com/GetTrained/Accessibility-Guide-for-Educators) provides resources and tutorials for AT (Microsoft, 2014).

The Web

The information superhighway is one of the most powerful tools in a teacher's arsenal, and this should not be underestimated by teachers of students who are differently abled. The Internet offers a vast array of possibilities for teachers and their students. With the proper connection and a fair amount of access, teachers have a world of information about disabilities and ideas that may bring success to their students at their fingertips. One excellent example is the Website LD Online (www.ldonline.org), which provides teachers with terms, expert advice, personal stories, and many more resources. Another site for teachers *and* students with learning disabilities is LD Pride Online (www.ldpride.net) with sections such as "Finding Your LD Pride" and checklists for identifying various learning disabilities. Teachers can also explore virtual tours of museums, download songs to explore, analyze the latest pictures or other artifacts from the Smithsonian, and much more. With the Internet, the notion of LRE has a new meaning: an entire classroom "can fly to Paris," tour the Louvre, and explore the countless treasures housed in this famed museum, as an example. This type of access to virtual fieldtrips can be of benefit to *all* children in a classroom, but, perhaps, even more so for students with special needs.

Despite the potential that the Internet offers, it does not come without certain drawbacks. A district's barriers to the Internet and determining the legitimacy of the information continue to be among the biggest concerns for teachers. For the most part, some districts have adopted an all-or-none policy, which has meant equal blocking of legitimate and illegitimate sites with Internet protection, often using blocking barriers known as firewalls (depending on the district). This leaves teachers with very little choices as to what Websites to use. Despite the great amount of irrelevant information on sites like YouTube or Wikipedia, teachers are often deprived of accessing legitimate information that these Websites have to offer. Teachers who do not have access to information at school should not ignore the possibilities of working at home to find out more information for their students, which could increase students' rates of academic success.

Technology in the Curriculum

As we have seen, the benefits of AT are vast, and teachers can effectively use technology to enhance the general learning of their students who are differently abled. Writing, reading, and mathematics are critical skills that all students must and should master as essential skills in their learning. In this section, we discuss different AT available to teachers in these three essential areas.

Writing

AT is designed to make hard, or seemingly impossible, tasks manageable. For students with disabilities, writing can often be the most difficult task of all. Since complications in writing are wide ranged and technology is evolving, finding the right AT device to incorporate into the student's accommodations can be time consuming. However, finding a fit can make a major difference to a student who is supported by special educational specialists (see Figures 6.2, 6.3, and 6.4). These specialists are more experienced with AT and other equipment, note-taking, composition, productivity, and cognition. For example, special keyboards and/or modifications on regular keyboards can enhance access for students with motor coordination problems, while text-to-speech programs assist those with visual impairments. Note-taking tools such as voice recording pens (electronic scribe pens) or apps can help students record complete lectures and download them to a computer. Composition tools—such as word processors—can help the student with outlining, formatting, spell checking, and correct use of grammar and punctuation. Productivity tools such as proofreaders

Figure 6.2 Student with visual impairment using computer with Braille computer display and a computer keyboard.

zlikovec / Shutterstock.com

Figure 6.3 Student with a visual impairment using an audio book player for the visually impaired, and listening to audio book on his computer.

Figure 6.4 A student recording a voice message on her app.

Table 6.6 Writing Solutions With AT

Low Tech	Mid Tech	High Tech
Modified pencils Templates Pre-written words Magnetic letters Big pen/pencils Printed graphic organizers Oversized ruled paper Slant board	Labeler Portable word processors Graphic organizers	Text-to-speech software Dictation (speech-to-text) software Oversized keyboard Word-predicting software Accessible computers Touchscreens

can assist the student in analyzing the text for style and appropriate sentence construction and can cross-check for plagiarism. A number of other tools are mentioned in Table 6.6.

Speech recognition software allow users whose strengths lie in oral composition to dictate words and then capture them on the screen. In the end, technology is helping students acquire essential skills. The regular classroom teacher will, however, be expected to use technology with the student if identified as part of his or her IEP program. As a reminder, regular classroom teachers are supported by special education specialists who should know much more about AT and matching the correct AT to individual students.

Creative writing is an essential component that students should be encouraged to develop. In a language arts class, it is not uncommon for teachers to have students write stories by having a student in a small group start a story and, then, have others "Round Robin" to finish the story. This type of exercise motivates creativity and participation—*if* all are able. Several activities can assist the teacher in helping all his or her students develop their creative writing.

Ms. Morris is a creative writing teacher with upper-grade level students. One semester she begins a lesson on how to write a story. She begins by putting several desks into a circle (4 to 6 students works well). Students take out a blank sheet of paper and write their names on the back. All students start to write a story about any topic. Ms. Morris uses a timer and at the end of a short period (around a minute or less, but she uses her judgment, depending on the class), the students must then pass their papers to the right. They continue the story started by the previous writer. The exercise continues until the paper ends up with the original author. This activity can bring excitement and liveliness into the classroom. However, the following year, Ms. Morris worries that her students with disabilities should not be deprived from participating in an exercise like this. When working with children with special needs, Ms. Morris modifies this lesson by incorporating technology (see Table 6.6). For example, she uses a computer lab set up to create stations within the room. Instead of passing papers, the students rotate from one station to the next. The computer keyboards are set with "typing helpers" and modified mice for two of her students. This exercise finishes when the students are back at their original station. Then, she asks the students to read the story aloud. Her students with special needs are allowed to use speech software, when they have difficulty reading. This exercise has several variations, such as the beginning, middle, and end exercise, where a student starts a story, another writes the middle, and another finishes the story. AT can assist by involving all students in this activity.

Reading

Reading is one of the most essential skills that students must have. Research shows that children who fail to learn how to read by first grade will suffer academically later in life (Heward, 2013). For the most part, formal reading instruction tends to happen mostly in elementary schools during the most crucial developmental years. In the upper grades, instruction tends to focus on content, sometimes leaving an instructional gap for many students with disabilities who need more attention in developing crucial reading skills. AT for reading can help to greatly increase the quality of reading instruction for students in all grades and content areas (see Figure 6.5). Text-to-speech technology helps students with difficulty pronouncing or decoding words to better understand a passage or text. For example, a student with good oral communication skills but who lacks the capacity for output (such as oral fluency or

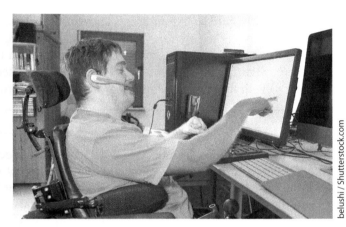

Figure 6.5 A student with special needs uses a computer with a wireless headset reaching out to touch the touchscreen.

writing) can use presentation technology tools (e.g., Prezi or Voki) that can help him or her to share his or her ideas with the class. AT for reading can help students with reading speed, understanding, and comprehension.

Young children develop a better concept of the alphabet by knowing the sounds of the letters and how they are used. Phonetics becomes an important tool as children use familiar sounds to decode and learn new letters and words. Phonetics is only one aspect that new readers need to learn. Young children also must learn the semantic, syntactic, and pragmatic side of a language. The best time for learning the sound and proper use of letters and words is early in life. Students with problems decoding and analyzing the meaning of words will have a difficult time learning such skills (Heward, 2013). Furthermore, students with difficulty in handwriting will miss out on a very important component, which is to learn the printed aspect of word. The act of writing is crucial to learning the environmental component of word, which means the ability to use the word in the proper social setting. As children grow older, this helps them understand the order of words, when words are used, and where the proper placements of words occur (Friend & Bursuck, 2015). AT can help children with exceptionalities overcome these barriers and other grammatical errors such as omissions or deletions of letters with available technology (see Table 6.7). Word synthesizer software can help a student learn and understand the proper sounds of letters and words. Spell-checkers, the thesaurus, and other software can assist students with the proper writing and use of a word, and grammar checkers (**IF** students use it) can help students with or without special needs with proper construction of sentences and other grammar errors such as omission and deletion of letters.

Table 6.7   Reading Solutions With AT

Low Tech	Mid Tech	High Tech
Large prints Magnifying glasses Highlighted text Simple word texts Printed graphic organizers Printed word-to-pictures examples Dictionaries and thesauri	Recorded text Handheld word processors Graphic organizers	Text-to-speech software Multimedia software Electronic graphic organizers Tactile-word processing software Audiobooks and digital TTS books Optical character recognition (OCR) Annotation tools Display control

Research has proven that students learn best when they are active and engaged (McKenney & Voogt, 2012). Ms. Olsen starts by introducing letters and words. She then asks students what are letters and words that they may have seen before. Next, the teacher asks the students in which place the letters and words are more likely to appear: names, cereal boxes, games, cartoons, movies, or television shows. This is the perfect activity to spark children's curiosity and encourage them to ask questions. Using technology, the teacher can use the Internet with students who have reading comprehension and decoding challenges. For example, the teacher provides the student with a letter or word, and the student uses the Web to find where, when, and how these letters and words are used. Furthermore, the teacher can use a word synthesizer to help the student properly pronounce the word.

Ms. Wang uses SpeechTRON (www.a1-speechtron.jaleco.com) or LingvoSoft (www.lingvosoft.com) to help Stephen understand the meaning and pronunciation of words. She also uses software games such as Smart Boarding School (www.smartboardingschool.com/spelling-6—8) and Funbrain (www.funbrain.com/games/rooting-out-words) that allow the student to rehearse the correct and incorrect use for letters and words. Electronic worksheets with word banks and fill-in-the-blank questions can replace the printed worksheet and can provide a manipulative (mouse or touchscreen) rather than constant writing. If the learning materials are already in electronic format, students can use text-to-speech tools, which read the instructions and questions aloud. They can then answer the questions using AT tools such as dictation technology and word prediction. While many writing assignments have been digitized—making the lives of many students with dyslexia much easier, worksheets are still mostly a pen-and-paper medium (see Figure 6.6). Ms. Wang tries to find quick ways to digitize worksheets and many other documents as accessible educational materials (or AEM). Literacy programs such as Kurzweil's (www.kurzweiledu.com/products/k3000-standalone.html) scanning and OCR functions are combined so that after a worksheet is scanned, students use the built-in text-to-speech feature to read the questions aloud before adding their responses.

Since some desktop software are expensive (and many of these programs rely on an external scanner to produce document images), Ms. Wang finds several inexpensive iPad apps such as ClaroPDF (www.claro-apps.com/claropdf) that can utilize the device's camera to create accessible worksheets.

Adobe Acrobat is a productivity tool familiar to teachers. Ms. Wang is innovative with using it to make educational materials accessible because she has figured out how to use the Acrobat program to scan worksheets directly to an editable PDF document, creating electronic versions that can be completed with various AT tools.

Figure 6.6   A word cloud of dyslexia

We also suggest reading Chapter 1 for further ideas on teaching literacy. Many suggestions in that chapter may strengthen students with special needs' literacy skills as well.

Mathematics

Mathematics is another basic skill that all students need to master. From telling time to knowing the distance of a road trip to knowing how much the weekly grocery shopping trip costs, we all use mathematics for many essential daily tasks, but students with special needs may experience difficulties in numerous areas of mathematical learning. AT has made significant progress in mathematics for those who have learning differences. Gone is the myth that only through paper and pencil can a student learn real mathematics (Haq & Elhoweris, 2013). Today, it is widely accepted that technology plays an important part in mathematics. Contrary to some myths, technology enhances problem-solving skills, helps develop better mathematical concepts, assists the student in drills, saves time, and improves the student's attitude of the subject (Haq & Elhoweris, 2013). Moreover, students who use technology in mathematics have shown better performance (Bottge et al., 2004; Roblyer & Doering, 2016). Watch Mathew Perterson, who has dyslexia, in his TED talk on teaching mathematics to those who cannot read words at www.youtube.com/watch?v=7odhYT8yzUM.

With AT, students with exceptional challenges can compute, organize, align, and copy mathematical problems without the need of paper and pencil; furthermore, visual and/or audio support can assist the student in setting up and calculating mathematical problems. Today, calculators exist with speech synthesizers, allowing the student to verify the accuracy of the number pressed. Students with writing difficulties can use electronic worksheets, which allow students to organize and align mathematical problems with more ease. Josue, in Mrs. Guadarrama's third-grade class, for example, uses the Coin-U-Lator (www.enasco.com/product/TB19071CQ) for money identification in addition to many free downloadable apps. In addition Josue can also use the MathPad app www.zurapps.com/all/index.php/mathpad/mathpad/) available for iOS and Android devices or download worksheets from worksheet generator sites such as the Math Worksheet Site (www.themathworksheetsite.com/).

Identifying basic geometric shapes can be a good example of where AT can be of great use.

In Mr. Green's class, the teacher asks students to identify basic geometric shapes by using online tools such as Geogebra (www.geogebra.org/). He plans a wide array of exercises for students—from identifying the basic geometric shapes in a worksheet to constructing the shapes with glue and construction paper. Students with disabilities, however, may have difficulty with some of these exercises. Gary, who has difficulty grabbing a pencil, can use a modified mouse and/or can identify basic geometric shapes with the help of software by simply clicking on the correct answer. Carla, who has difficulty with manual craft, can replace a glue and construction paper activity with three-dimensional (3-D) software to create the 3-D shapes. Carla can use 3-D software such as SketchUp: 3-D modeling for everyone. Furthermore, Mr. Green can allow her (and other classmates) to explore the complexity of creating more sophisticated shapes such as the construction of basic homes, cars, or airplanes. She can explore how basic shapes can make more complex shapes and can also help assist other children with difficulties in spatial skills.

Mathematics skills are vital, and AT is helping educators with the task of helping students learn these skills. Regardless of how many facts students know, it is imperative to apply this knowledge in meaningful ways. The students have an array of technology available at their disposal to achieve the following:

- **Virtual** simulations have become an integral part of the student's experience in the classroom. Teachers can use an array of software such as the various mathematical simulators created by PHET Lab (www.phet.colorado.edu/en/simulations/category/math) to help students explore scenarios where to use their mathematical knowledge. For example, students can use 3-D virtual models (e.g., SkyCiv at www.skyciv.com/free-truss-calculator/) to calculate the stress of bridges.

- **Problem-solving** is an important skill in mathematics, and having a sense of how to gather and use data is more important today than ever. Software such as Kidspiration for elementary level (www.inspiration.com/Kidspiration) or Geometer's Sketchpad for secondary level (www.mheducation.com/prek-12/program/MKTSP-HGA01M0.html) and scientific calculators can help students gain a better sense and understanding of numbers. These data-gathering instruments allow the student to make mathematical representations more meaningful so that the student can explore trial-and-error scenarios.
- **Mathematical representation** has become a norm in mathematics classes of today. Software such as Mutti Math (www.mattimath.com/) and other tools in the National Library of Virtual Manipulatives, (www.nlvm.usu.edu/en/nav/vlibrary.html) that allow students to create 3-D representations, are readily available. With the help of technology, students can see a graphical representation of many concepts.

The technology available to the mathematics teacher is abundant; therefore, careful consideration must be taken when assessing the use of technology in the class. Teachers must have a precise understanding of the learning objectives. Technology for mathematics classes is available in all arrays—from an abacus to spreadsheet software. Table 6.8 describes the most commonly used technology in the mathematics class. Math tutorials on YouTube and other sites provide expert explanations for students, and Chapter 4 in this text provides further information.

Table 6.8   Math Solutions With AT

Low Tech	Mid Tech	High Tech
Graph paper Manipulative	Non-scientific calculators	Scientific calculators MathLab software Electronic worksheets Electronic whiteboards Math notation tools Graphing tools Drawing tools Virtual manipulative tools

Self-Regulation

There are times when students with special needs (e.g., learning disabilities, attention deficit hyperactivity disorder [ADHD], autism spectrum disorder) struggle in their classes—not because of a deficit(s) but rather because of lack of strategies to regulate themselves (Guerra, Tiwari, Das, Cavazos Vela, & Sharma, 2017). Some students with special needs such as autism spectrum disorder and ADHD can begin to exhibit tics, for example, which are reparative involuntary movements or gestures that usually occur briefly in spurts. These can include tapping the finger on the desk and moving the leg repeatedly. Providing the students with a soft pad on which to tap his or her finger is a simple yet effective strategy. For the student who has a need to move his or her leg, teachers could make adjustment in seating to provide enough space. These strategies involve no technology, but there are technologies that can aid students, particularly those with special needs, in various target areas that contribute to school success.

Self-regulation is one such strategy that helps students train themselves to regulate their own behavior. Self-regulation is an umbrella term that includes self-management and self-monitoring (Gargiulo, 2014). Self-management entails students taking responsibility for their own behavior by accepting that "locus of control" is internal—for example, a student taking the responsibility for "off-task behaviors." Self-monitoring entails students identifying and regulating their own behavior. For example, a student running an experiment in science lab could self-monitor by using a checklist of steps involved to ensure accuracy and safety. Self-regulation is a central idea in positive behavior intervention support (PBIS).

There are many types of technology to help students with self-regulation, assisting them in improving their behavioral and academic performances (Bouck, Savage, Meyer, Taber-Doughty, & Hunley, 2014). Students can work with teachers and parents in monitoring behaviors. Smartphone app Class Dojo is a popular app that can help students monitor their on-task behaviors. This app works on both iOS and android devices, and the data can be transferred to a computer. Class Dojo also creates visual graphics that students can see to determine their

Table 6.9   Helpful Smartphone Apps

Apps	Function
Wunderlist	Cloud-based technology that allows users to create and share tasks
TickTick	Smart watch app that can be used to provide cues/reminders
Class Dojo	Can be used to create a behavior monitoring system for group of students/whole class
Upad	Allows users to take notes in their own handwriting
Any.do	Provides help with organizing and reminders; can be used to take notes
Remember the milk	A time management app that organizes schedules
Positive Penguins	User can type or speak about their thoughts to identify their feelings
Youper	Set and monitor goals related to overcoming social skills
Nearpod	A synchronous way to manage the flow of information
Class Act	User can get help from teachers in real time

progress. In many classrooms, teachers use clickers to monitor behavior. However, clickers can sometimes be intrusive. Self-prompting devices provide a viable alternative to clickers.

MotivAider (www.habitchange.com/) is a programmable device that helps users change their behavior by prompting them at certain intervals. The user can set the time interval and intensity of vibration that can only be felt privately by the user. This device could be easily clipped to belt or could be placed in the pocket. The MotivAider vibrates in the scheduled interval that is not noticeable by other students. This vibration reminds students of the target behavior. For example, a student with ADHD who goes off task easily can be reminded to go back on task every 10 minutes or so through MotivAider. Similarly, WatchMinder (www.watchminder .com/) is a device that appears to be a sport watch. WatchMinder can be programmed to set voice prompts at certain intervals. Students set voice or vibration prompts or both. These devices are easy to use and are rechargeable. Furthermore, there are many smartphone apps that could help students with self-regulation (see Table 6.9).

Universal Design

We have discussed some specific areas and tools for students with special needs, but there is an overreaching set of princi[ ] s of curricular practices that makes the curriculum more accessible to this popul[ ]n for Learning (UDL). As one educational program (South Carolina Assistive Tec[ ]ted,

> "Universal Design for Learning" is a relatively new term, but it incorporates age-old, basic principles of good teaching through different modes. It involves using technology that allows students to access educational materials through their strongest learning mode. Universal design provides equal access to learning, not simply equal access to information. It does not remove academic challenges; it removes barriers to access. (para. 35)

UDL has become one of the indispensable components in deciding what type of services and AT are required in the LRE (see Table 6.10).

UDL has its foundation in the architectural concept of universal design. Universal design advocates for the increase accessibility of buildings and structures—entrance ramps, corners at street level, automatic doors, and hands-free fountains and restrooms are all examples of universal design. The concept of universal design is credited to the late architect Ronald Mace (1941 to 1998), who was bound to a wheelchair. Mace is also credited with founding the Center for Universal Design at North Carolina State University www.projects/msu/design/cud. The Center for Universal Design specifies seven principles: equal use, flexible,

Question 3

> **Recognition Network:** The "what" of learning; how we gather facts and recognize what we read, hear, and see; how we identify what we learn.
> **Strategic Network:** The 'how' of learning; how we organize and express what we learn; performing complex math problems, recreating an historical event through a play, or writing a report are examples of strategic network.
> **Affective Network:** The "why" of learning; how learners are engaged and motivated; how they are challenged and excited about learning.

Center for Applied Special Technology (CAST). (2011). *Universal design for learning guidelines version*. Wakefield, MA: CAST. Retrieved from www.udlcenter.org/sites/udlcenter.org/files/updateguidelines.pdf

perceptible, low or no physical effort, intuitive in use, low error tolerance, and appropriate size and space for use (Turnbull et al., 2016). These principles are the basic guides that help design and produce easy accessible buildings that meet the accessibility need for a large portion of a population. Over the years, the concept of universal design has been used to provide and implement a wide range of services and products. Education is not the exception.

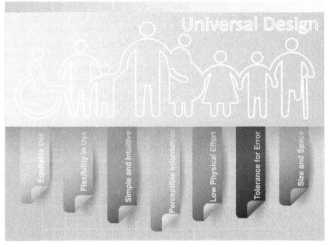

These principles of universal design can be used in the classroom. Equal use can be used to design curriculum material that meets the expectation of a mixed pool of learners, including those with learning disabilities. Flexible material can be used to accommodate different learning preferences. Perceptible curriculum and equipment can address the need of those with a visual disability. Cognitive impairment can be addressed with curriculum that promotes low error tolerance and low physical effort. Finally, issues of physical accommodation and factors as simple as font size can be addressed with size and space for use.

The Center for Applied Special Technology (CAST) is at the forefront and center of promoting universal design in the implementation of curriculum in schools, aligning educational initiatives with the use of technology. According to CAST, there are three main principles to the application of universal design in the school curriculum: multiple representations, multiple ways of action and expression, and multiple ways of engagement (Center for Applied Special Technology [CAST], 2011) (see Table 6.11).

The principle of universal design has emerged from our need to access the physical environment, which has benefited more individuals than originally intended. For example, ramps for buildings, initially designed for individuals with wheelchairs, have benefited elders with walkers, mothers with strollers, and so on. A teacher, as an advocate for his/her students with special needs, should ensure that technology is in place throughout the school building (e.g., restrooms, hallways). For example, automatic doors, sensing beepers in the hallways, or a "trapeze" design over a toilet can make a huge difference in the lives of students with vision or mobility issues. Simply being able to use soap and/or paper towel dispensers can be impossible without sensors for some. UD concepts have been applied specifically to help students with disabilities. An example is the access

Table 6.11 *Question 4* Design

Multiple Means of Representations	Multiple Means of Expressions	Multiple Means of Engagement
Provide the learner with various opportunities to gain information and knowledge.	Provide the learner with different avenues to express knowledge.	Motivate and challenge the learner to participate in multiple engaging activities.

to software and computers. Accessibility software and hardware in computers, such as accessibility control panels, are standard features, but issues such as easy seating for computer use are just as important for students.

The current challenge for teachers working with disabled students, especially those in inclusion, is the need to constantly modify the curriculum, instruction, assessment, and environment. Modifications are important, and will always be needed, as the majority of instructional materials continue to be designed without consideration for the classroom diversity (Roblyer & Doering, 2016). UDL attempts to erase this barrier by providing other ways to conceptualize accessibility. This can be achieved by exploring new ways of representing, expressing, and engaging. The following section explains the three main principles to the application of universal design in the school curriculum: multiple representations, multiple ways of action and expression, and multiple ways of engagement (Center for Applied Special Technology [CAST], 2011).

Multiple Representations

The traditional means of representing information and ideas has been the printed word. This includes work of fiction, nonfiction, and informational material such as textbooks. Over time, printed materials have proven to provide difficulties to those with visual impairment. It has also presented challenges to those with learning disabilities who have difficulties deciphering the meaning of words in textbooks and tests. Furthermore, different learners may prefer different means of obtaining the same information: pictures, audio, or video, for example.

The challenges that often cause the printed word to be problematic for the disabled have been addressed by advocating the use of digital text. In this format, textbooks or other printed material are scanned and digitized. Once in digital format, the learner can change the size of the font to his or her desire. Other learners can use text-to-speech software, creating an oral version of the text. Other software can render a visual representation of the text. Students with learning disabilities can use software that can modify and simplify the text with the additional help of electronic dictionaries and thesauruses.

Multiple Actions and Expressions

In the classroom, students are expected to display the knowledge they have learned. Traditionally, this has meant the production of printed reports, paper-and-pencil tests, and worksheets to demonstrate their understanding and acquisition of information. Multiple actions and expressions explore different and nontraditional ways to express the knowledge acquired: debates, plays, art, drawings, or oral reports. AT can be used with the disabled student to access software that can aid in the creation of multiple forms of expressions. For example, a student can use digital software or Web-based tools such as Toondoo to draw or create a comic strip or political cartoon. These would be more engaging projects for *many* students.

Multiple Means of Engagement

Traditional instruction relies heavily on teacher-directed instruction, textbooks, and worksheets. UDL encourages the teacher to explore and reassess the delivery and mode of instruction, considering learning modes such as cooperative learning, themed-based units, physical/kinesthetic activities, and student-centered activities that may provide greater learning motivation for students with special needs. Such methods of instruction can help the teacher recognize the true talents of his or her students with special needs, promoting learning that goes beyond the mere implementation of assignments for a grade.

For many decades, teachers have been perceived as the main source of knowledge in the classroom (Cowhey, 2006; Freire, 1970). Teachers utilizing technology can allow the student to become a knowledge producer rather than a knowledge recipient, and multiple forms of engagement can assist the teacher with that. For example, notes and worksheets can be replaced with WebQuests, having the student to investigate different angles of the same information. A student who is studying the battles from World War II (WW II) can read articles, visit museum Websites, and access other sources such as film clips, helping him or her to gain a better perspective about an event at his or her own pace. Multiple engagements have many benefits. Students with disabilities often experience delay in processing information and often have difficulty in keeping pace with the rest of their peers (Friend & Bursuck, 2015; Turnbull et al., 2016). The "one-shot" classroom experience is no longer a limiting factor for students who need variety and "replay."

Table 6.12 Turning a Traditional High School Algebra Lesson Plan Into a UDL

Traditional Lesson Plan	Possible Barriers	UDL Solutions
Goal: The students will be able to look at a pair of linear equations and tell what kind of solution to expect by reviewing advance organizer.	Attention Motivation Structure Organizations Memory	Relate the topic to a real-life example that students are interested in. Post the goal and organizer in the room.
Instruction: Explore the idea that there are only three possible relationships between a pair of linear equations when graphed on the same set of axes.	Auditory processing Visual processing Comprehension	Instruction: Use 2 "uncooked" pieces of spaghetti or 2 "pick up" sticks to demonstrate. Students drop them on the overhead. Teacher and students will consider the possible arrangement of the lines by "thinking aloud."
Independent practice: Students will graph different systems of equations and determine whether each system has no solution, one solution, or infinitely many solutions.	Working independently Confidence Comprehension Memory	Independent practice: Students may use self-monitoring checklist if needed. May work with partner or on computer with program that scaffolds this same instruction.
Extension: Think of a real-world situation that could benefit from graphing systems of equations to make future predictions. What data would you need to consider? Include equations and graphs as possible solutions are developed.	Motivation Confidence Attention Generalization Memory	Students have access to geoboards, floor grid, whiteboards, poster board, graphing calculators, and computers. Teacher circulates, questions, provides needed cues/prompts, and feedback.

Activity: Applying UDL

The three main principles of UD (multiple representation, expression, and engagement) can be successfully applied to any lesson plan (see Tables 6.11, 6.12, and 6.13) and with all students, but the disabled student can greatly benefit from this practice. We can illustrate this better by analyzing a WW II history lesson:

1. How would one incorporate multiple means of representation?
   Instead of using traditional textbooks, teachers can help students with disabilities by having students use Websites, audio and video selections, and electronic textbooks. This will better help visual learners. Students who experience difficulties with reading comprehension can greatly benefit from multiple sources of information available on the Internet. The History Channel Website, www.history.com, is an excellent source where students can gain information. A teacher should ask, "If I couldn't read well, how would I know?"
2. How could a teacher incorporate multiple actions and expression?
   In the past, students were often required to simply construct a written report. Today's students can express their knowledge in a variety of ways. For example, students with special needs who may have difficulty with written expression can benefit by creating a visual portrayal of WW II images using Ezvid (www.ezvid.com/) and Shortcut (www.shotcut.org/). A simple Google Slides presentation can become a collage of stories, and a simple written report can become a "newspaper article" with MS Word or Glogster. com, or a student can record a "newcast event" with him or her as the announcer. It is imperative for teachers to understand that the student who is differently abled can also be creative and have imagination.
3. How would you use multiple engagements?
   Traditionally, teachers presented the lesson by assigning students to read a chapter, take notes, and complete worksheets and tests. In the past, this has created many disadvantages for students with special needs who find it difficult to operate in the traditional instructional setting (O'Rourke & Houghton, 2006). The Internet can ease this burden for teachers, and WebQuests are excellent tools

Table 6.13   UDL Lesson Plan Template

Date: _____	**Subject:** _____
Grade Level: _____	**Theme/topic:** _____

Multiple means of representation:

(How are you going to present your content so that it meets the needs of all your students? Is the information represented in different ways (for example, utilizing, guided notes and graphic organizers in addition to a lecture formation or having several books that represent different reading levels)? Indicate how you will differentiate instruction for all students, including students in your class who have disabilities and students who are English language learners).

Multiple means of Engagement:

(How are you going to provide multiple pathways for students to actually learn the materials presented? Practice or active mental/physical engagement is required by students to make real learning happen. For example, some students may benefit from small-group learning opportunities; others may require more focused practice with precise feedback, while others might benefit from working independently. Some students will need to write, others will need to talk through ideas before they understand, while others may need to physically present what they are learning. Indicate how you will differentiate instructions for all students, including students in your class who have disabilities and students who are English language learners).

Multiple means of expressions:

(How will students demonstrate what they have learned? Again, the creation of many paths is key. Some students are good test-takers, while others are not. Tiered assignments, oral exams, building a model, making a video, and using portfolio assessment are examples of alternatives to traditional paper/pencil tests. Indicate how you will differentiate instructions for all students, including students in your class who have disabilities and English language learners).

Application:

(How would you plan a task so students apply this new knowledge in new ways? Indicate how you will differentiate instructions for all students, including students in your class who have disabilities and English language learners).

that teachers can use to engage the student. In another example, during a WW II lesson, the teacher can interest his or her student with the help of WebQuests to explore the lives of those who were children during WW II to get a better background of the conflict (www.gilderlehrman.org/history-by-era/world-war-ii/resources/children-home-front) and produce their own Google Slides presentation (www.wwiiwebquest.wikispaces.com/World+War+II+WebQuest). Instead of a traditional oral recitation of the paper in front of the class, these types of presentations can be rotated through a computer center where all students in the class view others' work. Students may also assume identities of historical notables, or, as mentioned above, a young person of the times and create a presentation from that perspective. Other types of presentations may include "moving maps" of how various invasions and battles changed during the war. Letting students "become the teachers" in an area of learning which is interesting to them (student choice) is more interesting ***and*** very empowering—especially to the student with special needs. A teacher who feels unable to support these types of products with his/her technical skills can easily go to the school or district technology specialist for assistance.

Although UDL is very well known in the field of architecture and special education, other areas can benefit from using it. Research has shown that English language learners (ELL) can greatly improve their language skills with the use of UDL (Lopes-Murphy, 2012), especially in the area of representation, engagement, and expression (King-Sears, 2014). As such, UDL is a useful tool for language acquisition for learners with special needs. The main goal for UDL is to bring lesson and instruction to the learner's academic level by providing access to the curriculum. With ELL students, exposure to the content is crucial, especially new vocabulary (Jang, Dunlop, Wagner, Kim, & Gu, 2013; Wallace, 2008), and this could apply to learners with special needs as well. Teachers can use technology and UDL to achieve this goal. An example of this is the use of digital texts. The use of digital texts with UDL as customary practice (Turnbull et al., 2016) is very common in subjects like science (Rappolt-Schlichtmann et al., 2013). Digital text is the electronic format of printed media that can be stored, changed, and manipulated. Digital texts not only provide access to the curriculum, they also provide information in a variety of representations and effective practice of new content (King-Sears, 2014). This can be crucial as students learn new vocabulary, practice the implementation of this new information, and express what they learn in different ways.

Teachers should have no trouble in accessing digital text; because of New IDEA requirements, publishers must comply with the National Instructional Material Accessibility Standard (NIMAS). In this format, texts are created with a source file in XML format. This allows the publisher to produce the final texts in a variety of formats such as HTML for the Internet, Braille for the blind, or Daisy for digital voice. Project Gutenberg (www.gutenberg.org) and Bookshare (www.bookshare.org) are two online libraries where students and teachers can find an extensive collection of digital texts.

Beginning a UDL Lesson Plan in Science:

PHOTOSYNTHESIS

PART I: THE SUN AND LIGHT
Not all of the light from the **Sun** makes it to the surface of the Earth. Even the light that does make it here is reflected and spread out. The little light that does make it here is enough for the plants of the world to survive and go through the process of **photosynthesis**. Light is actually energy, electromagnetic energy to be exact. When that energy gets to a green plant, a number of reactions can take place to store energy in the form of sugar molecules.

Remember we said that not all the energy from the Sun makes it to plants? Even when light gets to a plant, the plant doesn't use all of it. It actually uses only certain colors to make photosynthesis happen. Plants mostly absorb **red** and **blue** wavelengths. When you see a color, it is actually a color that the object does NOT absorb. In the case of green plants, they do not absorb light from the green range.

PART II: THE CHLOROPLAST
We already spoke about the structure of **chloroplasts** in the cells tutorials. We want to reinforce that photosynthesis happens in the chloroplast. Within this **cell organelle** is the chlorophyll that captures the light from the Sun. We'll talk about it in a bit, but the chloroplasts are working night and day with different jobs. The molecules are moved and converted in the area called the **stroma**.

PART III: THE MOLECULES
Chlorophyll is the magic compound that can grab sunlight and start the whole process. Chlorophyll is actually quite a varied compound. There are four (4) types: a, b, c, and d. Chlorophyll can also be found in many microorganisms and even some prokaryotic cells. However, as far as plants are concerned, chlorophyll is found in the chloroplasts. The other big molecules are water (H_2O), carbon dioxide (CO_2), oxygen (O_2), and glucose ($C_6H_{12}O_6$). Carbon dioxide and water combine with light to create oxygen and glucose. Glucose is used in various forms by every creature on the planet. Animal cells require oxygen to survive. Animal cells need an aerobic environment (one with oxygen).

PART IV: LIGHT AND DARK REACTIONS
The whole process doesn't happen all at one time. The process of photosynthesis is divided into two main parts. The first part is called the **light-dependent reaction**. This reaction happens when the light energy is captured and pushed into a chemical called ATP. The second part of the process happens when the ATP is used to make glucose (the **Calvin cycle**). That second part is called the **light-independent reaction**.

_____

Source: Biology4kids.com

Your Turn

After viewing the Photosynthesis lesson above, incorporate the three UDL main concepts:

1. How would you incorporate multiple means of representation?
2. How would you incorporate multiple actions and expression?
3. How would you use multiple engagements?

We hope by now that you have some good ideas. Here are some suggestions:

1. How would you incorporate multiple means of representation?
   In this instance, the students have multiple opportunities to gain information and knowledge. Using technology, they can learn about photosynthesis using many different avenues such as Prezi presentations,

Websites, electronic encyclopedias, or online videos—as only a few of the resources available to use. The teacher can also use cooperative learning by dividing the classroom into four groups: Group 1 Sun and Light; Group 2 Chloroplast; Group 3 The Molecule; and Group 4 Light and Dark Reactions. In a jigsaw configuration, each group will first research the Internet to find the information, which they will then present to the class using technology.

2. How would you incorporate multiple actions and expressions?

   In multiple expressions, students express their gained knowledge in different formats. In the case of a photosynthesis lesson, the teacher can have the students create a multimedia presentation. Platforms such as Moovly (www.moovly.com/) can allow the students to create presentations that will incorporate multiple modes of learning. In their presentations, they must incorporate video, audio, and text. One group, for example, in Mr. Conde's class created a "TV New Flash" format video for their presentation.

3. How would you employ multiple engagements?

   The idea of UDL is to have students involved in engaging activities. A lesson about photosynthesis is the perfect opportunity for students to do a meaningful project. The availability of light is vital for photosynthesis to occur. Students can put their knowledge to the test. Each group will be responsible for growing with a different amount of light. There are many ways to access or design tables using technology so that excellent data can be collected and displayed through various tables and figures. Digital cameras can record growth as well. At the end of a given number of days, each group will report their findings. The teacher can also have his or her students use virtual labs to simulate the process. With virtual labs such as Gizmos Photosynthesis Lab (www.explorelearning.com/index.cfm?method=cResource.dspDetail&ResourceID=395) and Bioman Biology (www.biomanbio.com/HTML5GamesandLabs/PhotoRespgames/photointeractivehtml5page.html), students can decide which kind of light (e.g., orange, green, blue, or violet) they will use and which plants (e.g., radish, spinach, or lettuce). Student can see how much a plant will grow using different lights after 30 days. Using a light scale developed by the University of Reading (www.reading.ac.uk/virtualexperiments/ves/preloader-photosynthesis-full.html), students can regulate the growth rate of Elodea and watch the plant grow in real time.

AT in the Classroom

Remember Stephen from the case study at the beginning? In order to be successful in the classroom, Mrs. Wang must recognize Stephen's ability by examining the effectiveness of different tasks. She can do this by considering the AT and support discussed by parents and professionals (IEP/ARD Team) dealing with his challenges. Students with disabilities may have a number of challenges. For example, we noted that students with cerebral palsy or muscular dystrophy have difficulty producing legible handwriting, lacking the dexterity to write legibly or at a productive rate. Students

wizdata / Shutterstock.com

with autism, Down syndrome, or a learning disability may have difficulty with fine motor coordination with dysgraphia and/or illegible handwriting. Students with difficulty producing legible handwriting often have difficulty producing final products, expressing ideas, and editing their own work.

It is clear that Stephen will need intensive means of instruction at different levels of academic intervention to improve his fine motor skills, especially in the area of writing. This goal can be accomplished by the use of RTI instruction, which is a multilayered approach to implement academic instruction and assessment (Byrd, 2011; Hoover & Love, 2011). Even before an IEP committee makes proper recommendations,

Stephen's teachers can implement some strategies that can help him improve and deal with his learning skills. Since it might be difficult for Stephen to draw diagrams, Mrs. Wang can have him use Inspiration (www.inspiration.com/) or Coggle (www.coggle.it) to create digital graphic organizers. This can help Stephen organize his ideas. Writing for Stephen can be a challenge. Besides using MS Word, he can benefit from utilizing Dragon Speech Recognition Software (www.nuance.com/dragon.html), which offer vocabulary prediction. In the end, teachers can be proactive about helping the student with his or her struggle. Mrs. Wang, according to RTI, should monitor the use of each AT to ensure that it is helpful for him. If it is not, she may modify small changes or she may have to go back to the ARD/IEP team to ask for other AT for him.

How does a student get the technology he or she needs? Let us revisit how AT arrives in the classroom for students in the beginning. To have a better understanding of the student's need and the proper implementation of AT, usually a nondiscriminatory assessment and evaluation process take place. This process includes an initial screening of the student's learning ability, an exhaustive assessment of the student's performance, the proper consideration of the LRE, related services needed, and the present level of academic performance. An IEP is developed with measurable goals and objectives, supplementary aids, modifications and accommodations, and a proper standardized assessment format.

The use of AT should be considered by the ARD (or IEP) team in the implementation and discussion of services for students with disabilities. The screening process should include the consideration of possible technologies to be used. For the teacher, an AT checklist such as the one listed can help the teacher and the IEP team evaluate the student's need. Such a checklist can help better identify the areas of strength and weaknesses. Usually, the AT checklist is also part of the overall process in determining the proper annual goals and objectives for the student IEP (see Table 6.1). In some cases, an AT checklist is also part of the original screening process.

Usually, the IEP teams make one of four decisions in determining the implementation of AT for a student with disability:

1. No AT is required.
2. AT is considered, but additional screening is needed.
3. AT is recommended, and a proper list is provided.
4. AT is recommended, but a full assessment evaluation is required. (In some cases, the IEP/ARD team might need further assistance in determining the proper AT for the student.)

AT can offer a better learning environment for the student. In doing so, the teacher must constantly evaluate and reassess the student's need for AT in accordance with the student's IEP goals and objectives. To accomplish this, the teacher can follow these steps:

1. Review existing information regarding the student's ability
2. Schedule meetings with members of the ARD (or IEP) team
3. Identify the problem
4. Prioritize potential solutions to be considered
5. Generate solutions
6. Implement a plan of action and assess its impact

An ARD (or IEP) committee must meet at least once a year but can be called at any time by a member (including the regular classroom teacher). If the classroom teacher believes that certain technology is needed or is not working, he/she should meet with the team to request change.

Such an exercise can help the teacher best assist in understanding the learning environment for the student. Teachers can make solid decisions about the proper implementation of AT when they have full knowledge of the resources available, the needs of the student, and a proper plan of action in assisting students with disability.

Activity: Implementing AT and the IEP

Let's look again at Stephen from the vignette at the start of this chapter. As noted, Stephen has cerebral palsy, and his condition affects his writing skills. (For the purpose of this exercise, we can also determine that Stephen is also confined to a wheelchair and has difficulty with his fine motor skills.) Also, remember that Stephen has a learning disability in the areas of writing and reading comprehension.

Using the AT checklist and Stephen's IEP goals and objectives, let's consider Stephen's proper needs for AT.

The above IEP goals and objectives suggest that Stephen will need assistance in the areas of reading, writing, and mobility. By referring to the AT checklist (see Table 6.1), Mrs. Wang can immediately deduce that Stephen will greatly benefit from a word processor with a spell-checker; she can use voice-to-text software that can help Stephen read and assist him with his reading comprehension, and software can be used that will assist Stephen with his writing and model production. However, as noted earlier, Mrs. Wang was not waiting for the ARD or IEP committee to make recommendations; she was knowledgeable enough to start implementing some RTI interventions with the proper use of technology.

Stephen's IEP Goals

Goal 1: Demonstrate independent reading skills.
Objective: When given a reading assignment, Stephen will accomplish with 70% accuracy:

1. identifying the implied main idea,
2. drawing conclusion and inferences, and
3. summarizing a reading selection.

Goal 2: Demonstrate independent writing skills.
Objective: When given a writing assignment, Stephen will with 70% accuracy:

1. write at least 3 complex and compound sentences per paragraph,
2. write 25 words per paragraph with no more than two spelling errors, and
3. use proper writing rules and mechanics,

Goal 3: Demonstrate use of fine motor skills.
Objective: When in the classroom, Stephen will with 70% accuracy:

1. write clear and legible letters, and
2. demonstrate the ability to draw, construct models, and produce crafts model.

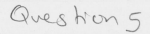

Differentiated Instruction

Differentiated instruction (DI) refers to a series of classroom practices that tailors instruction to a learner's styles, interests, and needs, taking into consideration the individual's prior knowledge, social exposure, and educational experience. If national, state, or district standards tell us what knowledge a learner must acquire, DI is the blueprint that allows teachers to create a more dynamic learning environment where the student can learn in a more purposeful way (see Table 6.14).

The premise behind DI is to introduce meaning and dynamics into the learning process. Guided by a constructivist approach, the belief behind DI is that learning occurs best when learners make meaning out of the information. DI is much more than distinguishing the heterogeneous component of the learning environment. It means taking into consideration the readiness, learning needs, and interests of *each* student (see Table 6.15). When implementing DI, teachers must consider careful planning and the dimension of the learning environment.

Table 6.14   Guidelines for DI

Content	Different levels of reading or resource materials, reading buddies, small-group instruction, curriculum compacting, multilevel computer programs and WebQuests, tape-recorded materials, etc.
Process	Activity choice boards, tiered activities, multilevel learning center tasks, similar readiness groups, choice in group work, varied journal prompts, mixed readiness groups with targeted roles for students, etc.
Product	Tiered products, students choose mode of presentation to demonstrate learning, independent study, varied rubrics, mentorships, interest-based investigations
Interest	Options in content, topic, or theme, options in the tools needed for production, options in methods for engagement
Profile	Consideration of gender, culture, learning styles, strengths, and weaknesses
Readiness	Identification of background knowledge/gaps in learning, options in amount of direct instruction, options in amount of practice, options in pace of instruction, options in complexity of activities, options in level of analysis/exploration of a topic

Table 6.15   Useful Tools for DI

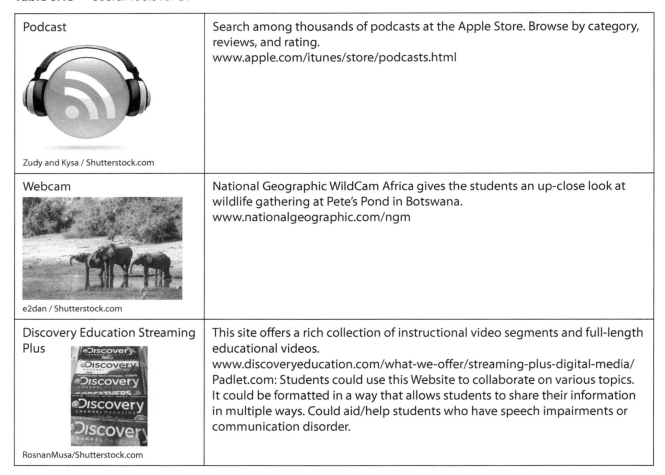

Podcast	Search among thousands of podcasts at the Apple Store. Browse by category, reviews, and rating. www.apple.com/itunes/store/podcasts.html
Zudy and Kysa / Shutterstock.com	
Webcam	National Geographic WildCam Africa gives the students an up-close look at wildlife gathering at Pete's Pond in Botswana. www.nationalgeographic.com/ngm
e2dan / Shutterstock.com	
Discovery Education Streaming Plus	This site offers a rich collection of instructional video segments and full-length educational videos. www.discoveryeducation.com/what-we-offer/streaming-plus-digital-media/ Padlet.com: Students could use this Website to collaborate on various topics. It could be formatted in a way that allows students to share their information in multiple ways. Could aid/help students who have speech impairments or communication disorder.
RosnanMusa/Shutterstock.com	

They can do this by considering the instructional dimension of DI. Teachers must take into account the content to be learned, process of instruction, and desired product. Furthermore, teachers must include the student's interest, readiness, and profile.

The goal of DI is to engage each learner by offering multiple ways for individuals—particularly those with special needs—to demonstrate learning and understanding (Heward, 2013). Over the years, technology has assisted the teacher with effective tools to achieve this. Furthermore, technology lets the teacher embrace the student's different learning styles. It provides an engaging and motivating learning environment with the opportunity for grouping so that they can use various products to demonstrate their learning. Technology facilitates the gathering of data, which helps teachers and students to monitor the progress of learning and guiding future instruction. DI attempts to captivate the student's interests, thus encouraging interaction, participation, and creativity.

When using technology, the first step for teachers is to gather and use data. By using data-driven decision, teachers can better understand the student's progress. Websites such as Texas Student Data System (www.texasstudentdatasystem.org/TSDS/TEDS/1718F/TSDS_PEIMS_Data_Standards) give the teacher a better understanding of how the student is performing in his or her class. With data, communication between parents, teachers, and students has become indispensable for success. As such, in recent years, online grading has opened a crucial line of communication. Websites, such as Engrade (www.engrade.com), help the teacher to create online grading, attendance records, assignments calendars, and progress reports, which can be shared with parents and students. With DI, giving students ownership of their own learning is also crucial. For example, creating a graph (www.nces.ed.gov/nceskids/createagraph/) helps students to visualize and understand their own learning.

Having students explore new ideas is very motivating with DI. Different Websites allow students to download podcasts, use virtual cameras, and access thousands of videos. It is important in motivation theory that students explore their interests. This allows the student to take ownership of the learning process, inspiring them to be engaged.

WebQuests were designed to help students learn to navigate the Web and locate information in meaningful ways. They can be designed as simply or more complex to match the needs of learners. Because they can be easily modified for students with special needs, they are considered a particularly motivating inquiry activity for this audience. For example, support hints (support notes) and more or fewer documents can be easily added, audio or video can be added for interest, cooperative group assignments can be made for motivation and/or support, and so forth. Here is a list of u*seful WebQuest tools* (see Table 6.16).

Collaboration and production is at the core of DI. Technology can definitely facilitate this. In the twenty-first century, technology provides endless possibilities for students with special needs to excel. A WebQuest is a perfect tool for collaboration and production. There are many advantages to WebQuests. First, they allow the student to learn about a topic by exploring information sources that build on his or her interests. Second, they make the student an expert in the topic. Third, they can be designed to promote higher-level thinking. Students are not just learning information but using it to create a product.

Table 6.16 Useful WebQuest tools

Concept to Classroom is a collaboration between Thirteen Ed Online and Disney Learning Partnership. This URL features Concept to Classroom's take on WebQuests. www.thirteen.org/edonline/concept2class/
This site is designed to serve as a resource to those who are using the WebQuest model to teach with the Web. By pointing to excellent examples and collecting materials developed to communicate the ideas, teachers experimenting with WebQuests will be able to learn from each other. A WebQuest is an inquiry-oriented activity in which most or all of the information used by learners is drawn from the Web. WebQuests are designed to use learners' time well to focus on using information rather than looking for it and to support learners' thinking at the levels of analysis, synthesis, and evaluation. The model was developed in early 1995 at San Diego State University by Bernie Dodge with Tom March. www.webquest.org/index.php
This "Explore More" site offers a number of WebQuests in various subject areas for middle and high school teachers along with other projects and lesson plans. www.iptv.org/exploremore

In the twenty-first century, teacher-centered instruction is only one of the many choices in instruction. Student-centered instruction has proven to be much more effective because the student becomes active and engaged rather than a passive listener. To comply well with DI, student-centered instruction is promoted. As such, blogging, presentation software, and digital storytelling are indispensable tools for the teacher. Blogging allows student and teachers to take the classroom to a different level. The classroom is no longer four physically defined walls but virtual spaces where new ideas and horizons can be explored. Blogging can increase a student's participation, motivation, and collaboration. In the case of special education students, this is a very important skill that they must master. Blogging gives the student with exceptionalities the opportunity for active participation. For instance, students with speech difficulties will not have the fear of interaction. Liam, for example, experiences speech aphasia from a head injury during a biking accident. He is no less intelligent than his peers, but he has trouble with word finding at times, especially during stressful situations. Blogging provides him with a tool to participate as an equal and for others to see him as a valuable resource.

Another aspect of the twenty-first-century classroom is the creativity of student products, which is at the core of DI objectives. New software and Web tools, such as word processors and drawing software, allow students to enhance the production of their work. The days of only paper-and-pencil reports are past. Today, teachers are encouraged to tap into all students' imagination and ingenuity. New technology, such as VoiceThread (www.voicethread.com), allows students to incorporate voice and sound into their final product. Furthermore, such creativity can be enhanced by creating digital stories, which students can use to display final presentations. Additionally, Web-based tools such as Polleverywhere and Kahoot could be excellent ways to engage students during lesson delivery.

Technology Strategies for Gifted and Talented

Gifted and talented (GT) is often defined as the category of individuals identified as possessing extraordinary qualities that provide the potential for high quality performance in intellectual activities, leadership roles, creative endeavors, and artistic performances with a high degree of commitment (Heward, 2000; Renzulli, 2011). Many teachers are surprised that these students are labeled as learners with special needs, but the definition of "needing special attention to obtain their maximum potential" fits GT students handily. According to Roblyer and Doering (2016), the primary concern for teachers should be to identify the students who merit these services not ordinarily available in the general curriculum. Comprehensive discussions of how best to service these students are provided by Heward (2000) and Renzulli (2011).

Roblyer and Doering (2016) observe that technology has increased the potential abilities of students, providing the student with greater freedom and independence. They find that technology integration for GT students should evolve around three major areas:

- **Virtual Communication**—the ability to electronically communicate with other cultures and people from other regions of the world should exponentially enhance GT students' potential for expression.
- **Research**—the ability of resources (e.g., the Internet and electronic databases) allows GT students to explore new ideas and events in greater depth so that students truly investigate a particular subject.
- **Independence**—the availability of various tools for interactivity and representation provides GT students with opportunities to explore new discoveries and display their creativity freely.

Finally, we all agree that GT students are highly creative and motivated students (Renzulli, 2011). Teachers must not only provide the tools and opportunities for these students to excel, but they must also provide the opportunity for cooperation and group work. When educating the GT learners, teachers tend to focus on the academic outcome of the student, often overlooking vital social skills components (Coleman, 2014), but socialization of GT students continues to be an area of concern (Coleman & Cross, 2014). According to Roblyer and Doering (2016), working in the creation of Websites or multimedia projects provides the opportunity for GT students to participate in the motivational tasks that they need, while providing them with the chance to develop important social skills needed in the workplace.

Final Strategies for Teachers

Teachers in the special and non-special education classroom face the ever-increasing challenge of meeting the needs of exceptional children (Roblyer & Doering, 2016), and the demand to provide these services is mounting (Pohl, 2013). Here are some suggestions that teachers can apply to meet these needs:

- Become familiar with the student's need(s) as soon as possible. If the student qualifies for special education services, it is important for the teacher to begin the process or review the IEP to ensure understanding and determine how to support the student most effectively. Contact the school special education administrator to learn about the student before he or she arrives in your classroom if the student has already been identified. Learn about and how to use any required technology as soon as possible.
- Continually survey the classroom with a checklist (see above for a checklist example) to see if the environment meets the needs of the student in terms of accessibility and AT.
- As with all good instruction, take care to match the technology to the individual learner's age level, interests, motivation, and other needs.
- Check often to see if AT is required or enhanced by the student's modification and accommodation. Employ RTI if small changes are required.
- Always use resources such as *Wave*, *Closing the Gap Solution*, and professional development training to check for Web accessibility. Watch for the latest technology (see Figures 6.7 and 6.8), and stay on the alert for new information/updates (Roblyer & Doering, 2016).

What can i help you with?

Figure 6.7 The latest technology includes home advisors, voice recognition, artificial intelligence devices, and the Internet of things concept, which refers to a network that will connect many types of electronic devices for data exchange, etc.

Figure 6.8 A group of children interacting with a robot

Conclusion

In this chapter, we provide an introduction to the basic concepts and implementation of AT for students with special needs. An underlying principle of AT is to provide independence and full participation of the student in the learning environment while minimizing any stigma that might occur as a result of being differently abled to provide a way for the learner to reach his/her full potential. AT is not cheap, and it adds substantially to the cost of educating a student. However, it may make a lifelong difference in the life of a child (and society) in untold ways. The teacher, who realizes the potential of students with special needs to become independent learners and contributing members of their communities, may, at times, need to become an advocate for a student in obtaining the technology. When implementing AT, the district, school administrators, teachers, and other professionals must be knowledgeable of the correctly applicable equipment, costs, usage, technology support, and various other services that go hand in hand with the technology. Communication and cooperation among members of the IEP/ARD team are crucial. Finally, a teacher must be knowledgeable on how to translate the IEP goals and objectives into the use of AT and be wholehearted in following through with its use in the classroom.

References

Abberley, P. (1987). The concept of oppression and the development of a social theory of disability. *Disability, Handicap & Society, 2*, 5–19.

Baglieri, S., & Knopf, J. (2004). Normalizing differences in inclusive teaching. *Journal of Learning Disabilities, 37*, 525–529.

Bottge, B. A., Heinrichs, M., Mehta, Z. D., Rueda, E., Hung, Y.-H., & Danneker, J. (2004). Teaching mathematical problem solving to middle school students in math, technology education, and special education classrooms. *Research in Middle Level Education Online, 27*(1), 43–68.

Bouck, E. C., Savage, M., Meyer, N. K., Taber-Doughty, T., & Hunley, M. (2014). High-tech or low-tech? Comparing self-monitoring systems to increase task independence for students with autism. *Focus on Autism and Other Developmental Disabilities, 29*(3), 156–167.

Byrd, E. S. (2011). Educating and involving parents in the response to intervention process: The school's important role. *Part of a Special Issue: Collaboration, 43*(3), 32–39.

Center for Applied Special Technology (CAST). (2011). *Universal design for learning guidelines version.* Wakefield, MA: CAST. Retrieved from www.udlcenter.org/sites/udlcenter.org/files/updateguidelines.pdf

Coleman, L. J. (2014). The power of specialized educational environments in the development of giftedness: The need for research on social context. *Journal for the Education of the Gifted, 37*(1), 70–80.

Coleman, L. J., & Cross, T. L. (2014). Is being gifted a social handicap? *Journal for the Education of the Gifted, 37*(1), 5–17.

Cowhey, M. (2006). *Black ants and Buddhists: Thinking critically and teaching differently in the primary grades.* Portland, ME: Stenhouse.

Education for All Handicapped Children Act of (1975). Public Law 94-192. U.S. Code. Vol. 20, secs. 1401 et seq.

Elbro, C. (2014). Dyslexia as disability or handicap? When does vocabulary matter? *Journal of Learning Disabilities, 43*(5), 469–478.

Freire, P. (1970). *Pedagogy of the oppressed.* New York, NY: Herder and Herder.

Friend, M. P., & Bursuck, W. D. (2015). *Including students with special needs: A practical guide for classroom teachers* (7th ed.). New York, NY: Pearson.

Gargiulo, R. M. (2014). *Special education in contemporary society* (5th ed.). Thousand Oaks, CA: Sage Publications.

Haq, F., & Elhoweris, H. (2013). Using assistive technology to enhance the learning of basic literacy skills for students with learning disabilities. *International Journal of Social Sciences & Education, 3*(4), 880–885.

Heward, W. (2000). *Exceptional children: An introduction to special education* (6th ed.). Upper Saddle River, NJ: Prentice Hall.

Heward, W. (2013). *Exceptional children: An introduction to special education* (10th ed.). New York, NY: Pearson.

Hoover, J. J., & Love, E. (2011). Supporting school-based response to intervention: A practitioner's model. (Sage Publications Inc. February 1, 2011). Retrieved from www.ezproxy.uhd.edu/login?url=www.search.ebscohost.com/login.aspx?direct=true&db=tfh&AN=57405584&site=eds-live&scope=site

Jang, E. E., Dunlop, M., Wagner, M., Kim, Y.-H., & Gu, Z. (2013). Elementary school ELLs' reading skill profiles using cognitive diagnosis modeling: Roles of length of residence and home language environment. *Language Learning, 63*(3), 400–436.

King-Sears, P. (2014). Introduction to learning disability quarterly special series on universal design for learning: Part one of two. *Learning Disability Quarterly, 37*(2), 68–70.

Lopes-Murphy, S. (2012). Universal design for learning: Preparing secondary education teachers in training to increase academic accessibility of high school English learners. *Clearing House, 85*(6), 226.

McKenney, S., & Voogt, J. (2012). Teacher design of technology for emergent literacy: An explorative feasibility study. *Australasian Journal of Early Childhood, 37*(1), 4–12.

Microsoft. (2014). Accessibility in education. Retrieved from www.microsoft.com/enable/education

Offen, K. (2013). Historical geography II: Digital imaginations. *Progress in Human Geography, 37*(4), 564–577.

O'Rourke, J., & Houghton, S. (2006). Students with mild disabilities in regular classrooms: The development and utility of the Student Perceptions of Classroom Support scale. *Journal of Intellectual & Developmental Disability, 31*(4), 232–242.

Pohl, B. (2013). *The moral debate on special education.* New York, NY: Peter Lang.

Rappolt-Schlichtmann, G., Daley, S. G., Lim, S., Lapinski, S., Robinson, K. H., & Johnson, M. (2013). Universal design for learning and elementary school science: Exploring the efficacy, use, and perceptions of a web-based science notebook. *Journal of Educational Psychology, 105*(4), 1210–1225.

Renzulli, J. S. (2011). What makes giftedness? Reexamining a definition. *Phi Delta Kappan, 92*(8), 81–88.

Roblyer, M. D., & Doering, A. H. (2016). *Integrating educational technology into teaching* (7th ed.). Boston, MA: Allyn and Bacon.

Scott, S. M. (2012). Go ahead . . . be social. *Distance Learning*, *9*(2), 54–59.

South Carolina Assistive Technology Program. (2017). SC Curriculum Access through AT. Retrieved from www.sc.edu/scatp/cdrom/atused.html Strickland, E. (2014). The end of disability. *IEEE Spectrum*, *51*(6), 30–35.

Turnbull, A. P., Turnbull, R., Whemeyer, M., & Shogren, K. (2016). *Exceptional lives: Special education in today's classroom* (8th ed.). New York, NY: Pearson.

Guerra, F., Tiwari, A., Das, A., Cavazos Vela, J., & Sharma, M. (2017). Examining teachers' understanding of attention deficit hyperactivity disorder. *Journal of Research in Special Education Needs.* doi:10.1111/1471-3802.12382

Valentine, J. (2007). How can we transgress in the field of disabilities in urban education? In S. R. Steinberg & J. L. Kincheloe (Eds.), *19 urban questions: Teaching in the city* (pp. 127–142). New York, NY: Peter Lang.

Wallace, C. (2008). VOCABULARY: The key to teaching English language learners to read. *Education Digest*, *73*(9), 36.

Wise, P. H. (2012). Emerging technologies and their impact on disability. *Future of Children*, *22*(1), 169–191.

Chapter 7

Technology to the Rescue: Helping English Language Learners Advance in English Proficiency and in Content Knowledge

Myrna Cohen, Laura A. Mitchell, Stephen White, Bernardo Pohl, and Colin Dalton
University of Houston - Downtown

Meet Mrs. Davidson

Mrs. Davidson worked with her five English language learner (ELL) students in different ways in order to have them practice speaking more. She noticed, however, that Binh, a student from Vietnam, was going through a silent period—a time when second language learners will not speak the new language at all in front of others. Mrs. Davidson, therefore, had Binh work on technology projects such as screencasts (see example at tube.sandi. net/video/videos/2564/beginning-esl-autobiography or at tube.sandi.net/video/videos/2565/beginning-esl-autobiography). In this way, Binh could use headphones and a microphone to speak her new language in private instead of speaking in front of others, which can be embarrassing and intimidating for students in the silent period.

Regreto / Shutterstock.com

Second Language Acquisition Principles and Technology

The ways in which technology can be effectively used to facilitate learning for all students are vast. However, using technology to teach English language learners (ELLs) can make the ELL teacher's job much easier than in the past. This is because technology offers many ways to implement best practices into second language

---

teaching. These best practices, often seen in the most popular ESL (English as a Second Language) teaching strategies, have been developed and adapted over the past decades and are based on the fundamental principles of second language acquisition that have been well researched and are widely accepted in the field. Teachers should understand these principles in ~~Question 1~~ sely for ELLs. Several of these principles are discussed in the following paragraphs.

Second language acquisition principle guide teachers of ELLs as they consider: (1) the level of English to use with their ELLs, (2) the sequencing of instruction that is most effective, (3) distinguishing among the different language domains to enhance proficiency, (4) the role of emotion in second language learning, and (5) why it is crucial to differentiate between conversational and academic language. An understanding of these principles will help teachers make decisions about the technology tools that are most effective for their ELLs and about using the technology tools to their students' best advantage. Note that ELL teachers need not speak two languages. Many effective teachers of ELLs are monolingual *but* have a good grasp of second language acquisition principles and the appropriate technology to support them.

One of the most important considerations for learning a second language is for the learner to have access to *comprehensible input* (Krashen, 1985), or *accommodated language*. This means that the learners are given "clues" to help them understand the message being communicated, in addition to having "just the words" of a new language. There are many ways to help make the new language *comprehensible* with clues. For instance, adding pictures, objects, gestures, intonation, and cognates (words that are similar in both languages) to spoken or written language can aid in the comprehension of a new language (see Figure 7.1). Consider an ELL hearing the sentence "The Arctic Circle is in the northern hemisphere, and the temperature there is ice-cold." Just hearing or reading this sentence may be hard to understand for a beginning ELL. However, the teacher could make this sentence much more *comprehensible* by displaying a globe or computer image of the world, pointing to the northern hemisphere, tracing the Arctic Circle with her finger, using the cognate *zero* (for temperatures below zero), and by shivering to indicate the ice-cold temperature. In addition, seeing the globe can activate the student's prior knowledge about the northern and southern hemispheres and the North and South Poles. In the original delivery of the sentence using only words, the student might be so clueless about its meaning that he or she might not even know if he/she had any prior knowledge of this area–it would simply be *incomprehensible*! Making the new language comprehensible to the learner is a key component of ESL strategies. Technology is an attractive way to accomplish this goal with its ready access to pictures, sound, video, illustrations, games, maps, and so forth.

Krashen (1985) affirms that the learner is best served by experiencing language that is slightly more difficult than his or her proficiency level. Krashen uses the term "i" (input) to indicate the *current* proficiency level of the learner. This is the level where language is produced and comprehended without effort. He uses the term "i + 1" to indicate the next higher level where the learner has to struggle slightly to use the language but where comprehension and production are possible with the appropriate accommodations. The "i + 1" level is a "slight stretch." Therefore, according to Krashen, the "i + 1" level of language is the most fruitful for the second language learner. If learners stay at their comfort level, they will be able to function easily in the new language at that level, but no further language progress is likely to take place. If the learner jumps to a level that is too far above the current level, he or she will not be able to comprehend the language, frustration will set in, and no language progress will occur. However, with the "i + 1" level, the learner will be able to stretch just enough to advance. For example, let us say that a learner knows the words "gift," "birthday," and "yesterday" and is familiar with the irregular past tense "gave." He will understand the sentence "Yesterday, he gave me a gift for my birthday" without difficulty

Syda Productions / Shutterstock.com

Figure 7.1 Technology is an attractive way to make the new language comprehensible with clues, such as pictures, sound, video, illustrations, games, maps, and so forth that are readily accessible.

and will not advance in his language proficiency because, for him, the sentence is at the "i" level. If a learner does not know the words "gift," "birthday," "gave," or "yesterday" and hears that sentence, he probably will not understand it at all because it is too difficult, and he will not advance. However, if a learner knows the words "gift," "birthday," and "yesterday" but is not familiar with the irregular past form "gave," he probably can figure out the meaning of the sentence by inferring the meaning of "gave" from the words "yesterday," and "birthday," and "gift." For this learner, the sentence is on the "i+1" level. This is the English language level for which teachers should aim as they work with their individual ELLs and as they choose technology tools to enhance instruction.

It follows that in order to teach at the "i+1" level, teachers need to know the current proficiency level of each of their ELL students so that teachers can stretch each student beyond his or her level. In Texas, for example, a great deal of effort has been invested in identifying and describing second language proficiency levels through the Texas English Language Proficiency Assessment System (TELPAS). These TELPAS levels are incorporated into the state's English Language Proficiency Standards (ELPS). The TELPAS has developed a rubric of Proficiency Level Descriptors (PLDs) that is an effective tool for Texas teachers. Four levels of language proficiency are described – (1) beginning, (2) intermediate, (3) advanced, and (4) advanced high – in each of the four language domains (listening, speaking, reading, and writing) (see Figure 7.2). Many excellent resources regarding the TELPAS and the ELPS can be accessed from the Texas Education Agency (TEA) Website (www.tea.state.tx.us).

Teachers can learn a great deal about their students' English language abilities in each language domain by referring to the descriptions of each of the four proficiency levels in that domain. For example, it should be clear that *listening* in English is quite different at each of the four proficiency levels. It is evident from the PLDs that a student at the beginning level of proficiency (1) in *listening* will struggle to understand simple English, even when the topics are familiar and even when extralinguistic clues are available (see Figure 7.3). The beginner most likely will not ask questions about what they are hearing but will rather remain silent. For instance, if Rosa, a third grader from Puerto Rico who just arrived in the United States without knowing any English, hears the teacher talk about the supplies the children need to bring to class each day, she will not understand, even if she is familiar with school supplies in Spanish and even if she may see examples of scissors, markers, and pencils. She probably will not ask questions of the teacher or of her classmates. This is typical of the beginner stage (1) in *listening*.

Once Rosa progresses to the intermediate stage (2) in *listening*, she will understand the main ideas (the gist) of her teacher as he talks about the daily schedule and the class rules because these topics are now familiar to her in English. However, when he explains and discusses with the class the traditions and history of, for example,

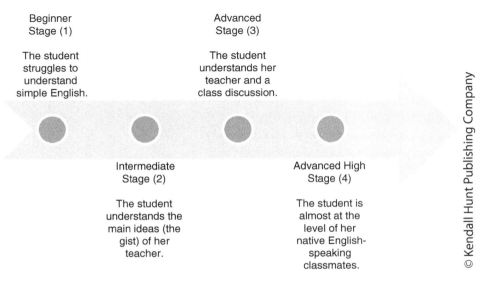

Figure 7.2 The four levels of language proficiency.

Thanksgiving, she will most likely not understand unless the teacher uses a number of pictures, cognates, short sentences, and other accommodated language. At this point, Rosa may ask her teacher or classmates to speak more slowly or to explain some words. This is typical of the intermediate stage (2) in *listening*.

Once Rosa reaches the advanced stage (3) in *listening*, she will understand her teacher and a class discussion about the solar system in English because she is somewhat familiar with the information, but she still may need to see some diagrams or three-dimensional models to aid her understanding. Even if the teacher speaks in long, complex sentences, she has a good chance of understanding him. This is typical of the advanced stage (3) in *listening*.

When Rosa reaches the advanced high stage (4) in *listening*, she is almost at the level of her native English-speaking classmates, although she may not understand idioms, subtle nuances, and very low frequency vocabulary. For example, when the teacher says, "If you follow the study guide as you prepare for the test, it will be a piece of cake," Rosa may be confused as to why her teacher is suddenly talking about cake. Because she has not yet mastered the many idioms and figurative expressions in English, she may think that there will be a party tomorrow after the test. This is typical of the advanced high stage (4) of listening.

In the PLDs, the four proficiency levels are described in detail for the language domains of *speaking, reading,* and *writing* as well as for *listening*. The PLDs can be accessed from the TEA Website (www.tea.state.tx.us/ student.assessment/ell/telpas). Teachers of ELLs who want to use technology effectively should understand what each of the four levels entail for each language skill so that the technology used for instruction is applied most effectively.

Another important consideration for learning a second language is related to the emotion (or affect) of the learner. Krashen (1985) proposes that if the learner feels comfortable, safe, and at ease, second language acquisition will be facilitated. On the other hand, if the learner feels tense, at risk, or anxious, acquisition will be hampered. He refers to this as the "affective filter." Technology, in particular, can contribute to a low affective filter because the learner can often be anonymous when he or she wishes; whereas, in a classroom, using a new language publicly can be anxiety-evoking for a learner. In addition, the game-like nature of so many of the technology tools adds enjoyable, pleasant connotations to learning.

Second language theory also recommends a preferable *sequence* of instruction. It is suggested that the ELL should experience the second language along two continuums. The first moves from *context embedded* to *context reduced*. This means that the teaching, at first, should provide many context clues or that it should be very accommodated. As the learner advances, the language should become less and less context embedded, having fewer context clues and should become less accommodated, or more context reduced. As seen in Figure 7.4 below, the horizontal continuum moves from context embedded to context reduced. In quadrant A, when discussing food groups and nutrition, the use of pictures and personal accounts would be used. In quadrant C, the ideas can

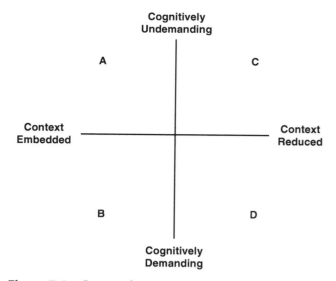

Figure 7.3 A student at the beginning level of proficiency (1) in *listening* will struggle to understand simple English, even when the topics are familiar and even when extralinguistic clues are available.

Figure 7.4 Range of contextual support and degree of cognitive involvement in language tasks and activities. *Source*: Reprinted from *Language, power, and pedagogy: Bilingual children in the Crossfire* (p. 68), by Jim Cummins, 2000, Great Britain: Cromwell Press Ltd.

be presented without pictures and first-person stories. The material can be presented in a more theoretical and abstract manner. The vertical continuum addresses how cognitively demanding the language is. The learner should first experience language that is less cognitively demanding and should gradually move to language that is more cognitively demanding (Cummins, 2000). Quadrant D is the ultimate goal, wherein students are operating with the language that is both context reduced and cognitively demanding. Teachers using technology need to be aware that their ELLs should gradually experience less context-embedded language if they are to advance in English. This is a challenge for teachers of ELLs because context-embedded language is common when using technology. Teachers and students may have to make a conscious effort to gradually reduce the context clues in order for the learner to become more proficient.

One of the major goals of ESL strategies is to facilitate ELLs' acquisition of *academic* language in English. Academic language refers to language that is context reduced and abstract. This is the kind of language mostly used in school. It is referred to as "Cognitive Academic Language Proficiency," or CALP. Language that is conversational and less school-like is referred to as "Basic Interpersonal Communication Skills," or BICS. Teachers can use technology to support their ELLs develop in both areas, but it is particularly helpful to employ technology for CALP, or academic language development (Cummins, 2000).

Lastly, second language learning is most effective when the language experienced is holistic in nature so that the learner is exposed to all four language skills: *reading*, *writing*, *speaking*, and *listening*. Technology is adept at allowing for this integration, as visual and auditory language is so accessible. Moreover, ESL strategies encourage the learning of the second language through the learning of content—whether it is social studies, mathematics, science, literature, or other subjects. The emphasis should be on the *meaning* of the ideas, not simply a focus on the language itself (and its rules). In this way, while concentrating on the *content*, the learning of language "comes in through the back door." In other words, the language is the "means" to an end (understanding the idea) but is not the "end" itself.

> Ms. Halloway is working on a unit about civil rights in her tenth-grade history class. The students are engaged in a heated discussion about the pros and cons of using violence when fighting for social justice. The students are captivated by this question. Marko, an ELL, is so drawn in by the discussion that his thoughts are all focused on the question of using violence. He has an opinion, and he expresses it without even realizing that he is talking in English. His motivation to express his ideas is so forceful that he is not self-conscious about his new language. Technology can be an effective way to advance this motivation to communicate without self-consciousness because the range of content is abundant, and its presentation can be so motivating that the learners may become less conscious of the language, making their second language acquisition a by-product.

In this chapter, we explore several possibilities of how to use technology for English language learners. It is important to understand *why* each technology tool is effective for ELLs so that teachers can make wise decisions about how or even *if* they should use the new tools for their ELL students. It is crucial to have an understanding of how to use comprehensible input, the affective filter, the suggested sequence of language learning, BICS and CALP, academic language, and holistic language. When reading about and evaluating the use of technology games, electronic publishing, e-readers, computer-assisted language learning (CALL), apps, social media, and personal communication tools for ELLs, one should keep in mind how all of these technology tools are supported by the second language principles described above.

Teaching English as Second Language with Technology Games

There are many advantages to using technology games when learning a language. It is a given that technology games invoke different reactions in different people. For some, these games are nothing more than a form of entertainment. However, others have discovered the great educational value of technology games, especially when it comes to ELL students. The Internet offers many sites where educators and students can find useful games for students, and when it comes to ESL classrooms, educators have an array of games to choose from. For a start, teachers can help ELL students build their vocabulary by using video and online games. One of the best sites for students to use for vocabulary building is Game Zone (www.english-online.org.uk/games/gamezone2.htm). This site offers over 20 games that provide the ELL student with practice to help build his or her vocabulary–from practicing the vocabulary of a food menu to learning the tools for gardening. ELL students can use games such as *The Garden Game* and *Which is the Bicycle?* to practice the basic vocabulary that they are required to learn at the beginning stage. The ESL game section of the English Club (www.englishclub.com/esl-games) is another good Website that can offer the students valuable grammar and pronunciation games. Finally, basic vocabulary games for ELL students can be found in Games to Learn English (www.gamestolearnenglish.com).

As learning progresses, teachers can use technology games to help their more advanced ELL students progress. At the intermediate level, ELL students are not only ready for vocabulary and grammar building, they are ready to engage in learning experiences online—platforms that can help students be fully involved in interactive experiences. In Tripping (tripppin.com), the ELL student can join Trip and his brother Pin in a world adventure by using the English language around the world. With DuoLingo (www.duolingo.com), students can use a variety of games to improve their conversational English. In this Website, ELL students can measure their learning level as they practice their talking and listening. The Website even offers an application that ELL students can use on their mobile phones. Moreover, the application tailors the exercises by knowing the student's native language. In addition to using this site to learn English, students can even use this site to learn other languages.

Video Games

ELL students can also greatly benefit from video games to learn English. Today's video games feature sophisticated plots, complex characters, vibrant settings, and realistic sound tracks. These modern video games allow players to control many aspects of the game, including the characters' appearances, actions, and even personalities. When students engage with the language of the game through the personas of the game's characters, their language learning anxieties are reduced. Krashen (1985), as noted earlier, refers to this aspect of successful second language education as lowering the "affective filter." The complex plots of the games require players to listen to and read detailed instructions in order to play. Additional reading and listening must be accomplished to comprehend the plot of the game and the characters' background information.

One of the greatest benefits is that video games offer the opportunity for role-playing. These video games, commonly known as role-playing games or RPGs, allow the students to immerse themselves in games as they take on the roles of well-defined characters. Usually, the player controls the outcome of different scenarios. RPGs require players to assume the role of characters in a fictional setting tasked with accomplishing a predetermined goal. Some of these are: creating or nurturing a society from mud huts to space travel in *Civilization Revolution,* designing bacteria and guiding them through a millennium of evolution in *Spore,* or managing an amusement park in *Thrillville: Off the Rails.* To accomplish these goals, players must read manageable amounts of material, including directions for playing the game, descriptions of the game's setting and characters, and information pertaining to the goal and plot of the game. Additionally, students must listen and respond to vast amounts of in-game dialogue, both directional and character based, to accomplish the task of the game. Playing as partners or in small groups supports the ELL learner, too.

Most RPGs offer complex stories about combat and war, where often the character is asked to save the world. The story is often a crucial part of the entertainment, offering developed tales about characters and places. The variety of RPGs available for ELL learners is huge, offering a selection for every taste and level. However, educators must be careful and choose age- and school-appropriate RPGs which they may use in class or suggest. Common Sense Media (www.commonsensemedia.org/lists/role-playing-games-rpgs-for-kids) offers a good variety of games, which includes the age appropriateness for each game. Another excellent Website where teachers can find a list of RPGs designated by age is AngelFire.com. There are many

RPGs that ELL students can use, from *Zelda* to *Dragon Quest*. However, teachers must also be careful about the cultural sensitivity issues that can arise from many RPGs in terms of religion and cultures.

Using Video Games for Academic Language Instruction

Video games provide a platform for ESL teachers to teach subject-specific academic language. Knowledge of subject-specific academic language (or CALP), as opposed to BICS, should feature prominently in the language goals of every lesson in a K–12 ESL classroom.

Language Arts in the ESL Classroom: Elements of Fiction

An example of teaching CALP through video games can be illustrated in the fields of literature and language arts. Video games provide the appropriate platform for teaching students the structure of a dramatic work (similarly found in novels, plays, and films), including exposition, inciting incident, rising action, climax, falling action, resolution, and denouement (or conclusion) of the plot. These commonly taught elements of a dramatic work stem from the nineteenth-century German novelist and playwright Gustav Freytag's (1863) analysis of the common patterns in the plot of stories and novels. Video games contain the *common elements* of fiction: plot, setting, characters, conflict, symbolism, flashbacks, foreshadowing, personification, style, and point of view. Conflict, a major literary element of the genre of fiction, clearly exists in video games. Themes of "Person vs. Self," "Person vs. Person," "Person vs. Society," "Person vs. Nature," "Person vs. Supernatural," "Person vs. God," "Person vs. Fate," and "Person vs. Machine" play out in novels, plays, *and* many video games alike. Similarly, character types exist in video game plots as they do in fiction on the page. Protagonists, antagonists, static characters, dynamic characters, foil characters, supporting characters, and minor characters have their entrances and exits on the virtual stage of video games. ESL teachers should provide students with a lesson on the elements of literature prior to playing the video game. After playing the game, students can use this language arts-specific academic language in their reading journals, just as they would after reading traditional literature.

Post-Game Reading Journal Entries

A reading journal provides students with a place to react to their experiences playing the game using the academic language taught prior to playing in conjunction with the language utilized during the game. Students can practice summarization skills, outline written character sketches (appearance, personality, behavior, motivations, and actions), reflect on the events of the game, or respond to specific teacher-generated writing prompts pertaining to the cultures, politics, metaphors, life lessons, and so forth expressed in the game.

In addition to regular diaries and journal entries, there are many tools the teachers can use to facilitate ELL students with their writing. For example, teachers can introduce the concept of electronic diaries, or e-Diaries, to students through their electronic devices such as desktops, laptops, tablets, and even mobile devices (see Figure 7.5). The most immediate benefit of using e-Diaries is that students can take advantage of grammar and spelling checkers as they write. There are many Websites that offer free account e-Diaries. Among the most popular sites are DearDiary.net, Penzu, MyEjournal, and DiaryLand. In addition, many e-Diary sites can be customized for the user. For example, FitDay offers users a customized e-Diary for those interested in tracking one's fitness life. In addition to writing down that "awesome moment" that one had in the gym, the Website allows one to track

Figure 7.5 Teachers can introduce the concept of electronic diaries, e-Diaries, to students through their electronic devices.

everything from calories intake to the daily steps counts. For the avid traveler, there is TravelDiaries, and for those willing to explore their deepest emotions, there is MyTherapyJournal. The other benefit of e-Diaries is that entries can be as private or public as the user wants them to be. Therefore, teachers can create public blogs for an entire class with very little effort, allowing an entire class or group of students to share their writing and feelings. The connection for ELLs is when learners write in their new language about things which are relevant.

Oral Language Activity: Reader's Theater and Video Games

ELLs require opportunities to reread texts to develop sight word vocabulary, reading fluency, and comprehension skills. Additionally, they require *scaffolded* (or supported) experiences to practice pronouncing new vocabulary and grammatical structures with character-specific inflection, expression, and varied volume. Reader's Theater, which requires students to read character dialogues in the form of a play, allows for the development of these interrelated language skills. Students can read teacher-generated or student-generated Reader's Theater scripts based on the setting, characters, and plot of a recently played video game (see Figure 7.6).

Figure 7.6   Teachers can provide beginning ELL students with the script from a play, and there are many online databases where teachers can download scripts.

Mrs. McAffee assigns her ELL students their Reader's Theater roles before the actual in-class performance, allowing them to rehearse their parts before performing in front of the class and thus lowering the affective filter. Reader's Theater helps students to further immerse themselves in the plot of a video game and reread its vocabulary and grammatical structures, thereby acquiring the language used in the game in a natural, fun way. She videotapes their performance so that they can later reflect on their speech in private and, also, so that she can maintain oral assessment data.

Reader's Theater gives students the opportunity to "live" the story. It offers opportunities for teachers to encourage learners to interact with each other in a variety of scenarios. For beginning ELL students, teachers can provide them with the script from a play, and there are many online databases where teachers can download scripts. For example, teachers can use the Reader's Theater section of ReadingA-Z.com. They can also find scripts from TeachingHeart.net. Scripts for Reader's Theater, according to subjects, can be downloaded at ReadingRocket.org, including scripts for science and mathematics. Finally, Aaron Shepard's Website (www.aaronshep.com) provides one of the most comprehensive online database of Reader's Theater scripts.

For advanced ELL students, teachers can enhance the Reader's Theater experience by allowing students to create their own scripts. For example, after playing a video, reading a story, or investigating a historical event, students create their own scripts and perform their own stories in front of the class. Teachers encourage ELLs to use free online script writing tools such as Plotbot.com. The Reader's Theater experience can be enhanced by adding extra features to the experience. For instance, music can be added as the students read the story. The teacher can also encourage students to create a slide show that can be played as the story is read.

Clearly, technology games and video games should not replace traditional methods of ESL instruction but rather should provide students with exciting supplements to relevant content area curriculum. It must be noted that not all technology and video games are suitable for classroom use. Obviously, violent games that award points for killing, maiming, or other violent/ antisocial acts should be avoided. Also, games and scripts devoid of language content should be avoided. Just as with literature offered in class, games and scripts should be age and school appropriate for both the lower grades and the upper grades. Beginning ELLs who are in middle and high school will benefit from technology and reading with simple English but that goes beyond "See Spot Run." Since video games mostly require students to read and listen, students should be encouraged to talk about their experiences after playing the game to practice pronouncing their newly acquired vocabulary and grammatical structures (see Figure 7.7). After participation in these types of activities, language practice should occur in writing in students' reading journals to link language learning across the *listening*, *speaking*, *reading*, and *writing* spectrum.

Figure 7.7 Since video games mostly require students to read and listen, students should be encouraged to talk about their experiences after playing a game to practice pronouncing their newly acquired vocabulary and grammatical structures.

Utilizing Electronic Publishing Platforms to Teach English as a Second Language

The purpose of language is to communicate with others. In the twenty-first-century world, many aspects of communication via publications have moved online. Therefore, ESL teachers should include aspects of electronic publication in their teaching. Electronic publishing platforms, both online and software formats, allow ELLs to acquire language in a natural environment with a low affective filter. Additionally, utilizing electronic platforms in the ESL classroom allows teachers to connect with students on their level and better obtain student buy-in, motivation, and participation (Wright, 2010).

Today's students in most parts of the world are part of the technology revolution. In fact, they cannot fathom a world before technology, and they cannot imagine living without technology. Teachers today find ways to integrate English language learning strategies with technology to motivate students to participate in learning activities. The suggestions below will open up the teaching and learning process for many teachers so that they can integrate their learning strategies with technology tools to meet the needs of the ELLs in their classrooms. Teachers of ELLs, however, must remember that the Digital Divide does exist, meaning that *all* their learners may not have had the experiences with technology that others may have had. Part of teaching ELLs may be teaching the technology terms and skills in the new language along with the content.

Digital Stories

ESL teachers can utilize digital storytelling platforms like Pinnacle Studio, WeVideo and Animoto to publish any manner of language acquisition projects. Mrs. Blaylock incorporates activities in her classroom where students create personal narratives; for instance, students document their family's sociocultural histories and traditions by using images, narratives, text, video clips, and music. Also, students can create traditional research projects utilizing a digital story platform. Moreover, research projects using a digital story format require students to interpret, analyze, and evaluate visual images—important visual literacy skills. Posting digital stories on social media Websites, podcasts, video blogs, and video posting Websites provides an incentive for students to produce their best work, knowing the far-reaching distribution of these online publishing platforms. This can also be shared with friends and/ or family members who were left behind in their previous country or who live in other areas across this country.

To see how meaningful these narratives can be, in one adult ESL class, students created digital narratives that they used to describe events that were very important to them.

Sadie created a digital narrative that combined her wedding ceremony with the important traditions in a pueblo in Oaxaca, Mexico. She described the events through pictures and videos that had been taken during their wedding while she narrated the story through her own emotions and experiences. Sadie described how her husband asked her if she would be willing to travel to Oaxaca to share their wedding with the community where he grew up. When she agreed, she did not realize that she would be inviting over 1,000 people to her wedding because everyone in the village attends weddings in the community. Sadie had the opportunity to learn about the local customs and traditions. It was good luck for their marriage to have a rooster wake them up on their wedding day. As they celebrated the wedding mass, a baby was baptized as a sign of prosperity. The women in the village made a beautiful bag for the couple to contain grain so they would not go hungry. As they left the church, bells were ringing to celebrate the mass, and people were shouting, "*Beso, Beso, Beso*" or "Kiss, Kiss, Kiss" just like in the movies. As Sadie told her story, she not only shared about an important event in her life, she gave her audience a glimpse into the cultural lives of a different country and a different place. She shared how much she valued the culture and life of her husband's family and community.

Younger students find empowerment as well in sharing their life events with others.

The process of developing a digital narrative gives ELLs opportunities to reflect about their culture and language so that they can learn more about themselves. Teachers provide reflective practice to the ELL students through the writing process. The teachers can implement reading responses to literature in order for the ELLs to reflect about their own life experiences. Mitchell, Miller, and Dalton (2016) described writing experiences that gave ELL students specific opportunities to reflect through literature. Using the grammar and spelling tools (and the translation tools, when needed) on computers is also an aid in writing in the new language for the ELL. Students can keep these reading responses in video journals or blogs. They respond to literature that is presented to them through class read alouds in their video journals (see Table 7.1). Once they have written several entries in their video journals, they may choose one entry to develop into a full story. As they write, the students utilize the writing process of revising, editing, and rewriting to prepare their digital narrative (Fletcher & Portalupi, 2001). They have peer and teacher conferences to complete their written story. When the story is ready to be published, learners put it into a storyboard. They create several squares to place the events of their story in order; then they place the story in the storyboard and add pictures to the storyboard according to how the events unfolded.

Table 7.1   Template for Video Game Character Sketch

Character	Appearance	Personality	Motivations	Actions	Allies	Enemies

The ELL students will be able to identify their own cultural identity through this writing process. They will also identify what is important to them through their culture and language. Nieto and Bode (2012) found that when students were able to identify their culture and identity, they discovered that they did not live in isolation and that others may have many of the same experiences as theirs. This encouraged the students to become a part of the classroom community because they realized that the students in their classroom had more in common with them than differences.

ELL students utilize the digital narrative process to use both their literacy and technology skills. They can write about connections that they make to literature while also learning new technology skills (see Table 7.2). They find different ways to tell their stories and use personal reflection to identify who they are and how they and their family came to be in the United States.

Facebook, the most pervasive online social networking service, boasts a membership of over one billion active members. Users create and manage a personal profile—including photos, personal information, contact information, interests, and life events to remain in contact with friends, family, classmates, and acquaintances. The platform also allows users to send messages, email, voice call, and video call to other users. When ELLs utilize this collaborative technology to interact with their peers in English, it becomes both an independent and collaborative natural English acquisition environment. The Facebook platform provides students with an effective publishing platform for audio and visual recordings of them performing speeches/presentations, original poems, Reader's Theater performances, and even songs. Additionally, students can publish their thoughts, feelings, and opinions on a variety of topics, including restaurants, films, music, politics, world events, and sports. Students can even publish, using appropriate privacy settings, a class Facebook page where they post photos and descriptions of class events, fieldtrips, and school activities (see Figure 7.8).

Teachers can now create closed groups in Facebook so others can participate in the community through invitation. They can create a class Facebook group for students to communicate with each other. This process allows students to post pictures, videos, and comments in a safe environment for the class. They can utilize informal language to practice fluency with language. The pictures, videos, and comments are

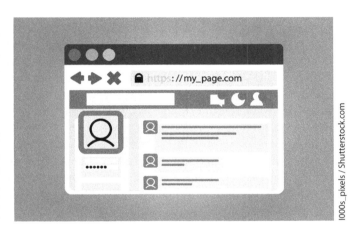

Figure 7.8 Teachers create closed groups in social media sites.

1000s_pixels / Shutterstock.com

Table 7.2 Here Is a List of Books About Students' Lives, Names, and Families

Writing prompt	Literature selection
How did you get your name?	Ada, A. F. (1995). Names and surnames. In *My Name is María Isabel* (pp. 7–12). New York, NY: Atheneum Books for Young Readers. Cisneros, S. (1980). My Name. In *The House on Mango Street* (pp. 10–11). New York, NY: Vintage Contemporaries.
Special memories of your family.	Cisneros, S. (1980). The House on Mango Street. In *The House on Mango Street* (pp. 3–5). New York, NY: Vintage Contemporaries. Cisneros, S. (1980). Hairs. In *The House on Mango Street* (pp. 6–7). New York, NY: Vintage Contemporaries.
What were some embarrassing moments in school for you?	Anaya, R. (1992). Seis. In *Bless me, Última* (pp. 59–67). New York, NY: Grand Central.
Who were the story tellers in your life?	Villasenor, V. (1991). Foreword. *Rain of Gold* (pp. 9–11). Houston, TX: Arte Publico.

safely shared only with those who are invited into the group. Teachers can also implement Messenger, one of the Facebook tools used to send private messages to the students in the group.

Business-Oriented Social Networking Services

Online business-networking platforms, for example LinkedIn, allows users to communicate with professional colleagues, customers, distributors, clients, classmates, and employees. Users build a contact network to find jobs, build a customer base, obtain information about a company, and congratulate colleagues' successes. In 2017, LinkedIn reported 500 million members in more than 200 countries utilizing the Website, which is available in over 20 languages. Despite these diverse language offerings, ELLs should set up an account in English. This activity can work with high school students with part-time jobs, designated career ambitions, and career-specific classes. Setting up an account, which includes developing a professional profile, provides students with a publishing platform to learn business English in a natural setting.

Wikis for Collaborative Writing

A wiki, unlike a blog, allows an online community of people to contribute to the content of an informational webpage on a specified topic. Since the webpage structure is present, a Web-based wiki allows students to easily create a webpage by concentrating on content rather than format. For example, the structure of the most commonly used *wiki*, Wikipedia, is already in place, and contributors can easily add or edit an existing article, thus making it an appropriate platform for collaborative writing projects. Students can write individual or group contributions to a wiki site and peer edit each other's writing at the same time. Also, students can add images, videos, audios, and links to other Websites to enhance the content of a wiki. Since contributions to a wiki appear instantly on the wiki Website and are accessible by anyone with an Internet connection, contributors are highly motivated to put forth valuable content using their best writing. Students keenly allow their peers and teachers to provide content input and editing advice. Wiki sites allow contributors and readers to track individual contributions to the sites, providing teachers with a valuable assessment tool. The history tool also allows teachers to track students' work continuously as they revise their writing, a valuable tool that permits teachers to monitor students as they continue to work through the writing process. Commonly used wikis in classrooms include PBworks (www.pbworks.com), Wikispaces (www.wikispaces.com), and Wetpaint (www.wetpaint.com).

Teaching English as Second Language with E-Readers

Advances in technology have been changing the ways in which we use language along all dimensions, including the ways in which we read. The popularity of electronic reading has been growing at a remarkable pace (Yoon, 2013). Electronic reading includes reading online documents from Websites or reading online versions of newspapers or magazines that once could only be accessed in printed form (see Figure 7.9). It also involves reading books (e-books) on screens that include not only personal computers, laptops, and tablets but also on e-readers such as the Kindle and the Nook. Debates are ongoing as to whether paper books will one day be obsolete, giving way entirely to electronic media or whether it is unreasonable to think that a complete takeover by online reading will ever occur. The answer to this debate is interesting, but the essential question for educators of second language students is how to maximize electronic reading options to enhance the ELLs' language development as well as their content knowledge through English.

Figure 7.9   Electronic reading includes reading online documents from Websites or reading online versions of newspapers or magazines that once could only be accessed in printed form.

In order to maximize e-reading experiences for ELLs, teachers would like to know whether or not students' attitudes toward e-reading differ depending on the purpose of the reading, the length of the text, or whether students' attitudes and ease with e-reading changes over time. As researchers investigate these questions, ELL teachers can benefit by some answers that are already emerging.

It seems that students' attitudes toward e-reading become more positive over time. Therefore, it would be wise for ELL teachers to start their readers with shorter texts and to gradually build up to longer ones. Teachers also should be patient and should not get discouraged if students at first do not seem to embrace e-reading. Students may need time to get used to the medium and to develop effective strategies for themselves. For example, Chou (2016) found that students who were not accustomed to e-reading were distracted by Internet possibilities; thus they were less focused when using e-readers than when using hard copy texts. However, students can be taught to resist distractions by skillful teachers. It is important to make students aware of the benefits of e-reading so that they can use e-readers on their own as well as when assigned e-reading in class. Advantages include having more access to numerous books (in the second and, perhaps, the first language) and texts, having up-to-date material, having remote access, and enjoying more portability (Chou, 2016).

Many resources are available for teachers who wish to encourage e-reading for their ELLs. For example, for teachers who engage their ELL students in independent reading, the International Digital Children's Library (IDCL) (www.en.childrenslibrary.org) is an excellent place to start. The library contains over 4,500 books in 59 languages. One important feature for teachers of ELLs is that it is easy to find books that are of interest to older students even though they are written in more basic English. On the IDCL Website there is a category of books that have received the distinguished White Raven label because of their universal themes and innovative style and design. Within the White Raven Catalogue on the IDCL site, there is a subcategory of "easily understandable" books that are of particular interest to mature readers who are at beginning English levels. These books allow ELLs to explore sophisticated ideas and themes in understandable English. The IDCL can be downloaded on iPhones and iPads at www.itunes.apple.com/us/app/icdl-for-ipad-free-books-for/id363731638?mt=8.

Another resource for free e-books is the Worldreader's Open Library. This library houses books with varied content and represents many cultures. Books are available in many languages, including English.

Mr. Horace's ninth-grade history class is comprised of 24 students, eight of whom are ELLs. Of the eight ELLs, five students are on the intermediate level, and three students are on the advanced level. Mr. Horace is responsible for integrating all of his students into this class so that the same learning objectives apply to all students. However, he needs to accommodate language for his ELLs and make it comprehensible for them, while not sacrificing the level or rigor of the content curriculum. The class is studying the Great Depression years and how that period affected different regions in the United States. The students are reading *To Kill a Mockingbird* by Harper Lee (1960) to better understand the Deep South during that time. The book will also provide background for his upcoming unit on civil rights. Because all students have tablets with e-reader apps, everyone in the class is reading the electronic version of the book, the features of which allow Mr. Horace to implement effective differentiated reading instruction for students.

Dimitri, an intermediate level ELL student in Mr. Horace's class, can listen to sections of the text in English while reading along silently. Moreover, he can look up unfamiliar key vocabulary words by clicking on them and by accessing the simplified versions of the words, pictorial illustrations of the words, or translations of the words into his first language. For very difficult passages, he can employ Google Translate which will present the entire selected passage in his first language. Fatima, an advanced level student from the Middle East, is lacking knowledge of the Deep South during this period in general, so she accesses the Internet to view short documentary film clips and explanations about this era. These clips also expand her vocabulary as she both hears and sees illustrations of key words such as "rural," "mansion," "segregated," "civil rights," "discrimination," and so forth. Tuyen, a Vietnamese student on the high-advanced level, is interested in the legal aspects of the novel. She wants to concentrate on the parts of the book that relate to the law. Mr. Horace helps her to identify the "legal" vocabulary words in the book such as "jury," "defend," "accuse," and "prosecute." She uses the Web search tool on her tablet to locate the sections of the novel where these words appear to help her highlight and compare these passages so that she can better understand the court system described in the book.

These students highlight sections of the book that they think are significant for either language or content so that they can easily return to them at a later time. They also enter comments and make notations using the note-taking tool on the tablets. Some students may enter questions that they would like to ask in class about different parts of the book. As Mr. Horace guides his ELL students through their reading of the text, he helps them use the technology tools wisely. For example, he emphasizes that they should not look up every unknown word; they should only look up the words that are essential for comprehending the important ideas. He encourages them to guess at what unfamiliar words mean before clicking on them and to see if they guessed correctly. He is conscious that they still need to develop inferencing skills in their second language and that these tools should not be overused. He also aids them choosing appropriate short videos to develop the prior knowledge necessary for comprehension of the text and of this period in American history. Mr. Horace remembers that years ago he invested a great deal of time figuring out ways to make English comprehensible for his ELL students. The e-readers offer multiple and individualized ways to do so and free him to invest his time helping his students individually in other ways.

Ms. Gino appreciates e-readers for her younger students. She teaches second grade and has several ELL students in her class. She provides them with opportunities to hear professional readings of the electronic books that she will read with her students in class by referring them to the Actors Guild Website (www.sagfoundation.org/childrens-literacy). She knows that many of her students whose first language is English most likely have family members at home who can read English books aloud to them, but this is probably not the case with her second language students. A few days before she is to read *The Rainbow Fish* by Marcus Pfister (1995) in class, she has her ELL students listen to the electronic book read by Ernest Borgnine, who was a famous American film and television star, while reading along with him silently. This allows her ELL students to have heard the text read with skillful expression and correct pronunciation of vocabulary prior to their encounter with the e-text in class. This activity will make the whole-class instruction effective for the ELL children because they have had the chance to build schema for the ideas and language of the book.

Kat Buslaeva / Shutterstock.com

Kathy Hutchins / Shutterstock.com

The descriptions of Mr. Horace's and of Ms. Gino's activities using e-readers need not be restricted to ELL students. Certainly, students whose first language is English can also benefit and enjoy these strategies. However, using e-books for ELLs in this fashion is essential for the language development and content knowledge of ELL students (see Figure 7.10).

Reading proficiency in a second language should best follow the sequence of *context-embedded* text to *context-reduced* text (see Figure 7.4). Electronic texts can be context embedded simply by the reader accessing related pictures, diagrams, graphics, and sound that provide him or her with clues to the meanings that go beyond the mere words of the language. In any effective ELL lesson, the teacher provides these extralinguistic clues to make the language comprehen-

Figure 7.10   Parents are encouraged to read with their students at home using resources provided by teachers.

sible. With e-readers, the ELL student is empowered to self-provide these clues on demand and to regulate the amount of context-embedded clues needed. It is the responsibility of the teacher to facilitate the ELL student in finding the optimal level of context needed to supplement the text so that the text remains challenging but not frustrating. Being able to do this enables ELL students to be self-regulated learners as they continue to pursue all forms of e-reading, which, undoubtedly, will become more sophisticated in time.

Question 2

Computer-Assisted Language Learning and Tools

Computer-assisted Language Learning (CALL) programs provide an effective learning environment so that students can practice language in an interactive way using multimedia content. Learning can take place either with the supervision of teachers or individually at one's own pace. As CALL becomes more engrained in the ELL classroom, many educators are interested in figuring out how to use CALL programs in meaningful ways for their students.

As we know, the ELL classroom is made up of various levels of proficiencies within the skills of *listening*, *speaking*, *reading*, and *writing*.

Consider Mr. Boone's classroom. Xochilt has just arrived in the United States. When she was given the language proficiency test, she scored a 1 in English and a 1 in Spanish based on a scale of 5. She has never attended a school. Clara is also a recent immigrant. Clara's oral proficiency test scores were a 5 in Spanish and a 4 in English based on a scale of 5. From these descriptions, one can see that Xochilt is a beginner with only listening and speaking skills in her native language, and Clara, who is an advanced high, is totally proficient in her native language. As an ELL instructor, how does one meet all the needs of teaching ESL when students come with such a wide range of language skills?

Web-based commercial programs can benefit the school and district by generating score reports and can aid the classroom teacher with individualizing instruction. For example, the tests that are administered to ELLs in Texas provide important results for teachers. These English Language Proficiency (ELP) scores align to language standards so that teachers can easily understand their ELL strengths and weaknesses and make sure that ELL students receive the right support. ELP scores help teachers analyze their students' proficiency gains and serve as a guide for differentiated instruction. The scores also support documenting and tracking ELL students' progress after they exit ESL programs. The reports can help classroom teachers set specific goals for each student by language domain, based on proficiency level and standards. The software options noted in the following paragraphs show how Web-based commercial programs can support students who are at beginning levels as well as those at advanced high levels by allowing the teacher to provide differentiated instruction while using authentic language for *listening*, *speaking*, *reading*, and *writing*.

Teachers of ELL children must become knowledgeable about the wide variety of educational software available to benefit the enhancement of all skills in learning a language. For example, numerous software programs can aid ELLs with survival and real-life reading skills. Students learn to read labels, menus, advertisements, job ads, job applications, banking forms, travel schedules, and maps on many of the software programs available. *Core Reading and Vocabulary Development* are designed for low-level literacy learners and ELL students who require a basic foundation in vocabulary, spelling, and comprehension. *Internet Pictionary Dictionary* (www .pdictionary.com) is an excellent Internet site that offers materials in five languages, including English. Learners build vocabulary through motivating activities that include flashcards, fill-in-the-blank games, word scrambles, spelling challenges, and so forth. Each activity can be chosen at a variety of levels, and all activities offer self-checks. This kind of site is excellent for individual practice and differentiated instruction. *Easy Writer Interactive Software* lets the learner read, choose, and edit compositions that ELL students from all over the world have written. *Longman English Interactive* is a four-level, video-based integrated skills software program that has engaging video, audio, animations, and extensive practice activities to develop essential skills for beginners to intermediate high (see Figure 7.11). *Exercise Generator Plus* is for busy teachers who want to produce professional looking paper-based reading and vocabulary activities, exams, and homework materials. Story World (www.eurotalk .com/en/store/learn/english/storyworld/cd and www.storyworld.us) brings to life well-known children's stories and songs to help them to build on their knowledge and use of English language and bilingual learning. *Road to Citizenship* was designed to help qualified people become U.S. citizens. As one can see, there are numerous software programs that can support the ELL teacher. Depending upon the student's needs, most likely there is a technology program that will help ELLs develop academic language and become more proficient in English.

Videoconferencing options that can enhance the educational experience for ELLs are numerous. These videoconferencing options offer the same opportunities for students regardless of where they live—in small towns, rural communities, or big cities. Students, irrespective of the location, can connect with other students across the United States and the world. One can even connect with experts to begin to develop not only essential communication skills but also an awareness of global issues. It is a truly valuable educational experience to talk with experts and peers face-to-face through Skype. Students in a classroom in Houston, Texas, can work with students in a classroom in Madrid, Spain. If the ELLs in the United States are Spanish speakers, *they* are able to become experts in the conversation for the classroom. While in the past, collaborative activities might have been limited to one classroom or one school, videoconferencing allows students from multiple schools around the world to work together on relevant issues. One benefit of such an exchange is that learners can receive different views and fresh ideas from students who are miles away. Students in schools with ELLs can benefit from communicating with ELLs in other schools to broaden their perspectives and, of course, the ELLs benefit from "teaching" their online peers about their cultures and experiences. Teachers can explore the Website of the international organization Teachers of English to Speakers of Other Languages (TESOL) (www.tesol.org). In doing so, they can network with other teachers of ESL around the world to initiate such partnerships.

The interactive electronic whiteboard is another tool that can help in demonstrations and that can accommodate different learning styles and language proficiency levels. Since the board can be used with any software, it is extremely adaptable for numerous uses and does not require acquisition of additional software. Its creative use is limited

sirikorn thamniyom / Shutterstock.com

Figure 7.11 Web-based commercial programs can help the classroom teacher with individualizing instruction, particularly with listening.

only by the imagination of teachers and students. It can interface well with a document camera and video camera. With the document camera, the presenter can show an object such as a story, and then the skills being taught can be highlighted. The board is excellent for lessons where the participants need printed copies of a brainstorming activity. Copies of the resulting document can be printed and distributed and/or can be saved for future work. With proper planning, preparation, and training, it is a powerful instructional tool that can be adapted for use with a wide range of subjects and ages. Many ELL learners may have limited vocabulary in the new language, but having them contribute visual examples will help increase their understanding (see Figure 7.12).

Whenever possible, teachers should provide learners with the opportunity to practice with technology. Computer skills should be a regular part of the learning process. In one of the classrooms described above, there were two students with very different language proficiencies. By using CALL programs, teachers can individualize instructions for each student, especially when they have a classroom with multiple levels of proficiencies. Using computers and other technology devices helps deliver material in class (video, clips, images, etc.) and aids learners in improving their language skills and sources of information. The more learners are exposed to technology, the more comfortable they feel using it. The benefits and features of technology support the teacher in preparing lessons, tracking students, and in using authentic language to help them become more proficient.

Figure 7.12 Many ELL learners may have limited vocabulary in the new language, but having them contribute visual examples by taking pictures with digital cameras will help increase their understanding.

Mrs. Keen is teaching the rectangle shape in her first-grade class. She gives out digital cameras to pairs of students in the classroom, and they take pictures of books, the whiteboard, and other real-life rectangular shapes in the school and post them on the interactive whiteboard showing their knowledge and offering many visuals for other students to see.

Tablets and Apps

Apps and online resources can make learning English fun. Instead of repeating common English phrases in a classroom setting, ELL students play games and complete exercises while learning the ins and outs of the language, even if they are far away from a teacher or school. For instance, the Internet *TESOL Journal* (www.tesol .org) created a site comprised solely of quizzes, tests, exercises, and puzzles for ELL students. With thousands of contributions from teachers, students can take advantage of exercises that suit their needs. Users are allowed to choose their level of difficulty in grammar, vocabulary quizzes, and even crossword puzzles. In addition, the site offers a range of podcasts and YouTube videos, including those that allow students to listen and read along.

When teachers look at how technology has changed education over the past decade they cannot help but be amazed by the sheer number of phone and tablet apps for educators that have absolutely flooded the electronic marketplace. There are so many apps for teachers released every month that even the most plugged-in educator would have a challenging time processing and utilizing them all. It is wise for teachers to keep up with professional notices that rate many of these.

As technology continues to become more and more popular, classroom attention spans are getting shorter and shorter. Keeping the attention of a student may seem difficult at times, but by using some of these apps, teachers can add a new dimension from the traditional classroom while still reinforcing the skills that are essential for ELLs.

Mobile digital devices like smartphones, tablets, and laptops have made it much easier for learners of ESL to immerse themselves in constant practice and speed up their learning process. Smartphones and tablets aren't just for games or social media. They can also prove to be great tools for English language learning or practice (sometimes, even those are games). There are limitless apps on the market for learners at any level.

ESL and TESOL teachers and learners can find a world of useful apps for every platform to help with such critical language learning processes as vocabulary building, reading comprehension, pronunciation, and more.

Mobile apps are just one part of the picture for ESL learners. Total immersion is the best way to learn a language. That means spending time conversing with native speakers and practicing vocabulary by speaking, writing, and reading will always be important. However, mobile apps for ESL and TESOL provide additions to the arsenal of teaching ESL.

What Can Apps Do?

To integrate apps into a lesson plan, teachers must understand exactly what they are capable of doing to support instruction. First, educational apps are multimodal. They incorporate written and oral language, moving and still images and audio, and the ability to move objects around the screen. Second, many apps enable users to collaborate. Students can connect their tablets to the same app and work in real time and design collective work. Third, it is interactive. If leveraged effectively, it can increase audience awareness by providing a wide readership. In turn, students invite critique in ways that extend beyond classroom walls.

Type of Apps

1. **Content**. The purpose of these apps is to help students consume content. Skills are typically assessed as levels of difficulty are completed. Many have game-like interfaces requiring users to beat the clock, play against opponents, or earn points. Additionally, some publishers create these as supplemental resources.
2. **Presentation**. Presentation apps incorporate a range of multimodal affordances allowing students to become active, creative producers of information. Whiteboards, note-taking, and concept mapping apps fall within this category. For example, multiple students can log on to BaiBoard, a whiteboard app, using their individual devices to create and revise content. This enables problem-solving to occur in real time while seated next to a classmate or with students in classrooms around the world.
3. **Productivity**. Productivity apps are characterized by how they support organization, management, and document sharing. They do not teach skills or present information. Qrafter, for example, can be used to scan quick response codes directing students to Websites, podcasts, or electronic information. Another example is !Homework, an app to help students organize assignments and allocate time effectively.
4. **Hybrid**. This type of app incorporates the characteristics of two or more of the app categories here. Edmodo, a password-protected social networking site for educators, incorporates features of both presentation and productivity apps. This app increases productivity by allowing teachers to store resources, share documents, and manage classroom activities such as attendance. The quiz, poll, and comment capabilities categorize Edmondo as a presentation app because they allow students to share perspectives and information.

Mr. Gomez had a variety of students in the same ESL classroom. Bianca who is in her second year in the ESL program moved here from Mexico but knew no English when she arrived. She was retained one year in her old school. Henri is a student who moved here two years ago from Haiti. He speaks Haitian-Creole and French and can read and write in French, although he was several years below grade level in these skills. Based on these two scenarios, the ESL instructor needs to have a variety of tools to meet the needs of these students as well as to differentiate for each student based on their levels of proficiency.

wavebreakmedia / Shutterstock.com

Although ESL lessons can be extremely beneficial, they often focus solely on the basics. Online resources and apps can supplement basic skills to allow students to learn slang and idioms. This creates more natural sounding dialogue and allows the student to better understand phrases and terms that are not available in a dictionary. Sites like manythings.org not only feature games, quizzes, exercises, and vocabulary words but also a collection of slang terms, English songs, proverbs, jokes, and American stories. Podcasts such as the Learn a Song Podcast, Jokes in English, and Listen and Repeat Podcast can also be enjoyable ways to not only learn the language but to "soak up" the culture as well. Since culture and language are strongly connected, this is an important part of learning English.

Convenience is another major benefit of utilizing apps and online resources. ESL students can learn on their own time and tailor a program to fit their needs. YouTube and podcasts allow the student to hear English language being spoken. The well-respected Voice of America (VOA) Special English program (www.learningenglish .voanews.com/programs/radio) offers streaming podcasts, Facebook lessons, YouTube tutorials, mobile phone applications, and webcasts—free of charge. These sessions read English newscasts slowly, and some of their lessons include issues like learning TV or movie English. There are some YouTube sites that even show clearly where to place the tongue in pronunciation of sounds. Apps are ideal for ESL students on the go.

Relying solely on a classroom approach to learning English can be unsatisfactory for certain types of learners. To maximize a student's ability to absorb new information, it is important to expose him/her to a variety of learning styles. Internet resources and apps are an effective way to teach all students, regardless of their learning needs. By choosing the type of resources or apps that work for him/her, the student can create a personalized program. Active learners can use chat rooms, games, or competitive tools. Reflective learners can use informative lessons, concentration games, and vocabulary tools. As for visual and verbal learners, charts, diagrams, video lessons, listen and speak apps, pictures, and reading exercises satisfy both types of learning styles.

The following apps are extremely useful tools to implement in ESL: (1) FaceTime is a video phone app built into the iPad, and it is an excellent way to have students practice speaking and listening. This app can be used to arrange various types of conversations with different speakers and can assist in arranging conversations between ESL students and English language native students; (2) Camera app, with the built-in camera lets a user record audio and video so that ESL students can use this feature to record themselves and then send the recording to others to seek feedback; (3) Conversation English app is dedicated to helping the user practice and improve conversational English skills; (4) Sentence Builder is aimed at elementary ages and assists children in learning to build grammatically correct sentences in English; (5) Intro To Letters app is an application that runs through all the letters of the English alphabet, introducing users to the structure and pronunciation through tracing, audio, digital flashcards, and phonogram puzzles; (6) IDaily PRO HD is an innovative app that turns English language news into valuable lessons in listening, grammar, and sentence structure with its custom dictionary, allowing users to save words and phrases that need clarifying; (7) Hello-Hello is an app which helps users with their conversational English, providing lessons chosen and selected from real-life scenarios, flash cards, note-taking exercises and more; (8) Phonetics Focus app, one of the iPad's most popular ESL applications, offers a phonetic typewriter, games, flash cards, audio recording and playback; (9) Puppet Pals HD is an app suitable for ESL K-10 students to practice their fluency and language skills; (10) The Cat in the Hat—Dr. Seuss app is appropriate for ESL K-2 students and assists students in practicing reading fluency through echo reading. This app offers students three different ways to read: Read to Me—Read It Myself—Auto Play. As is evident, there are numerous apps for the ESL classroom, and, no doubt there will be more in the future.

ELL students who immerse themselves in the new culture often have an easier time picking up on the cultural nuances that exist in all languages. For example, when a student lives in the new culture, he or she goes to the school cafeteria to get his/her lunch. The student will have the real-life experience of getting into line, picking up a tray, making food decisions, deciding on a drink, and hearing questions such as, "What side (order) do you want?" From this experience, the student will learn new vocabulary words in context. With the ease of video capture today, astute ESL teachers may stage and film some of these situations in their own schools to help their students. Online resources are not as powerful as real-life experiences, but they do offer opportunities that go beyond what can be traditionally learned in a book. Students can chat with native speakers and learn about holidays, sports, and pop culture. Apps and Internet sites offer stories, news, videos, and pictures about many practical topics that can add to understanding. There are many complex programs offered for teaching foreign languages that have value to the student and the teacher. These often include scenarios for going to school, renting an apartment, being in a restaurant, and so forth. Perhaps the greatest advantage of using online resources and apps for ELL students with limited resources is cost-effectiveness. There are thousands of Websites that offer free lessons, activities, and resources for ELL students. Even those students who do not own a computer can take advantage of the resources by using the Internet at a library or community center or from cell phones. While apps are sometimes available for a charge, the fee is usually never more than a few dollars. There are a considerable number of apps that are free. Athabasca University recently released a free app called Mobile ESL with 86 sections of lessons and activities.

When the right educational tablet application is integrated into a content-rich lesson, it provides multisensory access to that content, facilitating comprehension and allowing ELLs to participate more effectively in academic subjects. Apps can be used to scaffold activities that may otherwise be difficult for ELLs to understand. In addition, using multimedia apps to deliver content enhances traditional methods of delivery that are largely text based. This opens the door to critical thinking by lowering the language barrier and channeling the instructional focus to academic content. Some of the advantages of recommending language learning apps to students are: (1) convenience—the mobility of these devices provide students with the chance to study/review any day, any time, without the need to bring their books or class material; (2) efficiency—most apps are tremendously user friendly and well organized into topics, meaning that students do not waste any time looking for what they want to practice; and (3) engagement—language learning apps are the ideal tool to engage learners who are very tech-minded and naturally enjoy using gadgets and to engage learners who may not be tech-minded but who use applied technology in their daily lives. There are many useful apps that incorporate images, videos, audios, writing, and drawing to create interactive multimedia presentations and videos. Once we understand the synergy between teaching and technology, we can progress to effective integration. However, we must never lose sight of the fact that teachers' instructional design is the most critical component.

Teaching English as Second Language with Social Media

Social media technologies offer good opportunities for teachers of ELLs to find motivating tools to engage the students in the process of learning English. Social media is the organization and creation of innovative ideas that are shared with others through tools such as blogs, podcasts, and video sharing. Social media refers to the many ways that people communicate with each other to share information and can be as simple as writing a letter, drawing pictures, and/or sharing ideas in groups that use media tools to create interactive and global communication. These tools include Skype, Whatsapp, and Google Hangouts, to name just a few. Students of the twenty-first century, more than ever, use and follow social media to gain information, share ideas, maintain relationships with others, and keep up with relatives and friends. These social media tools are ones that ELL students may already know how to use in their first language, and they can find new uses for them to learn a second language. In fact, even when students use social media to enrich their first language, they are strengthening their second language. The reasoning behind this is that the richer the knowledge of one's first language, the better able he or she is to learn a second language (Cummins, 2000). Moreover, the skills that students have in social media communication in their first language will transfer over to their second language. For example, if there is a meaningful abbreviation like "LOL" in their first language that is prevalent in social media communication, they will recognize that there are such abbreviations in their second language as well.

The task for teachers in this technology age is to find ways to transfer the technology skills that students have for personal use into classroom learning environments. In the traditional classroom, communication may have consisted of teacher lectures, students taking notes, pen pals, letter writing, journal writing, and passing notes in class. With today's social media, the classroom communication may now consist of blogging, Facebooking, Instagramming, and social videos such as YouTube, Tumblr, and Myspace. The plethora of tools to choose from can create a conundrum for teachers as they decide how to use them in the classroom, yet teachers should recognize that these tools can lead to stronger communication skills for ELL students and should embrace them. For example, social media tools can bring ELL students who may be isolated from their peers because of language or cultural differences to a social learning environment that increases their communication and relationship skills.

In Mr. Robinson's middle school classroom, one sees literature circles (Daniels, 2002) with ELL students added into the groups. The students choose a novel that focuses on a social studies concept and their reading levels. They use social media tools to interact with the novel, individually through reading responses, while dialoguing about the novel, questioning each other about different parts of the book, and completing a project (such as a video) together. As the students work together, the ELL students receive excellent language support through social media tools to develop academic language by interacting with peers. For example, students in a social studies class are reading the book, *Roll of Thunder, Hear My Cry* by Mildred D. Taylor (1976). As they are completing their reading assignments at home, they post their reading responses to the group in their assigned blog. While writing their reading responses, they ask each other questions about parts of the book. As the ELL students participate in this process, they read the blog to see how the more advanced language students are using the concepts and the vocabulary words in the context of the book.

In setting up an online environment for a class, Ms. Nieto expected the students to communicate with each other through the messaging tool and to create presentation groups based on the topics they were choosing. A student asked, "How are we supposed to form a group when we are working online?" Following that comment, Ms. Nieto discovered that the students who used Facebook daily had not thought about how to transfer those skills into a classroom environment. When she suggested to the students that they contact each other using the tools in the online environment (much like they would do in Facebook), they were able to connect with each other and work with their groups. As teachers implement social media tools in their classrooms, they need to realize that the tools should be explicitly taught so that the students can transfer their everyday knowledge of the tools into an online class environment.

Monkey Business Images / Shutterstock.com

Blogs

Blogs are electronic journals where people share unique perspectives, news, and world events that are happening in their own lives. Blogs are connected electronically and linked to Internet news so others can read the entries and follow the links or connections that the authors make. Blogs reflect the personal journal writing and opinions of authors. Sometimes blogs can be used as a place to maintain personal information photographs or space to express personal opinions of current or world events. Inf○○○ are added on a regular basis. Followers of blogs can be family and friends. Journ○○○ looking for key words to identify trending topics or ideas. The owner of the blog ○○○○○○○ ○an read the blog. It can be maintained by a set of people or be open to the public. Those who have access can add comments to the blogs. Bloggers create communities of blogs by connecting links and blogs together. This allows groups to work together and to maintain connections when working at a distance. Some interesting blogs for ELLs may be family, travel, or food blogs. Students can create the blogs for real events or as information for class assignments. Often, teachers assign reflective journals as a part of the course assignments. Students can use a blog as an interactive journal between the teacher and the reflective journal entries.

In Miss Knight's English class, students create their own blogs to add their individual responses about what they are reading. The teacher may give prompts or questions for the students to respond to based on the reading selection. The teacher sets up the blog so that only the teacher and the student and/or the literature circle group can read it. The teacher also interacts in the blog by writing comments to students about the blog entries.

Wikis for Collaboration   Question 4

As stated previously, Wikis create collaborative spaces for groups of people to work together from a distance, so they can add information to a text and view, contribute, and edit content. Wikis can also build collaborative language groups for ELLs. This collective space gives groups the opportunity to maintain their creativity within the project without having to save, edit, or email new documents. They can add or change information in real time and work from a distance on the same text. The wikis tool allows teams to work on projects in real time. In a mixed class, even beginning ELLs can benefit by the collaborative process, as they can learn a great deal by observing how the English-proficient students use language and can apply their own knowledge to the process.

Facebook, Instagram, and Pinterest

Facebook, Instagram, and Pinterest are social media tools that allow for exciting and innovative ways to share life events with friends through photos, videos, and comments. Each tool has a unique approach to connecting people together. While Facebook focuses on groups of friends and sharing life events, people share their life events through a series of pictures in Instagram and Pinterest, which is a pin board-style photo sharing Website. Each of these tools allows for individuals to create groups of family, friends, and/or colleagues to share life events, interests, and hobbies. These tools focus on the relationship building of groups so that families can be connected from distances, friends can keep in contact with each other, and colleagues can keep up with the latest trends in their fields. The social messages that are shared throughout these social media tools connect people to each other and give them understandings and perspectives through shared comments, pictures, and other media. Students can also use their smart phones or tablets to participate in these social media experiences. Many ELLs feel isolated when leaving friends and family, and this may be a way to encourage keeping those ties.

Pinterest works much like fashion magazines. Readers create boards in Pinterest according to their own interests, and this can generate a following among other Pinterest readers. Pinterest followers will see what others have pinned, will add their pins, and will begin following various readers. The reader flips through the Pinterest boards much like they would flip through a magazine. When they find a recipe or a hair style, for example, that they like, they can pin it to their own personal boards. In this way, they save the recipe or hair style for later use while also connecting with others who may be interested in those same items. The Pinterest boards continue generating links and pins based on those interests. As this tool becomes more popular, teachers will find ways to use Pinterest to develop the students' interests and to motivate them to find more information about their topics. They can share their pins with others and continue to find more pins that may interest them. The special advantage of Pinterest for ELLs is that the topics are expressed with visual information in addition to written text, providing them with accommodated language. Boards can be private or public depending on how the reader sets them up. In a classroom, the teacher may create boards for the classroom community. The students can work on the classroom boards without having others outside of the classroom community viewing them.

Mr. Robinson uses social media in his middle school class in a way that helps his ELLs develop their literature knowledge and their English proficiency. Students are placed in literature circle groups, and, as they continue to read their novels, they may respond through social media tools from the perspectives of the characters in their books. For example, the students may want to take on the character's perspective of Cassie Logan in the book, *Roll of Thunder, Hear My Cry* (Taylor, 1976). Cassie is upset because the students in her school received used and unwanted books from the school for White children. An ELL student could take on the perspective of Cassie. The student may consider sending out a post about the injustice of receiving the used textbooks. The students in the literature circle groups can interact with each other through the social media tool in the way that they believe their characters would interact with other characters from the novel or from that time period. The students create authentic dialogue based on their character's voice and post this in social media tools. Writing in direct speech in dialogue form can be easier for many second language learners than writing in third person is. This format would thus be advantageous to ELLs. Moreover, students can find different photos or videos to illustrate what they want to say, thus making their language more context embedded. Students in this activity focus on how to understand the perspectives of their characters and find ways to give them a voice using these new tools. This creates a shift in thinking about the possibilities that "could be," while developing the voice and perspectives of characters in language that is comprehensible to ELLs.

Social Videos

Question 5

Social video tools such as YouTube, Tumblr, and Myspace have become strong teaching tools in the classroom. Students like the social video tools because they can learn at their own pace. They can watch a video, pausing or repeating it to get the information, or they can move through it quickly when they already understand the information. Students can also create their own videos and post them in YouTube, Facebook, or Instagram for others to see. When students have access to these tools in the classroom, the instruction can be tailored to their specific learning needs. Teachers can find materials for students based on their achievement levels, interest, or academic needs. When students view a video on a particular topic, they can often understand the content more easily than when teachers give a "one-shot" lecture on the topic, or a video can reinforce content they already know for even better understanding. Note that there are some videos that are not useful or are inappropriate, so part of a teacher's job is to create an index to direct students to videos that are appropriately connected to their topics.

Creating videos has become easier with the digital video editing tools that are available to students. They can create videos to demonstrate their understanding of concepts, topics, or as a reflective process in an autobiography. The videos can be used in different social media tools to share with others. This process has opened up the teaching process for students and teachers. It has literally *flipped* the classroom so that a student-centered classroom is created rather than a traditional, heavily lecture-based classroom. In flipped classrooms, students learn the content before they come to class. During their class time, the teacher and students respond to the content through classroom activities. This is particularly advantageous to ELLs as they can preview the class materials before going to class with the aid of simplified language, translations, added context, voice recordings, and so forth. They can then have a better understanding of what is happening in the lesson as they participate in the applied classroom activities.

Two teachers created a collaborative social studies project between two grade levels using social video tools. Ms. Rodriguez in a fourth-grade ESL class planned with Mr. Smith in a fifth-grade sheltered class. The students were reading different books about communities in the early 1600s. Both groups needed to create a project to demonstrate their understanding. The teachers decided to put the students into groups made up of two fourth graders and one fifth grader. The fifth graders knew how to use the digital story-telling tools very well and taught the fourth graders how to use the nuances of the technology. The fourth graders wrote the storyboards or scripts for the digital narratives and shared their work with their fifth-grade partners. The students worked in collaborative teams to create a digital narrative about communities.

In Mrs. Goldman's sixth-grade classroom, social videos are used to develop a deeper understanding of the science content that students are exploring. They search for videos that are based on their concept. They create a digital narrative that explains the science concept and how it is applied. The ELLs have opportunities to develop a concept map or a story dialogue of the scientist(s) who is famous for the concept while matching it with videos or photos that show how the concept is used in the real world. Students show not only their understanding of the science concept, but they also demonstrate their understanding of its application in real life. The videos and visuals provide them with the context clues that enrich their understanding of the academic language.

Personal Communication Tools for Sociocultural Enhancement

As noted, ELLs can connect with their family and home with different communication tools. Literacy includes cultural and linguistic diversity because of global literacies, connections, and migration. Many students may be connected globally because of their family's displacement from their home countries or because of travel or work (Giroux, 1993). They can find ways to connect with their friends and/or family through emails and instant messaging. The ELLs will also find that they can develop their home language through this family communication. Often, students will tend to develop their English language skills, especially reading and writing, but ignore those skills in their home language. For example, many times ELLs come to the United States with their parents and siblings, but their grandparents stay behind. By communicating with their grandparents in their home countries, the ELLs not only maintain personal relationships with their grandparents, they also develop necessary reading and writing skills in their first language. Students find that through videoconferencing, they can talk with their family members who live far away from them. The students can interview grandparents about when they were little children and perhaps develop a digital narrative about their grandparents' lives as a story to share with the class. The students can add pictures and video to the story as they also incorporate grandparents' voices from the interview, or the students can, for the same purpose, develop digital narratives with cousins or friends to get a peer perspective on "what's happening" in their former home. Of course, teachers who have as their aim sharing these types of family histories must be careful to gain approval from students, as some family histories and immigration journeys may have been from conflict, poverty, and so forth that students may not necessarily want to share with others.

Digital tools call for a new understanding of literacy and literacy development. The emergence of hybrid digital forms such as wikis, blogs, online databases, and online news calls for a visionary understanding of teaching in the classroom. Textual features require students and teachers to learn new technology proficiencies. In the classroom, students may be motivated to inform their technology and literacy groups based on friendship and interest groups. They may find opportunities to use videoconferencing, social media, and electronic communication to enhance personal communication skills. In their class, students create multimodal texts to communicate messages with family and friends. They may use a combination of text with visual, audio, spatial, and gestural modes to communicate.

Global Communication and Maintaining Culture

Many ELLs live in a society that maintains home and global connections. The ELLs find that they must maintain both their home language *and* English to communicate with all their family and friends. Young people may use their home language to communicate with parents, grandparents, and possibly aunts and uncles or others back home, but they may use English to communicate with their brothers, sisters, nieces, nephews, and friends in their new home. Often, they find that the personal communication with their family from their home country will be through videoconferencing such as Skype, Viber, or Whatsapp. As mentioned,

they may also use electronic communication such as email and instant messaging. At the same time, they feel enormous pressure to fit in with their school friends using English communication skills. Their context for communication often requires distance communication with family and direct communication with immediate family and friends.

Many of these traditions can be continued with digital conferencing tools. Parents and grandparents can video call with their children or grandchildren miles away while still, for example, maintaining the tradition of sharing Sunday with the family (see Figure 7.13). ESL teachers can encourage the technology skills needed for this type of communication, and students can later share these experiences with others in the class in English.

Figure 7.13   An ESL student video calls her *abuela* on a Sunday through Skype to share a birthday.

With the transition of the global society, many traditions have changed drastically. An important tradition in the Latino American home, for instance, is to visit the grandparents, or *abuelos,* on Sunday. Many families will spend all day together eating traditional foods, playing games such as *Lotería*, and visiting with each other. Now that Camila lives in the United States, she cannot visit with her grandmother on Sundays, but Camila video calls her *abuela* every Sunday through Skype, and her *abuela* can still share favorite recipes for traditional foods with Camila and give her advice on how to cook her favorite tamales or enchiladas.

Camila maintains her home language with her *abuela*, while learning new things about her family background and heritage and also sharing important events of her life with them.

Class Communication

Teachers can generate purpose and meaning within these contexts for personal communication for BICS and CALP. In a primary language arts classroom, students create their purposes and audiences for writing and developing multimedia products. The students work in small groups to decide which form of communication they will use to communicate with family members. They develop questions to interview various family members about a particular event in their lives (getting married, having their children, going to school, etc.) or about particular events that occurred in history. The group then interviews the family member through Skype, Viber, Whatsapp, or Zoom. This creates a purpose for communicating with family in various settings while also developing the communication skills in their home language.

To develop this further, ELLs can use a virtual tour to tell classmates and friends about their former home. Using Google Earth, they can collect pictures of their communities from a distance. As they create a virtual tour of their home, they can describe their home, school, and local community. The ELLs will be able to share a part of them with their new classmates and friends while also describing their identity. The ELLs utilize technology tools such as photos, video clips, and recordings from their homes. Dialogues can be recorded with digital software programs that explain their homes and communities. The virtual tours can also give the ELLs an opportunity to proudly share their former homes with friends and classmates whom they now have in their new country. Remember again that teachers should be sensitive to some situations in which an ELL may not want to share—or even remember—about his or her home country. Some families may not be documented; others may have lived in extreme poverty or may even be refugees from fighting or political violence. If that is the case, the teacher must certainly find alternative assignments.

ELLs can develop their BICS language skills by writing emails about more casual, general information. They can have pen pals within the class or school or students from other cities, states, or countries. They also text or write emails to their family and friends. Instant messaging is a tool that creates immediate responses. Students find information quickly by using this tool. They also develop good questioning strategies and learn how to write questions to find information.

Academic language is developed through the multimedia products that the groups of students complete. They may choose to create multimedia presentations of informational texts. They also choose to write an informational text, such as a nonfiction book, a brochure, or a class newsletter. Students can import lyrics of a favorite poem or song and then analyze the lyrics to find ways to incorporate them into a multimedia project. Music is an excellent teaching tool for language, and the availability of songs in many languages on the Internet is a dramatic addition to ESL instruction. Pairing ELLs with various partners can help the students share in the writing/reading strategies (see more in Chapter 17 on multicultural teaching for music ideas). By incorporating both partners into the writing process, both groups of students will contribute their ideas to the multimedia process.

Conclusion

Clearly, there are many technology tools currently available to enhance learning for students for whom English is their second language, and many more will become available in time to come. It is important for teachers of ELLs to understand how to evaluate the usefulness of current tools and of tools of the future. Table 7.3 summarizes the ways in which teachers can evaluate the effectiveness of technology tools for their students and reviews the principles of second language learning presented in this chapter.

Understanding how to best use technology for ELLs is imperative for all teachers in school districts whose populations include students for whom English is a second language. It is safe to say that most teachers will have second language learners in their classrooms at some time during their teaching careers. For example, in the Houston Independent School District, the largest school district in Texas and the seventh largest in the United States, 30.77% of the student population was determined to be limited English proficient in 2016 to 2017 (www.houstonisd.org/achievements). In a nearby district, Alief ISD, the home webpage of the district can be translated into 80 home languages. The potential for using technology to help advance ELLs in both content knowledge and in English language has never been more exciting. Teachers should embrace all that our growing technology has to offer and should use good judgment by choosing the tools that best support the principles of second language acquisition.

Table 7.3   Criteria to Choose the Most Effective Technology Tools

Criteria	Questions to ask
Engaging in learning	Does this tool engage my students? Are the topics and the tasks interesting to them? Do they have the prior knowledge necessary to comprehend the ideas?
Using language i+1	Is the English language in this tool just a little bit above students' current level in English so that they can make educated guesses for vocabulary or grammatical structures that are unfamiliar to them?
Integrating language and content	Does this tool add to the content knowledge of my students as well as to their English language development?
Integrating language skills: listening, speaking, reading, writing	Does this tool use several language skills?
Providing collaborative experiences	Can my students use this tool to work with other learners–either face-to-face or electronically?
Lowering affective filters	Will this tool be enjoyable to my students and will they feel comfortable and relaxed when using it?
Possible sequencing from context embedded to context reduced	Does this tool allow me to gradually expose my students to less context-embedded language?
Providing comprehensible input (accommodated language)	Will my students be able to access clues to the meaning of the content in addition to the language itself?

Resources

Here are collections of apps and Websites for the ESL classroom.

- Recommended by Scholastic: www.scholastic.com/teachers/articles/teaching-content/50-fab-apps-teachers
- Recommended by Mastersin ESL: mastersinesl.com/essential-esl-app-guide
- Recommended by ESL Kids Stuff: www.eslkidstuff.com/apps-for-esl-kids.htm

References

Chou, I. (2016). Reading for responding to literature: EFL students' perceptions of e-books. *Computer Assisted Language Learning, 29*(1), 1–20.

Cummins, J. (2000). *Language, power, and pedagogy: Bilingual children in the crossfire.* Clevedon, Great Britain: Cromwell Press Ltd.

Daniels, H. (2002). *Literature circles: Voice and choice in book clubs and reading groups* (2nd ed.). Markham, Ontario: Sternhouse Publishers.

Fletcher, R. J., & Portalupi, J. (2001). *Writing workshop: The essential guide.* Heinemann. Retrieved from www.ezproxy.uhd.edu/login?url=www.search.ebscohost.com/login.aspx?direct=true&db=cat02844a&AN=uhd.b3002320&site=eds-live&scope=site

Freytag, G. (1863). *Die technik des dramas.* Germany: S. Hirzel.

Giroux, H. (1993). *Border crossings: Cultural workers and the politics of education.* New York, NY: Routledge.

Krashen, S. (1985). *The input hypothesis: Issues and implications.* New York, NY: Longman.

Lee, H. (1960). *To kill a mockingbird.* New York, NY: Grand Central Publishing.

Mitchell, L., Miller, D. M., & Dalton, C. (2016). Finding Latino/a voices in the storytellingprocess: Preservice teachers tell their stories in digital narratives. *Journal of Family Strengths, 17*(1), Article 7. www.digitalcommons.library.tmc.edu/jfs/vol16/iss1/7

Nieto, S., & Bode, P. (2012). *Affirming diversity: The sociopolitical context of multicultural education* (6th ed.). New York, NY: Pearson.

Pfister, M. (1995). *The rainbow fish.* New York, NY: North-South Books.

Taylor, M. (1976). *Roll of thunder, hear my cry.* New York, NY: Puffin.

Wright, W. E. (2010). *Foundations for teaching English language learners: Research, theory, policy, and practice.* Philadelphia, PA: Caslon.

Yoon, T. (2013). Beyond the traditional reading class: The application of an E-Book in the EFL English classroom. *International Journal of Research Studies in Language Learning, 2*(1), 17–26.

Part II
Using Educational Technology for Best Practices in Schools and for Teacher Education

Chapter 8

Using Technology with Models of Teaching

Janice L. Nath - *Professor Emeritus*
University of Houston - Downtown

Meet Miss Givings

Sarah Givings, a first-year, fifth-grade teacher, had felt prepared to go into teaching. However, after her first six months, it seemed as if *she* was doing the majority of the "thinking work" in the classroom; that is, she was presenting all the information, while her students waited for her to assign their lower-level independent work. She had had good methods classes in her teacher education program for the content areas that she was currently teaching but something just wasn't working as well as she had envisioned for a learner-centered classroom. Was she falling back into the ways that some of her own teachers had used most often when she had been in school—that is, simply giving the students the information and then having them apply it in some way (most always through a worksheet or writing assignment)? The "kicker" had come this very afternoon, when Jorge in sixth period had noted on his way out of the room in a "stage whisper" (which she was surely meant to hear) that her class today had been particularly "boring and lame." What was missing? What could she do?

antoniodiaz / shutterstock.com

Models of teaching are exciting ways of having students learn because these instructional methods of teaching encourage *active* rather than *passive* student learning; that is, the learner is more active than the teacher in constructing knowledge. A model of teaching is a format in which almost any content area can be "inserted"—and, in addition, model formats can be modified to work for all school-age learners. One popular and well-known model of teaching, for example, is cooperative learning, which can be used in mathematics, science, language arts, social studies, music, and so forth. However, there are many more models of teaching that offer student-centered (rather than teacher-centered) learning, and many of these develop students' higher-level thinking abilities as well. Coupled with technology, these models offer teachers novel ways of teaching that actively engage students in stimulating instruction. This chapter will discuss the following models of teaching and their integration with technology: Concept Attainment, Cooperative Learning, Memory, Concept Development, Suggestopedia, and Case Studies.

Models of teaching have been examined at length by researchers such as Joyce, Weil, and Calhoun (2015). These and other educators (Kilbane & Milman, 2014) have noted that each type of model has a distinct purpose (i.e., creativity, social skills, forming or developing concepts, mastery, review, and so forth). A teacher who has knowledge of these models can use them wisely to create variety in his or her instruction and specifically to target the academic and social needs of a class.

These models of teaching can stand alone without technology, but coupled with technology, they can have a powerful effect on instruction. When the computer first began to be viewed as a future educational tool, Bruner (1960) noted that "what one does and how one teaches [with technology] depends upon the skill and wisdom that goes into the construction of a program of problems" (p. 83). The teacher who considers models of te_____ his/her repertoire of "solving student learning issues" will be rewarded with _____ gain in multiple areas of learning.

Concept Attainment

The Concept Attainment model has as its main purpose helping learners to form and remember concepts. It is based mainly on the work of Jerome Bruner, Goodnow, and Austin (1965), who purported that without the ability to *categorize*, human beings would not be able to identify objects/concepts in order to make sense of the world. Defining and learning concepts is part of categorization or organizing one's world.

Perhaps one of the first questions asked in beginning the process of creating a lesson with this model might be, "What do we mean by a concept?" The answer can be simple—"a thing or idea"—but that is, at times, much more complex in instruction. Gunter, Estes, and Schwab (2003) state that "Concepts are defined by the attributes we give them" (p. 82). A concept that an elementary teacher may want children to learn, for example, might be as simple as "general transportation," or he or she may want to narrow it down to "transportation without wheels" (hot-air balloons, sleds, helicopters, skates, etc.). Instruction may focus yet on another concept such as "walls", and, based on the content area, grade level, or purpose, the organization of the concept may be very different. In one lesson, instructors may wish students to touch on *all* types of walls, or he or she may want to narrow the concept to simply walls that are vertical structures made of concrete types of materials (wire, wood, stone, chain-link, etc.) or famous walls from an historical context (the Berlin Wall, the Great Wall of China, Hadrian's Wall, the Wailing Wall in Jerusalem, etc.). He or she may even consider the more abstract concept of walls which "one puts up to others" (protectionism, fear, isolationism, separation, etc.). Therefore, in planning, a teacher must consider that a concept has particular attributes and boundaries that make it unique, and he or she must decide ahead what those boundaries/attributes will be in order to have students obtain that exact concept through many offered examples and nonexamples. To give a very simple example of this process, let us consider the following common examples and nonexamples and ask ourselves, "Of what could the teacher be thinking here, or/what could this concept be?"

Examples	Nonexamples
Sprite	water
Mountain Dew	milk
Dr. Pepper	juice
7-Up	tea

By looking at the examples and the nonexamples, one can almost immediately see that the concept is "soda" or carbonated beverages. By the teacher offering examples and nonexamples *a bit at a time* (rather than just giving students a definition with a few examples), the learner engages with this idea and mentally builds a place in his/her mind for this category of drinks. The learner is likely to form a more permanent storage area for the concept because the information was not simply "served up" by the teacher. As the learner sees each example and nonexample, the brain engages in hypothesis testing to try to "make a category" and/or to fit in other known examples/nonexamples. Therefore, the learner could ask, "Is Coke an example?" or "Are Kool-Aid and lemonade nonexamples?" When the teacher confirms a student's input, the learner (and the class) firms up the category or concept even more clearly—or, conversely, realizes that his/her train of thought is going in the wrong direction, so a new pathway must be found. This is the beginning of forming a concept in this model.

Let's try another simple concept as Mrs. Clayborn might actually teach it as a "practice game" for students to understand the format and the rules of the game. After she sets the stage with a statement such as, "I have something that I am thinking of, and I want to see if you can guess what it is." She then adds, "I am going to give you some examples of 'it' and some nonexamples, or things that are 'not it'" (note that she could easily use visuals from technology to generate pictures of these examples and nonexamples as well [e.g., soda cans as in the earlier "game" or pictures of real fruit and vegetables if using those concepts]). For further directions, she gives the rules of "the game," which include not calling out without raising one's hand and not guessing the concept itself until cleared by the teacher to do so. She tells students that only examples or nonexamples may be given until she feels that most of them have a good idea of what the concept is. Mrs. Clayborn then puts the first two examples below on the board along with one nonexample. Learners may then participate by adding examples or nonexamples to "test their hypothesis" about the concept that Mrs. Clayborn is "thinking of." She adds the learners' responses to the correct side. This practice game is presented below.

Mrs. Clayborn begins by putting up two examples and one nonexample:
She writes on the board:

She writes on the board:	Examples	Nonexamples
	apple	beans
	orange	
A learner asks, "Is *lettuce* a nonexample?" The teacher confirms by placing it in the correct column (as a nonexample).		lettuce
Next, Mrs. Clayborn adds: (as a nonexample)		book
Callie asks about bananas as an example, and Mrs. Clayborn confirms it by writing it in the example column.	banana	
Jack also says:		pencil
		peas
Then the teacher asks where pears, cherries, and dog would go and writes them in the correct columns as students direct her:	pears cherries	dog
(Notice that a nonexample does not have to be "an opposite", but for a simple practice game, it can help the learner see the process more easily. Also, using "opposites" works well for very young children.)		

Mrs. Clayborn adds other examples as students brainstorm. By now, learners have certainly understood that the category was fruit, and they can test their hypothesis further by suggesting strawberries as an example or corn as a nonexample and so forth. Once Mrs. Clayborn has the sense that the class, fairly much as a whole, has the concept, she calls on one student to say it or asks the whole class to say it together—fruit!

One benefit of this game is that by the end of the process, the teacher will have an excellent idea of the overall knowledge of the class about this concept because students, once they have the concept, will list all examples they know. When prompted to add, "What other fruits do you know?" they may say, "Lemons, grapefruit," and so forth. This is valuable information for the teacher because it lets him/her know where to *start* teaching in terms of the concept. For example, if students did not respond well, she may want to delve into the concept from the beginning, or, if the game was too easy, move to fill in the blanks on obvious areas that students did not list or move to the more difficult areas of the concept.

Once a teacher has taught this model a time or two, the flow will become very easy; however, it is important for the learners' thinking processes that the teacher prepare and teach the model in this format for the model to work well. Again, the teacher first gives the general goal of the game (e.g., "Today we are going to play a game where I am thinking of something, and you are going to try to guess what 'it' is. I am going to give you some hints [examples] and some things that are 'not it' [nonexamples] or that don't include an idea of the concept."). Again, the teacher then gives the class some strict rules that should always include:

1. always raising one's hand if he or she has an example or a nonexample to try,
2. not shouting out what he/she thinks what the concept is (only offering examples or nonexamples), and
3. waiting for the teacher to "clear" an individual or the class to guess the concept.

These rules are very important for the teacher to follow, and Mrs. Clayborn makes sure that she redirects students during the practice game so that during the real game, students don't give the concept away early. Of course, students are often very excited to guess what the concept is when they think they know, so there will be some slips in the rules—especially in calling out the concept—but the teacher must be firm in saying, "I need to hear you give me an example or nonexample to test your hypothesis" (even if the learner should happen to guess the concept correctly). Reminding the class or individual of these rules often will prevent the game from being over before it starts. The teacher may say, "Remember you are not allowed to guess the concept until I ask for it, so try an example or a nonexample to see if you are still on the right track in your mind."

There are other important considerations in teaching this model's format. This is one of the main reasons for beginning with a simple practice game like the ones above. Students learn the format quickly, and, when learners break the rules during a practice game, the teacher can remind them before the "real game." Again, when the teacher thinks that a good many students have gained the concept, she or he can ask for an educated guess of the concept. A teacher can also control how long the game goes by: (a) giving more examples quickly, (b) having students caucus in groups to see if they can generate more examples/nonexamples/ideas, or (c) simply telling learners the concept if time or examples are running out and students are "stuck". Students are next asked to give examples and what they know about the concept ("milking it") when the concept is confirmed. Another important part of having students really think hard is to be sure *not* to give them the objective(s) of the lesson until *after* playing the game. If, for example, the teacher wrote on the board, "Today, you are going to identify shapes with corners" and then began right away by putting shapes upon the board for the game, students would not have to think hard at all about what the concept might be. They would guess it quickly—but the object of the model, of course, is to have students engaged in active thinking.

The teacher should also know that there are other phases in the thinking aspect of this game. The order of "the game" is listed below again but with more detail.

1. Give the goal and rules;
2. Play a simple practice game for students to see the game format (this should be very short and an obvious concept for all grade levels so that the instruction can move on to the "real concept" of the day) (there is an example at www.youtube.com/watch?v=GZO6lWdYMDs followed by an explanation at www .youtube.com/watch?v=5uQCqcEnHLs);
3. Give the examples and nonexamples, starting with two examples and one nonexample (so that the students can begin comparing and contrasting right away);
4. When the teacher "reads the audience" and feels that a number of students probably have an idea of the concept, he/she changes "modes" to give students words/pictures/real items to have students classify each as an example or nonexample (e.g., in the game above, the teacher might say, "On which side would I put grapefruit [as an example or a nonexample] or cabbage, kiwis, and onions?");
5. When the teacher sees that, indeed, most students have gained the concept, he or she has a student or the class tell what the concept is. If incorrect, the teacher would continue on, but, if correct;
6. Have students give *all* the examples that they know and can generate ("milk it"); and
7. Have students construct a list of the attributes that make up the concept;
8. If students (or the teacher) question some of the examples/nonexamples and their placement in a category, the class "talks it through" *after* the concept is revealed. For instance, if a tomato was given as a nonexample in the game above, the teacher might have "put it in the middle" and come back later to discuss it as a fruit, and it can be revealing how a learner may "defend" the item as an example or nonexample;
9. Have students reflect on and discuss the strategy(ies) that allowed them to "get it".

The advantages of integrating technology into this game are that, for almost all concepts, there are instant images, examples, and videos and/or animations available, and images are sometimes much more vivid and can convey more than words in print. The old saying that "a picture is worth a thousand words" is not misplaced here.

If Mr. Kumar in science class, wanted to teach the concept of "force" with relationship to movement, he might have to draw or comb through many magazines for pictures of images that fit the definition if it were not for technology. If he had to write or tell about the examples, he might also give the concept's attributes away by having to write descriptions (for instance, "a man kicking a ball" and "a statue just sitting on a stand" rather than letting students see the movement [or lack thereof] in the image that contributes to the definition). With technology, however, he might be able to offer pictures (as seen below) of force in nature, force in work, force in play, force in weapons, and so forth, and its many nonexamples rather than just give the formula and "talk about it". Mr. Kumar constructed the game below. He gradually offers the pictures in a PowerPoint with time for thought, and, as above, has students construct the concept as they try to guess what it could be.

Examples	Nonexamples

	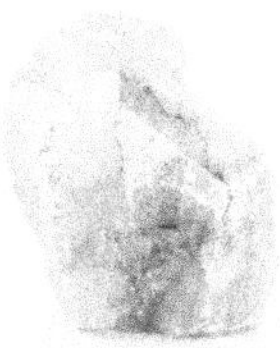

Images © Shutterstock.com

(Continued)

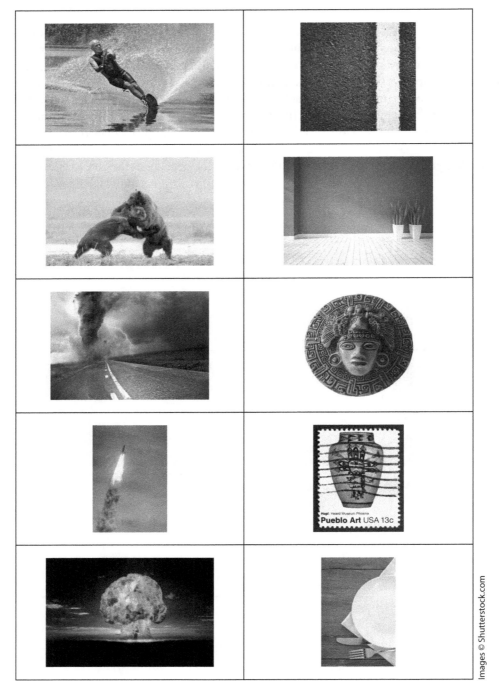

Images © Shutterstock.com

He offers pictures of the waterfall and the wave as examples first, as well as the chessboard as a nonexample. He then flips up examples and nonexamples one at a time, asking on which side each would go.

He may also create a presentation as the one shown below in the next example. Here, the teacher has added the example and nonexample pictures as she goes along to keep them firmly in the students' minds. This allows them to better see all of the examples and nonexamples together.

Not only are the images more vivid but these types of pictures can be easily put on a PowerPoint as a slideshow or on a Web-based presentation such as Prezi and shown to Mrs. Bostic's young learners as follows in her reading lesson. She did so as the class sits in a circle around the screen. See if you can guess the concept.

Slide 1

It (Examples)	Not It (Nonexamples)

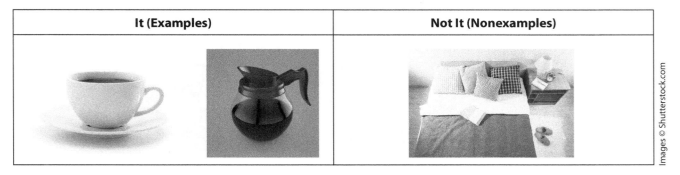

Slide 2

It or not it?

Slide 3

It	Not It

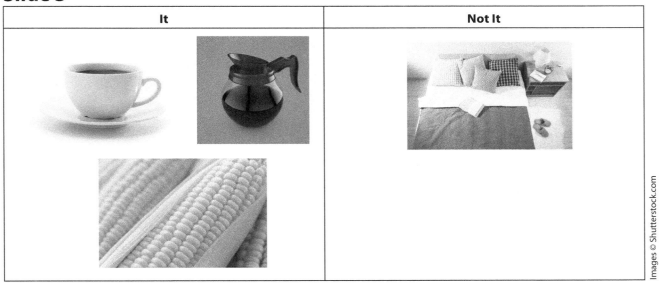

Slide 4

It or not it?

Slide 5

It	Not It
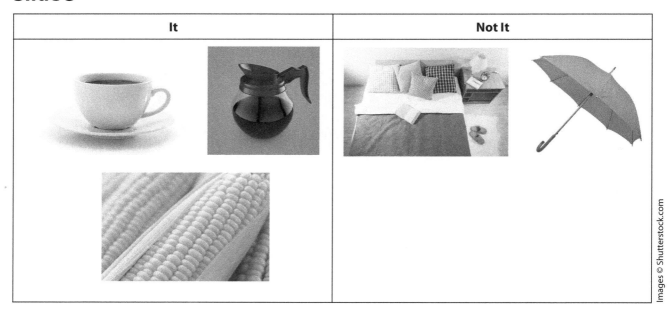	

Slide 6

It or not it?

Slide 7

It or not it?

Slide 8

It	Not It
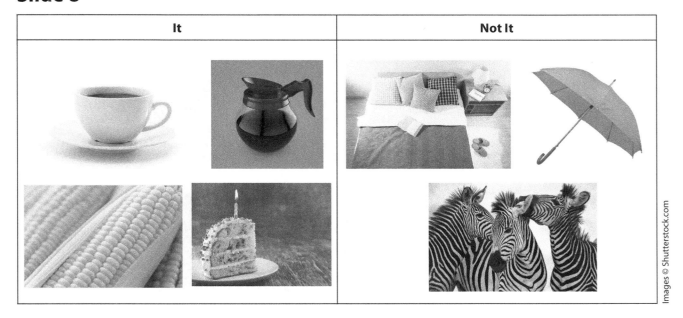	

Slide 9

It or not it?

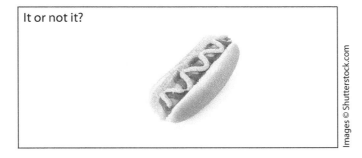

Slide 10

It or not it?

Slide 11

It	Not It
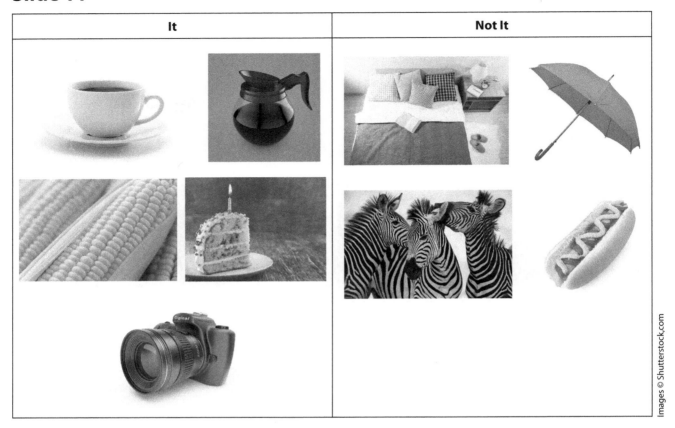	

Slide 12

It or not it?

Slide 13

It or not it?

Slide 14

It	Not It

Slide 15

It or not it?

Slide 16

It or not it?

Images © Shutterstock.com

Slide 17

It	Not It

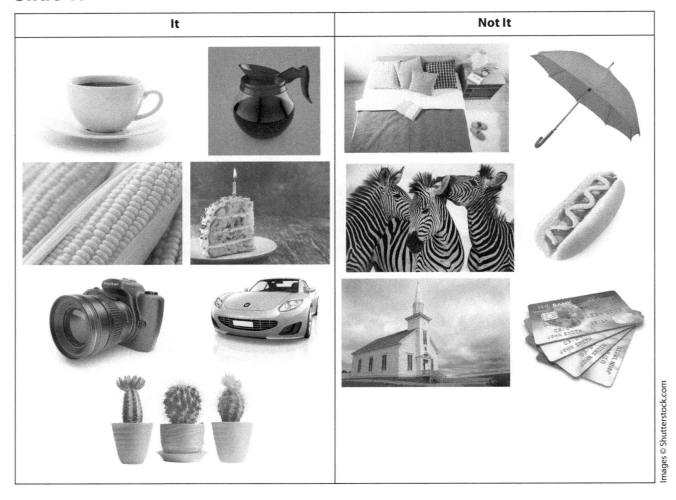

Images © Shutterstock.com

Slide 18

It or not it?

Images © Shutterstock.com

Slide 19

It or not it?

Images © Shutterstock.com

Slide 20

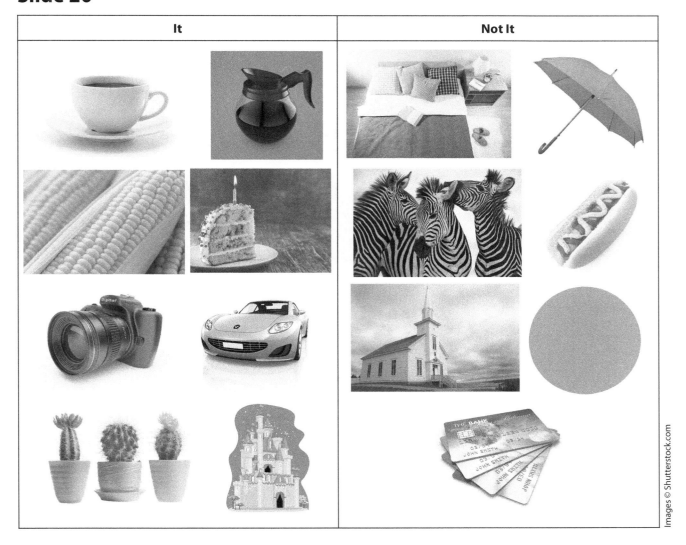

Slide 21—A Final Look

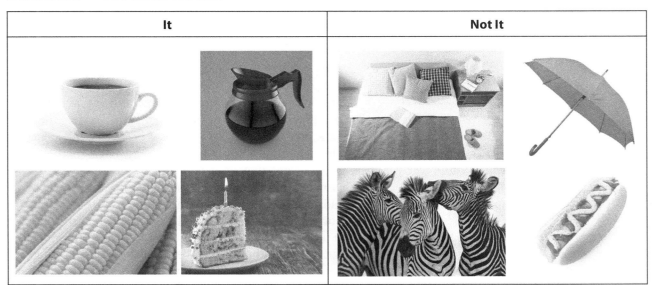

Slide 21 - continued

It	Not It

Slide 22

What else could we add to the list?

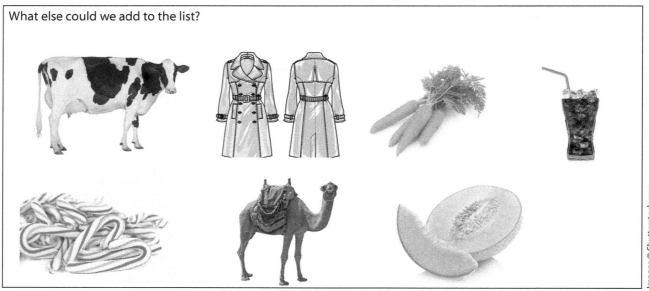

Mrs. Bostic is teaching the concept of words that have the /k/ sound but begin with the letter "c." She has chosen a number of images above that illustrate the /k/ sound for examples and other nonexample images that do not have this sound. When examining how children might think through this model, we can imagine that in the beginning of the game they might believe, when presented with the first few images, that the concept might be "things we eat or drink." They test their hypothesis by asking the teacher if pizza would be an example. She says that it is not. When Mrs. Bostic continues with the example of cake, learners may still believe it is food or drink. When the picture of the camera goes up as an example, however, they realize that it is something else entirely, and they begin to have to rethink their ideas. A teacher may design this game to show all nonexamples without a "c," but Mrs. Bostic knows students have already had some experience with this sound, so she puts in items as nonexamples that begin with a "c" but have blends or the /s/ sound (circle). When she puts the game into her computer center for children to review, she adds even more nonexamples like a chick, a check, and so forth.

Throughout this narrative on Concept Attainment, one sees the words "the teacher will," but groups of learners and individual learners also love to create Concept Attainment games for their peers, so it is beneficial to remember that "the teacher" could be a student, or, even better, groups of students who generate a Concept Attainment game (after they understand the format and have played several times).

Mr. Aldana assigned his seventh-grade groups to design a PowerPoint game for each of the geographic regions of Texas. They were to include examples of both words/phrases and pictures or even film clips. The group assigned the Coastal Plains area included pictures of oil wells in the Gulf, wind farms, rice fields, pine forests, big ships in the channel, fishing boats, the skylines of Houston and Corpus Christie, and so forth. Mr. Aldana made sure that each group kept their region a secret as they were working so that the other students would have to guess when groups made their presentations.

This is truly higher-level thinking at its best, and the computer or the Web is able to store these for further retrieval for interest, addition, review, and/or remediation.

How and When to Use the Concept Attainment Model

This model can be used in a number of ways during a lesson. Most often, perhaps, we see it used as a focus activity, for if the teacher uses direct instruction, he or she will have given away the concept; learners, as mentioned earlier, will not have to think as much. As a focus, the model puts the learner into a motivating game immediately. However, this model can be used during a lesson as students come to a concept in the middle of a lesson.

Mrs. Kiley, a high school geography teacher, had been talking about various ways that natural disasters influence the growth of cities and nations. She decided to insert a Concept Attainment game into the middle of her lesson on current "Ring of Fire" cities. She selected pictures of areas that had experienced disasters from long ago and the more recent past and included an unlabeled picture map of the country or state with the city marked to illustrate the concept of major earthquakes and volcanic eruptions as the focus of natural disasters. She included pictures of cities that have recovered and some that have not in her concept game. At the end of the game, she involved students in predicting where this type of disaster may occur again and had them discuss why some cities recovered from these types of disasters and some remained in ruins.

Finally, this model can also be used as an evaluation tool (closure).

After a fourth-grade class has read *The Secret Garden* (Burnett, 1911), Mrs. McNamera used this game to see how well students remembered the parts of the book, characters, plot, and so forth. She began with two of the more difficult examples and one nonexample, and students then offered examples and nonexamples to "fill in" the rest (following the format of "playing the game" discussed earlier). Using technology, she added a number of images downloaded from "Images for *The Secret Garden*" (following technology usage requirements/laws).

One suggestion for using this model is that students continue to develop a concept using a shared electronic folder to which students can add images from their own or school digital devices or from the Internet. Students can review these concept folders as often as desired or be directed to review them when the teacher sees that it could be needed.

Teachers constructing a Concept Attainment model can use the following steps to be sure that they isolate the concept well and have clear examples and nonexamples ready:

1. Select a concept and write a definition as to how the teacher wants it to be used. Make the definition of the concept very specific and clear so that examples and nonexamples can be generated (e.g., if the concept was vegetables, the game cannot change in the middle to be only "green vegetables").
   - Select attributes and boundaries that are then checked for clarity as an example or nonexample.
2. Develop examples and nonexamples for both a "practice" game and a "real" game using:

   | words | phrases | sentences | film clips |
   | pictures | tangible items | computer images | animations |

   - The teacher/leader should generate at least 10 of each (and place these into lesson plans to avoid having to scramble to remember these "on his/her feet"). After completing the list, one should go back yet again to ensure each clearly fits the attributes and definition of the concept.

3. Order the examples and nonexamples.
   * The examples and nonexamples should be arranged with the "most difficult" first to "easiest" so that students must think harder.
4. It is not necessary to "match" nonexamples, but this can be easier for younger children. Using opposites usually means students "get it" more quickly.

A Review of the Real Game

1. The teacher/leader of the game should present examples and nonexamples one at a time, but should always begin with at least two examples and one nonexample.
2. The leader should ask students to use their language of inquiry to "test their hypothesis" by offering their own examples or nonexamples. A leader should also ask players if they would like to be given another example or nonexample at times when they may be slower to play. To make sure of participation, the leader should call on individuals to contribute an idea, even if they are not raising their hands.
3. When it seems as if students may have an idea of the concept, the leader switches modes to present an example (or nonexample) and then ask players to classify it into the proper column.
4. If students become "stuck," the leader can have them use group caucusing to generate ideas.
5. When it seems that most students have gained the concept, the leader asks for an answer.
6. The leader then asks for all examples that the entire class knows ("milks it" for all the examples known by the entire group and everything known about the concept).
7. The leader asks for a good definition of the concept and its attributes and then checks for understanding.
8. The leader has players reflect on strategies that helped them "get there" or attain the concept.

There are many, many concepts that a teacher can use in this model for all areas of learning and all grade levels—early childhood to high school. The teacher can easily use this model in almost any content area to help students think in an active way. The example below shows a variation on the game in an early elementary science lesson on animals that live in the sea. For high school, it might be modified to show examples of microscope slides, figurative language, specialized vocabulary, and so forth.

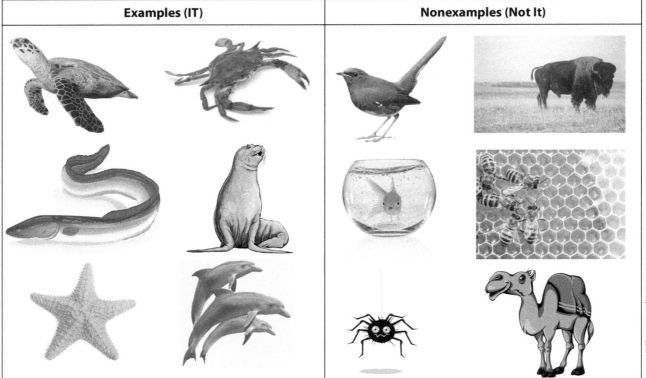

Examples (IT)	Nonexamples (Not It)

Images © Shutterstock.com

The following is another way to look at using this model for mathematics, remembering that the numbers would be introduced by starting with two examples and one nonexample. If only one example is offered at first, the learner's brain cannot start any kind of theory for a category—it could really be anything, which is frustrating for a learning situation. After some thinking time, the teacher would ask students to test their ideas about the concept. Then, as in the games above, the teacher would introduce more examples and nonexamples one at a time. The teacher may also want to add a "hypothesis" column when playing so that students can keep up with their ideas as they go. There are many variations on how teachers can use this model to fit their learners' needs. Teachers should use these variations to "make them their own" for their learners and for their content area, remembering to keep the general teaching format discussed in order to better engage the brain in higher-level thinking.

Examples	Nonexamples	Hypothesis
$1\frac{1}{2}$	55	Fractions; small numbers
$22\frac{1}{2}$	$\frac{4}{5}$	Numbers with 1 and 2
$131\frac{1}{3}$	$\frac{4}{3}$	Whole numbers with a fraction, eliminate small numbers
$28\frac{3}{5}$	1	Yes, that stands! Let's test more to be sure!
$5\frac{7}{8}$	34	Mixed numbers!!!

The following is a "writing starter" for language arts. Look carefully at each picture to see what it might have in common with the ones below it, remembering that a teacher/leader would begin with two examples and one nonexample and add the ones below one at a time. Think of them in terms of colored pictures (which they would be using technology).

(Continued)

You Can See An Example Here	You Can't See It Here

Images © Shutterstock.com

Students in this language arts class are using images to learn about similes, metaphors, and adjectives for the "color orange". Now when they write, they have these more vivid varieties in their heads (such as "orange as a cantaloupe," or "candy corn orange," or "the sun hung like an orange lifebuoy in the sky").

Students can also use text using their word/picture answers and write them onto the electronic whiteboard. Clip art images, photos, and so on, can also be used from software packages such as Kidspiration and Inspiration, both of which offer images, text boxes, graphic organizers, and much more. Students and teachers may also use videos (from YouTube or other sources) to enhance learning concepts in this model.

Mrs. Long, for instance, teaches a World War II Concept Attainment on the Allies and Axis powers using short film clips. On the example side, she selects short film clips from the Allies such as President Roosevelt declaring war after the attack on Pearl Harbor, Winston Churchill's "finest hour" speech, and clips of the Battle of Britain, D-Day, the flag raising at the Battle of Iwo Jima, the French Resistance, the bombing of Hiroshima, and so forth. On the nonexample side, she selects clips of Hitler's speeches, Hirohito's reviewing the troops, the attack on Pearl Harbor, the Bataan Death March, Mussolini's speeches, and more that identify the Axis forces.

This model gives teachers a great deal of important information and provides many other benefits for instruction. The most beneficial is active thinking on the part of the learners. Strategies that students use can be observed and strengthened, group work becomes enhanced as members see each other as resources, and, again, the teacher is provided, in the end, with all the knowledge a class knows about the concept. This allows him or her to build on that or teach further in order to fill in the blanks. Technology allows these concepts to come to life in vibr̶a̶ ̶̶̶̶̶̶̶̶̶̶̶̶̶̶̶̶̶̶̶̶̶̶̶̶̶̶̶̶̶̶̶̶̶̶̶̶̶̶ ̶̶̶̶̶ging in colors, images, lights, sound effects, transitions, time effects, animati̶ ̶̶̶̶̶̶̶̶̶̶̶̶̶̶̶̶̶̶̶̶

[handwritten note: Question 2]

Cooperative Learning/Grouping

There are many, many cooperative grouping "submodels," and each one offers the teacher a different goal or goals for his or her class. For example, Mrs. Avalos may know that, in addition to academics, she can also target students' social or emotional needs by selecting the right fit with a particular type of cooperative grouping structure. With technology, teachers can also include specific technology goals by using various peer groupings— pairs or small numbers of students—who work together on a particular assignment using computers, phones, digital cameras, clickers, and so forth. Working together not only strengthens social skills but meets the needs of technology instruction, particularly at times when there is not enough equipment for each student to have his or her own for an activity (Dockterman, 1994). Various submodels of cooperative learning can also work well with technology when students have outside-of-class assignments and members can work asynchronously (on their own time). The discussion in this section goes over some of the important planning issues of using technology with groups along with some of the submodels of cooperative learning that are particularly suited to technology integration.

When teachers begin to incorporate cooperative groups, they have several decisions to make. The first, of course, is "What are my goals academically?" and then, "What are my students' needs outside of academics?" Academic goals are excellent for cooperative grouping because the literature shows that most students learn well academically from being placed in groups due to the *active* (versus passive) nature of peers working with peers (Joyce, Weil, & Calhoun, 2015). Mrs. Krowley, for example, knows that when she teaches a topic, *she* learns it better—and her students are the same. She often sets up cooperative groups requiring that the students who are placed in small groups "teach each other" so that they become more actively involved with the materials. She also knows that this works because students can often explain something more easily to their peers on their own' level, and/or they can help to create more meaningful connections that may sometimes make more sense of materials than can an adult's explanation. Lessons involving technology are typically excellent for using pairs or small groups because one person in the group may be "an expert" who can help others to problem solve with the use of the technology. Group members can all move past the technology issues and on to the academic goals.

Let us examine some thinking processes for a group lesson with technology.

Mrs. Krowley knows that some students do not always do their independent work well alone, she sometimes creates a "group goal" so that the peers in the group will work together toward that shared goal. Teachers already understand that goals are "broad *but guiding* learning ideas" such as "Students will learn about conservation," or "Students will learn to use figurative language in their writing." Now, Mrs. Krowley must also decide on a social/emotional skill that his/her class(es) may need. For example, Mrs. Krowley notices that her middle school students need lots of reinforcement. She also knows that her own "teacher's public reinforcement" at this age level can be more embarrassing than effective; however, peer praise is avidly sought and *is* effective. Therefore, her social goal (alongside her academic goals) for students becomes, "The students will appreciate giving and receiving praise." She plans a "sub lesson" for social goals that goes alongside many of her cooperative group lessons.

Mr. Bradley also teaches this type of sublesson to his fourth graders. He begins his lesson by asking students what praise looks like, and students answer him by giving examples such as "That was cool," "Good job," "Great," "Awesome," and so forth. He has one student come up and Google "praise words" on the electronic whiteboard (where they find a site with 150 words of praise that could be used with classmates). He also asks them to try some more meaningful praise and uses as a reference a project that the class had completed not long ago. "Try to think of some examples of what your partners did on the last project that you really liked," he encourages. "For example, you might say, 'That image or picture you picked really made your poster stand out.'" The class follows with some good examples that coworkers could use. Then Mr. Bradley tells them that they were half done, because when someone gives praise, the receiver has to acknowledge it in some way. He goes on to say, "If someone says to you, 'Wow! I like that shirt,' and the first person does not acknowledge that compliment, it makes the one who gave the complement doubt his or her judgment or feel uncomfortable . . . so what are some ways we verbally acknowledge someone's compliment or praise?" Students think for a moment and say, "Thanks," "I appreciate that," or "That was nice," and so forth. Mr. Bradley asks that the student at the electronic whiteboard now go to a site on "how to take a compliment," and some ideas pop up on the site he had designated. Now Mr. Bradley asks the class to turn to their partners and practice using some of the words/phrases that they have generated (or some new ones). The first partners would give three praise words or phrases, and the second partners would acknowledge them. Then students would reverse roles. Mr. Bradley gives the class four minutes to practice this skill.

In the next phase of the social mini-lesson, Mr. Bradley asks students how we give praise nonverbally. After thinking about that for a moment, students reply that thumbs up, high 5s, silent cheers, a pat on the shoulder, fist in the air, and others show praise. The class is asked again to practice this with their partners. Now students have some concrete ideas to use during the group lesson. However, Mr. Bradley knows that "just knowing it and using it" are two very different things, so he tells the class that during the lesson, he will be looking for the "Social Skill of the Day (praise)," and when he sees it, he will give that group a point. At the end of the class period, the group with the most points would receive a prize. Mr. Bradley is now ready to begin his academic lesson.

Kilbane and Milman (2014) also suggest that teachers may even want to have students write and film a short "documentary" of their groups as they are role-playing how to be supportive when working in small groups. "They could ask students to model positive and negative examples of supportive feedback," these researchers continue, "and then later use these videos to reflect on and compare how they actually practiced these skills in reality" (p. 337).

Using groups with technology can be very successful, but the process must be highly structured. The format of using groups can provide good classroom management just through motivation. Technology provides interest and active learning when students are talking and learning for the sake of learning—simply because it is more fun! However, it can all fall apart if the teacher is not careful to structure each part of the lesson so that students feel that they have fair usage of technology and that time issues are carefully regulated. That is not to say that each member of a group will have a turn with the technology during every activity, but students must feel that they get their "fair share" (perhaps even later during the week). The younger the child, the more keenly this will be an issue. That is one reason Ms. Simms makes sure to have roles in her class for each group activity that she uses. A key role is the timekeeper of the group so that in "take turns activities," everyone has the same amount of time with technology, or it is understood that in the next activity, they will change roles and have equal time then.

Ms. Simms, an elementary teacher, uses a group learning project with her 20 third graders (and 5 computers) where each group of students must come up with a poster for a mammal of their choice. On the poster, children must download a picture of the mammal, and also, they must have a summary paragraph that includes the mammal's habitat, what it eats, what preys on it, and if its appearance changes season-ally. By assigning the role of timekeeper to each group, Ms. Simms makes sure that all students get equal time on the computer to download the information and a picture, which they will eventually print out and paste onto a poster. She also assigns to each group of students the role of a "checker", who is the person who will make sure that in each summary, each group member has the required information. The "qual-ity engineer" will make sure that the poster and its summaries/pictures are all finished in a way that is attractive and that each student's name is on his/her contribution. Finally, there is a "materials manager/presenter" whose role includes getting anything else the group needs for the poster as they work toward their joint project together, and, in the end, present it to the class.

For this grade level, the information and picture is glued onto poster boards, but Mr. Johnson may have his older students present their similarly structured slideshow on the electronic whiteboard. This encourages each student to do his/her best using peer pressure to move in a structured way to both an individual academic task and an interdependent task. Assigning roles provides a great deal of structure when using groups *and* technology.

As Ms. Simms gets ready for her lesson, she also plans carefully as to what her directions will be for groups. How will she get children into five groups around the technology if they are not already in long-term groups? Who will she put together this time? How will she make sure she creates diverse groups academically (and with computer skills) so there are no "win/win and lose/lose" groups? One of the best reasons for using groups is to make sure that students work with those who are different from themselves ethnically, academically, gender-wise, and so forth, so she carefully designs her groups with much thought. At times, she also may use as a reward having pairs choose their partners, but normally she structures her groups carefully. In doing this, she does not want confrontation as she directs children to work together. To prevent this, she begins by placing a color-coded card face down on each student's desk as she starts the technology part of the lesson. When all the cards have been passed out, she asks students to move into groups one by one with their matching colors ("If you have a red card, please move together in the right corner of the room now."). It seems that each card is the "luck of the draw," but Ms. Simms has carefully "stacked the deck" so that when a student complains that he/she does not want to work with someone in the group, Ms. Simms can say, "Well, next time the cards will probably come out a different way" (and she does make sure they do). This usually does much to deescalate the situation of "I don't want to work with him/her!" rather than pointing to students and saying, "You ARE working with him/her today, and that is that" (which often sets up a power struggle and starts the project off with a negative environment as one child gets farther into the confrontation and the other cringes or lashes out because he/she is an unwanted group member).

Ms. Simms also thinks carefully through how much time each student will need on the computer, if applicable, during the lesson and how groups will decide who goes first (she has them number off before they do anything, so she establishes the order and the roles using these numbers). It is sometimes difficult to plan for exactly the right amount of time for each group member's activities on and off technology, but thinking about this ahead of time will assure better classroom management and help members see that all "jobs" are valuable in a group effort. She also reminds them of the "first three, and then me rule," which means that if someone in the group doesn't know how to do something on the computer (or the answer to other questions), he or she must ask everyone in his or her group prior to all group members raising their hands to get the teacher's attention to ask for help. This ensures that each group uses its members as resources first and gives Ms. Simms more time to facilitate issues where no one in the group knows the answer. She also thinks about the seating situation with technology, and, in addition, she decides what work students will be doing when it is not their turn on the computer (or with other digital devices) so that engagement and management are main-tained throughout the experience.

Several chapters in this book, particularly about social studies, may mention projects where classrooms may work together from different locales—even from different countries--on a particular project. This is one aspect of group work that can be easily managed by today's technology. Again, to do this, careful planning must be a top priority. First, the teacher must decide if this should be synchronous (in real time) or asynchronous (at one's own convenience, such as with email). One issue when working with groups outside the school is timing. Times when groups may be available online to chat at the same time (in chat rooms, Google Hangouts, or Skype connections) must be considered carefully, especially if time zones are an issue (for example, in middle and high schools a teacher may want his or her different periods during the day to participate, but school may be over in different parts of the world by the time that some periods are in session). The types of technology available (and various firewalls which a school may have) must also be considered when connecting to other classrooms or other resources. Clear contributions for each participant need to be carefully thought out and set up prior to beginning. Equipment that *all* can use may also be of concern. Many students in U.S. classrooms may have availability to digital cameras, for example, where students in other countries (or other parts of the United States) may not have those same options. It also becomes a management problem when teachers have made plans for groups to be online, and, for a variety of reasons, an Internet connection is not made. Teachers must have a backup plan for groups to connect at a later time and an assignment or instruction ready for now. A calendar is also a must in planning these types of group adventures with mini- and final project goals clearly laid out and interim deadlines established. During communication times, time slots should be set forth clearly so students understand that they must complete their messages within a certain limit (especially if it is synchronous/real time). Depending on one's district, there may be course management tools such as Blackboard or Zoho.com that offer chats, connections, documents, discussions, email, meetings, projects, and wikis as well as business and productivity applications. Moodle.org offers its learning platform free as a "build for free."

Miss Verma, a high school social studies teacher, makes arrangements for her students to conduct a project with a counterpart class in India. First, she gives her students a brief time zone lesson of the two locations by asking students to try out Web-based time zone tools, such as Time Zone Converter or World Time Buddy. To manage the scheduling issue, she uses Web-based scheduling tools such as Doodle and Meeting Wizard to decide meeting times of the two classes. Then to remind teachers and students alike of events and activity dates, the Web-based Google Calendar is set up to share with all participants. Miss Verma also incorporates the project's Google Calendar into her homepages created on Weebly. Miss Verma thinks of the social studies content students will learn in their projects: knowing how to interact with people from a different culture, understanding how international time zones work, knowing how to manage big projects that involve many parties, and being able to conduct effective business scheduling that are important work force skills for her students.

Another area to consider for those using groups is self-evaluation. Some of the controversial issues of being in a group are: that not everyone participates equally (riding on coattails); some members may try to manage the team too forcefully; some may not share digital time well; all members may not adhere well to deadlines; and so forth. These should be carefully considered in group reflections. In the real world, without skills that make a group work well together, productivity is not high and negative feelings of working on a team are generated. Because preparing students to do well in the real world is of paramount importance, students need to reflect on their productivity skills so they can become better for the next time—and for the future. Luckily, there are some easy technology assessment tools that can help students look at this in a quick and metacognitive way. For instance, SurveyMonkey, Socrative, or Google Forms allows students to sign on quickly and record their answers so that the teacher can see if students are feeling positive or negative about their group and what areas they see as strong or, conversely, problematic. They can also rate their own participation.

Jigsaw

Mr. Stanton teaches world history, and he wants to use a submodel of cooperative learning called Jigsaw. He begins by explaining that today, each member of the well-established long-term group is "going away" to another group to become an expert in *one* area of the Mayas—the topic for today's lesson. In their new expert groups, they will be reading a brief summary, and each expert group will also be seated at one of the four computer stations in the classroom so that they will be able to get further information (for which URLs have been bookmarked) about "their piece of the puzzle" on the computer. The aim of the expert groups is to come up with the "most important information" about their assigned area (Group 1: Short history of the Mayas; Group 2: Religion; Group 3: Agriculture/economy; Group 4: Famous landmarks/ artifacts); Group 5 War; and Group 6: Geography of settlements. He continues to give all directions before asking students to move—since he knows they will be distracted once they begin moving. He then has students number off in their long-term groups. "I will have all the roles on the board for your expert groups," he tells them. "When you get to your new expert group, renumber in your new group, and then I will show you the roles for the day." Your mission in your expert groups is to design a way to teach your long-term group about the details of the readings and the information you found out from your computer. Everyone in your group should have the same exact memory model that you all design together (and/or other graphic organizers) to take back to your long-term group by the end of the time so that no member of the expert groups forgets to teach all the information that you found out in your expert group. That will be your individual responsibility when you get back to your original group at the end of this activity—to teach them your piece of the puzzle so that we can pass a test on *all* the information. For example, if a group felt like it was important to remember that most of the Mayan cities had pyramids, the group might download pictures of some of the major ones that are still available to see . . . or they may draw or download images of pyramids on a map of Mexico and other Central American countries indicating where the pyramids are located to show their group . . . or they might even construct a funny picture of many pyramids along with other information they find in their chapter to make a memory model. It is a group's decision as to how they design materials that will best be remembered. "Allright," he directs, "let's pack up our belongings, and all those who are 'ones,' come to Computer Station 1." He waits until that move is settled before calling the next station until all have been reseated in their expert groups.

There are some examples of a teacher using Jigsaw at www.teachingchannel.org/videos/literature-circle-prep-sfusd and www.teachingchannel.org/videos/groups-to-analyze-complex-texts. See if you can add a technology aspect to their lessons.

The flowchart on the following page demonstrates how students might move from original groups to expert groups and back.

Numbered Heads

Mr. Abboud plays Numbered Heads, another submodel of cooperative learning, with his young students in mathematics using images flashed up on the computer screen. This submodel uses the power of the total members of each group to support each other in the search for correct answers. This cooperative structure requires that students first number off in their groups and, if they do not already have a group name, give themselves one. They can also create a brief group "cheer" and a group handshake, both of which they offer each other when their team get a correct answer during the game for increased bonding. After asking a question or showing a picture on polygons in mathematics class for example, the teacher calls for (1) "think time" (in which there is a pause for students to silently come up with his or her individual answer) and (2) "talk time" (in which all group members agree on one answer), and then he calls out a group's name and a number. If that student knows the

An Example of Jigsaw for a Class of 24:

Expert Groups of 6

1. | Original/Home Groups of 4 |

2.

3.

4.

5.

6.

All 1's

Rauf Aliyev / shutterstock.com

All 2's

Rauf Aliyev / shutterstock.com

All 3's

Rauf Aliyev / shutterstock.com

All 4's

Rauf Aliyev / shutterstock.com

| Original/Home Groups of 4 |

Start in groups of 4 (6 tables). In original/home groups of 4 number off–1, 2, 3, 4 at each table.
Move Into Expert Groups
   All ones move to one area (where one laptop is positioned)
   All twos to another area (where one laptop is positioned)
   All threes to another area (where one laptop is positioned)
   All fours to another area (where one laptop is positioned)

Academic assignment
1. Read short information packet/chapter that is bookmarked (group members can use "round-robin" read-aloud if needed)
2. Retrieve addition information on the Internet
3. Design a memory model or graphic organizer to "take back" to original/home group (use clip art/graphics, etc.)

Examples of roles (be sure to have expert groups renumber)
1. Timekeeper and Praiser
2. Artist/graphic artist (can be done with technology)
3. Checker (to make sure everyone has a copy of the information from which they will teach [when they move back into their original group])
4. Gatekeeper (to be sure that everyone in the group contributes equally) and reflector (to determine "how we did/what could we do better next time")

Move Back to Original Groups
1. Renumber and reassign roles: timekeeper, gatekeeper, roundup (revisits big picture/main points), and reflector/ celebrator (roles can vary as to the needs of the assignment and the class)
2. Each member teaches the rest of their group (round-robin style) about what was discovered by their expert group and demonstrates the memory model they created. Afterward, the reflector of the group has the entire group give one suggestion about what they did well together and what they could work on the next time. He or she leads the group in a celebration of having completed all this material with everyone's help.
3. The quiz on this material is assigned for tomorrow. This activity. however, gives *all* members the chance to go back over the other chapters on their own once more, but the teacher knows that all students wiil have had an active experience with the material today. The "puzzle" of reading long sections alone was broken up into "doable" pieces in expert groups and put back together in original/home groups.

answer, he or she gains a point for the whole group. If not, Mr. Abboud goes to a different group. For a practice question, Mr. Abboud flashes the following picture up:

He then calls out "think time" and, after a short pause, "talk time," and, finally, he calls on the T-Rex group, Number 2. Steve, who is Number 2 in that group, answers, "A rectangle," and Mr. Abboud confirms that Steve's answer is correct and to have the T-Rex group give their handshake and cheer. He then proceeds to the real game in which he mingles real-life pictures of polygons with the shapes as seen below. He shows examples like these one at a time.

After each picture is shown, he calls the name of a new group and a new number within the group. After this "game", he announces the winning team and then has groups go to their assigned computer which has an assigned shape with bookmarked sites for groups to identify more examples and put them on a short PowerPoint to show the class the next day.

This submodel provides an excellent and supportive structure because students have their group members to consult if they don't know the answer. Peer reinforcement is built in (e.g., handshake, cheer, winner of round). Interdependence is enhanced, and students are actively talking about the question. The competition between groups provides motivation to get the answer right within each group.

A long history of research shows the positive results of using cooperative learning groups during instruction—both academically, motivationally, and socially/emotionally (Slavin, 1987; Stahl, 1994, Stevens & Slavin, 1995). This type of instruction can be joined with technology, but a teacher must structure these experiences to have the potential of the group experience and the technology work well together.

Ms. Tran recently learned of the interactive Website, Socrative (www.socrative.com), from a teachers' conference and eagerly tried it out with Numbered Heads. She had been inspired by a conference presentation where a high school AP (Advance Placement) teacher incorporated it into his physics lessons. The Web tool has the ability to quickly and interactively gather feedback from students by offering many possibilities for gauging opinions, testing understanding, and engaging all participants. Ms. Tran had used Quizlet, Cram, and Flashcard Machines to host online flashcards and quizzes for students before but thought the Socrative interface would be more appealing to adolescent learners. Ms. Tran modified this teaching strategy to fit her seventh-grade mathematics class. She liked being able to display the break down analysis of student responses in percentage as well as diagram formats. After implementing this interactive Website, one student found out that she could respond to Socrative by using her own smartphone rather than computers or proprietary hardware in real time such as a physical voting handset (e.g., clickers). This makes implementing this type of interactive Website even more convenient.

One feature of this site that groups can use with Numbered Heads is the Space Race that allows teams to compete. As teams answer electronically, and they can see immediately on a display who is winning.

There are good examples of this submodel on YouTube that can be found by typing in "Numbered Heads Together YouTube" on a search engine. One elementary example with Mrs. Hines (Numbered Heads Together 0001) is at www.youtube.com/watch?v=v8uYS48BIUw (or search for Mrs. Hines and Numbered Heads) and a high school example is at www.youtube.com/watch?v=ADmXhDuHpD4, although there are many more.

Group Role Play

Dockterman (1994) describes a cooperative learning submodel termed "group role play" that requires both cooperation *and* conflict that generates good discussion through dissonant points of view. A situation which requires a decision about a particular compelling issue is required. If background material is needed, it is taught or reviewed, and then each student is given a well-supported opinion (of which there are many), with the end objective being a whole group decision. Teams of about four students are given advisory roles or "put on a committee." For instance, for an environmental decision in a town or city through a "mayor's" office with a reelection on the horizon, there may be teams/committees of environmentalists, scientists, economists, reelection specialists, public advocacy, or others. Each group will have targeted information bookmarked that is coming from their perspective roles. Dockterman gives the following as one such scenario:

> *Dead fish! The headline glares at you from your desk. The danger forced you, the mayor of Alpine to close Snyder Pond. Could the nearby dump be polluting the pond and killing the fish? Or is it some other cause. . . .? Many people suspect the town dump! Who knows what the mining company is dumping there? Are Malaco and its jobs really good for Alpine? What if the company seeks to mine beautiful Gab's Gully? You are the mayor, and it's an election year.* (p. 41)

Part of the instructions for each advisory committee would be to summarize the materials on what their position should be and then rank their goals for a decision. In the case above, goals would be to win reelection, protect the environment, hold down costs, preserve the economy, and so forth. Based on their rating, groups then individually begin to form their case (based on the bookmarked or other information they find online) to the mayor. Cases are presented, and the class must then come to a consensus after much high-level, persuasive discussion. Even "reelection speeches" can be filmed as part of the lesson. As one can see, these types of role play can cover mathematics skills, language arts, science, social studies, and so forth. Students become invested in their positions, so involvement is more intense. There are a few software applications for these types of role play, but the teacher is able to create "cases" easily in his/her content area that support a particular class and bookmark resources for each group.

Memory Model

The memory model is one that is most useful in helping learners remember the vast amount of information that teachers ask of students throughout their schooling. Although there are some memory submodels that do not require technology, many of these submodels can be enhanced through its use.

One of the submodels that is very effective with technology, for example, is using ridiculous images. Teachers often use this submodel to help students remember vocabulary words. The word "litany" for instance might be depicted as the "mind jolter" seen below:

Images © Shutterstock.com

The vocabulary word "litany" means a form of prayer. The common elements that help memory to "click in" when the definition cannot be remembered is that someone has turned over a candle during prayer and set his knee on fire . . . or "lit-an-knee" (litany) = prayer. The ridiculous association picture pops readily to mind when the word is heard. Often the memory model will use a "play on words" such as this one above to associate the real meaning with the ridiculous. For another example, one may want to teach the word "discommoded." A picture of a frustrated person standing over a toilet will surely bring up the funny phrase, "'Dis' commode is broken, and so I am very annoyed." The definition of discommoded is annoyed.

One element that makes technology a boon to creating memory models is that these "ridiculous association" pictures may sometimes require artwork, and many students do not feel confident in their drawing. Using clip art, they can quickly search for art images that might help make up their ridiculous image. In doing so, they are seeing a number of images, which makes the word more likely to "stick in the brain." For example, there are more than 100 clip art images to choose from the "prayer category" above for litany on bing.com images and by clicking on "Clip Art." The artist creating the memory model has to examine each to see if the image is suitable for making into his/her or a group's imagine, so already the focus on the word *litany* as associated with a form of prayer, for instance, is making pathways into the brain through activity. If using small learning groups, there can be quite a bit of discussion as to the choices and arrangement of the items used. This also helps the image and vocabulary word to "stick" in the brain. If students are drawing, there may be quite a bit of erasing or starting over, but using technology is quick and easy. This can be used for many different concepts. For example, if Mr. Farr wanted elementary students in science to remember the terms for some "animal babies," he might help students design the following:

Bears: Tony Campbell

The ridiculous image presents three bear cubs with trash/litter all around because the term for a group of baby bears is a litter.

Another science class was studying "animal groups" and came up with a memory model for a group of caterpillars. One may be able to guess by looking at the picture below that a group of caterpillars is an army.

Similarly, a group of coyotes is. . . .?

. . . a band. When asked to remember that dogs, however, in a group were a pack, one group came up with a picture of dogs going into a suitcase (packing), while another came up with an image of a six-*pack* of soda with dogs coming out of it.

If Mrs. Bures was having her students remember the years of World War II in her social studies class, she might ask students to create "an image" for some major events using a rhyming scheme for numbers. This rhyming list stays the same for all numbers and is created by the class and used throughout the year.

    1 = sun
    2 = shoe
    3 = tree
    4 = door
    5 = hive
    6 = sticks
    7 = heaven
    8 = gate
    9 = dine
   10 = hen

Therefore, we might see a history memory model for 1939 as the following picture/ridiculous image:

One = sun, 9 = dine, 3 = tree, 9 = dine, and we have added to the "dine" a Polish sausage plus a Polish folk group to remind students one of the beginning events of WWII was the invasion of Poland by Germany in 1939. This could also be enhanced by an image of Hitler's moustache superimposed over "the diners at the table."

Mr. Wood, a science teacher, has his students use ridiculous images to help remember Newton's three Laws of Motion.

1st Law of Motion: An object at rest wants to stay at rest.

2nd Law of Motion: When two forces are acting on each other, the greater dominates. (2 elephants for the 2nd law)

3rd Law of Motion: Force exists in pairs. (three pairs of pears being pushed together to help remember this is the 3rd law).

Tips for Using Memory Models

As with all models of teaching, this model can be used with most content areas. It can also be used with and without technology. Teachers may want to investigate more usage of the model in other ways such as visualization, mnemonics, and silly songs (of which there are an amazing number as resources on the Internet). For example, many preservice teachers may remember their own teachers playing various Schoolhouse Rock songs, and many can probably still remember the lyrics to this day. Schoolhouse Rock still produces songs (and videos, and teachers can search for a plethora of songs in most content areas such as social studies, language arts, mathematics, and science or more specific areas within the content area [e.g., the rain forest]). Typing in the content area and/or the specific area such as math+fractions+songs will bring up a number of sites. Many Websites have animations to go along with the songs (e.g., David Williams' Rainforest Song—YouTube). Groups may create and film their own songs and/or animations to help remember content information which continues to enhance the memory process.

Indeed, there are many other ways to help students remember various things that we need to teach. With the ideas that have been introduced here, there are some factors to remember. The teacher must clearly understand that for the memory model to work, a memory connection must be meaningful for the learner. If the association doesn't "ring a bell" with the student, he or she cannot make the connection to put it into memory easily. Since teachers are often much older than those in their classrooms, students may have no idea of a connection that a teacher makes in terms of a concept. Therefore, the teacher should always give students an idea(s), but he/she should also give students time to generate their own so that there is a meaningful connection. Using groups is particularly supportive for creativity in generating these ideas.

Part of the reason that this model works is that learners pay more attention to the material, so an *activity* must also be in place during the lesson for this. Students must have some time to work on memory connections of their own. "Anything that captures students' attention and engages their mind has the potential to produce learning," notes Banikowski (1999). She continues with, "of course, the opposite is also true: No attention, no engagement, no learning."

This model works in a number of other ways as well. Banikowski (1999) also reminds us that "a picture is worth a thousand words", and the numbers and variety of pictures available through technology are vast. Humor is also an element that causes ridiculous associations to be caught in memory because these images are often funny and/or unusual (Whilte, 2012).

The more students use this technique and are directed to where it might be used, the more they may be able to see its application in other content areas and in life (for instance, even remembering homework assignments or a list for shopping). A social studies teacher, Mr. Barton, tells his class, "I know you are studying *Hamlet* with Mrs. Cole this term in English. We are going to use the same memory model format that you worked with in her class that helped you remember the story line and characters of *Hamlet* to remember the main events of the American Revolution in my class." The more that teachers can use these elements in memory models, the better chance students may have to access their memories of the vast amount of information that they learn throughout their time in school and onward.

Concept Development

Mrs. Brandenburg was planning to begin a unit with her high school English students on *Romeo and Juliet*. She knew that they already had some experience with the story, but she wanted to find out how much they knew. On the electronic whiteboard, she asked students to brainstorm what they thought of when they heard the title *Romeo and Juliet*. Students begin to "toss out" the following ideas, and Mrs. Brandenburg wrote them in as they did:

Romeo and Juliet

a play	Shakespeare	old English	sad	movie
stabbed	feuding families	died	young	

With this, the students began to taper off. Mrs. Brandenburg was surprised! She thought they would know more. She saved the brainstorm on her computer as 1st Period—*Romeo and Juliet* Concept Development and moved on with her next lesson on the play.

At the conclusion of the unit, she brought the brainstorm back up on the computer screen and asked the same question, showing them what they had known before. "What can you add now?" she asked. They contributed the following:

Romeo and Juliet

a play	Shakespeare	old English	sad	movie
stabbed	feuding families	died	young	Paris
Capulet	the nurse	Friar Laurence	Verona	Mercutio
Montague	street fight	the party	balcony	secret marriage
sleeping drug	banishment	"O Romeo, Romeo, . . .	poison	crypt/tomb
"star-crossed"	tragedy	wherefore art thou	sixteenth century	love at first sight
lovers	"sun hides its face	Romeo?"	men actors	comedy to tragedy
women's roles	in sorrow"	hatred	feud	Juliet's room
forced marriage	Capulet's house	orchard	Mantua	church
forbidden love	*West Side Story*	ballet	movies	*High School Musical*
Shakespeare	*Romeo & Juliet* (the	"Parting is such	love is as	swordplay
In Love	movie, 2013)	sweet sorrow"	"boundless	. . . "what light through
masks	themes	light/dark	as the sea"	yonder window
timing	fate/fortune	prologue	Justin Bieber	beaks . . ."
"Bye Bye"	"You Had Me at	timeless	songs	plaza/public square
party crashers	Hello"	Capulet's tomb	Tybalt	revenge
the prince	"Indian Summers"			

After listing, Mrs. Brandenberg looked at the list and asked if anyone else had anything else they could think of to add and made sure that students knew they could do so if they thought of anything as they went along through the model. She told them that she was going to read the list, and if anyone had another idea that she would add it. Also, if someone didn't know why a term was added or what it was, he or she should raise his or her hand, and they would revisit the reason the term had been added. She began to read the list and came to the word Mantua, when Brad held up his hand. "I don't know what that is," he said. "Who put Mantua up?" Mrs. Brandenberg asked, and Kaylynn said that it was her. "Can you tell Brad why you added that?" the teacher asked. "It was the place where Romeo got banished to by the Prince," Kaylynn told him, "you know, after Romeo killed Tybalt who had killed Mercutio." "Oh, okay," answered Brad, "I didn't remember that." Another student asked about "Indian Summers," and Nita told him that it was a series on TV about India in the 1930s that showed similar themes found in *Romeo and Juliet* about forbidden love between a British man and an Indian woman and another Indian couple who were of different religions. "You can't believe how Shakespearean it is," Nita told the class. The teacher moved on down the list, and there were a few more terms that were discussed and some that students wanted to add.

For the next step, Mrs. Brandenburg told students that they would be finding words/phrases/concepts that belonged together and give them a category name. They were to use all the words on the list. Mrs. Brandenberg asked them what might go with Verona, for example, and Angie said, "The balcony, the public square, Capulet's orchard, Capulet's house, and the tomb." "What could we call this category?" Mrs. Brandenberg continued. "It could be the settings for the scenes," another student chimed in, "so then we would add Mantua." "That's a very good idea," said Mrs. Brandenberg.

Settings

Verona
the balcony
the public square
Capulet's orchard
Capulet's house
the tomb/crypt
Mantua

She continued telling students to find their computer groups, because they would be working on the computer to use all these terms listed in this way. She emailed the list to the accessible class email so that students could pull it up at their stations and work on it. She also had cards at each station with roles and time limits so that all students would have some time on the computer. As they used each term, they used the cross out feature of MS Word. One group began classifying the terms in the following way (although other groups make other categories):

Romeo and Juliet

~~a play~~	~~Shakespeare~~	~~older English~~	sad	movie
stabbed	family didn't want	died	young	~~Paris~~
~~Capulet~~	~~the nurse~~	~~Friar Laurence~~	~~Verona~~	~~Mercutio~~
~~Montague~~	~~street fight~~		~~balcony~~	~~secret marriage~~
sleeping drug	~~banishment~~	"O Romeo, Romeo, . . .	poison	~~crypt/tomb~~
"star-crossed"	tragedy	wherefore art thou	sixteenth century	love at first sight
lovers	"sun hides its face	Romeo?"	men actors	comedy to tragedy
~~women's roles~~	in sorrow"	hatred	feud	~~Juliet's room~~
forced marriage	~~Capulet's house~~	~~orchard~~	Mantua	~~church~~
~~forbidden love~~	*West Side Story*	ballet	England	*High School Musical*
Shakespeare	*Romeo & Juliet* (the	~~"Parting is~~	~~love is as~~	swordplay
In Love	movie, 2013)	~~such sweet sorrow"~~	~~"boundless~~	~~. . ."what light through~~

Romeo and Juliet

~~masked ball~~	~~themes~~	~~light/dark~~	~~as the sea"~~	~~yonder window~~
timing	~~fate/fortune~~	Prologue	~~Justin Bieber~~	~~breaks. . ."~~
~~Elizabethan~~	~~"You Had Me at~~	~~timeless~~	~~songs~~	~~plaza/public square~~
party crashers	~~At Hello"~~	~~Capulet's tomb~~	~~Tybalt~~	*revenge*
~~the Prince~~	~~wedding~~	~~New Moon~~		
~~"How Do I~~				
~~Live Without You~~				

The following categories emerged from one group.

Settings	Characters	Themes
Verona	Romeo	revenge
the balcony	Juliet	fate/fortune
the public square/plaza	parents	light/dark
Capulet's orchard	Tybalt	roles of women
Juliet's room	the Prince	forbidden love
Capulet's house	Capulet	love at first sight
Capulet's tomb/crypt	Montague	
Mantua	the nurse	
Church	Mercutio	
	Paris	
	Friar Laurence	

Events	Author	Movies/Plays/Books/Songs
wedding	Shakespeare	*New Moon*
street fight	timeless	Justin Bieber songs
masked ball	sonnets	"You Had Me at Hello"
banishment	Older English	"How Do I Live Without You"
secret marriage	Queen Elizabeth	*Westside Story*
Juliet is buried	England	
Romeo takes poison		
Juliet stabs herself		

Famous quotes

". . . what light through yonder window breaks . . ."

love is "boundless as the sea"

"Parting is such sweet sorrow . . ."

For students to interact more with the important vocabulary words within *Romeo and Juliet*, Mrs. Brandenberg asked students to copy and paste a number of key word lists to word cloud sites such as WordItOut (www .worditout.com/word-cloud/make-a-new-one) or Tagxedo (www.tagxedo.com/). To extend even more, one student found the entire *Romeo and Juliet* play from the Shakespeare homepage at MIT (www.shakespeare.mit .edu/romeo_juliet/full.html) and created a word cloud of the entire play through a word cloud generator such as www.jasondavies.com/wordcloud/#. Some students liked the word clouds so much that they ordered custom-ized t-shirts with the word clouds online from sites such as www.spreadshirt.com/word+cloud+t-shirt. Several students expressed that these word clouds made learning English literature more artistic and educated fun.

Images © Shutterstock.com

Mrs. Brandenberg's class is was having so much fun with the words, phrases, and quotes in *Romeo and Juliet* that one student created a meme with a meme generator (such as makeameme.org) on the quote "Parting is such sweet sorrow. . . ."

Parting is such sweet sorrow...

Images © Shutterstock.com.

The bell was about to ring, so Mrs. Brandenberg had students save their work for the next class period so they could come back to it and finish up using all the terms on the brainstorm list. One group's categories are listed above, but other groups came up with some differences. The teacher let them make the list in the form above, or they could download or create a graphic organizer that suited their purpose. One group used a web for theirs, adding some other things as they worked (see next page).

The next day, Mrs. Brandenberg had them go straight to their group computer station and pull up their saved documents. Each group was to continue to work on using all the terms in the brainstorm. At the close of the time limit on this activity, the teacher asked each group to select two categories each to share with the class orally and to read all the terms underneath the category. If a group had already shared a particular category, the next group should try to pick a different one (if they had one or, if not, they could repeat). After completing this activity, each group was to take one of the categories they had chosen and summarize it by using all of the terms they had used underneath it. Mrs. Brandenberg gave them a time limit and set them to work. One group constructed the following summary from the category they created on turning points:

The main **turning points** of this play were key in having the fate of these two star-crossed lovers come out the way it did. First, they met and fell in love at first sight at a <u>masked ball</u>. They pledged their love and <u>were married secretly</u> by their friar. Romeo went to the plaza where he got into a <u>street fight</u> with some Capulets over sneaking into the party, and his friend is killed. Romeo, in retaliation, kills Tybalt (a Capulet). Because of this, he is <u>banished</u>, but, meanwhile, Juliet's <u>parents push her to marry Paris</u>. The friar <u>gives her a drug</u> that will make it look like she died, and <u>she is buried</u> in the family crypt. Romeo <u>doesn't get the message</u>, so he finds Juliet in her crypt and <u>takes poison</u> to join her in death. <u>Juliet wakes up and sees Romeo dead</u> and <u>stabs herself</u> with this dagger to join him. The Prince points out what the families have done though their hate and feuding to cause these tragedies.

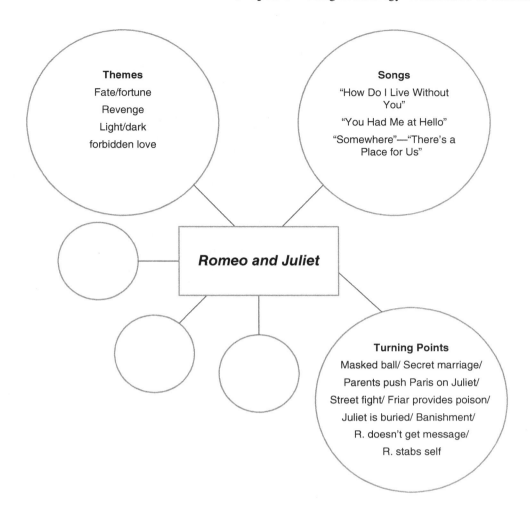

Another group wrote:

> Shakespeare is the author of the play, *Romeo and Juliet*. He lived in England during Elizabethan times in the later 1500s and early 1600s. He wrote many plays in sonnet form in older English, so it is difficult to understand some of what he is saying without studying it, but when we do, many of his ideas are timeless.

Each of the groups covered the main categories with each other. Mrs. Brandenberg asked them to remember how much they hadn't known about the play at the beginning and how much they knew now. She went back and reinforced a few idea[s] _____ students during the model. A few days later, she tested them on the play, and her _____ all learned *much* more than her classes from the past year before when she had n[ot] _____ model as a closure or employed as much exciting technology.

Question 3

Tips for Using Concept Development

Students must know something about the concept/subject before they can generate the number of terms needed to complete this model well. This is an excellent model to use as a focus activity—but only if students have some prior knowledge about it. If they do not, it is a very effective closure activity to sum up everything they have learned. The broader the topic, the more terms they will be able to add. One must also remember that younger children will not need to contribute as many examples as older students, and the teacher may need to help young children over time to do each phase according to their skills. Mrs. Knight, for example, has children pick out pictures of birds from her animal cards or from a technology folder in the class shared drive on the school network and then asks them to make their categories in stacks or by moving the pictures into another folder. Children usually do this based on colors or sizes. She does not require them to do very many, but she does ask them to orally give her a summary sentence about the categories.

Students can use technology to seek more information about contributions. For example, several students in Mrs. Brandenburg's class had not heard of the musical *West Side Story* or the song "Somewhere." They looked it up on the Internet to listen and view the lyrics. Others wanted to know how far it was from Verona to Mantua (where Romeo was banished), so they brought up an interactive map of Italy online with that information.

This method of forming and developing concepts can be used with all subjects and concepts within subject areas (including technology). "What comes to mind when we think of the *Internet*?" might be used to generate all the terms associated with that area of technology or "What do we know about *Word*?" Questions like this can remind students of broad associated terms, very specific terms, ethical areas, or historical information—among others.

This model can also be continued to increase higher-level thinking. This is based on Taba's (1962, 1967) belief that thinking can be taught. Asking students to predict consequences, explain unfamiliar phenomena, hypothesize, analyze, and so forth might be a next phase. For instance, an English teacher using this with *Romeo and Juliet* as above might ask if there are still arranged marriages in some cultures and, if so, what are the consequences for going outside family's wishes. Questions that could be asked of groups to delve into this area would be, "What would happen if . . . ," why do you think this would happen (supporting the predictions and hypotheses and determining links), and verifying predictions ("What would it take for this to be generally true or probably true?"). Are there modern-day interactions to support Shakespeare's story? Why does this story have such universal appeal even today? Other questions and verifications can be brought into play with consideration to the content area.

Teachers should also allow students to contribute terms that seem unlikely—*if* the student can make the connection to the concept. The only time a term should not be included in listing is when it is inappropriate or intended to create disruption. As with all the models, establishing time limits for each phase and providing role for each group members participation and success. Allowing for and/or providing for technology us[ ] Question 4 [ ]al listing has occurred) helps students to follow up on their interests genera[ ].

Suggestopedia

Suggestopedia is a model that was originally developed to teach foreign languages (Lozanov, 1978; Bancroft, 1995), but we must remember that much knowledge is "Greek" to learners when first presented. Suggestopedia, perhaps obviously, is based on positive suggestion and uses all the senses to relax the learner so that knowledge can "flow" in. This model is based on the belief that tension, stress, and boredom when trying to learn something new can actually prevent learning, which makes a good case for a more relaxed, joyful approach. For example, Ms. Jameson was teaching her fourth graders vocabulary dealing with the rain forest. She pulls up music and sound effects that are available on the Internet and selects one that is most appropriate. Then she writes her own suggestion story (see on the next page). She also brings in a "rain forest" scent (after checking for students' allergies) and some ferns and plants to enhance the atmosphere. By her chair, she has a spray mister bottle, which she sprays during her reading. While students are seated in a circle, she dims the lights asks them to close their eyes and "come with her on a journey to the rain forest." As she plays the soundtrack, she reads the story she has constructed to help them "see and feel" the vocabulary words. After her reading, she then goes over the vocabulary (humidity, vegetation, understory, emergent tree layer, and canopy) that she wants them to include in their own presentations, having them tell her what they think the words mean from her reading. As she talks about each word, she shows several images on her whiteboard. Finally, she divides them up into laptop computer groups and has them construct their own short stories using the vocabulary words and the idea that they are visiting the rain forest and replays the soundtrack as they work. Each group is also tasked with finding images from bookmarked sites. Each member of the group has a task, one of which is the presenter. At the end of the assigned time, each presenter reads his/her group's story as the soundtrack is played again in the background. There are many more aspects to Suggestopedia than are discussed here, but the main focus remains on creating an atmosphere for the learner where the teacher's suggestions create a total experience for learning. One major reason that this model seems to work well is novelty, context clues, and repetition—in addition to application. The learner is asked to become a part of the atmosphere. In learning a foreign language (as demonstrated later in French), the learner can actually take on a new persona; in the following example, students became visitors/naturalists in the rain forest.

Example of a Suggestopedia Reading for the Rain Forest:

Close your eyes and relax . . . and come with me to the rain forest of Central America. The first thing that overwhelms our eyes here is the green vegetation—the incredible number of growing plants! Everywhere you look the vegetation is green, and many of these plants have beautiful flowers. The green vegetation grows all year long because this forest is so warm and humid; that is, sticky and damp. We say that the humidity is very high because so much rain falls—almost 9 feet a year. How humid it is here! I am already sweating and my clothes are sticking to me. Most places in this state receive only about 1-2 feet of rain. There is so much rain that it cannot evaporate away, so the humidity (or moisture in the air) remains high all the time. Think about here when the humidity is high—you feel sticky, sweaty, and damp, and your clothes don't dry easily. In the rain forest, there is even more humidity, and that is one reason for some much vegetation. The vegetation gets so much moisture, and it never freezes here. Feel your body and feel how damp you feel. Look up and see all the green above you (and she continues with the "trip" into the rain forest and the other vocabulary).

The part technology can play in these types of lessons is providing an amazing number of resources for teachers and students. Remember, too, the definition of a model means that many content areas can be inserted into the framework, and in this model, the teacher's imagination can be limitless in constructing "suggestion scenarios" for his or her purpose. Mr. Cahill concentrates on creativity by pulling up shamisen music from Japan. He reads a number of haikus to students as they listen with their eyes closed to the poems. When he is finished, he asks students to tell him what the poems had in common, and students were able to talk about the form and the subject (often a "flash shot" of nature or emotion). He then set them to the task of writing their own haiku while listening to the music again. He found that their creativity was much increased from the year before when he simply told them what a haiku was and told them to write one. The uniqueness of the mood allowed them to think and visualize much more. Technology offers much to the teacher who wishes to create a special mood for his/her lessons. Almost any music can be found to match readings or as a background for other activities, and the teacher may record his/her presentation for review. In the example below, the teacher plays soft music in the background that "automatically takes the reader" to France.

Mr. Valdez, a social studies teacher, combines the Concept Development model with music from Africa after asking the question, "What do you think of when you hear the word "Africa"?" After students list their thoughts, he reads the list for review and questions, and then plays the same music as they categorize the terms and use the terms in a summary of a category. This makes a much more memorable event than just having students remember terms.

An Example of Suggestopedia for Reading in a French Lesson

Mes étudiants, please close your eyes and let the music carry you to a very special city, *la ville de Paris*. In this beautiful *ville*, we find ourselves walking along the river Seine, *la rivière Seine*, behind a couple holding hands. We hear them talking about their last night together before she must leave. *La rivière Seine* catches the reflection of the lights, and *la lune* is round and bright in the night sky and *les étoiles* sparkle above, too. *Cette jeune fille* and her young man talk about the times they have walked along *cette rivière* with *la lune* and *les étoiles* to light the sky. As we watch *cette jeune fille* and *le garçon* walk on, we look up at *la lune* and *les étoiles* and think what a lovely *ville Paris* is and how lucky they were to have found each other here—if only for a while. (The teacher lets the music continue to the end and then asks students to "come back to class" and open their eyes. She then asks them to describe the scene in English. Afterward, she asks them to create a scenario with the new vocabulary as they pick a soundtrack, then share with the class. Through the mood, they understand the French words for students, city, river, moon, stars, girl, and boy.)

Case Studies

The Harvard Business School has used case studies for many years (Shipiro, 1975), as have many business colleges and colleges of science throughout the country and around the world. Cases offer students an answer to the age-old question that they often have about what we learn in schools: "Teacher, when would we ever use this stuff?" The rationale is clear using this model because the case is a real-life application. However, few teachers have tapped into case study potential for school classrooms, especially in the younger grades. The case study normally involves discussion and problem-solving through a mini-dilemma or can be an extensive problem with information that unfolds step-by-step. Because cases are real stories/problems (or are based on real-life issues), students are often "caught" in the excitement of the inquiry. Of course, teachers can retrieve cases online or create their own scenarios that are cases, but they should involve real-life issues and be able to be solved using data and resources. An interesting part of using many cases is that there is not always an established "right answer", but there can be multiple solutions which involve creative thinking.

Technology offers an amazing tool for teachers to find case studies at appropriate levels for their learners and also to the inquiring minds of students who are searching for answers to unusual situations. Most cases begin with an article or situation. For example, in one secondary case (*Souvenirs* by Shagam, Decker, & Stanley, 1999), secondary science students are presented with "pieces" of the story as it unfolds about three young women returning from a vacation in New Mexico in which they participated in a "dig" at a Native American ceremonial site. One of the friends become ill on the plane home, and, as the scenario continues, she passes away, and another becomes deathly ill. Each subsequent scene brings new questions and issues to the readers. It becomes obvious that their lives must be put under a microscope to find what is happening. The scientific community becomes involved in the many aspects of this case, and students learn about the Centers for Disease Control and Prevention. Learners are placed in groups to represent the "players" who would be a part of this story: family, doctors, community health agencies, lawyers, etc. After the introduction of each piece of the scenario, the groups meet to dig for details, research using technology, and make decisions and/or presentations. Students are normally able to conclude that the hanta virus was contracted, but it is the learners who are active researchers who put the pieces of the puzzle together. Along the way, they discover how many groups and professions are involved and the problem-solving that accompanies a communicable disease—instead of simply being told about it. An exciting model such as this would not be available to learners without the wealth of information offered by technology nor would the presentations be as professional.

Mr. Ortega uses a case study of the eruption of Mt. Helens as his class final on his Earth Science unit (www.geobytesgcse.blogspot.com/2007/01/volcano-case-study-mount-st-helens-1980.html). Teachers can find the instructions and Web resources to be used by students on the site. Younger students can also use scenarios like this but modified to their age level. Application of skills, rationales for learning new skills, and problem-solving are all included in the case study model.

As noted, many cases are available for teachers at all levels. For example, Case Studies for Kids! (www.engineering.purdue.edu/ENE/Research/SGMM/CASESTUDIESKIDSWEB/index.htm) offers cases, tools and resources, teaching notes, and more. The teaching notes basically provide a lesson plan for teaching the case with many ideas on time management, various skills that are needed, assessment, and presentations.

Teachers can also create their own cases (even filming parts). Recently, a large urban area in Texas experienced "500-year" flooding in some areas of the city. Mrs. Coker had a number of students whose homes had been affected. She developed a case to have students research "what had changed" in their neighborhoods and how to negotiate the wide range of city services that might prevent flooding in the future. She encouraged students to use technology in their presentations to demonstrate problem areas and research and also to conclude with letters to the appropriate officials.

Case studies support inquiry-based learning, which, in turn, creates motivation "to have to know" the answer. One of the most popular television series "Law and Order" is, perhaps, one of the best examples of a case study. The program always begins with a short vignette of the crime. If one happens to see this beginning, it is very difficult to "let go mentally" of the situation because the viewer "just has to know who 'done it'" and solve the mystery. This is the type of "hook" that case study often creates for the learner.

Concluding Thoughts

There are a number of other models of teaching (along with their submodels) that can be used to engage students in active learning. Many of these, as we have seen with the models discussed here, can be combined with technology to enhance the learning experience in various ways. The use of models of teaching creates variety, promotes "minds on" thinking, increases students' curiosity to search deeper, and finds a way into many of areas of teachers' concerns (management, motivation, etc.). A teacher who is creative with this excellent combination of models of teaching and technology will motivate students and enrich his or her own practice in exciting ways for learners. The ideas for combining these two areas of effective instruction are part of what establishes teaching as a creative process and a satisfying endeavor.

References

Bancroft, W. J. (1995). *The western tradition of suggestion and Lozanov's archaeology/Suggestopedia*. Retrieved from files.eric.ed.gov/fulltext/ED382006

Bruner, J. (1960). *The process of education*. Cambridge, MA: Harvard University Press.

Bruner, J., Goodnow, J., & Austin, G. (1965). *A study of thinking (6th printing, 2009)*. New Brunswick, NJ: Transaction Publishers.

Banikowski, A. (1999). Strategies to enhance memory based on brain research. *Focus on Exceptional Children*, 0015511X, *39*(2). Retrieved from scboces.org/english/IMC/Focus/Memory_strategies2.pdf

Burnett, F. H. (1911, 1962). *The secret garden*. Philadelphia, PA: Lippincott.

Dockterman, D. (1994). Cooperative learning and technology. Retrieved from www-tc.pbs.org/teacherline/courses/math230/docs/clt.pdf

Gunter, M., Estes, T., & Schwab, J. (2003). *Instruction: A models approach*. Boston, MA: Allyn and Bacon.

Joyce, B., Weil, M., & Calhoun, E. (2015). *Models of teaching* (9th ed.). Boston, MA: Pearson.

Kilbane, C., & Milman, K. (2014). *Teaching models: Designing instruction for 21st century learners*. Boston, MA: Pearson.

Lozanov, G. (1978). *Suggestology and outlines of suggestopedy*. New York: Gordon and Breach.

Shagam, J., Decker, J., Stanley, E. (1999). *Souvenirs: A case study for the 90s*. Retrieved from files.eric.ed.gov/fulltext/ED460698.pdf

Shipiro, B. (1975). Participating in a case study. Retrieved from www.hbs.edu/teaching/Documents/HBS_Brochure_for_Companies_Regarding_Field_Cases.pdf

Slavin, R. (1987). Developmental and motivational perspectives on cooperative learning: A reconciliation. *Child Development*, *58*(5), 1161–1167.

Stahl, R. (1994). The essential elements of cooperative learning in the classroom. ERIC Digest (ED370881).

Stevens, R., & Slavin, R. (1995). The cooperative elementary school: Effects on students' achievement, attitudes, and social relations. *American Education Research*, *32*(2), 321–351.

Taba, H. (1962). *Curriculum development: Theory and practice*. New York, NY: Harcourt College Publishers.

Taba, H. (1967). *Teacher's handbook for elementary social studies*. Palo Alto, CA: Addison-Wesley.

White, R. (2012). Humor enhances memory. Retrieved from www.brainathlete.com/humor-enhances-memory

Chapter 9

Integrating Technology Standards for Teachers

Irene Chen, *University of Houston - Downtown*
Libi Shen, *Educational Consultant*

Meet Miss Brown

Miss Brown was considering a lesson on the life cycle of the plants with her third graders. She wanted students to be able to complete the following objectives in her science lesson:

- Students will follow an inquiry process to answer questions.
- Students will use an existing WebQuest to find information about the life cycle of the plants.

While preparing the lesson plan, he decided to use the National Science Education Standards (NSES) available online for the science content. However, she also remembered that the district encouraged all teachers to integrate the state technology standards in lessons.

Rawpixel.com / shutterstock.com

As Miss Brown sat down at her computer, she pulled up a split screen of the science education standards, the state technology standards, and even the national technology standards to integrate into her curriculum. She also considered the Common Core State Standards. This made her wonder if she had to refer to all of these standards in order to be a ***twenty-first-century digital teacher***.

Educational standards are set by a number of groups—national content area specialists' organizations (such as in mathematics and science), states, districts, and so forth. By setting guidelines in various content areas (including technology), they hope to ensure that students are taught "the essentials" for the specific subject. These standards are normally set up to progress in age-appropriate steps so that students will have the knowledge and skills they need from year to year to help them easily move up to the next level.

As a new teacher, one is likely to make the connections of how learning objectives are linked to standards through (1) certification exams, (2) professional knowledge, and (3) lesson planning. Teacher certification examinations often include questions directly related to the knowledge and skills of the standards, including technology. Interviewers for teaching positions may also ask professional knowledge questions about what children should "know and be able to do" at certain grade levels or in particular content areas where positions may be open. Because of the emphasis on students' state test scores (which connect back to standards), a teacher candidate can be sure that a school wants its new teachers to clearly understand how important these standards are for students to learn.

Teachers are also *routinely* asked to display objectives **and** specific standards for their lesson plans. They are often required to turn in these objectives and standards on weekly lesson plans to their principals or other administrator(s). This procedure is in place to help schools, districts, states, the nation, and, ultimately, children to be assured that their knowledge and skills are on level with what is expected by the experts who created these standards. On top of taking attendance, learning students' names, and maintaining classroom management, it is no wonder that new teachers like Miss Brown question how they can accomplish all that! The process becomes very automatic once teachers have worked with this requirement, and there are even programs and apps that list and "plug in" standards at the touch of a fingertip. In addition, many textbook companies now offer various standards as part of their teachers' editions as part of a state's purchase of the text.

The best way to ensure that the required standards are covered in the curriculum is to include them right from the start of any planning phase by determining specific learning objectives. Hill (1995) stated that,

> Good teachers have standards in mind when they set their lessons up, where the idea of a "standard" represents a specific idea of what the teacher expects a student to recall, replicate, manipulate, understand, or demonstrate at some point down the road—and of how the teacher will know how close a student has come to meeting that standard. Standards, in other words, are conceptually nothing new—but they did receive a new emphasis over the last decade, through state initiatives and through the passage of the Goals 2000: Educate America Act. (para. 1)

It is important to match learning objectives with the standards that are to be covered. For example, if a state standard asks that students *evaluate* their products before final submission to the teacher, then toward the conclusion of a lesson or a project, the teacher would need to have students go through a final checklist, peer check the project, or complete another activity designed to include self-evaluation as a part of the project or assignment. The best projects and lessons focus on one or two specific standards instead of trying to cover too many. Most standards are designed to be covered during a year's time. By looking at the objectives and standards, teachers develop instructional procedures, assignments, projects, and other components in their lesson plans. With these steps, learning outcomes are then easily measured through assessment. Connecting broader expectations with standards and objectives makes it easier to ensure that curricular goals are met and that students gain the essential knowledge and skills set out by the district, state, and others.

What Are Curriculum Standards, Benchmarks, and Technology Standards?

Some major educational developments during the past few decades are: (1) the pervasive impact of computers and the Internet in schools, and (2) the implementations of academic standards. Many researchers consider *A Nation at Risk* (National Commission on Excellence in Education, 1983) that was published over three decades ago as the initiating event of the modern standards movement. Later, with the passage of the *Goals 2000: Educate America Act* in 1994, U.S. lawmakers acknowledged the importance of high standards in improving education. Curriculum standards, for example, have emerged at the national level for those participating in the Common Core in order to convey the educational requirements in each subject area at each grade level that students are expected to learn and teachers are expected to teach. Again, these standards are broad statements that identify the knowledge and skills that students should acquire. The domains (or main fields) normally remain constant, but the difficulty of the content and the complexity of student work increase as the child progresses through the grade levels. This is called a spiraling curriculum in which learning is revisited but in a "wider and deeper" manner.

Each standard then provides specific information in a hierarchical view. The lowest levels of the hierarchy are offered as "benchmarks" (refer to Figure 9.1). A particular curriculum standard will contain many educational benchmarks which consist of keywords and directions that educators will use to further build their lesson plans. Benchmarks may be specific to a grade level or provide a learning target for a span of grades, such as grades

K–2. Each standard is an essential piece to ensure rigor and to challenge current student performance. Implementing curriculum standards requires a system of supports, which include benchmarks, grade-level expectations, curriculum, teacher professional development, and assessments. Most schools and school districts test students against these benchmarks so that teachers are held accountable for children to have learned the knowledge and skills set forth prior to official state testing.

An example standard with benchmarks from Technology Applications (TA) from the Texas Essential Knowledge and Skills (TEKS) for the elementary level reads:

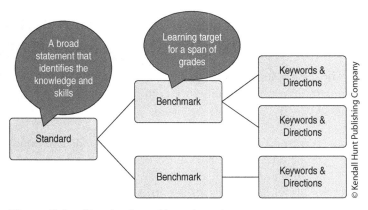

Figure 9.1 Standards and benchmarks.

Digital citizenship. The student practices safe, responsible, legal, and ethical behavior while using digital tools and resources. The student is expected to:

A. adhere to acceptable use policies (AUP) reflecting appropriate behavior in a digital environment;
B. comply with acceptable digital safety rules, fair use guidelines, and copyright laws; and
C. practice the responsible use of digital information regarding intellectual property, including software, text, images, audio, and video. (see www.ritter.tea.state.tx.us/rules/tac/chapter126/ch126a.html)

As one can see, the standard is supported by the benchmarks listed in detailed language below it.

Texas, along with Delaware, New York, and Massachusetts, were early adopters of standards. The TEKS, for example, are the state standards for what students should "know and be able to do" (Texas Education Agency, 2017a, 2017b). The TEKS include divisions for subject areas, such as English language arts, reading, mathematics, science, social studies, and, for our particular interest here, TA TEKS from kindergarten through high school levels.

National standards are created by a variety of national organizations, including the National Association for the Education of Young Children (or NAEYC), the National Council for the Social Studies (NCSS), the National Research Council (NRC), the National Council of Teachers of Mathematics (NCTM), and so forth. Unlike state standards, which all public schools in a particular state are required to use, national standards set by organizations are voluntary, and K–12 students are not officially held accountable to them (Great Schools Partnership, 2014). However, some states use national standards as guidelines for creating their own state standards or simply adopt them as state standards.

In addition to state curriculum standards and national curriculum standards of some subjects, the Common Core State Standards were launched in 2009 and now have support from 42 states, four territories, and the District of Columbia (National Governors Association Center for Best Practices and Council of Chief State School Officers, 2017). At this time, Texas, Indiana, Virginia, Minnesota, and a few other states have not adopted the Common Core Standards for various reasons, including the belief that they may have more stringent standards and may better understand their localized needs.

With the passing of No Child Left Behind (NCLB, 2001), stricter certification, higher expectations, and more stringent hiring policies for new teachers have been implemented by school districts across the nation. NCLB requires teachers to meet the criteria of "Highly Qualified Status" in subjects that they will be teaching. Standards are increasingly imperative in the practice of all teaching fields for establishing accountability for what is needed to prepare learners for their futures. In addition, NCLB, Title II Part D, or the Enhancing Education through Technology Act of 2001, requires that all teachers be technology literate and be able to integrate technology into content areas across the curriculum. More emphasis was placed on the technology literacy and integration requirements for students, teachers, and school staff so that national education could be enhanced through technology.

Why Is It Important for Beginning Teachers to Know Technology Standards?

The TEKS for TA are intended as a planning aid and a vehicle to support technology integration across the curriculum to help students develop twenty-first-century skills. In general, state curriculum standards impact teachers by:

- providing teachers with consistent goals and benchmarks to ensure students are progressing;
- providing teachers with consistent expectations for students who relocate to their districts from other states;
- providing teachers the opportunity to collaborate with other teachers as they develop curricula, materials, and assessments linked to high-quality standards;
- helping colleges of education and professional development programs to better prepare beginning teachers;
- promoting equity to ensure that all students are well prepared to collaborate and compete with their peers; and
- matching what is taught in the classroom to the standards so that students and parents will know what students should be learning and on what they will be tested.

Although improved student achievement is the most important goal, other unexpected outcomes of curriculum standards, such as teacher morale, are also important because, ultimately, they affect student achievement. Teachers should know what they expect of students so that they can more clearly plan for and address instruction with confidence.

As in the case of the International Society for Technology in Education (ISTE), many professional organizations have taken on the challenge of creating educational standards to be used on a national or, sometimes, an international level. Most states, like the state of Texas, adopt and modify these national or even international standards by soliciting the experience of teachers, subject matter experts, and leading thinkers in the field. They then incorporate evidence-based research, literature, and theories with feedback from the public (National Academy of Education, 2009, p. 8). With such close alignment as this, a beginning teacher can be assured that he or she is meeting separate state technology standards as well as national technology standards—as they are comparable (refer to Figure 9.2). A beginning teacher can normally follow one set of standards, knowing that the experts have examined all of them and merged many of them together.

Generally, TA standards describe **what** needs to be taught but not **how** to teach the content. This is important for beginning teachers to understand because each child is unique with his or her own pattern and timing of development. Teachers will need to plan curriculum to respond not only to their class as a whole but also to individual differences. Teachers are also expected to use information about typical development within a specific age span that is provided through standards and benchmarks to plan an effective learning environment and applicable experiences.

One way for states to ensure that teachers know about standards is through state certification exams. As noted, a number of questions on the state examination for teacher certification in Texas, for example, are closely related to technology (more specifically, Competency 9 of the Pedagogy and Professional Responsibilities/ PPR TExES [TEA, 2017a, 2017b, p. 14]). Prospective teachers are also expected to be capable of integrating technology skills when they walk into their first classrooms, so those who demonstrate excellent technology knowledge and skills (see Chapter 12 on e-portfolios) are in great demand in the hiring market.

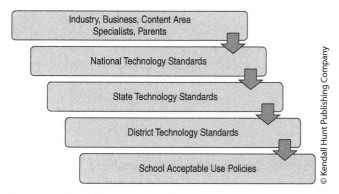

Figure 9.2 A flow chart on how the standards are developed.

© Kendall Hunt Publishing Company

Hopefully, beginning teachers will use the international, national, state, districts, and/or school technology standards as a foundation to implement their curricula. Many districts and organizations have lesson plans that provide excellent ideas for these types of activities, but they do not necessarily make sure that each teacher implements them (other than through the lesson plans they have turned in to administrators). It is every teacher's responsibility to do so. By using the required standards and many ideas already generated as resources, teachers can create solid objectives for their lessons; thus, students will learn the way they should learn for their individual needs and to prepare for the world ahead. Mrs. Brown, in the case scenario above, made copies of the various standards for her students' level so that she could cross-reference them and apply them to her plans. She noted that many were similar, but it helped to make some notes as she began to think ahead about her long-range plans for the year. Knowing exactly what was expected from the various experts helped her feel confident that she was preparing her students in the best possible ways.

National Educational Technology Standards

Computer technology has germinated, evolved, and advanced for more than four decades, but classrooms are often left behind because of initial cost and professional development for teachers. Teaching and learning need to change as society changes to match the needs of the workforce and social uses that are so much a part of the world today. These necessities address the demands of a wide base of affected adopters for using classroom information, and communications technology has emerged accordingly.

To examine more of the "big picture" of how these standards work, we can see that one way of ensuring that schools stay up to date is to have the national and/or state governments or influential organizations establish specific goals and directives pertaining to their focus (mathematics, science, etc.). Most of these types of standards ask teachers to integrate technology with a specific content area, but there are standards that center on technology alone as well. With this in mind, schools understand what skills and knowledge their students should have from the frameworks recommended by experts in the industry, education, and other fields (see Figure 9.2). The National Educational Technology Standards (NETS), for example, come from the ISTE. The American Association of School Librarians (ALA) also provides Information Literacy Standards for Student Learning (ILSSL) to help students become skillful producers and consumers of information. The International Technology Education Association (ITEA) provides Standards for Technological Literacy, which is intended to help educators define and recognize quality technology instruction. Among the three entities (ISTE, ALA, and ITEA), ISTE has the most commonly referred to set of standards (NETS) in schools and colleges of education across the United States and even worldwide for technology.

The standards for using computer technology in schools were first developed in the 1980s (Roblyer, 2000). Based on Bitter (as cited in Roblyer, 2000, p. 134), "some states set their own computer literacy standards, and various national groups recommended that students should learn some computer skills at each grade level." Later, ISTE has "worked in conjunction with the National Council for the Accreditation of Teacher Education (NCATE) to generate standards and a vision statement for how teacher education programs should address technology" (Roblyer, 2000, p. 135). ISTE provides a list of standards that are applied to learning, teaching, and leading in a technological society (see Tables 9.1 and 9.2). These offer teachers a framework for integrating technology in teaching and learning.

The first ISTE Standards for Students was released in 1998 under the name NETS. It focused on technology skills for students, while the second version was released in 2007 where the focus changed to integration of technology in the classroom. The ubiquitous access of today's technology requires distinct kinds of learning. The 2016 version aims to "develop lifelong learners" (Snelling, 2016).

By reviewing the ISTE Standards for students and teachers, it is noticeable that simply being able to use technology is no longer sufficient. Today's students should be able to use technology to analyze, learn, and explore. Digital skills are vital for preparing students to work, live, and contribute to today's society.

While knowing how to use the technology is still important, it is no longer the primary focus of the standards. The standards provide teachers with more guidance on assigning tasks that are authentic and relevant to learners,

Question 1

Table 9.1   ISTE Standards for Students (2016)

1.	Empowered Learner	Students leverage technology to take an active role in choosing, achieving, and demonstrating competency in their learning goals, informed by the learning sciences.
2.	Digital Citizen	Students recognize the rights, responsibilities and opportunities of living, learning and working in an interconnected digital world, and they act and model in ways that are safe, legal, and ethical.
3.	Knowledge Constructor	Students critically curate a variety of resources using digital tools to construct knowledge, produce creative artifacts, and make meaningful learning experiences for themselves and others.
4.	Innovative Designer	Students use a variety of technologies within a design process to identify and solve problems by creating new, useful, or imaginative solutions.
5.	Computational Thinker	Students develop and employ strategies for understanding and solving problems in ways that leverage the power of technological methods to develop and test solutions.
6.	Creative Communicator	Students communicate clearly and express themselves creatively for a variety of purposes using the platforms, tools, styles, formats, and digital media appropriate to their goals.
7.	Global Collaborator	Students use digital tools to broaden their perspectives and enrich their learning by collaborating with others and working effectively in teams locally and globally.

Source: www.iste.org/standards/standards/for-students

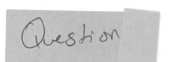

Question

Table 9.2   ISTE Standards for Educators (2017)

Learner	Educators continually improve their practice by learning from and with others and exploring proven and promising practices that leverage technology to improve student learning.
Leader	Educators seek out opportunities for leadership to support student empowerment and success and to improve teaching and learning.
Citizen	Educators inspire students to positively contribute to and responsibly participate in the digital world.
Collaborator	Educators dedicate time to collaborate with both colleagues and students to improve practice, discover and share resources and ideas, and solve problems.
Designer	Educators design authentic, learner-driven activities and environments that recognize and accommodate learner variability
Facilitator	Educators facilitate learning with technology to support student achievement of the ISTE Standards for Students.
Analyst	Educators understand and use data to drive their instruction and support students in achieving their learning goals.

Source: www.iste.org/standards/standards/for-educators

where tools and skills are a means to a purposeful end (see Figure 9.3). They emphasize the process of student learning over a continuum with rich and authentic assessment tools, resources, and standards-aligned content and curriculum to measure multiple levels and styles of learning. They seem to place emphasis on creativity and globalization, communication, collaboration, problem-solving, and decision-making. Teachers are expected to encourage students to look at real-world problems and use technology tools to solve them. Students are expected to be given more opportunities and take responsibility for their own learning that is meaningful to their lives.

Overall, the standards reflect twenty-first-century learning skills and appear to be very specific and measurable. There is a great focus on application and communication using technology within the global society. As of 2017, the ISTE Standards are used throughout the world and by educators in all 50 U.S. states (Snelling, 2016).

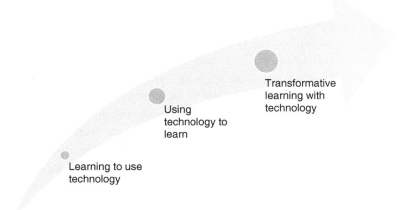

Figure 9.3 The ISTE Standards for Students evolved from learning to use technology to transformative learning with technology over two decades.
Source: Based on www.k12blueprint.com/news/new-iste-standards-students

State Technology Application Standards for Students and Teachers

States and school districts can also determine goals and standards that teachers and students must reach (see Figure 9.4). For instance, in Texas, it is important for teachers to be familiar with these resources: (a) Texas Long-Range Plan for Technology (LRPT), 2006–2020 (TEA, 2006a); (b) School Technology and Readiness Chart (STaR Chart) (TEA, 2006b); and (c) TA TEKS (TEA, 2017a, 2017b).

The passing of the federal NCLB Act in 2001 led to the 2002 update to the Long-Range Plan for Technology, 1996–2010 (TEA, 2006a) to make sure Texas goals and objectives were aligned with the federal plan. In view of the quick advances of information technology, Texas once again updated the Long-Range Plan for Technology, 2006–2020 in 2006 to set new strategies for all school districts in response. An electronic resource allows districts and charter schools to prepare and submit a technology plan to the state for review and approval in a completely online process called an ePlan.

Figure 9.4 The standards establish what students need to learn but do not dictate how teachers should teach. Decisions on how to implement standards are often made by classroom teachers.

An online resource tool called the Texas STaR Chart is used to assist Texas teachers in self-assessing efforts to effectively integrate technology across the curriculum (TEA, 2006b). The STaR Chart focuses on four areas of Long-Range Plan for Technology, 2006–2020: (a) teaching and learning; (b) educator preparation and development; (c) leadership, administration, and instructional support; and (d) infrastructure for technology. One can access the charts at: www.txstarchart.org/.

While Technology Applications Standards for All Teachers (see Table 9.3) are expected of **all** Texas teachers, Technology Applications Standards for All Beginning Teachers (see Table 9.4) are expected of **all** beginning Texas teachers. Both sets of standards are incorporated into the Texas Examination of Educator Standards (TExES) PPR test.

Table 9.3 Technology Applications Standards for All Teachers (in Texas)

Technology Applications Standards for All Teachers

Standard I. All teachers use technology-related terms, concepts, data input strategies, and ethical practices to make informed decisions about current technologies and their applications.

Standard II. All teachers identify task requirements, apply search strategies, and use current technology to efficiently acquire, analyze, and evaluate a variety of electronic information.

Standard III. All teachers use task-appropriate tools to synthesize knowledge, create and modify solutions, and evaluate results in a way that supports the work of individuals and groups in problem-solving situations.

Standard IV. All teachers communicate information in different formats and for diverse audiences.

Standard V. All teachers know how to plan, organize, deliver, and evaluate instruction for all students that incorporates the effective use of current technology for teaching and integrating the Technology Applications Texas Essential Knowledge and Skills (TEKS) into the curriculum.

Source: www.tea.texas.gov/WorkArea/linkit.aspx?LinkIdentifier=id&ItemID=2147484175&libID=2147484174

Table 9.4 Technology Applications Standards for All Beginning Teachers (in Texas)

Standard I. All teachers use and promote creative thinking and innovative processes to construct knowledge, generate new ideas, and create products.

Standard II. All teachers collaborate and communicate both locally and globally using digital tools and resources to reinforce and promote learning.

Standard III. All teachers acquire, analyze, and manage content from digital resources.

Standard IV. All teachers make informed decisions by applying critical-thinking and problem-solving skills.

Standard V. All teachers practice and promote safe, responsible, legal, and ethical behavior while using technology tools and resources.

Standard VI. All teachers demonstrate a thorough understanding of technology concepts, systems, and operations.

Standard VII. All teachers know how to plan, organize, deliver, and evaluate instruction for all students that incorporates the effective use of current technology for teaching and integrating the Technology Applications Texas Essential Knowledge and Skills (TEKS) into the curriculum.

Source: www.tea.texas.gov/WorkArea/linkit.aspx?LinkIdentifier=id&ItemID=51539612985&libID=51539612985

The Performance Descriptions of the STaR Chart categorize teachers' technology skills into (a) early technology level, (b) developing technology level, (c) advanced technology level, and (d) target technology level. The system assists the state and districts in the measurement of efforts to improve student learning through the use of technology. It helps schools identify needs for ongoing professional development and raise awareness of research-based instructional goals. It also assists teachers in assessing needs and setting goals for the use of technology in the classroom to support student achievement. More details can be found at: www.txstarchart.org/standards.html.

TA TEKS for Students from the Kindergarten to the 12th Grade

As noted, many states have developed their own set of TA for students based on ISTE Standards. The TA curriculum developed in Texas, for example, has the following six strands:

- Creativity and innovation;
- Communication and collaboration;
- Research and information fluency;
- Critical thinking, problem-solving, and decision-making;
- Digital citizenship; and
- Technology operations and concepts.

The latest Chapter 126 TEKS (available at www.ritter.tea.state.tx.us/rules/tac/chapter126/ch126b.html) contains subchapters for the elementary level, the middle school level, the high school level, and other TA courses.

Integrating Appropriate Technology Applications

In addition to national and state standards, future teachers are expected to become familiar with what "developmentally appropriate" means in terms of technology through professional organizations such as NAEYC, NCSS, NRC, and NCTM. The national councils of these organizations each make recommendations regarding technology use for their content area. Central to their recommendations is the concept that development and learning are influenced by multiple social and cultural contexts. Knowing what is typical at each age and stage of development is crucial. This knowledge helps teachers decide which experiences are best for learning and development, so it is essential for teachers to note the following three important concepts:

Question 3

Developmentally appropriate practice (or DAP). Teachers use knowledge about child development to create a program that is suitable for the age and stage of development as well as the individual needs of children. (See Chapter 5 in this book for further information on the use of technology with young children.)

Age-appropriate practice. Teachers use information about typical development within a specific age span to plan a learning environment and experience.

Individually appropriate practice. Teachers understand each child is unique with his or her own pattern and timing of development.

Individual Appropriateness

Developmental Appropriateness ⟷ Age Appropriateness

© Kendall Hunt Publishing Company

Figure 9.5 The three anchors of appropriate technology applications.

Technology also offers options for students with special needs. Some of these students may benefit from the less constrained and more engaging task situations possible with computers and other assistive technologies. Students with physical challenges can become much more engaged in learning using assistive technologies. When planning technology-based activities for students with high-incidence disabilities, it is important to consider how the learning will be structured and how much direction and guidance should be given to a student (Wong & Law, 2016). (See Chapter 6 for further information on the use of technology with children who have special needs.)

As noted, the Texas legislation requires that all students should be technology literate by the time they leave the eighth grade. In the years preceding the eighth grade, students may need instruction and support to use these skills, although many students will be able to perform the skills ahead of the target years. Teachers must, however, remember that children come from many backgrounds which may not have provided them with early access to technology.

Joe Salinas was a teacher candidate who was excited to begin his semester with fourth graders. He was currently involved in his fieldwork as a university senior and was asked to teach several lessons by his teacher education program. As he opened a conversation about planning the science lesson, his mentor teacher reminded him to include technology. He began to ask himself, "How do I know what fourth graders ought to be taught in technology?" When he asked his mentor this question, she told him that, luckily, the experts had researched it well and provided them with standards. In addition, the district provided them with benchmarks. She gave him the Websites, and he began to put together the science content with the technology. When he taught the lesson, he felt like the match had been a good one. Students were challenged but successful in both areas.

Chris Howey / Shutterstock.com

Best Practices of Integrating Technology Standards

While national technology standards set goals, as noted, they do not define how the standards should be taught or which materials should be used to support students because local needs and support for technology vary. It is up to the states to define the full range of support appropriate for these students. States and localities often take different approaches to implementing the standards and providing their teachers with the support they need to help students successfully reach the standards. However, decisions on how to implement the standards are most often made by classroom teachers. Teachers usually know about what works well in their classrooms for their particular students (Dean, Hubbell, & Pitler, 2012). This is a rationale of why the standards establish what students need to learn but do not dictate how teachers should teach. Instead, schools and teachers decide how best to help students reach the standards. Again, TA standards describe **what** needs to be taught but not **how** to teach the content. Teachers are expected to use information about typical development within a specific age span provided through standards and benchmarks to plan a suitable learning environment and applicable experiences for their classrooms, although the [illegible]y online) to support them.

Question 4

Very Young Children

When used intentionally and appropriately, technology and interactive media are effective tools to support learning and development (see Figure 9.8). NAEYC is the organization that offers key messages for teachers of young children (see Table 9.5). NAEYC has suggestions for effective classroom practice for preschoolers and kindergarteners in terms of using technology tools and interactive media. NAEYC's Key Messages (2012b) for technology and interactive media serve as tools in early childhood programs for children from birth through age 8.

For very young children, play is an important vehicle to develop self-regulation and promote language, cognition, and social competence. Children's experiences shape their motivation and approaches to learning. When children are appropriately challenged, development and learning advance. Baby software, designed for children ages 6 months to 2 years old, is nicknamed "lapware" because the parent holds the child while he or she plays (see Figure 9.6). Baby software lets tiny fingers "whack away" at the keyboard without destroying data (see Figure 9.7). Most lapware programs reward babies or toddlers for doing what comes naturally by responding with a variety of sounds and dancing shapes whenever they touch the keys (see Figure 9.9). It teaches them cause and effect, which is important for babies and young children to grasp.

For the many benefits of technology, there are also some concerns for its use with young children. Excessive screen time is linked to a host of childhood problems, including poor school performance, attention issues, sleep disturbance, obesity, and more (Gray et al., 2015; Page, Cooper, Griew, & Jago, 2010). Mobile touch devices and screen devices are so omnipresent that it is becoming harder for parents and teachers alike to figure out how and when to set limits. Because the explosion of smartphones and tablets is relatively new, most of the research on the harmful effects of technology on young children is associated with television, but emerging studies are beginning to raise concerns about the time and appropriate use of smartphones, iPads, tablets, and other types of digital media (Page et al., 2010) (see Figure 9.10). Teachers stay vigilant on these issues and keep up on the latest research for best practices. Chapter 5 in this book offers more details about technology use with young children.

Table 9.5 NAEYC's Key Messages for Technology and Early Childhood Programs

NAEYC's Key Messages for technology and early childhood programs
• When used intentionally and appropriately, technology and interactive media are effective tools to support learning and development. • Intentional use requires early childhood teachers and administrators to have information and resources regarding the nature of these tools and the implications of their use with children. • Limitations on the use of technology and media are important. • Special considerations must be given to the use of technology with infants and toddlers. • Attention to digital citizenship and equitable access is essential. • Ongoing research and professional development are needed.

Figure 9.6 An example of "lapware."

Figure 9.7 The finger of a toddler selecting the correct letter on a touchscreen tablet with learning software.

Figure 9.8 Toddler and children focusing on the computer.

Figure 9.9 A cartoon robot asks children to write text on the board.

Figure 9.10 *Little Red Riding Hood* in digital format.

Although the American Academy of Pediatrics recommends that children under age 2 avoid TV and computer screens, the goal can be unrealistic in practice because TVs, DVD, video games, PCs, and telephones fill our lives as well as those of children. Some educators tend to be cautious of using technology for babies and toddlers because the child is, too often, a passive observer of the action (see Figure 9.11). Manufacturers of digital media for young children distance their products from video and television by marketing educational apps and games as "educational", but Goodwin and Highfield (2012) found that only 4% of the apps marketed as educational for young children promote open-ended and constructive learning.

It is of great importance that teachers use resources and information to carefully evaluate equipment or software that they already have available or that they request. There are rating systems for movies (Motion Picture Association of America) and video games (Entertainment Software Rating Board), which are tools for parents and educators when deciding if the content is appropriate for their children, but there is still not a universal rating system for software applications and tools. Some organizations such as Common Sense Media offer Certified App Review Programs where they review apps for Apple and Android platforms. Parents can set ground rules for children with Google's Family Link app. Teachers can have parents view lists of approved applications from these institutes when picking media resources.

The NAEYC (2012a) also recommends that young children explore digital materials in the context of human interactions with an adult as mediator and co-player (see Figure 9.12). As with shared book reading, teachers use shared technology time as an opportunity to talk with children, use new vocabulary, and model appropriate use. Most educators agree that unlike software for preschoolers that aims to teach reading, numbers, or other complex skills, software for young children is meant to be simply fun, and it is not designed to be a substitute for play between parent and child.

Figure 9.11   An example of passive screen time.

Figure 9.12   Teacher as a co-player.

Miss Clay, a daycare teacher, understands that during the earliest years, infants and toddlers interact primarily with people. Whenever technology tools are used, she makes sure to allow children to explore digital materials with an adult as mediator and/or a co-player. Her young children are drawn to push-button switches and controls. The classroom is surrounded by toys and technology tools that infants and toddlers might use that are safe, sturdy, and not easily damaged.

As with shared book reading, Mrs. Clay uses shared technology time as an opportunity to talk with children, use new vocabulary, and model appropriate use. Since children need to freely explore and try out everything in the environment in the early years in today's world, this includes the exploration of technology tools and interactive media.

In the daily classroom and at school events such as parents' nights, Miss Clay is always there, holding her cameras to make digital audio or video files to document her students' progress. She is often able to share examples of children's growth with parents.

She uses technology as an active and engaging tool to provide toddlers with access to images of their families, friends, animals, objects in their environment, and a wide range of different images of people and things they might not otherwise encounter. Among her favorite activities is sharing her collection of photos of children from other countries.

Miss Clay tries to avoid passive screen time for toddlers in her class. She does not think that infants and toddlers learn from docilely watching videos. She also believes that if infants are distressed, they need the comfort of a caring adult, not an electronic toy.

She noticed that some of her students watched videos for hours at home. She works toward persuading parents not to use TVs or videos for hours as a baby-sitting tool. Instead, parents should mediate or play digital materials with very young children to provide human interactions.

How does she persuade busy parents not to allow children watch TVs or videos for hours as a baby-sitting tool?

Kindergarten through Eighth-Grade Students

Most states start their curriculum framework and technology standards from the kindergarten year and, again, require that all students should be technology literate by the time they leave the eighth grade. These states publish specific guidelines which are intended as a planning aid and a vehicle to support technology integration across the curriculum to help students develop twenty-first-century digital knowledge and skills.

Table 9.6 Category Comparison between Computer Literacy and Technology Applications

Categories of Computer Literacy	Categories of Technology Applications
• Email and Internet • Network and computing skills • Word processing • Graphics and presentation • Spreadsheets and databases	• Creativity and innovation • Communication and collaboration • Research and information fluency • Critical thinking, problem-solving, and decision-making • Digital citizenship • Technology operations and concepts

As might be expected, different entities may view concepts in different ways. Some states define the "twenty-first-century digital knowledge and skills" as a set of basic computer literacy, while others describe the skills as TA skills (see Figure 9.13 and Table 9.6). Both act as a key for the students of today and tomorrow. Fluency with TAs may require more intellectual abilities than the rote learning of software and hardware associated with computer literacy, but the focus is still on the technology itself (ALA, 2017). This section will first discuss the skills from the computer literacy perspective and continue the discussion from the TA perspective.

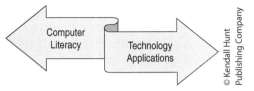

Figure 9.13 Two views of "Twenty-first-century Digital Knowledge and Skills."

© Kendall Hunt Publishing Company

Many states view twenty-first-century digital knowledge and skills as **basic computer literacy,** and they publish computer skills scopes and sequences that represent reasonable expectations of student skills that they expect all educators to make a part of how their classroom functions to improve student learning. The states and districts that view twenty-first-century digital knowledge and skills as **basic computer literacy** provide specific information in the following five computer literacy areas shown above in Table 9.6:

• Email and Internet
• Network and computing skills
• Word processing
• Graphics and presentations
• Spreadsheets and databases

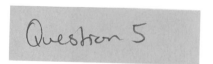

In the area of **email and Internet**, from the kindergarten year through the eighth grade, students grow from: following a Web link; using the browser; using Internet bookmarks; creating bookmarks; sending and replying to email; sending and reading attachments; and managing address books. They move on to evaluating search tools, finding information and using appropriate search strategies, and, finally, to assessing the quality of Internet resources.

In the area of **network and computing skills**, from the kindergarten year through the eighth grade, students develop skills from starting up and shutting down a computer and handling CDs and other media to logging on to the network. They continue with launching programs, copying and pasting between windows, switching among open windows, and managing directories to navigating file systems and local area networks. They complete basic troubleshooting skills by the eighth grade.

In the area of **word processing**, from the kindergarten year through the eighth grade, students improve skills from keying in letters and sentences, editing by inserting and deleting letters, and formatting text (e.g., changing sizes, fonts, colors, cutting, formatting page layout with margins and tabs, adding headers and footers). They progress to using outline tools for prewriting purpose and using a combination of tools to create publication quality documents.

In the area of **graphics and presentations**, from the kindergarten year to the eighth grade, students grow from drawing using computer programs, taking pictures using digital cameras, inserting clip art, creating multimedia presentations, and importing pictures to using appropriate animations or transition to enhance presentations. They move to being able to create self-timing presentations, save graphics in a variety of format, and capture and utilize digitized videos.

Mrs. Rodriquez's preschool students are curious about the world around them and about learning. They are finding out their ability to create and communicate using crayons, markers, and their bodies to represent ideas and experiences. In addition to crayons, markers, paints (and other art materials), blocks, dramatic play materials, and miniature life figures, Mrs. Rodriquez uses digital technologies to provide her preschool students one more outlet for them to demonstrate their creativity and learning. Most of her students are eager to use the two tablets and one desktop she has in the classroom to explore touch screens loaded with a developmentally appropriate interactive media.

Han, a student who comes from a lower socioeconomic status (SES) family with several siblings, is not eager to use the tablets. Mrs. Rodriquez notices that Han has not developed the fine motor skills of coordinating the small muscle movements of his fingers in coordination with his eyes when using the computer mouse and keyboard.

Mrs. Rodriquez allows Han a little more computer time to provide opportunities for him to explore and feel comfortable using a traditional mouse and keyboard.

Keyboarding is a foundational skill largely related to motor skills. The standards Mrs. Rodriquez looked up indicate that based on the child's developmental readiness, it may be appropriate to begin keyboarding training in grades 2–4.

Is it too early to "correct" Han's mouse and keyboarding problems? What else can Mrs. Rodriquez do to bridge the digital gap for preschool students like Han?

In the area of **spreadsheets and databases**, from the kindergarten year through the eighth grade, students begin early by locating data in a spreadsheet or a chart, being able to enter data, and locating a spreadsheet cell by its column and row. Students move forward to being able to insert simple calculations, create formulas, format data, print spreadsheets, use absolute and relative addressing, and differentiate between records and fields in a database.

It is hoped that future teachers will begin to grasp the general scope and sequence of teaching technology to children. Again, these scopes and sequences are aligned with state technology standards, which are then aligned with ISTE standards. Teachers need to integrate directly or indirectly each of the stated skills into lessons in ways that are appropriate. Similar to other content areas, individual learners may need remediation and/or challenge. If a student does not have the knowledge and skills he or she should have obtained in earlier levels, the teacher must make sure that a foundation is established before going on. If a learner has already mastered the standards well, the teacher should provide accelerated instruction.

In addition to the five computer literacy areas discussed above, keyboarding and the teaching of the ethical, human, and social issues are two areas that need teachers' attention. Keyboarding is considered a foundational skill largely related to motor skills (see Figure 9.14). Most states recommend that it is appropriate to begin keyboarding training in grades 2–4, based on the child's developmental readiness. Therefore, Mrs. Rodriquez may want to wait until later to enhance Han's keyboarding skills, as he may not be developmentally ready as a preschool student. Most states

Figure 9.14 When using a mouse, the small muscle movements of a child's fingers coordinate with eyes.

also suggested that the ethical, human, and social issues related to uses of technology should be addressed as appropriate each time they arise in the classroom. More about this area will be addressed in Chapter 10. Educators are to model and practice Internet safety at all times.

As mentioned earlier, Table 9.6 illustrates how "twenty-first-century digital knowledge and skills" can be viewed by some states as basic computer literacy skills, while other states describe the skills as TA knowledge. An analysis of the more recently required technology competencies of Texas and a number of states reveals an emphasis by some on **TA** over **computer literacy**. Fluency with applications requires more intellectual abilities than the rote learning of software and hardware associated with computer literacy. According to the American Library Association (2017),

> "Fluency" with information technology may require more intellectual abilities than the rote learning of software and hardware associated with "computer literacy," but the focus is still on the technology itself. Information literacy, on the other hand, is an intellectual framework for understanding, finding, evaluating, and using information—activities which may be accomplished in part by fluency with information technology, in part by sound investigative methods, but most important, through critical discernment and reasoning. Information literacy initiates, sustains, and extends lifelong learning through abilities which may use technologies but are ultimately independent of them. (para. 11)

Individuals are faced with abundant information choices in their academic studies, in the workplace, and in their personal lives.

> The uncertain quality and expanding quantity of information pose large challenges for society. The sheer abundance of information will not in and of itself create a more informed citizen without a complementary cluster of abilities necessary to use information effectively. (ALA, 2017, para. 6)

In view of the complexity of information applications, Texas (and other states) design its curriculum framework and standards from the perspective of **TA**. The TA curriculum (TA TEKS) starts with the kindergarten year and requires, as many of these do, that all students should be technology literate by the time they leave the eighth grade. Texas, like most states, publishes specific guidelines which are intended as a planning aid and a vehicle to support technology integration across the curriculum to help students develop tomorrow's digital knowledge and skills.

Table 9.7 illustrates the growing expectations of the TA TEKS in terms of **creativity and innovation** through various age ranges. Note that in the creativity and innovation strand of the TA TEKS, students in K–5, according to the spiral curriculum, are expected to create original products using a variety of resources, while students in the sixth grade are expected to **add personal and group expressions** to their work. Students in the seventh grade add **presentation of their work,** in addition to the expectations for the sixth-grade students. Furthermore, eighth-grade students are expected to also **publish their work** as a supplement to the expectations of the sixth- and seventh-grade students.

Table 9.7 Expectations of Creativity and Innovation Competencies for K–8 Students

	Kindergarten-Grade 2	Grades 3–5	6th Grade	7th Grade	8th Grade
(1) Creativity and innovation.	(B) Create original products using a variety of resources;	(A) Create original products using a variety of resources;	(B) Create original works as a means of personal or group expression;	(B) Create and present original works as a means of personal or group expression;	(B) Create, present, and publish original works as a means of personal or group expression;

Note: Adapted from "Chapter 126. Texas Essential Knowledge and Skills for Technology Applications" by L. Chen in 2017. Copyright 2017 by Texas Education Agency.

Table 9.8   Communication and Collaboration Expectations Within Technology Standards for K–8 Students

	Kindergarten-Grade 2	Grades 3–5	6th Grade	7th Grade	8th Grade
(2) Communication and collaboration.	(C) Format digital information, including font attributes, color, white space, graphics, and animation, for a defined audience and communication medium.	(C) Collaborate effectively through personal learning communities and social environments.	(C) Read and discuss examples of technical writing.	(C) Create products using technical writing strategies.	(C) Create and publish products using technical writing strategies.

Note: Adapted from "Chapter 126. Texas Essential Knowledge and Skills for Technology Applications" by L. Chen in 2017. Copyright 2017 by Texas Education Agency.

Table 9.8 shows the growing expectations of TA TEKS in terms of **communication and collaboration** through various age ranges. Note that in the communication and collaboration strand of the TA TEKS, students in K–2 are expected to **format digital information** for a defined audience, and students in grades 3 through 5 are expected to **collaborate** effectively through personal learning communities and social environments. Later, in the sixth grade, students are expected to read and **discuss technical writing**. Technical writing is a written form of professional communication used in a variety of technical and occupational fields, such as engineering, health science, chemistry, finance, and biotechnology. On that foundation, students in the seventh grade should begin to **create products** using technical writing strategies. Furthermore, eighth-grade students are expected to also **publish** their work as a supplement to the expectations of the sixth- and seventh-grade students.

Table 9.9 highlights the growing expectations of the TA TEKS in terms of **research and information fluency** through various age ranges. Note that in this strand, K–2 students are expected to **manage information** to build a knowledge base regarding a task, and students in grades 3 through 5 are expected to **collect and organize information** from a variety of formats, including text, audio, video, and graphics. Students in the sixth grade should be able to **discuss and use search strategies**, including keyword(s) and Boolean operators in addition to the expectations for the grades 3 to 5 students. On that foundation, students in the seventh grade should be able to **evaluate** various search strategies in addition to using search strategies.

As for communication and collaboration, seventh-grade students **create personal learning networks** to collaborate and publish with peers, experts, or others by using digital tools such as blogs, wikis, audio/video

Table 9.9   Research and information Fluency Expectations Within Technology Standards for K–8 Students

	Kindergarten-Grade 2	Grades 3–5	6th Grade	7th Grade	8th Grade
(3) Research and information fluency.	(B) Use research skills to build a knowledge base regarding a topic, task, or assignment;	(B) Collect and organize information from a variety of formats, including text, audio, video, and graphics;	(B) Discuss and use various search strategies, including keyword(s) and Boolean operators;	(B) Use and evaluate various search strategies, including keyword(s) and Boolean operators;	(B) Plan, use, and evaluate various search strategies, including keyword(s) and Boolean operators;

Note: Adapted from "Chapter 126. Texas Essential Knowledge and Skills for Technology Applications" by L. Chen in 2017. Copyright 2017 by Texas Education Agency.

(rather than simply participating in those activities). They are able to form technical writing strategies when creating products instead of simply creating and discussing the products. They **use and evaluate** various search strategies, including keyword(s) and Boolean operators, rather than simply discussing and using various search strategies as most sixth-grade students do. Eighth-grade students are expected to also **plan** their search strategies in addition to using and evaluating search strategies. In the tables below, one can see how the standards advance in difficulty through the grade levels.

Nathan, a third grader, watched how his brother, who goes to a community college, uses digital technologies at home. Nathan emulates the usage, first through imitation, and then later he does not even have to count on his brother's help, for example, in using apps from his cell phone or doing things on the Internet.

Nathan loves to go to school. Among all things, he likes how his teacher, Mr. Washington, provides digital microscopes and other digital tools for science investigation and how he installs geometry software that allows the class to explore the concept of shape by stretching, bending, shrinking, or combining images. Like most third graders, Nathan does not like drill and practice. Nathan has found that on the days they have technology, he is more excited than ever to be at school.

What do the standards mean to Nathan?

Table 9.10 summarizes the expectations of TA TEKS in terms of **critical thinking, problem-solving, and decision-making** through various age ranges. Note that in this strand, K–2 students are expected to identify **what is known and unknown and what needs to be known** regarding a problem and **explain the steps to solve the problem**; **evaluate** the appropriateness of a digital tool to achieve the desired product; and **evaluate** products prior to final submission.

Table 9.10 Critical Thinking, Problem-solving, and Decision-making Expectations Within Technology Standards for K–8 Students

	Kindergarten-Grade 2	Grades 3–5	6th Grade	7th Grade	8th Grade
(4) Critical thinking, problem-solving, and decision-making.	(A) Identify what is known and unknown and what needs to be known regarding a problem and explain the steps to solve the problem;	(A) Identify information regarding a problem and explain the steps toward the solution;	(A) Identify and define relevant problems and significant questions for investigation;	(A) Identify and define relevant problems and significant questions for investigation;	(A) Identify and define relevant problems and significant questions for investigation;

Note: Adapted from "Chapter 126. Texas Essential Knowledge and Skills for Technology Applications" by L. Chen in 2017. Copyright 2017 by Texas Education Agency.

Students in grades 3 through 5 are expected to identify information regarding a problem and explain the steps toward the solution like K–2 students. They should also be able to **collect, analyze,** and **represent** data to solve problems using tools and **evaluate technology tools** applicable for solving problems.

Mr. Washington provides simple digital microscopes and other digital tools for science investigation (see Figure 9.15). As noted, he installs geometry software that allows Nathan's third-grade class to explore the concept of shape by stretching, bending, shrinking, or combining images. These science and math investigation tools are used by students to collect, analyze, and represent data to solve problems, and these practices are aligned with TA TEKS. By complying with standards such as the TA TEKS, Mr. Washington offers lessons that are motivating and developmentally appropriate in Nathan's class.

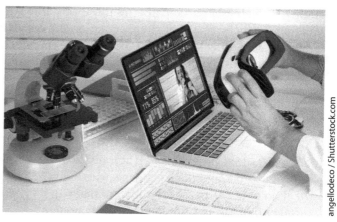

Figure 9.15 Laptop, microscope, and other tools for science investigation.

Students' **critical thinking, problem-solving,** and **decision-making skills** in the sixth grade are to plan and manage activities to develop a solution, design a computer program, or complete a project; **collect** and **analyze** data to identify solutions and make informed decisions; **use multiple processes** and **diverse perspectives** to explore alternative solutions; **make informed decisions** and **support reasoning;** and **transfer current knowledge** to the learning of newly encountered technologies. Students' critical thinking, problem-solving, and decision-making skills mature in the sixth grade and are refined in the seventh and throughout the eighth grade. In other words, students should all be literate with problem-solving and critical-thinking skills by the time they leave the sixth grade.

As Table 9.11 illustrates, children's **digital citizenship responsibilities** grow along with ages as well. Note that in the digital citizenship strand of the TA TEKS, students in kindergarten through the second grade are expected to **adhere to AUP,** reflecting appropriate behavior in a digital environment. As they grow older, from the third grade through the fifth grade, students are to adhere to AUP, reflecting **positive social behavior** in the digital environment. In addition to being expected to adhere to AUP, students starting in the sixth grade are asked to also **understand** copyright principles, including current laws, fair use guidelines, creative commons, open source, and public domain. Students starting in the seventh grade are asked to understand and **practice** copyright principles, including current fair use guidelines, creative commons, open source, and public domain, while students starting in the eighth grade are expected to also understand, **explain**, and practice copyright principles, including current laws, fair use guidelines, creative commons, open source, and public domain.

Table 9.11 Digital Citizenship Within Technology Standards for K–8 Students

	Kindergarten–Grade 2	Grades 3–5	6th Grade	7th Grade	8th Grade
(5) Digital citizenship.	(A) Adhere to acceptable use policies reflecting appropriate behavior in a digital environment;	(A) Adhere to acceptable use policies reflecting positive social behavior in the digital environment;	(A) Understand copyright principles, including current laws, fair use guidelines, creative commons, open source, and public domain;	(A) Understand and practice copyright principles, including current fair use guidelines, creative commons, open source, and public domain;	(A) Understand, explain, and practice copyright principles, including current laws, fair use guidelines, creative commons, open source, and public domain;

Note: Adapted from "Chapter 126. Texas Essential Knowledge and Skills for Technology Applications" by L. Chen in 2017. Copyright 2017 by Texas Education Agency.

Table 9.12 Technology Operations and Concepts Within Technology Standards for K–8 Students

	Kindergarten-Grade 2	Grades 3–5	6th Grade	7th Grade	8th Grade
(6) Technology operations and concepts.	(A) Use appropriate terminology regarding basic hardware, software applications, programs, networking, virtual environments, and emerging technologies;	(A) Demonstrate an understanding of technology concepts, including terminology for the use of operating systems, network systems, virtual systems, and learning systems appropriate for grades 3–5 learning;	(A) Define and use current technology terminology appropriately;	(A) Define and use current technology terminology appropriately;	(A) Define and use current technology terminology appropriately;

Note: Adapted from "Chapter 126. Texas Essential Knowledge and Skills for Technology Applications" by L. Chen in 2017. Copyright 2017 by Texas Education Agency.

As Table 9.12 illustrates, children's **technology operations and concepts** grow along with ages as well. Knowing and using basic technology terms is also expected. From kindergarten through the second grade, students should be able to **use appropriate technology terms** such as hardware and software and use appropriate tools for input, output, and storage. They know how to **open** an application and **create, modify, print, and save** files (see Figure 9.16). They also know how to use the online "help" function and demonstrate basic keyboarding skills (see Figure 9.17). School-aged children can **evaluate** the usefulness of acquired digital content. They can use simple **search strategies** to access information regarding a topic and develop habits to adhere to **AUP** reflecting appropriate behavior in a digital environment.

According to the TA TEKS, older children, from the third through the sixth grades, should be able to follow the rules of digital etiquette; respect the intellectual property of others; use search strategies such as keywords and the Boolean identifiers *and*, *or*, and *not* and other strategies appropriate to specific search engines; validate and evaluate the relevance and appropriateness of information; draft, edit, manipulate files using appropriate file management system; and publish products in different media individually and collaboratively. They should also be able to troubleshoot minor technical problems with hardware and software using online "help".

The sixth-grade students should be able to **identify, create, and use files in various formats,** such as text, raster and vector graphics, video, and audio files. They create original works as individuals or in groups. Students understand and use operating systems; perform more advanced troubleshooting techniques, such as resolving software compatibility and verifying network connectivity; and demonstrate effective file management strategies such as conversion. Sixth graders use technology to discuss trends

Figure 9.16 Common multimedia file type icons.

TAW4 / Shutterstock.com

Figure 9.17 School-aged children need to know how to seek online help.

Jakub Krechowicz / Shutterstock.com

and possible outcomes and create a research plan to guide inquiry as well. They use productivity tools, including word processors, spreadsheet workbooks, databases, and digital publication tools. More importantly, this level creates nonlinear media projects using graphic design principles and that integrate two or more technology tools to create a new digital product. They can also discuss how technology has changed throughout history and the relevance of technology to daily living. They **understand** the negative impacts of inappropriate technology use, including online bullying and harassment, hacking, intentional virus setting, invasion of privacy, and piracy of software, music, video, and/or other media. Rather than simply protecting and honoring individual privacy, just as with their younger counterparts, they venture into the direct implications of these issues. The expectations for seventh-grade students are very similar to that of the sixth-grade students. The differences are in the expectation for the seventh graders to **discuss trends** and **make predictions** instead of just discussing possible outcomes.

Students from the 9th through the 12th Grades

Adolescence is viewed as a transitional period between childhood and adulthood. The age at which particular changes take place varies between individuals, but adolescence is also generally regarded as a time for rapid cognitive development (Luna, Marek, Larsen, Tervo-Clemmens, & Chahal, 2015; Mills, 2016) (refer to Figure 9.18). Piaget (1964) describes adolescence as the stage of life in which the individual's thoughts start taking more of an abstract form, and their ability to think more deductively and logically emerges. This allows the individual to think and reason in a wider perspective.

By the time the individuals have reached about age 15, their basic thinking abilities are comparable to those of adults. These improvements occur in five areas during adolescence:(a) attention, (b) memory, (c) processing speed, (d) organization, and (e) higher-level cognition (Daddis, 2011; Graca, Calheiros, & Barata, 2013; Sylwester, 2007). They gain more in the areas of behavioral autonomy, cognitive autonomy, and emotional autonomy.

In gaining **behavioral autonomy**, adolescents are developing the ability to regulate their own behavior, to act on personal decisions, and to self-govern (Sylwester, 2007). With **cognitive autonomy,** they partake in processes of independent reasoning and decision-making without excessive reliance on social validation. With **emotional autonomy**, they develop more mature emotional connections with adults and peers. During adolescence, there is a high emphasis on approval of peers due to adolescents' increased self-consciousness. In general, adolescents think more quickly than children. Their thinking is also less bound to concrete events than that of children because they have also developed the skills of hypothetical and abstract thinking (Sylwester, 2007). The thoughts, ideas, and concepts developed at this period of life greatly influence one's future life. Where does technology come into play in these changes? Simply being able to use technology is no longer enough. Today's teenagers need to be able to use technology to analyze, learn, create, and explore.

Figure 9.18 New family communication concept by technologies.

The TA TEKS cover computer literacy in grade K–8; there are many other areas in which students should grow throughout their K–12 experience in order to enhance the use of technology in learning. There are technology-related courses designed for high school students to prepare for successful transitions to post-secondary education and employment beyond the eighth grade.

Regardless of whether students choose to enroll in college or look for employment after high school, they need to acquire additional technology skills beyond basic computer literacy. The world's best companies are redesigning themselves to increase productivity, quality, variety, and speed, which can only be accomplished by "tech savvy" employees. Digital age skills are vital for preparing students to work (refer to Figure 9.19),

Figure 9.19 Scientists using microscopes and computers tablets in a laboratory.

live, and contribute to society. The following courses are often offered as electives on the high school level (ninth grade and above) for students who have built a computer literacy foundation in grade K–8. These are the areas in which students can grow throughout high schools to bridge the gap from high school to work or high school to colleges:

Computer Science I, II, & III	3-D Modeling and Animation
Digital Forensics	Digital Communications in the Twenty-First Century
Game Programming and Design	Digital Video and Audio Design
Mobile Application Development	Web Communications
Robotics Programming and Design	Web Design
Digital Design and Media Production	Web Game Development
Digital Art and Animation	Independent Study in Technology Applications

In the two-semester Computer Science II Honors/AP course, for instance, students usually learn Java programs and object-oriented programming, array lists, Boolean logics, nested control structures, and other concepts. The course description typically indicates that "The course will develop the skills using Java as a means for learning programming. The types of problems solved by means of programing will vary (i.e., mathematics, science, finance, and graphics)."

High school students who are enrolled in career and technical education programs also have opportunities to take additional technology-related courses, including animations, audio/video production, graphic design and illustration, touch system data entry, business information management, virtual business, computer maintenance, telecommunications and networking, computer programming, and Web technologies. Industry has considerable influence in the standards in courses such as these. These courses offer school-to-work opportunities for students to earn portable job skills; prepare students for jobs in high-skill, high-wage careers; and increase students' opportunities for further education, including education in colleges or universities.

Historically, women have played a crucial role in computer programming, and the first computer programmers were, in fact, mostly female (Eveleth, 2013). Ada Lovelace (1815-1852) is often recognized as history's first computer programmer, due to her work on Charles Babbage's proposed mechanical general-purpose computer, the Analytical Engine (see Figure 9.20).

Nevertheless, the proportion of women represented in the information technology (or IT) field has declined ever since, so that in 2013 Sydell stated that only about 20% of all U.S. computer programmers are female. Computer programmers were expected to be male and antisocial (Eveleth, 2013). The articles of Eveleth and Sydell (as well as others) provide bases for a positive correlation between perceived gender gaps in ability and career choices (see Figure 9.21).

pantid123 / Shutterstock.com

Figure 9.20   A cartoon caricature to portray Ada Lovelace, history's first computer programmer.

RedPixel.PL / Shutterstock.com

Figure 9.21   "Computer programmers are expected to be male and antisocial" (Eveleth, 2013).

Lately, in addition to formal school curriculum, there are informal "boot camps" and training, internship, and other opportunities funded by corporations to expand all students' access to computer science to increase participation in the IT professional field, especially by women and underrepresented minorities. Among the informal initiatives, Code.org® (www.code.org/, 2018) has a vision that all students in every school should have the opportunity to learn computer science. Code.org organizes the annual Hour of Code campaign, which, in 2017, engaged 10% of all students in the world and provides the programing curriculum for K-12 computer science in large school districts in the United States (Code.org, 2018). GirlsComputingLeague (www.girlscomputingleague.org) and Girls IntoComputing (www.tnmoc.org/learn/girls-computing) are just two organizations that target school girls by offering scholarship, recognition, and opportunities to encourage female students to engage in coding.

Conclusion

States' legislation requirements that all students should be technology literate by the time they leave the eighth grade is an important one for emphasis in this chapter. High schools also offer technology-related electives courses in which students can expand their knowledge and skills from the ninth grade through the twelfth grade to bridge the gap from schools to work or K–12 to colleges. If teachers know what is expected, they can easily plan for the grade level they will teach to ensure that students finish each year with the knowledge and skills they need. Future teachers should know the national ISTE and state TA TEKS in Texas (or their comparable standards in other states) that both describe what K–12 students should know and be able to do with technology. Prospective teachers should also understand the ISTE, the state level Technology Applications Standards for All Beginning Teachers, and Technology Applications Standards for All Teachers, which are the standards for evaluating the skills and knowledge that educators need to teach, use for work, and learn in an increasingly connected global and digital society. In addition, when teaching content areas, teachers also have recommendations from teachers' councils and associations, such as the NAEYC for early childhood and the NCTM for mathematics education.

Technology standards were developed to provide benchmarks and guidelines for helping beginning and current teachers develop strategies for using technology in effective and meaningful ways with their students. They also reflect the importance and the infusion of twenty-first-century technology skills to assist and guide students to be productive, responsible citizens and to emphasize the importance of lifelong learning with changing technology.

Good teachers commit to a professional life of staying current with new devices, apps, software, and instruction methods both about technology and teaching their content with technology. Teacher education programs introduce the basics of standards to beginning teachers, but ongoing exposure and familiarity with relevant details in various fields of specialization is a part of continuing professional development for educators. New teachers must become familiar with standards at all phases—from field testing in the work setting to professional development in their best use and application–so that technology becomes the norm in their classroom.

Beginning teachers must know their technology for today, but they must also know that they are the agents of change in this process for the future and are at the active center of the lifelong learning process. Technology cannot replace the teacher nor can it be used as a replacement for basic understandings and intuitions. Teachers must make prudent decisions about when and how to use technology and should ensure that the technology is enhancing students' learning and thinking. Technology should become a tool to enhance all other learning and skills.

References

American Library Association. (2017). *Information literacy competency standards for higher education*. Retrieved from www.ala.org/acrl/standards/informationliteracycompetency

Code.org. (2018). About us. Retrieved from www.code.org/about

Daddis, C. (2011). Desire for increased autonomy and adolescents' perceptions of peer autonomy: "Everyone else can; Why can't I?" *Child Development, 82*(4), 1310–1326.

Dean, C. B., Hubbell, E. R., & Pitler, H. (2012). *Classroom instruction that works: Research-based strategies for increasing student achievement* (2nd ed.). Alexandria, VA: Association for Supervision and Curriculum Development (ASCD).

Eveleth, R. (2013). Computer programming used to be women's work. Retrieved from www.smithsonianmag.com/smart-news/computer-programming-used-to-be-womens-work-718061

Goodwin, K., & Highfield, K. (2012). *iTouch and iLearn: An examination of "educational" apps*. Paper presented at the Early Education and Technology for Children Conference, March 14-16, 2012, Salt Lake City, Utah. Retrieved from www.academia.edu/1464841/iTouch_and_iLearn_An_examination_of_educational_apps

Graca, J., Calheiros, M., & Barata, M. (2013). Authority in the classroom: Adolescent autonomy, autonomy support, and teachers' legitimacy. *European Journal of Psychology of Education, 3*, 1065.

Gray, C., Gibbons, R., Larouche, R., Sandseter, E. B. H., Bienenstock, A., Brussoni, M., & Tremblay, M. S. (2015). What is the relationship between outdoor time and physical activity, Sedentary behaviour, and physical fitness in children? A systematic review. *International Journal of Environmental Research and Public Health, 12*(6), 6455. doi:10.3390/ijerph120606455

Great Schools Partnership. (2014). *The glossary of education reform*. Retrieved from www.edglossary.org/learning-standards

Hill, C. (1995, September 6). *Re: Education: Developing educational standard page*. [Electronic mailing list message]. Retrieved from www.cartman.mofet.macam98.ac.il/~dovw/aa/0066.html

International Society for Technology in Education. (2016). *ISTE Standards for Students*. Retrieved from www.iste.org/standards/standards/for-students

International Society for Technology in Education. (2017). *ISTE Standards for Educators*. Retrieved from www.iste.org/standards/for-educators

Luna, B., Marek, S., Larsen, B., Tervo-Clemmens, B., & Chahal, R. (2015). An integrative model of the maturation of cognitive control. *Annual Review of Neuroscience, 38*-51. doi:10.1146/annurev-neuro-071714-034054

Mills, K. L. (2016). Possible effects of Internet use on cognitive development in adolescence. *Media and Communication, 4*(3), 4. doi:10.17645/mac.v4i3.516

National Academy of Education. (2009). *Standards, assessment, and accountability: Education policy white paper*. Retrieved from www.files.eric.ed.gov/fulltext/ED531138.pdf

National Association for the Education of Young Children. (2012). *Key messages of the NAEYC/Fred Rogers Center Position Statement on Technology and Interactive Media in Early Childhood Programs*. Retrieved from www.naeyc.org/files/naeyc/file/positions/KeyMessages_Technology.pdf

National Commission on Excellence in Education. (1983). *A nation at risk: The imperative for educational reform. A report to the nation and the Secretary of Education, United States Department of Education*. Washington, DC: National Commission on Excellence in Education.

National Governors Association Center for Best Practices and Council of Chief State School Officers. (2017). *Common Core State Standards Initiative: Standards in your state*. Retrieved from www.corestandards.org/standards-in-your-state

No Child Left Behind (NCLB) Act of 2001, Pub. L. No. 107-110, § 115, Stat. 1425 (2002).

Page, A. S., Cooper, A. R., Griew, P., & Jago, R. (2010). Children's screen viewing is related to psychological difficulties irrespective of physical activity. *Pediatrics, 126*(5), 1011–1017.

Piaget, J. (1964). PART I cognitive development in children: Piaget. *Journal of Research in Science Teaching, 2*(3), 176.

Roblyer, M. D. (2000). The national educational technology standards (NETS): A review of definitions, implications, and strategies for integrating NETS into K-12 curriculum. *International Journal of Instructional Media, 27*(2), 133–146.

Snelling, J. (2016). *New ISTE standards aim to develop lifelong learners*. Retrieved from www.iste.org/explore/articleDetail?articleid=751

Sydell, L. (2013). Blazing the trail for female programmers. Retrieved from www.npr.org/sections/alltechconsidered/2013/04/29/178810467/blazing-the-trail-for-female-programmers

Sylwester, R. (2007). *The adolescent brain: Reaching for autonomy*. Thousand Oaks, CA: Corwin Press.

Texas Education Agency. (2006a). *School Technology and Readiness Chart*. Retrieved from www.tea.state.tx.us/WorkArea/linkit.aspx?LinkIdentifier=id&ItemID=2147501875&libID=2147501869

Texas Education Agency. (2006b). *Texas Long-Range Plan for Technology, 2006–2020*. Retrieved from www.txstarchart.org/docs/TxCSC.pdf

Texas Education Agency. (2017a). *TExES™ Pedagogy and Professional Responsibilities (PPR) EC–12 (160): Test at a glance*. Retrieved from www.cms.texes-ets.org/files/2114/8717/0543/ppr_EC_12_160_TAAG.pdf

Texas Education Agency. (2017b). *Texas Essential Knowledge and Skills*. Retrieved from www.tea.state.tx.us/index2.aspx?id=6148

Wong, M. E., & Law, J. S. (2016). Practices of assistive technology implementation and facilitation: Experiences of teachers of students with visual impairments in Singapore. *Journal of Visual Impairment & Blindness, 110*(3), 195.

Chapter 10

Technology Legal and Informational Literacy Essentials

Sue Mahoney - *Retired,* Irene Chen, and Janice L. Nath - *Professor Emeritus*
University of Houston - Downtown

Meet Mrs. Mehta

Mrs. Mehta was working on Google Slides for her presentation to her class on frogs. She really wanted to catch the attention of her young students by using a picture of Kermit, the Frog (see Figure 10.1). She downloaded a picture from the Web and was ready to insert it into her presentation when she remembered that she should think about the copyright rules covering the use of the image. Can she use the image in her slideshow?

michaeljung / Shutterstock.com

Harmony Gerber / Shutterstock.com

Figure 10.1 Kermit the Frog is a popular Sesame Street puppet character.

Technology Responsibilities

Technology encompasses numerous powerful and exciting tools, but with these tools comes the responsibility of using them legally, ethically, and appropriately. It is important in many ways that all parties—parents, teachers, and students—comply with the acceptable use policies (AUPs) developed by their school district. Teachers should introduce the school's AUP to their students (and to their parents) because it provides them with appropriate guidelines for Internet use. Classroom teachers should also be mindful that they are role models for students and that they should always model the legal, ethical, and appropriate use of technology.

Classroom teachers have multiple responsibilities to their students when integrating technology into the curriculum. These responsibilities include knowing:

- the content and how best to present it to ensure student mastery;
- the tools available and how best to include them in the content presentation;
- relevant ethical responsibilities associated with using technology tools in a manner that conforms to the teachers' ethics code and for being in compliance with international, federal, state, and school district rules and guidelines;
- the legal responsibilities regarding copyright laws and plagiarism; and
- how to communicate effectively and appropriately with students and parents. Not all families have computers and/or Internet access, and teachers must be cognizant of this fact. These students and their families are experiencing the Digital Divide or the technology gap.

Check Your Knowledge - Super YouTube video

You are preparing a lesson on Hawaii and have just found a fantastic video clip about volcanoes. Can you use it in your classroom? Could you also put it in a presentation that you are giving at an upcoming conference? What things do you have to think about when you want to use media?

Content Knowledge

Content knowledge is key when preparing lessons and using resources properly. The district and state curriculum requirements (e.g., the Texas Essential Knowledge and Skills, or TEKS, in Texas and Common Core requirements in many other states) provide guidelines for what content information is to be taught in the classroom. The curriculum and the lesson content guide the type of and ways that technology that should be used with lessons, but technology "for technology's sake" should not guide the lesson content. Many states have separate technology knowledge and skills requirements outside the content areas that must also be integrated. Required state assessments and other formative and summative assessments determine if teachers have taught and students have learned both the content areas and the technology knowledge and skills that have been set forth.

Figure 10.2 Available resources in the Web-based environment.

New teaching tools—software, Web-based applications (refer to Figure 10.2) and new advances associated with the Internet, phone apps, and many others—arrive in the marketplace on a continuous basis for use with content areas and for technology knowledge and skills. It is the responsibility of each teacher: (1) to examine and evaluate any new resources that may be of benefit to instruction, individual students, or to the school in other ways; (2) to seek professional development opportunities and resources when appropriate; and (3) to comprehend and follow the legal and ethical issues associated with using these tools.

Social and Ethical Issues of Integrating Technology for Learning

Ethics refers to a moral duty and obligation to try to do what is right (Merriam-Webster, 2007). There are many issues in the use of technology which not only concern laws but also doing what is right for all users, particularly students. For example, the Digital Divide, as just mentioned, is an economic and social inequality according to categories of persons [Question 1] ess to, use of, or knowledge of information and communication technologies. The Digital Divide is normally the result of inequalities between individuals, households, businesses, or geographic areas, and this inequality is most often due to different socioeconomic levels.

The Digital Divide exists for many students, as many are also first-generation immigrants from developing countries and/or live in lower socioeconomic status (SES) situations. According to research, one of the major barriers to raising student literacy levels and computer skills is a lack of parental assistance at home (Daugherty, Dossani, Johnson, & Oguz, 2014). Past research also shows that computer-based information, communication, services, and instruction are less available to those who are poor, live in rural areas, are members of minority racial/ethnic groups, and/or have disabilities (National Telecommunications and Information Administration, 1999). To tackle this challenge, educators must work collaboratively and creatively with school districts and grant funding sources for solutions.

To help bridge the Digital Divide gap, teachers can serve as the advocates for their technologically disadvantaged students. Training for teachers in integrating technology and the particular impact of the Digital Divide can be emphasized. Future teachers can brainstorm solutions on how they can assist in bridging the gap, but they must always consider if the assignments (especially homework) they are giving will be equitable for students being able to complete them (and complete them in equitable ways—quality-wise). There are other places besides home where students can use technology (such as public libraries), but parents may not be able to always take children there, and older students may often need to work during public library hours. Teachers must also consider if parents are able to receive technology communications, and, if not, phone or paper alternatives are required.

Educators can extend their connections with other appropriate agencies and organizations to offer computer literacy training courses to parents and community members. For community adult computer courses, acquiring basic computer skills such as surfing the Internet, setting up and using email, learning basic keyboarding, word processing skills and data entry, are taught. Participants experience the value of technology utilization as a tool for life. Schools can encourage faculty and staff involvement in community service in this way, too, as a means to bridging this gap and, perhaps, to bring in parents to the schools in afterhours classes.

There are a number of ways that a teacher may try to help gain more technology for his or her students—from business donations of old equipment to writing large and small funding grants. This type of advocacy for the preparation of students may need to occur if one's district cannot support large budgets for technology. However, a teacher must always be sure to follow district guidelines in seeking equipment or funding from the outside. The more that can be obtained, the more students will be able to develop their technological knowledge and skills. A district may provide funding and help obtain grants, but it may also be up to the teacher, at times, to initiate the process.

New Literacies

The meaning of literacy commonly signifies interpretation of a written text. *Visual literacy, graph literacy,* and *media literacy* are relatively new phrases amid the rising wave of multimedia technology. Visually pleasing, accurate charts enable users to easily find critical information or recognize important relations between data. *Visual literacy* is the ability to ma[Question 2]resented in the form of an image. *Graph literacy* is the ability to read and u[Question 2]aphically. The skill of reading and understanding tables, diagrams, flow cha[Question 2]ts is an essential skill in the contemporary workplace. The third term, *media literacy* refers to the ability to read, analyze, evaluate, and produce communication in a variety of media forms, including audio and video. Media literacy is critical in everyday life: information that is viewed on TV and on the Internet is used for decisions, including transportation, medical, grocery shopping, financial, and many others.

Information literacy is "the set of skills needed to find, retrieve, analyze, and use information" (American Library Association, 2014, para. 1). This term encompasses all three kinds of literacies—visual literacy, graph literacy, and media literacy:

> It allows us to cope by giving us the skills to know when we need information and where to locate it effectively and efficiently. It includes the technological skills needed to use the modern library as a gateway to information. It enables us to analyze and evaluate the information we find, thus giving us confidence in using that information to make a decision or create a product. (para. 6)

It is important to note that information literacy skills are relevant to all content areas in K-16 educational settings. Teachers must stay abreast of the ever-changing teaching and learning landscape to continue to produce "learners who not only know how to think, but know how to problem solve within a diversified information and communication technology universe" (National Forum on Information Literacy Skills, 2017, p. 1). With these new concepts, guidelines, laws, and regulations have and will continue to be developed and refined. These laws and guidelines continue to change and grow at the international, national, state, and local levels that govern everything from electronic bullying to the usage of copyrighted materials, including materials used under fair use and plagiarism.

Technology Standards

The International Society for Technology in Education (ISTE) is a nonprofit organization whose purpose is to assist educators and educational leaders in advancing technology use for learners (www.iste.org). To this end, ISTE has developed standards for educators and students. These standards identify the skills and expertise both groups need to function in today's digital environments. During 2016, ISTE adopted new student standards that focus on skills and expertise that students need to function in today's digital world. These standards focus on creating an individual as an empowered learner, a responsible digital citizen, a knowledge constructor, an innovative designer, a computational thinker, a creative communicator, and a global collaborator (ISTE, 2016). Updated educator standards were introduced in 2017. These standards focus on how educators can help students become empowered learners (ISTE, 2017). ISTE's goal is for these new standards to continue to empower teachers to further develop their teaching practices and collaborate with other educators and students, leverage technology usage in the classroom, inspire students to become responsible participants in the digital world, and promote authentic learning activities that correspond to student learning styles and capabilities as well as continued professional development, use of data-driven instruction, and leadership (ISTE 2017).

States and school districts may have their own set of technology skills and standards that teachers and future teachers must meet. Teachers must equip children with various technology skills (along with content) in specific terms, and this technology knowledge of teachers is often first measured through certification testing for preservice teachers and state and district testing for children. For example, the Texas technology components of the TExES™ Pedagogy and Professional Responsibilities (PPR) EC-12 (Texas Education Agency, 2017) exam are found in Competency 9 (Nath & Cohen, 2011) and in the Technology Application (TA) Standards I–V. These documents identify the knowledge and skills required for beginning teachers.

Teacher and Student Behaviors/Practices

Professional and appropriate behavior is a requirement for all teachers in many areas of their lives, including their technological actions. Likewise, students should also practice appropriate behavior in the face-to-face classroom *and* in the digital environment. This section discusses some important topics and resources relating to these topics. It is critical that teachers and students be aware of the issues involved in these areas and engage in "best practices" for all parties involved. Many s........................certification sanctions and even ....vior with technology (see Figure ....

Question 3

Figure 10.3 Proper teacher and student online behavior: respect, ethics, honesty, and integrity.

Stuart Miles / Shutterstock.com

Acceptable Use Policy (or AUP)—This is a written agreement among involved parties that provides guidelines for behavior on the Internet or intranet, which is a network that uses technology to share information or computing services within an organization. Most school districts have developed an AUP (see Figure 10.4).

This policy about acceptable use with school technology includes what the school district will do to protect students from inappropriate online materials, student practices with regard to Internet usage, and parental understanding that the school district will do its best to provide a secure, safe environment for its students—but that sometimes students venture to inappropriate Websites. Very often, parents must a sign a permission slip prior to their children using a school computer.

Figure 10.4 Acceptable Use Policy equals Terms of Use Guidelines for Internet or intranet use in a school.

Netiquette/Online Manners—Because electronic communication does not include the body language so necessary to the full understanding of some messages and because the writer is often in a hurry in today's busy world, messages sent via email, text message, or discussion board can be easily misunderstood. Knowing the proper etiquette for communicating in the online environment can make a difference in how a message is perceived. This is particularly true of teachers who are writing to parents, colleagues, administrators, and, sometimes, students, but school-age learners also need to be taught how to avoid conflicts and misunderstandings. Proper online communication includes the following conventions:

- Always identify oneself (include title and/or place where one teaches, especially if writing to parents or other administrators) (e.g., Sincerely, Jane Smith, Katie's Teacher at Sandy Creek Elementary).
- Use appropriate language.
- Refrain from using sarcasm.
- Avoid obscenity.
- Do not be offensive online with language or pictures. Keep a high standard of behavior for the online environment.
- Do not use all caps because this means that the sender is "SCREAMING" at the person receiving the message.
- Use spelling, punctuation, and grammar check tools on your messages.
- Be alert to copyright and plagiarism issues.
- Be respectful and sensitive to others in both copying and sharing messages and regarding diversity issues.
- Use emoticons appropriately and be cautious with using humor—sometimes humor does not translate to text properly, and different cultures see humor (and sarcasm) in different ways.
- Avoid forwarding spam and/or suspicious messages with possible viruses.
- Avoid forwarding "chain letters" (from the teacher's message box in particular).

While the previous guidelines are important, here are a few others that should also be used:

- Be respectful to the recipient of your message (Steber 1994–2012).
- Be aware that acceptable and/or casual language can vary from audience to audience (friends, teachers, parents, a colleague) (Steber 1994–2012).
- Be respectful of your reader—make messages meaningful and concise without unneeded graphics or attachments. If attachments are pertinent, be mindful of their size and required download time (Steber 1994–2012).
- Use your virtual diplomatic skills to direct angry or off-topic discussions back to the discussion topic (Steber,1994–2012).

Teaching the use of emojis may be fruitful, as Lowell (n.d.) in *Psychology Today* tells us that "They are everywhere these days because they increase the precision and nuance of our often super-brief and open-to-misunderstanding communications" (para.1). For example, Ms. Kohl sent out a quick reminder to her students' parents that she needed them send some classroom supplies in the next week, if possible. Because she did not want to indicate that she was upset, she attached a "Smiley Face" to it.

> Emily, a student teacher, was asked by her mentor teacher, Ms. Jefferson, to send out reminders to students' parents about the school Open House next Tuesday. Ms. Jefferson said it was fine for Emily to send the reminder from her email account with the sender's name as "Ms. Jefferson". Should Emily follow Ms. Jefferson's advice since she is her mentor?
>
> Emily noticed that most teachers remind students to follow netiquette guidelines at the beginning rather than in the middle of the semester. What is the rationale behind this instructional decision?

According to proper online communication (netiquette), Emily must "always identify oneself." Even though Ms. Jefferson, her mentor teacher, said it was fine for Emily to send the invitation from her own email account with the sender's name as "Ms. Jefferson", she still had to send the message to students' parents to remind them of the school open house from her own email account with her own identity or *clearly* indicate this was not Ms. Jefferson's letter. For instance, she could sign her name and add "for Ms. Jefferson" or begin the letter, "Ms. Jefferson has asked me to send a reminder . . ." (signed Emily Vargas, Student Teacher).

Netiquette refers to the etiquette for students to follow when going online for email, chat, and discussion forums. Netiquette guidelines are usually introduced to students early on in the school years to clarify expectations, set up class norms, to explain to students what technology behaviors are acceptable and what are not, and to put into effect online behavior guidelines. Some teachers even invite students' input to create an honor code so that they become invested in it. A savvy teacher will know that particular assignments or situations are times when students may need reminders, so he or she does so again prior to those times.

Computer and Cyber Ethics—The Computer Ethics Institute provides a forum and resources for the identification, assessment, and responses to ethical issues associated with the advancement of information technologies in society. The institute has also published the Ten Commandments of Computer Ethics (www .computerethicsinstitute.org/images/TheTenCommandmentsOfComputerEthics.pdf) which provides guidelines for ethical behavior in the computer world (Computer Ethics Institute, n.d.):

1. Thou shalt not use a computer to harm other people.
2. Thou shalt not interfere with other people's computer work.
3. Thou shalt not snoop around in other people's computer files.
4. Thou shalt not use a computer to steal.
5. Thou shalt not use a computer to bear false witness.
6. Thou shalt not copy or use proprietary software for which you have not paid.
7. Thou shalt not use other people's computer resources without authorization or proper compensation.
8. Thou shalt not appropriate other people's intellectual output.
9. Thou shalt think about the social consequences of the program you are writing or the system you are designing.
10. Thou shalt always use a computer in ways that ensure consideration and respect for your fellow humans.

These rules of etiquette for the computer have expanded over time to include concepts relevant to the expanded use of computers, the Internet, and the ongoing innovations that appear daily in the technology world.

Teachers and students need to be constantly alert to their actions and the actions of others regarding ethics in today's world. Teachers and students need to be appropriate in all their communications—they must think before they send any communication, and, when in doubt about the appropriateness of the message, not send it. School districts have policies about responsible computer use, communication with parents and students, and social media use. Teachers and future teachers must familiarize themselves with these policies! They must also not post inappropriate comments or pictures on their social media pages, even though it is "outside school." To be hired and to keep one's job, they must act responsibly and use good judgment!

Bullying and cyberbullying are unacceptable practices for students and teachers, whether it is perpetuated face-to-face or through electronic technology. Either type of bullying is an unsolicited aggressive behavior toward another person (see Figure 10.5).

Student- and school-related abuses of computer and communication tools are widely reported in the media. In 2012, the word *sexting* was listed for the first time in Merriam-Webster's Collegiate Dictionary (Plafke, 2012). Sexting is the act of sending sexually explicit messages, primarily between mobile phones. "Staff must not use social networks to communicate with students" is the guidance given in some schools' e-safety policy, nor should staff "have students classed as 'friends' or the equivalent." In recent years, Facebook, MySpace, and other social networking sites have sometimes been involved with cyberbullying issues which, in turn, have been blamed for incidents of teenage students' fear, embarrassment, and other problems (including harming themselves) in some states. A number of recent lawsuits have looked at the role a school or teachers could have played in preventing students from being cyberbullied and causing them anguish (even to the point of committing suicide). This is a serious issue that includes the teacher being aware of inappropriate pictures and/or messages sent to and about students and of monitoring behavior that might indicate that a student could be a bully or is being bullied. Two resources available are:

Figure 10.5 Bullying, It's So Not Cool! sign.

- Stopbullying.gov (www.stopbullying.gov) provides information about the types of bullying, who is at risk, how to prevent it, how to respond to it, and how to get help immediately. This Website contains information that is relevant to students, educators, parents, and the community.
- Cyberbullying Research Center (www.cyberbullying.org) is an organization that is committed to providing the public with information about cyberbullying among adolescents. The Website has resources for educators, parents, and teens. The center also has several publications available about cyberbullying and the center's research about cyberbullying.

It is important for teachers, parents, and guardians to closely monitor children's use of electronic devices, computers, and cell phones alike and to note any behavior that seems inconsistent or out of the ordinary.

Hinduja and Patchin (2014) list the following as red flags that a child maybe becoming a victim of cyberbullying if he or she,

- unexpectedly stops using their device(s)
- appears nervous or jumpy when using their device(s)
- appears uneasy about going to school or outside in general
- appears to be angry, depressed, or frustrated after texting, chatting, using social media, or gaming
- avoids discussions about what they are doing online
- becomes abnormally withdrawn from usual friends and family members. (p. 7)

And, the following items are some red flags that a child maybe cyberbullying others if he or she,

- quickly switches screens or hides their devices when others walk by
- uses their devices at all hours of the night
- gets unusually upset if he/she cannot use their device(s)
- avoids discussions about what they are doing online
- uses multiple online accounts or uses an account that is not his/her own.

For a full list see www.cyberbullying.org/cyberbullying-warning-signs.pdf.

It is also a good practice to remind older students to keep a clean online presence of themselves if they have social network profiles on sites such as Facebook or Twitter. Recruiters often use the Web as a place to search for talent and conduct employment background searches for job applicants. Any hint of an inappropriate posting can cause one to not be hired in the first place or an employee to be sanctioned, including teachers. One must also remember what he or she may not consider offensive could be to others. If in doubt, a teacher or prospective teacher should not send or post.

Maintaining a respectable and appropriate Web presence is critical, as what is posted to the Web does not disappear but remains to be uncovered at a future date. Also, teachers must always remember that their technology belongs to the school district, and the district has a right to monitor emails and school computers (including search histories). Downloading or searching inappropriate sites can be cause for a teacher to be fired and/or, in worst-case scenarios, prosecuted. This is particularly true of anything that may be associated with pornography.

Academic Dishonesty and Plagiarism

Academic dishonesty is present in any classroom, in any school, in any university—but now it goes beyond cheating on a test. Due to technological advances, there are different types of dishonesty, such as claiming someone's work as your own, paying for someone else to do an essay, or not citing the sources used to create one's own work. Statistics have shown in high school that more than 70% of students inside a classroom admitted to cheating (Rodrigues, 2011).

The question that needs to be addressed is why are these students cheating? Are students aware that it is against school rules and that plagiarism outside of school can be considered a crime? If so, do they still find it acceptable?

It is now commonplace for students to bring personal digital devices (PDAs) and/or smartphones into the classroom (BYOD), which gives them swift access to the Internet. While this technology is a benefit for students conducting research for a project, it can also be detrimental for educators who need to assess students' content mastery. Some students say they cheat because "this is my safety net" and/or "it is no big deal" (McMahon, 2007). However, we also know that later on, it cannot only cost grades but also the loss of a student's professional program (such as becoming a teacher), embarrassment, loss of a job, or many other detrimental actions.

Plagiarism is defined as the act of using another person's words or ideas without giving credit to that person (Merriam-Webster.com). To plagiarize is to:

- steal and pass off (the ideas or words of another) as one's own
- use (another's production) without crediting the source
- commit literary theft: present as new and original an idea or product derived from an existing source (Merriam-webster.com).

When using someone else's materials, ideas, and so on to create documents, credit must be given to the sources used. Many teachers and instructors have spent an abundance of time explaining plagiarism with regard to assigned papers. The Online Writing Lab (OWL) at Purdue University (www.owl.english.purdue.edu) is a useful resource for both students and teachers. The scope of information provided on multiple writing and writing-related topics, including plagiarism, is outstanding. The OWL lists some common examples of plagiarism:

- If you buy, steal, or borrow a paper and turn it in as your own.
- If you hire someone to write a paper for you, then turn it in as your own.
- If you use a source too closely when you are paraphrasing information.
- If you build on someone's ideas without citing or giving proper credit.
- If you copy from another source without giving proper credit.

More and more school districts and universities subscribe to plagiarism checking services such as TurnItIn (www.turnitin.com) to check students' papers against its huge database of previous work, dissertations, theses, newspapers, and other paper and online sources over the Internet for similarities. The Originality Check feature provides a summary of matching or similar areas of text found in a submitted paper. The higher the similarity percentage, the greater the amount of text in the submission that appears as matching (to have been copied) against information in the database repositories.

For those schools who have not subscribed to TurnItIn or other plagiarism checking services, teachers can try out other plagiarism detection Websites such as Grammarly (www.grammarly.com), PaperRater (www.paperrater.com), and Dupli Checker (www.duplichecker.com), for occasional searches.

Some teachers make it a requirement that students submit "originality reports" generated from TurnItIn to accompany all major class papers. Instructors can also set up a view to see all class papers with similarity indices (or SI) in class assignment inboxes. Some schools are more general about the SI in order to call a paper "clean" or "original," while others give specific percentage numbers. Teachers not only have to become familiar with technology-based plagiarism checkers, but they can educate their own students about how to avoid plagiarism by using free cartoons, games, and other interactive Internet resources (see Additional Resources at the end of the chapter for recommended sites). After these activities, students should have less of an excuse to say that they do not know they have committed plagiarism. Part of the technology knowledge that can be taught from a very early grade level and onward is having students give credit when it is someone else's work.

Multimedia must conform to the same guidelines as a research paper which means citations and references are required. Quotation marks with a citation on the slide/screen and a full reference in the Credits/References at the end of the document are required if text is quoted verbatim. There are several formats that various organization use. For example, educators most often use American Psychosocial Association (APA) style, which can easily be found in one's search engine or at www.owl.english.purdue.edu/owl/resource/560/01. Using information from a source requires that the source have a citation in the document with a full reference at the end of the document. In summary, when creating any kind of document, credit must be given to the author, photographer, artist, musician, Website, or others in the document.

Teachers should incorporate anti-plagiarism mindfulness in their classrooms by doing the following: include the school's academic honesty policy and penalties associated with plagiarism in the course syllabi as well as explain plagiarism at the beginning of a semester and refresh students' memory multiple times throughout the year as they venture into projects where students might be most apt to plagiarize. The school librarian would also be a relevant resource for reinforcing the anti-plagiarism mind-set. Teachers and students should also be aware of the school district's policy and the guidelines for handling any plagiarism incidents that occur.

Authors, software creators, artists, composers, and others are paid and/or recognized for their efforts, and they have the right to agree to let others use their work (see Figure 10.9). Most will agree to use for teachers in schools, but they *must* be asked. Many persons make their living selling excellent products to schools, so they can ask for compensation for usage. Taking that from them is really a form of stealing. When others claim that something is their own work, the value of the creator's work is diminished. If there is financial or other type of recognition lost, it is doubtful that their creative efforts will continue. This includes copying others' text-books or chapters in textbooks without permission by the publisher. Even at the college or university level, the librarian is also an excellent resource for plagiarism rules, copyright issues, fair use guidelines, and other guidelines and can usually be emailed for advice.

Software Issues

Question 4

When **purchasing software**, one is **purchasing a license**, and with the license comes **terms of use**. The options can include purchasing a single license and a license for a network. Both of these state the number and guidelines of installations that can be made. Simply because a license has been purchased does not mean that one can install the software on as many machines as desired. This unauthorized copying is termed piracy. The limitations of the contract must be followed on installations, even for school use.

There are also several other types of software available:

- **Freeware** is copyrighted software that the author allows for free use. The author retains the copyright, which means that a user must conform to the author's copyright guidelines (Webopedia, 2017a).
- **Shareware** is also copyrighted software that is distributed free of charge, but the author of the software requests a small fee if a user likes the software and uses it regularly. Shareware is inexpensive, often produced by a single programmer, and is offered directly to users (Webopedia, 2017b).

- **Public-domain** software (refer to Figure 10.6) is software that is not copyrighted. It is free and can be used without restrictions (Webopedia, 2017c). For instance, the public-domain software BLAST (Basic Local Alignment Search Tool, www.blast.ncbi .nlm.nih.gov) allows high school biology teachers to perform similarity searches against constantly updated databases of proteins and DNA.

Figure 10.6 Creative Commons Public Domain Logo.

- **Open-source software** is software in which the source code is available to the general public for use and/or modification from its original design free of charge (refer to Figure 10.7). It is usually developed in collaboration with other programmers and is under a license defined by the Open Source Initiative (OSI). Not all open-source software is distributed under the same licensing agreement (Webopedia, 2017d). More information about OSI can be found at www.opensource.org. Mozilla Firefox, the Web browser used by many educators and students alike, is a free and open-source Web browser developed by the Mozilla Foundation. Another open-source software example is Moodle (www.moodle.com). Used by many school districts, Moodle can be customized as a learning management system (LMS) for students without any licensing fees.

Figure 10.7 The Open Source Initiative helps users identify open-source software.

- **Creative Commons** is a nonprofit organization that provides free copyright license tools that allow authors to customize the copyright terms for their creations (www.creativecommons.org) (refer to Figure 10.8).

Using the Internet, educators can more easily find quality shareware or freeware products while still preserving the ability to find obscure niche software. Major download sites, such as CNET's Download, rank titles based on user reviews, editors' reviews, and a few other ways. There are also user blogs and forums that assist individuals to spread news about titles they like.

However, educators also must note that a limitation of open-source resources, freeware, and shareware programs is potential instability and/or poor quality. When looking for open-source resources, freeware, and shareware programs, educators should be cautious of the credibility of the hosting servers from where they plan to download the program so that a computer virus, such as Trojan Horse, will not become a threat to one's computer.

Figure 10.8 Creative Common's CC button.

Which Is It? Trademark? Patent? Copyright?

Mashups are combinations that bring together different content into one place. They can combine pictures, audio, text, maps, and videos from various sources. **Remix**, a related term, refers to combing multimedia elements in ways that were not originally intended by the creators. Mashups can be music pieces, videos, audios, games, word clouds, Web contents, and even books.

Some mashups that teachers often use are blogs on Blogger, Edublogs, or WordPress on which teachers can post materials, such as video helps or instructions on assignments necessary for students to complete work while at home. The electronic presentation on Prezi in class that teachers use typically pulls information and materials from several sources.

Mashups can be included in reports and assignments to provide a visual representation. Students can create mashups as class projects for assessment to replace the traditional written reports or presentations. Mashups rely on open and discoverable resources, open and transparent licensing, and open and remixable formats. However, most publicly available data used in mashups today (such as graphics from Flickr or videos from YouTube) are not designed for educational purposes. Educators must be keenly aware of issues of plagiarism and copyright infringement in the mashups they present to their students and the mashups created by students. For the future generation of Americans to become more aware of intellectual property at an even younger age, schools need to begin educating children as early as possible on the nuances of intellectual property, innovation, and patents.

[Question 5] that trademark, service mark, patent, and copyright are not synonyms (refe...... g definitions come from the United States Patent and Trademark Office (USF......

- A **trademark** is a word, phrase, symbol, and/or design that identifies and distinguishes the source of the goods of one party from those of others.
- A **service mark** is a word, phrase, symbol, and/or design that identifies and distinguishes the source of a service rather than goods (Figure 10.10).
- A **patent** is a limited duration property right relating to an invention, granted by the United States Patent and Trademark Office, in exchange for public disclosure of the invention. The USPTO can issue design, utility, and plant patents.
- A **copyright** protects works of authorship such as writings, music, and works of art that have been tangibly expressed (see Figure 10.9).

Each of these terms has a set of criteria which must be followed in order to be in compliance with its governing agency: the United States Patent and Trademark Office (an agency of the Department of Commerce) (www.uspto.gov) and the U.S. Copyright Office (a division of the Library of Congress) (www.copyright.gov). More often than not, students and teachers are concerned about copyright issues. Therefore, it is expected that students and teachers be aware of the legal issues surrounding the use of copyrighted materials.

Teachers play a key role in students' lives and should model the appropriate behavior regarding the literacies, ethics, and laws that revolve around schools, classrooms, the community, and society as a whole. Let us return to Mrs. Keith at the beginning of the chapter. She is practicing a good teaching strategy of engaging students' attention by inserting the picture of Kermit the Frog in a presentation, but she has to model proper online behavior to her young students when downloading a picture from a source to which she has legitimate access, citing the source properly in her presentation. If she does not cite the source of the graphic, she should not use it.

Figure 10.9 The many aspects of copyright.

Truffelpix / Shutterstock.com

Figure 10.10 A fictional logo using the service mark symbol.
Source: Sue Mahoney

esbeauda / Shutterstock.com

Figure 10.11 Common infringement symbols: copyright, registered, trademark, and patent.

The **1976 Copyright Act** (www.copyright.gov/title17) provides guidelines for use of copyrighted materials. The following information comes from the document, ***Copyright Basics***, provided by the U.S. Copyright Office in Circular 1 (www.copyright.gov/circs/circ01.pdf). Copyright is a form of protection provided by U.S. laws to authors of "original works of authorship", including literary, dramatic, musical, artistic, and certain other intellectual works. Section 106 of the 1976 Copyright Act generally gives the owner of the copyright the exclusive right to do and to authorize others to do the following:

- Reproduce the work in copies or phonorecords
- Prepare derivative works based on the work
- Distribute copies or phonorecords of the work to the public by sale or other transfer of ownership or by rental, lease, or lending
- Perform the work publicly, in the case of literary, musical, dramatic, and choreographic works, pantomimes, and motion pictures and other audiovisual works
- Display the work publicly, in the case of the literary, musical, dramatic, and choreographic works, pantomimes, and pictorial, graphic, or sculptural works, including the individual images of a motion picture or other audiovisual work
- Perform the work publicly (in the case of sound recordings) by means of a digital audio transmission

Circular 40 (www.copyright.gov/circs/circ40.pdf) provides information about Copyright Registration for Pictorial, Graphic, and Sculptural Works. Copyright protection comes into existence at the time the work is created in a fixed, tangible form. Prior to March 1, 1989, the use of a copyright notice was mandatory on all published works, but after March 1, 1989, the use of a copyright notice is optional. A copyright notice includes the copyright symbol © (see Fig. 10.12), the owner of the copyright, and a date—for example:
© John Smith 2019.

What is protected by copyright? Protected are original works of authorship that are fixed in a tangible form of expression. Works created in one of the following categories are considered to be copyrightable:

- Literary works
- Musical works, including the accompanying words
- Dramatic works, including any accompanying music
- Pantomimes and choreographic works
- Pictorial, graphic, and sculptural works
- Motion pictures and other audiovisual works
- Sound recordings
- Architectural works

Tyler Olson/Shutterstock.com
© 2019, John Smith

Figure 10.12 Notice the copyright that John Smith has for this photograph both on the top right corner and on the right edge of the picture.

Copyright law allows educators the use of copyrighted materials under the fair use guidelines, Section 107. Limitations on exclusive rights: Fair Use (www.copyright.gov/title17/92chap1.html#107). The doctrine of fair use has evolved through multiple court decisions and is continuing to evolve with court decisions and the evolution of ways to use/create media (see Fig. 10.13). This doctrine allows for the reproduction of materials for the purpose of criticism, comment, news reporting, teaching, scholarship, and research. Four factors are to be considered in determining whether or not a particular use is fair.

1. The purpose and character of use, including whether such use is of commercial nature or is for nonprofit educational purposes
2. The nature of the copyrighted work

Arcady / Shutterstock.com

Figure 10.13 Fair use copyright rubber stamp.

3. The amount and substantiality of the portion used in relation to the copyrighted work as a whole (see Table 10.1)
4. The effect of the use on the potential market for, or value of, the copyrighted work.

To copy or not to copy? These elements must be carefully weighed. A chart such as the one below may help to tip the educator's decision one way or the other (refer to Table 10.2).

An Attribution (BY) licensee can be obtained, if the work is correctly referenced to the author, to copy, distribute, display, and perform it.

Educators can refer to the Fair Use Checklist put out by the Copyright Advisory Office at Columbia University (2017) Libraries (www.copyright.columbia.edu/content/dam/copyright/Precedent%20Docs/fairusechecklist.pdf) for a checklist of items to consider before copying a copyrighted document. Another very handy series of charts to help judge whether copying is Fair Use or not is shown at www.home.moravian.edu/public/reeves/library/ Fair%20Use%20Flow%20Chart.pdf. The distinction between what is fair use and what is infringement in a particular case is not always clear or easily defined, and, in recent times, cases have been taken to court for these decisions. The law calls for a balanced application of these four factors: purpose, nature, amount, and effect. The Copyright Advisory Office of Columbia University (www.copyright.columbia.edu/basics/fair-use.html) calls this a "balancing test" and states,

> To determine whether a use is or is not a fair use, always keep in mind that you need to apply all four factors. For example, do not jump to a conclusion based simply on whether your use is educational or commercial. You still need to evaluate, apply, and weigh in the balance the nature of the copyrighted work, the amount or substantiality of the portion used, and the potential impact of the use on the market or value of the work. This flexible approach to fair use is critical in order for the law to adapt to changing technologies and to meet innovative needs of higher education (para. 3).

Table 10.1 Amount Desired to Be Copied. *Modified table used under a Creative Commons BY license from the Copyright Advisory Office of Columbia University,* author, Dr. Kenneth D. Crews (formerly of Columbia University)

Amount Desired to Be Copied	
Favoring Fair Use	**Opposing Fair Use**
• Small quantity is to be copied. • Portion used is not central or significant to entire work. • Amount is appropriate for favored educational purpose.	• Large portion or whole work is to be used. • Portion used is central to or "heart of the work."

Table 10.2 Effect *of the use upon the potential market.* Used under a Creative Commons BY/NC license from the Copyright Advisory Office of Columbia University, author, Dr. Kenneth D. Crews (formerly of Columbia University)

Effect of the use upon the potential market	
Favoring Fair Use	**Opposing Fair Use**
• User lawfully purchased or acquired it for consumable purposes (many teacher workbooks can be bought *for the purpose* of copying). • Only one or few copies will be made. • No significant effect is made on the market or potential market for copyrighted work. • No similar product is marketed by the copyright holder. • There is no licensing mechanism.	• Could replace sale of copyrighted work. • Significantly impairs the market or potential market for copyrighted work or derivative. • Reasonably available licensing mechanism for use of the copyrighted work. • Affordable permission is available for using work. • Numerous copies will be made. • The copier will make it accessible on the Web or in other public forum. • Repeated or long-term use.

Let's apply the "balancing tests" on Miss Brown's scenarios. Miss Brown, a mathematics teacher, thinks a shareware tutorial software program that she uses in class can be helpful for a group of disadvantaged children that she volunteers to mentor after school in a community center. Should she request to purchase as many individual copies of the software as needed in the community center as required by the software company? Can she use the school software CD to install a copy for the community center?

Miss Brown's school purchases one copy of a typing tutorial program, which is housed in the library. It is checked out to individual students to take home for 2-week periods. This is permissible and, if so, under what conditions?

Miss Brown should check the software company homepage and the documents that come with the shareware tutorial software program and the school AUP to see if she can install the software program in the community center where she volunteers. The typing tutorial program should be checked out to individual students to take home for 2-week periods only if the software is removed from school and home computers after use.

Let's apply the "balancing tests" on Jason's scenario.

At one time or another, most teachers and students have found that "perfect piece" of video, music, or art for a presentation and hoped that the use of it fell into the category of "fair use." Jason, a student in the high school Web design class, finds a photo online dramatizing a pre-Columbian Viking landing in America. Since the school symbol is the Viking, he uses this photo as a graphic element on the school's Web page—giving credit to the site from which it was copied. Is this Fair Use? Why or why not?

Jason also takes a video class alongside his Web design class. His class produces a student video yearbook to add to the school homepage that they sell at community events to raise money for equipment for the school. They use well-known popular music clips. The money all goes to the school, and the songs are fully listed in the credits. Jason does wonder, however, if this is covered under Fair Use? Why or why not?

School districts are liable for any copyright violations committed by their staff and students, and the area with the greatest potential for liability is the district's public Website. Even though Jason plans to give credit to the site from which the Viking photo is found, it is still not a good practice to add the graphic element on the school's Web page without written consent from the original graphic owner. Again, using well-known popular music clips on a video yearbook to add to the school homepage without written consent is not permitted, even if it is for a good cause. There is not always a clear line between fair use and infringement. The best rule of thumb is that when in doubt, get permission from the copyright holder in writing. Many authors, composers, photographers, and others allow this through their Websites. The key concept that should be taken away from this section is that copyright is important! Copyright violation can result in civil and/or criminal sanctions as well as substantial fines depending on the nature of the violation.

When teachers are looking for high resolution stock photos for illustration, or other visual need, they can first try out royalty-free sources such as Morguefile. There are also stock photo services such as Shutterstock or iStockphotos that charge by annual subscription fees or download fees per picture (see Figure 10.14). Stock photos are copyrighted images.

Figure 10.14   Educators can purchase stock pictures online.

For instance, with Shutterstock, users must purchase permission to use an image or subscribe to a photo service much like subscribing to a magazine in order to use these images. If a user has a license for a software package that includes clip art/photos, the user can use the clip art/photo images that are associated with the software usually without any additional charges, depending on how they are being used. The user should always review the software licensing agreement for the "terms of usage" to insure that images are used within the limits of the licensing agreement.

If using an image from a Website under Fair Use, it is imperative that the source information be included under the image in a small font size (e.g.,—Source: www.complete.url.information.com).

If one uses personal photos in a document and he or she is the owner of these photos, a notice of copyright should be included in the information with the photos. This information should be in a small font size underneath or to the side such as in Figure 10.12 and include a notice of copyright, for example, © 2019, John Smith.

Two pieces of federal legislation, the Digital Millennium Copyright Act of 1998 (DMCA) and the Technology, Education, and Copyright Harmonization (TEACH), were created to govern issues related to digital distance education. If one is participating as a teacher in digital/online delivery of materials, he or she should check with school district resources to be sure to comply with the institution's requirements.

Best practice dictates that teachers and students be acquainted with copyright laws, fair use doctrine, and any future laws pertaining to copyright. It is also best practice to ask for permission in writing to use copyrighted materials when creating multimedia documents. Again, the school librarian is a useful resource for what is allowed.

Students and teachers must be mindful of copyright laws. Copyright law can change, and teachers serve as models for proper copyright protocols.

Citations and Reference Guidelines

As mentioned, there are a number of styles for citing and referencing others' work. The *Publication Manual of the American Psychological Association*, currently in its sixth edition, is used as the formatting guide for documents created in the field of education. Among many, the APA Website (www.apastyle.org) provides resources and guidance for users. Typing in "APA electronic citations" or "APA electronic references" will bring up a number of sites and examples in a search engine (also see Table 10.3).

According to current APA guidelines (2014), if citing an entire Website and not a specific document found on that site, it is sufficient to include the Web address (URL) in parentheses in the text. However, the guidelines change when citing a particular document or information from a Website, and this requires a listing in the reference list as well as an in-text citation.

Music and video must also be properly cited and referenced. The following examples are from the *APA Style Guide to Electronic References, Sixth Edition (2012)*.

Table 10.3   The Online Writing Lab (OWL) at Purdue University. More can be found at www.owl.english.purdue.edu/owl/resource/589/2/

Citations and References are required when you . . .
- use words or ideas presented in a magazine, book, newspaper, song, TV program, movie, Web page, computer program, letter, advertisement, or any other medium
- use information gained through interviewing or conversing with another person, face-to-face, over the phone, or in writing
- copy the exact words or a unique phrase from a source
- reprint any diagrams, illustrations, charts, pictures, or other visual materials
- use or repost any electronically available media, including images, audio, video, or other media

Music recording, full album
Writer, A. A. (copyright year). *Title of album* [Recorded by B. B. Artist if different from writer; Medium
    of recording: CD, mp3, record, cassette, etc.]. Retrieved from www.xxxx (Date of recording if different
    from album copyright date)
Music recording, single track on an album
Writer, A. A. (copyright year). Title of song [Recorded by B. B. Artist if different from writer]. On *Title
    of album* [Medium of recording: CD, mp3, record, cassette, etc.]. Retrieved from www.xxxx (Date of
    recording if different from album copyright date)
Music recording, single track, republished
Lennon, J., & McCartney, P. (2000). I want to hold your hand [Recorded by The Beatles; mp3 file]. On
    The Beatles 1. Retrieved from www.amazon.com (Original work recorded 1963)
Streaming video (*e.g., YouTube video*)
Author, A. A. [User name]. (year, month day). Title of video [Video file]. Retrieved from www.xxxx
User name. (year, month day). Title of video [Video file]. Retrieved from www.xxxx

The person who posts a video is credited as the author. If the person's real name and user name are both
available, the real name must be provided in the format: Author, A. A., followed by the user name inside brackets. If the real name is not available, one must include only the user name without brackets.

Citations and/or references are critical in any document created. If there is a resource that needs citing and
it is impossible to figure out how to do it, the school librarian can be asked for assistance (refer to Table 10.3).
Sometimes Websites offer citation assistance. For example:

• Van Gogh Gallery—www.vangoghgallery.com/ Scroll to the bottom of the Web page . . . "How to Cite
  this Page"
• Wikipedia—www.wikipedia.org/ Although Wikipedia should not be used as a primary and the only
  reference for researching a subject, if used it should be included in the references. Wikipedia provides
  citation help in its menu: Tools > Special Pages > Page Tools > Cite This Page.

Driven by the rapid expansion of published and online literature, a new generation of online citation genera-
tors, or citation management software, are available for authors to record bibliographic references (Table 10.4).
These online tools facilitate the creation of bibliographies or reference sections. Citation generators work by
asking users to fill out Web forms to take input and format the output according to guidelines such as MLA from
Modern Language Association, APA from American Psychological Association, and the Chicago Manual of
Style. The excuses used by students who plagiarize are sometimes that they do not know how to cite properly.
These sites prevent problems.

Table 10.4   A List of Citation Generators for Students

Citation Generators	Web Address
Citation Machine	www.citationmachine.net
EasyBib	www.easybib.com
Citation Builder	www.lib.ncsu.edu/citationbuilder
KnightCite	www.calvin.edu/library/knightcite
RefME	www.refme.com/us
BibMe	www.bibme.org

When the citation process is made easy by introducing the citation generators, hopefully, instances of plagiarism should decrease. Nevertheless, teachers must beware that not all citation generators are created equally. For instance, some citation generators target APA style formats, while others may be more accurate with MLA or other styles. Teachers are recommended to find the citation generators that best fit the practices of their subject areas and produce the most accurate bibliographies.

It is imperative to remind teachers and students alike that citations and references are required in any type of document created. If the information required for a specific citation/reference is not readily available, it is a definite responsibility to locate the information and properly cite/reference any source used.

Confidentiality

Part of an ethical conversation about technology revolves around the plethora of data that teachers collect on students, including grading. There is student and parent information on a teacher's technology tools that cannot be shared with others. Much care must be taken to ensure that none of this type of information be seen and/or taken. This could occur, for example, when a teacher leaves his/her screen on where others (including other parents) may view it. A student and his/her parents, according to the Family Educational Rights and Privacy Act (FERPA) (www2.ed.gov/policy/gen/guid/fpco/ferpa/index.html), have rights to see the education records of their child—but not those of other students. When in doubt what types of records a teacher may give out, he or she should consult the FERPA guidelines. The teacher must always secure his or her computer with passwords and be very mindful of clearing the screen of sensitive information being used when he or she has others around. The placement of the screen is also important if a teacher is working on sensitive data during the time that a class may be in the room.

Records can be easily lost with technology, so a teacher should ask what backup system a school district uses to be sure that grades and other important information will remain secure. If personal backup is allowed, the teacher must follow strict protocols to ensure that the information is never compromised.

Technology Safety—An Ethical Issue

There are really two main issues that teachers must think about under the heading of safety—child safety and "machine" safety. Teachers have the responsibility to protect expensive school equipment, which means that rules for use must be established so that the equipment is not severely damaged and can be used year after year. Teachers must also secure the equipment so that it does "not disappear." To avoid having viruses take over, the teacher must have students avoid going onto certain sites and/or accepting certain emails while on school equipment. If the teacher controls the password, he or she should make sure that it remains secure and that machines needing a password are locked at the end of the day (if required).

Almost everyone who has used the computer or other devices has been in a situation that has caused physical discomfort. Teachers are also responsible for making sure that the technologies they have in their rooms for children are set up for comfortable physical use. This includes the height of the chair, the work surface, and a possible document holder. Obviously, students come in all sizes, so they should be taught to properly adjust (if possible) the seating and eye-to-screen length to their physical attributes. The lighting is another critical issue, particularly glare. Windows and/or overhead lights can quickly cause eyestrain, so the tilt of the screen and its placement is important. The brightness of a screen can be adjusted as well. Too long in any position can create painful situations, so teachers must consider time limitations of computer use in terms of age appropriateness. Teaching proper posture can also help alleviate pain. Securing all cords and electrical hazards must be a consideration in classrooms for people's safety, and rules for foods and liquids around technology should be established for equipment safety. Teachers can prevent a host of issues from occurring by being thoughtful about the placement of screens and other equipment. Being able to see students' screens easily is a first step in careful monitoring.

Mental health is important for students as well. Many districts install firewalls that do not allow certain things to be viewed. A teacher must still check to see if that which he/she presents or that which students are viewing is safe and age appropriate. An appropriate part of ethical technology is addressing sending scams and viruses to others intentionally. Scams ("phishing") are a regular part of the Internet today, and people lose a considerable amount of money by being lured in. Cyber predators or cyber stalkers often target children of all ages as well. Teaching children to never give out personal information to those online who are unknown is a critical part of technology safety. If a child suspects that someone who is unknown is trying to "get too close," teachers should help children see how important it is to report it to an adult to have them check it out, particularly if someone wants to "meet up". It is imperative that students, as well as teachers, comprehend the seriousness of cyberstalking and phishing. Some tips for stifling these actions include always logging out of your computer, good password management, limiting online sharing by using privacy settings on online accounts, using updated security software, and maintaining updates.

Hacking has also become a part of technology that can cause financial and informational loss. Some hackers do it for the challenge, while others, usually students, do it to change information such as grades or cause havoc to a school. Students should be taught that there are stiff penalties for those who are caught breaking into school systems, but schools may not often enforce them with young students. This, says Kassner (2013) in his article "Hackers: From Innocent Curiosity to Illegal Activity," is one of the prime reasons that students continue to the next level of hacking. Hacking for any reason should be considered as serious misconduct.

A racially charged item was placed on Jefferson High School's Facebook page. The district began at once to investigate who was responsible. The district network administrators suspected that the campus Facebook was hacked by a group who called themselves "the Jeff Electronic Army" or JEA. The district network administrators had experienced some previous incidents with hacking the past year when some desperate students hacked into the district electronic grade book system to bump up their grades. When the current suspected hacking behaviors were detected, district network administrators used "packet sniffers," a program that can see all the information passing over the network to which it is connected in order to monitor their networks and perform diagnostic tests or troubleshoot problems. With both experiences, the district decided to take measures to prevent more incidents by assigning IT personnel to set up stronger firewalls, follow hacking forums to pick up on all the latest methods, encourage institute-wide users to change passwords frequently, install proper scanning software programs, and run attack and penetration tests to detect vulnerable points in the network that can be easily accessed from both external and internal users. The district encourages schools and teachers to make user-awareness campaigns to make all network users aware of the pitfalls of security and the necessary security practices to minimize hacking risks. They also want to send out the message to potential hackers that modern technology is so advanced that tools can be used to track "digital footprints" of hackers' online activities; therefore, it is better "not to even think about it!"

Snapchat has gained quick popularity, and the concept of volatile, self-vanishing images also became trendy, so many other social media companies, such as Instagram and Wickr, have come up with the same concept packed in their own apps. The vast usage of image-sharing applications has communicated that their users are primarily millennials, young people who were born between 1980s and early 2000s, and the primary usage is sending fun content. They usually can view but not necessarily download images or videos, and they can also select different copyright options for images or videos.

With all the fun of these types of communication, there comes a responsibility to the users. Other problems that have risen include inappropriate content being posted, personal information being compromised, and the uses of defamation and gossip about others give out. Again, current and future employers may have access to job applicants' social media files which, if inappropriate, can hinder users in their careers. Educators originally were concerned that that the apps' self-deleting nature encouraged sexting. However, it doesn't seem to stop there. Read Mr. Adams' story below.

A mashup photo posted to Snapchat by Wilson, who is in the twelfth grade, has sparked outage.

The image shows Mr. Adams, the school's softball coach, in business attire, standing in an empty room with nooses drawn around him.

"I saw it on Snapchat and Facebook," said a boy who attended high school with Wilson. "I've heard a lot of people trying to figure out what Wilson's intentions were behind it—whether or not it was a threat, or whether or not he was just joking."

Some parent expressed outrage about the pictures.

School leaders knew who had posted the photo. Wilson told them that it was meant to be a joke. He thought that his scribble would only be available for a short time for his four friends before the temporary photo became inaccessible.

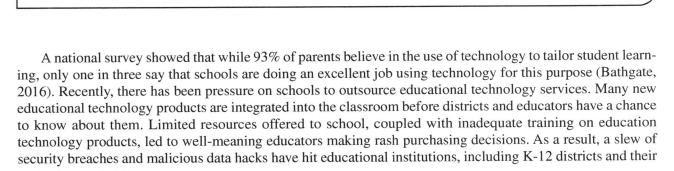

One person forwarded to another, and it seemed like the photo was on everyone's social media after just a couple of days. There was no way to erase the photo.

"Personally, that's not a joking matter," said Mr. Adams. "Whether it was a threat, or the kids were just thinking it was cute and fun; it wasn't to me."

The superintendent sent parents the following statement:

"The school district along with the sheriff's office has initiated an investigation. This kind of picture on social media will not be tolerated in the school system."

A national survey showed that while 93% of parents believe in the use of technology to tailor student learning, only one in three say that schools are doing an excellent job using technology for this purpose (Bathgate, 2016). Recently, there has been pressure on schools to outsource educational technology services. Many new educational technology products are integrated into the classroom before districts and educators have a chance to know about them. Limited resources offered to school, coupled with inadequate training on education technology products, led to well-meaning educators making rash purchasing decisions. As a result, a slew of security breaches and malicious data hacks have hit educational institutions, including K-12 districts and their technology providers.

Loosing personal data is also at risk in today's times, so it is important to be able to assess what particular vendors' privacy practices are. One important consideration is to ask if the vendor has a privacy policy, request a copy, and analyze it to see if it is well written and reflects what the vendor does and does not do with data. Another suggestion is to ask a vendor for a list of references and check those to discover if previous and current clients have or have had incidents with the vendor.

If a teacher is careless with passwords and that carelessness lead to data breach incidents, then all cost associated with the breach could fall on the district. Providing school employees with training on privacy expectations from vendors, cybersecurity threats, and operational precautions could save districts considerable resources, including money and personal time.

Most recently, one of the education technology companies, Schoolvilla, had records of thousands of students exposed. Schoolvilla, like Edmoto, is a network that enables teachers to share content, distribute quizzes and assignments, and manage communication with students, colleagues, and parents.

A cybersecurity researcher found that Schoolvilla had inadvertently exposed personally identifiable student data (including students' social security numbers, parents' names, and home information) and test scores through the company's database backups.

Among the districts affected was Carter Middle School, where 600 former and current students' records were exposed. While Schoolvilla scrambled post-attack to patch up the problems with their servers, parents were sometimes the last to know. Some read about these incidents on the news before receiving physical letters from the district.

Each state has laws mandating how schools and districts notify parents and staff after security breach incidents. When the privacy breach was first found, the school had followed protocols.

Mr. Goyle, the middle school principal, noted that the limited resources offered to schools coupled with inadequate training on education technology products led to well-meaning educators making rash purchasing decisions of Schoolvilla. "Working in the district, you are really under pressure to address the areas of technology growth," said Mr. Goyle. "That pressure has caused the schools to acquire Schoolvilla without a thorough plan or understanding of the product's capabilities."

The incident underscores "how important it is to have a good vendor when you're dealing with these outsourcing relationships," Mr. Goyle added. "This incident offered us a real lesson in the importance of software terms of service." He thought professional development covering contract review and negotiations could help but also pointed out that most districts lacked the budget for it.

In recent years, experts have witnessed a spike in "ransomware" attacks across all sectors of the economy, public and private. News media has reported that massive cyberattacks have crippled the IT systems of several hospitals across the United States, forcing some to redirect emergency patients and locking clinicians out until a ransom had been paid. Ransomware attacks have also infected airlines, banks, and utilities across the world. Obviously, ransomware does not discriminate, because K-12 school systems across the country are also being targeted with "ransomware", which has forced them to spend money they did not have; it also put their operations at grave risk.

A big headache was waiting for Dr. Clements, the superintendent of the York Bay Public Schools, as he arrived at work on a Monday. His district was under a cyberattack. A computer virus had infiltrated the district's student-information servers and encrypted substantial amounts of data, making it inaccessible to district employees and schools. The perpetrators had left a message demanding a ransom in exchange for a decryption key.

After the district was hit by the ransomware attack, York Bay Public Schools' IT director immediately shut the servers down to stop the spread of the virus. He then discussed with his supervisor whether to pay the nearly $10,000 ransom. The IT director figured that the alternative to paying up would be to rebuild the district's data systems from backups.

Some districts have been forced to weigh the ethics of paying money to untrustworthy and anonymous criminals against surviving for weeks without access to lesson plans, learning software, or student records, but Dr. Clements said he would not consider paying the ransom. Even if his district paid the ransom, he said, there would be no assurances that the hackers would unlock the data. "Paying," said Dr. Clements, "would only empower a criminal group."

"Paying the ransom should be a business decision," said the school board president, who held a different opinion. "What's it worth per day to not have access for our 32,200 students?"

School networks are large, and the types of data collected by schools are sensitive. If not handled well, ransomware can be a long-term problem for educational organizations. With school budgets already stretched, finding the money to support cybersecurity may require cutting spending in other areas of the budget.

Law enforcement agencies like the FBI generally discourage hacked organizations from paying ransoms because doing so only emboldens criminal enterprises. They *urge victims* to *report* and suggest school districts to take a number of defensive measures (www.ic3.gov/media/2016/160915.aspx) to avoid ransomware attacks including:

- Regularly back up data and verify the integrity of those backups.
- Secure backups. Ensure backups are not connected to the computers and networks they are backing up.
- Scrutinize links contained in emails and do not open attachments included in unsolicited emails.
- Only download software—especially free software—from sites you know and trust.
- Ensure application patches for the operating system, software, and firmware are up to date, including Adobe Flash, Java, Web browsers, etc.
- Ensure antivirus and anti-malware solutions are set to automatically update, and regular scans are conducted.
- Disable macro scripts from files transmitted via email. Consider using Office Viewer software to open Microsoft Office files transmitted via email instead of full Office Suite applications.
- Implement software restrictions or other controls to prevent the execution of programs in common ransomware locations.
- Focus on awareness and training.

For additional resources, visit:

khanacademy.org/partner-content/nova/cybersecurity/cyber/v/cybersecuity-101

pbs.org/wgbh/nova/labs/lab/cyber/1/1/

staysafeonline.org

wired.com/video/category/security

Keeping students, teachers, and equipment safe is an ethical responsibility. Schools must do all they can to maintain the integrity of their technologies and ensure the safe usage of those resources.

The Web – Visiting, Citing, Safety, Creation, Evaluation, and More

The Web is a major component in today's classrooms. Reviewing some key concepts regarding the Webpages and Internet usage will be helpful. Materials or content on the Web are protected under the copyright law and cannot be freely used or modified without permission from the copyright holder. Website content is protected under copyright law whether or not it carries a copyright notice. Permission from the copyright holder is required, in writing, if a work is being used beyond fair use.

What does it take to view a Web page? Web pages (.html documents) can be read with a browser (e.g., Firefox®, Safari®, Microsoft Edge). HTML documents can be read without Internet access. This means that a teacher can create Web pages for his/her students to use in the classroom without Internet access. Each Web page has a URL (Uniform Resource Locator) which is the address of documents and other resources on the World Wide Web and includes the following:

www.copyright.gov

1. http://—**http** stands for **hypertext transfer protocol** and defines how messages are formatted and transmitted (Webopedia, 2017e).
2. www—stands for World Wide Web and often today is not needed when entering a URL into the address box of the browser
3. copyright—is the domain name which is used to identify an Internet protocol (IP) address
4. The domain suffix (.xxx) located at the end of a homepage (or main address) indicates which domain the Web page belongs to (Webopedia, 2017f) (see Figure 10.15):
   • gov—government agencies
   • edu—education
   • org—organizations (nonprofit)
   • mil—military
   • com—commercial business
   • net—network organizations
   • ca—Canada (e.g., as countries have two letters)

Figure 10.15   A few popular domain names are shown.

What should teachers consider before using a Web page or Web resources with students? Whether teachers realize it or not, each time they visit a Web page or Web resource they are evaluating it, depending on what one is looking for and how he/she will use the information provided (see Table 10.5). If one does this automatically when he/she is on the Web, it must be at a heightened level for each Web page students are to use in the classroom. All Web pages should be previewed before having students use them. Depending on the age of the audience, it is preferable to have students click on a link to go to a Web page rather than having them enter the URL and possibly entering it incorrectly—a URL incorrectly entered can sometimes direct a student to a Website that is inappropriate! When using Web resources the teacher should consider the following:

• Rich content
• Accuracy of the information
• Source of the information (reliable source or someone who just created a Web page for fun)
• Page design which includes colors scheme, fonts, page layout, and graphics
• Navigation
• Copyright date. Is the date current?
• A listed contact person or Web master for the Website
• Inappropriate elements: bias, inappropriate language, violence, and inappropriate graphics and advertisements
• Appropriateness for audience (does content and the way it is presented work for your audience)
• Stimulation factor (on target to maintain interest level versus overly stimulating for age group)
• Readability or one's particular age group

Table 10.5   Web Resource Evaluation Checklist

Criteria	Quality		
	High Quality	**Medium Quality**	**Low Quality**
Rich Content			
Accuracy of the information			
Sources of the information			
Page Design			
Graphics load quickly			
Navigation			
Copyright date			
Contact person or Web master			
Free of inappropriate elements			

Source: author

Teachers may want to educate students to be flexible when they encounter broken links on Web pages. Due to the dynamic nature of the Web, outdated online materials and inaccessible links are almost unavoidable. Teachers can demonstrate to students how to self-help by finding substitute materials, access cached information, or apply advanced search techniques for other alternatives. At the same, teachers should also remind students to update Web page information and ensure accuracy of the information they have posted on the Web as a courtesy to viewers who visit the information they have posted.

Appropriate protocols need to be followed when a teacher wants to use Web resources that are not available through the school intranet. Each school district has its own classroom guidelines, as well as Internet security firewall specifications that monitor and control what teachers can use and access in their classrooms. Many popular Websites are blocked by the school district's filters. If appropriate online resources are available that are not accessible in the classroom, the school librarian is a useful resource for facilitating access to these resources. School librarians are very knowledgeable about district guidelines and copyright laws. In some instances, the teacher may be required to download a file on a jump drive or external hard drive to be able to use a resource in the classroom. When doing this, the teacher should follow copyright laws and, if required, request permission from the copyright holder to use the resource in the classroom.

File Formats

A file format is how a document is saved, depending on the software being used to create the document. When doing a "save as" in any software, the program defaults to its native file format (e.g., Microsoft Word [.docx], Excel [.xlsx], and Windows Live Moviemaker project file [.wlmp]). Most software also gives the user additional file format options for saving the document. For example, Microsoft Word will allow a document to be saved in multiple file formats including RTF (rich text format) and PDF (portable document format). As a rule of thumb, one should always save the document being created in its native format and then do a "save as" and save in a different format if that is needed.

Audio, graphic, and video files are key components of many Web pages and multimedia documents. Files are saved in different formats and often the format chosen depends on how the file will be used. It is important to remember that when using someone else's work, in any of these file formats, copyright/source information is required when using them in multimedia documents and, depending on how they are being used (for education or for commercial), may require a royalty fee to the owner of the document being used.

Some file formats use lossless or lossy compression when saving documents. Lossless compression (e.g., PC platform—WinZip) reorganizes a file so that the file size is smaller, but it can only reduce the size of a document a specific amount. Lossy compression methods, such as MP3 for audio and JPG and GIF for graphics, remove file data from the document, which cannot be retrieved once deleted (see Figure 10.16). To ensure that a document in its original form is not lost, one should always work on a copy of the original as a safeguard against disaster. Lossy compression is often used with graphic, audio, and video file formats. For instance, the popular photograph format, jpeg, is a lossy format. Photographs that are saved with .jpg extension will lose its sharp quality over extensive editing (Figure 10.16).

Figure 10.16   A sharp JPG photograph may become grainy after extensive editing.

To reach a larger audience, proprietary video formats should be converted to popular formats such as MP4, WMV, and MOV. For instance, digital stories created with apps or software should be output to a common video format before distributing to students' families. In addition, electronic brochures or newsletters created with Microsoft Word or page layout software also need to be saved as a PDF document when sent to a long listserv of recipients. The PDF format conversion usually protects the contents from being changed and keeps the file sizes smaller. Documents can be accessed by almost everyone using Acrobat Reader, a free PDF viewer from Adobe, and the format also keeps the contents in the right format during transmission.

Webopedia offers a comprehensive list of graphic formats (2017g) and file extensions (2017h). The Website's search feature will also allow a search for a specific format. Table 10.6 is a partial list of more commonly used file formats.

Table 10.6   A List of Commonly used File Formats

AVI: Multimedia audio/video
DOC or DOCX: Microsoft Word document
BMP: Bitmap formatted graphics are most often clip art. This type of graphic is usually created using paint software.
EPS (Encapsulated postscript file): Generic vector/raster graphics file format
EXL or EXLS: Microsoft Excel document
GIF: A graphic file format that can have 256 colors.
HTML (hypertext markup language): Web page document
JPG or JPEG (Joint Photographic Experts Group): Lossy compression graphic format used for photographic images that can support 16 million colors.
MIDI (.mid): MIDI stands for musical instrument digital interface.
MOV (.mov): QuickTime video clip
MP3 (.mp3): Windows-compatible audio format
MP4 (.mp4): Video file
PDF (Portable document format): PDF documents can be read with Acrobat Reader⁻ (free download from Adobe).
PICT: Graphic file format developed by Apple Computer and supports 8 colors. PICT2, a newer version of this file, supports 16 million colors. Both of these graphic file formats are supported by Apple Macintosh computers.
PNG (Portable Network Graphics): Lossless bitmapped graphics format that supports transparency and opacity. This file format does not support animation.
PPT or PPTX: Microsoft PowerPoint document
PSD: Adobe Photoshop document
Real Audio (.ra, .ram, .rm): RealPlayer is required to play this type of streaming audio file.
RTF (Rich text format): Generic word processing file format that can be opened by any word processing software.
WAV (.wav): Windows-compatible audio file format. Uncompressed WAV files can be quite large.
WMV: Windows media video

Teachers can convert individual media files such as M4A audio file output from iPad audio recording apps to the popular MP3 format by going through free online media converter sites such as www.online-convert.com or www.media-converter.sourceforge.net.

It is a good practice for teachers to use the file formats recommended by their schools or districts when creating tests, worksheets, handouts, and other course materials. For example, when using a Web tool to generate a worksheet, teachers may have to be creative in order to save the document for future use (e.g., taking a screen shot of the page, copying and pasting the information in a word processing document) or saving the Web page as a PDF document. A file that cannot be accessed by recipients, whether colleagues, students, or students' families, can cause teachers headaches. They can also be students' models in terms of *media literacy*. Teachers and students should know what kind of file formats go with various documents and use the appropriate file format when creating documents. This may entail creating a document in a software package and then converting it to a generic file format so that it can be viewed/used by individuals who do not have the software used to create the document. Knowledge about various media formats also helps teachers to become more effective media users. For instance, digital sound files must be structured so that a media player can read them.

Conclusion

A tremendous amount of responsibility comes with using technology tools, especially in schools. The user, whether administrator, teacher, or student, needs to be committed to using these tools responsibly, legally, and ethically. Doing this is important as a user, but it becomes even more essential if one is a teacher in a classroom and is modeling technology and its usage for learners.

All classroom teachers have an ethical responsibility to use technology tools in a manner that conforms to the teachers' ethics code. They also have the responsibility of being in compliance with federal, state, and school district laws and/or guidelines. Professional development is one key component of staying abreast of technology and its guidelines and use. Opportunities are available for staying current on these use issues for teachers through their school district, online courses, software tutorials, and YouTube videos, to name a few. Likewise, students can take advantage of online tutorials and how-to blogs for learning new software or refreshing skills and for maintain knowledge for safe and ethical/legal use.

Technology is a tool to help facilitate student learning and in managing teachers' work. Because technology is evolving, the associated rules and laws will also evolve. This means that teachers and students must stay current on the changes associated with any given technology and its associated components.

Additional Resources

Academic Integrity
www.ryerson.ca/academicintegrity/students/tutorial-episodes
This site has effective animated episodes on certain issues with academic integrity.

Blog Basics: Copyright and Fair Use
This site introduces protections that apply to work posted online.
www.gcflearnfree.org/print/blogbasics/copyright-and-fair-use0?playlist=Blog_Basics

Cheating: Pressures, Choices and Values
www.hrmvideo.com/catalog/cheating-pressures-choices-and-values
This resource is about students' academic cheating.

Cheating—at school
www.cyh.com/HealthTopics/HealthTopicDetailsKids.aspx?p=335&np=286&id=1427
This Website is very informative about the breakdown of examples of academic cheating.

BYU Copyright Licensing Office
This tutorial includes a short instructional film followed by some interactive scenarios.
sites.lib.byu.edu/copyright/about-copyright/tutorial

Copyright and Primary Sources
The Library of Congress explores copyright and Fair Use in a question-and-answer format.
www.loc.gov/teachers/usingprimarysources/copyright.html

References

American Library Association. (2014). *Introduction to information literacy.* Retrieved from www.ala.org/acrl/standards/informationliteracycompetency

American Psychological Association. (2012). *APA style guide, APA style guide to electronic references* (6th ed.). [Kindle version]. Washington, DC: Author.

American Psychological Association. (2014). *APA style.* Retrieved from www.apastyle.org

Bathgate, K. (2016, October 20). *National survey shows strong parent support for technology in the classroom; Suggests gaps and opportunities in implementation.* Retrieved from www.marketwired.com/press-release/national-survey-shows-strong-parent-support-technology-classroom-suggests-gaps-opportunities-2168298.htm

Computer Ethics Institute. (n.d.). *The ten commandments of computer ethics.* Retrieved from www.computerethicsinstitute.org/home.html

Copyright Advisory Office of Columbia University. (2017). *Fair use checklist.* Retrieved from www.copyright.com/wp-content/uploads/2015/04/CR-Teach-Act.pdf

Daugherty, L., Dossani, R., Johnson, E., & Oguz, M. (2014). *Using early childhood education to bridge the digital divide.* Retrieved from Rand Corporation Website: www.rand.org/content/dam/rand/pubs/perspectives/PE100/PE119/RAND_PE119.pdf

Hinduja S., & Patchin, J. W. (2014). *Cyberbullying fact sheet: Identification, prevention, and response.* Cyberbullying Research Center. Retrieved from www.cyberbullying.org/Cyberbulling_Identification_Prevention_Response.pdf

International Society for Technology in Education. (2016). *ISTE Standards for Students.* Retrieved from www.iste.org/standards/for-students

International Society for Technology in Education. (2017). *ISTE Standards for Teachers.* Retrieved from www.iste.org/standards/for-educators

Kassner, M. (2013). *Hackers: From innocent curiosity to illegal activity.* Retrieved from www.techrepublic.com/blog/it-security/hackers-from-innocent-curiosity-to-illegal-activity

Lowell, A. (n.d.). *Why do we use emojis?* Retrieved from www.psychologytoday.com/blog/contemporary-psychoanalysis-in-action/201605/why-do-we-use-emojis

McMahon, R. (2007). *Everybody does it: Academic cheating is at an all-time high. Can anything be done to stop it?* Retrieved from www.sfgate.com/education/article/Everybody-Does-It-2523376.php

Merriam-Webster. (2007). *Ethics.* Retrieved from www.wordcentral.com/cgi-bin/student?book=Student&va=ethics

Nath, J. L., & Cohen, M. D. (Eds.). (2011). *Becoming an EC-6 Teacher in Texas: A course of study for the Pedagogy and Professional Responsibilities (PPR) TExES.* Belmont, CA: Wadsworth/Cengage Learning.

National Forum on Information Literacy. (2017). *Information literacy skills.* Retrieved from www.infolit.org/information-literacy-projects-and-programs

National Telecommunications and Information Administration. (1999). *Falling through the net: Defining the digital divide.* Retrieved from www.ntia.doc.gov/report/1999/falling-through-net-defining-digital-divide

Plafke, J. (2012). *Merriam-Webster inducts "F-bomb", "sexting", "mancave", and others into the 2012 dictionary.* Retrieved from www.themarysue.com/merriam-webster-2012-dictionary-inductions-f-bomb

Rodrigues, A. (2011, June 10). *Seniors cheating in high school sociology case study.* [Blog post]. Retrieved from www.sociologyseniors.wordpress.com/2011/06/10/students-cheating-in-high-school-sociology-case-study-adriana-rodrigues/

Steber, G. (1994–2012). *Core rules of netiquette.* Learning@CSU. Colorado State University. Retrieved from www.writing.colostate.edu/guides/guide.dfm?guideid=4

Texas Education Agency. (2017). *TExES™ Pedagogy and Professional Responsibilities (PPR) EC-12 (160) Test at a Glance.* Retrieved from www.cms.texes-ets.org/files/2114/8717/0543/ppr_EC_12_160_TAAG.pdf

United States Copyright Office. (December 1998). *The Digital Millennium Copyright Act of 1998, U.S. Copyright Office Summary.* Retrieved from www.copyright.gov/legislation/dmca.pdf

United States Copyright Office. (May 2012). *Circular 1, copyright basics.* Retrieved from www.copyright.gov/circs/circ01.pdf

United States Copyright Office. (September 2015). *Circular 40, Copyright Registration for Pictorial, Graphic and Sculptural Works.* Retrieved from www.copyright.gov/circs/circ40.pdf United States Patent and Trademark Office. (2013). *Trademark, patent, or copyright?* Retrieved from www.uspto.gov/trademarks-getting-started/trademark-basics/trademark-patent-or-copyright

Webopedia. (2017a). *Freeware.* Retrieved from www.webopedia.com/TERM/F/freeware.html

Webopedia. (2017b*). Shareware*. Retrieved from www.webopedia.com/TERM/S/shareware.html

Webopedia. (2017c). *Public domain*. Retrieved from www.webopedia.com/TERM/P/public_domain_software.html

Webopedia. (2017d). *Open source software*. Retrieved from www.webopedia.com/DidYouKnow/Computer_Science/open_source.asp

Webopedia. (2017e). *HTTP—HyperText Transfer Protocol*. Retrieved from www.webopedia.com/TERM/H/HTTP.html

Webopedia. (2017f). *Domain name*. Retrieved from www.webopedia.com/TERM/D/domain_name.html

Webopedia. (2014g). *Graphics formats*. Retrieved from www.webopedia.com/quick_ref/graphics_formats.asp

Webopedia. (2017h). *File extensions*. Retrieved from www.webopedia.com/quick_ref/fileextensionsfull.asp

Chapter 11

Employing Technology to Facilitate Assessment of Student Learning

Ronald S. Beebe, Irene Chen, and Janice L. Nath, *Professor Emeritus*
University of Houston - Downtown

Meet Mr. Johnston

Mr. Johnston uses peer editing in his high school English class to increase students' understanding of how best to create various genres of writing. His typical practice had students exchanging papers during part of the class, yet this did not afford enough time for many of them to provide feedback to their peers. Generally, most students received editing comments from only one or two students—with little quality feedback provided by the peer editors. Frustrated by the amount of time in class needed to exchange papers and the lack of substantive comments among his students, Mr. Johnston looked for a technological tool that could both shorten the time to receive feedback as well as engage more students in the peer-editing process. He decided to explore the use of Dropbox as a platform for students to upload their work but also to gain access to the writing of classmates. Mr. Johnston thought exchanging edited documents through a shared cloud space (such as Dropbox) would allow students asynchronous access to writing assignments for peer editing as well as free up instructional time in class to focus on the essentials of writing and editing.

racorn / Shutterstock.com

As part of the planning for implementing this idea, Mr. Johnston spent time with the students in class to develop good peer-editing skills. Because he would not be available to provide in-class guidance during the editing process and to insure consistency in the online peer-editing comments, he developed a rubric clearly describing the editing requirements and the intended focus of student comments. He also arranged for students to use the computer lab at school in case they had limited access to the Internet and to insure compatibility with the word processing program.

As a result of using this technological adaptation, Mr. Johnston found the number of thoughtful comments regarding the construction of a thesis, development of an argument, and consideration of an audience increased as well as the number of students providing feedback on individual assignments. Students noted an appreciation for the additional time to carefully review peers' work and the ability to extend their feedback beyond simple spelling and grammatical errors had improved their own writing skills.

Beginning to Think about Assessing with Technology

Technology provides various opportunities to assess student learning and work that can provide both formative and summative outcomes. Blogs, wikis, shared workspaces (e.g., Dropbox, Google Docs, Smartsheet, and SharePoint), and other types of asynchronous discussion formats offer platforms on which to base new ways of assessment practice. Although much has been made of implementing technology for delivering content, it affords an excellent option for assessment of student work. While these options present students with engaging means of demonstrating knowledge and understanding of content, the use of these formats requires careful thought and planning to avoid becoming a set of "bells and whistles." Additionally, teachers need to plan for time to inform and instruct students on how to use the technology—for example, assisting students in navigating a wiki page so they can easily add or edit text, make comments, and post to the wiki page's discussion forum or know how to access SharePoint files, upload documents, and so forth.

When employing technology in the classroom, teachers should first consider the purpose of its use. As Wiggins and McTighe (2006) note, the development of assessments should be driven by whatever knowledge and skills learners are to demonstrate in the lesson's goals and objectives. By considering the nature of the information to be assessed, alignment of the assessment with the learning objectives should provide "a good fit" with the instrument or product that will be used. A teacher who is designing ways to determine how well students are able to attain the objectives could begin by asking reflective questions such as "Why am I using this as an assessment?" and "Can this set of concepts be adequately addressed through traditional forms of assessment (written tests, essays, etc.)," or "Is there a technology assessment option that could be used to make the assignment more engaging for the learner and the teacher?" These types of questions help to ensure that the evaluation of student learning outcomes remains of primary importance. As a well-developed tool, technology allows students multiple ways to exhibit knowledge and skills not easily replicated in the classroom in a single assessment—and often at higher levels of creativity and thought.

The goal of "intentionally reflecting" on the use of a technological platform should be to prevent a teacher from using technology "just to use technology." Teachers must think carefully about their assessment of students, including both the assessment of *technology knowledge and skills* and the assessment of the *content* using technology. This chapter focuses on guidelines that may help with the use of technology in assessment. We begin with a brief narrative on types of assessment, its place in instruction, and on planning in order to establish the context for the examples provided that relate to technology. The next section will offer examples of those which are asynchronous (working/communicating at one's convenience)—discussion boards, shared workspaces. Other types of examples and their use also will be discussed, including rubric generators, performance assessments, e-portfolios, and others.

The Assessment Cycle

Assessment does not occur in a vacuum—as noted, it aligns closely with the goals of instruction. In writing an effective lesson plan, teachers include an assessment section because they (and students) want to know if learners "got" the concepts and/or skills of the lesson objectives and to what degree (or how much or how well did they "get it"). This will direct the next step in teaching. A helpful framework for understanding the place of assessment in classroom instruction is provided in Figure 11.1. In this perspective, assessment occurs in tandem with instruction and can provide either formative or summative feedback to students. The results of formative assessment, assessing in the midst of instruction (or "How are we doing so far?"), may lead teachers and learners back to review what has been taught so that corrections can be made (if needed)—or the result may show that the learner is right on track. This type of assessment may even

Cheryl Casey / Shutterstock.com

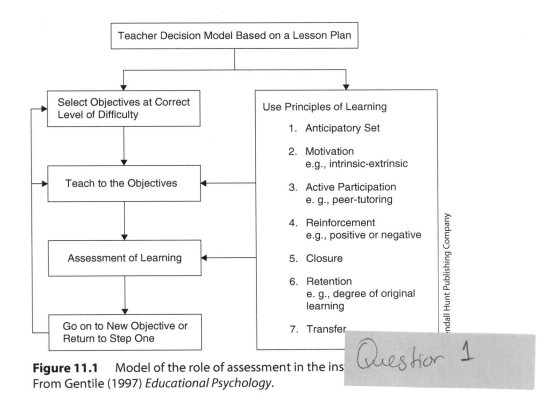

Figure 11.1 Model of the role of assessment in the ins~~tr~~ From Gentile (1997) *Educational Psychology*.

Question 1

indicate that the level of the original objectives has not been established appropriately; that is, the objective may have been too advanced or even too easy. Re-teaching may need to occur at that moment, or, if students overachieved, the teacher may need to consider moving on to lessons that are more difficult.

Summative assessment, on the other hand, occurs at the end to make a final judgment on what has been learned over an entire course of instruction. Judgments are made upon a whole project, a grading period (such as 6 weeks), a course, a semester, or another unit of instruction or time.

Figure 11.2 illustrates the place of assessment in the teaching–learning cycle. Traditionally, teachers start from the objectives or skills to be learned (the top box), develop a lesson plan based on those objectives, and create assessments (e.g., tests, essays, projects) to measure and evaluate student mastery of concepts

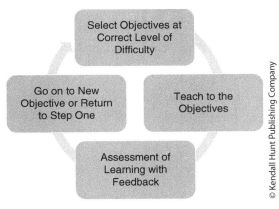

Figure 11.2 An abbreviated version of the assessment cycle.

taught. Whether objectives or outcomes are determined first, assessment serves to inform both teacher and student what has been learned and what still requires further instruction—as well as what has been retained. Subsequently, teaching and learning follows a process of instruction, assessment, and feedback, that, when repeated, should indicate the level of m~~astery of the learning~~

Second Part of Question 1: ②

Types of Assessment

We have already heard the terms formative and summative assessments. Assessment can be evaluated in both modes. Again, **formative assessment** provides an opportunity for students to attempt to demonstrate knowledge and understanding of learning objectives *during* the process of instruction and receive feedback (teacher or peer) as they work toward the mastery of the concepts. **Summative assessment** views students' final products as representative of their level of mastery of the learning outcomes at the completion of instruction. **Self-assessment** is the process of examining one's own work carefully to evaluate aspects that are important to one's learning so that he or she can self-correct. Much learning can progress when all three work in concert; one advantage of technology in assessment is that it often provides instantaneous feedback to both the learner and the teacher (see Figure 11.3).

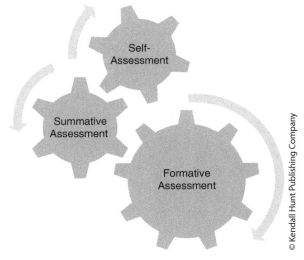

Planning and Teaching for Student Success

The Importance of Feedback

Students need and want good formative assessment so that they will know if they are progressing as expected or if they need to correct their knowledge and/or skills before a final summative assessment (often a "final grade") occurs. Feedback, or determining how one is doing in an effort to reach a goal, is a major part of the successful learning process (Wiggins, 2012). Consider the following exchange between Carl and his teacher, Ms. Fortrain, in the case study below.

Figure 11.3   Three major types of assessment of children and adolescence.

Carl received a grade on his Prezi project from Ms. Fortrain. The only information about the project that Carl found was a "C" at the top of the page, but there were no other comments. Carl asked his teacher after class, "What did I do wrong? I thought I had completed this with some good ideas! I really liked what I presented. I was excited by this project!" Ms. Fortrain replied, "Well, it just didn't have the information presented in the way I wanted it." "But I worked on it a couple of weeks during class time," Carl countered, "and you never said anything about what I was doing wrong. This isn't fair!"

When teachers assign larger projects or complicated tasks (particularly with technology), it is important to schedule feedback that affords students the opportunity to submit work and receive information on what is correct and what still needs improvement before assigning a summative grade. As Wiggins (2012) notes, "Adjusting our performance depends on not only receiving feedback but also having opportunities to use it" (para. 26). In the scenario above, Carl was engaged in his project and invested the time in completing his lengthy Prezi presentation, thinking that all was going well. Best practice would suggest that Ms. Fortrain circulate among the students to offer informal feedback on their work in progress during class time, establish several mini deadlines, and provide some formal feedback early in the project prior to summative assessment. In this case, timely feedback would have helped Carl redesign his work to receive a grade that he felt was more reflective of his efforts.

In discussing feedback, several areas are important to consider. One area of importance that we have seen above is the necessity of planning for and providing feedback early and often whenever assigning technology projects or other types of technology assessments. Many types of technology assessments are creative in nature and can be very subjective in grading. Planning for frequent feedback for corrections is crucial; in addition, clearly defined rubrics should be provided to students at the start of the project or task to be completed. This allows students to gain an understanding of expectations and ask questions before starting the assignment. In this way, the development of rubrics also can be used as an instructional tool by engaging students in conversations regarding what a completed project or task should look like. Another area to be discussed in more detail is how teachers can use technology to give feedback in simple and timely ways in the midst of or after instruction.

Interim Deadlines

Technology projects are becoming quite prevalent as assessments across content areas. To best ensure student success and reduce student frustration and possibly failure, thoughtful planning is essential. As with any authentic or project-based assessment, it can be quite helpful with technology assessment projects to divide them into logical units with a due date established for each section (these are known as gateways or interim deadlines). This prevents students from receiving a low final assessment because of their inability to begin and maintain momentum (so that work is not started and completed on the night before a final due date). It also provides an opportunity for the teacher to offer feedback throughout the process. Last minute work typically does not represent what a student knows or can do but what a student can produce right before the final due date. Just as "cramming" for an exam does not always produce results that demonstrate a student's mastery of the material, neither does a project that is hastily produced. Because technology projects often combine new technology skills with new content, this can end up as a disaster at the last moment, particularly when the student realizes too late that he or she may not have the technology expertise required of a project. Gateways assure that students are making progress and are provided ample direction through appropriate and timely feedback.

Helping Students Think at Higher Levels

A significant consideration in the design of assessments is determining the level of learning that is the target of both instruction and assessment. Bloom's taxonomy provides such a framework. Originally, the taxonomy was composed of six levels (knowledge, comprehension, application, analysis, synthesis, and evaluation); however, it has been revised (remembering, understanding, applying, analyzing, evaluating, and creating) to better reflect the process of learning (Anderson, Krathwohl, & Bloom, 2001). Bloom's taxonomy provides a convenient means of determining the focus of an assessment relative to student learning outcomes (Miller, Linn, & Gronlund, 2013). Most types of traditional assessment positions learners as recipients of knowledge where learning is measured and documented at the lowest levels of Bloom's taxonomy as knowledge and comprehension (Robles & Braathen, 2002). This type of assessment does not allow for higher-order thinking skills (HOTS) such as analyzing, evaluating, and creating (Speck, 2002). On the other hand, alternative forms of assessment assume the role of students as inquirers who are actively engaged in the learning process. In this case, assessment activates learning at higher-order thinking levels and embraces collaboration (Anderson, 1998). Although technology often is used as "an electronic worksheet," it is poised to take on a much greater role in producing higher-level thinking. Technology can be used to support student-centered activities, hands-on experiences, creation, and exploration. Technology can also provide a myriad of electronic resources such as student response systems (e.g., www.todaysmeet.com, www.socrative.com), critical thinking (e.g., www.inspiration.com/inspmaps), and creativity (e.g., www.toontastic.withgoogle.com). This makes technology use an effective teaching and learning platform to encourage students' higher-order thinking. An important part of planning with technology is designing assessments that will help students reach those higher levels of thought.

Assessment strategies need to be diverse and provide multiple opportunities for learners and teachers to evaluate learning. The traditional Scantron® "fill in the bubble" tests tend to dominate our thinking about technology assessment practices (see Figure 11.4), but there is a plethora of assessment practices with technology that provide useful alternatives—both for "quick checks" and for very deep and thoughtful assessment.

Figure 11.4 Student filling out answers to a test with a pencil on a Scantron answer sheet.

Thinking through Assessment

Mr. Beaumont was teaching a unit on Texas history. Students were asked to design a multimedia project in groups. Each group was tasked to put together a plan of their design during the first phase of the project. Although some groups were on target, many were not at the level of his expectations regarding the content. "Oh, my," he thought, "it's time to reteach this material before students are too far along in their project designs." He had set up mini deadlines at several points throughout the duration of the project, and he was glad that he had required these formative measures so that students would be much more successful when the project was completed.

goodluz / Shutterstock.com

There are some general guidelines that can inform the use of technology when designing assessments. As noted, one of the first aspects to consider is the purpose of the assessment: What is the exact knowledge and understanding that students are to demonstrate through the assignment? Related to this is a determination of the type of assessment—that is, whether the task is to provide formative, summative, or self-assessment of specific learning outcomes. In the above example, Mr. Beaumont, based on information gathered through formative assessment, decided to reteach the materials before the students were too far along in their project.

"Assessments become formative when the information is used to adapt teaching and learning to meet students' needs" (Boston, 2002, para. 2, as cited in Frey & Schmitt, 2007). While not exhaustive, guidelines for designing formative assessments include: (1) designing assessment activities that are relevant to students, (2) providing clear instructions for the assessment and its relationship to learning targets, (3) providing descriptive feedback to assist students in understanding where improvement is needed, (4) allowing students several opportunities to demonstrate learning, and (5) encouraging students to self-assess (Chappuis, 2005; Guskey, 2003).

Technology: Strategies and Resources

Because technology standards exist, many teachers feel that they are almost required to include technology in every lesson; however, it should not be used just for the sake of introducing a technology component into the lesson plan or classroom environment if that would not be the best choice for learners. One ideal spot for technology, as noted, can be in assessment—*if* it is appropriately matched to the learners and the lesson. Consideration of the goals for using technology in the assessment process will aid in the development of clear guidelines, improvement of students' understanding of the role of the assessment in learning, and can create a setting where instructive feedback can be provided. Effective assessment techniques can improve a teacher's understanding of student needs and help establish a more learner-centered classroom.

When incorporating technology into the assessment process, teachers should consider which specific types of technology tools (hardware, software, and peripherals) can be used to enhance student knowledge and understanding and inform instructional strategies. The next section will offer examples of technology tools that can be integrated for individualized instruction—formative, summative, and self-assessments. These include but are not limited to rubric generators, online discussion forums, shared workspaces, online test creators, online education/competition games, e-portfolios, interpretive exercises, performance assessment, storyboarding and prototype tools, and data analysis and presentation tools.

Rubric Generators

Creating expectations for work *prior* to an assessment creates a contract with learners that sets up an informative and fair system of grading. This often prevents a teacher from grading an assignment by comparing it to others' work rather than comparing it to the stated objectives—which students may or may not have met. Constructing

Table 11.1   Some of the More Widely Used Rubric Generators

> RubiStar
>   www.rubistar.4teachers.org
> TeAchnology
>   www.teach-nology.com/web_tools/rubrics
> RCampus
>   www.rcampus.com/indexrubric.cfm
> Aannenberg Learner
>   www.learner.org/workshops/hswriting/interactives/rubric

appropriate and useful rubrics is an essential process for many types of assessments, and there is a multitude of Web and electronic resources that can be used to generate rubrics (see Table 11.1 for some of the more widely used Websites). Generally, rubric-generating Websites provide "ready-made" rubrics for a wide variety of subjects, including content areas, observation, peer appraisal, and so forth. For some examples, type in "peer assessment rubrics images" to see a number of grade-appropriate rubrics. This is a useful resource: www.pinterest .com/sramauge3/rubrics. A "smile meters" allows audience to rate peer performance by filling in an appropriate "smile" for each category–a squiggly face (meaning "Keep Working!"), a smile ("Almost there!") or a BIG smile and crazy hair ("Awesome!"). For a sample look, visit www.pianimation.com/download/free_teacher_resources/ studio_aids/Smile-O-Meter%20Cards.pdf.

To build a rubric using rubric generators, users will first choose a rubric template from a variety of categories, much like choosing an MS PowerPoint template.

The creation of one's own rubric provides students with assessment that matches instruction actually given in the classroom (see Figure 11.5). Teachers must be cautious about adopting prefabricated rubrics; for rubrics to be effective assessment tools, they need to reflect the specific learning goals and outcomes of the

> Mr. Jefferson, a U.S. history teacher, wanted to evaluate students' digital stories on the topic of the American Civil War. A "product rubric category" might be the best choice from a list of those which might include oral projects, work skills, art, writing, or science. He will then decide what criteria to use as row titles. Good rubric generators allow users to manipulate the computer mouse to pick and choose the row titles from a pull-down menu. In the case of Mr. Jefferson's digital stories, the following list of row titles was available for him to choose from:
>
> - Point of View—Awareness of Audience
> - Point of View—Purpose
> - Dramatic Question
> - Voice-Consistency
> - Voice-Conversational Style
> - Voice-Pacing
> - Soundtrack—Originality
> - Soundtrack—Emotion
> - Images
> - Duration of Presentation
> - Grammar
>
> Most teachers prioritize and list the most important criterion first. Once the rubric is being generated by the rubric generator and after the submit button is clicked, a rubric will be displayed on the screen. At this point, Mr. Jefferson can copy and paste to save the rubric to his word processor program. After pasting the rubric to his word processor program, Mr. Jefferson can further edit the rubric by making changes such as adding text, changing text, or deleting text. Additional rows and columns can be added to the rubric to provide more spaces to type up comments for each criterion or overall comments for the project.

The American Civil War Project				
Student Name: _____				

CATEGORY	4	3	2	1
Point of View— Awareness of Audience	Strong awareness of audience in the design. Students can clearly explain why they felt the vocabulary, audio, and graphics chosen fit the target audience.	Some awareness of audience in the design. Students can partially explain why they felt the vocabulary, audio, and graphics chosen fit the target audience.	Some awareness of audience in the design. Students find it difficult to explain how the vocabulary, audio, and graphics chosen fit the target audience.	Limited awareness of the needs and interests of the target audience.
Point of View— Purpose	Establishes a purpose early on and maintains a clear focus throughout.	Establishes a purpose early on and maintains focus for most of the presentation.	There are a few lapses in focus, but the purpose is fairly clear.	It is difficult to figure out the purpose of the presentation.
Dramatic Question	Realization is dramatically different from expectation.	Realization differs noticeably from expectation.	Realization barely differs from the expectation.	Realization and expectation do not differ.
Voice— Consistency	Voice quality is clear and consistently audible throughout the presentation.	Voice quality is clear and consistently audible throughout the majority (85–95%) of the presentation.	Voice quality is clear and consistently audible through some (70–84%) of the presentation.	Voice quality needs more attention.
Voice— Conversational Style	Uses a conversational style throughout.	Uses a conversational style the majority (85–95%) of the time	Uses a conversational style most (70–84%) of the time.	Presentation style is primarily monologue.
Voice—Pacing	The pace (rhythm and voice punctuation) fits the story line and helps the audience really "get into\" the story.	Occasionally speaks too fast or too slowly for the story line. The pacing (rhythm and voice punctuation) is relatively engaging for the audience.	Tries to use pacing (rhythm and voice punctuation), but it is often noticeable that the pacing does not fit the story line. Audience is not consistently engaged.	No attempt to match the pace of the storytelling to the story line or the audience.
Soundtrack— Originality	Choice of the music is originally creative.	Choice of over half of the music is originally creative.	Some choice of the music is originally creative.	None of the choice of music is originally creative.
Soundtrack— Emotion	Music stirs a rich emotional response that matches the story line well.	Music stirs a rich emotional response that somewhat matches the story line.	Music is there, and not distracting, but it does not add to the story.	Music is distracting, and inappropriate OR was not used.
Images	Images create a distinct atmosphere or tone that matches different parts of the story. The images may communicate symbolism and/or metaphors.	Images create an atmosphere or tone that matches some parts of the story. The images may communicate symbolism and/or metaphors.	An attempt was made to use images to create an atmosphere/tone, but it needed more work. Image choice is logical.	Little or no attempt to use images to create an appropriate atmosphere/tone.
Duration of Presentation	Length of presentation was 4–5 minutes.	Length of presentation was 3 minutes.	Length of presentation was 2 minutes.	Presentation was less than 2 minutes long OR more than 5 minutes.
Grammar	Grammar and usage were correct (for the dialect chosen) and contributed to clarity, style, and character development.	Grammar and usage were typically correct (for the dialect chosen), and errors did not detract from the story.	Grammar and usage were typically correct, but errors detracted from story.	Repeated errors in grammar and usage distracted greatly from the story.

Figure 11.5 A glimpse of the assessment rubric used by Mr. Jefferson to evaluate the American Civil War projects.

assignment designed by the teacher. However, there are many available on the Internet which can be matched or manipulated to fit one's assignments.

Engaging students in the process of creating a rubric can be a powerful instructional tool. For example, Ms. Webster was developing a lesson plan to instruct her English composition students about creating a persuasive essay. Rather than lecturing on the basic principles of a persuasive argument, she decided to have the students engage in a conversation about what they believed to be the critical elements of a persuasive essay. Ms. Webster used this process to assess students' prior knowledge and check for misconceptions as well as guide the conversation by adding relevant information. Similarly, Ms. Webster could use a rubric generator and have students discuss the appropriateness of the categories and descriptions. In either case, rubrics can be both a useful instructional strategy and informative assessment tool.

Whether Web-based templates or teacher-created rubrics are used, there are basic guidelines that should be considered when designing rubrics. First, it is important to consider the nature of the assignment or task to be evaluated. Some factors to consider are:

- What are the key learning outcomes related to the content the student will need to demonstrate?
- What critical thinking skills should students be able to employ?
- What is the nature of the learning reflected in the assignment; that is, does it require assessing a product, a process, or both?

Next, the rubric needs to address specifically the learning outcomes to be assessed based on a clear definition of quality levels. This needs to reflect a continuum from low to high, describing mastery of the outcomes being assessed. These are usually word descriptor phrases such as "high quality"/"below expectations" or "excellent"/"marginal", or they can be numerical (1 to 4) or letter grades. Figure 11.6 provides an example of a rubric designed to assess a writing assignment. In this case, the assignment and its associated rubric relate to a product of student work. The left-hand column describes the learning goal to be evaluated (e.g., Focus, Organization, etc.) and includes a definition of that goal. Generally, it is advisable to limit the number of quality levels to three or four, as rubrics with fewer levels do not provide adequate feedback, and those with more become cumbersome to employ. Each of the levels needs to contain a concise description of the level of mastery demonstrated by the student's product. As mentioned, levels may reflect grade distributions (e.g., A, B, C, D) or descriptive terms (e.g., not evident, partial evidence, substantial evidence) and should be indicated in the top row of the rubric. Remember that an effective teacher would also try to make the rubric as objective as possible by further explaining areas of the rubric about which students may have any questions or concerns.

Here are links to several online examples in various subject areas with numbers and letters to reflect grade-appropriate descriptions based on specific assignments:

Science Experiment

www.rubric-maker.com/samples/science_experiment_prim.pdf

Skit

www.rubric-maker.com/samples/skit_elem.pdf

Teamwork

www.rubric-maker.com/samples/teamwork_elem.pdf

Behavior Performance Observation checklist

www.fcit.usf.edu/assessment/classroom/Behavior%20Observation%20Checklist.pdf

Type in the key term "student performance checklist" through Pinterest to find plenty of samples that you can use for models.

Numerous Websites provide free templates to create rubrics at all grade levels and subject areas. Some of the more widely used Websites are listed below:

- pblchecklist.4teachers.org/checklist.shtml
- schrockguide.net/assessment-and-rubrics.html
- www.teacherplanet.com/rubrics-for-teachers?ref=rubrics4teachers

	Emergent (1)	Developed (2)	Mastered (3)	Exemplary (4)
Focus The single controlling argument is made with awareness of a specific thesis.	Thesis of the paper is unclear. The paper is poorly developed.	No apparent thesis but evidence of a specific argument. There is some evidence of development in the paper.	Thesis is clear; there is some evidence of a specific argument. The development of the paper is clear.	Thesis is distinct; the argument for the thesis is well defined. The development of the paper clearly supports the thesis and argument.
Content The presence of ideas developed through facts, examples, anecdotes, details, opinions, statistics, reasons, and/or explanations.	Superficial and/or minimal content provided.	Limited content with inadequate elaboration or explanation.	Sufficiently developed content with adequate elaboration or explanation.	Substantial, specific, and/or illustrative content demonstrating strong development and sophisticated ideas.
Voice and Audience Awareness The presentation clearly demonstrates a connection with the intended audience and communicates the author's interest.	Communicates lack of awareness of audience and lack of interest of the author in the topic.	Viewpoint is vague; does not seem to address a specific audience. Author's presentation is natural but lacks engagement with the topic.	Presentation is somewhat connected to an audience. Author shows some engagement with the topic.	Presentation clearly identifies and connects to a specific audience. Author shows clear interest and engagement with the topic.
Organization The order developed and sustained within and across paragraphs using transitional devices, including introduction and conclusion. APA style is utilized correctly.	Minimal control of content arrangement. No evidence of APA style.	Confused or inconsistent arrangement of content with or without attempts at transition. Limited use of APA style.	Functional arrangement of content that sustains a logical order with some evidence of transitions. APA style is utilized with minor imperfections.	Sophisticated arrangement of content is evident with subtle transitions. APA style is utilized correctly throughout.
Style The choice, use of, and arrangement of words and sentence structures that create tone and voice.	Minimal variety in word choice and minimal control of sentence structures.	Limited word choice and control of sentence structures that inhibit voice and tone.	Generic use of a variety of words and sentence structures that may or may not create writer's voice and tone appropriate to audience.	Precise, illustrative use of a variety of words and sentence structures to create consistent writer's voice and tone appropriate to audience.
Conventions The use of grammar, mechanics, spelling, usage, and sentence formation.	Minimal control of grammar, mechanics, spelling, usage, and sentence formation.	Limited control of grammar, mechanics, spelling, usage, and sentence formation.	Sufficient control of grammar, mechanics, spelling, usage, and sentence formation.	Evident control of grammar, mechanics, spelling, usage, and sentence formation.

Figure 11.6   An example rubric for a writing assignment.

Because rubrics can be employed to assess both product and process, they are an excellent resource for evaluating projects that incorporate technology aspects. Oral communication is an increasingly important aspect of the curriculum and one which may include the use of technology (e.g., Prezi, Vine, Instagram, YouTube, and even smartphone videos) and generally requires assessment of both content and delivery. Some educators compile collections of rubrics for future teachers to refer to, such as:

www.uwstout.edu/soe/profdev/rubrics.cfm

www.schrockguide.net/assessment-and-rubrics.html

Mr. Kohn wanted his chemistry students to present the results of their titration experiments as though they were at a research conference. He needed to assess both the product (in this case the results of the experiment) and the process (delivery of the results). Such presentations often are evaluated with a rubric that provides students with feedback on the correctness of the work and an evaluation of their presentation skills. Mr. Kohn also wanted to include specific feedback regarding the organization and creativity of Prezi and other visual effects used in the presentation.

Figure 11.7 provides an example of a presentation rubric which assesses both the product and process of an oral presentation assignment. Note that a new row and a new column are added through the word processing program to the rubric originally created by a rubric generator.

Name of presenter _____

	0	1	2	3	Score and Feedback
Abstract	Not present	Does not provide a clear overview of the experiment; lacks reference to: purpose and method	Provides an overview of the experiment but is missing reference to one of the following: purpose or method	Clearly provides an overview of the experiment: states purpose and describes method	
Problem Statement	Not present	Does not provide a rationale for the experiment	Provides a partial rationale for the experiment	Provides a complete rationale for the experiment	
Procedure	Not present	Presents clear procedural steps but does not discuss instruments or data analysis	Presents clear procedural steps, discusses instruments, but does not describe data analysis	Presents clear procedural steps, discusses instruments, and explains data analysis	
Findings	Not present	Presentation of results is not clear; missing complete discussion of the findings	Presentation of results is clear, but discussion of the findings is not presented logically	Presentation of results is clear; discussion of findings is logically presented	
Delivery	No eye contact with audience; reads from notes; low volume or monotone delivery	Minimal eye contact; mostly reads from notes; uneven volume, little inflection	Good use of eye contact but occasionally reads from notes; satisfactory delivery	Eye contact with entire audience; rarely looks at notes; delivery includes appropriate volume and inflection changes	

(Continued)

	0	1	2	3	Score and Feedback
Presentation	Demonstrates no interest in experiment; does not inform audience	Demonstrates minimal interest in experiment; informs audience on some points	Demonstrates some interest in experiment; informs audience on most points	Demonstrates consistent interest in experiment; informs audience on all points	
Prezi and other visual effects	Either confusing or cluttered; buttons or navigational tools are absent or confusing	Includes combinations of graphics and text but buttons are difficult to navigate; some buttons and navigational tools work	Includes a variety of graphics, text, and animation; adequate navigational tools and buttons are included and work	Includes a variety of graphics, text, and animation that exhibits a sense of wholeness. Creative use of navigational tools and buttons	
				Total	
Comments:					

Figure 11.7   Sample oral presentation rubric.

Online Discussion Forums

One area where technology provides a useful platform for assessment is in group discussion activities. For example, whole class discussions are often difficult to assess strictly from an observational perspective. Further, engaging all students in class discussions is not always feasible, nor do all students interact in the same way. For example, extroverted learners are more likely to offer lengthy responses as they tend to think through the question verbally; on the other hand, introverted learners will ponder a response and often participate once the original discussion on the topic has ended. Some students are reluctant to participate at all, and, oftentimes, teachers do not realize that they do not call on everyone. In many thoughtful technology-related responses, it becomes clear whether or not all have responded.

In using a technology platform, students can demonstrate their knowledge and understanding of concepts as they engage in dialogue focused on the specific learning outcomes identified for the assessment. This can be done in a variety of ways. Online discussion boards, for example, afford an opportunity for all students to participate in a manner that is appropriate for their learning style and provide clear written data to inform assessment of student learning. In addition, a discussion board allows for interaction among students; this not only encourages students to learn from each other but also employs peer assessment skills.

What might such an assessment look like? Mrs. Kator wants to assess the level of student understanding of a specific text in her high school government course and to engage students in a dialogue about what that text means. The first step is to develop clear instructions for engaging in the discussion forum (formative) (Figure 11.8) as well as a specific rubric (summative) that will be used to assess student contributions (see Figure 11.9).

Posting Guidelines

In order to be prepared for the class discussions each week, a discussion thread will be used to provide comments on the assigned reading(s) for the upcoming class. Each thread will have a specific prompt to guide reflection on the readings to allow for the expression of your perspective on the readings. These posts should be approximately 250–300 words in length and do not require any reading outside of the assigned material for that week.

In addition, you will respond to two posts of your classmates. These posts should be approximately 75–100 words in length and provide a substantive comment on the selected post. In other words, "Great ideas!," "I agree!," and "Ditto" are not insightful. Responses may compare or contrast the author's ideas with your posting or offer a comment on the insights the author provided you, and so forth.

Figure 11.8   Sample guidelines for a discussion forum.

Objectives	Low Performance	At or Below Average	At or Above Average	Earned Points
Knowledge of Topic	**0 points** —Answer does not display an understanding of the topic. —Answer does not incorporate any aspect of the readings for the week.	**1–2 points** —Answer displays a basic understanding of the topic. —Answer incorporates personal experience but makes no connection to readings and/or video. —Does not post response in a timely manner.	**3–4 points** —Answer displays a good/excellent understanding of the readings/topic for this week. —Incorporates the readings and/or video into answer. —Posts response in a timely manner.	
Responding to Classmates' Questions and Comments	**0 points** —Does not respond to classmates' responses for the week. Or —Response is very vague and offers no real contribution to the discussion (i.e., "I agree").	**1–2 points** —Responds to 1–2 classmates' responses for the week. —Response offers additional explanations or elaboration to classmates' response. —Does not respond to classmates in a timely manner.	**3–4 points** —Responds to at least 3 classmates' responses for the week. —Response offers additional explanations or elaboration and incorporates personal experience and/or the readings into answers. —Responds to classmates in a timely manner.	
			Score:	

Figure 11.9 Sample rubric for assessment of discussion forum.

Haubenreich suggests at the end of his article that "the future of the debate over whether education belongs in the Constitution remains bright" (p. 453). Based on your reading of his argument, does the right to an education belong in the Constitution? What would such a "Constitutional right" guarantee and how would that be enforced? Or, do you believe education should be governed by states/localities? Provide support for your response from the article. Please follow the guidelines on Reflection Postings.

Figure 11.10 Sample discussion forum assignment.

Once the general guidelines and rubric for the discussion process are provided, the next step is to provide specific instructions to guide the students in terms of the assignment. Figure 11.10 gives Mrs. Kator's directions.

The design of this type of assessment lends itself readily to either a formative or a summative approach to evaluation of student work. Teacher feedback in the discussion forum is one way to identify misconceptions and lack of understanding as well as indicate when students demonstrate mastery of the material. The discussion forum thread below is an example of how the thread engages students in dialogue about a specific understanding of the assigned reading noted in Figure 11.11. In this thread, the teacher provides feedback confirming the correctness of the student's interpretation but also points to the contrary position. The interaction that follows extends the students' conversation on the topic. This "extended conversation" illustrates the way in which the technique of class discussion can be modified using technology to enhance the teacher's insight on student learning. Note that this example provides the actual text posted; it has not been edited.

As can be seen in this example, after providing specific guidelines describing the nature of the initial post of a student along with a clear presentation of the quality of responses, the students engaged in an informed discussion of the topic and indicated their areas of agreement and disagreement. Reviewing all the posts from a class thus gives the teacher an opportunity to determine the level of student comprehension of the assigned concepts. The teacher is now able to answer such questions as: (1) are there areas of knowledge that

Student 1: RE: The "right" to an education
I believe that the right to an education should belong in the constitution. This constitutional right will guarantee that everyone will have a fair chance at an education with no excuses. I don't think education should be governed by states or localities because everyone should all be on the same page. I don't think it's fair how some state laws are less lenient than others.
Instructor: RE: The "right" to an education (response to Student 1)
An interesting perspective, and valid. The issue, of course, is not only one of local control (which has been the historic rule) but also of funding. Those who believe that government is already too big may oppose more federal oversight. Nevertheless, there is something to be said for national standards for K–12 students.
Student 2: RE: The "right" to an education (response to Student 1)
I agree with you that it is unfair that standards differ from state to state. I also think that the every student has the right to have a good education regardless of where they are from.
Student 1: RE: The "right" to an education (response to Student 2)
Yes, I feel that it is very unfair that the standards can differ from state to state. It shouldn't be harder for one state than the other so I don't think that makes sense in any way. . . . I feel like no matter anyone's culture or where they reside, it should be an equal opportunity for the right of an education.
Student 3: RE: The "right" to an education (response to thread)
I agree with both of you in that it is unfair that standards are different from state to state. This brings about the problem of disadvantagement on [sic] some states. I am also with you in that as students of the United States, it should be a right to have a good education regardless of where one is from, one's class, race, gender, religion, sexual preference, ethnicity, sex, intelligence, location, etc.
Student 4: RE: The "right" to an education (response to thread)
I agree with what you said. If we get more teachers and staff in schools to feel that education is an important factor for life, I think there could be a major turnaround in the learning ability levels and graduating rates can increase.

Figure 11.11 A sample of students' responses on the discussion forum.

require additional emphasis, (2) have students demonstrated mastery of the concepts so that the next concepts can be addressed, (3) are there particular students who may need some individual attention, and so forth. Understanding student work both in terms of student mastery of concepts and effectiveness of instruction is an outcome of developing an appropriate rubric that allows for objective judgment of the product being assessed. Of course, technology can ensure that the teacher quickly assesses every student and that students are both able to share opinions with others and to judge how their opinions and writing align or differ with others.

Shared Workspaces

Another technology platform that is useful in assessing student knowledge and understanding are shared workspaces (e.g., Dropbox, Google Docs, and Wikispaces). Time constraints often affect the ability of students to engage in collaborative projects while in the classroom. Often, conversation and learning occur outside of the normal school day, and creative ideas cannot always develop within a given timeframe for a class. Shared workspaces provide students an accessible platform to pursue work initiated during class when further thinking and planning around topics is required.

One option is to incorporate shared workspaces in the assessment process because these can provide a means for the development of student-generated texts focused on content, peer editing, and higher-order tasks involving evaluation skills. Developing authentic assessments which require students to demonstrate not only what they have learned but to evaluate that information regarding important constructs and principles is essential in promoting critical thinking and deep learning. As with discussion forums, shared workspaces can be used for both formative and summative assessment purposes separately or at the same time.

Mrs. Mathis wanted to develop an assessment that incorporated collaboration and demonstration of understanding algebraic principles of solving for an unknown. Rather than constructing a traditional test that identified what she saw as important concepts and specific paths for solutions, her idea was to have the students create a "text for future students" based on their understanding of the concepts and their application. She decided to use a wiki as the platform, as it permitted creation of separate pages and opportunities for student-generated text, track edits made, and a space for comments. Further, the wiki platform tracked the contributions, edits, and comments of each student, which allowed for a keener understanding of students' knowledge and assessment of the level of collaboration. Following guidelines similar to those for a discussion forum, Mrs. Mathis created a section on a wiki page that provided a clear rationale for the project and learning outcomes, her posting requirements, and the tasks involved (see Figure 11.13). In addition to presenting a focus for the students, she created template sections with specific headings. The process would involve students creating problems, developing clear solutions, editing what other classmates presented in terms of accuracy, and providing comments supporting the created problem, solution process, and what was corrected or edited (see Figure 11.12). Figure 11.14 gives a snapshot of the students generating the text for the template.

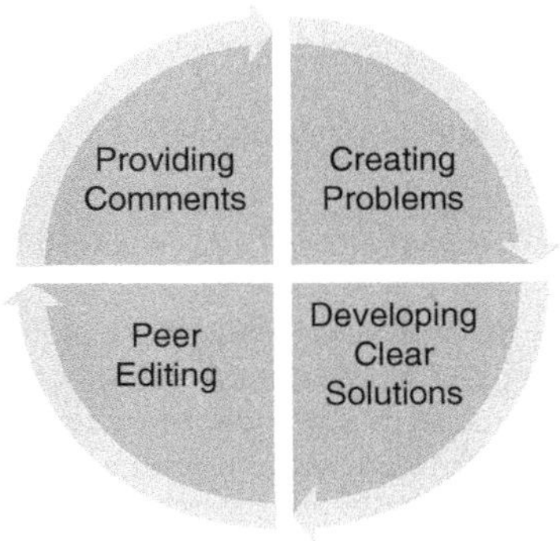

Figure 11.12 The process students follow on a shared workspace.

The comments in italics and bold (see Figure 11.14), indicate additions made by three classmates (based on the different font style) to the original author's contribution. As illustrated, the project provides the teacher with a clear indication of the students' understanding of the concept of solving for a single unknown. Additionally, Mrs. Mathis is able to view the thinking processes of the student editors in terms of the nature of the added comments. Here, the student editors extend the description of the steps needed to solve the problem as well as indicate the potential problems of one of the alternatives (see Figure 11.15).

Chapter: Solving for an Unknown

The purpose of this chapter is to provide a discussion of the various strategies that can be used to solve for an unknown. Each strategy should be clearly described, including procedural steps leading to a solution.

---

1. Create a problem that requires a solution for a single unknown, for example: $5x + 8 = 38$.
2. Provide alternative means of solving the problem, including the steps required and an explanation of how the steps lead to the solution.
3. Write a brief narrative that explains the approaches used and how they are related.

Figure 11.13 Sample wiki page with a rationale section and a template.

Chapter: Solving for an Unknown

The purpose of this chapter is to provide a discussion of the various strategies that can be used to solve for an unknown. Each strategy should be clearly described, including procedural steps leading to a solution. Be sure that x is a whole number.

1. Create a problem that requires a solution for a single unknown.
   $3x - 7 = 5$
2. Provide alternative means of solving the problem, including the steps required and an explanation of how the steps lead to the solution.

First, you need to make the equation simpler. To do that, add 7 to each side of the equal sign.
$3x - 7 + 7 = 5 + 7$
Then, the equation looks like this $3x - 0 = 12$, which is the same as $3x = 12$
Next, in order to solve for x divide each side of the equation by 3 like this $\dfrac{3x}{3} = \dfrac{12}{3}$
Now you know that $x = 4$

Another way to solve for x would be to divide each side of the equation by 3 first. This would look like

$\dfrac{3x}{3} - \dfrac{7}{3} = \dfrac{5}{3}$ which would then leave $x - \dfrac{7}{3} = \dfrac{5}{3}$

Then, add $\dfrac{7}{3}$ to each side $x - \dfrac{7}{3} + \dfrac{7}{3} = \dfrac{5}{3} + \dfrac{7}{3}$ and then solve $x - 0 = \dfrac{12}{3}$ or $x = 4$

3. Write a brief narrative that explains the approaches used, and how they are related.

The first approach seems to be the simplest and does not require fractions. In the first example, $3x$ is isolated by adding seven to each side of the equation, since this still leaves each side equal. Once that is solved, then each side is divided by three so that the solution for x is found. In the second example, the division step is done first, then the step to isolate x. **The problem with this strategy is the inclusion of fractions.**

Figure 11.14 Sample wiki page entry for an algebra class.

Next, in order to solve for x divide each side of the equation by 3 like this $\dfrac{3x}{3} = \dfrac{12}{3}$

I think the steps are correct, but there does not seem to be a connection between the two equations. So I inserted this step to show how to get from $3x = 12$ to $x = 4$

and then solve $x - 0 = \dfrac{12}{3}$ or $x = 4$

This set of steps did not seem complete. I think you just forgot to add this, or you thought that we would know the answer from the previous strategy. Now, the entire solution is complete.

The problem with this strategy is the inclusion of fractions.

While I agree that both ways get the same answer, I think having to work with fractions is hard. I would just do it the first way.

Figure 11.15 Sample discussion posting.

It should be noted that collaborative projects such as this one require a certain amount of scaffolding of student thoughts in order to fully complete the assignment. Often the initial chapter drafts are not as detailed but, with appropriate feedback to provide guidance, students move beyond simple, brief comments. In this case, Mrs. Mathis began each chapter with an outline of key tasks that required explanation. Starting with a clear presentation of the concepts to be mastered, each "chapter" in the text followed a specific outline, requiring students to present solutions and support them with a narrative. In addition, a teacher can also provide sample work to communicate his or her expectations. Creating a typical test allows for assessment of student knowledge and understanding of the learning goals focused on that particular lesson, but the process of peer editing affords insight into students' higher-order thinking and their ability to apply learning, synthesize new interpretations, and evaluate the "worth" of their peers' contributions to the text.

	0	1	2
Problem	No problem provided	Problem provided, but the equation does not use whole numbers for x.	Problem provided is correct.
Procedure	No procedure provided	Procedure is incomplete; does not address all steps.	Procedure is complete; addresses all steps.
Narrative	No narrative provided	Narrative does not completely describe the steps in the solution.	Narrative completely describes the steps in the solution.
Editing	No editorial changes or comments	Editorial changes are incorrect or do not add to the text.	Editorial changes provide correct information and add to the text.

Section	Score
Problem	/2
Procedure	/2
Narrative	/2
Editing	/2
Total Points	/8
Comments:	

Figure 11.16 A scoring rubric for the student-generated "wiki" project.

The incorporation of wikis in the assessment process can be designed to meet most grade levels where text is appropriate and can incorporate all levels of Bloom's taxonomy. At higher grade levels, the use of student-generated text can address critical thinking, evaluation, and transfer of concepts to other areas. For example, in a social studies class, an "understanding the concept of freedom of speech" wiki could then support a debate regarding whether restrictions on cyberbullying violates an individual's freedom of speech and how that relates to slander or defamation of character. For their posts, as well as any substantive editorial changes, conversations can be generated in the comments section that extended the material to the students' contexts. In this way, the assessment becomes relevant to the students, and the learning outcomes for the assignment are integrated into the students' experience.

Teachers can use the student-generated text to reflect on instruction in terms of addressing misconceptions, misunderstandings, and missing information. Feedback becomes an active, participatory process that informs teaching and learning and provides a dialogue that works to close the assessment loop (instruction, demonstration of learning, feedback, and demonstration of mastery) (Hatzipanagos & Warburton, 2009).

In the case of this example, in addition to a formative assessment standpoint, there was a summative aspect as well for Mrs. Mathis. Rather than administering a series of exams that may not accurately assess what students know because it is not in a format related to their learning style, this project was designed to provide an authentic assessment, reflecting the students' ability to communicate their mastery of course concepts. Again, a simple rubric was employed as a means of communicating to each student his or her level of mastery (see Figure 11.16).

Online Test Creators

Technology affords several advantages when considering creating more traditionally designed tests. As with rubrics, most textbook publishers now provide electronic test banks focused on key concepts and learning outcomes, and, in some cases, these are aligned with state and/or national standards. While useful, it is important to be aware that some test bank items may focus too specifically on "page memory" rather than concept understanding, so teachers should carefully read items before using them in a test. Teachers must also be cautious to use items *only* if they have been covered in class or as directed in a class assignment. Otherwise, students should not be held accountable for them.

Most learning management systems (LMS) offer test generator platforms that allow teachers to create a variety of test formats (e.g., multiple choice, short response, true/false, essay). Blackboard, for example, provides options for both tests and surveys as well as an option to generate teacher-constructed pools of items for both options of these. Tests are designed to provide assessment feedback measuring student performance; surveys are not graded and provide anonymous feedback, addressing such areas as student preferences, reflection on experiences, and so forth.

Mr. Blackwell wanted to evaluate how well students understood mathematics concepts presented in class but did not want to use instruction time to give students exit tickets. Since his school had recently purchased a Blackboard license, he thought students could complete an exit ticket online. Using the test generator, he created a short quiz that focused on the key concepts presented during class. Students were then asked to complete the quiz online as part of their homework (or if computer access was a problem, after school or during their free period in the library). The test generator allowed Mr. Blackwell to provide the correct response as well as insert specific comments if the student gave an incorrect response. All of this could be entered into the test format in Blackboard so that students received immediate feedback when completing the quiz (see Figure 11.17). Additionally, he could review the quizzes in order to plan for the next day's instruction. Using this technology approach for formative assessment freed valuable class time, provided self-assessment information for students, and focused Mr. Blackwell's instruction. Besides, LMSs such as Blackboard immediately generate test reports that include the standard deviations, median, mean, highest score, lowest scores, and other relevant descriptive statistic data for the entire class. Mr. Blackwell can easily use these reports to reteach topics on which students have not performed well.

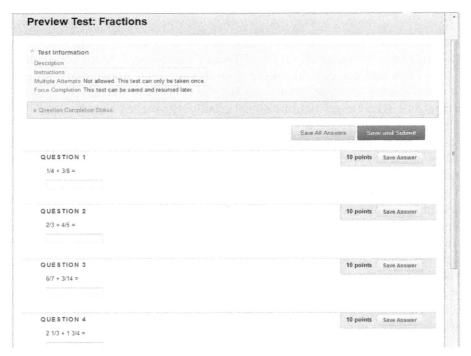

Figure 11.17   Screen shot of a test in Blackboard.
Source: Ronald S. Beebe

It is important to experiment with online test formats to narrow the focus of the assessment. In some cases, it may be best to use multiple-choice items that employ carefully constructed distracters that inform the teacher of the conceptual mistakes students have made. Mr. Blackwell could have created multiple-choice test items for the exit ticket that used distracters which highlighted specific errors. For example, Question 2 could have been constructed as:

$\frac{2}{3} + \frac{4}{5} =$ (a) $\frac{6}{8}$ (b) $\frac{6}{15}$ (c) $\frac{22}{15}$ (d) $\frac{8}{15}$ (e) $\frac{22}{8}$ which would indicate errors in the process of adding fractions:

(a) that the student added across numerator and denominator, (b) that the student found the common denominator but added numerators, (c) the correct response, (d) that the student multiplied across numerator and denominator, or (e) that the student cross-multiplied for numerator but added denominators.

In a different vein, a new generation of online learning tools, or, as others might call them, memorization tools, was first introduced to allow users to create "sets" of terms customized on the Web for their own needs. These sets of terms can then be studied under several study modes. Table 11.2 shows a list of online quizzes and accompanying interactive resources that can be created within minutes by teachers and students. When using these online learning tools, such as www.quizlet.com, www.sporcle.com, www.cram.com, and www.flashcardmachine.com, students can choose to review the content as flashcards, tests, or other formats.

Some quiz generators such as Cram and Quizlet have features to enhance study experiences such as shuffle, read, alphabetize, front first, integrating illustrations, and "read" with computer-synthesized voices (See Table 11.3). These online quizzes and interactive resources range from children's books, middle school foreign languages, and U.S. history to college calculus. For instance, a sixth-grade gifted teacher can assign students to create electronic flashcards and exchange them for the unit review of social studies. Adolescents often enjoy challenging their peers with such activities, and they can also be used to support competitive groups in the classroom as described below.

Table 11.2 Teachers Can Assign Students to Create Flashcards and Exchange For Unit Review

Group 1	Use www.quizlet.com	Chapters 9, 10, 11
Group 2	Use www.cram.com	Chapters 12, 13, 14
Group 3	Use www.flashcardmachine.com	Chapters 18, 19, 20
Group 4	Use www.sporcle.com	Chapters 15, 16, 17

Table 11.3 A Sample List of Online Quizzes and Interactive Resources

Categories	Quiz titles and URLs
Children's Books	Can you match the names of these Roald Dahl characters? www.sporcle.com/games/CatStarcatcher/dahlightful
Children's Books	Can you name the popular children's books based on their opening lines? www.sporcle.com/games/farishta/childrens_opening
Elementary Science	Fourth-grade science on Scientific Inquiry Vocabulary www.quizlet.com/13554243/hills-elementary-science-grade-4-flash-cards
Young Adults Books	Can you name the missing words from these titles of Young Adult books? www.sporcle.com/games/khands/missing-word-young-adult-books-a-z
Learn Spanish Language	Vocab 14A: La música y el baile www.flashcardmachine.com/machine/?topic_id=3103505&source=pub
Middle School Computer Literacy	Computer Literacy 101 www.quizlet.com/22756154/computer-literacy-101-chapter-8-flash-cards
High School Social Studies	Advance Placement (AP) U.S. History Review www.cram.com/flashcards/ap-us-history-review-4738708
Higher Education	College Educational Technology www.cram.com/flashcards/educational-technology-4677895

Online Education/Competition Games

Activities like role-playing and Reader's Theater easily lend themselves to using technology as an assessment tool. The incorporation of technology-based education games in the assessment process can be designed to meet all grade levels and can incorporate all levels of Bloom's taxonomy. In addition, numerous software and Websites offer students opportunities to create game shows (see Figure 11.22), board games (see Figure 11.21), word searches (see Figure 11.20), and puzzles (see Figure 11.19), among other assessment options (see Figure 11.18). These types of platforms can be used in class or as projects as well as for review of material. They provide students with an engaging and creative way to demonstrate concept understanding along with instant feedback—either individually or in groups.

In addition to the above for early elementary grades, word recognition associated with pictures provides a video game style format to learning basic vocabulary (refer to Figure 11.21). In this example, students can click on the picture and the associated word is highlighted (or vice versa), which allows students to self-assess their vocabulary knowledge. This type of activity is more exciting than a worksheet and can engage the student with some "bells and whistles" for immediate feedback for both the students and the teacher. There are times when immediate feedback such as this is useful on lower-level objectives, particularly in formative assessment, although the advantages of technological assessment can offer much higher levels of thought for students.

Students and teachers can create diagrams, games, and quizzes.

    www.classtools.net

Students and teachers can generate their own e-learning quizzes, games, and applications with no coding.

    www.contentgenerator.net

Students and teachers can create several types of games online by using this Website.

    www.superteachertools.net

Students and teachers can create lesson puzzles, word searches, and other types of education games for presentations and printouts.

    puzzlemaker.discoveryeducation.com

Students and teachers can turn photos and video clips into interactive media and animations.

    www.animoto.com

Figure 11.18   A sample of Websites that allow users to create education puzzles and other types of games.

Figure 11.19   Animal word search game that can be created using an online generator.

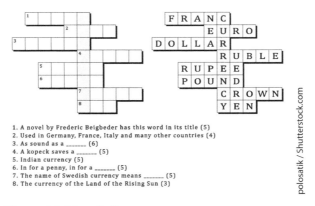

1. A novel by Frederic Beigbeder has this word in its title (5)
2. Used in Germany, France, Italy and many other countries (4)
3. As sound as a _____ (6)
4. A kopeck saves a _____ (5)
5. Indian currency (5)
6. In for a penny, in for a _____ (5)
7. The name of Swedish currency means _____ (5)
8. The currency of the Land of the Rising Sun (3)

Figure 11.20 Online generators can create a crossword for world currency and related vocabulary words.

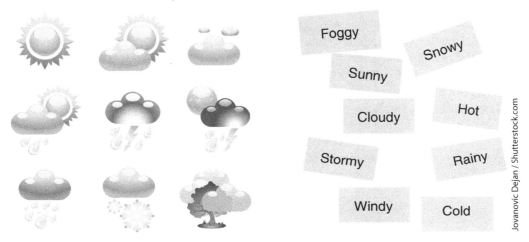

Figure 11.21 Sample picture vocabulary matching game.

History Review				
The Civil War	**US Geography 1860-65**	**19th Century Political Parties**	**Transportation**	**US and World Affairs 1860-65**
5	5	5	5	5
10	10	10	10	10
15	15	15	15	15
20	20	20	20	20
25	25	25	25	25
SCORE BOARD				

Figure 11.22 A "Jeopardy-style" review for history.

Electronic Portfolios

A teacher can also use portfolios to assess students' mastery of certain content topics. Generally, there are four common types of portfolios, each with a specific purpose: (1) best work, (2) representative, (3) developmental-growth, and (4) summative (see Figure 11.23).

Consequently, it is important to determine the purpose of the portfolio, as that will indicate what types of artifacts should be selected. Additionally, clear guidelines for construction of the portfolio, its evaluation, and a determination of who will place artifacts in the portfolio should be decided before starting to build the portfolio. Using portfolios, students develop ownership of their work, especially if they are selecting the artifacts as well as reflecting on the quality or perspective the artifacts represent. A "developmental-growth" portfolio, for example, can provide opportunities for learners to see how they have progressed in their mastery of concepts and typically incorporates student-selected work. Similarly, students and teachers can use a "best work" portfolio to showcase student work both for a class and parents. A "best work" portfolio can also designate both the student and the teacher to be contributors to the selection of artifacts. Portfolios also encourage student ownership of their learning and work through the process of identifying artifacts, evaluating their work, and reflecting on the learning demonstrated. A well-designed portfolio project should yield valid and reliable results, even though no written test is conducted. How can this be done? A well-planned portfolio project guideline is the key. A project should be designed to last for a set period of time in order that the student demonstrates progress and mastery over this time period. For this process to unfold properly, careful planning must occur prior to the beginning of the project and development of the portfolio.

According to Miller et al. (2013), "Portfolios also foster student skills in evaluating their own work. Self-evaluation is a critical skill in developing independent learning ability and one that is often emphasized and reinforced by asking students to include some form of self-evaluation and thoughtful reflection on each entry in their portfolios" (p. 284). In addition to self-assessment, portfolios can be an effective way of communicating with parents by showing concrete examples of what their child can do. Technology provides a convenient means of assembling student portfolios. A multitude of [Question 3] rtfolio platforms to meet a variety of needs (e.g., www.weebly.com, www.opr_____n/us). In addition, with the increasing

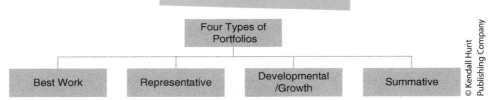

Figure 11.23   Four types of portfolios.

© Kendall Hunt Publishing Company

Mrs. Green was looking for a way to have her seventh-grade students describe a variety of activities that they would complete during a unit on the environment focused on the theme "Reduce, Reuse, Recycle, Renew", She had previously required students to create posters or tri-fold presentations, and then they would participate in a gallery walk to observe the various work classmates had completed. After one gallery walk, a student asked, "How can we keep all of this information? There's just not a good way to store it, and some of the parts will get lost." Mrs. Green agreed that the posters and tri-folds were not the best method of creating a representation of the work in the unit. She spoke with her technology resource specialist who suggested using an electronic portfolio platform based on a Google app (www.sites.google.com/site/eportfolioapps/Home). This would allow her students to use a variety of Internet-capable devices to create, upload, and publish their work as well as serve as a convenient archive for later use.

proliferation of smartphones, there are several free apps that can be used to create and maintain portfolios (e.g., www.evernote.com, www.voicethread.com, www.kidblog.org, www.google.com/drive) with some that are free specifically for teachers (e.g., www.play.google.com/store/apps/details?id=com.openschool.app&hl=en).

More about the applications of e-portfolios in teacher education will be addressed in Chapter 12, including many details that could also apply to school-age student portfolios.

Interpretive Exercises

Interpretive exercises, an innovative test question format, are considered an effective format to ask HOTS questions (see Figure 11.24). To help schools and parents better prepare students, most states publish their released state-mandated exams for public school students that were taken in previous years (such as the released exams published by TEA [Texas Education Agency, 2014]). By reviewing the released exams, it is obvious that the percentage of interpretive exercise type of questions is increasing. Examining the first ten questions in the 2014 fourth-grade TEA-released STAAR mathematics test, one will note that all ten questions are asked in the formats of a clock, a number line, a column chart, a coin diagram, a data table, a fraction bar, or other types of graphic illustrations. For a look at other released STAAR tests, one can visit www.tea.texas.gov/student.assessment/ STAAR_Released_Test_Questions. Technology makes it particularly easy for teachers to generate many of these examples from photographs or clip art for understanding and practice (see Figures 11.25, 11.26, 11.27, 11.28).

Josh gives the same number of breadsticks on each plate in his restaurant. The table below shows the number of bread sticks in different numbers of plates.

Number of plates	15	30	45	60
Number of breadsticks	45	90	135	180

Which statement describes the relationship between the number of plates and the number of breadsticks?

A.   The number of plates × 3 = the number of breadsticks
B.   The number of plates + 30 = the number of breadsticks
C.   The number of plates × 5 = the number of breadsticks
D.   The number of plates + 60 = the number of breadsticks

Kelvin Wong / Shutterstock.com

Figure 11.24   A sample question for fourth-grade students using a data table.

nicemonkey / Shutterstock.com

Figure 11.25   A fourth-grade math question asks students to tell time by presenting a clock picture.

Shapiro Svetlana/Shutterstock.com

Figure 11.26   A fourth-grade question asks students to interpret a picture of math manipulatives.

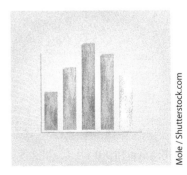

Mole / Shutterstock.com

Figure 11.27   A fourth-grade math question asks students to read a column graph.

An interpretive exercise consists of a series of objective items based on a common set of stimuli or introductory material. It is a special type of question in that the student is expected to answer by interpreting or understanding the presented visual materials. This type of question typically asks for interpretation of graphs, poems, cartoons, diagrams, charts, stories, passages, pictures, or data tables (see Figures 11.29, 11.30, 11.31, 11.32). To answer the questions, students must comprehend, analyze, apply, or synthesize the information presented. Miller et al. (2013) note:

> The series of related test items may also take various forms but are most commonly multiple-choice or true-false items. Because all students are presented with a common set of data, it is possible to measure a variety of complex learning outcomes. Students can be asked to identify relationships in data, to ~~~~~~~~~~~~~~ *Question 4* appraise assumptions and ~~~~~~~~~~~~ ications of data, and the li~~~~~~~

Figure 11.28 A fourth-grade math question asks students to answer a money question that is presented with coin graphics.

Here are five guidelines for interpretive exercise style questions:

- Relevance (or relevant to subjects)
- Similarity (or similar to what you are teaching in class)
- Brevity (of short length)
- Answers not provided (or students have to think to get the answers)
- Multiple questions (or a series of objective items based on a common set of stimuli)

Thanks to modern desktop publishing programs such as MS Publisher, productivity tools such as MS Office Suite, and graphic editing utilities tools such as MS Paint 3D, it has become easier for classroom teachers to create assessment items as interpretive exercises (see Table 11.4). When combined with graphic editing programs such as MS Paint 3D, scanners, and digital cameras, teachers can be very resourceful when it comes to creating the introductory materials for interpretive exercises in the classroom to prepare students to become familiar with the formats of standardized tests, particularly state exams or other commercial tests.

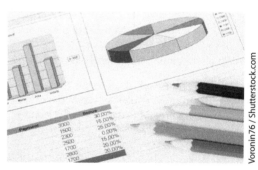

Figure 11.29 MS Excel is an effective tool for creating the data sets, tables, diagrams, and charts for the introductory materials of interpretive exercise.

Figure 11.30 Newspaper articles can be used in the introductory material of interpretive exercises.

"I see we're split between those who like my new tie, and those who welcome unemployment."

Figure 11.31 Newspaper cartoons can be used in the introductory material of interpretive exercises.

Figure 11.32 Many types of graphic organizers can be used in the introductory material of interpretive exercises.

Table 11.4 Technology Tools Used to Create the Stimuli of Interpretive Exercises

Technology Tools	Types of stimuli for interpretive exercises
MS Word	Graphic organizers, poems, passages, data tables, stories, clip art, shapes, number lines
MS Excel	Graphs, data tables, pie graphs, column graphs, bar graphs, charts
WWW	Pictures, data sets, stories, cartoons, news, charts, maps, photographs
Other	Photographs taken by digital cameras, newspapers scanned by scanners, graphics edited with MS Paint 3D

In many of the figures above, Shutterstock.com images have been used to generate images. An account to use their photographs can be created for teachers and students for a charge, but they have almost limitless subjects. In creating many of these assessments, educators must be wary of issues of plagiarism and copyright infringement in tests and other instructional materials that they create for students and in class projects created by students. For future generations of Americans to become more aware of intellectual property at a young age, teachers need to demonstrate respect for property laws. More about the legal and ethical essentials of educational technology are addressed in Chapter 10.

Performance Assessment

Traditional assessment techniques are of two general forms: selection and supply. Multiple-choice, true-false, and matching items are called **selection test items**. When answering selection test items, students respond to each question by selecting an answer from the choices provided. Essay questions, short answer, completion questions, or "fill-in-the-blank" questions are **supply test items** that require the student to construct a response. Both *supply test items* and *selection test items* are forms of **traditional assessment**.

On the other hand, extended supply items such as book reports, portfolios, experiments, and class projects are usually referred to as **performance assessments** (also **alternative assessment** or **nontraditional assessment**). Traditional assessment activities like fill-in-the-blank and multiple-choice quizzes are quickly losing popularity, and, in their place, lear_____ative higher-level assessments that are more authentically testing the learne_____nt. Performance assessment is gaining acceptance in K-12 classrooms (Mille_____archers note:

> Performance-assessment tasks are intended to closely reflect long-term instructional goals and require students to solve problems of importance outside the confines of the classroom or to perform in ways that are valued in their own right. Written essays are one example of a complex-performance task that reflects the instructional goal of effective communication more than a selected-response test could. Other examples include open-ended mathematics problems requiring extended responses, laboratory experiments in science, the creation of a piece of art, oral presentations, projects, and exhibitions of student work. (p. 36)

After several decades of computer application in schools, technology has infiltrated all aspects of education. Yet, teachers still talk about "doing a technology lesson" as though teaching with technology is somehow different from "everyday" lessons. Performance assessments require students to demonstrate specific abilities, and, for most teachers, assigning technology-based performance assessment projects can be an easy way to integrate technology because students learn technical skills from each other and genuinely enjoy collaborating on the projects. Miller et al. (2013) believe that

> Like essay questions, performance assessments should be used primarily to measure those learning outcomes that cannot be measured well by objective test items. . . . Performance assessments are better suited for applications with less structured problems where problem identification; collection,

organization, integration, and evaluation of information and originality are emphasized (e.g., where is the best place to locate a restaurant?). They are also essential for learning outcomes that involve the creation of a product (e.g., painting) or an oral or physical performance (e.g., the presentation of a speech, the repair of an engine, or the use of a scientific instrument). (p. 285)

Technology, especially the Internet, can be a powerful tool to be incorporated into students' performance projects. Reader's Theater, as mentioned, offers an entertaining and engaging means of improving fluency, enhancing comprehension of the text, building vocabulary, improving public speaking skills, increasing self-confidence, and exposing students to different genres. Reading teachers have used this strategy for decades to blend students' desire to perform with their need for oral reading practice. The strategy can be modified for all grade levels. What is Reader's Theater? It is a way to involve students in reading aloud as part of classroom instruction. Students "perform" by reading scripts created from age-appropriate books or stories. They can do so with or without costumes or props. With a technology "twist", students can record their own "theaters", edit with Audacity or other audio editing tools, post to and distribute through safe podcast sites such as Podbean (www.podbean.com) to have audio sound, and create audio effects as one hears in radio broadcasts. When technology is used in support of projects such as this, it can, in turn, contribute to students' sense of authenticity and to the "real-life" quality of the task at hand. This is a technology-enhanced performance project that affords opportunities for both formative and summative assessment of students' knowledge and skills.

Another way in which performance assessment can occur is to develop activities that employ a variety of information.

Mrs. Lambert's elementary science class is separated into groups. Each group is responsible for one day's weather report per week. Each report rotates group members to serve as the reporter, the digital camera operator, data collector, the graphic arts director, and an "on the street" person who dresses appropriately, comments, and so forth. At the end of the week, the reports are merged and viewed, and predictions for the weekend are given. Just as with Reader's Theater, students could use various "props" such as green screens, Google Slides, and the like to enhance the "real-world" feel of the assignment. Similarly, these activities could also be recorded and edited for a "professional" presentation.

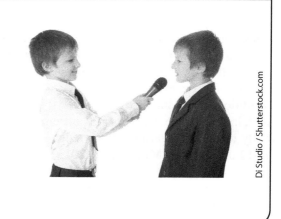

Di Studio / Shutterstock.com

With the flexibility of student performance projects, teaching, learning, and assessment can be enmeshed in a single technology-based performance assessment activity. Technology makes it possible for students of performance assessment projects to aspire to produce inexpensive copies of multimedia materials with quality appearances. Table 11.5 describes technology-based performance projects ideas for elementary, middle, and high school levels.

Not everyone agrees that technology integration improves student learning. Some argue that research results have been mixed. Yet, overall, the evidence seems to support the belief that appropriate use of technology results in higher student achievement (Nusir, Alsmadi, Al-kabi & Sharadgah, 2013; Devlin & McKay, 2016). The ease with which technology-based performance assessment projects can be integrated with instruction has made them particularly appealing to teachers and students. These thoughtfully planned performance assessment projects can engage students to a much higher degree than traditional assessment and lead to the development of twenty-first-century skills such as complex thinking, creative problem solving, and collaboration (Miller et al., 2013).

Table 11.5 Technology-based Performance Projects Ideas (Based on U.S. Department of Education, 1995)

Grade Level	Performance Assessment Project Ideas
Lower Elementary Grade Level	Students create multimedia reports that include not only text but also digitized photographs and sounds as well as artwork. Tenkaly (2017) offers "10 Technology Enhances Alternatives to Book Reports." Among them are: have students create a cartoon version of a book; have students create a video (www.creaza.com; or www.xtranormal.com); ask them to create an virtual advertising poster (www.glogster.com); have them share reading logs (www.goodreads.com); have students record an audio podcast on a book (www.audacity.com; www.mashable.com/2005/12/03/gcast-free-podcast-hosting/#NVmV9raVBgqM; or www.podbean.com); have learners create a time line of events (www.capzles.com); ask them to share wikis (www.wetpaint.com; www.pbworks.com); instruct them to create a book talk (www.viddler.com); or have students create a slide show (www.voicethread.com).
Higher Elementary School Grade Level	In a fifth-grade bilingual class, students engage in a semester-long project in which they develop multimedia documentaries of the lives of minority group members who have achieved prominence within the students' local community.
Middle School	Students can experience an increased sense of communication with external communities not only by obtaining information from external sources but also by creating documents describing school activities for their school homepage. Students must conduct and videotape interviews and compose written highlights from the interviews. Students can create songs using Garageband or Audacity or create YouTube videos. Zaption (www.blog.zaption.com/post/146724427719/zaption-joins-workday) allows questions to be embedded in a video.
High School	Students in an architecture and design class use computer-aided design (or CAD) programs to plan and design a home for a hypothetical family with specified needs and financial resources.

Storyboards and Prototypes

Increasingly, teachers are requiring students to create electronic products such as computer games, technology-based performance projects, electronic portfolios, animations, digital stories, coded objects, videos, 3-D designs, Websites, electronic presentations, and many other complex and multifaceted projects for major course grades. The concepts of storyboards and prototypes that have a long-standing history in industry settings can also be introduced as gateways to technology-based class projects as a part of formative assessment (before a complete project is submitted).

Figure 11.33 Original cartoon figures and pictures—drawn with pencil.

Mila Basenko / Shutterstock.com

The digital storyboarding process was developed at Walt Disney Productions during the early 1930s and is still widely used by movie and animation studios. A storyboard is similar to a comic strip—a series of rough sketches (or even clip-art images) that show how a media sequence will look. The user or viewer can visualize the layout and sequencing for the sake of planning and communication. In the storyboarding process, technical details such as sound effects, dialogues, and captions can be described either in picture or in the notes (see Figure 11.33). The initial storyboard may be as simple as slide titles on yellow sticky notes, which are then replaced with illustrations and sketches by hand. Modern storyboarding tools, whether in the form of Web-based tools or apps, help to inspire students and organize thoughts (see Figure11.34 for a list of storyboarding sites and apps). Teachers can distribute a storyboard template

ACMI (Australian Centre for the Moving Image) Online Storyboard Generator
www.generator.acmi.net.au/storyboard

Storyboard That: Online Storyboard Generator
www.storyboardthat.com

Figure 11.34 A list of storyboarding Web tools and apps.

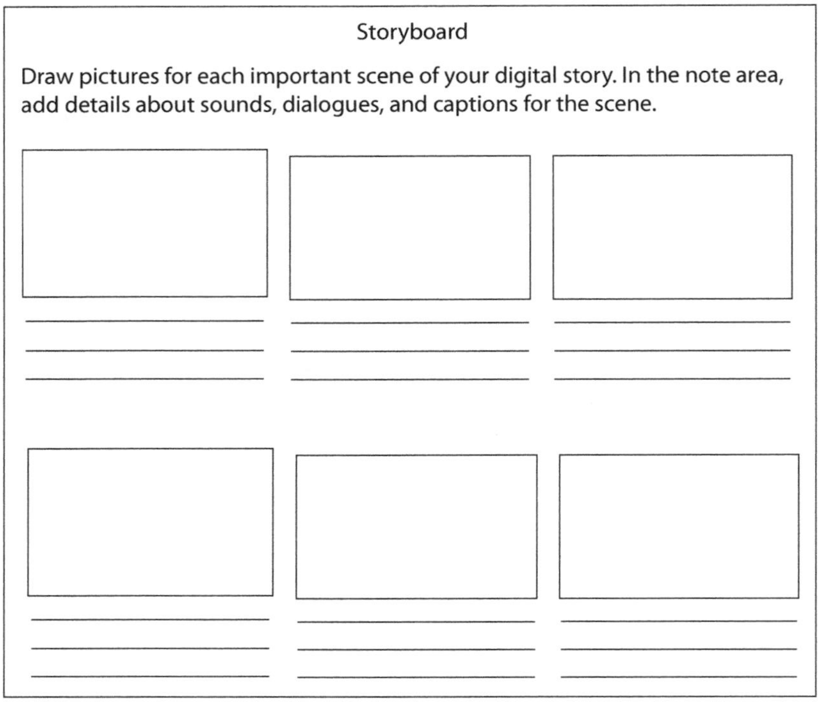

Storyboard

Draw pictures for each important scene of your digital story. In the note area, add details about sounds, dialogues, and captions for the scene.

© Kendall Hunt Publishing Company

Figure 11.35 A storyboard template that can assist with project planning and communication.

as seen for students to illustrate and fill out, which can assist with project planning and communication among team members and from team members to teachers (see Figure 11.35). For instance, at the start of the project, teachers can ask the class to turn in a storyboard template to communicate initial digital project ideas with her (see Figure 11.36). This should help students to receive useful feedback to launch the project in the right direction. Alternatively, students can draw stories by using MS PowerPoint to easily rearrange scenes when in the Slide Sorter View.

The idea of a prototype can also be introduced as a gateway to technology-based class projects such as programming, robotics, or other electronic projects. A prototype is an early sample, model, or release of a product built to test a concept or process or to act as a

lucadp / Shutterstock.com

Figure 11.36 This prototype diagram illustrates the phases of a mechanical project: sketch, project on a computer, prototype with a 3-D printer, and the final product.

semi-completed product to be replicated or finished. Creating a prototype is the step between the formalization of ideas and the final evaluation of a project. While the project is under way, teachers can ask to see a prototype of the project, which can contain the major working structure of the project without full multimedia details, programming, or model completion.

With the visualization capabilities of technology tools such as storyboarding and prototype tools, project expectations can be communicated to guide students and formative assessment can be accomplished.

Data Analysis and Presentation Tools

Good formative assessments present useful data in the form of feedback to students and teachers. With the increased use of smartphones, android tablets, laptops, and iPads in the classroom, an audience response system (e.g., www.iclicker.com) can offer teachers the opportunity to quickly assess student learning in the midst of instruction. Several of the more widely format-compatible Websites provide options for students to reply anonymously, support images and video prompts, give either typed or free-hand responses, and download a record of questions and responses (e.g., www.todaysmeet.com, www.padlet.com, www.socrative.com, www.getkahoot .com) (see Figure 11.37) . These browser-based platforms provide quick, accurate assessment of student learning, opinions, and feedback to the class at large. Poll Everywhere (www.polleverywhere.com) is specifically designed for smartphones and tablets allowing for text messaging and integrates with various word cloud platforms to display responses (e.g., www.wordle .net, www.tagxedo.com, www.tagul.com). There are a vast number of graphic organizers for use that offer students and teachers assessment possibilities (both formative and summative). Interactive graphic organizers (www.my.hrw.com/nsmedia/intgos/html/igo.htm and www.vrml.k12.la.us/graphorgan) provide "fill in/ type in" spider maps, main idea charts, conclusions charts, sequence chains, and many more options.

TeacherVision
www.teachervision.com/lesson-planning/graphic-organizer

Thinkport
www.thinkport.org/graphic-organizers.html

teAchnology
www.teach-nology.com/worksheets/graphic

Figure 11.37 A list of graphic organizer Websites.

These types of assessment tools generate student engagement with the material, while at the same time reflect their understanding of concepts; similarly, teachers receive immediate feedback on student comprehension in the midst of an instruction time period.

In addition, teachers can use technology to monitor assessment results that inform instruction. Most districts use some form of electronic grade book that operates similar to an Excel® spreadsheet that generates statistics on student achievement. Understanding trends among different learners, different classes, and across departments allows teachers to modify instructional strategies, confer with colleagues, and implement changes in curriculum, instruction, and assessment. Charts and graphs can also be generated for use in the classroom with students to illustrate progress over a marking period or the school year. For some, this can be a motivational strategy to encourage high performance; however, each teacher will need to judge whether this is appropriate information for her or his particular class.

Learning Analytics

As more teachers are required to document students' learning through online grading systems and more tests are administered and recorded online, the recent growth of data generated by the computer systems that collected them has surpassed the ability of many schools and districts to make sense of it all. With LMS such as Eduphobia, ITSlearning, Moodle, and Google Classroom, many learning result reports are automatically generated by the computer system and become easily accessible for teachers. Some reports conduct item analysis to analyze the difficulty levels of test items while others provide description statistic numbers such as mean, median, mode, maximum, minimum, and standard deviation on the entire class. Most of these reports are cloud-based, meaning they are stored somewhere on a server for educators to retrieve.

In an age when schools are under growing pressure to improve students' academic performance and increase instructional efficiency, learning analytics promises to be an important lens through which to view and plan for change in instructions. Simply explained, learning analytics is the science used to improve future learning by examining current assessment data. The very first International Conference on Learning Analytics and Knowledge that took place in 2011 provides a more detailed definition, "Learning analytics is the measurement, collection, analysis and reporting of data about learners and their contexts, for purposes of understanding and optimizing learning and the environments in which it occurs" (First International Conference on Learning Analytics and Knowledge, 2011, p. 1).

The data from assessments can help teachers, students, parents, and other stakeholders make decisions about teaching and learning. The goal of assessment should be, above all, to support the improvement of learning and teaching.

The reports generated by K-12 LMS systems can categorize the report in several ways, including teacher breakdown, student category breakdown, and student individual report. The most common are teacher breakdowns, which compares teachers of the same level to one another. Student category breakdowns allow a teacher to view each question categorized by response and the number of occurrences of each answer. Finally, the student individual report allows the teacher or student to view a breakdown of which questions test takers answered incorrectly and which questions they answered correctly. For example, personnel from the district could download each question to the state-mandated STAAR exams and align them with the appropriate Texas Essential Knowledge and Skills (TEKS) Standards. Many campuses have created a "BMAT" on which teachers use their professional judgment to label each question as "Basic, Mastery, Advanced, Transfer" (or BMAT), so that the report can be further analyzed to see how students did on questions labeled "B," "M," "A," or "T." Figure 11.38 shows that the students have achieved the Mastery level for the hypothetical Question 6. Figure 11.39 compares the students' performance for the individual teacher and state average by each answer for Question 6. Figure 11.40 shows the report's recommendation for Question 6.

❑ Adjust pacing ❑ Rewrite the question	❑ Realign the curriculum ❑ Modify level of questions	❑ Modify item distractors ❑ Other: _____

Question 6

Levels of Questions with Expected Student Performance

≥ 95%	✓ ≥ 85%	≥ 65%	≥ 40%
B	M	A	T

Figure 11.38 A sample BMAT breakdown for a question.

Data Analysis

Answer	State Stats	Teacher Stats	Aligned
A	52	46	
B	3	13	
C	17	24	
D	28	17	

Figure 11.39 The data analysis report compares individual teacher and state average by each answer for a question.

Possible Outcome(s) from This Analysis		
❑ Adjust pacing ❑ Rewrite the question	❑ Realign the curriculum ❑ Modify level of questions	❑ Modify item distractors ❑ Other: _____

Figure 11.40 The data analysis report's recommendation for a question.

Ms. Romero, a third-grade teacher, reflected on how learning analytics reports generated by her district's LMS help her become a more effective teacher as follows:

Data from assessments help us create our small groups, identify students who have not yet mastered state standards, and determine who needs remediation. In the district I work in, teachers are given access to an Eduphoria LMS. We can see how students did in each assessment. The Eduphoria reports can be broken down by percentage scores, and teachers are informed if students passed the assessment or received advanced placement. If we want a detailed Eduphoria report, we are able to see how each student did for each TEKS. I use this information to see which TEKS need to be retaught and which students need additional help. In the last assessment, we noticed that more than half of my students did not master TEKS 2.5D. Therefore, I retaught this concept in a mini lesson to the whole class. I used different approaches for remediation mini lessons. Sometimes, I included technology, games, and videos to see if that could help my students understand the material better.

Besides using Eduphoria, I also use IStation reports—an intervention for Tier 2 and 3 students—but all students have access to it. At the beginning, middle, and end of the school year, students take a test to measure their growth. IStation runs a report on what skills students did not master and also provides lessons to give students extra support. Using IStation for interventions provides detailed lessons to complete for extra help.

When I evaluate how my students did, I highlight each of my student's weakness, and I use this to plan my small group interventions. I also look at the students' strongest area and pair them with students who need additional help in that area. Those students become my peer tutors. Reports like these help me plan my lessons, and I am able to see how effective my teaching is. I can also monitor to see if my students were making progress. The district also allows us to see how the whole grade level did, and teachers can then work together as a team to see how we can help each other. I think tools like these help us become effective teachers.

New Technology-Based Assessment Tools on the Horizon

Research suggests that teachers spend one-quarter to one-third of their time on assessment-related activities (Stiggins & Conklin, 1992). Considerable technology progress has taken place in the past decade to give teachers more tools for summative, formative, and self-assessment. A number of technology trends have been developing for decades and soon will be integrated by educators or implemented in most LMS. We are starting to witness the convergence of several growing technology trends used to enhance educational assessment and evaluation to achieve the goal of "good" assessment. Specifically, this section discusses technology-based tools for video feedback, co-creation, goal-tracking, scheduling, and other interactive tools.

The goal of assessment should be, above all, to support the improvement of learning and teaching. Descriptions such as "timely," "fair," "specific," "meaningful," "constructive," and "immediate" all describe "good" assessment feedback given by teachers to students.

Pennebaker, Gosling, and Ferrell (2013) explain that in the history of the study of learning, the role of feedback has always been central. When people are trying to learn, they must get some information that tells them whether they are correct in their knowledge and/or skills. Both the mastery of content and the mastery of how to think require trial-and-error learning. They also argue that one important self-regulatory method to improve performance is to give students frequent testing along with rapid, targeted, and structured feedback on their performance so that they can adjust their learning and studying strategies in time to improve their performance.

For students to be active partners and become involved in the assessment process to make effective decisions based on feedback, a teacher's *immediate* feedback at an interim deadline is critical. In addition to verbal comments given to students in person or written comments, there are technology-based alternatives. Technology has moved past only simple and quick "correct or incorrect" feedback on lower-level assignments and games. It is common for teachers to share comments with students by using the track changes feature of word processing software. For decades, teachers have recorded their talks as audio files and saved them in audio cassettes, CDs, or emailed them to students to review. Vocaroo has been one of the most popular cloud-based voice recording tools that teachers employ to leave asynchronous verbal comments. Teachers call Vocaroo's toll-free number to record audio files, which are stored online. The process is intuitive and effective. At the end of the recording, Vocaroo generates URLs for teachers to send to students through emails or pasted to students' work or evaluation rubrics. To view a demonstration of how to use Vocaroo audio feedback, visit: www.youtube.com/watch?v=zQ3tMOx-o6E.

Another cloud-based voice recording site, Voice Spice, allows teachers and students to record, morph, and share recordings by downloading audio files.

Some teachers use screen casting such as Jing, a free screen casting tool, to record screens to give video feedback to students. To watch a tutorial video of how to use Jing for video feedback, visit: www.youtube.com/watch?v=teRPg139zVU.

In recent years, a video feedback mechanism has been built into many LMSs and other education platforms for teachers to provide brief videos created with screen captures, webcams, cameras, or other means. This

---

Here is a narrative written by Mrs. Ejiro about her recent experience of integrating an online collaboration tool with a video discussion tool.

***

This activity is designed for fifth graders and pertains to their science subject.

Earth Day was this past 22nd of April, and it is important for students to know how to care for our planet.

The first video discussion tool I decided to use was MeetingWords as a collaboration tool. This tool is an interactive notepad or word document. Many students are able to contribute to the documents at the same time and are able to chat with each other if needed. In the MeetingWords space, my fifth-grade students were allowed to post interesting facts, reflections, discussions, links to video, etc. I decided to keep it simple since fifth graders are starting to use more advanced technology, and I don't want to overwhelm them. They were also able to chat with each other if they needed clarification or just some extra assistance with the project.

Here is the link to the MeetingWords Project of my class: www.meetingwords.com/fPrlVqizBp.

The second part of this activity was to use FlipGrid to record students' responses to the prompt which asked students to volunteer their time to help clean our homes. Students could upload a video of themselves participating in such activities or describing what they did. With this tool, students can record their responses to a prompt or activity instead of posting to a common discussion thread. Students are also able to reply to other students' responses.

As far as analyzing data, MeetingWords provides a time-slider that allows the creator of the pad to see who contributed and what was typed. This aspect can be used by teachers to ensure that students are not playing around or writing inappropriate things. It helps to monitor the project and encourage students to maintain good Netiquette. An example of this can be seen here, look for the time-slider at the top of the screen: www.meetingwords.com/ep/pad/view/fPrlVqizBp/latest.

FlipGrid also provides assessment data for analysis and feedback. Teachers can view how many times students posted, the number of replies, dates, likes, and much more. The purpose of these two activities is to get students to collaborate with each other and learn from each other. Not all assignments are understood the same by every student. Some students may be creative, while other prefer to post simple discussions. As educators, we provide the tools for them to use.

link provides sample video feedback for a student's writing project through the instructor using a webcam: www.youtube.com/watch?v=YBXF-A_pstk. Here is another sample of video feedback for a student's math test using a webcam:

www.youtube.com/watch?v=Jqu8JaSzZfs.

Educators at Monash University reflect on the impact of giving video feedback to students: www.youtube .com/watch?v=18cVKli7jMg.

MeetingWords, a Web-based text editor, can be used for teacher/student and student/student communication. With MeetingWords (www.meetingwords.com) multiple users can work at the same time, with everyone's changes reflected instantaneously to all others. Furthermore, every writer's contributions are marked with their individual color codes. All persons who work on that project are provided with the same URL and will be able to access the same pad that contains the joint project whether on campus or away from campus.

FlipGrid (www.info.flipgrid.com) allows teachers to post a prompt or question, and students can then record a video reply in response, even from their phones. Students can view and revise their video before they submit the final version. Teachers are pleased because they have an easy and unique tool to use to collect assignments and assess them on their iPads or other devices, and it is more gratifying than grading paper-and-pencil tests.

Miss Wellington wrote about her recent experience of using "I Done This" and Goalscape to facilitate goal setting and coordination as follows:

Setting goals at an early age can help students because they are able to monitor their education, they can gain confidence, and it can help improve their own ability. The tracking tools that I selected are "I Done This" and Goalscape.

I geared my project to second-grade reading. Currently, my school is following the Teacher College Reading and Writing Project. This program is very goal oriented, and students are always working on a new strategy which becomes their goal. The students work independently and with a reading partner to become fluent readers, master new strategy, and develop a love for reading. My students read independently for a total of 30 minutes. During this time, I go around and conference with individual students. I target an area in which students need to improve and practice with them. At the end of my conferences, I leave them with an artifact and make sure they know what they are working on. I also allow my students to evaluate themselves as readers and set goals for themselves. Usually, students set the goal to reach a certain reading level, but I help them develop more precise goals. This is the reason why I choose goal-tracking tools—because I would like to take what I learn here and actually apply it to my classroom.

"I Done This" is a goal-tracking tool which is very interactive. It reminded me of Facebook and Twitter. With this tool, students can create an account using their email address. They are able to set goals, monitor their progress, and look at what other students are doing as well. It also allows students to mark their goals as achieved or state what is blocking them from achieving their goals. Students are also allowed to comment on other goals. As a teacher, you can pull a report on each student's progress and their activity. It allows you to see the report as a graph and export to Excel.® One is also allowed to receive reminders of students' activity and receive emails of what the students post. Based on the data provided, I was able to see that student R was very involved in the class. He had more activity and was awarded the "most verbal" title. You can see that he had 16 entries. Student A was less involved, and she only had five entries. This tells me that she is not setting goals for herself and not providing her peers with feedback. These reports help me see who is having difficulty setting goals and who needs more help. I can also see who is accomplishing their goals.

Goalscape is also a great tracking tool. With this tool, students can also create goals and subgoals which help them achieve their main goal. The students are able to track their progress by adjusting the accomplishment bar. As a teacher, you can also assign which students need to accomplish which goal. As you add more goals, your wheel increases in size, and, as goals are accomplished, the color of the wheel turns blue. It is a simple way to track students' mastery.

Here is a Goalscape I have created:

www.connect.goalscape.com/#/goal/D9A86E8E-5AE7-D5BD-460E-89D7E371D297/note (To view the page requires newer Web browsers with the Adobe Flash player).

Group work coordination such as "I Done This" (www.idonethis.com) makes it easy to track and celebrate the progress that colleagues make at work every day. The program emails members at the day's end and asks, "What'd you get done today?" and then compiles members' replies. The next morning, group members receive a digest that shows the group's accomplishments from the previous day.

In schools, goal-tracking tools can be used to replace spreadsheets, mind mappers, and outliners to define goals and plan activities for work projects and sports campaigns. Goal-tracking tools such as Goalscape (www.goalscape.com) is an innovative way to assist students in setting goals, enhancing motivation, and prioritizing activities or assignments. Unlike other industry-grade project management software, Goalscape is easy to use so that teachers and students alike are better organized and more focused.

Online scheduling tools have a rapidly growing user base. It takes the tediousness out of finding the right date and time for a group of people to assign work or collaborate in other ways. Due to the nature of working in teams, group members can sometimes find that they are not working effectively, which negatively affects their progress. One common problem identified by individuals working in teams is how difficult it is to ensure that the group gets off to a good start. It may be beneficial to decide on jobs or subtasks for each member and develop an agenda and a time line. Good scheduling tools simplify group projects and topic assignments. Online scheduling tools such as Doodle, Omnipointment, or Framadate lets users post a "poll" (a tabular display of possible available topics or time slots), invite participants through emails, and allow them to vote transparently and democratically for their preferred activities or time slots.

Summary

This chapter addresses a number of ways in which technology can be used to improve and evaluate student learning outcomes. Assessment should be viewed as both a means of evaluating the students' knowledge and understanding as well as providing opportunities for higher-level, critical thinking activities. Additionally, the assessment tools employed can provide feedback to the teacher regarding student misconceptions, confusion, or lack of mastery of requisite skills. This leads to potential changes in (and more effective) instructional strategies. Technology platforms are varied, and it is important for the teacher to carefully consider the purpose of the assignment and whether using technology will enhance student mastery. Shared workspaces, such as Google Docs, Dropbox, blogs, and wikis, offer creative and engaging opportunities for students to demonstrate mastery of learning outcomes. In addition, these platforms can be designed to deliver formative feedback, peer appraisal, self-assessment, and teacher response. Other technologies, such as game generators, e-portfolios, audience response systems, and word clouds provide exciting options for students to self-assess as well as provide feedback during class time that can be used to modify instruction. Finally, assessment results can be easily analyzed using electronic grade books (e.g., learnboost.com) and spreadsheet programs such as Excel® to modify instruction and track student achievement. The electronic assessment tools available to teachers now provide them with rich, quick, and creative alternatives.

References

Anderson, L. W., Krathwohl, D. R., & Bloom, B. S. (2001). *A taxonomy for learning, teaching, and assessing: A revision of Bloom's taxonomy of educational objectives*. Complete edition. New York, NY: Longman.

Anderson, R. S. (1998). Why talk about different ways to grade? The shift from traditional assessment to alternative assessment. In R. S. Anderson & B. W. Speck (Eds.), *Changing the way we grade student performance: Classroom assessment and the new learning paradigm* (pp. 5–16). New Directions for Teaching and Learning, No.74. San Francisco, CA: Jossey-Bass. doi: 10.1002/tl.7401

Chappuis, J. (2005). Helping students understand assessment. *Educational Leadership, 63*(3), 39–43.

Devlin, M., & McKay, J. (2016). Teaching students using technology: Facilitating success for students from low socioeconomic status backgrounds in Australian universities. *Australasian Journal of Educational Technology, 32*(1), 92–106.

First International Conference on Learning Analytics and Knowledge. (2011). Retrieved from www.tekri.athabascau.ca/analytics

Frey, B. B., & Schmitt, V. L. (2007). Coming to terms with classroom assessment. *Journal of Advanced Academics, 18*, 402–423.

Gentile, J. R. (1997). *Educational psychology* (2nd ed.). Dubuque, IA: Kendall Hunt Publishing Company.

Guskey, T. R. (2003). How classroom assessments improve learning. *Educational Leadership, 60*(5), 6–11.

Hatzipanagos, S., & Warburton, S. (2009). Feedback as dialogue: Exploring the links between formative assessment and social software in distance learning. *Learning, Media and Technology, 34*(1), 45–59.

Miller, M. D., Linn, R. L., & Gronlund, N. E. (2013). *Measurement and assessment in teaching* (11th ed.). Upper Saddle River, NJ: Pearson Education, Inc.

Nusir, S., Alsmadi, I., Al-kabi, M., & Sharadgah, F. (2013). Studying the impact of using multimedia interactive programs on children's ability to learn basic math skills. *E-Learning and Digital Media, 10*(3), 305. doi:10.2304/elea.2013.10.3.305

Pennebaker, J. W., Gosling, S. D., & Ferrell, J. D. (2013). Daily online testing in large classes: Boosting college performance while reducing achievement gaps. *Plos ONE, 8*(11), e79774. doi:10.1371/journal.pone.0079774

Robles, M., & Braathen, S. (2002). Online assessment techniques. *Delta Pi Epsilon Journal, 44*(1), 39–49.

Speck, B. W. (2002). Learning-teaching-assessment paradigms and the online classroom. In R. S. Anderson, J. F. Bauer, & B. W. Speck (Eds.), *Assessment strategies for the on-line class: From theory to practice* (pp. 5–18). New Directions for Teaching and Learning, No. 91. San Francisco: Jossey-Bass.

Stiggins, R. J., & Conklin, N. (1992). *In teachers' hands: Investigating the practice of classroom assessment.* Albany NY: SUNY Press.

Tenkaly, K. (2017). 10 technology enhanced alternatives to book reports. Retrieved from teaching.monster.com/benefits/articles/8529-10-technology-enhanced-alternatives-to-book-reports

Texas Education Agency. (2014). STAAR Released Test Questions. Retrieved from www.tea.state.tx.us/index4.aspx?id=25769814834&menu_id=793

U.S. Department of Education. (1995). Technology supports for project-based learning. Retrieved from www2.ed.gov/pubs/SER/Technology/ch8.html

Wiggins, G. (2012). Seven keys to effective feedback. Retrieved from www.ascd.org/publications/educational-leadership/sept12/vol70/num01/Seven-Keys-To-effective-feedback.aspx

Wiggins, G., & McTighe, J. (2006). *Understanding by design* (2nd ed.). Upper Saddle River, NJ: Pearson Education.

Chapter 12

E-Portfolios for Teachers and Students

Tina Nixon, Janice L. Nath - *Professor Emeritus*, Irene Chen
University of Houston - Downtown

Meet Tanya

Tanya Gleason walked into her first interview for a teaching position. She remembered that her professors in her teacher preparation program had told her that having a portfolio was worthwhile for hiring purposes, so she even ran a hard copy of her portfolio (in case the technology at the interview site would not interface to open her e-portfolio). She also had a cheap flash drive and a disk to leave when she finished the interview in case there wasn't enough time to show everything she wanted the principal and/or the grade-level interviewing committee to see during her scheduled interview time. She felt very confident because her teacher education program had made teacher candidates present their e-portfolios orally for the last three semesters before she graduated. This had given her considerable confidence in talking about her educational experiences and how they fit with best teaching practices. After the preliminary questions, the principal began with the serious questions. "I may have a third-grade reading/language arts position," Mr. Beck announced. "Can you tell me some ways that you might assess students in these areas?" Tanya quickly flipped to a running record that she had completed in one of her methods classes. "Let me show you what I did in my field experience that I would like to continue to use," she told him, as she showed the principal on her iPad which she had also brought with her. "I am impressed," said the principal. "You've obviously used lots of technology here. The last three candidates I interviewed didn't have portfolios—much less electronic ones." She got the job.

When Tanya was in her first year of teaching, there was so much to do that she wanted to put off keeping up with her professional portfolio. However, she did create a new folder and added several professional development certificates that she had acquired and evidence of activities in which she had participated that year. She also scanned in some of her students' best efforts and replaced a few of her lesson plan examples with others that were even more exciting. When she was working on this, she thought of a few more ideas that would make these lessons even better, and she added those ideas to her reflections.

At the end of her first year, Tanya's husband was suddenly transferred to a new city. She found herself in a similar situation in another interview (see Figure 12.1), but she was well prepared to "show and tell" about her teacher training and her experiences in her first year of teaching. She got the job (again).

Figure 12.1 Teacher candidate using an iPad to show a potential employer her e-portfolio.

Monkey Business Image / Shutterstock.com

A portfolio is often used as an assessment tool in both business and academic environments. In academia, a portfolio is defined as: "a selection of a student's work (such as papers and tests) compiled over a period of time and used for assessing performance or progress" (Merriam-Webster Online, 2018). To add to this, educational researchers (Avraamidou & Zembal-Saul, 2006) assert that it should be a ***deliberate*** collection of work rather than simply a scrapbook collection. At the collegiate level, portfolios have been used to assess the level of competence of students ***and*** as a road map to assist students academically (Gambrel & Jarrott, 2011). Chen and Light (2010) believed that as an assessment tool, the student portfolio is considered unique because, over time, it captures evidence of student learning. This may happen in multiple formats and contexts that can be captured in this type of documentation. In addition to an e-portfolio being used as a form of assessment, portfolios can also be used to highlight what those who have created them have learned, and this may also encourage prospective teachers to integrate both their formal and informal learning (Chen & Light, 2010).

Most universities use teacher candidate portfolios in multiple ways. Teacher educators (in addition to using them for self-assessment in their own instruction) want to:

- monitor their potential teachers' progress throughout a time period (such as a course or field experience) or throughout a program;
- have an assessment tool at the end of various semesters (which often matches their state's certification requirements);
- have teacher candidates become reflective about their growth;
- have a way for preservice teachers to tangibly highlight their experiences in the job market upon graduation.

Wray (2008) found that shifting from a perspective of seeing portfolios only as a tool for employment to a resource to evaluate professional growth was more beneficial to learners. The reflective growth involved in this shift will be discussed in detail later in this chapter.

With the advancement of technology, the standard portfolio (see Figure 12.2) has now evolved into an electronic format. This electronic format has become known as the electronic portfolio, or e-portfolio. Compared to its hard copy predecessor, the e-portfolio is often seen as more accessible, capable of holding more information in various formats, and easier to update and modify. Many universities are requiring learners to create an e-portfolio as a way to reflect on their work, provide more thorough assessment, and to provide teacher candidates with a means of displaying their academic work to potential employers. Other researchers (Nath, Cohen, Hill, & Connell, 2012) also discovered that many teacher candidates found the process of creating a portfolio to be a valuable study tool for their state certification tests. Real-life connections were realized as teacher candidates targeted, wrote about, and included personal examples from their field experiences and other assignments regarding the required state competencies. By the time future teachers had completed their portfolios, which were solidly based on the state competencies, teachers-to-be had become so familiar with the competencies that they had been "well absorbed"—with very little formal study needed prior to taking state certification tests in professional development.

Research shows that while e-portfolios can be very beneficial to college students, concerns may also arise. Ali (2005) suggested that planning must take place before a university can begin to implement the e-portfolios, and he provided nine steps to consider in overcoming these concerns. Students should be familiar with these concerns and address them when creating

Figure 12.2 Portfolios of the past. Hard copied material compiled into a notebook.

their portfolios without the complete expectation that their professor(s) must always guide the process for them. Normally, professors will set parameters and will guide the process to some extent, but teacher candidates should also use the following points to better direct their own roles in their portfolio development and completion:

- define the aim(s) of one's portfolio (i.e., a course grade, future hiring, professional development, etc.)
- consider the technology that is currently available to be used
- consider the type of technology that one would like employ use and decide how to learn the necessary skills, if possible
- know and define one's audience when considering the creation and presentation of a portfolio
- become empowered to "show what you know"; do not be shy about showing one's work and professional life to the best advantage (It might help somewhat to think of it as a tool to help "market" one's knowledge and expertise.)
- plan for ongoing review and correction/revision of the portfolio
- incorporate a feedback mechanism into the portfolio from those who will view it (peers, experts, interviewers, etc.)

Prospective teachers should always begin by familiarizing themselves with their university's (or teacher preparation program's) expectations and work toward the process of building their portfolio as a responsibility to themselves. Thinking and planning ahead will make the portfolio more complete and certainly a less stressful, more reflective process. To start the process, e-portfolios for future educators should include (but not be limited to): a title page, table of contents, a short résumé, samples of their work and of their students' work (from field experiences), reflections, a letter to viewers, and a comment box for individuals viewing the document (Ali, 2005).

Teacher candidates are sometimes required to create "showcase" e-portfolios in their teacher education courses. Visit the following URL to find the e-portfolio of Michelle, a teacher candidate, who has created hers on the Padlet platform:

www.padlet.com/michelleangelinagarcia96/s0owi1e49jmy

Also read what Michelle wrote when she reflected on the creation of the e-portfolio:

When creating my portfolio, my strategy was to include chapter projects that were quite fun to make. The projects did require time, but it was really nice to sit down and create something original. I was able to use things I learned in other classes and include that knowledge in the projects. The projects I included are mainly ones that can easily be used in the classroom for fun, interactive activities. Another strategy I used when creating my portfolio was to show my progression in the class. I realized that the projects started off simple, and, as the semester went on, they were more detailed and required more skills. The portfolio has helped show that technology in the classroom can be used for many different things. It also shows that I was able to use more difficult technology to create many new things. This portfolio will be a nice factor when applying for future jobs because I will be able to easily showcase my work rather than searching for the projects years after I created them. The portfolio is easily accessible and can be added on to at any time.

Before moving to a Web-based tool like Padlet, many education students created their e-portfolios using PowerPoint, then zipped the files and uploaded them to a platform for the instructor to view. Many students worked hard to create a creative product, but the lack of technical skills in terms of saving and formatting material as well as properly zipping them into a sharable file caused much of the content to be lost. Using a platform such as Wix, Padlet, Weebly, etc. still requires some technical skills, but documents can be easily shared as a Web link (URL) or a QR (quick response) code, a type of barcode. The result can be a valuable tool both in gaining technical knowledge and in storing projects overtime that students or teachers can retrieve and display.

It is worth noting that one can click on the hyperlinks on the Padlet project to reach the projects hosted on other sites. The images within the e-portfolio also hyperlink to the project hosted on other sites. For instance, a click on the Voki URL links to Michelle's Voki, which teaches the mathematics concepts of mean, median, mode, and range. A click on her Kahoot game image will guide users directly to the Kahoot site. In addition, in her e-portfolio, Michelle of the above case story has also given short descriptions to the projects to explain them to viewers. For instance, for the word "cloud project," she wrote, "The word 'cloud' covers the many factors of the Declaration of Independence" along with the word cloud image. The short descriptions provide contexts to the projects.

While this information may be important, Gambrel and Jarrott (2011) show that e-portfolios should support evaluations and student learning similar to the traditional portfolio process. In a music classroom, Mills (2009), for example, observed that using e-portfolios provided a rewarding experience to learners. Mills also found portfolios to be both formative and summative, depending on the learning environment. She describes the main strength of a learning portfolio as encouraging the students who created them to reflect on and assess the quality of their own individual work. The portfolio gives students wide boundaries to represent their own learning. When a teacher candidate directs a role in e-portfolio development, he or she is taking ownership and building a document that encompasses who he or she is as a learner and as a future teacher. This is beneficial to creators of portfolios because they also learn from the process of the work they put into their documents, which provides an additional set of skills (Ritzhaupt, Parker, & Ndoye, 2012).

Some teacher education programs have "portfolio presentation days" where teacher candidates participate in mock interviews using their portfolios. By seeing how their peers use many types of artifacts and design elements, the teacher candidates are better able to critique their own work and see more clearly how they compare to others. More importantly, they may be better able to judge the quality and impact of their work on others. Sometimes a professor's evaluation of a student's work can be perceived as somewhat biased by that student, but when the student is able to contrast his/her own portfolio presentation directly with excellent examples, mediocre examples, or poor examples, the understanding of these evaluations can become much clearer. An excellent factor regarding portfolio assessment is that it is not based on "one test" but that it can evolve over time and is easily modified with expert, peer, and self-feedback. Growth is the aim for teacher educators and their preservice teachers—rather than one-shot efforts such as final papers or exams.

As noted, teacher candidates may also develop additional technology skills as they put together their portfolios. They may include an array of multimedia resources that support student-created material. These skills allow prospective teachers to showcase their work in different platforms for different audiences (Ritzhaupt et al., 2012). For most schools, technology is a needed skill, and teacher candidates can use their portfolios to their advantage over the job competition by demonstrating technology competence (and even superiority) in their portfolios to distance themselves above others in comparison for teaching positions. Although portfolios can be more time-consuming to develop and assess, they offer significant benefits to students and are, therefore, worth the investment of time and effort (Mills, 2009).

In another area associated with improvement during the process of portfolio development, teacher candidates should consider discussing the expectations of their portfolio with their instructors. Wray (2008) discovered in her study of university students that many of them found that discussion with their professors about their portfolios allowed them to make connections between the artifacts and their educational philosophy. Students also benefited when the instructor spent time discussing the different artifacts students could use within their portfolio (Wray, 2008). In one's education program, there may be a menu of suitable items and/or many student choices to include as headings or as artifacts to demonstrate mastery, but selecting the best can often evolve through multiple conversations with professors (and peers). Artifacts are support for a heading, and they should clearly show that a person has "done something concrete" that applies to the heading or category. For example, under the heading of Classroom Management, Jon Martin, a university senior, selected to demonstrate his knowledge and experiences by including the following artifacts: a classroom management plan which he had constructed, a picture of a workable management chart that he and his mentor used during his field experiences, a write-up of an interesting student management incident with a reflective resolution, and others.

Ritzhaupt et al. (2012) suggest that e-portfolios in both preservice and inservice teachers' perspectives serve them in three ways: representation, reflection, and revision. Representation refers to the work that the creator of the portfolio produces which documents his/her skills. Reflection is the author's description that summarizes his/her perspective on the learning gained in producing the artifact. The last "r" is revision. This stage refers to authors reexamining their products to reassess what they have put together and to make changes as needed. For preservice teachers during a semester, it can seem difficult to keep up with revisions as new assignments become added, but the revision step is essential in having an excellent product without the pressure of having to complete revisions at the end and to incorporate improvements to new assignments along the way. One professor commented on this when a prospective teacher who had been in his class asked him for a reference. "I couldn't do it," he told a colleague. "She misspelled a very common educational term on her first assignment (assess), the same word on the second assignment, and on the last one...and everywhere in between. If she would have revised the first couple of times, she would have seen this and corrected it after the first or second time. As it was, she never did, and a principal who saw her artifacts would never hire her. It would be embarrassing if she used her misspelled word within a school setting."

E-portfolios are viewed by many as being a positive tool for prospective teachers in teacher education programs. Researchers (Strudler & Wetzler, 2005), however, discovered that the demands of creating an e-portfolio have caused some students to shy away from taking this process to heart. Streamlining the process and making the e-portfolio sustainable was suggested. In addition, some teacher educators see benefit from requiring the technology with which teacher candidates should be familiar and which they have used in the past, while other professors may want to use the portfolio experience to help their students learn new technology skills. Although it may require some extra individual time and effort, taking the extra step to learn new skills can be profitable in many ways to the prospective teacher (see Figure 12.2).

In one study conducted by Wray (2008), some students enjoyed the process of creating an e-portfolio but wanted more direction as to what to include within the portfolio. An idea that seems to help this development is to create an "empty shell" at the beginning of the portfolio process with all the required titles/slides but with no documents/artifacts yet. This can even be done in PowerPoint with a "slide shell" (see Figure 12.3).

As the timeline for completion progresses, documents/artifacts can be "slotted into" the shell and other slides added or deleted as needed to fill out the compete portfolio. This would be similar to creating a table of contents and adding pages/slides for each heading or filling in an outline at the beginning of a paper or other project.

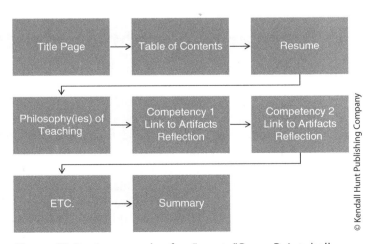

Figure 12.3 An example of an "empty" PowerPoint shell.

Students' Ownership of Studies/Motivation for Self-Improvement

Stacey Barnes, a recent college graduate, was nervous about her upcoming interview for a fourth-grade teaching position. Stacey had worked hard throughout her years in college and wanted her academics, as well as her positive student teaching experience, to show in her interview. She knew it was important to dress appropriately and to answer each interview question both clearly and precisely. The job description stated specific qualifications for each candidate, and Stacey also wanted to ensure that she addressed ways in which she met the requirements. Stacey prepared for her interview in some important areas; however, she did not take time to critically review her educational portfolio to ensure that it provided accurate examples and information that would support her as being the best candidate for the position. Her professors had given her feedback, but with student teaching and a host of graduation activities, she had not taken the time to go back and address their comments. When Stacey opened her portfolio to share examples with the interview panel, a few of her documents did not open, and she had to say weakly, "Well, this *was* a lesson plan I did". . . or "I *had* some examples of some student work here." In the interview, it became clear that a few of her documents really did not support her interview responses, some of the documents were out of order, and not all of her reflections showed that she understood how to apply what she had learned in her undergraduate studies. One member of the grade-level team even asked her about a slide that did open, "Is that something you actually did, or you just copied and downloaded it?" (which she, unfortunately, had done and had to say so). Stacey also saw how this "came over" to the panel when they asked about how she might incorporate various learning styles into her teaching, and she just showed them a copy of Gardner's Multiple Intelligences chart. She had also neglected to label a few of the artifacts that she had included, so when one team member asked about a particular picture, Stacey became flustered and said, "Uh, I think this was something I did in my first semester field experience." She quickly realized that she needed to have prepared a better portfolio that showed her as a positive and organized teacher-to-be.

Borysevych.com / Shutterstock.com

E-Portfolios for Teacher Education Students

Several formats have been used to create e-portfolios (Ittleson & Lorenzo, 2005); these formats include Web-based, text-based, graphic, or multimedia elements. Additional formats may include electronic media such as CD-ROM or DVD (Ittleson & Lorenzo, 2005). Although CD-ROMs, DVDs, and flash drives are often used, many universities are using a more Web-based format. This format allows the students to easily share portfolios with potential employers and to also turn them in as an assignment. Unlike other formats, students no longer have to purchase disks or flash drives and make multiple copies of their portfolio. The concerns of scratching a disk or losing a flash drive are also eliminated because with the online format, students can provide a uniform resource locator, or URL. Students can also create QR codes which they can attach to their business card or résumé that will immediately direct users to their site. Some universities do require "hard copy" versions, so portfolio creators must always remember to back up their portfolios—regardless of how they is created. This can be done on a different computer, on a separate flash drive(s), a cloud backup, emailing it to one's own or a second email, and so forth. A portfolio is a valuable document, and it is devastating to reach the end of a semester (or even several semesters of work) to find that one has lost the only copy of a portfolio on a disk or flash drive to an electronic glitch, leaving it somewhere, theft, or so forth.

Among other teacher education programs, the University of Idaho uses a Web-based platform called WordPress. WordPress is also commonly used at many colleges and universities. Using Web-based formats may eliminate the concern of who owns the e-portfolio. With newer cloud storage tools such as Google Docs and Dropbox, which allow the inclusion of video, pictures, and texts, teacher candidates now have several ways to build an e-portfolio. Now, they cannot only build quality e-portfolios, but they also have the opportunity to provide a clearer picture of what they have learned (see Figure 12.4). However, some Web-based portfolios are not easily viewable from schools with strong firewalls to the Internet, and there is often information included that one would not necessarily want to be posted for public viewing (i.e., addresses, phone numbers, work addresses, pictures, and other information found on résumés/curricula vitae or other portfolio artifacts). It is always best to know for certain who may have access and how before posting on a Website.

Figure 12.4   Teacher candidate confidently interviewing for a teaching position.

Some students may choose to use platforms that are more Web-based and provide them with the experience of creating a Website. Programs such as Weebly, MyFolio, and Silk, may offer this type of experience for students. Others may include edu.gloster, Google Sites, WordPress, Blogger, Prezi, and, Wix. Students may benefit from the ability to drag and drop photos and hyperlink material. If students want to include videos, it is important to understand how to embed or link the videos to their host platform. While searching for examples via Google, one of the authors of this chapter discovered that many of the links to student portfolios did not work. Students should check their links to ensure the material is up to date and working at all times if they decide to use this format.

A Principal's Reflections

I remember interviewing a few candidates for a third-grade teaching position I had at my campus. I'd gone through several candidates, and many of them did not meet our needs. What I remember the most is that one of the teachers presented a portfolio to provide examples of her teaching experience. She provided examples of lesson plans, rubrics, and evaluations from her previous teaching positions. I allowed her to guide us through the process, and she did a great job until the very end. She was adamant of showing us an example of a teaching strategy we use here in the district. She asked if she could access the video from her Dropbox account via her laptop (see Figure 12.5). As we all sat, waiting to see this video, the teacher struggled to get the video working for us. She cited problems with the network, so I asked if she would provide the link to her site so we could view it later. We really liked this candidate, so we didn't mind viewing it later. When we went to view the video later, the link still did not work, and we received an error message saying: "The Page You Requested Was Not Found." I am not very knowledgeable in the area of technology, so I didn't push any further to see the video. The video was not the determining factor in our hiring decision, but it did play a major part in our decision.

Figure 12.5   Dropbox is an electronic tool that may be used for file storage.

E-portfolios for K–12 Students

Not only are portfolios used for teacher candidates, but a portfolio may also be used in the K–12 classroom by teachers. Portfolios are becoming increasingly popular in the K–12 environment. Teachers are using tools such as Seesaw (www.web.seesaw.me) to collect, share, and assess student work that are designed to share with both students and parents. Seesaw is a Web-based tool and application (app) that can be used on *multiple operating devices which allows users to insert images or take images* within the tool. It also allows students to record and/or upload video. Teachers can share the content with partner teachers, and they can also set up an account that allows parents to view their child's work. Many teachers find this tool useful because they feel it allows them to collect work samples throughout the year. They can use the work to show growth or lack of growth in students. Students can work in the tools collaboratively and "publish" their work when projects are complete.

Another tool that is being used in the K–12 learning environment is a personal "start page" tool called Symbaloo (www.symbaloo.com) that allows users to navigate and bookmark sites throughout the Web in a cloud. This allows easy access on any device.

Typical Items in a Job-Seeking E-Portfolio for Educators

There are similarities and differences in e-portfolios, but, as mentioned earlier, many of the items within the portfolio may depend on the degree program. For example, an engineering portfolio may differ greatly from an educational portfolio. Although the artifacts within the portfolio may differ, the required material may be very similar. For example, a standard e-portfolio may include the student's objective(s) and/or philosophies. A quick summary that clearly states future objectives is necessary to guide readers as they review the material included within the portfolio.

If the student is using the e-portfolio to pursue employment, it may be important to include (but not be limited to) the following items:

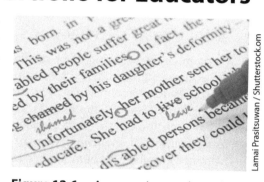

Figure 12.6 A preservice teacher edits and revises her portfolio documents to make sure they show her best efforts.

- title page
- table of content
- letter of interest in a particular position (if applicable)
- teaching philosophy(ies) (general and specific to content areas)
- a résumé
- artifacts
  - detailed lesson plans
  - relevant work examples or meaningful assignments of the teacher candidate
  - work samples of students (for some examples, see Figure 12.6 and Figure 12.7)
  - multimedia PowerPoints, technology games, and other items that one has created
  - assessments
  - pictures of relevant items (completed projects, bulletin boards, etc.) done by the teacher candidate

Figure 12.7 Work sample of the students.

- pictures of meaningful school experiences (following district policies)
  - observations/critiques by other professionals
  - other examples of learning and/or mastery
- a list and short description (if needed) of appropriate organizations to which one belongs
- certificates for completing trainings or professional developments (refer to Figure 12.8)
- references (that are requested for permission *before* posting with each person's title, phones, and emails) and possible letters of recommendations (although most applications are now taken online rather than in letter format)
- summary and/or reflections. You may find some

Figure 12.8 Certificate of training completion.

examples at www.uleth.ca/education/resources/eportfolios/sample-portfolios (look under Teacher Samples).

Providing a résumé provides an overview of what the learner has accomplished, but the artifacts within the portfolio provide examples of that work for potential employers to review. It is important that one includes his/her most significant work in an e-portfolio and introduces it well to the viewer(s) (refer to Figure 12.9 for the title page for a social studies teacher's portfolio). These may be assignments on which one received rave reviews, or it may, surprisingly, include one's best reflections about what was learned from a negative situation to show thoughtfulness and the ability to self-correct for growth. Running a spell/grammar check program (and/or having items reviewed for errors) is critical to being hired if using a portfolio. Principals will see glaring errors as a warning sign that a potential employee may not have the ability to teach school students proper grammar and spelling if he or she cannot present "clean" examples for an important job interview. They may also worry that, once hired, letters and notes sent home and to other colleagues and administrators may appear unprofessional.

Additional points to consider:

- Know that this portfolio not only shows one's knowledge about teaching but also one's technology skills. A principal can be impressed with the technological ability of the candidate by the examples that are selected, and technology expertise is valued in schools.
- Make sure that documentation is easily readable (i.e., font size, style, and so on).
- Keep page layouts the same rather than having some in PDF formats and others in Word formats.

Figure 12.9 A title page for a social studies teacher's portfolio.
Source: Janice L. Nath

- Include detailed information/artifacts about one's classroom management. It can confidently be stated that there have been few interviews for teaching positions which have failed to ask about this area.
- Rich, detailed lesson plans as artifacts indicate a teacher who has the potential to produce excellent lessons. Shallow lesson plans show a teacher who is unqualified or uncaring about the details of the classroom.
- Include any appropriate volunteer projects, professional honors, and professional organizations of which one is a member. Outside (but appropriate) activities indicate a person who is well-rounded and who may go above and beyond to interact with the community.
- Title page pictures and pictures working in various field experiences can present a compelling addition to a portfolio. It shows that "I have been in schools. . . . I have some experience with students/children," or it may show someone's interest and commitment to a content area. The title page for a social studies position in Figure 12.6 shows a teacher's experience and interest in other lands.
- If choosing to include photos in the body of the portfolio, consider capturing how one works collaboratively with teachers and students. Also for the cover, select photos carefully in terms of one's clothing and grooming. Prom pictures, glamour shots, or those with low necklines, low pants, or very short skirts for women do not convey that everyday look that will be recognizable or connect with a school atmosphere. Including pictures of one's family and children may lead a principal to think in two opposing ways: "Oh, this person has children so he/she will understand students and parents well," or, on the other hand, a principal may think, "Oh, no! Small children mean lots of outside activities . . . and the teacher may be absent a lot when those children are sick!" There is no need to give away one's family situation one way or another, and a main objective of a title page picture is to positively reconnect a face to a name when a principal has many interviewees. In addition, one must take into account other issues or concerns that may arise. For example, posting a title page with recent pictures taken with a fiancée may lead to a principal's thoughts of too many impeding wedding plans, and so forth. Some districts may have hair or beard restrictions for males, so men would want to consider a picture that matches those restrictions. Appearing ready to walk into a classroom in the district where one applies is the best choice for photographs. As one can see, each part of the portfolio sends a message to the viewer. Much thought must be put into each addition.
- A short, concise résumé (or curriculum vitae [CV] as it is known in academia) is important for principals in a portfolio (see Figure 12.10 for a sample résumé). They will want to quickly and clearly see a teacher candidate's qualifications. There are many formats (and professors may add different requirements to which students should adhere), but "simple" is best. For example, when listing prior employment or experiences, include a short and very concise description of the work done. If one was a server in a restaurant, that is sufficient rather than "seated patrons, took drink orders and served them, attended to guests needs, took food orders and interfaced between them and the kitchen, and so forth."
- Putting careful thought into one's philosophy must also be considered. One way to direct this is to examine a school's "mission plan" (their philosophy) for the school where one will interview. This is usually available on the district or school Website. If the candidate's and the school's philosophies agree, all is well. If not, there could be problems and discomforts in working there. This can also happen in an interview. For example, if a principal clearly states that frequent testing and high test scores will be required for children starting in their young childhood program at this school and the teacher candidate realizes that this may not necessarily agree with his or her own philosophy for this age group, it could be predicted that it may not bode for a good working relationship. How one feels about children, the basic purposes of schools, what students should be able to do when they finish their schooling, how teachers go about their work to accomplish goals, and so forth are essential to know about one's own philosophy. These thoughts will guide one's practice, and a portfolio can be used to set these down so that a teacher candidate can speak well to them and find a good "school match." A statement regarding the candidate's philosophy should be no more than about a 1 ½ -2 pages as principals will probably not have time in an interview to read through a lengthier one. The philosophy statement should come to the point in a powerful way to make a clear impression. This should be professionally stated and carefully edited.
- Teacher candidates should plan to keep this portfolio as a way of life—there are many unhappy stories of teachers who have lost all their records of past experiences and professional development, excellent student examples, and so forth during weather disasters, moves, and other situations; therefore, backing up data and keeping multiple copies may serve to be beneficial throughout one's career.

Jane Doe
100 Main Street
Great Town, TX 77777
222-333-3456 (c)
333-444-6789 (h)
DoeJ@inter.net

> **University((ies), college(s), high school with dates attended and locations with the most recent first. Include the city and state.

Education

2015–2018	State University, College Town, TX
2017	B.A.I.S. with EC-6 Certification/expected Spring
2014–2015	City Community College, Big Town, TX
	A.A.
2013–2014	Middletown Community College, Middletown, TX
2013	Littleton High School, Little Town, TX
	Graduated

> Give a VERY brief description of your duties.

Employment information (list most current first);
Student Teaching: Spring, 2018—Oak Harvest Middle School (6th Grade); Alamo Elementary School (2nd grade), Big Town, TX
Field experience: Spring, 2017— 60 hours at Pine Tree Elementary (3rd grade), Big Town, TX

  *Active part of the classroom with mentoring children, helping in small groups, creating bulletin boards, taught four lessons, participated in Science Fair Week

Giant Burger: June-Aug. 2009—Little Falls, TX

  * Full-time summer work as waitress and cashier

Honors/Other Information

Literacy Club	2015–18	President, 2017
I Am Smart International Society	2013–14	
Dean's List	2015–16	
Volunteer, Special Olympics	2012–13	

*I speak moderate conversational Spanish.

> Include a minimum of three references with titles, addresses, emails, and phones. These should be related to employment or education (not personal friends or relatives), and each should be asked if she/he would be comfortable being listed.

References
Mrs. Johanna Smith
Mentor teacher/third grade; Spring 2016
Brown Elementary School, Langram ISD, South Oak, TX
234-567-6789 (c) 234-567-8901 (w) SmithJ@inter.net

Mrs. Kayelynn Jones
University Supervisor for Student Teaching, Spring 2017
Department of Education, State University, College Town, TX
345-678-91011 (c) 456-789-1011 (w) kjones@statecollege.edu

Figure 12.10   A sample résumé.

Here are more e-portfolios of teachers and teacher candidates on a variety of platforms:

Wixsite:

  www.klbean.wixsite.com/standardsportfolio

Google Sites:

  www.sites.google.com/site/stephanieladner/Home

Weebly:

  www.ostergrenm.weebly.com/

Adobe PDF:

www.mcgill.ca/edu-e3ftoption/files/edu-e3ftoption/cindyportfolio.pdf

Eduportfolio:

www.eduportfolio.org/53787

Students' E-Portfolios:
Slideshare:

www.slideshare.net/TechnologyLab/student-e-folio-example

Blogspot:

www.pesbrooklyna.blogspot.com/

Google Sites:

www.sites.google.com/a/apps.edina.k12.mn.us/lindseya19041/home

www.sites.google.com/a/lajunta.k12.co.us/4acre-s-a-p-eportfolio/

Weebly:

www.mrszvi.weebly.com/eportfolios.html

Wikispaces:

www.jesseportfolio.wikispaces.com/My+Parents+opinions

Concerns with E-Portfolios

Some first-year teachers may have concerns with "negotiating their identity" through their e-portfolios (Hallman, 2007). These students will add additions or make modification to their portfolio after it is turned in for a grade to make themselves more marketable during their job search with K–12 schools. One student stated:

> You know that the professor wants us to be all reflective and represent ourselves as inquirers. But you know what? I don't really think that's what schools want. You know, I want to look confident, not like I'm questioning everything. (Hallman, 2007, p. 474)

The above thought is interesting because an aspiring teacher recognizes there are two different objectives he/she must accomplish. The first objective is to meet the academic requirements of education courses and of a program, and the second objective is to obtain a teaching position. Preservice teachers should understand that universities have an ethical responsibility to ensure that their students work to meet the learning objectives for each course and that they must often demonstrate this to accreditation entities. While the expectations may appear extraneous to students, it is important to adhere to those expectations to meet the course requirements. Many educators, including those in schools, highly value those who can reflect critically and well in order to grow, but some may see too many negative examples as a detriment. However, if students want to make themselves more marketable in different ways for a specific opportunity, then they can modify their portfolio, as needed, after they have met the academic requirements.

Hallman (2007) also found that students should consider their target audience and how they can best portray themselves when writing for multiple and, perhaps, conflicting audiences. Again, a future educator can be challenged with this and must determine if he or she wants to be considered as more of a reflective, inquisitive student or an already completely competent student. The answer is that a principal will want to see both. Knowing this information may be a challenge because, as Hallman (2007) showed through her research, it may be difficult to see how the content of the e-portfolio could move smoothly from coursework for a university to a K–12 hiring tool. It is, perhaps, wise to see the portfolio process as "never ending." Very similar to a high fashion model's portfolio (where photos are constantly replaced with those of higher quality or those which are more relevant to a particular job [sportswear, evening attire, jewelry, the hands, etc.]), a teacher's portfolio will grow and change with added experiences and different audiences. Technology offers this option at the touch of a button. One can save a particular version (clearly labeled) and create a copy with revisions quickly and easily.

As mentioned earlier, students may also want more direction as to what should be included within their portfolio. For example, in the study conducted by Wray (2008), it was found that students wanted their professors to provide an outline of everything that should be included within their portfolio. Students stated this would give them a clear direction on what to include so that they could work on that rather than compiling unsubstantial miscellaneous material. Providing an outline may be both beneficial and detrimental, depending on one's perspective. Having a set outline may provide a guide to students who struggle with what to share. It may force students to consider resources and materials that are common at other major universities, which can then be used to level the playing field when competing against students from other universities for the same job. Although the benefits may help students, they may also hinder students from thinking outside the box, which may impact how they present themselves to potential employers (Hallman, 2007). Teacher candidates may be less inclined to look for opportunities to be creative and take risk to produce the best portfolio because they may want to show they are meeting all predetermined guidelines for their college or university. It may be of help in courses that do not necessarily require a portfolio as an end-of-course assignment to ask if the professor could still cue students as to if his/her major assignments could be used later on for a teacher education program portfolio. Future teachers should certainly ask.

Tension surrounding time and worth, validity and reliability, and autonomy and compliance are a concern for some who are creating a portfolio (Reis & Villaume, 2002). Many university students and professors may feel that there is not quite enough time allowed between the beginning of the course and the end for students to deliver. It may be felt, too, that this short interlude does not provide a reasonable amount of time for teachers/professors to provide quality feedback to preservice teachers who may need to improve their work. Be that as it may, a good guideline to professors *and* students is to establish many intermediate deadlines throughout a course to ensure that a portfolio will not be completed a few days before (or worse, the night before) the end of class and that a prospective teacher has been able to use feedback along the way to adjust the product over the semester (or the program). It is also the future teacher's responsibility to meet these deadlines and to make modifications as directed for the grade and for the interview. A prime concern of educational programs is having their students obtain positions, but, in the end, it is the teacher candidates *themselves* who are responsible for making sure they have a superior product that demonstrates their own worth.

Some education students may find that the increased options of technology may be overwhelming. With a variety of applications, Web tools, and media outlets at their fingertips, determining which one(s) to choose may prove difficult if the students do not know how to use them in presenting their work in the best light. Peer and program support should be sought in order to grow. Additionally, students may not know what operating systems their evaluators will use to review their material. If a student uses a Mac operating system to create documents in the Pages software, a reviewer using a PC that operates the Microsoft Office Suite (Word, Excel, PowerPoint, etc.) may not have access to open a document because it is not supported by that system. This is part of the formative process that teacher candidates must check as education students. If a portfolio is to be presented in a course(s) on university equipment, the student should check early to see if his/her computer will interface with that system (even checking the equipment in the presentation room itself). Not being able to open documents, for example, creates stress for all parties because it may mean the teacher candidate does not receive a grade until he or she goes back to quickly fix the portfolio. The student may not receive a grade at all if it is too late, or the professor may have to hold up class grades to wait on the corrected portfolio. If often creates a stressful situation that could be avoided if all was checked earlier.

Matching a school district's format is not as controllable. Many districts have extensive firewalls, so all files and documents should be on a disk or flash drive instead of connecting to the Web to open. Connections to one's documents and navigation must be designed and tested with clear indicators of where to "click on" to navigate to the document or go back "home" to the table of contents. Not knowing if one's technology will be "a match" at a school is another reason for running a hard copy to back up the electronic copy for interviews. If the technology does not interface, the interviewee still has access to the information, and the school interviewer can still see much of a candidate's skill. The portfolio (electronic or hard copy) can act as a safety net or prompter in an interview for candidates who momentarily forget an answer they want to give.

Another issue in portfolio creation is showing one's own work. Education students must always be ethical and never use other students' work, replicating it as their work (unless, of course, there was a group assignment/project--in which case, that should be made clear). Portfolio creators can use viewable portfolios as a means to compare one's own work with someone else's or as an example to spur one's thinking process—but they should never represent the work of others as their own. Many universities use plagiarism tools which search for these issues, and, if found, plagiarism can be grounds for removing someone from a teacher preparation program. Clearly referencing other's work is acceptable, but presenting someone else's efforts as their own is an unethical decision that can cost a grade and, possibly, a career.

Periodically checking that the links and attachments included in e-portfolios are working properly will help to ensure that it is ready for anyone at any time to view. Having a portfolio current and ready avoids the considerable stress of interviewing or being evaluated.

Mrs. Freeman moved due to her military husband's orders in August—one week before school started. Because of the timing and not knowing necessarily where they would be living, she felt that obtaining a teaching position at this late date would be impossible. As luck would have it, however, the superintendent of the district was a new neighbor who greeted her in front of her new house during the moving in process. "What do you do?" he asked. "Well, I am a teacher, but I'm probably not going to be able to work this year. I'll have to fill out all of my records for this district." "What kind of documentation do you have?" he asked. "I have my portfolio with all my information handy," she replied. "Go get it," he told her, and after looking through it on his computer, he came back out and asked, "Can you start in three days? We can work with this! I have just the perfect match for you still open at one of my schools!"

apveanz / Shutterstock.com

Campus-Wide Por ~~Question 2~~

As mentioned previously, campus-wide portfolio platforms such as TK20 are beginning to play an integral role in the way universities assess and receive state, regional, national, and/or specialty accreditation. TK20, as an assessment tool, provides information that assists units at all levels in: measuring and improving student learning outcomes; facilitating continuous improvement of academic and support services; and accumulating, generating, communicating, and disseminating institutional information to support assessment of student learning (TK20 Assessment Solutions at Work, 2014).

The percentage of teacher education programs in the United States who use portfolios to assess students is at least 90% (Ritzhaupt et al., 2012). While the assessment is necessary for student growth, it is also important for universities to receive and maintain accreditation in various areas. Banister, Vannatta, and Ross (2006) conducted a study on the best e-portfolio system and integrated three systems into the university setting. When considering the types of platforms, they found it is very important for any university considering a portfolio system to consider:

- What are the critical functions and how do they relate to their college?
- What types of reports need to be generated?
- What type of storage environment do students need?
- How and when will students be introduced to the portfolio? (Banister et al., 2006)

Another concern with using cloud-based platforms such as TK20 was the difficulty they posed to teachers. (Banister et al., 2006, p. 86). This especially raised concern because one of the primary reasons for a university to use an e-portfolio system is to enable the collection of data for its national accrediting body.

As stated, the security of student data can also be of concern with the e-portfolio (Ali, 2005). If a portfolio creator makes the work accessible to anyone via the Internet, he or she can sometimes run the risk of losing control over who has viewing rights. Teacher candidates may not have the option to make their information completely private; therefore, it is very important to use a system that will allow him or her to provide more personal information to reviewers only.

Web-based Portfolio Platforms

Learners may consider using other software or Web-based tools when developing their portfolio. Tools such as Padlet and Symbaloo may provide a unique visual for perspective employers. Blogs may also be an option. They provide a timeline for learning. Each entry is time stamped, with the most current information on top. While a blog is an option, it may not be the best choice.

Padlet and Symbaloo are Web-based tools that look like a "wall." Imagine walking into a house with blank canvas; then one has the opportunity to showcase one's life visually and with video. Padlet and Symbaloo both allow a user to add images, videos, and text to represent his or her artifacts. Potential employers will not have to watch a slide show presentation or open a zipped file; instead, they can open either the tool and navigate it similar to the way they would navigate applications (apps) on their smartphones.

As noted, the e-portfolio is often a cumulative project with a final presentation or summative evaluation at the end of a series of professional development courses, at the end of the student teaching semester, and/ or the completion of the teacher education program. E-portfolios serve other purposes in higher education. Most often, they are implemented at the level of an individual student, a course, or a program; these types of e-portfolios help make individual learning visible (Mayowski, 2014). In other universities, e-portfolios are used as tools to assist with academic advising, curricular development at the department level, or career planning and development (Reese & Levy, 2009). A number of institutions of higher education have used e-portfolios as components of their assessment and accreditation processes, which must be continuously updated and reported. Web services such as TK20 make collections of campus-wide student data possible. Recent development of learning analytics provides more advanced methods to analyze student learning, which, in turn, provides more tools for institutional researchers and university assessment directors when they report accreditation reports.

One example is the Florida State University Career e-portfolios. Florida State University has implemented the e-portfolios institution-wide, to help meet accreditation requirements of the Southern Association of Colleges and Schools Commission on College (SACSCOC). Academic administrators have found the career e-portfolio to be a valuable component in the accreditation process (Mayowski, 2014).

Many teacher education programs in the United States are accredited by the Council for the Accreditation of Educator Preparation, or CAEP. According to CAEP (2016),

> CAEP calls upon all educator preparation providers to create a culture of evidence to inform their work. Such a culture is built on an infrastructure that supports data collection and monitoring, the participation and feedback of appropriate stakeholders, a focus on the results of quantitative and qualitative measures, and a practice of using evidence to increase the effectiveness of preparation programs. (p. 6)

In response to the request for "a culture of evidence," many teacher education providers use portfolios as the source of evidence for content or pedagogical knowledge or skill. Furthermore, teacher candidates are often asked to align their e-portfolios with state standards or their program's own conceptual framework for professional teaching practice for e-portfolio design. The most frequent evidence contained in e-portfolios includes reflective statements, lesson plans with reflections, items related to unit planning, student or pupil assessments and results, other student work, an education philosophy, and formal or informal feedback teacher candidates have received from cooperating teachers and supervisors. Other components include résumés, teaching video with self-assessments, and teacher work samples.

E-portfolios are evaluated by those responsible for the preparation of educators, sometimes through a panel that might include the teacher candidate's adviser and supervisor. Good teacher preparation portfolio assessments are expected to capture information on the candidate's knowledge and teaching performance, including impact on student learning and diversity.

Using E-Portfolios for University Accreditation

As seen earlier, one major use of e-portfolios by universities is to share information and receive reaccreditation from their states or professional organizations (Ittelson & Lorenzo, 2005); therefore, student portfolios have become even more important to such universities. The student e-portfolio provides a variety of documentation that supports student success and achievement to accrediting agencies. Portland State University, for example, requires all of their students to create an e-portfolio. This document links student learning outcomes to its institutional portfolio, which is then publicized for internal and external audiences to display the students' educational experiences (Ittleson & Lorenzo, 2005). This is one way for a state (or national accrediting agency) to assure that a teacher education entity is providing a solid program for its students. Universities, therefore, may ask students to provide a copy of their portfolios (or provide access) for this purpose, and students should understand that this allows an accreditation team a method of determining if their program is providing a quality experience.

Examples of How In Service Teachers Use E-portfolios

It is important to remember that teacher portfolios should not stop after students graduate from their initial certification program. As a reflective tool, a portfolio provides a substantive and concrete way to document one's own growth as an inservice teacher. In addition, many graduate programs for educational leadership or other degrees require their students to produce a portfolio of some type during their last course or even for admission. Before the popularity of the e-portfolio, the student might only compile materials such as coursework records and a practicum log.

An Internet search using Google by the authors of this chapter resulted in several examples of e-portfolios created by teachers who were seeking a new teaching position or a different type of teaching position (such as an instructional specialist). Many of the e-portfolios included examples of:

- Certifications
- Résumés
- Recommendations and evaluations
- Classroom management plans
- In services or professional developments attended,
- Specifically targeted lesson plans and/or teaching experiences

Many teaching assistants at the collegiate level also use e-portfolios for promotion or placement into teaching positions. Among the many other artifacts that may be used in an in service teaching portfolio include:

- Student work samples (may include video footage)
- An overall philosophy of teaching (which may have changed with classroom/school experience)
- A short philosophy of teaching various contents such as mathematics, reading, social studies, science, and so forth and/or should be inclusive of age level ranges (early childhood, elementary, middle school, high school) that one may teach (This should answer the interview question of "How do you plan to teach _____ [content] in your classroom if you have a ___ grade class and why?")
- Observations
- Reflections
- Critiques/evaluations
- Unsolicited but substantive letters from students, parents, or colleagues (rather than simply, "I love you, Miss Jones).
- References (with titles and current emails and phone numbers, *after* obtaining permission to use them as a reference)
- Other evidence of strengths that one might bring to the position

Carlos Ramos had really wanted a fifth-grade classroom his first year, but there was not one available. However, in his third year of teaching, he heard about a position in a neighboring school. In his interviews, the principal made it clear that mathematics was going to be the focus for the particular classroom fifth-grade class she had open. "How, in general, do you plan to set up your mathematics classroom, and what might I see on a typical day if I slipped into the back of the room?" Carlos pointed out that he had a formal philosophy statement on teaching mathematics in his portfolio that she could read later, but since he had already thought about it and written it in professional wording, he was easily able to talk about his belief in the use of manipulatives, student-centered activities, real-world problems, and other areas that he felt were necessary for children's understanding of mathematics. He spoke of allowing for exploration time with manipulatives and the need for cooperative group support in mathematics, and then he clearly described a "typical math lesson" based on one that he had placed in his portfolio. He also told the principal, "I did note on your Website that there is a high percentage of English language learners here. If you look at my résumé in my portfolio, you will see that I speak conversational Spanish. There are notes from three of my colleagues about different situations where that was really helpful to them with parents and a few notes from parents and children, although they are in Spanish."

wavebreakmedia / Shutterstock.com

Thinking Ahead

Preservice teachers in education programs should select a tool that will be easy to access and update. While *easy* is the key, students should not settle on the quality of the tool they use because hiring committees may miss the quality of their work—based on the restrictions and/or the representations of their e-portfolios. A simple Google search will produce several examples of student-created e-portfolios. It will be beneficial to review what others have created and to note if the formats seem limiting or not. Another option is agencies that provide courses for students who need to learn how to select programs and create a competitive e-portfolio. Students may benefit from taking these courses.

Most district applications also require references, and, as noted above, a portfolio is the place to maintain a current list. The best references are those from someone who has seen a teacher candidate with children in the classroom (field supervisors, mentors, principals, and so forth) or in other situations (coaching, tutoring, etc.). A school district wants to know information about how a potential teacher interacts with students and as a team member in a school with others, and many people (including most professors who do not teach in field-based courses) cannot answer all those types of questions, although they may be able to say that a particular teacher-to-be is "a wonderful person and was a fabulous student." A reference cannot be a family member or peer/friend. This negates the validity of the reference. If a teacher candidate (or teacher) feels that a certain educator would make a good reference, he or she should be sure to ask at that time if the person would serve now (and perhaps later on). If a reference is from several years past, it is essential that the contact information be checked and possibly updated. Choosing references wisely will ensure that the portfolio is more value as a hiring tool.

As one can see, a portfolio is an excellent place to store information for filling out a job application. Most of this information is tedious to keep up with (particularly after a number of years [e.g., years of coursework and addresses of former professors, employers, references, and/or supervisors; dates of professional development workshops completed; awards or professional organizations in college or elsewhere; and so forth]). Maintaining this type of information in a portfolio from the beginning (in college) and keeping it current later on guarantees that one will not need to spend hours locating it when it comes time to fill out applications.

Using E-Portfolios with Texas Teacher Evaluation and Support System (T-TESS)

Texas is just one state that has moved into the use of inservice teacher portfolios as a tool to provide evidence of competence in teaching. The need for keeping an up-to-date e-portfolio for the classroom and for various other certifications does not stop at graduation from a teacher education program. Teachers use e-portfolios to fulfill the demands of many other professional requirements. Teachers-of-record are assessed by their campus school principals or assistant principals for annual performance reports. School administrators come into classrooms to observe teachers in action with their students to evaluate their interactions, content knowledge, improvement over weaknesses, and many other professional practices. The Texas Teacher Evaluation and Support System (T-TESS, www.teachfortexas.org) is a new evaluation system that is being implemented in K–12 school systems in place of the former evaluation system known as the Professional Development and Appraisal System (PDAS). Other states employ similar evaluations. This newly designed system in Texas is founded on the idea of continuous growth in educators by using a holistic approach to evaluate teachers through observations of their work and progress with students. Texas Education Agency or TEA (TEA, 2017) states, ultimately, that T-TESS is a process that looks for teachers' best practices and continuous improvement.

The details of this evaluation system consist of four domains which are viewed collectively at the end of an evaluation year and are scored using a rubric that is presented to teachers through professional learning and goal-setting meetings. The performance level is determined through classroom observations, walk-throughs, and-evidence that teachers provide. Administrators are trained and must pass rigorous tests to receive their T-TESS evaluator certificates. Then, an administrator or a designee (who is also certified) will train teachers who are evaluated using this system. Prior to the first observation, teachers and their evaluator(s) have a goal-setting meeting to predetermine goals that will be evaluated at the end of the year during the summative conference. The performance levels are: Distinguished (the highest), Accomplished, Proficient, Developing and Improvement Needed (the lowest). The T-TESS rubric is anchored in PROFICIENT.

During the summative evaluation, it is the teachers' time to showcase both his or her achievements and students' achievements that occurred throughout the school year through evidence. Teachers can review the depth of growth they must achieve/pursue throughout the school year. TEA has also provided an area that includes "Possible Sources of Evidence" for each dimension. In addition to teacher observations, the evidence teachers provide for Domain 4 can be a huge undertaking. Many teachers find that e-portfolios fulfill this requirement by establishing an e-portfolio as an online repository of documents compiled throughout the school year. Using an e-portfolio is not a requirement, but many teachers have expressed the ease of sharing their electronic tools from one centralized location. Teachers can develop an e-portfolio based solely on Domain 4 to ensure they have collected evidence that will allow them to earn an acceptable summative rating. Teachers have the autonomy to choose the tool they would like to use, but some of the more popular tools are Google Docs within the Google Apps for Education (GAFE), Padlet, and Symbaloo. The example below provides a visual to help teachers prepare the e-portfolio prior to the yearly summative evaluation.

For instance, for Dimension 4.3, to receive an "accomplished" rating in T-TESS, the teacher:

- Leads colleagues collaboratively on campus to identify professional development needs through self-reflection.
- Fosters faculty knowledge and skills in support of the school improvement plan through professional learning communities, grade- or subject-level team leadership, committee membership or other opportunities beyond the campus (TEA, 2017).

Possible examples:

- Professional learning sign-up sheets in Google
- Teacher reflections in Google forms/Padlet
- Images from the professional learning event on Twitter

- School social media pages
- Weekly Smore (online newsletter)

Teachers use the following evidence to prove committee involvement (district, campus, regional, state):

- . PTA sign-up sheets
- Email communication/correspondence
- Team meetings by grade level or subjects
- Curriculum writing team communication
- TEPSA planning meeting notes

Examples:
Sample Teacher E-Portfolio for T-TESS on Padlet: www.padlet.com/drtinanixon/58323c1fe9yx
Or try out Padlet QR Code:

Sample Teacher E-Portfolio for T-TESS on Symbaloo:
www.goo.gl/X1XfDN

Formatting the Final Products

The visual presentation of a portfolio makes a statement to the viewer. It may say, "I really care about the work I do, I am aware of technological design and its impact, and I pay attention to detail . . . and I will probably do so with instruction for my students," or it may, unfortunately, indicate the opposite. In current times where there are many "slick" Websites, the overall design of a portfolio becomes important, particularly when there is a competitive teaching market. Below are some hints that may help to make a good presentation.

- Use a simple color scheme without too many clashing colors.
- Use one basic background theme or template consistently throughout (there are many that relate to classrooms that can be downloaded free or purchased). A school theme can be very attractive but is not necessary; however, a common template helps to unify the portfolio. Making sure that titles and navigation buttons are in the same place on each slide helps the reader to see organization. Selecting a style that fits one's own personality will also send a message to the viewer.
- Use titles or subtitles on *each* slide so that it is easy to identify each one when modifying or searching for the right examples to show. If a document is continued onto the next slide, indicate that in its title (e.g., Competency 3, continued).
- Use title fonts that are not too big (over 40, for example); 36 or 32 are big enough to not overpower the slide). Do not use font that is so small that it is difficult to read.
- Select a font style that is easily read. Ornate script can be hard to read in a formal document. Also, select a font that "matches" one's desired grade level. For example, Comic Sans maybe attractive for teachers of the younger grades but may appear too elementary for future high school teachers.
- Do not run print/typing into template borders or margins.
- Use dark type on a light background. Light type on a dark background is often difficult to read when the lighting conditions are not good.

- Using some sound and special effects in opening or closing slides may be fine, but an "overdose" is distracting for the viewer, especially when sound and blinking text is used in a school area.
- Take a camera/phone camera *everywhere* during field experiences or other relevant activities to snap shots that show work with children or work within school settings. A picture really is worth a 1,000 words, and these types of artifacts confirm that a teacher candidate clearly has child-related or school experiences (but do be cautious to follow district policy in taking photos or videos of children). Label any pictures to explain why they are part of the portfolio (Under one photo taken with girls doing crafts, a teacher candidate wrote, "I was a Girl Scout leader for three years, during which time I prepared craft and badge projects and lessons for 15 young girls each week. I also organized successful three-day campouts each summer with the girls and parent volunteers.") Saving pictures and video can be easily done in a folder, on YouTube, Flickr, Slideshare, or on a cloud.
- Think ahead about filming video clips when there is an exciting lesson activity or lesson coming in order up to arrange for videotaping. Be sure that the video is stable (not jerky) and the sound is at a level that can be understood well by viewers. Ask if the school or teacher education program might have a video tracking device as discussed earlier.
- The name of the teacher or teacher candidate should be the main focus on the title page. Make it the largest font on the title page.
- If a meaningful quotation is used on the title page to sum up one's views on education, citing this quote is mandatory if it was written or spoken by someone else.
- Be sure that is obvious where a reader should click to go to the next page or navigate to another artifact (particularly if there is a pull-down menu). Instructions may be needed if it is not initiative. Navigation button need to be placed in the same spot on most slides.
- Use formal English and formal phrasing (use "children" or "students" rather than "kids," etc.).
- Run Spell/Grammar Check each time the portfolio is modified.
- Check navigation on each page to make sure the user can get back to the Table of Contents page easily and that each linked document opens.
- Include VoiceThreads when and where it might add to the presentation, especially if there may not be an opportunity to show important aspects of the portfolio or the portfolio may be sent afar.
- Have a second (or third set of eyes) go through the portfolio. Peer checking can be very valuable to check for errors or other issues.
- Make it "one's own" so that it will be a pleasure to work on it and can be seen as a true picture of one's own personality.

Integrating E-Portfolios with K–12 Students

Teacher candidates can easily integrate the e-portfolio techniques they have acquired in their teacher education programs when they have classrooms of their own. Teachers in K–12 will find that e-portfolios offer some of the same benefits to their students as they do students in higher education. Students of our generation are digital natives (see Figure 12.11). Most of them already have social presence on social media outlets such as Facebook, Twitter, Snapchat, and Instagram. In their own ways, they have created their own portfolios, but teaching them how to transfer these skills into school is the goal.

K-12 teachers are not unfamiliar with collecting student work. Quite often upon entering a school, one can find pictures covering classroom walls, outside on doors, and in the hallways of school buildings.

Figure 12.11 A student holding his phone with Instagram app.

WoraweeMeepian / Shutterstock.com

Teachers understand the importance of showcasing their students' work (see Figure 12.12). They know how students feel when they enter the classroom and can point out to their parents their "story about the first day of school," or their depiction of the Mona Lisa in their eighth-grade art class. Students feel a sense of pride and ownership when their work is displayed.

Figure 12.12   A school hallway showcasing students' projects.

Teachers in K-12 integrate e-portfolios for educational purposes. For example, Karlin, Ozogul, Miles, and Heide (2016) found that e-portfolios allow for students to not only self-regulate their learning but to curate and showcase their previous work and talent while, at the same time, expressing their individuality and creativity—all within a digital space which can be easily shared with peers, teachers, parents, and others. As we have identified earlier, e-portfolios can provide opportunities for teachers to monitor student progress and identify strengths and areas of improvement. An e-portfolio is also a way to differentiate instruction because it allows students to create work using a variety of tools.

Jaden is a ninth-grade student at Cliff High School. He is nervous about the e-portfolio that he is expected to create in his second year of Spanish class. Since he had not used an e-portfolio in his middle school, he is nervous that the material he is considering gathering will not meet the expectations for the assignment due at the end of the semester. The Spanish teacher told students to "get together and help each other"—rather than giving specific guidelines or suggestions. Jaden took it upon himself to look into some options because he didn't really know anyone in the class yet. After researching online tools for creating e-portfolios, he found a site called Wix that appears student-friendly and allows him to record video, add links, and drop items onto the Web pages. He has not had any Web design courses, so he reviews different YouTube tutorials to know how to "get around". After reviewing the tutorials, he decides to incorporate other tools such as Flipgrid, Adobe Spark, and Padlet. Now he has the tools for the portfolio, but, unfortunately, Jaden is still unsure about how to begin. His teacher did not provide a clear purpose for the portfolio nor did he provide clarity of how it would be assessed. He also did not mention if there are specific pieces that should be included within the e-portfolio. Jaden is feeling overwhelmed and upset about what his grade will be.

If you were Jaden's teacher, what would you do differently to motivate him to not only survive but to excel in the class? Jaden's Spanish teacher might be able to provide better guidance to students by integrating the e-portfolios across a number of weeks, giving clear instructions, showing samples, providing evaluation rubrics, giving intermittent due dates to provide immediate feedback instead of one single due date, inviting students to provide peer comments, and creating opportunities to allow students to reflect on their work and learning.

Quality e-portfolios that showcase what students can do can further their academic career or get them a job (Davis, 2015). If done well, portfolios can aid students in self-regulation, reflection, and ownership of learning. If poorly structured, as shown in Jaden's case, students may feel overwhelmed or feel like portfolios are a waste of time. Good K-12 e-portfolios should be a part of the instruction process. Davis (2015) lists the following "essentials" that school teachers must be aware of prior to starting the e-portfolio process in their classroom:

- know the purposes
- select tools to empower students

- select a variety of content
- empower portfolio review and publish to an audience
- know the timeline
- empower metacognition
- relate portfolios to coursework
- do not overwhelm students
- link paper and e-portfolios
- consider the portfolio's longevity
- engage teachers in effective portfolio use

Having a clear **purpose** allows teachers to outline how they want the portfolios to look, making sure that the format is consistent with the school's technology levels, suggesting the kinds of topics to include, including how often it will be used for assessment, and so on. School teachers should also determine if they want to the portfolios to be a collection of work to be reviewed summatively, or if they would like to informally assess the work throughout the semester or year.

For younger grades, the work may only be a collection of previously assessed work compiled into one electronic document such as MS PowerPoint. For older grades, the requirements can be for students to publish Web pages or other cloud-based platforms such as Google Slides. The types of **tools** that teachers choose for use with students are equally important. There are a number of tools that appear "fun" on the Internet or in an app store that may not be user-friendly or age-appropriate for younger students. Tools such as Seesaw are suitable for students in their primary years of school, but a program such as Google Sites would be overwhelming for students in grades K-2. While we want to give students the autonomy to choose which tools may work best for them, educators also must use some discretion in tool selection.

When teachers select a variety of **content**, it is important to ensure that the material aligns with and relates to the curriculum for students to make a connection with the rest of their learning activities. Many teachers started with asking students to scan current works, such as text and photographs, into digital formats. In addition to print media, teachers can encourage learners to use videos, screencasts, hyperlinks, audio recordings, and a variety of other content formats. An e-portfolio that contains only scanned text and photographs is missing the authentic students' voices that can easily come across with audios and videos (Davis, 2015). When choosing content formats, it is also a good practice for learners to find alternative ways of expression to showcase strength. For instance, students struggling with writing could record video journals as part of their portfolios.

As mentioned earlier in the chapter, an e-portfolios is a collection of student work. In the K-5 classroom, the collection in a student's e-portfolio may look different than the work included in a portfolio for a student in grades 6-12. Teachers in the upper grades may require students to create specific portfolios for the subject area in which they teach, while students in K-5 classrooms may include a collection of each of their subject areas or in a specific area.

Educators know that having an audience for work improves student engagement, and that is one of the reasons why school hallways are lined with students' artwork. The twentieth-first century teachers are now expected to facilitate learning while students act out, record, or visually manipulate tools, which may be in person or electronically. Teachers must find ways to capture their mastery of content so it can be shared with a variety of individuals invested in the students' academic success. For example, parents want to know how their child is progressing in school. It is not uncommon for teachers to send work home either by the child or electronically by email. When parents attend conferences, they would like to see a collection of their child's work.

Teachers who are technology leaders have set up tools such as Google Classroom or Seesaw so that parents can see a collection of their child's work by logging into a site, accessing an app, clicking on the pop-up notification, or scanning the QR code(barcode) when a new assignment is posted. However, privacy should always be protected, and age-appropriate safeguards should be considered. The Digital Divide, which often separates those who have access to technology at home, must also be considered.

For a quick introduction, follow this URL:

www.youtube.com/watch?v=pzlrtDR84KY

To see a learning journal overview, follow this URL:

www.youtube.com/watch?v=tlw-tUKvnNc&t=9s

Evaluating the E-Portfolio

Rubrics

While some educators see portfolios as excellent qualitative measures to replace paper-and-pencil tests, it is important to know that the subjective nature of portfolio assessment can make it an unreliable measure. Rubrics should not only be used to grade a learner's e-portfolio but should also be used to guide its process of development. Following a rubric set by a professor, as a reminder, can initiate a document that teachers-to-be may use to create a timeline that will allow them to complete their portfolio in a timely manner. The rubric should be written thoroughly without much room for the students' own interpretation in terms of a grade—if it is to be graded objectively by the professor. Teacher candidates may want to examine their portfolio rubrics given by a professor carefully (and early) *and* ask questions up front about documentation as they go through the process—rather than wait until the end to ask if particular assignments/documents will match the criteria for specific areas and to confirm that the writing and technology is up to expectations. (refer to Figure 12.13 for a non-example of a teaching portfolio title page). Again, scrambling for documentation is stressful and often produces a substandard portfolio that one will not want to put into use for professional purposes. Collecting and saving work to go toward possible use in the portfolio throughout the semester (and even throughout one's teacher education program) can be a valuable way to obtain quality artifacts in the end. Barrett (2003) suggests: (1) determining levels of performance in the rubric; (2) determining the criteria by addressing the components/elements that will be assessed individually; and (3) determining the content descriptions. This is a valuable reminder for future teachers to take into consideration for their future students.

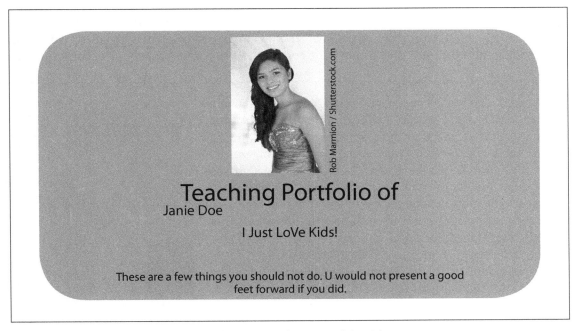

Figure 12.13   A nonexample of an effective teaching portfolio title page.

Peer Grading

Involving one's peers in the assessment of one's work has been seen to a beneficial process (Ali, 2005). Not only will the teacher candidates learn from the feedback of their peers, but they may also learn from the feedback they provide to others (see Figure 12.14). This research also calls for peer review to be an essential part of the process of the development of the portfolio. Peer assessment should be ongoing throughout the development of the portfolio. Peer review assessments can be either structured or nonstructured, meaning feedback can either be guided by a rubric—or just given based on the reviewer's perspective. Oral presentation of portfolios in class can

Figure 12.14 Peer reviews are beneficial.

also provide value when peers are required to rate or list comments on their fellow students' presentations. As they view others' portfolios, new ideas for their own portfolios are generated, and these comments can act to improve what the presenter may not have seen when originally constructing the work. If done orally, an opportunity to vocalize views and to "practice an interview" is provided—as previously mentioned. This also gives practice time in quickly locating important examples/artifacts that one may want to show in a real interview. A principal or a grade-level team will not want to wait for a teacher candidate to flip through numerous slides to try to locate a specific one about which he or she wants to talk in the short time scheduled for the interview. Go to www.mcgill .ca/edu-e3ftoption/files/edu-e3ftoption/cindyportfolio.pdf. Flip through the example of Cindy Salib's portfolio to assess what elements you find valuable and what might be added or changed to make a better presentation. Jackie Gerstein also has a portfolio through Weebly.com at jackiegerstein.weebly.com in a completely different style.

Self-Assessment

It is also crucial for education students to self-assess their work, especially if there is a supplied rubric. If the material that a student is presenting in his or her portfolio does not meet the required objectives/goals (of a particular course, an interview, etc.), the material should be removed, or the teacher candidate can ask professors if it is acceptable to include. There may be additional artifacts or material that could bring an additional level of understanding or simply make the portfolio stronger. Seeking approval and guidance from professors (or one's teacher education program) *ahead* of deadlines is always the safest path. Turning a rubric into a checklist is also recommended. This allows one to quickly assess whether or not each required item is included. See a number of examples of portfolios at www.csuartstudent teaching.com/portfolios. Scroll down to select portfolio examples.

Claudia Gomez, as she began her portfolio in her junior year, thought of the process much like a grocery list or a school supply list that she might take to the store. When at the store, each item on the list was of some importance, so she would spend time "walking up and down each aisle" until she found the item. As she found the item, she might draw a line through it or put a check beside it to show that she could move on to the next item on the list. If she didn't find the item right away, she might skip it and come back to it. If the store did not carry the item, she might draw a circle around it to say she needed to look for this item later in another store. This helped her mind-set in making sure she completed all the requirements of her portfolio. She also knew that, as when one goes to the store, there are always some extras that end up as treats in the basket. She wanted to make sure that even the items that might not have been on "the list" were special enough to be included, so she would save them as well. Whenever she did an assignment that could be used in her portfolio in her education classes, she mentally and physically cross-checked her portfolio list.

This method might be a good one to begin assessing one's own portfolio. A rubric is a good checks and balances system. Taking the time to really understand what is being asked within each section of one's portfolio will help to create a valuable document—both for a grade, for further professional development, and for the hiring process.

As a note, quality is of foremost importance. If one is asked to supply a lesson plan, he or she should not supply a short lesson plan template but should make sure to have detailed plans listed for each subject that will be required to be taught. One must be sure that each artifact included within the portfolio is labeled and is introduced with a title and header. An evaluator needs to know *why* the item is relevant, so one must take the time to explain where the item was obtained. For example, Jayme Chang included this as a description for one of her artifacts:

> I taught this math lesson in a fourth-grade class during my student teaching at Pine Hollow Elementary. I began with a mini lesson on number talks and then led the class in a lesson on long division. I was also evaluated on this lesson by my student teacher mentor on January 23, 2018, and I have included my observation scores (click here to see my evaluation). The best part of this lesson came after I carefully divided students into groups to use manipulatives because they had great discussion and were all successful at their task.

When using a portfolio for an interview, one should remember that it is valuable to look at the Website of the school/district and add something that shows one can relate to the particular students/staff/demographics/ and/or the area.

As an important reminder, each link in the e-portfolio must be working, and the material (audio and/or video) should also be clear and easy to view and hear. Visual design is important in the overall message, and attention to detail is always noted by assessors in the teacher education program and by hiring administrators. First impressions through the portfolio do matter.

One of the chapter's authors recently met with a principal at an elementary school, and the administrator stated, "I welcome candidates who want to show samples of their work during an interview. I do caution them to be mindful of the time and try not to provide *too* much information at once [a good reason to have a disk or flash drive to leave with them for later viewing]. Strategically, they should work the information from their portfolio into their answer for the interview question."

Some additional hints for the portfolio process are included below:

1. Save all artifacts from one's teacher education program. This will eliminate the need to reproduce or recreate them if they become useful or needed at a later date.
2. Ensure that the artifacts represent you and the work you have completed well. Do not include generic material that is standard for the course and will be well known to all educators unless you can meaningfully tie it to your own personal application in some way. Ask, "Have I shown that I have actually applied this concept in some way?" A downloaded picture or clip art image from the Internet is not enough unless accompanied by one's own thoughts on why it is an applicable artifact. However, unless it can be shown that an artifact is applied or created in some way, it should be a last choice. It is also critical not to use examples provided by your academic program as your own. Again, remember to be ethical when compiling artifacts for your portfolio. Ensure the work you compile is your own.
3. Include your name and dates on the material. This will provide some validity and ownership to your artifacts. This may reduce/eliminate the reproduction/use of your work by other students, too.
4. If choosing to use pictures, make sure that they are "professionally related" and are not snapshots from a party, date, or something that does not represent school professionalism (see Figure 12.15). If the picture includes students, be sure that permission is granted to use them. During your work in schools, try to take many pictures of artifacts that may

Figure 12.15 Take pictures whenever possible of work involved in schools, with children, or is educationally related.

pikcha / Shutterstock.com

make an impact (bulletin boards you may have created, student work, involvement in a field day or special project, etc.). Try to take a few pictures where your face is seen, but students' backs are to the camera in case a district would not allow students' faces to be in photographs.

5. Including some student notes will be of interest, but they need to be more than just "You are the BEST, Mr. King!"

The best way to bring all of this altogether in a successful portfolio is to establish deadlines on a calendar for tentative dates on which you want to complete each stage of your portfolio (see Figure 12.16). Some professors may include this for you with interim deadlines, but others may leave this open to the student.

Figure 12.16 Establish a calendar with deadlines.

David is a fourth-grade elementary teacher with many years of experience who is applying for a new position as an instructional specialist and who understands the importance of collecting student work samples to show parents their child's academic achievement throughout the school year. David has worked in the elementary environment and has witnessed the influx of technology into his classroom. His work examples often include both formative and summative assessments. Some of his assessments derive from online collaborative transcripts through Web tools such as Google Docs, backchannel applications, or Websites. David also has had the opportunity to provide audio and video examples of student assessments to parents during parent conferences and/or open houses. David wishes that he had the same technology resources available when he was in his undergraduate teacher education program to collect work samples for his own records as he has now. He feels that is a powerful statement to show a child's work at the beginning and at the end when they leave his instruction. He also noted that having audio and video available helps others understand clearly when a child is not making progress so that other professionals or parents, for example, can step in quickly. He also uses examples that include student work via a mobile device, such as a Galaxy tablet or an iPad. David originally looked at creating a portfolio as a means of collecting data on his students. Now that he is pursuing an advanced degree in teacher education, he has found the material he has collected through the years will serve to be beneficial when he goes through the application process for an instructional specialist position with his current employer.

Additional Resources for Teachers

We have provided a further list of possible tools for portfolio creation below. Please use the URLs to access the tools or you can use the QR code to scan the resource using a mobile device or computer with a QR reader.

Title	URL	QR Code
Digital Student Portfolios	www.goo.gl/zKXQTV	

Title	URL	QR Code
Digital Portfolios	www.goo.gl/4X3S5t	
ISTE: Which e-portfolio tool is best for you?	www.goo.gl/J9E2oi	
Google Sites examples of K–12 e-portfolios	www.goo.gl/JHmJfY	
Ten Tools to Create Student Portfolios	www.goo.gl/54XKWu	

A Quick Summary of Tools for Creating E-Portfolios

There are a number of tools that educators can use with students or that teacher education students can use to create their own portfolios. We have provided a list of possible tools below, but remember that technology is always advancing, so new tools may come on the market at any time. Please use the links to access the tools.

Padlet: www.padlet.com/blog/portfolios

Symbaloo: www.symbaloo.com?

Prezi: www.prezi.com

Digication: www.digication.com

Googlio: www.sites.google.com/site/googlioproject

KidBlog: www.kidblog.org/home

Edublog: www.edublogs.org

Wix: www.wix.com

Seesaw: www.web.seesaw.me

Book Creator: www.bookcreator.com

Google Sites: www.google.com/sites

WordPress: www.wordpress.com

Weebly: www.weebly.com

Evernote: www.evernote.com

Final Thoughts

A portfolio can be a valuable asset before and during one's career as a teacher. Understanding how to create a portfolio and what to include in a portfolio can make a huge difference. Starting this process early, so that one can become familiarize with software programs well before it is time to start integrating collected work will be an advantage. Not only do the artifacts paint a picture of the teacher candidate or teacher, but also the reflections and critiques reveal whether he or she has met the established learning and performance outcomes. One's portfolio can be used not only for evaluation and self-evaluation "along the way" but also for growth and improvement throughout a teacher's career. A portfolio can also be a valuable tool for teachers to track student work as they move from grade level to grade level. It can be a tool that allows parents and students to share successes from the beginning of the school year to the end of the school year and anytime in between. For students who have not shown much success, the teachers can use the data to create intervention strategies to help support the areas in which the students need additional help. There are many ways to complete this task, but the authors believe that it is a document well worth the time and effort—for now and the future.

References

Ali, S. (2005). An introduction to electronic portfolios in the language classroom. *The Internet in Support of Learning to Teach TESL Journal, 11*(8). Retrieved from www.iteslj.org/Techniques/Ali-Portfolios.html

Avraamidou, L., & Zembal-Saul, C. (2006). Exploring the influence of web-based portfolio development on learning to teach elementary science. *AACE Journal, 14*(2), 178–205. Chesapeake, VA: Association for the Advancement of Computing in Education (AACE). Retrieved from www.learntechlib.org/p/21982

Banister, S., Vannatta, R. A., & Ross, C. (2006). Testing electronic portfolio systems in a teacher education: Finding the right fit. *Action in Teacher Education, 27*(4), 81–90.

Barrett, H. C. (2003). Evaluating electronic portfolios. Retrieved from www.electronicportfolios.com/ALI/rubrics.html

Chen, H. L., & Light, T. (2010). *Electronic portfolios and student success: Effectiveness, efficiency, and learning.* Washington, DC: AAC&U Association.

Council for the Accreditation of Educator Preparation. (2016). CAEP accreditation handbook (Version 3 – March, 2016). Retrieved from www.caepnet.org/~/media/CAEP%20Accreditation%20Handbook_March%202016.pdf?la=en

Davis, V. (2015, April 30). 11 Essentials for excellent ePortfolios. *Edutopia.* Retrieved from www.edutopia.org/blog/11-essentials-for-excellent-eportfolios-vicki-davis

Gambrel, L. E., & Jarrott, S. (2011). The bottomless file box: Electronic portfolios for learning and evaluation purposes. *International Journal of ePortfolio, 1*(1), 85–94.

Hallman, H. L. (2007). Negotiating teacher identity: Exploring the use of electronic teaching portfolios with preservice English teachers. *Journal of Adolescent and Adult Literacy, 50*(6), 474–485.

Ittleson, J., & Lorenzo, G. C. (2005). An overview of eportfolios. *Educause Learning Initiative*, 1–27. Retrieved from www.educause.edu/ir/library/pdf/ELI3001.pdf

Karlin, M., Ozogul, G., Miles, S., & Heide, S. (2016). The practical application of e-portfolios in K-12 classrooms: An exploration of three web 2.0 tools by three teachers. *TechTrends, 60*(4), 374–380. doi:10.1007/s11528-016-0071-2

Mayowski, C. (2014). Eportfolios for accreditation? Prevalence, institutional characteristics, and perceptions at United States Regionally Accredited Institutions. Doctoral Dissertation, University of Pittsburgh. (Unpublished).

Merriam-Webster Online. (2018). Portfolio [Def. 5]. Retrieved from www.merriam-webster.com/dictionary/portfolio

Mills, M. (2009). Capturing student progress via portfolios in the music classroom. *Music Educators Journal, 96*(2) 1–8.

Nath, J. L., Cohen, M. D., Hill, L., & Connell, M. (2012, Feb.). *We think they work: What do students really think about electronic portfolios?* Paper presented at the annual conference of the Association of Teacher Educators (ATE), San Antonio, TX.

Reese, M., & Levy, R. (2009). Assessing the future: E-portfolio trends, uses, and options in higher education. *ECAR Research Bulletin, 4*, 1–12.

Reis, N. K., & Villaume, S. (2002). The benefits, tensions, and visions of portfolios as a wide-scale assessment for teacher education. *Action in Teacher Education, 23*(4), 10–17.

Ritzhaupt, A. D., Parker, M. A., & Ndoye, A. (2012). Qualitative analysis of student perceptions of eportfolios in a teacher education program. *Journal of Digital Learning in Teacher Education, 28*(3), 99–107.

Strudler, N., & Wetzel, K. (2005). The diffusion of electronic portfolios in teacher education: Issues of initiation and implementation. *Journal of Research on Technology in Education, 37*, 411–433.

Texas Education Agency. (2017). TTESS—Texas Teacher Evaluation and Support System. Retrieved from www .teachfortexas.org

TK20. (2014). Assessment solutions at work. Retrieved from www.tk20.com

Wray, S. (2008). Swimming upstream: Shifting the purpose of an existing teaching portfolio requirement. *Professional Educator, 32*(1), 1–16. Retrieved from www.files.eric.ed.gov/fulltext/EJ802013.pdf

Chapter 13

Using Technology to Study for Certification Exams

Jane Thielemann-Downs, *Retired, University of Houston - Downtown*

Hsin-Hui Grace Lin, *University of Houston - Victoria*

Kwanglee Chu, *Questar Assessment*

Mei-Chih Mandy Wang, *University of Houston - Downtown*

Meet Jessie

Born as a member of the Millennial Generation, Jessie takes the Internet for granted, accepting the utility of devices and services such as smartphones, Google apps, Venmo, online shopping, Snapchat, FaceTime, Facebook, and streaming videos. He prefers frequent and quick interactions with digital content and is constantly multitasking. Educator preparation programs nationwide are facing a new youth culture of digital natives like Jessie.

This semester, Jessie is student teaching in a middle school while, at the same time, preparing for his state certification exams. He knows how critical it is for him to pass his state-required certification exams before the end of the semester because many school districts will not even interview (much less hire) a teacher candidate who has not passed the tests. Jessie and other teacher candidates should become familiar with all the available technological resources to accomplish their goals of becoming certified teachers, including the myriad of resources available to study electronically.

mimagephotography / shutterstock.com

The typical college student of today is a digital native, so it is important to take advantage of the wide variety of technology tools available for preparing teacher candidates for state certification examinations. Digital natives, fluent in acquiring and using technological tools and learning this technology quickly with an intuitive understanding, seem to use technology tools as an extension of their brains (Black, 2010). When researching and learning a topic, they easily handle multiple streams of information. Digital natives prefer frequent and quick interactions with content, and they display exceptional visual-literacy skills. These are essential skills when navigating the digital technology used today (Black, 2010). Nontraditional students who may not have grown up with technology in the same ways will find it to their advantage to "jump in", both in terms of resources for studying now and for when they are in classrooms with technological test prep packages for their own students.

It is upon these characteristics that this chapter was developed—as numerous resources are available to assist and support today's preservice teachers in preparing for certification examinations. Specifically, this chapter describes: (a) the reason why adding technology is useful in preparing for certification exams; (b) the effective approaches for using technology to study; and (c) an overview and description of national and state online resources available for study, including: videos, preparation manuals/textbooks, test-at-a-glance overviews, tutorials/test simulations, interactive practice exams, and general guides/tips for test-taking. The TExES (Texas Examinations of Educator Standards) are discussed in detail, and this chapter also describes information about the Praxis, the national teacher certification exam used for licensure in many states. In addition, the national trends and statistics concerning teacher certification are presented.

Using Technology-Based Sources

Most technology-based source materials described within this chapter can be accessed any time—during evenings, weekends, or daily breaks (refer to Figure 13.1). These materials can be viewed repeatedly as needed and cover a wide range of subject content, best teaching practices, and practice questions. The user's ability to control the learning media is important to success. Therefore, in order to take advantage of this material, teacher candidates must become familiar with these technology-based resources and use them to meet individual test preparation needs.

Figure 13.1 Studying electronically for certification exams can be done on one's own time.

Effective Approaches to Study

Effective learning does not just "happen." In order to make the most of preparation for certification exams, preservice teachers must create a specific plan for successful examination completion. First, teacher candidates should determine when their educator preparation program *will allow* them to take a specific exam, for most have criteria and coursework that must be completed prior to testing. When cleared, the teacher candidate should then register for that examination several weeks or months in advance, choosing a test date that allows plenty of time for review and study of the material (refer to Figure 13.2). If teacher candidates have just completed coursework on a particular exam, they should not wait too long; important information may not be as fresh on their minds later on. TExES examinations registration bulletins can be downloaded free of charge (www.cms.texes-ets.org/registrationbulletin). The Praxis Information Bulletin can also be found online (www.ets.org/praxis/about/bulletin). States, such as Florida, California, and New York offer their own state-administered teacher certification exams. Many other states, however, accept Praxis test result.

In the United States, the Praxis Series test (developed by Educational Test Services [ETS]) or National Evaluation Systems tests (developed by Pearson) for teacher licensure tests are most commonly used. States like Texas (TExES), New York (NYSTCE), or Florida (FPE) have developed their own teacher license tests. Preservice teachers should become familiar with their own state tests. For example, people in Texas can go to the ETS Website and download the TExES testing information at www.cms.texes-ets.org (Texas Education Agency, 2017e). Most of the downloads for preparation materials are free.

Second, teacher candidates should become familiar with the content for each of their required tests by reviewing the online test preparation manual carefully. The manual will give a "test-at-a-glance" summary of the content divided into major subject areas and competencies. Test takers should then

Figure 13.2 Digital natives use electronic devices and Web-based calendars to plan for exam study and registration deadlines months in advance.

Table 13.1   Synchronous Communication Tools for Group Meetings

Zoom	www.zoom.us
Google Hangouts	hangouts.google.com
GoToMeeting	www.gotomeeting.com
WebEX	www.webex.com
Skype	www.skype.com
UberConference	www.uberconference.com
FaceTime	Facetime.com

gather and organize various study resources that meet each individual's own learning style. Finally, a study schedule should be created that distributes test preparation and practice into multiple study sessions over a specific time period.

Teacher candidates may choose to work within online media to interact with peers to discuss ideas, share strategies, voice concerns, provide mentoring, and support one another (Sternberg, Kaplan, & Borck, 2007). Forming a study group in order to share test tips and discuss the exam's content is an effective test preparation tactic. Different online technology applications can be used to support the varied models of learning. For example, members of the study group may choose to use asynchronous (not at the same time) communication tools (e.g., email, threaded discussion boards, newsgroups), which would allow each member of a study group to contribute at his or her own convenience.

Check out these test taker forums:

www.texas.teachers.net

www.pinterest.com/explore/teacher-certification

www.inspiretexas.net/scholarships

www.240tutoring.com

www.magoosh.com/praxis

Group members may alternatively choose to use synchronous technologies (e.g., webcasting, chat rooms, and desktop audio/video technology) to approximate face-to-face learning within the study group (refer to Table 13.1). If constant discussions and exchange of information is needed, synchronous platforms may be more effective than asynchronous platforms. However, if each member has to wait, think, or work on individual tasks before forwarding to the next person, the asynchronous platform may work better. Some groups may choose to schedule a meeting with Doodle scheduling or meet at a central location with an electronic whiteboard (such as a school or university) in order to discuss the material together.

Study groups work well for a number of reasons. First, they create a responsibility to participate, so they assure that some studying will occur. They also require members to actively participate through teaching and explaining the material to other members of the group. When one must teach certain material, it is more likely to be retained. For example, using Google Docs, teacher candidates can share notes with all parties at the end of study sessions via computers, phones, or tablets. More minds working together come up with more ideas to help remember the materials that may, in turn, resonate better with a learner (Sternberg et al., 2007).

Preparing for Computer-Administered Testing

In recent years, there has been increased movement toward computerized testing. The move toward adaptive assessments was designed to produce the most precise estimate of student achievement and growth and greater detail in diagnostic feedback. **Computer-administered testing (CAT)** is an assessment model in which candidates answer questions

versus

(multiple-choice questions) that are part of a computer program. In most cases, individuals who take these exams can often receive their scores immediately or very quickly after testing. While there are clearly advantages to administering tests via computer, there are also possible drawbacks in that a certain level of technological literacy and comfort is required (Stone & Davey, 2011; www.texes.ets.org/cat).

Online Resources: Videos

Since almost all certification exams, including those in Texas, are now given using a **CAT** (computer administered testing) system, successful candidates must be familiar with this system of testing (although there are still alternative testing methods using pencil and paper and other methods for those with special needs). An effective way to become familiar with CAT is to use a similar technology-based system for preparation; future test takers can begin the familiarization process by first viewing a video which explains the computerized testing experience (www.texes.ets.org/cat) (Texas Education Agency, 2017d) (refer to Figure 13.3).

The video presents important information specific to the CAT experience, including the following:

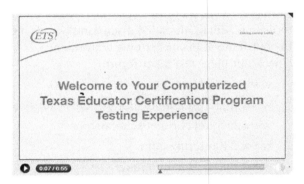

Figure 13.3 A video to introduce the TExES CAT presented by TEA and ETS.

- The first screen contains the examinee's personal data and photo. If this information is correct, click "continue."
- Several information screens are shown culminating with a confidentiality statement. Clicking "continue" signifies agreement to the terms.
- The examination clock will begin when the examinee starts the actual test. The clock will appear in the upper right-hand corner of the screen. If it is distracting, it can be clicked off.
- The test has no tutorial; however, basic navigation instructions and question type information is available by clicking "help."
- There are directions at the beginning of each section of the test. Some additional resource information, such as the periodic table and mathematics reference materials, is also available during sections of some tests.

It is also important to note that additional tutorial videos are available from Educational Testing Service (ETS) concerning alternate character toolbars for certification exams in Languages Other Than English (LOTE)

EC-12—French (610), German (611), and Spanish (613) (www.cms.texes-ets.org/texes/acttutorial/#altchar). Tutorial videos are also available from ETS concerning the use of graphing or scientific calculators, since an online calculator is now part of the testing software for some of the TExES tests (Texas Education Agency, 2017a). In addition, on the ETS Praxis Website, there are the Praxis® test familiarization videos that include important information one should know when preparing to take a Praxis test: study and test preparation tips, walk-throughs of a testing center, and a demonstration of what it's like to take a Praxis test (www.ets.org/praxis/prepare/video).

Online Resources: Test Preparation Manuals

Education Testing Service (ETS), a national testing company, is currently contracted to create and administer teacher certification exams for dozens of states in the United States. In Texas, for example, ETS develops and administers Texas Educator Certification Exams (TExES™) to individuals seeking educator licensure/certification. ETS has developed a preparation manual for each TExES certification exam (Texas Education Agency, 2017b). For a complete listing of preparation manuals, visit www.cms.texes-ets.org/texes/prepmaterials/texes-preparation-manuals. Although the TExES is highlighted, other certification exam sites such as the Praxis practice tests might be helpful for those teacher candidates who want to have more practice before taking the real exams. It might also be wise to consider whether or not one might be considering a move to a state which requires a different certification exam. It is always more effective to take examinations while teacher preparation is fresh in one's mind.

Texas Examinations of Educator Standards™ (TExES™) Program

Preparation Manual

Pedagogy and Professional Responsibilities EC–12 (160)

Figure 13.4 TEA TExES Preparation Manual.

The test preparation manuals (refer to Figure 13.4) are available free for downloading from ETS. These manuals are designed to help examinees become familiar with the test competencies, the test question formats, and appropriate study resources. Each preparation manual gives an outline of the test, a list of the domains and competencies that will be tested, strategies for answering multiple-choice questions, sample test questions, and an answer key with rationales. In addition, ETS also provides **Supplemental Guides** for the **Bilingual Target Language Proficiency Test** (BTLPT) Spanish and LOTE French, German, Latin, and Spanish EC-12 tests. These supplemental guides provide a preview of the actual test screens used in the computerized tasks encountered in these tests. The guides provide information about the introductory log-in screens, general regulations and policies, and general directions. However, it is important to note that only a limited number of sample questions are provided in the ETS preparation manuals; therefore, teacher candidates should seek further practice with additional questions from other resources.

The BTLPT is a special type of certification test that presents some challenges for teacher candidates who want to teach in bilingual education classrooms. There are four domains in the test: listening, reading, oral, and written. This Spanish oral test assesses teacher candidates' knowledge by combining content, best practices, language, and culture. For types of questions testing oral expression, test takers are typically asked questions such as: "What could you do to develop critical thinking in students?" and are given one minute to prepare and one minute to record the answer. To practice delivering the answers orally, teacher candidates in the past have used stopwatches to keep the time (www.online-stopwatch.com). However, some Millennials like Jessie may resort to simple and free podcast sites such as Yodio and PodBean to rehearse their time-measured answers (refer to Figure 13.5).

Rawpixel.com / Shutterstock.com

Figure 13.5 A podcast device.

Online Resources: Test-At-A-Glance

Each of the **test preparation manuals** for the TExES includes a **Test-At-A-Glance** chart which provides a quick overview and description of the test's content. The Test-At-A-Glance charts outline the areas of content (domains) to be tested, the number and types of questions, and the weight percentage of each. Each of the domains is further defined by a set of competencies or standards which detail the knowledge and skills needed by the teacher candidate. The approximate percentage of the test allotted to each domain is usually shown in table or pie chart form. If a teacher candidate is taking an exam other than the TExES, it will be worthwhile to look at the similar information about that test to see if there are areas that count more for passing. This will help to know what exactly to expect as listed with the competencies and, perhaps, direct the exam-taker to concentrate a bit more on those areas which are heavily weighed.

Online Resources: Test Preparation Textbooks

Many commercially made test preparation textbooks and manuals are available to preservice teachers (i.e., Barron's, Research & Education Association, Mometrix Test Preparation). These textbooks can be easily obtained online through Websites such as Amazon, and they typically provide an outline of the domains and competencies to be tested as well as sample practice questions. Most test preparation textbooks focus exclusively on practice questions, usually providing a complete practice exam experience to the reader. However, a few of the test preparation textbooks focus on content as well as practice questions.

Figure 13.6   Preparing to Teach Texas Content Areas: The TExES EC-6 Generalist and the ESL Supplement (2nd ed.).

    Content area test preparation guides differ from most preparation manuals in that they provide an overall summary of the content knowledge tested on the exam. This information, drawn from a wide range of teacher preparation textbooks, research articles, and education documents, offers the examinee a review of the material typically taught during professional development courses. For example, Nath and Ramsey's (2011) TExES E-C 6 Generalist preparation text, **Preparing to Teach Texas Content Areas** (refer to Figure 13.6), offers a comprehensive review of the eight content areas taught from early childhood through the sixth grade: language arts and reading, mathematics, social studies, science, art, music, health/physical education, and theatre arts. Each content area section contains a content summary, sample lesson plans, and prompts, as well as practice questions. This comprehensive test preparation textbook also helps students understand many of the basic theories and methodologies behind best practices typically applied to each content area. The book concludes with preparatory information and a content summary of material for the ESL supplemental certification.

    A **content book** for preparing for the Pedagogical and Professional Responsibilities (PPR) exam edited by Nath and Cohen (2011) is also available. This text, **Becoming an EC-6 Teacher in Texas: A Course of Study for the Pedagogy and Professional Responsibilities (PPR) TExES**, offers a complete course of study for the PPR exam that is specifically built around the Texas standards for teacher certification, including: human growth and development, student diversity, planning and instruction, learning theory, classroom environment and management, communication, student engagement, technology, assessment, home/school relationships, and laws, ethics and structure of education in Texas. Each chapter, devoted to a specific competency, provides detailed pedagogical and theoretical background, best teaching practices, and practice questions. Many preparations books like this one are available as e-books as well.

Figure 13.7   TExES Exam #231: Preparing for Teacher Certification in English, Language Arts & Reading Grades 7 to 12: A Complete Content Review for Texas Teacher Certification.

    There are some preparation books for upper-level content as well. A **content-based book** for high school English teachers, for example, is also available on Amazon.com. This textbook, **English, Language Arts and Reading 7–12 for Exam 231** by Thielemann-Downs (2014) (refer to Figure 13.7),

13.6 Nath, Janice L.; Ramsey, John M., Preparing to Teach Texas Content Areas: The texes Ec-6 Generalist & The Esl Supplement, 2nd, © 2011. Printed and Electronically reproduced by permission of Pearson Education, Inc., Upper Saddle River, New Jersey.

offers a complete review of the current high school English curriculum in the areas of American, British, multicultural, and young adult literature, literary and poetic elements, basic grammar and spelling rules, methods and strategies for teaching reading comprehension, literature interpretation, and writing as well as speech and business communication. This text includes 90 multiple-choice practice exam questions and four practice essay response prompts. Helpful information with regard to essay development, length, and scoring is also provided.

Other books are available from online searches, depending on one's content area. University or department libraries may also have practice books to use.

Online Resources: Tutorials/Test Simulations

Online Tutorials are more interactive and specific than a textbook. A tutorial seeks to teach by example and to supply information to complete a certain task. ETS provides video tutorials to orient students to the TExES test and to practice using specific tools before the test day (Texas Education Agency, 2014c). ETS also provides tutorial webinars for specific tests. A tutorial presented by the Texas Education Agency (TEA) and ETS is available for the Spanish BTLPT (www.cms.texes-ets.org/texes/prep-materials/test-familiarization-videos/; refer to Figure 13.8). Visit the following resources to view sample TExES Questions:

Bilingual Target Language Proficiency Test (BTLPT) Spanish What's New

Presented By
Texas Education Agency
and
Educational Testing Service (ETS)
2010

TEXAS EDUCATION AGENCY
TExES/ExCET · TExMaT · TASC/TASC-ASL

www.testprepreview.com/texes_practice.htm

www.texespractice.com

www.texestestquestions.com

Figure 13.8 The BTLPT webinar presented by TEA and ETS.

Visit the following resources to view TExES tips:

www.mo-media.com/texes

www.ultimatetexesguide.com/preview.html

Tutorials and interactive exams are also available from commercial companies to help prepare preservice teachers for certification exams.

For example, **240Tutoring** (see Figure 13.9) is an online resource (2018) for teachers preparing for their certification exams. 240Tutoring offers instructional content developed to address the

Figure 13.9 240Tutoring is an online resource for teachers preparing for their certification exams.

specific knowledge of each test area. The instructional content is an in-depth, comprehensive review of the subject knowledge tested. 240Tutoring also offers practice questions as well as an assessment feature that provides feedback about a test taker's strengths and weaknesses (www.240tutoring.com).

Online Resources: Study Tips Booklets

ETS and the TEA also offer test strategy and tips booklets that contain general information about preparing for and taking the TExES™. These booklets are in PDF format and can be downloaded at no cost from the TExES homepage at www.cms.texes-ets.org/files/4313/1404/6045/studytips_0607.pdf.

The booklet, ***Study Tips: Preparing for the Texas Educator Certification Tests*** (refer to Figure 13.10), contains useful information on preparing for multiplechoice tests and constructed-response tests. The instruction, tips, and suggestions contained here can help the teacher candidate become a better prepared test taker. Most teacher candidates already know from their own experiences in taking tests that good preparation is an important component of success.

Figure 13.10   TEA Study Tips: Preparing for the Texas Educator Certification Tests.

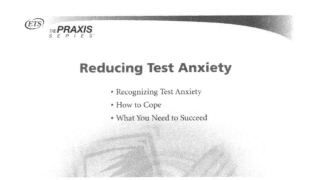

Figure 13.11   Reducing Test Anxiety presented by ETS.

The **Reducing Test Anxiety** booklet (refer to Figure 13.11) provides practical help for people who suffer from test anxiety. Although designed specifically for Texas Educator Certification test takers, it is useful for anyone who has to take a test. This guide reviews the major causes of test anxiety and offers practical advice on how to counter each one (www.ets.org/s/praxis/pdf/reducing_test_anxiety.pdf). Also, Apple's 2017 App of the Year, *Calm*, may be another way to help with anxiety prior to stressful exams (www.itunes.apple.com/us/app/calm-meditation-to-relax-focus-sleep-better/id571800810?mt=8) and apps for children and anxiety are available as well (www.coping-skillsforkids.com/blog/apps-to-help-kids-with-anxiety) for times when children one's classroom may feel stressed.

Online Resources for Content (STAAR)

There are a number of state tests for various grade levels required of school students that have been released in Texas for teachers to use in terms of content. Some of these are under the old testing system in Texas (the TAKS [Texas Assessment of Knowledge and Skills]). Teachers can take these test themselves to see if they know the content that they are going to be required to teach and can be used to practice for their own content tests. One only needs to type in "TAKS test released" and/or "STAAR tests released" for a number of grade level and content area tests choices to be displayed (www.tea.texas.gov/student.assessment/STAAR_Released_Test_Questions). A future elementary teacher, for example, may want to take the released tests up to the sixth grade, since elementary certification is often early childhood through the sixth grade.

The State of Texas Assessments of Academic Readiness (*STAAR*™) EOC (End-of-Course) tests mastery of the Texas Essential Knowledge and Skills (TEKS) by high school students for a given course and determines college and career readiness. Even though students entering the ninth grade must pass all five exams to graduate from high school, these EOC assessments are helpful to teacher candidates who may be preparing for a specific content exam as a way to self-assess weaknesses and strengths for the high school content that they hope to teach. The level for the state certification tests may be higher than the released tests, but these will aid in practice for each subject area listed.

Required high school STAAR EOC assessments include the following subjects:

- Algebra I
- Biology
- English I (combined reading/writing)
- English II (combined reading/writing)
- U.S. History

As mentioned, sample released tests from past years are available online, and immediate online scoring is available for some tests that are digitally interactive. Sample booklets containing released test questions are

---

13.11 Copyright © 2006 by the Texas Education Agency (TEA). All rights reserved. This image is reprinted by permission of the copyright owner. All other information contained within this publication is provided by the authors. No endorsement of any kind by Educational Testing Service should be inferred.

also available for downloading in PDF format. These tests are easily accessed through the TEA Website and some school district Websites. To obtain the STAAR test booklets, visit the high school section on this Website: www.tea.texas.gov/student.assessment/STAAR_Released_Test_Questions.

Various companies also have online ordering for practice STAAR tests. Those who are taking the EC-6 Generalist test, for example, may want to order the sixth-grade tests (for students) to practice questions that they may see on their own EC-6 Generalist test for content in mathematics and reading.

Testing Policy (in Texas) for Retaking Certification Examinations

Candidates are limited to five attempts to take a certification test for Texas teacher examinations. The five attempts include the first attempt to pass the examination and four retakes. The five attempts include any of the test approval methods (PACT, EPP, out of state, charter, and CBE), and all attempts taken before September 1, 2015 counts as one attempt. If a candidate chooses to register again for the same test after completion of the fifth testing attempt, scores will not be counted towards certification, and candidates will assume responsibility for test fees paid. The TEA firmly enforces the educator certification examination retake policy. Information can be found on the Texas-ETS Website (www.cms.texas-ets.org/home-new/#retakechange).

"The Texas Education Agency (TEA) implemented this change to Texas Education Code §21.048 in response to HB 2205, 84th Texas Legislature, 2015."

Currently, the Praxis does not have a limit on attempts. They do have a limit on how many days between attempts a test may be taken (21), and the test taker is charged for each retake. See all their policies at www.ets.org/s/praxis/pdf/praxis_information_bulletin.pdf. This highlights the recommendation that certification seekers take seriously their preparation, including collecting-materials and allowing plenty of time to study the contents, before taking the tests. Policies do change, so it is beneficial to stay up to date on retakes, fees, days required between retakes, and so forth to avoid situations where one must pass an exam to be hired or to keep a position.

Out of State Certified Educators

Many states are able to recognize teaching credentials from other states temporarily by giving teachers some time to become certified by their new residential state. For example, educators certified in other states who are seeking certification in Texas must apply for a review of their credentials. They may or may not be required to complete further professional work. The application process involves several steps described below:

- Create a TEA Online Account
- Complete application and pay a nonrefundable fee
- Submit official transcripts from all universities and colleges one has attended
- Submit copies of all certificates, front and back

Educators who have completed the review of credentials and are found to be eligible may be issued a **One-Year Certificate**. During the one-year period of this nonrenewable certificate, the educator must complete all appropriate tests. Once all Texas requirements are completed, educators may apply online for a **Standard Certificate**. It is important to note that educators who have completed a certification exam that is found to be comparable to a Texas test may request an exemption from the Texas exams.

Praxis Series Tests

*The **Praxis Series** tests* are currently required for teacher licensure in approximately 40 states and U.S. territories (refer to Figure 13.12). These tests are also used by several professional licensing agencies and by several hundred colleges and universities. Since the ***Praxis Series*** tests are used to license teachers in many states, teacher candidates can test in one state and submit their scores for licensure in any other *Praxis*™ user state.

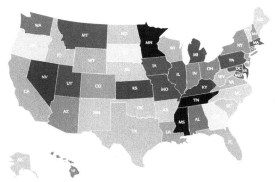

Figure 13.12   The Praxis Series tests are currently required for teacher licensure in approximately 40 states.

Hamik / Shutterstock.com

The official *Praxis* (test preparation) guide is published by ETS, the company that actually makes the tests. These preparation texts are available in three formats: e-book only, e-book with downloadable interactive practice tests, and paperback with CD containing interactive practice tests. The e-book/paperback text includes hundreds of authentic Principals of Learning and Teaching (PLT) scenarios and Praxis II® questions, so the practice experience: simulates the real exam; gives sample Praxis I (PPST) essays with actual scorers' comments; offers comprehensive outlines of PLT study topics; and presents sample case studies. The test preparation guide also provides detailed coverage of the Praxis II Elementary Education Content Knowledge (0014) and Curriculum, Instruction, and Assessment (0011) tests. For further information type into your browser "Praxis Official Guide Second Edition." You may also find a content study guide at: www.store.ets.org/store/ets/DisplayProductDetailsPage/productID.5082145000/CategoryID.3552300.

Future Trends in Teaching, Learning, and Teacher Certification

Currently, the three major trends in teaching and learning are: (1) alternative credentialing, (2) experimentation in new teaching models and learning spaces, and (3) student-driven personalized learning (Morrison & Camargo-Borges, 2016). These trends, in turn, have resulted in a change in focus in how to train and prepare future teachers.

Alternative Credentialing

Alternative credentialing means using different methods of assessment for learning (with a traditional degree as a metric). Instead of obtaining a degree, however, a person's learning is recognized by obtaining credentials (Morrison & Camargo-Borges, 2016). Online courses provided by the Massive Open Online Courses (MOOCs) are aimed at unlimited participation and open access via the Web. It was first introduced in 2006 and has emerged as a popular mode of learning. Many MOOCs provide interactive user forums to support community interactions among students, professors, and teaching assistants (Morrison & Camargo-Borges, 2016). For example, Open edX, founded by Harvard University and MIT is an online learning destination and MOOC provider. Open edX is an open-source platform that powers edX courses such as computer science, languages, engineering, psychology, writing, electronics, biology, or marketing and is freely available to people worldwide. For instance, Arizona State University offers four TESOL certificate classes in a series through Coursera to those who seek to become certified teachers.

Experimentation in New Teaching Models and Learning Spaces

In response to digital technology and culture, traditional education models have undergone a mass transformation. As a result, there are various types of new teaching and learning models. In the K-12 sectors, school modules aim to adapt to the changing culture and improve a system that can better serve students adequately. Examples of new models include Khan Academy founder Sal Khan's Lab School, a school designed to "investigate and explore new methods of learning and teaching." Facebook founder's (Mark Zuckerberg). The Primary School project, is geared to low-income children, is where healthcare and education are combined under one roof. A change adapted by higher education institutions is to reinvent their learning spaces from a traditional learning model (instructor-focused) to one that is student-centered. Programs such as Purdue University's IMPACT include new classrooms and active learning spaces that support blended learning; Vanderbilt University emphasizes creating new learning spaces, and the University of Central Florida's large-scale program has increased the number of students it serves while lowering costs by offering students F2F (face-to-face) courses along with an ever-widening menu of online and blended courses (Morrison & Camargo-Borges, 2016).

Student-Driven Personalized Learning

The new trend of learning methods is turning institutionally driven learning to personalized learning (see Figure 13.13). Personalized learning focuses on learner-driven formats, where learners control their learning and become not simply consumers of content but active creators, building knowledge through collaboration and connectivity, for example, via smartphone apps. Not only are students in control of when they learn, but they demand that they contribute to their learning through discussions and collaboration and creating content while doing so (Morrison & Camargo-Borges, 2016). For those teacher candidates who want to take charge of their test preparation, there are online study communities such as the forum on TexasTeachers.org (www.texas.teachersoftomorrow .org/study).

To better facilitate student-driven personalized learning methods requires information exchange and collaborative work among students and teachers. In progressive schools across the country, students and teachers are sharing information and connecting with others through social media.

Figure 13.13 The growing dependency on technology has great impact upon the classroom and teacher certification.

In education, collaborative learning has become a powerful tool. Each day students and teachers test out ideas and theories, learn facts, and gauge the opinions of others. Students learn to explore their own "kid-specific" social networking sites, on their blogs, on schools' sites, and, of course, on Facebook and Twitter. Educators have discovered that they can attract students' attention outside the classroom—using the online social world (Barseghian, 2011). See Chapter 16 for more information on employing social networking for instruction.

Sites like TeacherTube, PBS Teachers, Edmodo, Edublogs, Edutopia, and countless others are comprised of teachers' sharing success stories, asking for advice, and providing support to others.

This growing use and dependency on technology has great impact upon the classroom. Pens and pencils are far from obsolete, but forward-thinking educators use interactive tools to attract students' attention. Teachers are using Guitar Hero to teach music, Geo-Caching for high-tech scavenger hunts, Google Maps for teaching literature, Wii in lieu of P.E., Voice Thread to communicate, ePals to learn global languages with native speakers, Voki to create avatars of characters in stories, and Skype to communicate with peers from all over the world. Moreover, programs like Digital Youth Network focus on teaching students to create podcasts, videos, and record music; and Adobe Youth Voices teaches learners how to make and edit films and connects them to documentary filmmakers (Barseghian, 2011). Tech-savvy teachers are threading media-making tools into the curriculum with free (or inexpensive) tools like comic strip-creation site ToonDoo, Sound Slides for audio slide shows, VideoWin Movie Maker, and VoiceThread to string together images, videos, and documents, to name only a few.

It is worthwhile to note that there are reports available each year to help educators find the best technology tools and apps for classroom teaching. In 2016, the top 20 technology tools were Sight Words, Noodle, Quizalize, BoomEssays, Photos For Class, Kahoot!, Haiku Learning, Essayroo, Write About, Google Cardboard, Versal, Noisli, Formative, Emodo, Wikispaces, Schoology, Planboard, Creaza, Studysync, and Socrative (Kopp, 2016). Teachers who wish to keep up with the new tech tools can use these reports to do so.

Students in high school and college are using electronic portfolios (also known as e-portfolios, digital portfolios or online portfolios) to showcase their work on Websites that Information on portfolios is covered in depth in Chapter 12 of this text. Link to their assignments, achievements, and course of study, using photos, graphics, spreadsheets, and webpages.

Changing Student Demographics

Another growing trend is the changing demographics in America's public schools. Latino children represent a particularly urgent call to action in early childhood education. Comprising more than 38% of U.S. three- and four-year-old children enrolled in school (NCES, 2014)—a statistic that is rapidly growing—makes it important to address the fact that many Latinos start school with limited English-language skills. Latino children enter kindergarten about 6 months behind their non-Latino peers academically (Bridges & Dagys, 2012). The achievement gap persists as children advance through school, often culminating in low academic outcomes.

Although the overall high school dropout rate reached a new low of 7% in 2014, compared to blacks (7%), whites (5%), and Asians (1%), the Hispanic high school dropout rate still had the highest rate of 12% (Krogstad, 2016).

As classrooms across the country become increasingly culturally and linguistically diverse, teacher preparation and training programs must respond to these changes. The demand for ESL and bilingual certified teachers is growing each year, and many educator preparation programs in Texas and California have changed their program's focus in response to the demands (Bridges & Dagys, 2012). Currently, most districts in a number of states require that their teachers test for ESL certification either before being hired or at least by the second year of employment. ESL certification does not require that a teacher speak another language. Test preparation (both online and in hard copy) for this area also exists (as noted earlier in the chapter), and many programs highly recommend that teachers take the test for this as soon as possible to make themselves more eligible for employment.

Summary

In sum, the digital revolution has made a great impact on teaching and learning. Digital technology leads a wide range of new teaching and learning formats, such as e-modules, sophisticated simulations and serious games, and online collaborative learning. Technology allows flexible learning options and makes lifelong learning possible. This chapter provides information about the multiple streams of information that future teachers can use to prepare for teacher certification exams and current trends to give more direction to their future careers. Most of these materials are easily accessed any time—evenings, weekends, or during daily breaks. These materials can be viewed repeatedly as needed and cover a wide range of content, best practice sessions, and practice questions (www.texes.ets.org/registrationbulletin). Finally, an important fact for teacher candidates like Jessie to consider is the

Figure 13.14   The changing demographics in America's public schools.

changing job market for certified teachers (see Figure 13.14). As classrooms across the country become increasingly culturally and linguistically diverse, teacher preparation and training programs have responded to these changes (Bridges & Dagys, 2012; Lynch, 2015). Changing ways of teaching and learning, changing student demographics, and changing job market trends have all merged to create a demand for certified teacher candidates who have obtained up-to-date technological skills along with a depth of knowledge and understanding in best pedagogical practices.

References

240Tutoring. (2018). *240 Tutoring*. Retrieved from www.240tutoring.com

Black, A. (2010). Gen Y: Who they are and how they learn. *Educational Horizons*, Winter, 92–100.

Bridges, M., & Dagys, N. (2012). Who will teach our children? Building a qualified early childhood workforce to teach English-Language Learners. *New Journalism on Latino Children*. Institute of Human Development (NJI). Retrieved from www.latinoedbeat.files.wordpress.com/2012/09/njlc-brief-092412_pages.pdf

Kopp G. (2016). 20 EdTech tools for educators to use in the classroom this year. *School Administration*. Retrieved from www.blog.capterra.com/20-edtech-tools-for-educators-to-use-in-the-classroom-this-year

Krogstad, J. M. (2016). Five facts about Latinos and education. Washington, DC: *Pew Hispanic Center*. Retrieved from www.pewresearch.org/fact-tank/2016/07/28/5-facts-about-latinos-and-education

Lynch M. (2015). Four ways digital tech has changed K-12 learning. *THE Journal: 21st Century Learning*. Retrieved from www.thejournal.com/Articles/2015/05/20/4-Ways-Digital-Tech-Has-Changed-K12-Learning.aspx?p=1

Morrison K., & Camargo-Borges C. (2016). The opportunities and challenges of using digital learning environments in educational organizations. In A. Montgomery & I. Kehoe (Eds.), *Reimagining the Purpose of Schools and Educational Organizations* (pp. 161–172). Springer, Cham. www.doi.org/10.1007/978-3-319-24699-4_12

Nath, J., & Ramsey, J. (2011). *Preparing to teach Texas content areas: The TExES EC-6 Generalist and the ESL Supplement* (2nd ed.). Boston, MA: Pearson.

National Center for Education Statistics (NCES). (2014). *Percentage of 3- and 4-year-old children enrolled in school, by race/ethnicity and state*. Retrieved from www.nces.ed.gov/programs/digest/d15/tables/dt15_202.25.asp

Sternberg, B., Kaplan, K., & Borck, J. (2007). Enhancing adolescent literacy achievement through integration of technology in the classroom. *Reading Research Quarterly, 42*(3), 416–420.

Stone, E., & Davey, T. (2011). *Computer-adaptive testing for students with disabilities: A review of the literature*. Princeton, NJ: ETS. Retrieved from www.ets.org/Media/Research/pdf/RR-11-32.pdf

Texas Education Agency. (2017ba). *TEC home*. Retrieved from www.cms.texes-ets.org

Texas Education Agency. (2017b). *TExES test preparation manuals*. Retrieved from www.cms.texes-ets.org/texes/prepmaterials/texes-preparation-manuals

Texas Education Agency. (2017c). *Test preparation tutorials*. Retrieved from www.cms.texes-ets.org/texes/acttutorial

Texas Education Agency. (2017d). *Interactive CAT test demonstration*. Retrieved from www.cms.texes-ets.org/texes/prepmaterials/test-familiarization-videos

Texas Education Agency. (2017e). *Interactive practice tests*. Retrieved from www.cms.texes-ets.org/texes/prepmaterials/texes-preparation-manuals/interactive-practice-test

Texas Education Agency. (2017f). *Test retake policy*. Retrieved from www.cms.texes-ets.org/tasc/registration-information/test-retake-policy

Thielemann-Downs, J. (2014). *TExES exam #231: Preparing for teacher certification in English, Language Arts & Reading grades 7-12, a complete content review*. Createspace: Amazon.

Chapter 14

Transformative Learning: Preservice Teachers Becoming Reflective Practitioners through the Utilization of Technology Tools

Christal G. Burnett and Laura A. Mitchell
University of Houston - Downtown

Meet Ms. Tijerina

Ms. Tijerina, a new teacher in fifth grade (see Fig. 14.1), noticed that her students' scores on their last mathematics benchmark test were not as high as she had hoped. She knew that she had been going through the material more rapidly, which meant that she had been "ditching" the use of manipulatives so that she could use more pencil-and-paper activities. As she was reflecting on the students' test scores, she asked her teammates, who also taught mathematics, about what they were doing in their classes. Through this reflective conversation, Ms. Tijerina realized that she should not have omitted the step of working with the manipulatives. She decided to create a lesson with the students using manipulatives and technology and video record the activity interactions. She would review the video recording to see how the students

Figure 14.1 A teacher observes her students during their work to gain insight on their thinking.

were interacting with the manipulatives and with their teammates to understand how they were learning the math concepts. After observing how the students worked with the manipulatives and their teammates, she created some new lessons that better taught the objectives. Once she felt that they had mastered the concepts, she gave them a pencil-and-paper test to see if they mastered the mathematics benchmarks.

Introduction

Throughout a teacher preparation program, preservice teachers receive guidance as they consider curricular, management, and assessment decisions based on educational theory and best practices. During field experiences and student teaching, teacher candidates are shown how and why they must purposefully think about the decisions they will make in the classroom as they prepare to assume their roles as certified teachers of record. In the teacher preparation classroom, preservice teachers review related theories, develop skills, and gain an understanding of how such information should influence their practice—often encouraged by their program's assignments to reflect on lesson plans, teaching incidents, assessment results, and so forth.

During this time, some preservice teachers begin to develop their own reflective practices, which they will hopefully implement in their future classrooms. Reflective teaching requires that constructive criticism come not only from support personnel (e.g., mentors, university supervisors, principals) but from oneself as well.

The term "induction" is used to refer to a period during which a new teacher completes an introductory period, which is normally equivalent to one's first year as a teacher. In order to assist new teachers during their induction year in transitioning into a new role, some districts (and even some universities or other teacher preparation programs) assign them induction mentors. The purpose of these mentors is to serve as a support system and to provide peer evaluation to help new teachers.

Beyond the induction year, in the early years of the teaching career, teachers must develop the practice of automatically assessing the quality of the educational practices they use and the educational experiences they provide their students. The inservice teacher cannot simply rely on trained personnel to initiate dialogue regarding his/her strengths or weaknesses of teaching in the classroom; rather this must begin to occur internally. For teachers of record, there is no longer a university professor, field supervisor, or mentor teacher in the back of the classroom to observe and offer suggestions for improvement. Even a principal is only there a very limited amount of time during the year, so the teacher must be his/her own assessor for all educational interactions that occur each day. Self-evaluation should grow into a moral commitment to examine one's actions and to improve. This can occur in three areas: (1) before action (such as in the planning or mental rehearsal stage); (2) in action or when a teacher is in the middle of instruction or another professional situation and realizes "in midstream" that things could go in a better direction and then moves to do so; and (3) after action (when a teacher finishes a lesson or other interaction in teaching and looks back upon it for improvement; Cunningham & Moore, 2011).

One of the most difficult aspects of the teaching profession is the professional isolation from colleagues that it imposes on its practitioners (Danielson & McGreal, 2000). Teachers spend most of their days alone in their own classrooms with their own students. Few opportunities are available to casually observe, discuss with, and learn from other teachers or other educators such as specialists or professors. Little time is available to consult with one's colleagues about a difficult dilemma. As Danielson and McGreal state, (2000)

> The isolation of teachers has been well documented. On their evaluation forms after a workshop, many teachers will write that the opportunity to discuss issues with their colleagues was the most beneficial aspect of the day. Teaching is highly complex, and most teachers have scant opportunity to explore common problems and possible solutions, or share new pedagogical approaches with their colleagues. (p. 24)

The awareness of who we are, what we bring to the classroom, who we teach, and the most appropriate practices needed to provide an excellent and equitable educational experience to students must be much more heightened. Nonetheless, the task of reflecting on each and every decision made, the action that was taken (or was intended to be taken), and the words uttered—and the consequences of such practices—is vital in knowing how to teach the content which students must acquire and to address the whole child and his/her development in all areas. In other words, teachers must not only be their own toughest critics but must also become knowledgeable in ways to address the issues that are uncovered through their own intentional and reflective teaching practices.

Background

Reflective Practice: Definitions and Perspectives

Thinking is a natural process of the human psyche. Thinking is also what makes people, in general, human. Everyone is always thinking about something. Even when one says, "I don't want to think about it," thinking is happening. Some people do their best thinking in the shower, driving to work, or right after they wake up from a deep sleep. Dewey (1933) described the differences between random thought and reflective thought as "a consecutive ordering in such a way that determines the next thought as its proper outcome" (p. 13). Reflective thoughts are consecutive and with consequences. They grow from one another and support one another through consecutive thought patterns. This might be termed the "If . . . then" process of thought for teachers. When thoughts are connected, they become reflective thoughts. For example, Mr. Gaston thought to himself, "Karla has been acting upset all day. *IF* I call on her today, *THEN* she is likely to withdraw completely. . . ." Mrs. Salinas was in a conference with parents, and she perceived that they were becoming very defensive. "*IF* I will just listen a moment," she told herself, "*THEN* I will give them a chance to vent their frustrations with the situation, and we can go on from there."

In order to manage reflective thought, people often write in a journal, discuss their thoughts with others, contribute to a weblog (blog), record their audio reflections, and so forth. Through journaling and other reflection activities, they become observers of their own learning environments.

Schön (1983) described reflective thinking as a process of using prior knowledge, expertise, and experience to reframe a problem. When reflective practitioners find patterns or view actions from different perspectives, they may arrive at a new idea or a different solution. Many people, for example, may accept a particular practice as a tradition that has been established by an authority. They accept the everyday reality as "that's how it should be because (most often) that is the way it has always been done." Schön, however, described how *reflective* practitioners experience a disequilibrium or difficulty in the everyday practice under question. They begin to ask: "Why didn't this work? Why do we do it this way? Could there be an even better way?" The traditional practice that once seemed effective and efficient is now a problem that needs a solution. Schön suggested that approaching such situations requires a process that involves action that is persistent and with careful consideration. This reflective process necessitates intuition, emotion, and passion to follow through with necessary changes that will cause the reflective practitioner to approach the problem with new perspectives.

Argyris and Schön (1974) believed that reflective practitioners must integrate thought with action. The traditional way of doing things becomes what is termed the "Theory in Use" (p. 3). They found that when reflective practitioners integrated knowledge or expertise with competence and rigor, the reflective practitioner moves from solving problems from Theory in Use ("what is") to Theory in Action ("what can be"). Reflective practitioners become competent in taking action to learn from the situation and then take action to solve the problem. Zeichner and Liston (1996) applied this theory to teachers. They found that when teachers think about their teaching, they look at problems in the classroom (or even everyday practices that may not be as effective as they could be) from different perspectives or angles, ask themselves and others questions about their own teaching practices and actions, and examine their motives and attitudes within the context in which they work. Table 14.1 lists 22 common themes found in teacher candidates' weekly reflective journals (Doyran, 2013).

The surge of interactive technology in recent times opens the doors for preservice and inservice teachers to find useful technology tools to support their engagement in reflective practices throughout the teaching process (see Figure 14.2). By utilizing electronic journals, blogs, and social media, reflective practitioners can evaluate the teaching events they experience. They use the technology tools to document the problems they encounter throughout the teaching process, identify the problems

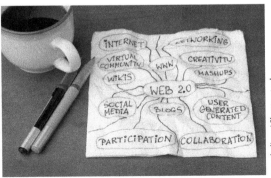

Figure 14.2 A concept web shows a variety of ways and technology tools to facilitate reflective practices.

Table 14.1 Common Themes Found in Teacher Candidates' Reflective Journals (Doyran, 2013)

1. Self-awareness
2. Awareness related to students
3. Awareness related to teaching profession
4. Awareness related to schools
5. Methodological issues/theory
6. Preparing and grading exams
7. Positive and negative factors affecting the preservice teachers' performance while teaching
8. Motivational factors
9. Personality factors which influence the teaching-learning process
10. Professional factors related to teachers
11. Classroom management and how difficult it can be
12. Teacher roles/characteristics in the classroom and while teaching
13. Different roles mentor teacher should have
14. The importance of time management
15. Peer pressure while teaching
16. Peer motivation while teaching
17. Mentor teacher pressure (as they are observing and giving feedback and grades)
18. Feedback received from peers
19. Feedback received from the mentor teachers
20. Feedback received from the supervisor at the university
21. Rules and regulations at school
22. Effective blackboard use

that evolve from the event, and determine solutions to the problems. Using tools such as blogs and interactive journals (synchronous, or "real time", and asynchronous, or "any time") provides computer-mediated communication for teacher reflection with teams on the problems they experience. Teachers collaborate together by writing about or recording the event, sharing the reflections with each other, and developing solutions to the problems with colleagues as a team.

Technology tools allow effective practitioners to move from a technical, traditional format to an intuitive, conscious choice of being. Greene (1978) described this process as being "wide awake" or conscious and noted that a teacher's decision-making must be based on research, knowledge of the youth in the classroom, and self-awareness. Greene summarized the transformative process that teachers experience when they are examining their practice in the following way: the teacher facilitates the teaching process with students, reflects about what worked or did not work, and adjusts the process to meet the needs of the students (see Figure 14.3). When Ms. Tijerina, for example, realized that her students did not do well on the mathematics benchmark tests, she reflected on what she had done during the teaching process. She collaborated with her colleagues to discover what might be missing from her lesson and used technology tools to capture the data. This reflective process moves teachers from thinking about what **they** as *teachers* are doing in the teaching process to reflecting about what works for the *students* in the classroom.

As noted, teachers break from the traditional or mechanical ways of teaching by asking questions—particularly "why" questions (see Figure 14.4). This questioning process requires teachers to attend more fully to their own professional lives and to question **what is** to **what could be** in the **ideal** teaching and learning process (refer to Figure 14.4). Technology tools create a space for the teachers to shift from their regular thinking processes in teaching and move to a more collaborative space with a team of teachers. This creates the transformative teaching process where the teacher actually becomes the learner by closely examining data from an educational incident.

Intentional inquiry is an important part of the reflective process. Teachers will begin to self-question by realizing a situation or a problem is not working or is not right for students in some way. This could occur in any area of their practice—with a child's learning or management, with a parent, colleague, or administrator, and so forth. They experience disequilibrium or dissonance and deliberately ask, "Why didn't this work?" Then, they begin asking, "What could I have done differently in this situation?" Schön (1983) called this **reframing the problem** or situation. Once reflective practitioners can reframe the problem, they **question the existing**

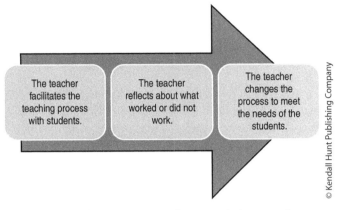

The teacher facilitates the teaching process with students.

The teacher reflects about what worked or did not work.

The teacher changes the process to meet the needs of the students.

Figure 14.3 The teacher facilitates the teaching process, reflects, and changes the process to meet the needs of learners.

framework, see patterns within the framework, and look for new ideas. This inquiry process leads the practitioners to **possible changes or solutions**. They **test their new solution** to see if it works, and, if it does not, they **repeat the questioning cycle** for other solutions.

Reflective practitioners reframe the problem or conflict in a way that may create a surprise or even elicit an "aha" for the problem or solution (Schön, 1983). Reflective teachers also want to see if the new solution is an ethically sound practice by knowing best practices and researching, if needed. The solution needs to be compared with their own values and perspectives to see if they now have a new perspective through which to view the situation. They need to know if it "feels right" for their personality and teaching styles and *is* right for learners. If it is, the reflective practitioners will adapt their situation to a new framework of knowledge.

Teachers who are reflective practitioners follow this process while also exploring their own personal motives and context in which they work. They question their perspectives and beliefs about the students they teach (see Figure 14.5). They examine their own personal assumptions and biases to know what and why they believe. This personal reflection leads teachers to look into their own stories so that they can understand who they are and why they respond as they do in different situations. This personal introspection allows teachers to take ownership of their own teaching practices so that they keep what is important to them while making needed changes. They are able to use inquiry on their own teaching practices and actions to make their practice better for students, colleagues, parents, administrators, and themselves.

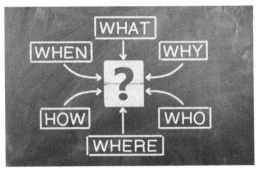

Figure 14.4 Teachers break from the traditional or mechanical ways of teaching by asking questions.

Figure 14.5 Reflective practitioners question their perspectives, beliefs, teaching practices, and actions.

Teacher candidates may begin to follow this process, too. A level of self-doubt is common when teachers (or teacher candidates) ask themselves some of the following questions:

- Am I really a good teacher (or going to be a good teacher)? Why or why not? What can I do about it if the answer is negative in any way?
- How does my teaching style compare to the styles of colleagues?
- Are my lessons engaging, and are they increasing academic performance?
- Are my classroom management skills as effective as those of other teachers in my school? Are they good for children?
- Can I communicate effectively with parents?
- Can I address the needs of *all* learners and students with various learning styles?
- Do I have biases which become oblivious to students in the classroom? Is my classroom a positive place for all students?

Although difficult at first (especially when one is totally honest with oneself), this type of questioning can become a way of life with practice. Some have likened it to performing on stage, while, at the same time, sitting in the audience at a play and judging how that performance is progressing (Osterman & Kottkamp, 1993). Teacher education programs encourage this practice to become automatic through adding reflection components to many assignments during courses of study to self-evaluate.

When coupled with technology integration, a teacher must ask introspective questions such as these and many more:

- Are students really different learners than when I was in school, and must I use technology in different ways to reach them?
- Am I not using technology (or not using it to its full potential) because I don't know how, don't feel comfortable, and/or need more training?
- Am I making good choices in the technology I use, or am I just using technology as an electronic overhead projector or for drill games?
- Am I assuming that all children and their families have (or have had) access to technology?
- Have I made technology use safe in my classroom?
- Would I know if there were cyberbullying incidents occurring with my students?
- Am I aware of the latest technology integration strategies?

Obtaining proficiency in technology and reflective teaching practices is as important for the preservice teacher as acquiring content area knowledge and classroom management skills (see Figure 14.6). Proficiency in the use of technology is no longer preferred, but required. Today's teacher must be able to manage administrative tasks, such as taking attendance and submitting lesson plans electronically, using the educational hardware and software available on campus for instruction and resources, and becoming familiar with possible educational opportunities of social media and common electronic devices like cell phones and tablets. For example, Ms. Long knows that best teaching practices include grouping, so she uses a search engine on her computer to type in "cooperative learning groups methodology YouTube," which resulted in numerous pages of ideas and videos of these models. Not only does the integration of technology enhance the students' acquisition of content and increase their development of the twenty-first-century skills required for the workforce, it also facilitates the process of reflective teaching for teachers who engage in reflective practices on a regular basis to enhance the educational experiences of their students.

Preservice teachers can utilize electronic devices such as cell phones, digital cameras, and tablets by carrying them into the classrooms.

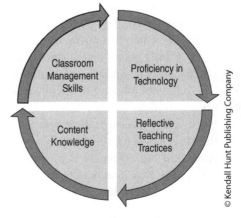

Figure 14.6 Professionalism in teaching has many facets, including obtaining proficiency in technology and reflective teaching practice.

© Kendall Hunt Publishing Company

Figure 14.7 Preservice teachers utilize cell phones, digital cameras, tablets, and other devices to observe their mentor teachers and/or their own teaching practices.

Connectivity with the Internet gives them the flexibility to upload data, take pictures, or create documents within the real time of teaching. They can send this information to colleagues, students, and/or parents for feedback. The preservice teacher learns how to transfer personal knowledge of electronic devices, social media, and media to use in their teaching process, and preservice teachers not only observe their mentor teachers with whom they work, they can also observe their own teaching practices through digital recordings.

Data are the subject of reflection and more easily captured, reviewed, and analyzed when teachers use electronic devices to facilitate reflection on their teaching practices. Tasks that once took weeks to organize and complete, such as scoring and analyzing certain types of assessment or videotaping a teaching episode, can now be done instantaneously. For example, by using apps and some online services such as Google Docs (with the Flubarro extension [www.flubarr]), teachers can easily create assignments and auto grade them without having to always take stacks of papers home.

Preservice teachers, by definition, are novices who should show sufficient growth in the areas of critical thinking and "effective reflection" on their paths toward becoming autonomous teachers during their teacher preparation programs (Loughran, 2002). A number of educational researchers have studied this area. Rodman's

Malek, a senior education major, had just finished his last student teaching lesson. He and three other student teachers at the school were sitting in the lounge reminiscing about how scared they had been in the beginning. In regard to management, they had, at first, not noticed half of what was occurring in the classroom, "My mentor sat down with me almost every day, and we 'went over it,'" Malek said. "I did lots of soul-searching! Now, my class can't get away with anything! I see every trick. In the beginning I was just so focused on getting the information out that I couldn't even think of anything  else. Now, if you search multi-tasker in the dictionary, you'll see a picture of me!"

Participating in reflective practices with supportive educators such as mentors and supervisors during the preservice years helps future educators develop professionally and personally so they can move into self-sufficient reflective practice. As well, their familiarity and deeper understanding of the importance of reflective teaching carries over to their appointment as inservice teachers (Ward & McCotter, 2004). Using electronic modes, such as audio, video, and data, to reflect on one's teaching, interactions, and beliefs helps to facilitate the reflection process and broaden the scope of information acquired through such a process.

(2010) study showed that preservice teachers' reflections demonstrated a better understanding of how to apply good theory and strategies to create stronger educational opportunities for students. They shifted from an egocentric perspective to being able to consider how their actions impacted the students; their reflection, in general, exhibited a more student-centered perspective. This shift in perspective should be a natural growth progression.

When preservice teachers learn about and practice reflective teaching during their field assignments, they carry that experience with them into the classroom as novice teachers. For example, they find ways to utilize electronic devices in a manner that others, who may be less technically experienced, may not have used. The energy that novice teachers bring into the classroom is invaluable because they can remind many experienced teachers of the importance of reflective practice while using electronic devices. Preservice teachers develop skills by reflecting about their teaching experiences, observing their mentor teachers, and observing students *with intentionality* in the classroom. A preservice educator begins the transformative practice of teaching by developing the practice of reflecting; these skills are then utilized as he or she enters his/her own classroom as a teacher of record.

Seeing Through Others' Eyes

To make such discoveries about one's own self, an educator must engage in the practice of "withitness." First coined by Kounin in 1970, the term "withitness" refers to a teacher's awareness of what is happening in the classroom at all times (USCRossierOnline, 2017; Gettinger & Kohler, 2011). Originally used in the context of classroom management, the implications of "withitness" touch nearly every aspect of teaching. Extending the idea of "withitness" to teachers purposefully monitoring and analyzing their own practices and beliefs about education is not a stretch but rather a first step toward incorporating reflective practices in teaching.

Becoming a reflective educator involves intense introspection on the part of the individual, and, therefore, some may mistake reflective teaching for an isolated undertaking rather than a continuous "loop" (or loops) of inquiry (refer to Figure 14.8). However, there is much more of a collaborative nature required to partake in reflective teaching practices. In fact, there may be (and should be) many of these loops occurring at the same time about multiple areas of teaching (e.g., instructional methods, management, efficiency, working with parents, technology integration, and many more). Effectively reflecting on one's beliefs, teaching, and classroom practices requires not only one's own teaching but gaining an understanding of how others perceive the educational practices as well.

Brookfield (2002) argues that critical reflection must incorporate the perspectives and experiences of others. He states that teachers must consider four lenses when examining their own teaching: (1) the autobiographical lens, (2) the students' perspectives, (3) colleagues' experiences, and (4) theoretical literature (refer to Figure 14.9). The information gleaned from critical reflection based on the use of these four lenses not only allows educators to make more informed judgments about their teaching practices, but teachers gain confidence and a newfound engagement in their teaching practices through consulting other sources as a part of reflection.

As a preservice teacher, the teacher candidate learns about and is encouraged to participate in reflection as

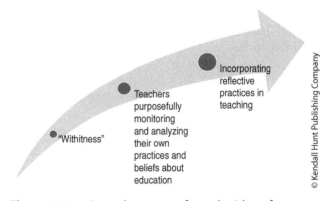

"Withitness"

Teachers purposefully monitoring and analyzing their own practices and beliefs about education

Incorporating reflective practices in teaching

© Kendall Hunt Publishing Company

Figure 14.8 A teacher moves from the idea of "withitness" and reflective practices to incorporating more effective practices into teaching.

kiri11 / Shutterstock.com

Figure 14.9 Brookfield's (2002) four lenses of self-examination.

Figure 14.10 In addition to Brookfield's (2002) four lenses, the family lens should also be considered.

a requirement of a university course or program requisite, usually as part of the fieldwork experience. Teacher candidates, as part of the teacher preparation process, normally have at their disposal their peers, cooperating teacher, and university supervisor who will encourage and remind them to use reflective practices. Once certification is obtained, however, the inservice teacher must provide a personal impetus and seek out feedback from students, colleagues, administrators, and students' families for information regarding their instructional practices. This requires preservice teachers to follow the training and experiences they learned during their teacher preparation programs and to recognize the confidence in teaching that they now have. According to Rodman (2010), preservice teachers who receive the opportunity to witness and develop reflective teaching practices are more likely to apply good theory to their practices and move away from teacher-centered reflection toward student-centered reflection. They develop the confidence and the efficacy in themselves to make decisions for the benefit of their students. The preservice teacher discovers the responsibility of being the teacher with open-mindedness and wide-awakeness as described by Greene (1995). Greene believed that when teachers began the reflective process, they were expected to make good choices and decisions for learners. These are based on their own training and experiences and that of other respected experts in the educational system.

Autobiographical Lens

Perhaps the most obvious piece of being a reflective teacher is that of consciously thinking about one's own teaching and practice through one's past experiences from "the self" perspective (Figure 14.11). Although no singular definition of reflection exists, all descriptions incorporate the act of self-reflection and problem posing (Loughran, 2002). The most basic type of reflection requires educators to consciously think back on their teaching or other educational interactions, identify ways that facilitate and impede student learning, and make changes to improve the educational interaction in the class and better meet students' needs. Davis (2006) warns that self-reflection must be productive reflection, requiring the practitioner to move beyond mere description of what occurs in the classroom to an analysis of teaching and learning and then to action. Productive self-reflection, according to Davis, includes two indicators: knowledge integration and analysis. Teachers demonstrate knowledge integration during reflection when they notice and reflect on four aspects of teaching: (1) instruction, (2) learners and learning, (3) content area knowledge, and (4) assessment. She also holds that reflection must not be teacher-centered but must include a student-centered focus aimed at understanding how students learn and how the instruction addresses those needs.

Figure 14.11 Teachers use conscious introspection to improve teaching.

Aside from reflecting on different aspects of teaching, the ideas of time and purpose must also be considered to practice effective reflection. Although reflection means analyzing past actions, it is important to engage in meaningful reflection at different stages throughout the process. As a reminder, reflection can occur at different times in the teaching process. Reflection-on-action includes analyzing the practice *after* it occurs, while reflection-in-action occurs *during* practice (Schön, 1983), usually during a moment when realization occurs that a change in midstream could be more fruitful. Reflection on future action occurs when teachers practice thinking ahead about what *will* or *could* happen, and they try to change it before mistakes are made. Loughran (2002) notes that the type of information one can collect differs as a result of anticipatory, retrospective, and contemporaneous reflection. Although the teacher reflects on the same situation, the change of time, perspective, experience, and framing yield different sets of information that enhances understanding and allows for effective change in practice to occur. Participating in video self-analysis, for example, can help verify one's recollection of a lesson or interaction and make a more accurate assessment of classroom management, identify mannerisms, and improve overall teaching. Dye (2007) as cited in Snoeyink (2010), notes that analyzing a video of oneself helps teachers "revise their internal representations of their own performance, thus more accurately identifying their own performance gap" (p. 102). In today's world, digital video recording devices make this extremely easy.

The Student Lens

The basis of all reflection in teaching is to enhance the educational experiences of the students in the classroom. If students are not learning, it makes no difference how well the teacher believes he or she is doing—it is not enough. An observant and reflective teacher can make educated decisions in planning and conclusions regarding the success of a lesson, particular classroom practices, or interactions; nonetheless, the most accurate information about the students' perception of the success of an educational experience comes from the students. Teachers should evaluate the success of their actions not based solely on student achievement on assessments or the students' perceived level of engagement but also include opportunities to solicit information from students about their educational experiences.

Figure 14.12 Expressions teachers can use for feedback with younger children.

One aspect that should also be included is the socio-emotional environment in the classroom. If students are to provide full attention to the learning activities, their affective filter must be minimally triggered. Although the affective filter hypothesis was proposed by Krashen (1984) and was specific to second language acquisition, the idea that the learning environment will affect a student's level of anxiety, motivation, and self-confidence transfers across all learning environments. Teachers must constantly reflect on the environment they create and address issues that may arise. Creating opportunities for students to submit feedback on how enjoyable, comprehensible, or relatable a lesson or activity was can help the teacher modify or design future learning experiences.

Again, technology in today's classrooms can make this easy. Younger children can complete an end-of-the-day online survey where they choose the appropriate "face" or "emoticon" (emotional icons) which describes how they feel and tell the teacher (through an automatic recording) why they feel that way. The teacher can also set up an anonymous and/or confidential messaging option in the online classroom workspace to allow students to provide feedback about the lessons, activities, or student interactions which they may not feel comfortable stating to the teacher face to face.

Essential to obtaining accurate, honest feedback from students is to build a trusting rapport with them. If the teacher shows interest and fairness and explains how the feedback is used to enhance the classroom experience, students will tend to provide useful comments. Some suggestions for eliciting student feedback include using interviews or student focus groups to receive whole class feedback in a face-to-face fashion. These arrangements can easily be adapted to online or electronic collection through a survey tool such as SurveyMonkey, Socrative, Google Forms, or learning management software similar to Blackboard Learn or Moodle. Teachers can solicit student feedback through the use of response forms such as the Critical Incident Questionnaire (CIQ) which

Brookfield's Critical Incident Questionnaire

Please respond to the following questions about this week's classes:

1. At what moment did you feel most engaged with what was happening?
2. At what moment were you most distanced from what was happening?
3. What action, taken by anyone (teacher or student), did you find most helpful?
4. What action, taken by anyone (teacher or student), did you find most puzzling or confusing?
5. What about the class surprised you the most? (This could be about your own reactions to what went on, something that someone did, or anything else that occurs.)

Adapted from Brookfield, S.D. (1995). *Becoming a critically reflective teacher.* San Francisco: Jossey-Bass.

Figure 14.13 Critical Incident Questionnaires (CIQs) solicit student feedback about strong and weak areas of a lesson.

Figure 14.14 Students use a classroom response system or cell phone apps to provide instantaneous feedback to the teacher.

requires students to comment on the strong, weak, and unique moments in the classroom (Brookfield, 1995). Students provide the teacher with insight into their perspectives about the learning experiences on a weekly basis through a CIQ which allows them to share their opinions freely and maintain anonymity (see Figure 14.13). Reflecting on what learners have to say quickly and easily through technology will help teachers to become more attuned to the classroom environment.

Classroom response systems (CRSs) solicit responses from students using clickers that allow educators to poll their students on questions of their choice given a multiple-choice format (see Figure 14.14 and Figure 14.15). If the campus does not have a CRS, a software-based audience response tool may be used as an alternative. Web-based audience response and polling tools function in a similar manner, but the information is transmitted through the Internet, and students can use their cellular or smartphones, tablets, or laptops to submit their answers. The results are tabulated synchronously and can be discussed immediately, if desired. There are several free Web-based audience response tools as well as options that include a monthly charge for the service. The teacher who uses technological data such as these can immediately determine what students know and/or how they are experiencing the learning environment.

The Peer Lens

As mentioned earlier, the teaching profession can, at times, seem like an isolated and lonely profession. Throughout the school day, teachers are involved in instruction in their classroom except for planning and lunch. There are very few opportunities during the school day to communicate with colleagues—and even fewer opportunities to have a colleague observe one's teaching practices or vice versa. Nonetheless, having the input of a colleague who has a familiarity with the campus culture, student body, and common habits of teaching, can be invaluable. Aside from receiving a different perspective on teaching and learning issues, communication

> **Web-based Audience Response Tools**
>
> ClickerSchool: www.clickerschool.com
>
> Echo360: echo360.com
>
> Poll Everywhere: www.polleverywhere.com
>
> QuestionPress: www.questionpress.com
>
> Socrative: www.socrative.com
>
> Top Hat: www.tophat.com
>
> Kahoot: www.kahoot.com
>
> Verso: www.versolearning.com/
>
> Mentimeter: www.mentimeter.com
>
> Google Forms: www.google.com/forms/about

Figure 14.15 Web-based audience response systems can be used with personal electronic devices such as laptops, cell phones, and tablets.

with a colleague helps to build support—a major factor in teacher retention. To gain information through the peer lens, a teacher must be willing to initiate dialogue with colleagues in the field; this dialogue can occur in face to face or virtual forums.

The main goal is to open lines of communication and collaboration with other educators. First-year, and occasionally teachers who are new to a school, are usually assigned a mentor who provides an instant opportunity to discuss ideas or dilemmas related to improving one's educational practices. Another collaborative space, a professional learning community (PLC), is a group of educators working collaboratively to seek answers to their questions, share what they discover, and act upon their new knowledge to enhance a school's effectiveness in the education of its students (Hord, 1997). If educators reflect on the "big ideas" of a PLC (e.g., ensuring that students learn, creating a culture of collaboration, and focusing on the results), then teachers will be more reflective in their practices to evaluate the effectiveness of learning in their classroom (DuFour, 2004). Peer coaching, Critical Friends Groups, and structured group problem-solving, along with intentional investigative improvement, collaborative dialogue, and structured communities of practice (CoP) construct ways for teachers to interact with peers for the sake of improving education. Partner or group collaboration such as peer coaching, even as a preservice teacher, can foster the development of reflective practices, which, in turn, can produce an inservice teacher who enters the first years of teaching understanding the importance of reflection and actively seeking support from peers (Kurtts & Levin, 2000). Collegial feedback and collaboration can be easily facilitated through electronic means by creating online CoPs. These can be particularly effective when group members are not in close physical proximity with one another or to allow for asynchronous communication which allows for different schedules. Lave and Wenger (1991) proposed the idea of a CoP as a group of people sharing a common interest and a desire to engage in and contribute to practices of their community (as cited in Lee & Brett, 2013). The rapidly growing networking platforms and spaces easily provide for virtual communities of practitioners. Blogging, wikis, discussion boards, and social networking spaces allow for the formation of CoPs and PLCs where educators can discuss topics of interest and concern with the goal of finding solutions to implement and improve the education of their students in classrooms around the world (Salazar, Aguirre-Muñoz, Fox, & Nuanez-Lucas, 2010). Just as with face-to-face group dialogue, it is important to join online collaborative communities that provide for a safe space to discuss questions and concerns as well as contribute to the development of others. It may be to one's benefit to join an online community where information can be shared with a broader audience as well as maintain a semblance of anonymity. Remaining anonymous allows a teacher to speak freely without having to censor the posting to avoid judgment or identification by coworkers or to worry about being connected to controversial topics occurring on their particular campus.

Like professional learning communities, peer coaching, and CoPs, anonymous online platforms for educators give teachers opportunities to bring their questions, concerns, and ideas to a group of educators who will provide insight through the peer lens. In online discussion forums such as the Teacher Chatboards section of Teachers.net (www.teachers.net) and the Communities section of Edutopia (www.edutopia.org/community), educators connect on an anonymous platform while staying connected with a large network of educators. For instance, as of November 2014, some topics that are relevant to new teachers or teacher candidates in the Communities section of Edutopia are:

- 5 Quick Classroom-Management Tips for Novice Teachers
- What I Wish I'd Known as a New Teacher
- Avoiding New Teacher Burnout

The initial post of the discussion topic titled "Avoiding New Teacher Burnout" was dated October 7, 2014. Within 3 weeks, over 1,300 people reviewed this Edutopia online discussion thread created by a new teacher with the question, "Daily, I see teachers that are in the 'burnout' stage of teaching . . . I see students suffering due to the fact that their teachers have given up. I am asking for advice on how to avoid the 'burnout' stage. Any advice?" (Gadawg01, 2014).

One English teacher responded by stating that education is a profession that people pursue because of their love for children, not because of the "extravagant" money or lifestyle. She advised new teachers to write down reminders of exactly why they got into the profession in the beginning. From there they can learn to appreciate the teaching profession all over again (t_ngo, 2016).

A teacher shared a tip that he had set a goal each day to leave by 5 pm—no matter what! He found that since he knew he was leaving at 5:00, he prioritized things much better (Thomas, 2016). Another teacher commented that burnout mostly happens when people feed into negativity. It is much easier to look at everything that is *not* going one's way, and people often tend to bond over what is *not* going right. She suggested that new teachers avoid those teachers who are going through a burnout because the negative attitude becomes contagious. It is a good idea for a new teacher to maintain a positive outlook—regardless of how bad things are. Most importantly, they should have good work-life balances and try not to take too much work home. They should also avoid bringing personal life/problems to work (Edutopia, 2016).

When facing "burnout," "becoming overwhelmed," or needing to talk about other common or confidential issues, new teachers sometimes can be embarrassed, may not feel safe talking to other teachers on their campus, or simply may not be able to find an understanding adult with whom to have a discussion. Anonymous online forums such as the above provide a safe channel for novice and mentor teachers to share experiences. Regardless of the space used, a teacher must remember, however, to always remain professional with any dialogue.

Terry Heick (2015) is a teacher who blogs on reflection. He gives an example of how Twitter can become a trigger for him. He notes that, "If I read a tweet, interpret what I believe to be its meaning, find relevance in its message, and think—even briefly—about how I relate to it and it to me, I'm approaching reflection." He gives the following example of his reflection process after receiving a Tweet on assessment:

Tweet: 10 Assessment Tools for the Flipped Classroom

My reaction: What are the strengths and weaknesses of assessment in a flipped classroom? What tools am I aware of that could work here? Do I need a tool–is this worth clicking on? Should I save to Pocket without clicking? Click and read? RT (ReTweet) without reading? Read, then RT? Favorite with or without reading? How am I spending my time right now on social media? Am I bumming around, or should I be more intentional–this tool or idea for this need I have tomorrow.

He also notes that there are hashtags for teacher reflection (# reflectiveteacher hashtag).

Apran Chokshi (2017), a high school social studies teacher, shares hints in his blog about ways to adjust instruction based on formative data (www.teacherreflections.com/author/anchokshigmailcom/):

> This year using tools like Pear Deck, Actively Learn, and Canvas helped generate data that gave me deeper insights into individual students' performance which then helped me differentiate instruction.

The Theoretical Lens

Although Schön's (1983) book, *The Reflective Practitioner*, was in a way a reaction to the contemporary focus on book knowledge rather than technology, there is relevance to being abreast of current research and literature when reflecting on one's teaching practices. University educators, administrators, psychologists, classroom teachers, and others seek to inform others about their studies and findings on a myriad of topics about teaching and learning. More informed, accurate decision-making occurs when a teacher incorporates researched-based practices in the classroom. Whether the concern relates to lesson planning, strategies to use with students with exceptionalities, how to provide a comprehensible education to an English language learner, or ways to strengthen classroom management, information from strong educational research should be incorporated into the decision-making process. The ease of being informed in current times through technology makes reflection on best practices amazingly easy.

One of the most obvious ways to build knowledge about the field is to subscribe to journals related to education and particular fields within education. As students, preservice teachers typically have access to their university library's electronic journals and books. Using databases such as Education Resources Information Center (ERIC) (www.eric.ed.gov) or Educational Full Text (www.ebscohost.com/academic/education-full-text) puts a wealth of knowledge at one's fingertips. Professional organizations or societies such as the National Council of Teachers of English (www.ncte.org) (*Voices from the Middle*), the National Association for Bilingual Education (www.nabe.org) (*Bilingual Research Journal*), or Kappa Delta Pi (*New Teacher Advocate*) may also maintain associated journals, and many organizations offer a membership discount for students. Many of these journals are electronic. Even without joining the organization, there is often information available to the public on the Website. Most organizations now have additional ways to stay connected by following them on Facebook, Twitter, LinkedIn, Google+, Pintrest, or YouTube. A number of organizations have annual conferences as well, and many now have electronic connections to papers, presentations, or addresses by experts at these conferences for members.

Additional ways to stay informed about current research and trends in the field include participating in professional development, joining email listservs or discussion boards, and subscribing to e-newsletters. Many educational organizations and leaders now offer webinars that can serve as professional development opportunities and, occasionally, as mentioned, keynote presentations from conferences are available on the Web as well. Subscribing to really simple syndication or rich site summary (RSS) feeds allows a teacher to have data from his or her favorite Website monitored automatically without the need to visit the sites individually. By checking a favorite Website with educational information, a teacher can get an aggregator (feed reader) such as FeedReader or ReadKit (which can read the feeds) and subscribe to the RSS feeds of one's choice. See Table 14.2 for a small sample of sites with RSS feeds that inform about current research in the field.

Table 14.2   A List of Sites With RSS Feeds that Inform About Current Research in the Field

Institutes	Web Addresses
Institute of Education Sciences' What Works Clearinghouse	www.ies.ed.gov/ncee/wwc
National Association for Multicultural Education	www.nameorg.org
Autism Speaks	www.autismspeaks.org
U.S. Department of Education	www.ed.gov/feed

RSS, rich site summary.

RSS feeds list the most recent additions to the Website's content in reverse chronological order and include the title and the first line of text. By clicking on the title, the reader is immediately connected to the content. To identify sites with RSS feeds, look for the RSS symbol, typically an orange square with white radio waves, on the Web page (see Figure 14.16).

The Family Lens (Refer to Figure 14.10)

Introspection, peers, and theory from communities of educators are not the only areas that should be considered as part of reflective practice. Families of students have specific goals, needs, or desires for their children, and each can provide feedback to the teacher regarding the family's perception on how the teacher is meeting their needs. Families can also provide important information about their child which can be taken into account by the reflective teacher. Ideally, the family member(s) and teacher will meet, and this process can be facilitated by online scheduling tools such as SignUpGenius (www.signupgenius.com) or Doodle (doodle.com). However, engaging in electronic communication can aid family/teacher interactions as well. Surveys or questionnaires, which solicit information about the child, can be disseminated through email, the teacher's Web page, or social learning platforms like Edmodo. Educators can encourage feedback from families by engaging them in classroom activities and posting information online. Parent/teacher conferences can have an optional electronic option for family members who are unable to visit the campus. Such conferences can occur through Skype, FaceTime, or other online collaboration software. Although a teacher may choose to engage families in electronic communication, it is important to note that the same amount of professionalism and caution is required in any communication between the school and the family—electronic or otherwise. Additionally, each educator must check with his or her district to see which of these video sites, if any, are blocked by school firewalls. By opening the lines of communication between the family and the teacher and by explicitly asking for feedback from family members of the students, teachers can incorporate the familial lens into their reflection as well, always keeping in mind that teachers cannot automatically assume that all families have digital access (the Digital Divide).

Figure 14.16 RSS feeds provide links to the most recently updated content on the organization's Web site. Sites with RSS feeds insert the RSS symbol on their Webpage.

FaysalFarhan / Shutterstock.com

Reflective Practices to Consider

As with many aspects of being a strong, effective teacher, becoming a reflective practitioner requires preparation and practice. Although many educators may engage in a reflective teaching practice "here and there", for the most part reflective teachers are not born but created through their own sense of responsibility for themselves, their students, their profession, and for society. Reflective teaching is an ongoing, continual process which one develops and modifies over time. Incorporating reflective teaching practices allows educators to strengthen the education provided to students by maintaining a heightened level of awareness of their interactions with students, peers, and families. Simply reflecting on the day's events is not the totality of reflective teaching. Zeichner and Liston (1996) propose five features of a reflective teacher which include:

- attempting to solve a problem in their practice,
- acknowledging and questioning the assumptions and values they bring to the class,
- recognizing the cultural and institutional environments in which they teach,
- participating in curriculum development and school change, and
- being responsible for furthering their professional development.

By participating in a variety of reflective teaching practices, the teacher increases the possibility of properly modifying his or her lessons and other teaching practices.

Dewey (1933) also added the ideas of open-mindedness, responsibility, and wholeheartedness to reflective teaching. Accordingly, a teacher must take responsibility for reflecting and for the consequences of one's actions. Teachers must do this wholeheartedly to maintain focus on what is best for the learner, considering all possibilities with an open mind—even the possibility that they themselves could be wrong.

As noted, engaging in reflective practice takes time and requires a collaborative environment. Educators must reflect within themselves, collect feedback from students and families, identify colleagues who are willing to participate in the ongoing collaborative effort, and stay well-read in current educational research. One way to facilitate the process is to incorporate multimedia technologies in the reflective process. In the following section, we present a description of common reflective teaching practices along with more examples of ways to facilitate such practices through the use of technology.

Journaling

There is an emerging body of literature that addresses the use of multimedia tools, computer-supported collaborative learning, and other Web-based products as options for reflective practice for teachers. Studies such as those by Kajder & Parkes (2012) and Killeavy & Moloney (2010) explore the use of weblogs and videologs as tools for reflective practice. The blog is a Website, or the contents of the Website, that contains personal commentary, or reflections, while a vlog is a blog that has video content. Both studies found that these forums can be used to reflect on one's own teaching as well as solicit feedback in a peer-review setting. While Killeavy and Moloney's study was less definitive regarding the benefits of weblogs, they suggest that establishing a sense of community is important to promote contributors' willingness to share. As well, they suggest that using blogs instead of print journals is beneficial for individuals or communities in rural or distant areas. Stronger support for the use of blogs and vlogs was found by Kajder and Parkes (2012) who also identified the benefit of electronic journaling in creating online CoPs that were vast and had a broader physical range. It was noted that Web-based tools captured more raw, "thinking in the moment" entries than printed reflection. As a contributor to a blog or vlog, a teacher has access to a larger CoP, allowing for the possibility or varying points of view, constructive critique, and viable solutions to enhance the students' learning experiences. Electronic journaling is available through emails, blogs, vlogs, word processing, and Webpages; all allow for electronic journaling to occur. Some options also allow the teacher to include images, audio and video, and links to additional content. Again, confidentiality is paramount when sharing, and professional guidelines must always be followed. When considering the type of medium to use, teachers may want to consider their comfort level with the tool, the expectations or guidelines they view of a particular medium, and their willingness to explore technology that may enhance their own reflections. Shoffner (2009) discovered that her students had certain beliefs about the capacity and/or expectations of different electronic resources. For example, does a particular tool require an entry of a specific length? Is this forum more (or less) confidential than another? Who will be reading this entry, and is it okay to use less formal language and structure in one forum versus another? Kadjer and Parkes' (2012) study revealed that blogged reflections were more "surface" in nature, while vlogged reflections were more "pedagogical" in nature. Sample surface level reflections include more logistical comments: "I started class by calling them 'to order,' taking role, and speaking a couple of minutes on business matters. I reminded them of homework due the following day and went over the plan for today's class" (p. 237). Pedagogical level reflections such as "I knew that they were learning because when we would do the criticism part of it—after listening—they knew what they needed to do next" (p. 239) focus more on how students are learning. Although the preservice or inservice teacher may consider these factors, the best tool to use is the one that will yield the most feedback to make changes to enhance the students' education. See Table 14.3 for a list of sample reflection blogs.

Table 14.3   A List of Sample Teaching Reflection Blogs

A Principal's Reflections	www.esheninger.blogspot.com/
Reflections of a High School Math Teacher	www.teachhighschoolmath.blogspot.com/
Mrs. Manners ELA 6	www.sites.google.com/a/austinisd.org/mannersela6/blog
Student Teaching Blog	www.publish.illinois.edu/uistudteachbmh/

Whether a teacher is creating a reflection blog, producing a class blog, or having students create multiple blogs, she should choose one effective blogging platform that works best for her and her students' needs.

- Blogger (www.blogger.com)—A general purpose blogging platform. It works well with Google Apps for Education
- WordPress (www.wordpress.com)—An industry standard
- Kidblog (www.kidblog.org)—Built specifically for elementary and middle school teachers with built-in security measures
- Edublogs (www.edublogs.org)—Created for K-20 student and teachers

Video Recordings

One of the hardest tasks of reflection is to step out of the role of teacher and observe oneself from a third person perspective. Video recording of the classroom permits the teacher, and perhaps, a colleague(s) to see how teaching and learning transpires during the school day. Peer video analysis, as described by Harford, MacRuaire, and McCarten (2010), shows the peer-videoing analysis as a transformative process during which pairs of teachers record, then view each other's practices in a way that promotes dialogue and a shared learning experience. An alternative to peer recording is to set up a camera in one's own classroom and provide the video to colleagues or upload it to a limited access site where individuals in a community of practice can view it and provide feedback (see Figure 14.17). In both cases, the colleague can provide feedback electronically or face to face, and the teacher can view himself or herself to analyze the captured teaching practices. The two sets of feedback can be discussed and positive changes made. In peer coaching communities, peers are trained to become trusted colleagues who build professional relationships without the fear of evaluation from superiors. Also, in videoing, one must remember to follow district rules for filming students, although filming for professional development is often allowed for self-evaluation.

Figure 14.17 A vlog can be posted to password-protected blog sites.

If peer recording is not feasible, there are motion-tracking swivel smartphone docking devices that will swivel to follow people around the room like a human cameraman would. Here's how it works. Once a teacher puts the swivel camera into place, he or she will grab hold of a small marker device and start recording himself or herself. As he or she moves around, the dock rotates and pans vertically to follow that marker with some fairly impressive results. The teacher can create hands-free videos with iPhones, iPod Touches, and pocket cameras. Videos can be streamed to store and share through the cloud immediately. A few popular swivel camera brand names are as follows:

Swivl (www.swivl.com/)
Jibagot (www.jigabot.com/)
Soloshot (www.soloshot.com/)

Some teacher candidates choose to set up a password on their reflective e-journals, vlogs, or blogs to allow access to a selected few while others share reflective contents to the general public through YouTube and other social networks. This can be accomplished on monologue, documentary, dramatization, or interview formats. See Table 14.4 for a list of representative reflective vlogs of student teachers or new teachers.

For instance, Nicholas Provenzano (with screen name "Nerdycast"), who is a high school English teacher, kept a vlog by creating a YouTube channel via www.youtube.com/channel/UCmqHm-Zo9dp3OxGiUjkKBgw.

Table 14.4   A List of Representative Reflective Vlogs of Student Teachers or New Teachers

Vlog Formats	Titles	URLs
Monologue	JenniferReed1220's channel	www.youtube.com/watch?v=6bK3mmT6J3E&feature=youtu.be
Documentary	Bonnie Wagner High School English	www.youtube.com/watch?v=vp-qOlf6tc4
Documentary	Year-long Teaching Documentary of Jennifer McNickle	www.youtube.com/watch?v=e6wAMC41ZXQ

This YouTube channel is a "platform" to help him organize his weekly reflection videos. In the **monologue** format, he reflected through his webcam about the first semester of teaching, plagiarism, adjusting lessons, the value of a holiday party in the classroom, and other topics relevant to teaching. He gives a rationale for taking time as a busy new teacher for keeping the vlog (Provenzano, 2014):

> The videos are short (I limit my posts to 4 minutes), but the reflections are meaningful, and that's what makes this medium so powerful for me. . . . I grow as an educator the more I think about my practice— and that's what is best for my students.

The **documentary** of a student teacher's reflection is a nonfiction video intended to document some aspect of a student teacher's life to honestly record for the purposes of instruction or to maintain a historical record. The line blurs between documentary and **dramatization,** in that with dramatization, the video is *organized to center on the reflection of a teacher.* With the **interview** format, the student teacher has a conversation with a second person about his or her experiences.

Often in the preservice teaching experience, prospective teachers have missed or lost opportunities to reflect on an event because they did not see it or observe it due to their main focus being on themselves. As noted, being aware of everything going on in the classroom ("withitness") comes with experience. When reviewing teaching experiences through technology tools such as video recordings, however, one may see the body language or the faces of the students. They may then begin to understand that the teaching process is not just about how they teach the lesson but how the interactions between themselves and the students create the learning process. The reflective process, through the use of technology tools, leads to development in the teaching process and will provide teachers with opportunities to participate in the transformative process of growing as teachers. The Teachthought staff (2013) suggests that students can become a part of this when teachers create as one of their classroom jobs a "videographer of the day" to take a few minutes of footage of learning. This provides the students and the teacher with highly insightful feedback.

Besides asking students to be "videographer of the day", video recording can go high tech as well with a new generation of technology that consists of mobile, wireless video and audio recordings that work together to record components of the classroom.

Teachers have used screen capture (also called screenshot, or screen-cap) images taken by the computer user to record the visible items displayed on the monitor. Screen captures display still images, while a step above and beyond are lecture captures, which refers to the process of recording the content of a procedure, lecture, conference, or seminar in video format for viewers to remotely access, either in real time or asynchronously. The lecture capture may use any combination of microphones, cameras, screen captures, slideshows, and/or document cameras. Products such as Camtasia, Screencast-O-Matic, and Jing are used to create lecture captures.

With the increasing demands of video contents for flipped classes and tutorials, teachers who provide lecture captures to students routinely had to set up generic mobile multimedia carts loaded with videotaping equipment to move around from class to class. Now, as discussed above, self-capture products such as Swivl combine robotic mobile accessories, apps, and cloud solutions for making video capture in class more professional. The recording robot automatically follows a speaker and provides wireless audio. The app and cloud options provide a storage and sharing solution. If one has not seen a product like this, simply visualize the robot wireless vacuum cleaners in TV commercials that roam around the house to clean the floors.

Know Your Students

Another step in the reflective process for teachers is to know their students well. Often, teachers need to know their students' personal lives so that they can make connections to the students and the learning process. When the teacher makes personal connections to the students in the classroom, students become more engaged in the learning process. An exciting tool that teachers can use to learn more about their students is digital storytelling or digital narratives. Students and teachers can use software programs such as MS Movie Maker, and iMovie to have them make a video or movie. These digital processing tools help the students create an action movie with personal photos, home movies, and a written script to describe personal events. The students develop their narrative by telling their autobiographical story. The teacher who assists their students in creating their stories learns about the students in the process. What begins as an introspective process for students, easily transforms into a reflective process for the teacher as consideration for how one's teaching meets the needs of each student and guides the teacher in gathering information about the students to incorporate into future lessons and educational activities.

Teachers also find the discussion tools in programs such as Edmodo, Weebly, and Blackboard as a way to participate in the reflective process when students complete their reading reflections. Students can respond and read their classmates' responses to questions about the content that the teacher is presenting in the classroom. Through discussions, the teacher can begin to see how to create a better understanding of the content for each student. The students respond to the discussions by describing their current knowledge about the topic, providing examples of what they have learned, and, finally, stating whether or not they agree with the content or the question that was presented to them. By sharing these reflective thoughts in discussion boards, the students have opportunities to organize and publish their thoughts in a more formal way. They have an audience of their peers who will read and respond to their thoughts. This furthers the change of stance from a teacher believing that a learner is unable or unwilling to learn to the teacher's "problem-solving stance" that he or she has just not found the "right fit" yet for teaching a particular student(s).

Peer Coaching and Technology

As noted, interpersonal interactions with peers such as through peer coaching have been found to help beginning teachers develop as reflective practitioners and encourage feedback from peers. Additionally, new teachers develop reflective practices that are more focused on how their practices affect their students' learning than more self-centered concerns (Kurtts & Levin, 2000).

Peer coaching is another collaboration tool for the preservice or novice teacher, whereby the teacher finds another teacher as a partner to meet with on a regular basis. This can be on a formal schedule with professional development training, or it can be in an informal setting such as with a friend or colleague. Many preservice teachers develop a network with classmates in their teacher preparation program which leads to the development of trusting relationships among a smaller cohort of their peers. These relationships last beyond the teacher preparation program and become the basis of support and collaboration as they graduate from preservice teacher to novice teacher.

Peer coaching allows for teachers to meet together and talk about their teaching practices, issues with students, and evaluation of their curriculum. As we have seen, peer coaching sessions can be face to face, virtual, or online. Coaching sessions give the teacher an opportunity to reflect with a colleague in a safe manner without the anxiety of being observed, scored, or evaluated by an administrator or supervisor. Rather, they can honestly share concerns they may have with a trusted colleague who watches, listens, provides data, and supports them to enhance problem-solving. This format works well because the teacher himself or herself selects an area for examination (e.g., Am I calling on *all* my students or just some? Am I asking higher-level or just lower-level questions? What is my "travel pattern" around the room, and am I near all students at some point during the lesson? What type of oral feedback am I delivering to students?). The teacher also selects the method of data collection by the peer, and the two colleagues plan and talk through the objective(s) of the lesson and the observation. The colleague views the lesson (face to face or electronically), collects the data *only* as specified by the teacher, and presents it to him/her without judgment; then they reverse roles. One reason that peer coaching works so well is that the teacher is not only able to see himself or herself through the lens of another educator, but he or she is also in a peer's classroom where ideas (both positive and negative) may emerge and be stored for reflection.

Mrs. Casagrande had Mrs. McNamera as a partner. When Mrs. Casagrande sat in to tape and observe her peer's classroom, she made note of an exciting activity in language arts that fully engaged students, which she decided to employ the following week. As she watched the video before sending it to her peer, she also noted that Mrs. McNamera called on her boys much more often than she did the girls. Although that wasn't what Mrs. McNamera asked to her check on her data sheet, Mrs. Casagrande thought to herself, "Hum-m-. I wonder if I do that, too?" and stored that into her "things to watch for" in her own teaching.

Using technology, the teacher and the observer can view lessons multiple times, even reviewing them together to focus on critical areas. Because the last step of feedback without judgment can be difficult, special development training can be obtained. Both partners must see the process as an honest, trusting, open-minded, self-searching way to improve one's practice. As a professional development activity for a teacher or an entire school, this is an exceptional reflective tool.

Video Conferencing

Video conferencing is an important collaboration tool. Teachers can use video conferencing to share with colleagues in other schools or in other cities. They can talk about the teaching practices that they are doing in their classrooms, describe problems that they may have encountered with students, and find solutions with other teachers. Teachers can use Zoom, Skype, WhatsApp, or HangOuts from Google+ as free connectivity tools. These tools allow teachers to call in or connect through computers in one place for a video conference and share with each other. These moments of sharing are invaluable to novice teachers as they discover that others are there to support them and that they can collaborate together to solve problems in their classrooms.

Mind Mapping

Whether one terms it semantic mapping, concept mapping, or mind mapping, these representations provide visual relationships and connections between a set of ideas and concepts (refer to Figure 14.18). Placing one's thoughts or ideas in a visual form has been shown to aid in developing a deeper understanding of a lesson that one plans to teach as well as to aid in cultivating reflective practices regarding pedagogical instructional decisions (Blackwell & Pepper, 2008). These researchers found a significant difference in the amount of reflection that occurred as related to decisions about instruction between preservice teachers who used concept mapping during lesson planning and those who did not. An analysis of kindergarten teachers' semantic maps by Lim, Cheng, Lam, and Ngan (2003) revealed evidence of reflective thinking

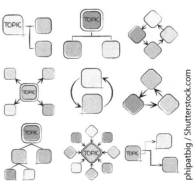

Figure 14.18 Sample mind maps. Additional examples can be found in Figures 14.2, 14.4, and 14.19.

as demonstrated through a change in perspective and attitude, as shown through connections and links in their maps, toward the content and teaching curriculum.

Although these studies focused on the use of mind maps to facilitate lesson planning, the use of such maps can be used in various aspects of teaching, such as classroom management and assessment. Plotting out a behavior management plan or designing a lesson is more easily accomplished through the use of a Web-based concept map tool or software. Electronic mind mapping allows for the addition, subtraction, revision, and/or saving of ideas and topics related to the teaching task at

Coggle	www.coggle.it
Bubbl.us	www.bubbl.us/
Popplet	www.popplet.com/
Gliffy	www.gliffy.com/
Lucidchart	www.lucidchart.com/pages/ usecase/education

Figure 14.19 Web-based Concept Map Tools.

hand. Creating and analyzing one's own sematic map will facilitate reflective practices as the teacher rearranges the map to reveal new understanding. Some mind mapping tools such as Inspiration (www.inspiration.com) and Kidspiration (www.inspiration.com/kidspiration) can be purchased while other programs provide free services with the opportunity to purchase packages with more features. Concept maps can also be created using a graphic organizer with MS Word. Figure 14.19, created with SpiderScribe, lists free mind mapping programs available online.

Using Reflection to Assess and Analyze the Data

In the current climate, in order to prove, support, or request anything such as additional resources for students, a teacher must include in his/her rationale the appropriate data. Collecting data about one's teaching or students' progress is important to gain the big picture about curriculum, assessment, and the quality of the educational experiences of the students. Often, teachers are responsible for collecting important data, submitting reports, and discussing those reports with parents. Since there is a push to show the quantitative (the hard numerical) data, many times the qualitative (descriptive) data and the reflective process of understanding how the data can inform the teacher about his/her own teaching practices are omitted. In the beginning case study when Ms. Tijerina realized that her students did not do well on the mathematical benchmark test, she had some choices to make about her own teaching practices. She could have responded to her students' failures as if it were their fault. Perhaps the students had not studied well or were not listening. Maybe they did not complete the homework assigned the night before. She could have even thrown up her hands and said that her students could not learn the material. Instead, she looked at the test scores to understand exactly *where* they were failing. Technology offers a number of quick ways to determine this information, and, in this case, her district allows her to sign in to reports from the district benchmarks to access this quickly. When she saw that most of the class failed to answer certain questions correctly, she realized that it was her teaching process rather than the students' learning process that needed correcting. She then went to her colleagues (possibly in peer coaching sessions) to discover how she could improve the teaching process. Once she reflected with her colleagues about the lesson (which she could easily do online), she found what was missing and learned what she could do to improve the lesson. Returning to her math class with new plans and ideas about how to reteach the materials, Mrs. Tijerina made a second attempt to create a learning environment where her students would be successful. Once she retaught the materials, she gave them the test again to assess their progress. This reflective practice puts the assessment and evaluation much more solidly on the teaching process. By collecting the data and reflecting on the lesson, Ms. Tijerina was able to pinpoint where the problems were in the learning process.

Teachers can also use reflection on assessments to understand why students are not progressing in the learning process. When teachers meet with content specialists to discuss the progress of their students, they must take into account the stories behind the numerical data. What have they learned about themselves as well as about their students that play a role in the educational process? Assessment in the classroom should encompass formal and informal, formative, and summative assessment. Teachers must reflect on the performance of their students as well as their own performance (from the autobiographical lens as well as from the student lens). An additional assessment at the heart of reflective practices is the student portfolio. Physical portfolios often take space that many teachers do not have, so creating an electronic version of the students' work not only saves space but also allows the portfolios to be easily transported. The teacher can review the portfolio to gauge student progress and ask students to reflect on the artifacts as well. Student feedback can be submitted electronically (in a discussion board, in an online classroom space, or in Dropbox) or as a hard copy. As teachers read the students' reflections, this will inform their own reflections as well about the learning that occurred. Other information about student portfolios can be found in Chapter 11, while information on teacher portfolios (another reflective tool) can be found in Chapter 12.

Conclusion

All teachers, in order to truly be effective, must participate in reflective practices throughout their careers. Part of professional growth includes developing one's skills to reflect during the planning phase, during implementation, and after the lesson or other educationally related incidents. While a main focus of reflective teaching is the lesson, all professional educational interactions and activities should be included in a teacher's reflective practice.

A common misconception is that reflective practice is an individual, isolated task. As we know, teachers spend the greater majority of the school day in isolation from their colleagues; however, a more collaborative nature for reflection is necessary. It is important for teachers, both preservice and inservice, to take into account reflection from various points of view, which include the autobiographical, peer, student, theoretical, and family lenses (see Figure 14.10). Consulting and incorporating feedback from these entities allows for a more thorough reflection; however, collecting such data can be difficult to facilitate. The advent of technological tools such as online classroom spaces, social learning platforms, electronic survey tools, social media sites, and CRSs adds a level of ease to soliciting and collecting data from different entities. Additionally, there is ample accurate information available via the Internet from reputable educational sites that allow preservice and inservice teachers to apply stronger teaching strategies as a result of their reflective practice.

These electronic tools and processes allow teachers the time and venues to develop reflection. Reflective practice is an ongoing practice that teachers need to develop beginning in their preservice training and continuing throughout their years in the classroom. When teacher candidates initially practice reflection in the preservice stages of teaching, they begin to learn the transformative process of their own teaching practice. By utilizing technology tools, such as blogs, journaling, or videos, they capture the teaching experience immediately and accurately. These teachers can then review the experience by themselves or with others to make adjustments or improve the teaching experience through reflective practices.

If teachers truly want to educate the generations of students who will pass through their classrooms, they must incorporate reflective practices as a part of their daily activity. The information gained as a result should inform future action which should, in turn, create stronger educational experiences for their students. The reflective cycle continues endlessly until the teacher steps out of the classroom for the final time with the assurance that he or she has always resolutely sought the best for students.

References

Argyris, C., & Schön, D. (1974). *Theory in practice: Increasing professional effectiveness.* San Francisco, CA: Jossey-Bass.

Brookfield, S. D. (2002). Using the lenses of critically reflective teaching in the community college classroom. *New Directions for Community Colleges, 118,* 31–38.

Brookfield, S. D. (1995). *Becoming a critically reflective teacher.* San Francisco, CA: Jossey-Bass.

Chokshi, A. (2017). *Reflections from 2016–2017.* Retrieved from www.teachereflections.com

Cunningham, D., & Moore, L. (2011). Interacting and communicating with other educators: In J. Nath & M. Cohen (Eds.), *Becoming an EC-6 Teacher in Texas: A study for the Pedagogy and Professional Responsibilities (PPR) in Texas* (pp. 466–497). Belmont, CA: Cengage.

Blackwell, S., & Pepper, K. (2008). The effect of concept mapping on preservice teachers' reflective practices when making pedagogical decisions. *The Journal of Effective Teaching, 8*(2), 77–93.

Danielson, C, & McGreal T. (2000). *Teacher evaluation to enhance professional practice* [e-book]. Alexandria, VA: Association for Supervision and Curriculum Development.

Davis, E. A. (2006). Characterizing productive reflection among preservice elementary teachers: Seeing what matter. *Teaching and Teacher Education, 22,* 281–301.

Dewey, J. (1933). *How we think*. Chicago, IL: Henry Regnery.

Doyran, F. (2013). Reflective journal writing on the way to becoming teachers. *Cypriot Journal of Educational Sciences, 8*(1), 160–168.

DuFour, R. (2004). What is a professional learning community? *Educational Leadership, 61*(8), 6–11.

Dye, B. R. (2007). Reliability of pre-service teachers' coding of teaching videos using a video-analysis tool. Unpublished Master's Thesis, Brigham Young University, Provo, UT

Edutopia. (2014). *Avoiding new teacher burnout*. Retrieved from www.edutopia.org/discussion/avoiding-new-teacher-burnout

Gadawg01. (2014, October 7). *Re: Avoiding new teacher burnout* [Online forum comment]. Retrieved from www.edutopia.org/discussion/avoiding-new-teacher-burnout

Gettinger, M., & Kohler, K. M. (2011). Process-outcome approaches to classroom management and effective teaching. In C. M. Everston & C. S. Weinstein (Eds.), *Handbook of classroom management: Research, practice, and contemporary issues* (pp. 73–95). New York, NY: Routledge.

Greene, M. (1978). *Landscapes of learning*. New York, NY: Teachers College Press.

Greene, M. (1995). *Releasing the imagination: Essays on education, the arts, and social change*. San Francisco, CA: Jossey-Bass.

Harford, J., MacRuaire, G., & McCartan, D. (2010). 'Lights, camera, reflection': Using peer video to promote reflective dialogue among student teachers. *Teacher Development, 14*(1), 57–68.

Heick, T. (2015). *What it means to be a reflective teacher*. Retrieved from www.teachthought.com/pedagogy/the-many-sides-of-reflection-in-teaching

Hord, S. (1997). Professional learning communities: What are they and why are they important? *Issues . . . about Change, 6*(1), 1–8. Retrieved from www.sedl.org/change/issues/issues61/Issues_Vol6_No1_1997.pdf

Kajder, S. B., & Parkes, K. A. (2012). Examining preservice teachers' reflective practice within and across multimodal writing environments. *Journal of Technology and Teacher Education, 20*(3), 229–249.

Killeavy, M., & Moloney, A. (2010). Reflection in a social space: Can blogging support reflective practice for beginning teachers? *Teaching and Teacher Education, 26*, 1070–1076.

Krashen, S. D. (1984). Bilingual education and second language acquisition theory. In California State Department of Education, Office of Bilingual Bicultural Education (Ed.), *Schooling and language minority students: A theoretical framework* (pp. 63–91). Los Angeles, CA: Evaluation, Dissemination and Assessment Center California State University. (ERIC Document Reproduction Service No. ED249773)

Kurtts, S. A., & Levin, B. B. (2000). Using peer coaching with preservice teachers to develop reflective practice and collegial support. *Teaching Education, 11*(3), 297–310.

Lave, J , & Wenger, E. (1991). *Situated learning. Legitimate peripheral participation*. Cambridge, England: Cambridge University Press

Lee. K., & Bret, C. (2013). What are student inservice teachers talking about in their online communities of practice? Investigating student inservice teachers' experiences in a double-layered CoP. *Journal of Technology and Teacher Education, 21*(1), 89–118.

Lim, S. E., Cheng, P. W. C., Lam, M. S., & Ngan, S. F. (2003). Developing reflective and thinking skills by means of semantic mapping strategies in kindergarten teacher education. *Early Child Development and Care, 173*(1), 55–72.

Loughran, J. J. (2002). Effective reflective practice: In search of meaning in learning about teaching. *Journal of Teacher Education, 53*(1), 33–43.

Osterman, K. F., & Kottkamp, R. B. (1993). *Reflective practice for educators: Improving schooling through professional development*. Newbury Park, CA: Corwin Press, Inc.

Provenzano, P. (2014, September 25). *The reflective teacher: Taking a long look* [Online forum comment]. Retrieved from www.edutopia.org/blog/reflective-teacher-taking-long-look-nicholas-provenzano

Rodman, G. J. (2010). Facilitating the teaching-learning process through the reflective engagement of pre-service teachers. Retrieved from www.ro.ecu.edu.au/ajte/vol35/iss2/2/

Salazar, D., Aguirre-Muñoz, Z., Fox, K., & Nuanez-Lucas, L. (2010). On-line professional learning communities: Increasing teacher learning and productivity in isolated rural communities. *Systematics, Cybernetics and Informatics, 8*(4), 1–7.

Schön, D. A. (1983). *The reflective practitioner: How professionals think in action*. New York, NY: Basic Books.

Shoffner, M. (2009). "Because I know how to use it": Integrating technology into preservice English teacher reflective practice. *Contemporary Issues in Technology and Teacher Education, 9*(4), 3he71–391.

Snoeyink, R. (2010). Using video self-analysis to improve the "withitness" of student teachers. *Journal of Digital Learning in Teacher Education, 26*(3), 101–110.

t_ngo. (2016, November 13). *Re: Avoiding new teacher burnout* [Online forum comment]. Retrieved from www.webmail.uhd.edu/owa/redir.aspx?REF=uaVu3U6xrfIH7sMlc6pDr2ZEIa8DbRUw7y4-ao1C0J6C2ylO5bnUCAFodHRwOi8vd3d3LmVkdXRvcGlhLm9yZy9kaXNjdXNzaW9uL2F2b2lkaW5nLW5ldy10ZWFjaGVyLWJ1cm5vdXQ, www.edutopia.org/discussion/avoiding-new-teacher-burnout

Teachthought Staff. (2013). *20 things you can do in (about) 10 minutes for a smoother running classroom.* Retrieved from www.teachthought.com/pedagogy/20-things-you-can-do-in-about-10-minutes-for-a-smoother-running-classroom/

Thomas, J. S. (2016, November 13). *Re: Avoiding new teacher burnout* [Online forum comment]. Retrieved from www.teachthought.com/teaching/20-things-you-can-do-in-about-10-minutes-for-a-smoother-running-classroom www.edutopia.org/discussion/avoiding-new-teacher-burnout

Ward, J. R., & McCotter, S. S. (2004). Reflection as a visible outcome for preservice teachers. *Teaching and Teacher Education, 20*(3), 243–257.

USCRossierOnline. (2017). *Teacher withitness.* Retrieved from www.rossieronline.usc.edu/blog/teacher-withitness

Zeichner, K. M., & Liston, D. P. (1996). *Reflective teaching: An introduction.* Mahwah, NJ: Lawrence Erlbaum Associates.

Chapter 15

Governance and Administration of Technology Use in Schools

Viola M. Garcia - *Professor Emeritus*
University of Houston - Downtown

Meet Ms. Vela

Ms. Vela asked her fourth-grade social studies students to work on a group project. One group approached her about bringing their own technology devices to school to investigate and identify the contributions of people of various racial, ethnic, and religious groups to their state. The teacher is unsure whether the school policy allows this. Further, she does not know if all devices are acceptable or if there is a ban on specific types of devices or Websites. She is puzzled as to how to respond to the students and how to proceed with the unit of instruction.

wavebreakmedia / Shutterstock.com

Governance and Administration of Technology Use in Schools

Technology use in schools is advancing faster than could ever have been imagined—even a decade ago. In order to address the needs of students in an ever-changing school environment, it is important that teachers are familiar with and comply with policies, procedures, and administrative and district practices related to technology use in schools. Teachers should understand and be assured that policies and procedures have been carefully developed with many considerations taken into account to help them and their students (especially with safety issues) (Figure 15.1). Policies also help students and parents know the rules and processes so that they can help teachers successfully integrate instructional technology and implementation opportunities for students in their classrooms.

jurgenfr / Shutterstock.com

Figure 15.1 Beginning teachers must learn about technology governance and policy decisions.

Decision Makers and Decision-Making for District Information Technology

There are a number of issues with which school districts must deal when making decisions about technology: budgeting, instructional and infrastructure needs, piloting, training, safety, repairing/upgrading equipment, and many more (refer to Figure 15.2). To effectively support teaching and learning, one overarching responsibility of school boards, superintendents, and administrative leaders regarding technology integration in schools is to set the expectations for daily implementation and use of technology in schools. Districts' educational technology findings are used in professional development of teachers in educational technology, increasing access to technology in pre K-12 schools, the integration of technology into the K-12 curriculum areas to increase academic success, and students' technology literacy. All of these fall under the umbrella term "technology governance issues." Districts may rely on administrators to deal with many issues or appoint a school technology governance team. Some overreaching questions among many then become: how do superintendents and school board members determine what to purchase, why, and, at what point, and how might some districts determine that the latest "bring your own device" (BYOD) is the most suitable solution? (Figure 15.3)

School leaders should engage administrators, teachers, and content area and technology experts in decisions such as these regarding technology use. In this collective, collaborative process, assessment of needs can be conducted in school districts to review existing technologies and to determine plans for relevant and future technology implementation. It will be every teacher's responsibility to participate during the collection of data and/or, at times, to serve on committees to ensure that good decisions are made about technology for themselves and their learners. Every student will be using technology in the future, and the equipment and training are an extensive investment in that future.

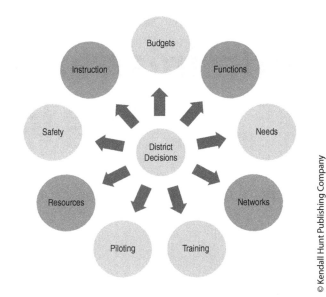

Figure 15.2 Multiple factors are considered in making decisions about technology in a school district.

Figure 15.3 Policies guide teachers when considering "bring your own device" options.

After analyses are conducted (see Figure 15.3), collective recommendations and multiyear action plans can be developed. It is critical that the plans be aligned with instructional needs, strategic plans, and goals and expected learner outcomes that enable teachers to work collaboratively to accomplish the end goal(s). An action plan can then be developed to motivate and promote creativity and cultivate high levels of engagement and commitment to meet the goals of the plan that will lead to teacher and student success.

A teacher's awareness, engagement, and knowledge about the decision-making processes and the district's technology plan help frame his or her decisions about technology use in the classroom.

Information Networks for Decision Makers

Will every teacher be a decision maker for technology use and implementation? At first, perhaps, the beginning teacher will only be responsible for decisions in his or her own classroom. However, there will be a growing responsibility for teachers to become part of school, district, state, and even national efforts to help students attain technology literacy and skills. How will teachers know what decisions must be made and how to judge if the decisions are good ones? District policies and procedures provide guidance to teachers along with state and national standards and those developed by national content area organizations (see Chapter 9 for more).

The Technology Leadership Network (TLN) was founded by the National School Boards Association (NSBA) in 1987 to provide an innovative way for school board members, district administrators, and technology specialists to investigate and have access to best practices shared by school districts across the country so as to make well informed decisions (Technology Leadership Network, 2014). As might be expected, a number of information networks have been created over the years to provide similar resources for decision makers. The Technology Innovation Showcase (www.nsba.org/services/technology-leadership-network/recognition-programs/technology-innovation-showcase) sponsored by NSBA yearly highlights six companies that represent innovative solutions in one of four K-12 areas: teaching and learning, administrative operations, parental outreach, and community engagement (The Technology Innovation Showcase, 2017). Another such resource is Project RED (2017a and 2017b). The national research and advocacy plan, Project RED (Revolutionizing Education), provides technology research, support, and guidance to K-12 institutions. The project's One-to-One Institute mission is to "transform education by personalizing learning through universal access to technology." The focus of the Institute is the implementation of one-to-one technology in K-12 education environments. Project RED resources for education professionals to work through the technology implementation processes are available at www.one-to-oneinstitute.org/other-resources and www.one-to-oneinstitute.org/one-to-one-institute/teacher-professional-learning.

> With the belief that technology can make a substantial impact on schools and students, three research organizations—The Greaves Group, The Hayes Connection, and One-to-One Institute—established Project RED: Revolutionizing Education. Initially, these organizations conducted a national survey of technology programs in 1,000 schools, which is the first and only national research focusing on academic results and the financial implication of education technology. The findings showed that if effectively implemented, technology programs can lead to improved student achievement and significant return on investment (Introducing Project RED, www.projectred.org).

Project RED has provided and archived a number of webinars. These serve superintendents, finance directors, curriculum directors, technology directors, principals, and educators. Some of the seminar topics include: *Financial Implications & Impact of Technology-Transformed Schools, Transformational School Leadership for the Digital Age, Teaching and Learning in the 1:1 Environment, Standards and Curriculum, Device Selection for 1:1,* and *Creating the Appropriate Infrastructure for 1:1.* In addition, resources were created to help district leaders make decisions about technology integration and use in schools. These resources include: (a) the International Society for Technology in Education (ISTE), which serves educators and leaders throughout the world, (b) *Discovery Education* (2018) (www.discoveryeducation.com), which offers a variety of lesson plans and teacher resources (www.discoveryeducation.com/what-we-offer/community/explore-your-community.cfm), and (c) virtual field trips by grade level and subject (www.2.ed.gov/free/index.html; U.S. Department of Education, Office of Planning, Evaluation, and Policy Development [US DOE, 2017]). One of the main purposes of ISTE is to describe the use of technology in classroom settings, regardless of the funding source. Surveys were conducted to determine the availability of computers, the use of technology for instructional and professional activities, and perceived barriers to the use of technology. Resources continue to be developed to provide guidance on technology use to new and practicing educators in schools. These information resources are invaluable to teacher candidates and beginning teachers. When investigating acceptable use policies and related information about the use of technology tools, these resources and many others provide the foundation for teachers' technology integration in instructional planning and implementation.

Policies on the Use of Technology Tools

School policies address a growing number of technology issues that are reviewed periodically and are clearly outlined in faculty, student, and parent handbooks. New teachers should note that such policies are normally accessible to all (often via the district Website). Initial considerations are given to such topics as digital citizenship and responsible use policies by all users, including students, teachers, and administrators. Policies are quite often developed to level the playing field for those students with limited exposure or experience (the Digital Divide, which makes access to technology difficult or impossible for some students and families) with any of the technology devices used in the district. Students' limited familiarity with technology could otherwise be a major stumbling block in technology integration (Figure 15.4). There is also a need to address homebound students and/or student assignments given for after school because some students may not have access to the technology in their home and are put at a great disadvantage when they are not able to complete required assignments. Homework assignments that require Internet research, flipped classroom modes of instruction, and the use of e-textbooks force administrators and teachers to consider issues of equity in a new digital environment. In an effort to equalize opportunities, school districts have forged new relationships with broadband and other Internet service providers. These are critical components in providing cost-effective access for such out-of-school needs. Teachers can be reassured that conversations and collaborations among school district administrators, municipal, county, and state agencies seek to provide technology resources to more students and families. They want to assure: (a) that contractual arrangements and specifications are met, (b) that installation of hardware or connectivity is not disruptive of instructional processes, and (c) that hardware and software technologies are:

- intuitive
- user-friendly
- supported structurally
- supported administratively, and
- supported technologically and:
  - are not cost prohibitive,
  - provide a seamless process for implementation, and
  - have transitions which include plans for impending iterations of upgrades and changes.

Figure 15.4 Limited familiarity with technology may be a stumbling block in technology integration.

Each one of these areas involves important policy considerations with which new teachers must become familiar and which are intended to guide technology-related decisions they make in the classroom, such as the one faced by Ms. Vela in the scenario at the beginning of the chapter.

Policies That Link Technology to School Budgets

With BYOD, which dramatically increases devices tapping into school servers, many districts find their current bandwidth inadequate in supporting students and teachers. Other new teaching and learning devices and applications keep bandwidth demands even higher. In the next few years, the potential of newer devices, such as wearable technology, fitness trackers, and medical devices that students and teachers bring with them, will be even a bigger drain on bandwidth.

"Bandwidth" refers to the channel capacity at which information can be reliably transmitted over a communications channel. The term "bandwidth hog" refers to heavy Internet users who use significantly more bandwidth than other users on the same network. Basically put, "bandwidth hogs" generally download more content than other users. Which do you believe are the biggest "bandwidth hogs" on campus: tablets, mobile phones, or traditional computers? According to a 2017 study conducted by the Association for College and University Technology Advancement (ACUTA) and Association of Colleges and University Housing Officers-International (ACUHO-I), on college campuses, the top bandwidth-consuming devices are desktops and laptops as they are used to access video, audio, and rich media applications (State of ResNet Report, 2017). Smartphones have recently surpassed tablets and rank second in bandwidth-consuming devices. Although the study is the survey result of 360 U.S. colleges and universities, it sheds light on the ever-increasing demands for more bandwidth on campuses.

Because bandwidth is expensive, its budgeting has become one growing area of concern with technology. Many district business administrators experience major concerns for Wi-Fi management budgeting. To address the problem, schools are turning to wide-area network (WAN) optimization technology that classifies Internet traffic and gives certain applications higher priority. Unlike firewalls, which let schools restrict students' access to specific sites, the technology differentiates important cloud application traffic from lower-priority recreational traffic like YouTube to ensure critical applications receive higher priority. This eliminates unnecessary bandwidth costs.

Districts' educational technology findings are used for many different areas of spending that must be considered carefully. Not only does the equipment and software require major research and thought but the support of technology and the professional development of teachers is crucial for increasing access to technology in pre K-12 schools, the integration of technology into the K-12 curriculum, and expanding students' technology literacy.

Many large districts have grant writing offices which support teachers by investigating, organizing, and disseminating information about grant opportunities or funds available for different initiatives, including technology purchases and implementation. Teachers may work with the grant writing expert(s) to submit a funding proposal to acquire monies to support their work. It is not unusual for teachers to write small grant proposals to obtain technology tools necessary to achieve their class goals using such devices as iPads, scientific calculators, projectors, probeware (for science), and so forth. Inasmuch as teachers participate in such initiatives, there are basic technology requirements that the school district must provide. Budgeting and the economics of providing the necessary infrastructure, hardware, software, staff development, and contracts for Internet safety (such as protecting students from cyberbullies, pedophiles, scams, and identify theft) are major costs. These costs need to be considered when planning for teachers and students to access the Web while at school or away from school. Smart budgeting also includes contractual assurances that upgrades, technical support, and security are provided and that upgrades are seamlessly integrated. The overall budget must include apps purchases, updates and access to licensing agreements, software purchases, and considerations for recurring or replacement costs. These are all expensive matters, as are plans for new costs, contingency costs, and pilot costs, which should be reflected in the budget functions of a school district regardless of the size of the district (Figure 15.5).

Then, of course, there is the cost of educator training to enable effective usage that must be folded into the budget. With the initial interest in technology implementation in the United States, the federal role in supporting technology has been relatively consistent to date (US DOE, 2003).

Figure 15.5   The initial costs, recurring costs, contingency costs, and pilot costs of computer hardware and software are reflected in school budgets.

> The vast majority of direct federal funding for educational technology comes from two sources, the E-Rate program and a state formula grant program operated by ED that is dedicated to educational technology. From fiscal years 1997 through 2001, the state formula grant program was known as the Technology Literacy Challenge Fund (TLCF) program; No Child Left Behind, the 2001 reauthorization of the Elementary and Secondary Education Act, replaced the TLCF with the new Educational Technology State Grants (also known as the Enhancing Education through Technology or EETT) program. (p. 3)

Knowledge about sources of funding helps teachers plan for grant writing opportunities (www.tech.ed.gov/funding). A great deal of money for educational technology initially came from the Title I program, as many local districts and schools chose to use their Title I allocations for technology-related expenditures. Analyses of the TLCF program revealed that the percentage of funds to high-poverty districts declined between 1997 and 2000, and this funding is no longer available. An analysis of all E-Rate applications and discount approvals through January 2000 indicated that public schools were the primary recipients of the program, receiving 84% of the discounts. The outlook for public schools continues to look promising as the Federal Communications Commission (2017) increased the cap for the E-rate program to $3.9 billion in funding year 2015. *Federal Funding for Educational Technology and How It Is Used in the Classroom: A Summary of Findings from the Integrated Studies of Educational Technology* (US DOE, 2003) summarizes the three final reports produced by the Integrated Studies of Educational Technology (ISET) (Integrated Studies of Educational Technology et al., 2003).

Findings revealed that:

> Technology is now considered by most educators and parents to be an integral part of providing a high-quality education. There is concern, however, that not all students, particularly students in rural schools or schools with a high percentage of minority or poor students, have equal access to educational technology, both in terms of the availability of equipment and the successful integration of technology into the classroom. (p. 3)

Even though the federal government continues to support technology integration in schools, it is wise for new and experienced teachers to know and learn how to access various available funds and to seek grants to support technology initiatives. These technology resources are highly motivating to students who have grown up using technological devices and who expect to learn via virtual and electronic sources.

Teacher candidates should know about investigating grant and funding opportunities for technology resources so they are prepared as beginning teachers to tap into those resources. This proactive approach gives new teachers the advantage of providing innovative ways to engage students in instructional technology approaches. These are a few technology grant sources available to teachers:

The Universal Service Administrative Company

www.usac.org/sl

Funding Digital Learning, Office of Educational Technology, U. S. Department of Education

www.tech.ed.gov/funding/

Positive Learning

www.positivelearning.com/blog/2016/2/11/7-ways-to-get-funding-and-grants-for-technology-in-your-classroom

DreamBox Learning

www.dreambox.com/blog/technology-grants-for-teachers-for-2016

Policies on Administrative Needs and Functions

There are many other parts of a teaching position that a teacher must carry out besides day-to-day instruction. Some college students may remember that their teachers kept class grades in a spiral or bound grade book which was highly guarded. However, very few teachers today rely on the trusted traditional grade book or attendance rosters. Teachers today rely on electronic management systems to enter grades, attendance, anecdotal records, reports, and many other forms of data. What assurances can teachers expect regarding the integrity of data systems that they rely on for every day work? The security and backup of Web-based portals for data access, data management, and other use have generated sophisticated off-site and cloud-based resources for fail-safe systems and necessary data retrieval. These systems include student data management systems, teacher evaluation portals, parent portals, finance management data sharing systems, energy conservation systems, child nutrition services, transportation services, building maintenance, heating and cooling, and scheduling systems, to name a few. These are just some of the examples of the dependence and sensitivity to complex systems that are electronically managed and, if jeopardized, provide serious limitations to safe and secure settings for the administrative functions required of today's educators.

Instructional technology integration can best be accomplished and used effectively if student data systems and resources are available to teachers and administrators. These resources include but are not limited to hardware, software, and technical support (Figure 15.6). In addition, technology solutions are used to prepare for a variety of administrative and emergency situations. These allow for employees, students, parents, the community, and local law enforcement officials to be notified of emergency situations. These events, including violence that can place schools in a lockdown mode (such as with an

Figure 15.6 Safe and secure settings for the administrative and technology functions are essential.

active shooter situation), also cover weather or other types of disasters, requiring district preparedness that extends well beyond evacuation charts and emergency drills. Good, effective communication and timely response to such emergencies is of paramount importance to minimize potential danger and to ensure the safety of the faculty, staff, students, and the surrounding community. While current modes of texting or email notifications are used, vigilance about future needs and real-time responses are ongoing endeavors for school district administrators and technology specialists and teams to consider. These are but a few examples of the structural and administrative support that teachers receive in an attempt to create a secure environment to do the necessary and important noninstructional requirements of their job. Teacher candidates and beginning teachers can be assured that these safe and secure support systems are continually being reviewed and upgraded by their districts to match current and future threats.

Supporting the Professional Development of Teachers

Imagine being a first-year teacher, or even an experienced teacher, and having your principal announce that teachers are expected to use iPads for all instruction. Or, imagine that students will not be issued textbooks, and they will have to now use e-books. This could be very exciting, but do you know what instructional technology training is available in your district to prepare for such initiatives? How would you find the quickest way to learn to use iPads for instruction? Are there workshops, webinars, one-to-one sessions, or other forms of support? Providing teachers with opportunities to work one-on-one with technology and professional development specialists, master teachers, and support staff is critical to meet new technology integration requirements. This support helps teachers improve their craft so that they, in turn, can best plan for the optimum student learning opportunities.

Instead of a one-size-fits-all workshop model, professional development should encourage teachers to create structures where they participate in developing professional activities that address their own needs and interests (refer to Figure 15.7). It is best if teachers do this in collaboration with school leaders. This type of professional development is most productive and beneficial. Pilot programs are a critical part of setting up successful implementation of technology that allows teachers in school districts to pretest processes, products, software programs, and strategies before their full implementation in school classrooms. This provides for glitches to be resolved and for both teacher and student focus groups to give critical feedback for continuous improvement to meet instructional objectives. Professional development policies must provide teachers time for planning, implementation, assessment, and review of goals, instructional frameworks, and best practices.

A layered approach to technology initiatives not only considers teachers' professional development and school integration but also administrative training (Figure 15.8). Principals, assistant principals, and instructional leaders need to understand the new technology's intended use, the time frames for implementation, and the expected learner outcomes. With this preparation, they can support and guide teachers in these new initiatives. In this way, principals can tap into existing talent at the district level and among teachers to increase support and confidence among reluctant users and to encourage calculated risk-taking among the teacher leaders in their schools to support new initiatives. Bringing employees together at all levels in this training process further supports common goals and their successful implementation.

Figure 15.7 Professional development promotes personal development.

A vital aspect of professional development for teachers to successfully incorporate instructional technology requires adequate time for production and preparation. Some of the techniques, strategies, or resources may take several hours for even an experienced teacher to program, to identify links, to bookmark, practice, upload to the Internet, and so forth. Often, even installing and setting up some software is tedious and time consuming, leading many teachers to avoid technology integration completely. The issue of allowing for time and technical support cannot be overstated in having teachers feel prepared and confident. A good integration plan will proactively schedule for this preparation time.

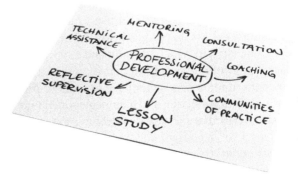

Figure 15.8 A layered approach to professional development.

Ultimately, when talented teachers effectively execute the intended strategic instructional goals and objectives, there can be higher likelihood of student success. When a school district makes the decision to equip students, generally seventh grade and up, with iPads or similar devices (where every student gets his/her own device), the implementation plan must include the preparation of teachers to (a) understand the goals and objectives of the initiative, (b) become familiar and experienced with the tools, and (c) prepare for the intentional, organized, deliberate and focused use of those tools for the instructional and academic growth of students. Faculty development and support of the technology integration plan, as mentioned, should include individualized opportunities for the professional development of teachers. A key component of the successful integration of new initiatives is that an informed, collective workforce (who practices personalized training) promotes successful and supportive student-centered, instructional services.

When a new teacher is presented with innovative technology initiatives by a principal, the teacher should be informed as to where to access the training, how to prepare to implement the new initiative, and what additional training is available to support the students. In addition to training for new initiatives, prospective and new teachers should become familiar with data systems to support effective instructional practices. There are often teachers in each school who are known to be "tech savvy" and with whom others can consult above and beyond the technology specialist. Informal or formal technology committees, where teachers are helping and teaching others, are very productive for schools. Teachers can also take it on themselves to "learn by doing" or simply self-teaching themselves, but resources should always be available when needed.

Connecting Data Systems to the Best Instructional Practices

A strong professional development plan and a technology integration plan must be appropriately aligned with the district's strategic plan and instructional goals and objectives that guide teaching and learning. Alignment produces an environment by which all levels of the school district are strategically organized with its instructional initiatives and provide support before, during, and after implementation of the new or ongoing plans. Even with the best laid plans, adequate resources must be made available. When they are not, teachers' lessons must be adapted accordingly. or technology integration must be reconsidered. Future teachers who practice connecting data systems to instructional practices are prepared to teach because they can systematically link data about their students' strengths and needs to appropriate instructional approaches in a systematic, coherent fashion.

Teacher Training for Use of Student Data Systems

Students primarily use technology to gather, organize, analyze, and report information, but this has not dramatically improved student performance on standardized tests. These findings lead to the conclusion that future efforts should focus on providing students and teachers with increased access to technology along with training in pedagogically sound best practices, including more advanced approaches for technology-based assessment and adaptive instruction. (Davies & West, 2014, p. 841)

How does a teacher know how well students are learning? Luckily, as mentioned above, technology can often help easily collect various types of data through data systems that teachers and district personnel can use to make good instructional decisions, but teachers must know how to collect and use that data. One area in which training and support is most beneficial is in building collaboration and structural designs to support teachers' understanding and use of student progress measures through data collection and data management reviews. A variety of structures that include overarching data management committees, team meetings, and training opportunities help teachers in this regard (Figure 15.9). In these group structures, teachers can refine their knowledge, skills, and/or strategies to approach data gathering, information seeking, and alternate solutions to

Figure 15.9 Teachers can receive guidance on technology use and practices via videoconferencing.

challenging scenarios. Implementing professional opportunities in collaborative environments builds participation and inclusion at all levels to support student success.

Utilizing a management system by which course materials, resources, instructional links, management tools, and content are systematically organized for ease of the teacher's management and the students' use is imperative for implementing best instructional practices. Improving and supporting teaching and teachers' use of instructional technology gives more students informed, adaptable teachers who, in turn, support students to their utmost potential. Measures of effective teaching now include aspects of technology integration and use that include comprehensive measures to support student growth. Many school districts have taken steps to methodically plan, implement, review, reassess, and redesign or redirect important aspects of such data system initiatives and processes that engage teachers at the district and campus levels.

Teachers can be confident that improvements in these management systems continue to occur and to be investigated. A series of reports (US DOE, 2009, 2010, 2011, 2017) by the U.S. Department of Education over the years describes attempts to connect student data management systems and instructional practices. The *Teachers' Ability to Use Data to Inform Instruction: Challenges and Supports* (US DOE, 2011) describes teachers' thinking about data that could guide districts' efforts to provide appropriate initiatives to prepare and support teachers in their expected use of student data as a basis for improving their effectiveness. The findings reveal that while teachers were adept at finding information in a table or graph, corresponding written text provided minor challenges. Difficulties in evaluating written statements about data that required basic mathematical calculations, for example, suggest that teachers may have misconceptions about their students' performance. A promising aspect of the report indicates that the teachers "appeared quite sensitive to the fact that students will do better on a test if they have received instruction on the covered content and had their learning assessed in the same way (e.g., same item format) in the past" (p. x). The *Use of Education Data at the Local Level: From Accountability to Instructional Improvement* (US DOE, 2010) documented a dramatic increase in the proportion of teachers with access to a student data system between 2005 and 2007 and provides a picture along with the *Reimaging the Role of Technology in Education* (2017) of increased local practices in implementing data-driven decision-making provided in the earlier reports. Quite simply, technology can currently provide a way for large amounts of information to be taken on student achievement, but this data is can sometimes be complicated for teachers to understand and apply back to instruction effectively. Helping with this factor should be a part of technology comprehension for which districts prepare teachers.

Important findings in the report include the assertion that data-driven decision-making is an ongoing process. This process is not a one-time event centered on the acquisition of a data system. This supports the thinking about system-wide innovations and long-term strategies as part of a continuous improvement process. Other findings reveal that teachers need data from recently given assessments and diagnostic information on students' learning needs and that the use of this type of data should be a regular part of teachers' practice. Continuing from earlier, this requires that schools provide time for teachers to meet with colleagues to discuss and use data according to the *Use of Education Data at the Local Level: From Accountability to Instructional Improvement* (US DOE, 2010). It is suggested that there be positions that are funded for instructional coaches who help teachers connect data to alternative instructional approaches. Further, the coaches provide modeling of data-driven decision-making for continuous improvement in their own operations.

The development of models of how to connect student data to instructional practices and to enhance teachers' assessment interpretation and data use skills also require time and support. The US DOE 2007 and 2008 reports on *Teachers' Use of Student Data Systems to Improve Instruction* provide evidence of increased teachers' access to and use of data from student data systems through a secondary analysis of data from teachers and district technology coordinators as part of the US DOE National Educational Technology Trends Study (US DOE, 2008). This allows teachers to use these systems to provide information to students and their parents in tracking individual student test scores and monitoring student progress. The *Implementing Data-Informed Decision Making in Schools: Teacher Access, Supports and Use* (US DOE, 2009) report from the U.S. Department of Education draws on case study findings resulting from interviewed district staff members as well as principals, whereby teachers were given a set of scenarios involving hypothetical student data to probe teachers' understanding of student data taken from the U.S. Department of Education's National Educational Technology Trends Study. The findings revealed that even though data systems were used in school improvement efforts, they were having little effect on teachers' daily instructional decisions at times. This was because neither teachers nor administrators were able to see a comprehensive record of students' longitudinal and up-to-date educational experiences and performances. Another important finding is that few of the data systems incorporated resources (such as instructional materials, model lesson plans, and formative assessment results) linked to frameworks and curriculum guides that could provide teachers a more comprehensive process by which to operate. These reports illustrate the progress that continues to be made and the initiatives yet to be incorporated to build more effective and efficient use of data systems intended to improve instruction. Nevertheless, beginning teachers must include time in their busy schedules to understand and receive training on the use of these complex data management systems. Once they learn how to use these systems, they can link data about their students to instructional practices that are most appropriate to their needs.

Mrs. Ash teaches eighth-grade mathematics. She has an average of 25 students in each of her classes, so it seems an overwhelming task at times to know where each of these students is in terms of the concepts. She does know that just teaching lessons "to the middle" or based on how her textbook chapters are arranged is not effective teaching for many students in her classes. Two years ago, her district invested in a data management system that is starting to pay off in helping her to target individual areas of need. District mathematics committees have designed benchmark tests to be given at designated intervals, and the data management system allows teachers to have the scores of each student and each concept quickly in her hands. During the first year, the district provided training on how to use the system, and this year she is able to run her data and understand it. From the beginning of the year, she was able to see the progress of each of her students. She and her grade-level colleagues meet after each benchmark test to generate new strategies to help students who are struggling on the concepts tested. The grade-level committee also asked the district for some blog space so that mathematics teachers throughout the district could communicate and share ideas for improvement. At the semester break, she compares students' scores from last year and is clearly able to see that she is more effective in reaching students with individual needs—because she now has a way to see what those needs are.

Instructional Technology Resources

The members of the graduating classes of the 2030s are mere toddlers today; however, current technology trends which have accelerated since their birth reveal that they will rely only on an address and GPS for directions rather than on maps (see Figure 15.10). They will buy and sell on sites similar to eBay as frequently if not more often than through shops and stores. Their "books," newspapers, classified ads, photo albums, or need for cash will be replaced with personal devices and a variety of online options. In the core areas of English language arts and reading, mathematics, science, and social studies, there are tools and resources already available to expand students' knowledge, skills, and approaches to learning and knowledge-seeking. In the future, these will have expanded in ways that we are not able to articulate today.

A brief summary of existing resources in the core instructional areas provides a hint of what these young learners will encounter in classrooms of the future. Teacher candidates can refer to chapters in this text focused on technology for each of the content areas and for other areas such as English as second language

Figure 15.10 Today, we do not know technological advances that will be available to the class of 2027.

(ESL) (see Figure 15.11), early childhood, and special education for more details. Subsequent sections of this chapter provide a general overview of instructional technology resources currently available in the core content areas. Future teachers should know the instructional technology resources available in the different content areas so that they can engage students in new and creative ways. Future students and their families will have used multiple electronic devices at home, and new teachers should respond to these changing environments because there will be an expectation from parents, students, and the community who will provide jobs to do so.

Figure 15.11 Instructional technology resources are available in all content areas.

Science Resources

In the area of science, electronic opportunities abound to engage students in self-initiated inquiries and discoveries (Figure 15.12). "I'm more interested in arousing enthusiasm in kids than in teaching the facts. The facts may change, but that enthusiasm for exploring the world will remain with them the rest of their lives" are passionate comments attributed to Seymour Simon (Musleah, 1996, para. 4). Simon, author of more than 250 highly acclaimed science books, provides sciences resources and a Website which includes free downloads of materials for educators to use as well as multiple resources for students (www.seymoursimon.com). Monthly newsletters, blogs, books, and electronic resources provide the latest materials.

Figure 15.12 Interactive science resources are readily available for use in today's classrooms.

General science technology tools, tools for instruction in chemistry, biology, physics, environmental and earth science, space astronomy and astrophysics, and medicine and nanoscience are bountiful (refer to Figure 15.13 for an example). These go beyond YouTube channels and apps which already provide virtual labs, simulations, digital libraries, short films, and scientific lectures. There are many other resources via iPads and Chrome books on topics from science, technology, engineering, mathematics (STEM) to gaming (Edtechteacher, 2018) (www.edtechteacher. org/tools/science). The National Institutes of Health (www.sis.nlm.nih.gov/outreach/k12.html), National Science Teachers Association (www.nsta.org/publications/ freebies.aspx), and the National Education Association (www.nea.org/tools/lessons/stem-resources.html) are a few helpful science resources for K–12 teachers. See many more suggestions in Chapter 3 of this book.

Figure 15.13 Thermometers for science experiments can be preprogrammed.

Social Studies Resources

Even though WebQuests are currently popular resources (as are virtual trips to countries and historical sites students are studying), using the Internet to research a country and/or historical sites is commonplace in the area of social studies. There has been an explosion of online search engines and databases such as The Library of Congress (www.loc.gov/teachers) and the National Archives (www.archives.gov/education), which have databases that center around American history and culture. Provisions for expanded communication options for teachers and students include the use of podcasts by which students could use iPods to create radiocasts of information they research. They use blogs to host online discussions to respond to other teachers or students and their discussion questions. Pen Pals is a hallmark social studies tool long used to help students understand and engage with other cultures. Reliance on a postal service and communication via "snail mail" letters has been replaced with the use of email with students in a country, region, or area that students are studying. Refer to Figure 15.14 for an example of how, by communicating via email and social network sites, social studies students could render aid to people recovering from natural disasters. This traditional mode of exploration and understanding is likely to be replaced by video and virtual experiences. These methods allow students to ask questions firsthand and to "experience" the culture through someone their own age. Videoconferencing that allows students to talk with experts or a guest speaker provide real learning opportunities. Teachers can facilitate and plan for these rich activities. They should check school policies or with the principal about enabling the use of necessary technologies, planning for the experiences, and supporting students with additional resources they may need. This happens during exciting lessons but also far prior to that in technology planning committees, training, and so forth to support today's teachers with these types of technological capabilities. More resources are available in Chapter 2 for social studies.

Figure 15.14   Social studies students could render aid to people recovering from hurricanes or other disasters.

English Language Arts and Reading Resources

In the area of English language arts and reading, opportunities via e-textbooks, adaptive reading sites which provide leveled books, and so forth promote student development to grow into more difficult texts as they become better readers and writers. These tools, which often contain graphics, video, sound, and animation, allow teachers to provide differentiated instruction to an ever-changing population of students with more diverse needs and interests. Other resources include the use of text-reading software. Teachers with students who have special needs and English language learners will want to provide opportunities for students to "hear" the written word or to use the translation options to optimize language acquisition for non-English speakers. These tools are also beneficial for students who may experience a lag in language development. Other helpful tools allow for creations of story boards, the use of interactive libraries, dictionaries, word play and phonics-based games, opportunities for read alouds, online language arts games, grammar and letter writing resources, vocabulary development games and activities, and fluency and comprehension resources. Technology resources in this content area can be used to accommodate students with learning disabilities, English language learners, different learning styles, and variations in student interests and academic performance. The teachers who interact with colleagues, attend training, and commit to staying current technologically will be able to provide such resources for their students. For more ideas, see Chapter 1 for literacy, Chapter 6 for special education, and Chapter 7 for ESL.

Mathematics Resources

The National Council of Teachers of Mathematics (NCTM) (2018) notes in its position on the role of technology in the teaching and learning of mathematics that "It is essential that teachers and students have regular access to technologies that support and advance mathematical sense making, reasoning, problem solving, and communication" (para. 1). The organization highlights the increasing importance of statistics, modeling, and discrete mathematics and the need to update curriculum pathways to prepare students mathematically for their futures. There are many mathematics resources for teachers, students, and parents—for both elementary mathematics and advanced mathematics. A site such as "The Math Forum" (www.mathforum.org/library) is an example of the tutoring and support system that provides students fast and easy ways to find answers to questions. From the elementary assistance provided by such Websites as *Learn Your Tables* (www.learnyourtimestables.com) to the more sophisticated free online scientific calculators for complex calculations, technology resources are plentiful in this content area. Online magazines and publications provide mathematics-related news articles, podcasts, and mathematics puzzles designed along "real-life" scenarios (see Figure 15.15). There are numerous interactive Websites that allow students to practice and find solutions to difficult problems (Figure 15.16). These Websites provide step-by-step solutions that help students learn and understand how to solve mathematical problems. Some include PBS (www.pbslearningmedia.org), mathematics lessons online, *All About Fractions, Math is Fun, FunBrain Math Practice and Challenges, JAVA Flash Cards,*

Money Sense Problems, PBS LearningMedia for Students (2018) (www.pbslm.lunchbox.pbs.org/student-experience), and videos from Khan academy to name a few. Students' ability to learn on demand or as needed will be greatly enhanced by enriched resources that are illustrated and already available.

Finding Other Resources for Content and Technology

Many content areas or general teaching organizations have conferences and newsletters that almost always include ideas for technology integration (refer to Figure 15.17). There are also conferences strictly for teaching with technology that are often geared for both classroom and university teachers. These face-to-face or online conferences often provide exciting demonstrations. Some districts will fund membership fees and travel to these regional, state, national, and international conferences. New teachers should take full advantage of these opportunities whenever possible.

Figure 15.15 Teacher candidates should subscribe to educator resources on the use of technology.

Online Learning

New teachers should be aware of the possibility that they may either be required to use online management systems or teach online and/or flipped classes in the future. These initiatives, when supported by district administrators, provide exciting opportunities for teachers to expand their reach to students outside their own classroom. Auyeung (2004) explains that both students and teachers benefit from a virtual environment in which they exchange ideas, views, and comments. Blackboard Learn technology, for example, uses communication tools such as Discussion, Email, Course Portfolios, Wikis, and Chat capabilities. These provide a variety of options for the organizational needs and internal and external communication within a school or within a school system. The Blackboard tracking tools assess whether the tools and content are used and how they are used. Teachers can see the frequency and entry points by which particular resources are used by students. The teacher can then use this analysis for future development of coursework in targeted and strategic ways that promote and facilitate communication and collaboration. Teachers, schools, and school systems can establish an online presence: (a) to post critical information, (b) to conduct online surveys and dialogues, (c) to elicit critical information from the teachers and students about how the programs are going, and (d) to share educational

Figure 15.16   Student engagement and curiosity is increased with technology resources.

Figure 15.17   Networking meetings and conferences allow teachers to share ideas about technology integration.

insights and strategies to improve programs and collaborative relationships. This existing management technology has the capacity to transform every aspect of a school's mission, goals, and objectives. As an example, opportunities for online professional development abound, as do educational applications to improve programmatic initiatives.

While Web-based instruction has been more ubiquitous in higher education institutions than in public education, states have initiated online or virtual networks and classrooms to meet the varied needs of small, rural, and financially challenged school districts or homebound students. While public schools can learn from the work in higher education, caution is required in generalizing to the K-12 population because the results are, for the most part, based on studies in other settings (e.g., medical training, higher education). Regarding virtual networks, the Levin *(2016) U.S. K-12 Educational Technology Policy: Historical Notes on the Federal Role* reveals that the *Enhancing*

Education Through Technology program is among one of the largest federal programs seeking to improve student achievement through the use of technology. This program is funded by the federal government, and this report supports the relationship between state educational technology program activities and the overarching goals and purposes of the No Child Left Behind Act of 2001 (2018). Findings in the report indicate that many states have technology standards for teachers that specify the knowledge and skills that teachers need for using technology for both administrative and instructional purposes. Both teacher and student preparedness to use technology cannot be minimized in future endeavors to expand virtual or online options for teaching and learning.

Learning Management Systems

One new technology initiative in schools is the introduction of learning management systems (LMS). Popularized in higher education by companies such as Blackboard and Canvas, LMS software companies are now working their way into K-12 to provide educators with a digital space for classroom activities—from documentation and tracking of student learning to the delivery of online teacher professional development. Among the LMS leaders that are slowly carving out a place in K-12 are Epsilen, Moodle, Cornerstone, Eduphobia, CourseNetworking, Agilix, and Desire2Learn.

AISD's Inspirit Project

Arthur Independent School District (AISD), one of the largest school districts in the nation, has recently received a multimillion-dollar grant to renovate its technology infrastructure. AISD has launched Inspirit to provide resources so that all two hundred of their schools create a personalized learning environment online for the twenty-first-century learners. The Inspirit Project also enables teachers to effectively facilitate instruction, manage curriculum, collaborate with their peers, and engage today's digitally wired students through one digital learning platform.

In a public announcement, AISD explains that this comprehensive initiative has three main drivers.

About the Inspirit LMS

As part of the **Inspirit Project, AISD** has launched a K-12 digital learning platform, the **Inspirit LMS,** that will eventually become the center of collaboration, personalization, curriculum, instruction, and communication for all HISD staff, students, and parents.

What is a digital learning platform?

A digital learning platform is an online software environment that can be used by educators and students to give everyone involved in education the information, digital tools, and resources that they need to learn together, both inside and outside the classroom.

How will the Inspirit LMS benefit teachers?

The Inspirit LMS helps AISD teachers manage time more effectively and personalize instruction for students. Teachers find that many of the routine tasks they do every day—from planning and delivering coursework to assessing and reporting student progress—are automated. Inspirit LMS also makes it easier for them to share resources with colleagues and students and develop multimedia instruction.

How will the Inspirit LMS benefit students?

To succeed in today's global workforce, students should be exposed to the technology, resources, and tools they will use in the real world. The Inspirit LMS allows students 24/7 access to instructional material, coursework, and digital textbooks from any device—on campus or away from campus. With the Inspirit, students have a safe space for independent learning, options to submit homework and projects, the ability to collaborate and communicate with classmates, and the ability to reflect on their learning through blogs, discussion boards, and e-portfolios.

"Some parents just don't understand what qualifies as an urgent question and what does *not*."

Mr. Watkins (a fourth-grade teacher) heard his phone ring while he was in church on Sunday morning. After running outside to answer the call, he found that it was Ian's father who asked what Ian should bring to the field trip next week. Ian's father thought it was an "urgent" call, because he was planning to go to the grocery store in the afternoon to pick up a few items that Ian might need to bring on the trip.

Ellie's mother called Mr. Watkins at 10:30 on Tuesday night to ask if Ellie should have done the fiction or fact worksheet in Chapter 3 in the reading workbook. He received several more calls from parents in the next few days–even late into the evening and early in the morning before school.

The school district has just redesigned the school's homepage. One major difference is that teachers' contact information, which used to be easily accessible through the "faculty" tab, was moved to another page that many parents could not find. Because of the change, Mr. Watkins ended up having to answer many phone calls on his personal cell phone on his time away from school. He regretted giving out his personal mobile phone number during the "meet the teacher" night at the beginning of the school year.

Mr. Watkins described this situation to the technology specialist and was advised that he should try out Remind. Using a parent communication app can be a great solution for protecting teachers' privacy while keeping parent emails and messages organized. Two of the most popular communication apps for teachers are Bloomz (bloomz.net) and Remind (remind.com).

Independent organizations such as iKeepSafe (www.ikeepsafe.org) help certify that companies like Remind are demonstrating compliance with federal and state-specific laws for student data privacy. The certifications they give to products, such as the iKeepSafeCOPPA Safe Harbor badge, iKeepSafeFERPA badge, and iKeepSafe California Student Badge make it easier for schools to navigate those laws and make the best decisions. This facilitates school districts in signing up for their teachers to use parent communication apps. This means that the days have passed when teachers were limited to weekly backpack notes and a shared phone in the office for the activity notification and student issues. Teachers in current times have connected with parents on their smartphones, but that has raised the kind of inconveniences that Mr. Watkins has experienced.

The next semester Mr. Watkins made the sign-up process for his new app part of "meet the teacher" night in the first week to ensure that parents and students are onboard. After implementing Remind, Mr. Watkins found that getting students and parents signed up takes very little time because Remind gives a specific code for students and parents that can be used to join the class of a particular teacher. Both Bloomz and Remind are efficient when teachers need to send out group messages. Both apps (available for Android and on iPhone systems) also keep teachers' private information secured. Among other features, at the beginning of the school year teachers can upload student information and schedule when to send out announcements through desktop computers on both Bloomz and Remind in advance.

Even a number of popular textbook publishers and assessment creators have also entered the LMS arena, creating a variety of options for schools to choose from. For example, Pearson's SuccessNet offers digital instruction resources and assessments as an alternative to the curriculum the company is already producing in hard copy. SuccessNet offers less features than a typical LMS, as it simply has resources and assessments, but currently lacks the tracking and documentation aspect that makes many LMS platforms so popular. Pearson also offers SuccessNet Plus, a more traditional LMS. SuccessNet Plus has all of SuccessNet's features with the addition of planning, instruction, and tracking programs, as can be found in most traditional LMSs. Additionally,

Pearson offers an Online Learning Exchange (OLE) feature that helps teachers connect to subject-specific media, documents, and other resources that can supplement curriculum. Pricing of publishers' LMS can be either based by per student or per building.

While LMS platforms are typically purchased for entire schools, teachers can sign up for a free solo account that gives them training classes and a few gigabytes (GBs) of storage. Since most teacher candidates already have experiences using LMS through their teacher training years in colleges or other programs, it is usually not difficult for them to transition from the student's role in an LMS system to that of a teacher.

Implications for Future Practice

To keep up with the quickly changing needs and requirements of technological innovations in schools, teacher preparation programs and school districts need to support teachers in new initiatives. Students in future classrooms will be no less inquisitive or creative than students in former years; however, technological tools will allow administrators and teachers to inspire and motivate student learning through creative uses of technology resources. Teachers will continue to blend content knowledge and pedagogical knowledge, but they will have access to electronic forms of assessment and record keeping to design and create learning experiences to maximize learning, skills, attitudes, and knowledge creation. It will be important for teachers to model and demonstrate confidence in the use of digital age tools that support research and learning. An understanding of district policies will guide teachers and students in the use of digital resources in such a way that they are used

Figure 15.18   Teachers participate in communities of learning to develop their own technology skills.

appropriately and that they promote learning and collaboration. All educators should aspire to grow professionally in the use of digital tools and resources and participate in communities of learning to develop their own technology skills (refer to Figure 15.18 to see that participating in a webinar is a way to participate in a community of learning). Our future, and the future for young people, depends on the enthusiasm of educators to embrace educational technology in its many facets to inspire connected learners.

References

Activities with rigor and coherence—ARCs. (2018). Retrieved from www.nctm.org/ARCs

Auyeung, L. H. (2004). Building a collaborative online learning community: A case study in Hong Kong. *Journal of Educational Computing Research, 3*(2), 119–136.

Davies, R. S., & West, R. E. (2014). Technology integration in schools. In J. M. Spector, M. D. Merrill, J. Elen, & M. J. Bishop (Eds.), *Handbook of research on educational communications and technology* (pp. 841–853). New York, NY: Springer.

Federal Communications Commission. (2017). FAQs on E-rate program for schools and libraries. Retrieved from www.fcc.gov/consumers/guides/universal-service-program-schools-and-libraries-e-rate

Integrated Studies of Educational Technology. (2003). *Federal funding for educational technology and how it is used in the Classroom: A summary of findings from the integrated studies of educational technology.* U.S. Department of Education, Office of the Under Secretary, Policy and Program Studies Service. Washington, DC.

Levin, D. (2016) *U.S. K-12 Educational technology policy: Historical notes on the federal role.* Retrieved from www.edtechstrategies.com/blog/federal-history

Musleah, R. (1996). Unveiling the panorama of the universe for young learners. Retrieved from www.nytimes.com/1996/02/18/nyregion/unveiling-the-panoramas-of-the-universe-for-young-readers.html

National Council of Teachers of Mathematics. (2018). NCTM Position. Retrieved from www.nctm.org/Standards-and-Positions/Position-Statements/Strategic-Use-of-Technology-in-Teaching-and-Learning-Mathematics

The No Child Left Behind Act of 2001. (2018). Retrieved from www2.ed.gov/nclb/overview/intro/execsumm.pdf

Project RED. (2017a). *One-to-One Institute Web site.* Retrieved from www.one-to-oneinstitute.org/introducing-project-red

Project RED. (2017b). *Revolutionizing education.* The Greaves Group, The Hayes Connection, One-to-One Institute Web site. Retrieved from www.projectred.org

Reimaging the role of technology in education. (2017). U.S. Department of Education Technology Plan Update. Retrieved from www.tech.ed.gov/netp

State of ResNet Report. (2017). Retrieved from www.acuta.org/ACUTA/Member_Services/ResNet_Survey/ACUTA/MemberServices/ResNet_Survey.aspx?hkey=8c787ad7-6a85-4a23-9b8d-37dc26685a41

Technology Leadership Network. (2014). www.nsba.org/services/technology-leadership-network. Reproduced with permission. Copyright © 2014, National School Boards Association.

Technology Leadership Network. (2018). National School Board Association. Retrieved from www.nsba.org/services/technology-leadership-network

U.S. Department of Education (2003). Federal funding for educational technology and how it is used in the classroom: A summary of findings from the integrated studies of educational technology. Office of the Under Secretary, Policy and Program Studies Service. Washington, DC.

U.S. Department of Education: Technology Plan Update. (2017). Retrieved from www.tech.ed.gov/files/2017/01/NETP17.pdf

U.S. Department of Education, Office of Planning, Evaluation and Policy Development. (2008). *National educational technology trends study: Local-level data summary.* Washington, DC: Author.

U.S. Department of Education, Office of Planning, Evaluation and Policy Development. (2009). *Implementing data-informed decision making in schools: Teacher access, supports and use.* Washington, DC: Author.

U.S. Department of Education, Office of Planning, Evaluation, and Policy Development. (2010). *Use of education data at the local level from accountability to instructional improvement.* Washington, DC: Author.

U.S. Department of Education, Office of Planning, Evaluation and Policy Development. (2011). *Teachers' ability to use data to inform instruction: Challenges and supports.* Washington, DC: Author.

U.S. Department of Education, Office of Planning, Evaluation and Policy Development. (2017). *Federal Resources for Educational Excellence.* Retrieved from www2.ed.gov/free/index.html

Part III
Technology Supporting Educational Psychology and Culturally Responsive Teaching

Meeting the Cognitive, Behavioral, and Social-Emotional Needs of Students Through the Use of Technology in the Classroom

C. Matthew Fugate and Franklin S. Allaire
University of Houston - Downtown

Meet Mrs. Soliz

Mrs. Soliz is a second-year, third-grade teacher. As is often the case with new teachers, she felt that her first year had provided her with many unexpected challenges. However, she was able to successfully meet those challenges and now feels more comfortable and confident as she begins her second school year. One of the things that she wants to focus on this year is how to better integrate technology tools and strategies that will support the cognitive, behavioral, and social-emotional needs of the students in her classroom. Although she understands the importance of connecting instructional strategies and experiences to the lives of her students, she is uncertain as to how to take the long-standing principles of developmental and educational psychology and present them in ways that will match the technology interests of the learners in her classroom.

mimagephotography / Shutterstock.com

Educational psychology is the study of teaching and learning. Because so much of what preservice teachers experience in education preparation programs involves specifics related to methods of teaching within the content areas, it can be difficult to grasp the fact that in educational psychology, there are no set of "absolutes" for individual learners or a specific class. When discussing issues such as teaching, learning, student motivation, emotional well-being, and other behaviors, there are *many* tools for teachers to employ that have potential to work, but there is no one predetermined magic answer that can provide an exact set of guidelines that direct a teacher to "do this, not that." Rather, the purpose of studying psychology related to education is to build an extensive understanding of the principles of how students develop *intellectually*, *behaviorally*, and *social-emotionally* through the learning experiences in which they are engaged—all with a knowledgeable teacher's support. More specifically, understanding the educational psychology behind teaching and learning, "[gives] educators the information they need to think critically about their craft and make teaching decisions that will work for their students" (Slavin, 2018, p. 4). Educational theories generated over many years of research can provide teachers with sound ideas that have a high probability of working, but because each learner and each teacher is an individual and each learning situation can be a bit different, a teacher who is equipped with a wide range of theories of learning is more apt to be able to make a match that is productive.

The principles of educational psychology can be traced back to the works of Plato and Aristotle who saw knowledge and understanding as traits that could be enhanced through learning experiences, interactions with others, and maturation (Grinder, 1989). This philosophy of learning has been expanded upon throughout the generations into the modern-day theories of cognitive, behavioral, and social-emotional development derived from educational theorists such as Jean Piaget, Lev Vygotsky, B. F. Skinner, and numerous others who have provided us with the foundations for understanding how students learn and the importance of being a knowledgeable and "intentional" teacher. Indeed, in their 2000 report, the National Research Council stressed that

> Children need opportunities to initiate activities and follow their interests, but teachers are not passive during these [child-] initiated and directed activities. Similarly, children should be actively engaged and responsive during teacher-initiated and -directed activities. Good teachers help support the child's learning in both activities. (pp. 8–9)

To support this position, researchers such as Epstein (2009) highlighted several characteristics of intentional teaching that support both student-directed and teacher-directed activities. In essence, the intentional teacher establishes a classroom environment in which students' interests are valued and respected while providing them with opportunities to expand upon those interests in a safe and supportive setting where setbacks are viewed as additional opportunities for learning and growth.

Twenty-First-Century Skills

It is estimated that as many as 5 million K–12 students participated in some form of online and/or virtual learning experience during the 2015–2016 school year (Besnoy, 2017)—a trend that will likely increase with time. Additionally, continued advancements in technology have increased the need for people to have the ability to create, innovate, and design as "traditional 'strong-back' jobs [are being] replaced by 'strong-mind' careers" (Slavin, 2018, p. 9). Further, there will be very few jobs or daily living tasks in the future that do not require some technological knowledge. As a result, the ability to work collaboratively and work with technology is more important than ever and requires that students be provided more opportunities to interact with technologies that support collaboration, problem-solving, and critical and creative thinking skills. Innovations in social media have addressed these needs by breaking down the four walls of the classroom and allowing students from different cities, states, and countries to work together in real time. While many teachers may be digital immigrants, the students in their classrooms are digital natives. The vast majority of today's students have never known a world without smartphones, tablets, and the integration of the Internet in their everyday lives. In addition to their almost innate understanding of technology tools, the proliferation of social media has created a population of students who are "wired" for the twenty-first-century classroom. Therefore, it is important that teachers capitalize on these skills to address the many needs of the students and of the world that they inhabit.

Motivation

To be successful in this new educational landscape, the twenty-first-century student needs to be an independent learner, computer literate, an effective communicator, and interested in online/technology-based learning experiences (Slavin, 2018). There are several advantages to these types of learning experiences, including increased options for self-paced, independent learning that breaks down the barriers of the classroom and allows students the freedom to work from locations outside of the traditional school setting. The skills required to do so are not, however, innate. They require training and support, particularly for those students who may perform better in a face-to-face environment, lack the necessary skills to communicate effectively in an online environment, and/or lack effective time-management skills.

Integral to this acquisition of skills is student motivation—the internal process that activates, guides, and maintains behaviors over time. Simply put, for a student to learn and acquire new skills, he or she must be motivated and interested to do so. This motivation may come in one of two forms: *extrinsic*, which relies on external factors such as rewards, social pressure, and/or punishment; or *intrinsic*, which relies on internal, personal factors such as needs, interests, and/or curiosity. It is important to note that it is impossible to tell just by looking at a student whether (s)he is being extrinsically or intrinsically motivated. Students can internalize and externalize their causes for motivation; therefore, these tendencies are independent of one another, and, at any given time, a student may be motivated by some of each. A perceptive teacher should determine what various technologies spark which type of motivation in his or her students.

Technology Instruction to Support Cognitive, Behavioral, and Social-Emotional Development

Technology-centered learning experiences might be classified into three categories—with technology functioning as a (1) replacement, (2) amplification, or (3) transformation of the pedagogy (Hughes, 2005). It is tempting to integrate technology into any curriculum "just because"; however, doing so can often lead to frustration for both teachers and students. Teachers must always remember their own experiences when technology for them has been both exhilarating and/or frustrating so that they can relate to students' experiences. Technology is a strategic tool in the teachers' toolkit, and professional discretion should be used when choosing what technology to use with students and how it is presented and employed in learning situations.

Like any strategy, teachers need to consider several key factors before integrating technology into their classrooms. These include, but are not limited to: (1) purpose [What will this technology do for my students and my teaching? What impact do I want this technology to have on learning and student success?]; (2) teacher/parent/student comfort level [Am I comfortable using this technology? How much training will my students and parents require to use this technology effectively?]; (3) access [How much access do I have to this technology in my school? Do my students have access to this technology outside of my classroom?]; and (4) age-appropriateness [Is this technology appropriate for the ages of my students? Is this technology appropriate for the abilities of my students?].

In this chapter, we have chosen three modalities through which to explore the intersection of technology-integrated pedagogy and principles of educational psychology: (1) the flipped classroom, (2) digital storytelling, and (3) social media/networking integration. These technologies can be used independently or collectively to replace, amplify, or transform traditional teaching strategies and learning experiences to create an environment that fosters and emphasizes twenty-first-century skills of collaboration and creative and critical thinking.

Flipped Classroom

The flipped (or inverted) classroom is a pedagogical approach to instruction in which lessons and/or materials are uploaded and accessed by students on the Internet instead of being presented in the classroom. This strategy has emerged as an extremely popular, technology-infused model and is the subject of a growing body of educational research (Talbert, 2016). Growth in the flipped learning model has been due, in part, to increases in technology-literate educators, professional development and support networks, and the emergence of smartphones as one of the ubiquitous pieces of technology that both K–12 students and teachers access on a regular basis (Jensen, Kummer, & Godoy, 2015; Kim, Kim, Khera, & Getman, 2014; Strayer, 2012). By having students review materials online before class as an introduction and after class for review, in-class time can be used for activities and discussions. The Flipped Learning Network (www.flippedlearning.org), with more than 12,000 educator members, notes that the "resulting group space (classroom) is transformed into a dynamic, interactive learning environment where the educator guides students as they apply concepts and engage creatively in subject matter." Effective use of the flipped classroom can address factual, conceptual, and metacognitive knowledge described in Bloom's revised taxonomy of learning (Milman, 2012). Additionally, when properly structured, flipped classrooms can positively impact cooperation between students, innovation, in-class student/teacher interactions, and higher-order thinking skills (Kim et al., 2014; Strayer, 2012). Review the Flipped Classroom section of Chapter 3 in this book for the *Nine Design Principles for Flipped Classrooms* suggested by Kim et al. (2014).

Digital Storytelling

Advances in the availability of low-cost, technologically advanced, and user-friendly digital cameras and photo/video editing tools have the potential to influence educational practices. K–12 educators are taking advantage of these advancements, in addition to the proliferation of smartphones, tablets, and laptops in schools by enhancing or transforming lessons through digital storytelling. Digital storytelling is a strategy that applies twenty-first-century technology to go beyond traditional storytelling using digital graphics, images, videos, and music along with the students' own voice. Online resources such as the Center for Digital Storytelling-Storycenter (www.storycenter.org), Digital Underground Storytelling for Youth (DUSTY; www.dustyotec.weebly.com), and Storybird (www.storybird.com) offer various levels of professional development, strategies, recommendations, and support for teachers interested in using digital storytelling with their students. The Center for Digital Storytelling (2005), a nonprofit community arts organization, offered seven elements for digital storytelling to guide those interested in creating and sharing personal narratives (see textbox). Effective use of digital storytelling has many benefits, including generating student motivation, enhancing creative thinking, improving concentration, facilitating student collaboration, enhancing student organization of ideas, breaking down complicated topics, helping students comprehend complex content, and allowing students and teachers to present content in meaningful and adaptive ways (Barrett, 2006; Malita & Martin, 2010; Robin, 2008; Yang & Wu, 2012).

Seven Elements for Digital Storytelling

- *Point of view*: What is the main point of the story and what is the perspective of the author?
- *A dramatic question*: A key question that keeps the viewer's attention and will be answered by the end of the story.
- *Emotional content*: Serious issues that come alive in a personal and powerful way and connects the story to the audience.
- *The gift of your voice*: A way to personalize the story to help the audience understand the context.
- *The power of the soundtrack*: Music and/or other sounds that support and embellish the storyline.
- *Economy*: Use just enough content to tell the story without overloading the viewer.
- *Pacing*: The rhythm of the story and how slowly or quickly it progresses.

Source: The Center for Digital Storytelling. (2005). Retrieved from www.digitalstorytelling.coe.uh.edu/page.cfm?id=27&cid=27&sublinkid=31

Social Media

Social media is no longer in its infancy and has become an essential part of our day-to-day lives. The dramatic increase in social media use, particularly among K–12 and college/university students, has been fueled by increased access to high-speed Internet connectivity, advancements in smartphone and tablet technologies, and the proliferation of social media-based applications (Freeman, 2016; Nielsen Company, 2012, 2016). The Pew

Internet Project (2016), an initiative of the Pew Research Center that has studied the use of social media sites since 2007, has found that 86% of 18- to 29-year olds who regularly engaged online also used social networking sites. These researchers identified Facebook, Instagram, and Twitter as the top three networking platforms with 76%, 51%, and 42% of users, respectively, using these sites on a daily basis.

Advocates for the use of social media in educational settings point to increased opportunities to expand learning beyond the classroom and connect students with people and events around the world in new and meaningful ways. The use of social media sites as educational tools has the potential to build a community of learners, while simultaneously addressing students' digital nativity as highly connected, creative, and collectively-oriented individuals. It can also serve as a pedagogical approach that creates and supports social and situational constructed learning environments (Freeman, 2016; Friesen & Lowe, 2011; Tess, 2013).

The Children's Online Privacy Act (COPRA) prevents Websites from collecting private information about children under the age of 13 without their parent's permission. However, a 2010 study by the Kaiser Family Foundation study found that 75% of seventh through twelfth graders surveyed reported having a social media profile (Rideout, Foehr, & Roberts, 2010). Obviously, students want to be on social media and will find ways to access it. Due to safety and privacy concerns, some schools and districts are prohibiting the use of particular social media outlets such as Facebook and Twitter and recommending using sites such as Edmodo, Blackboard, Seesaw, and Google Classroom. For example, the Texas Education Agency TEA has a Social Media Training Module with specific language in its Educators' Code of Ethics that addresses teacher/student contact through social media (Standard 3.9). Although social media is to be discussed as a motivating instructional tool, consultation with school and/or district administrators before using social media with students is highly recommended.

To provide some focus, this chapter is divided into three sections, starting with cognitive, then behavioral, and finally social-emotional development. Each of these sections provides background and general principles of these areas of psychology grounded in the literature. This is followed by explanations of how each of the three strategies—flipped classroom, digital storytelling, and social media—can be used by teachers to address the needs of their students.

Using Technology to Support Cognitive Development

"The demands made on our cognitive system by the technology surrounding us changes at an alarming rate and to function effectively in today's society, we have to keep up with these developments and adapt our ways of thinking" noted Taylor (2005, p. 12). Indeed, we are living in an age where the learners of today only know a world of mobile technology and where their access to information is as easy as reaching into their pockets or bags and pulling out their smartphones. This instant access has a direct effect on how children live and communicate in their daily lives. A 2015 study by Common Sense Media found that children ages 8 to 12 years old spend an average of 6 hours per day interacting with technology, *excluding* the time spent with technology for school and homework. That amount of time increased to an average of 9 hours per day for children 13 to 18 years of age. Therefore, it is important to understand what this increased dependency and proliferation of technology has on the cognitive development of today's students. However, to do so, we must first have an understanding of some basic foundations of cognitive development in education.

Constructivist Learning

Jean Piaget (1896–1980), one of the pioneers of cognitive development, is also one of education's most unlikely influencers. A biologist by training, Piaget began to observe his own three children, noting the differences in the ways that they thought about and interacted with the world around them. Through detailed observations as they grew and developed, Piaget identified four distinct stages of cognitive development associated with approximate ranges in age—each characterized by the emergence of new abilities and ways of processing information—the sensorimotor stage (birth–2 years); preoperational stage (2–7 years); concrete operational stage (7–11 years); and formal operational stage (11–adulthood).

The universality of Piaget's theory has been challenged by more recent researchers who have shown that development can take place at earlier or later periods in life dependent upon the circumstances and personal interactions of the individual (e.g., Baillargeon, 2002; Feldman, 2012; Kuhn, 2006). Nevertheless, his work has provided the foundation for constructivist learning—learning by doing—an influential concept in modern educational systems. Constructivism is built upon the concept of *schemes*—the cognitive framework that individuals use to organize their understandings, perceptions, and experiences. It is through the process of *adaptation* that children are then able to adjust these schemes or categories as they interact with the world around them. These adjustments are made through *assimilation* (the incorporation of new information into current schemes) and *accommodation* (the modification of existing schemes to account for new information). It is through the process of accommodation that *disequilibration*, an imbalance of what is understood through existing schemes during the presentation of new information, can occur as students begin to modify their thinking, resulting in new skills and understandings. Disequilibrium is an innate desire to "put things straight" in one's mind when confronted by information that just does not seem to fit in one's current state of knowledge. Teachers who are knowledgeable of this concept can often use technology to tap into this need to categorize and make sense of new learning. For example, look at the real images below that teachers can now easily offer through technology for examination by students.

The student will not necessarily be given the attributes but will be asked to compare images to determine what similarities and differences reinforce his or her own schema for "fish" and to create a new schema for penguins in Figure 16.1 and Figure 16.2. These images and, perhaps, audio can be carefully selected by the teacher and can be either simple or complex for younger or older students. These compare and contrast experiences can be prepared for many different topics. The difference from times gone by is that the Internet now offers all types of realistic images instantly for teachers and/or learners to access (see Shutterstock.com, for example).

Figure 16.1   See if you can "accommodate" a new category here. Teachers can offer all types of questions to encourage organization of cognitive schemas, such as which one does not belong and why? If children have not had experiences with penguins before, then a new schema must be constructed (accommodation) in their minds—such as "birds that swim underwater".

Figure 16.2   See if you can "assimilate" the last image into the one you already have for birds. Can it fit into a subcategory for "birds that can't fly", such as ostriches and kiwis?

Sociocultural Learning Theory

Unlike the individualistic view of growth proffered by Piaget, Lev Vygotsky (1896–1934) emphasized the influence that interpersonal interactions and culture had on cognitive development. He built this sociocultural theory on two key ideas: the first being that cognitive development could be understood through historical and cultural contexts of students' individual lived experiences (Crain, 2010); the second is the dependency of development "on the sign system that individuals [have] grown up with: the symbols that cultures create to help people think, communicate, and solve problems" (Slavin, 2018, p. 33).

Three primary concepts of Vygotsky's sociocultural theory of cognitive development are the zone of proximal development (ZPD), scaffolding, and cooperative learning. Similar to disequilibrium in Piaget's theory, the ZPD is often associated with "teachable moments"–the point of readiness to learn a skill that a student cannot accomplish on his or her own but can with the assistance of a more competent peer or adult. This assistance is known as *scaffolding*, a systematic method of diminishing assistance that gradually moves the student from his/her current level of understanding to an independent capability to use the new skill. Finally, through *cooperative learning groups*, students of varying abilities can benefit from the social interactions of guided learning within their individual ZPD, allowing them to hear each other "think aloud" as they co-construct new knowledge and understanding. The combination of technology and the classroom have allowed for a seamless integration of Vygotsky's key concepts. Virtual assistant tools such as Siri and Alexa now allow teachers and students to ask and find answers immediately and to generate new questions that arise during the learning process. YouTube currently provides scaffolding for almost every "how to" project imaginable. Further, many classrooms institute the "First Three Then Me" rule for social support in learning and using technology that requires students to first ask three of their peers when they have questions about technology use before calling on the teacher for help. These tools and practices give students opportunities to build academic relationships with other members of their classroom and give them the opportunity to seek out new resources of information. A recent study by a council of distinguished scientists noted that beyond academic development, the skills students need to be successful in the classroom and in life can be grouped into three areas (Blad, 2017):

- **cognitive skills** including executive functions such as working memory, attention control and flexibility, inhibition, and planning, as well as beliefs and attitudes that guide one's sense of self and approaches to learning and growth;
- **emotional competencies** that enable one to cope with frustration, recognize and manage emotions, and understand others' emotions and perspectives; and
- **social and interpersonal skills** that enable one to read social cues, navigate social situations, resolve interpersonal conflicts, cooperate with others and work effectively in a team, and demonstrate compassion and empathy toward others. (p. 10)

Other Psychological Connections

Creativity versus creative thinking. As mentioned previously, the ability to think creatively is increasingly valued. Before moving forward, it is important to differentiate between creativity and creative thinking, clearing up a common misconception that creativity is only associated with the ability to excel in artistic endeavors. Creative thinking abilities have long been associated with cognitive development and traits related to divergent thinking (i.e., fluency, flexibility, originality, elaboration) and with information processing (e.g., using existing knowledge as a basis for new ideas, questioning norms and assumptions, finding problems) (Davis, 2004b). These creative thinking abilities have been encouraged and emphasized by researchers across disciplines (e.g., Craft, 2012; Hui & Lau, 2010; Sawyer, 2011) and have long been documented as a predictor of future performance in the workplace (e.g., Tierney, Farmer, & Graen, 1999; Torrance, 1972, 1981), a factor in healthy emotional development, interpersonal relationships (e.g., Russ, 1998), and in gaining advancements in careers in science, technology, engineering, art, and mathematics (Plucker, Beghetto, & Dow, 2004; Sternberg, 1999). The importance of the development of creative thinking skills in gifted and talented students has been a focus of educational researchers for many years (e.g., Cramond, 1994; Fugate, Zentall, & Gentry, 2013). However, as noted here, it is important that these skills be developed for all students if they are to be successful in the twenty-first century.

Computational thinking. Supported by the basic principles of cognitive development set forth by Piaget and Vygotsky, computational thinking is the development of an understanding of computing competencies. These skills elevate students from merely using technology to becoming producers of information technology (Yadav, Hong, & Stephenson, 2016; Yadav, Mayfield, Zhou, Hambrusch, & Korb, 2014). Computational thinking is built upon three primary concepts: *algorithm*—breaking down problems into a smaller, more manageable sequence of steps; *abstraction*—evaluating the potential for transferability of a solution to other problems; and *automation*—determining the effectiveness of using technology to more efficiently solve the problem at hand (Wing, 2006).

Although traditionally thought of in the context of computer sciences, Yadav et al. (2016) emphasized the value of computational thinking across content areas in elementary and secondary education settings. This belief has been supported by researchers who found that the inclusion of computational thinking in a sixth-grade mathematics classroom significantly increased students' understanding of mathematical principles over students in a similar classroom with a curriculum that did not include this practice (Calao, Moreno-Léon, Correa, & Robles, 2015). This finding emphasized the effect that computational thinking can have on overall achievement, in addition to simply increasing general problem-solving ability. Additionally, Mishra and Yadav (2013) noted, "Computational thinking can foster creativity by allowing students to not only be consumers of technology but also build tools that can have a significant impact on society" (p. 11).

New Literacies. Literacies are "the social practice that comprises inter-related and dynamically connected symbol systems, technology (digital or not), knowledge, and skills, mutually evolving based on changing ideas about purpose, task, and context" (DeSchryver & Yadav, 2015, p. 414). Other researchers identified the need for students to develop the ability to adapt to become literate in technologies that have yet to be developed to meet future needs (Leu, Kinzer, Coiro, Castek, & Henry, 2013). This highlights the importance for teachers to be able to use new literacies and computational thinking as a framework for creating learning experiences that provide a foundation for skills that scaffold creative thinking (DeSchryver & Yadav, 2015).

Meet James

James is a student in Mrs. Soliz's classroom. He has been identified as dyslexic and, therefore, has been struggling in reading. This has influenced his grades across all subjects. Mrs. Soliz knows that James likes to play video games and interact with various forms of technology. She has also noticed that his oral comprehension is quite advanced. She wants to find some ways that she can integrate technology to help James become more academically successful without having to rely so heavily on assignments that require him to read from a textbook or write using pencil and paper.

Littlekidmoment / Shutterstock.com

Practical Applications to Meet Cognitive Developmental Needs

Flipped Classroom

The flipped or inverted classroom is a strategy that addresses both the individual and social cognitive development needs of students. It does so by transforming the traditional teacher-centered and lecture-style classroom to one that is student-centered and activity-based, enhanced by the addition of Web-based videos. Building upon the principles of computational thinking, the two facets of the flipped classroom—Web-based instructional videos and a student-centered classroom—address cognitive development in different but cooperative ways, allowing students to not only be consumers of the information being taught in the classroom but using that information to analyze problems and construct new understandings.

Much fanfare has been made about the use of Web-based videos to replace traditional in-class lecture and notes. The sophistication and user-friendliness of video editing software has made it easier for teachers and students to create their own videos for flipped classroom use. Additionally, Websites such as YouTube (www.youtube.com) and TeacherTube (www.teachertube.com) have made it easy to share teacher- and student-generated videos locally, nationally, and internationally.

For example, reading books out loud and asking questions about what was read is standard practice in many elementary classrooms. A very popular book for elementary students is Eric Carle's *The Very Hungry Caterpillar*. Elementary teachers can extend and expand a reading experience lesson through video. An elementary teacher could record him- or herself reading *The Very Hungry Caterpillar* and asking questions. This video would be available to both students and parents online. The video could be watched multiple times by students and parents, giving them more time to absorb what they are seeing and hearing. It also gives them more time to think about the questions that the teacher is asking.

For those teachers looking to edge slowly into the flipped classroom pool, there are a number of excellent videos already online that can be used at the elementary and secondary grade levels. Classic books for elementary students are available online. For example, there is both an animated video and a video of Eric Carle reading *The Very Hungry Caterpillar*. For secondary teachers and students, videos covering civics, economics, history, mathematics, science, and other content areas can be viewed and shared from Websites such as Khan Academy (www.khanacademy), Crash Course (www.thecrashcourse.com), and Bozeman Science (www.bozemanscience.com).

The use of videos posted on the Internet gives students several more degrees of flexibility that are missing from traditional lecture-style classrooms (Bishop & Verleger, 2013; Butt, 2014; Crews & Butterfield, 2014; The Flipped Learning Network, 2014). The ability to view content both before and after class and review as necessary has been shown to decrease student anxiety and to have positive impacts on student engagement, class participation, and overall course interest (Bishop & Verleger, 2013; Butt, A., 2014; Crews & Butterfield, 2014; Kim et al., 2014; Strayer, 2012).

YouTube videos also have features that allow viewers to tailor the viewing experience to fit their personal needs. YouTube viewers can modify the size, opacity, color, and font of the subtitles/closed captioning. Subtitles are also available in nine different languages, including English, and will auto-translate to over 50 different languages. Viewers can also adjust the speed of the video. This is ideal for students who are watching and taking notes on the content simultaneously. For an example, see CrashCourse video "Vectors and 2D Motion" with Spanish subtitles/closed captioning: www.youtube.com/watch?v=w3BhzYI6zXU.

Although these features are not exhaustive in terms of differentiation, they do provide users the opportunity to tailor the learning experience to their individual ZPD through scaffolding tools that support their growth. This ability to personalize the learning experience creates buy-in and ownership by the students and can lead to higher levels of engagement and, ultimately, understanding of the content.

With lectures and notes that are taking place outside of class, face-to-face time with students can and should be modified to create active learning experiences. Active learning strategies can include problem-based learning, peer-assisted learning, cooperative learning, collaborative learning, and peer tutoring (Bishop & Verleger, 2013) (see Figure 16.3). These strategies can be particularly useful as a means to move away from paper and pencil assignments, worksheets, and reading sections of a textbook.

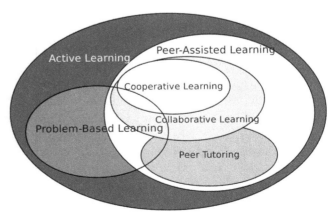

Figure 16.3   Active learning.
Copyright © 2013 by American Society for Engineering Education. Reprinted by permission.

Teachers can use a variety of assignments to engage students in a face-to-face setting, including but not limited to independent and small-group projects, project/problem-based activities, portfolios, long-term projects, in-depth readings, digital storytelling, discussions, and debates. Kim et al. (2014) explained, "student-centered learning environments necessitate applying more active learning strategies to classroom teaching" (p. 4). Accordingly, the transformation that must take place in and out of the classroom takes careful planning to effectively use both videos and face-to-face meeting time. Researchers such as Crews and Butterfield (2014) have shown that "students value active learning and interaction during face-to-face meetings; including peer interaction through small groups and discussion" (p. 44).

Regardless of the exact strategies employed, research into flipped classrooms shows that effectively combining Web-based videos and group-based interactive learning activities inside the classroom can have positive impacts on student interest, participation, and test scores when compared with traditional classrooms (Abeysekera & Dawson, 2014; Bishop & Verleger, 2013; Crews & Butterfield, 2014; Kim et al., 2014; Strayer, 2012).

Flipped classrooms encourage independent and active learning by providing a flexible and differentiated learning environment for students. "Although students expressed frustration with an environment full of varied and unexpected activities," Strayer (2012) noted, "they both adapted their learning strategies and came to see value in helping each other learn with a cooperative approach" (p. 183).

Digital Storytelling

Digital storytelling is another application of technology that addresses the cognitive needs of learners by supporting active learning through student-centered learning strategies and the social construction of knowledge. "At its core, digital storytelling allows computer users to become creative storytellers through the traditional processes of selecting a topic, conducting some research, writing a script, and developing an interesting story" (Robin, 2008, p. 222). Four student-centered learning strategies for instruction have also been identified (Barrett, 2006): (1) student engagement; (2) reflection for deep learning; (3) project-based learning; and (4) the effective integration of technology.

Digital storytelling has become a relatively popular project that encourages and supports students' active learning, process skills, cooperation between peers, and language development. There are a few reasons for the increase in its use in classrooms. As a project-based strategy, it is flexible and adaptable to just about any content area or age group. It is also inexpensive when compared with other technology-driven strategies. Digital storytelling projects no longer must rely upon desktop and/or laptop computers. Technology has progressed to the point where handheld devices, such as smartphones and tablets, have hardware and software comparable to laptop computers. Additionally, Websites and apps, such as Animoto (www.animoto.com) and Storykit, which are available through the app store, enable students to create digital storytelling in the palm of their hands. An article by Kapuler (2013) in the online magazine Tech & Learning (www.techlearning.com) lists 50 Websites and apps for creating digital stories.

Digital storytelling uses constructivist strategies such as collaboration, creativity, cooperative learning, flexibility and autonomy, interpersonal and group skills, and active engagement in reflective thinking, sharing, and evaluation (Di Blas, Garzotto, Paolini, & Sabiescu, 2009; Hung, Hwang, & Huang, 2012; Malita & Martin, 2010; Sadik, 2008; Yang & Wu, 2012). Research into its use and benefits has shown that digital storytelling has the potential to go "beyond the capabilities of traditional storytelling by generating student interest, concentration, and motivation, facilitating student collaboration and organization of ideas, helping students to comprehend complex learning content, and presenting knowledge in an adaptive and meaningful manner" (Yang & Wu, 2012, p. 340).

Digital storytelling gives elementary and secondary students opportunities to express themselves individually and collectively. While some coaching in the use of technology may be necessary, digital storytelling projects could be used effectively in elementary grade levels for projects ranging from sharing information about their families to exploring the planets of our solar system and celebrating Black History Month. Additionally, an entire sixth-grade class could work together to create a digital story about their school. As students mature, the sophistication of their projects can also increase. Digital photos and visual and audio downloads enhance storytelling. Secondary grade level digital storytelling projects can create exciting opportunities for students to express themselves and showcase their artistic and musical interests (see an example at www.youtube.com/watch?v=6U-JxoCeDyY).

The act of telling a story combined with a constructivist framework and effective integration of technology makes digital storytelling ideally suited to address students' cognitive development as well as positively impact their motivation and attitude toward learning. Along with helping to develop twenty-first-century skills and become better users of technology, digital storytelling has also been shown to improve academic achievement. In a three-year experimental project, researchers found evidence that effective use of digital storytelling in the classroom can improve listening skills, comprehension, language acquisition, and oral fluency (Di Blas, Garzotto, Paolini, & Sabiescu, 2009). Additionally, project-based learning with digital storytelling effectively enhanced problem-solving competence, thinking capacity, and the learning achievement of students (Hung, Hwang, & Huang, 2012). Watch www.youtube.com/watch?v=rKeJ9KVzb1k for an example.

Social Media

It may be hard to believe, but social media has many educational applications and can be a powerful, active learning tool for improving student engagement and motivation to support cognitive development. As Tess (2013) has pointed out, "the task of defining social media is made more challenging by the fact that it is constantly in a state of change. [Social Networking sites] evolve as developers create new or enhanced features that will meet the demands of users" (p. A61). Sites such as Facebook, Twitter, and Instagram cater to a broad audience of social media users. As mentioned earlier in this chapter, it is important to learn what policies your school and district have in place regarding social media use.

There are also social networks for niche markets, such as education. Edmodo (www.edmodo.com) and Class Dojo (www.classdojo.com) (see Figure 16.4), for example, cater to parents, students, and teachers with functionality along the lines of most mainstream online social media sites, allowing users to send messages, update information, create and join groups, and host or share content.

Some schools and districts have set up their own in-house social media networks to provide ways for students, teachers, parents, and schools to communicate with each other on everything from grades and assignments to upcoming athletics competitions. How teachers use social media depends greatly on the grade level. Social

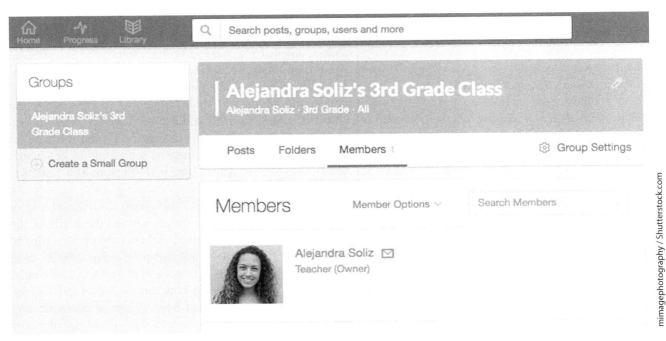

Figure 16.4 Screenshot of an Edmodo page set up by Mrs. Soliz for her third-grade class.
Source: Franklin S. Allaire

media may simply be another avenue that an elementary teacher will use more for parent communication. For secondary teachers, social media can extend learning experiences similar to the flipped classroom with teachers posting videos, assigning work, and engaging students online through discussion boards.

Ralph and Ralph (2013) stated, "although actively used by students in their personal lives, the use of social media as a teaching resource in . . . education has not been as widespread as expected" (p. 451). Research into social media has expanded almost as fast as social media use itself. However, there is some disagreement as to the benefits and drawbacks of using social media to engage students. Advocates for the use of social media in the classroom, sometimes referred to as *connectivists*, see these interactive tools as a replacement and/ or enhancement technology that continues in the social constructivist tradition, placing dialogue and social exchange as central to both the learning process and cognitive development. Bull et al. (2008; as cited in Fewkes & McCabe, 2012) explained,

> the informal learning that occurs in the context of participatory media offers significant opportunities for student engagement in formal learning settings. The experience with communication technologies that teenagers today possess must be tapped by educators and connected to pedagogy and content (p. 93).

Similarly, educational researchers (McLoughlin & Lee, 2010; Tess, 2013) have argued that social media can address the core beliefs that social constructivists hold dear—that learning is cooperative and that knowledge is socially constructed. The use of social media tools has benefits for student-centered instruction and can become the foundation for inquiry-based activities and collaborative learning groups (Tess). Others (Ralph and Ralph, 2013) stressed the importance of teacher professional development in the use of these recent technologies, noting that without proper training, instructors "risk losing the [students'] attention, interest, excitement and joy [of learning]" (p. 450) through inappropriate or ineffective integration.

As with any technology, there will always be questions about whether it can be shaped for educational purposes. Nonetheless, instructors have been making use of social media to improve student engagement in and out of class. Instructors are using the three most popular social media sites (i.e., Facebook, Twitter, Instagram) in a variety of ways to connect with students and share course-related content (Fewkes & McCabe, 2012; Freeman, 2016; Pew Research Center, 2016; Ralph & Ralph, 2013; Ravenscroft, Warburton, Hatzipanagos, & Conole, 2012; Tess, 2013; The Nielsen Company, 2016). For example, instructors can set up Facebook pages and/or groups for specific courses.

Twitter and Instagram have been making their way into the educational realm as well. In her online article entitled "How School Districts are Leveraging Twitter to Become Rock Stars," Jenkins (2017, www.eschoolnews.com) provided suggestions on how innovative educators, schools, and districts can use Twitter effectively. She stressed that "schools should be turning to the social media giant more than ever to share news, gather feedback, benefit from other educators' expertise, react instantly to breaking news—and sometimes just lighten the mood." Schools share sports schedules and scores, lunch menus, and photos of events happening in and around the school. *Hashtags*—a word or phrase preceded by a hash or pound sign (#) and used to identify messages on a specific topic—are also becoming a popular way to connect with individuals in specified interest areas. An online list of 60 popular education Twitter hashtags (www.gettingsmart.com) suggests searching for key words and phrases such as #BlendedLearning, #Education, #NTChat (New Teacher Chat), and #PersonalizedLearning to help one get involved in important conversations.

Aside from the top three social media platforms, Facebook, Twitter, and Instagram, individual and/or groups of teachers are also connecting with students and expanding the classroom beyond the walls of the school through services such as Class Dojo, Edmodo, YouTube, and Remind.com. Teachers employing a flipped classroom model and/or incorporating digital storytelling into their curriculum can post video content onto YouTube and require students to view and leave comments as part of the peer review process. Additionally, content-specific Websites are building in social media-like functions to create a community of learners locally, nationally, and internationally. For example, the citizen science Website Project Noah (www.projectnoah.org) allows users to follow one another, send messages, and share and comment on content. The use of social media in classrooms is an important and emerging trend that has the potential to energize students and support their cognitive development.

For Discussion: James (from the case study presented earlier)

1. Which modality—Flipped Classroom, Digital Storytelling, or Social Media—do you think would best help James to be successful? Why?
2. Compare and contrast each modality in terms of helping James with his dyslexia.
3. Explain how each modality could help Mrs. Soliz achieve her goal of supporting James' academic success without having to rely so heavily on assignments that require him to read from a textbook or write using pencil and paper?
4. What factors should Mrs. Soliz consider before using any of the three modalities to support James' academic success?
5. How could Vygotsky's sociocultural theory concepts of ZPD, scaffolding, and cooperative learning be used to address James' academic needs in each of the three modalities of learning described in this chapter?

Using Technology to Support Behavior Development

One of the fundamental questions of education is quite simply, "What is learning?" Although the question itself is simple, the answer is more complex. In its most basic form, learning is the activity or process of gaining knowledge or skills that change one's behavior by studying, practicing, being taught, or experiencing something. Learning involves the acquisition of any abilities that are not innate (e.g., growth, reflexes) and is dependent upon the feedback that is received from the environment.

Because it is tied to experiences and the environment, learning is a continuous process and can occur in one of two ways—intentional or unintentional. *Intentional learning*, also referred to as *purposeful learning*, is goal directed and occurs through information presented in a classroom that includes student interaction and feedback. In an intentional learning environment, it is the questions asked, the way data are organized, the connections made, how solutions are adapted to the problem, and the reflections made about the learning experience that guide the process. "Whether intentional learning occurs is likely to depend on both situational and intrinsic factors – on what the situation affords in goal-attainment opportunities and on what the student's mental resources are for attaining those goals" (Bereiter & Scardamalia, 1989, p. 363).

In contrast, *unintentional* or *incidental learning* results from unplanned formalized activities and can occur through observation, repetition, social interactions, and problem-solving (Kerka, 2000). We often consider these to be "teachable moments," those times when students will ask a question that is outside of planned instruction but provides opportunities to deepen understanding, or when researching a topic on the Internet leads to new and unexpected knowledge. There are two important benefits to this type of learning in the classroom (Wang, 2014). First is that it efficiently uses time that may not have been designated for learning. Second, this type of learning is often done "with a pleasure instead of pressure" (Wang, 2014, p. 1998).

Motivation

Regardless of whether the learning that occurs is intentional or unintentional, it cannot occur if the learner is not motivated to do so. "Motivation," Slavin (2018) tells us, "is what gets you going, keeps you going, and determines where you're trying to go" (p. 248). Motivation is guided by five basic questions (see the following textbox) and may be extrinsically driven—relying on external factors such as rewards, social pressures, and/or punishment. On the other hand, it may be intrinsically driven—relying on internal, personal factors such as needs, interests, and/or curiosity. As critical as motivation is to learning, it is often difficult to assess, as it hinges on a number of factors, including but not limited to personality, ability, type of learning task, the incentive to learn, anxiety, the educational environment, and interactions with the teacher. As stated earlier, it is often impossible to tell whether a behavior is intrinsically or extrinsically motivated just by looking at the person, and indeed, (s)he may be motivated by each type or a little of both at any given time. Although many theories are associated with students' motivation to learn, we will focus on two in particular—the self-determination theory and the expectancy-value theory.

Five Basic Motivation Questions

1. What **choices** do people make about their behavior?
2. How long does it take to **get started**?
3. What is the **intensity** or level of involvement in the chosen activity?
4. What causes a person to **persist** or to give up?
5. What is the person **thinking and feeling** while engaged in the activity?

Self-Determination Theory

Self-determination theory concentrates on students' need for competence, autonomy, and relatedness (the desire for an emotional bond with others) by focusing on the choices that people make without external influence. Self-determination theory "addresses such basic issues as personality development, self-regulation, universal psychological needs, life goals and aspirations, energy and vitality, non-conscious processes, the relations of culture to motivation, and the impact of social environments on motivation, affect, behavior, and well-being" (Deci & Ryan, 2008, p. 182). Classroom teachers who support student self-determination and autonomy are associated with greater student interest and curiosity, personalized instruction, creativity, a preference for challenge, and establishing a supportive and caring environment. In short, when students are given the authority to make choices based on their interests, they tend to internalize educational goals and make them their own. The right technology choices are also important to this. When students can access answers that interest them, the classroom supports relatedness, as is true for the teacher who presents real-life rationales and examples—a strongpoint of today's technology. Many technology programs help students to succeed by assessing their level of skills and knowledge and presenting work that allows them to succeed and grow. These can be optimum choices for students. View www.youtube.com/watch?v=m6fm1gt5YAM for futher explanations.

Expectancy-Value Theory

Expectancy-value theory is based on the belief that one's efforts to achieve are dependent upon their expectancy of some type of reward (Slavin, 2018; Wigfield & Eccles, 2000), taking the curiosity, interests, emotions, and anxieties of the student into account as they relate to the perceived challenge of the task. Slavin also noted that a task that is too easy or, in contrast, too challenging might result in diminished motivation. "If some students believe that they are likely to get an A no matter what they do, then their motivation will not be at a maximum. Similarly, if some students feel certain they will fail no matter what they do, their motivation will be minimal" (p. 254). Again, many technology programs have been designed to take this need for appropriate challenge into account by pretesting to determine students' current levels of understanding and then gradually increasing in difficulty as they progress through the activities. Most educational technology companies have also taken into account external motivation through rewards with "bells and whistles" that follow a correct answer.

Because interest plays a significant role in this theory of motivation, a teacher must distinguish between personal interests and situational interests. *Personal interests* tend to be associated with the person directly and are long-lasting. When personal interests are addressed in the classroom, the student tends to seek out new information and, in the process, develops a more positive attitude toward school. Situational interests are short lived and tend to be associated with a text or activity that maintains the student's attention for a brief period. In their Four-Phase Model of Interest Development, Hidi and Renninger (2006) stated that interest increases when a student feels competent; therefore, even if (s)he is not initially interested in a particular area of study, an interest may be developed as he or she experiences success (see Figure 16.5). Classroom teachers who support interests and curiosities can make connections to the content being taught with students' experiences, interests, and/or hobbies and incorporate them into (a) the class lesson and discussion; (b) infuse instruction with humor and personal anecdotes; and/or (c) create surprise. Most lesson plans require that a teacher, for example, includes a focus activity (or "hook") and a variety of connections (e.g., past or present learning, culture, locale, rationale). Technology provides an excellent pathway for these areas, including but not limited to pictures, videos, and games. One teacher (www.scienceteachingjunkie.com/2013/08/you-gotta-have-hook_15.html) recommends starting

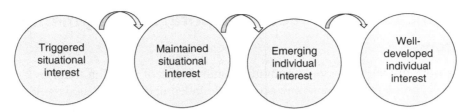

Figure 16.5 Four-Phase Model of Interest Development.
Source: Matthew Fugate

class with one of Mr. Parr's science songs for example (www.youtube.com/user/ParrMr). Sites such as www
.powtoon.com/blog/13-simple-ways-integrate-technology-lesson-plan offer many more ideas to whip up interest.

Creativity and Behavior Development

Davis (2004b) suggested that personality, cognitive abilities, and biographical traits work together to produce
creativity. He conducted an analysis of the creativity literature from 1961 to 2003 with the goal of identifying
the recurrent personality traits of creative people. Although not all traits applied to all creative people, he identified 16 positive high frequency traits (e.g., independent, risk-taking, high energy, curiosity, humor, artistic,
emotional). It is interesting to note that many of the traits that Davis identified play a significant role in the
theories of motivation that we have discussed so far in this chapter and should be considered when developing
technology experiences in the classroom.

Programmed Instruction

B. F. Skinner (1904–1990) was a behavioral theorist who posited that a behavior followed by a pleasurable
consequence (e.g., praise, success) is more likely to be repeated. This theory is known as *operant conditioning*.
Programmed instruction, the process of presenting new information to students in a controlled sequence of
steps, is based on Skinner's work and allows students to progress through learning materials at their own pace
with feedback provided when each step is completed--a process known as *shaping* the desired behavior. The
inclusion of technology as a tool for learning supports this model of instruction by allowing teachers to:

- break tasks down into small, manageable steps;
- present material in a manner that requires the student to respond correctly before moving on to the next step;
- inform the student of the correctness of his/her response; and
- in some instances, base the next step on the correctness or incorrectness of the previous step.

Meet Blanca

Mrs. Soliz is concerned about Blanca. Blanca started out the year doing well,
but as they move into the second half of the year, she seems to be working
below her ability level and has lost some of her excitement about school. From
her teacher preparation classes and the subsequent professional development
she has received since stepping into her own classroom, Mrs. Soliz knows
that students can experience times when they underachieve. Mrs. Soliz has
spoken with Blanca's mother and nothing seems to have changed at home,
so she feels like there may be something in the classroom environment that
has created this change in Blanca's class work. Mrs. Soliz wants to see if
there is something that she can do in class and feels that integrating strategies such as flipped classroom and digital storytelling will allow Blanca to
express herself in nontraditional ways, may increase her motivation, and
get her back to the quality of work that Mrs. Soliz knows Blanca can do.

Practical Applications to Meet Behavioral Developmental Needs

Flipped Classroom

The flipped classroom model "represents a unique combination of learning theories once thought to be incompatible – active, problem-based learning activities founded upon a constructivist ideology and lectures derived from direct instruction methods founded upon behaviorist principles" (Bishop & Verleger, 2013, p. 2). Structured properly, the flipped classroom model is well suited to support the challenges of student motivation, expectancy-value, and self-determination.

If planned and executed effectively, activities such a peer reviews, small- and whole-group discussions/debates, individual and small-group projects, and portfolios will enable students to be both self-directed and self-motivated (Crews & Butterfield, 2014; Jensen et al., 2015; The Flipped Learning Network, 2014). For example, a project that could be effective at elementary and secondary grade levels is to invite students to create songs or raps based on content covered in class. The Science Rap Academy (www.youtube.com/playlist?list=PLvgILFwoRX2min-PEDNXfk25KULkKfy7S) is a YouTube channel features content-related rap videos created by students. Rap videos about DNA (www.youtube.com/watch?v=VrTGclugG0k&index=6&list=PLvgILFwoRX2min-PEDNXfk2), light pollution (www.youtube.com/watch?v=pxy4TAXBbdA&list=PLvgILFwoRX2min-PEDNXfk25KULkKfy7S&index=9), metals, asthma, and others are examples to get students' interest and creative juices flowing.

Qualitative data gathered in the form of student surveys and interviews show that even students who preferred in-person lecture to online videos *still* preferred interactive class activities over in-person lectures. Placing students at the center of the learning experience and basing activities, at least in part, on their interests and experiences automatically builds value into coursework. When students value the work they are doing, they are more likely to be motivated and self-directed.

Despite today's students being digital natives, watching videos on the Internet for educational purposes is still a hook that can be used to motivate students. In a flipped classroom environment, students must prepare for the learning experience using the materials provided to them before coming to class (Jensen et al., 2015). However, this presents one of the biggest hurdles for instructors in terms of implementation—student motivation (Abersekera & Dawson, 2015; Butt, 2014, Kim et al., 2014). Researchers have noted that student-centered learning activities in class relied on students completing the pre-class groundwork requirements; in turn, this leads to "the perennial problems of student preparation: how do teachers know if students have prepared, what they know and if the preparation was useful?" (Abersekera & Dawson, 2015, p. 2). Additionally, variations in students' abilities, learning styles, as well as access to required technology could affect the amount of time and effort required by each student to prepare for the in-class learning experience (Jensen et al., 2015).

As educators, we want all students to be self-motivated. In a flipped classroom, this self-motivation—to prepare for class by watching assigned videos—becomes even more critical. In a perfect world, students would watch and re-watch assigned videos, watch any optional supplemental videos provided, read the accompanying chapter from the textbook, and come to class prepared and ready for the activities tied to these learning materials. In the real world, however, "successful face-to-face interaction . . . depends on the extent to which students have prepared before engaging with the in-class activities" (Kim et al., 2014, p. 29). In short, students may be better prepared for the flipped classroom experience at some points than they are at others.

Researchers have noted that issues relating to organization and pre-preparation are skills that students need to develop for themselves (e.g., Butt, 2014; Crews & Butterfield, 2014, Kim et al., 2014; Strayer, 2012). They offer several suggestions that could act as an incentive to encourage pre-preparation. Quizzes (either in-class or online), online discussion boards, and YouTube video comments with low-stakes grading are some of the tools consistently mentioned in flipped classroom research as ways to extrinsically motivate students to watch videos prior to class. Some researchers question whether such a "penal" approach to student motivation (in terms of watching videos or other material) encourages self-motivation and self-directed learning. However, qualitative data in the form of student interviews have shown that students themselves felt that the incentives were entirely appropriate and useful (Bishop & Verleger, 2013; Butt, 2014; Kim et al., 2014). Along those lines, Butt (2014) also noted the need "to have informal extension activities available in-class to those who feel they are being held back by those who haven't done sufficient pre-preparation" (p. 41). Perhaps the best approach is for the instructor to remember that the excitement and interest of students in pre-class online activities is dependent on excellent choices which are interesting, spark curiosity, engage student connections, are fun, and so forth. For example, a fifth-grade teacher could assign his class to watch a film clip about Hurricane Katrina that overwhelmed the city of New Orleans in 2005, causing severe damage. He could ask them to predict the amount of money that it cost to rebuild and to add additional infrastructure to prevent future flooding in hard hit areas. Students could then watch a film clip about Hurricane Isaac, which again overwhelmed much of the city in 2012. Students would be asked to consider the damage that resulted from this storm to determine how much money was spent in recovery from Isaac and whether the solutions that had been implemented after Katrina had worked. Students would then be tasked with considering the effects of Hurricane Harvey on Houston and the Gulf Coast area and come to class with environmentally sound ideas to discuss what could be done to improve the situation in the future.

Digital Storytelling

Before we discuss more theory for using digital storytelling as a strategy, watch the following example which won a prize for its construction: www.youtube.com/watch?v=vsuHabO2TYA. As you read, keep this video in mind and relate how it fits with the following information in this section.

There is evidence that the popularity of digital storytelling is due to the ways in which it supports students' behavioral development. The role of the teacher in this process cannot be understated. "Constructing a successful digital storytelling project requires instructors to pose problems that are deeply connected with the course content" (Yang & Wu, 2012, p. 340), so while students enjoy the autonomy that digital storytelling affords them, in reality, it is highly structured and carefully crafted and tailored to support specific student interests, course content, and active learning strategies.

Behavioral development support through digital storytelling comes from the way in which the project is constructed and executed in the classroom. Digital storytelling offers students quite a bit of autonomy to express themselves creatively. Students are encouraged to choose photos, videos, and music for digital storytelling, along with providing their own voice, that represent themselves and their life experiences. As we know, motivation is a critical element in learning. "A multi-media rich digital story," according to Robin (2008), "can serve as an anticipatory set or hook to capture the attention of students and increase their interest in exploring new ideas" (p. 224). Researchers have found that opportunities for self-examination through digital storytelling can hook students in and motivate them even more (Di Blas, Garzotto, Paolini, and Sabiescu, 2009; Robin, 2008; Sadik, 2008; Yang & Wu, 2012). As a social tool, it encourages sharing with others and helps teachers to know their students more thoroughly.

It has been found that students often prefer to create stories that are rooted in real-life activities experienced by the entire class (e.g., field trips, science experiments, sports games) (Di Blas, Garzotto, Paolini, and Sabiescu, 2009). Indeed, motivation and engagement increase when digital storytelling is based on these types of life experiences (Sadik, 2008). Another advantage to the teacher in selecting real-life experiences is not only increased interest in the activity itself but also the "long lasting effect of the experience being reinterpreted by the storytelling activity" (Di Blas et al., p. 3). For instance, a student who has struggled with mathematics in the past may create a digital story that relates his or her own personal journey, allowing an opportunity to be introspective and highlight the ability to be resilient and overcome his/her difficulties in this area.

The Oregon Writing Project at the University of Oregon YouTube channel (www.youtube.com/user/projectdirect2010/videos) has videos explaining the digital story process complete with hints, tips, and an example with second- and third-grade students (www.youtube.com/watch?v=rUZXBc6yRhU). The Website, *Educational Uses of Digital Storytelling*, provides several examples of how digital storytelling can be integrated across the curriculum, allowing students to express themselves through digital narratives (www.digitalstorytelling.coe.uh.edu). The grade level and content need not be restricted to storytelling. The following site gives examples of many topics for children: www.sites.google.com/site/ipadmultimediatools/digital-storytelling-project-examples.

Social Media

As mentioned, there is some disagreement as to whether social media is an effective pedagogical tool. However, it is now being harnessed by innovative educators and institutions as a method of engaging and supporting students' active learning. Social media is being "repurposed for educationally relevant activities that have impacts on real-world academic outcomes, namely student engagement (offline) and grades" (Junco, Elavsky, & Heiberger, 2013, p. 3). A study by the Pew Research Center (2016) revealed that 62% of U.S. adults receive their news from social media. Further, 79% of all Internet users regularly accessed Facebook (with three quarters reporting daily use); 32% used Instagram; and 24% used Twitter.

As we look to integrate social media and education, we should be aware of some concerns regarding the effects its use can have on student behavior. First and foremost, young adults are already spending an enormous amount of time in front of a screen. In addition to the statistics on children presented earlier in this chapter, The Nielsen Company (2016) reported that adults (18+ years old) spent an average of 5 hours and 30 minutes (22% of their media time) per week on social media either though their smartphones, tablets, or computers—an increase of 36% from their 2015 survey (p. 6). Assigning even more time can be questionable if not constructed well.

One of the biggest challenges in education is getting students to "buy-in" and see value in a strategy that an instructor or institution has adopted. Social media penetration has created an automatic buy-in of sorts for students and can make integration easier for instructors. Those who do integrate social media, either as a standalone technology-based enhancement or as part of another pedagogical strategy, have "argued that one of social constructivism's foremost tenets can be applied to teaching with social media [and that] social networks can become the impetus for inquiry-based approaches . . . collaboration . . . active participation, learner self-direction, and personal meaning construction" (Tess, 2013, p. A62). Additionally, the use of social media in educational settings has been found to increase motivation, achievement, and positive social interactions (Ralph & Ralph, 2013).

The results of the actual use of social media for educational purposes have shown that not all social media platforms are created equal. In their study, Junco, Heiberger, & Loken (2010) concluded "that using Twitter in educationally relevant ways had a positive effect on student engagement" (p. 10). Similarly, Tess (2013) noted that Twitter could be an effective tool for classrooms, particularly in terms of improving contact between instructors and students, promoting active learning, providing an avenue for prompt feedback, and maximizing time on task; Facebook, on the other hand, has produced mixed results. McCarthy (2010) concluded her study by suggesting that Facebook was ideal for use with a flipped classroom. She noted increased engagement and self-direction with most students (92%) who appreciated the interactive discussions with their peers that occurred online. More studies will likely identify issues as educators work toward positive integration into the curriculum.

The saturation of social media into student populations makes its integration for learning extremely attractive to educators. As stated in the previous section, how social media can and will be used in education depends greatly on the grade level. For elementary age students, social networking can be an effective communication tool with sites like ClassDojo offering ways for parents to connect directly with their child's teacher and school (see Figure 16.6).

For Discussion: Blanca (from the case study presented earlier)

1. Which modality—Flipped Classroom, Digital Storytelling, or Social Media—do you think will best help Blanca? Why?
2. In what ways can technology in the classroom support positive behavioral development in students? What are the drawbacks to using technology to support behavioral development in students?
3. Compare and contrast each modality in terms of providing elementary/secondary students with alternative ways of expressing themselves.
4. Consider the self-determination and expectancy-value theories of motivation. How could each be used to motivate Blanca?
5. What factors should Mrs. Soliz consider before using any of the three modalities to support Blanca's behavioral development?

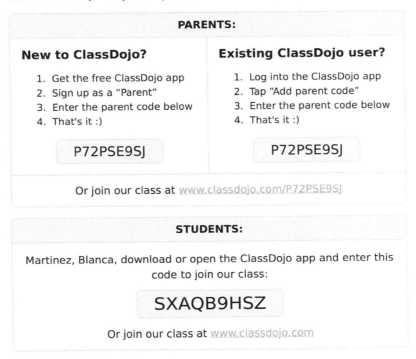

Figure 16.6   An invitation to Blanca's parents from Mrs. Soliz to connect with her third-grade class through ClassDojo.

Using Technology to Support Social-Emotional Development

As discussed previously, Vygotsky saw learning primarily as a social process. Despite this, schools focus more on the cognitive aspects of academics, often foregoing social-emotional competencies. As a result, learning may be challenged by occurrences of bullying and other antisocial behaviors that can lead to depression, anxiety, and, ultimately, a decrease in *emotional intelligence*. Educational researchers (e.g., Iaosanurak, Chanchalor, & Murphy, 2016) have noted the connection between cognitive and emotional intelligences stating, "emotions can aid intelligence and shape thinking through motivation and by alerting one's attention to what is important in a particular context" (p. 1640). Slavin (2018) emphasized the importance of understanding students' social development and the value that it had on the ways teacher's motivated, taught, and communicated with students. Certainly, when students believe that they are in a safe environment where they feel that they are understood and that their views and perspectives are honored, self-concept and *self-efficacy*—their belief in their own abilities—increase, making them more motivated to take academic risks.

Social and Emotional Learning

The integration of social and emotional learning (SEL) into the curriculum has been found by researchers to raise students' awareness of themselves and others; develop more positive attitudes and values; increase responsible decision-making; and cultivate positive social interaction skills (e.g., Durak, Weissberg, Dymnicki,

Taylor, & Schellinger, 2011; Payton et al., 2000). Further supporting these findings, Iaosanurak, Chanchalor, and Murphy (2016) examined the effects of a technology-based SEL intervention program, evaluating the effects of participation in the program on the group, as well as differences between genders. The students worked in cooperative learning groups using digital stories, online discussion forums and learning journals, and mind mapping software. The researchers described the learning process as encouraging "learner-to-learner interaction as well as dialogue and group collaborative reflection, problem-solving and decision-making on social and emotional issues" (p. 1645). They found that there was increased self-awareness, self-control, and self-concept for the group. Additionally, these researchers noted that the girls made significant gains in empathy (e.g., awareness of the feelings of others) and responsibility (e.g., ability to compromise; accept one's own mistakes; acceptance of the ideas of others; helping others) over the boys in the study. The interesting aspect of this study was the fact that the researchers used technology not as a *tool for learning* but to facilitate and support the students' understanding of emotional intelligence through collaboration, social interactions, and "scaffolds that [worked] in conjunction with technology" (p. 1657).

Identity Development

Adolescence has always been marked as a period of identity development for students. Erik Erikson (1902–1994) identified several conflicts that humans go through as they move through life. One of those conflicts that he called *Identity versus Role Confusion* generally occurs between the ages of 12 and 18 years. It is during this time that social relationships with peers take on a greater significance as children begin to explore their independence and sense of self. Erikson felt that those who received proper encouragement and reinforcement through personal exploration would emerge from this stage with a strong sense of self and a feeling of independence and control, while those who remained unsure of their beliefs and desires would feel insecure and confused about themselves and the future (Slavin, 2018).

With the advent of social media, this conflict has become even more pronounced as anxiety about "who they are"—that is, who children see themselves as being—becomes a matter for public comment. Turkle (2011) noted the paradox that social media has created in the lives of today's children.

> Networking makes it easier to play with identity . . . but harder to leave the past behind, because the [Internet] is forever. The network facilitates separation . . . but also inhibits it . . . [adolescents] start to resent the devices that force them into performing their profiles; they long for a world in which personal information is not taken from them automatically (p. 169).

This process of deciding what will be revealed through their online *identity disclosure* is further complicated by comparisons they make to the experiences posted online by their peers, forcing them to make decisions about how much of their own personal lives they will reveal to others. The potential to achieve *microcelebrity* status, what Nussbaum (2007) identified as the phenomenon of being well-known by a small group of online followers, increases as children become aware of being watched by an invisible audience who reinforce their behaviors through a series of comments and "likes," which can, in turn, alter their personal perceptions of themselves.

Tensions

Price, Wardman, Bruce, and Millward (2016) looked at the effects that social media participation had on high school–aged girls who were identified as gifted and talented. Specifically, they wanted to better understand what it meant to be a gifted girl in the age of social media. These researchers identified four "tensions" that were present in the lives of the study participants.

- **Tension 1: real versus air brushed.** The researchers identified the conflict that the girls in this study often faced as they tried to navigate between their lives as school leaders and being social media consumers. The result was a minimizing of their online and real-life personas, being conscious of keeping their online profiles authentic to whom they presented themselves to be in public.
- **Tension 2: public broadcasting versus private relationships.** One of the girls equated the one-sided, *parasocial* relationships fostered through social media to watching a television program where people

could merely be observers of the lives of others without any reciprocity of sharing their own lives. The girls also noted the role that instant messaging and chats played as a new way of supporting their social-emotional needs. These tools allowed them to communicate with a small group of friends and have serious conversations about events in their lives without the stigma or embarrassment that might be experienced if they were to have these same discussions in a face-to-face setting. This, in turn, allowed them to develop deeper, more personal relationships with these peers.

- **Tension 3: my time for them versus my time for me.** Price et al. noted that these girls found value in the time that they spent online. However, that time could go by so quickly and without realization of the *amount* of time that had passed. This could then lead to feelings of anxiety as it created a potential for them to lose their own sense of self. Reporting feelings of being overwhelmed, one girl recounted, "Sometimes I just want to shut it off . . . I mean it is a powerful thing and it's a scary thing" (p. 171).
- **Tension 4: viewing life versus living life.** Finally, although these girls saw value in social media as a way to keep up with the events going on in the lives of their friends and family, they also reported the potential for feelings of isolation and anxiety related to this increased connectivity. Time spent online viewing the world through a social media lens sometimes replaced living life in the real world. One girl summarized it this way, "When I go away . . . and I don't have Facebook, I actually start to feel anxious about what I have missed . . . I feel so disappointed in myself that I've let social networking affect me in such a way . . . I was happier without it. It was less complicated" (p. 171).

Though this study looked at a very specific participant group, the experiences reported by these girls may be generalizable to a larger population of students. The potential for the use of social media in education cannot be denied; however, the positive and negative outcomes on students' social-emotional development should be considered as teachers work to create new educational experiences for their technology-savvy students.

Meet Michael

Michael is a quiet student who seems reluctant to share in class. Mrs. Soliz is concerned because he has only gotten quieter since his parents divorced, and he and his mom had to move to a new apartment. Since that time, his mom has had to get a second job and is not home with him as often. Because of this, Michael's grandmother has been helping much more often at the house. He is very self-conscious about his parents' divorce and has privately expressed to Mrs. Soliz that he is afraid the other kids in the class will make fun of him. Mrs. Soliz has spoken with Ms. Collins, the school counselor, about his situation. She knows that Michael is very creative and has subsequently has suggested that Mrs. Soliz help Michael find ways to express his feelings through the work he is doing in class.

pixelheadphoto digitalskillet / Shutterstock.com

Practical Applications to Meet Social-Emotional Needs

Flipped Classroom

The flexibility of online video content coupled with a social constructivist framework for face-to-face meetings makes flipped classrooms ideal for supporting SEL. As stated in previous sections of this chapter, most students respond positively to the flipped classroom model (Butt, 2014; Crews & Butterfield, 2014; Jensen et al., 2015; Kim et al., 2014; Strayer, 2012).

The flipped classroom's use of videos from the Internet serves students' behavioral *and* social-emotional development needs. Because it gives students a greater degree of autonomy than in a traditional classroom, the addition of videos as a learning tool "satisfies their need to feel in control and independent" and thereby increases motivation; while in-class, socially interactive learning strategies supported SEL by creating "a sense of relatedness [that] comes from belonging or association with a social group in a given context" (Abysekara & Dawson, 2014, p. 4). Together, they give students the skills they need "to feel competent to master the knowledge, skills and behaviours (sic) necessary to be successful" socially and emotionally (p. 4). Students felt that the flipped classroom environment was more open and that the other students in the class valued their contributions. As a result, researchers (Kim et al., 2014) noted the benefits of using flipped classroom assignments as a way for students to develop self-regulation and goal-setting skills through feedback from peers—a vital component of SEL.

The development of students' positive attitudes as well as their social and emotional well-being does not happen on its own in a flipped classroom. Videos take time to be constructed or located and must be coordinated carefully with structured assignments that support students' active learning (Bishop & Verleger, 2013; Butt, 2014; Crews & Butterfield, 2014, The Flipped Learning Network, 2014). Fortunately, videos found on sites such as YouTube (youtube.com), SchoolTube (schooltube.com), and TeacherTube (teachertube.com) can be used to begin a flipped classroom environment. However, when used as a tool for SEL, students can benefit not only academically but also social-emotionally as they view the contributions of others with whom they can relate—others who look like them and can serve as role models for their future. In this way, students can develop a greater sense of self-awareness and positive attitudes toward school

Digital Storytelling

Digital storytelling can be an effective strategy for content-related exploration and knowledge and skills acquisition. The act of putting together content-related digital stories has been shown to increase student motivation for a subject area, increase knowledge retention, and improve listening and speaking skills (Hung, Hwang, & Huang, 2012; Robin, 2008; Sadik, 2008; Yang & Wu, 2012). Digital storytelling can be an even more powerful strategy when used for self-exploration. Just like in-depth interviews, digital storytelling can be an opportunity for students to learn more about themselves and their peers. However, instead of exploring personal connections to subjects or viewpoints on collective experiences through a transcript, students can construct creative, thought-provoking, multimedia presentations.

The popularity of personal narrative in digital storytelling has been noted because it involves students sharing their personal experiences (Robin, 2008).

> Each of us, at one or several points in our lives, has taken stock of ourselves and asked, 'Who am I?' The question invites reflection on the complex nature of our identity and awareness that while we are an amalgam of identities we are greater than the sum of our parts. (Allaire, 2014, p. 40)

Based on personal connections to an event and/or life experience, students' narratives presented through digital storytelling provide an opportunity to learn about themselves and others. "The sort of 'reflecting upon experience' involved in the production of personal narrative can range from a seemingly direct rendering of memory into words, to a self-aware evaluation and interpretation of experience, often constructed in interaction with another" (Davis, 2004a, p. 1).

When students can construct and tell their own stories, they can reflect upon their own identity and take ownership of what makes them both unique as individuals as well as members of a collective group. Research has shown digital storytelling projects to be excellent creative outlets for secondary students. However, they can be even more important to elementary students who do not yet have the advanced vocabulary to express their thoughts, ideas, and feelings. Digital storytelling's focus on music and images enables younger students to tell others things they may not yet be able to verbalize.

Despite the potential for digital storytelling to be deeply personal and emotional to both the storyteller and the audience, peer interaction and feedback are important aspects of the digital storytelling and SEL processes (Huang, Hwang, & Huang, 2012; Sadik, 2008; Yang & Wu, 2012). The digital storytelling protocols and procedures make it clear that sharing with peers is an integral part of the process. Additionally, students should be asked to work beyond simple comprehension of the stories during peer review, "to provide a critical perspective on their use of vocabulary, structure, logic, and plot, by providing critical feedback" (p. 347). From a content management standpoint, the peer review process creates opportunities to receive feedback on the quality of writing, speaking, and media used in the creation of digital storytelling. In some cases, students may use instructor-generated rubrics to grade each other and encouraged to use word processing programs to edit other students' scripts (Kajder, 2004; Yang & Wu, 2012).

This sharing of stories of students' cultural identities can also work to create a sense of community and belonging within the classroom. Belonging is one of Maslow's hierarchical psychological needs which he believes motivates human behavior (McLeod, updated 2016). The act of narration helps to build and reinforce a sense of self for students. Reading or listening not only helps students to recognize the differences that exist between individuals but also the similarities that link them to one another. For example, an elementary teacher can do a class-wide digital storytelling to help students get to know each other and increase the sense of community in the classroom. High schools, on the other hand, could do digital storytelling projects with incoming freshmen classes, as well as outgoing senior classes, to build a sense of community at both the beginning and end of the high school experience.

Qualitative interviews with students using digital storytelling to explore personal narratives showed that many found the process therapeutic (Davis, 2004a). As students analyze their own experiences and the experiences of others in their classroom, they can begin to ask deeper questions about individual and collective identity as suggested by Davis such as: Who can tell a story? How do others respond to the telling? How is one's story silenced by prevailing ideologies? These questions are relevant to constructing identity in the multiple worlds in which we act and the stories that we tell.

Social Media

There have been countless articles in newspapers, magazines, journals, and online regarding the dark side of social media, particularly cyberbullying. Cyberbullying is a serious issue for many students, teachers, families, and schools. Cyberbullying is real, and it can have a dramatic negative impact on students' identity, motivation, behavior, attitude, and self-esteem. The Cyberbullying Research Center (www.cyberbullying.org) found that in 2016, 33.8% of surveyed students aged 12 to 17 years reported being cyberbullied at some point in their lifetime and that adolescent girls were much more likely to be cyberbullied (36.7%) as compared to their male peers (30.5%). Before any teacher undertakes the use of social media for educational purposes, he or she must consult with the school, district, state, and content-specific professional organization's social media/ networking policies. Students are going to use social media regardless of whether it is incorporated into the classroom. Educators, however, have some leverage over how they have their students use it for learning and how they should treat each other on platforms such as Facebook and Twitter when used in an educational setting. Teachers must be constantly vigilant for signs that a student is being cyberbullied (see Chapter 10 of this edition) to prevent psychological harm.

As noted in previous sections, social media can be a powerful tool for education when used ethically and effectively. Not only does it have the potential to unlock a treasure trove of knowledge far beyond the walls of the classroom, it also has the capability to engage students who might otherwise not participate in the active learning process. In their study, Ralph and Ralph (2013) noted that, "social media in the classroom often results in positive psychological effects" (p. 450). They found that shy students in particular "have expressed that they liked using Facebook because it allowed them to think before responding" (p. 453)–rather than being required to answer immediately in face-to-face situations. In this way, social media becomes a differentiation strategy that can be used to address the needs of learners who may require additional wait time to process material and/or those who suffer from overwhelming anxiety in face-to-face situations. Along those lines, Towner and Muñoz (2011) explained that, "social media . . . has the potential to improve the quality of relationships between instructors and students in terms of personalization of communication" (p. 53).

Although some social media platforms do not have methods of dissent built into their architecture, instructors are still using them to facilitate lively discussions. Educators are using the comments section of course-related YouTube, TeacherTube, Edmodo, Facebook, and Twitter pages as online discussion boards and facilitating debates among students (Fewkes & McCabe, 2012). They have found that "students were engaged and when asked to answer questions using Twitter, they felt less pressure even if the answer was incorrect"

(Ralph & Ralph, 2013, p. 454). Additionally, it has been suggested that Twitter's 280-character limit can make for faster communication and, therefore, maximize time on task (Tess, 2013). Since then, Twitter has doubled it limit, so it will be interesting to see if these advantages still hold true.

It is important to note that with all the discussion that is happening with regard to connections (i.e., student–student, student–teacher, teacher–teacher), there is a great deal of concern as to whether we are "too connected." Over the past several years, social media has grown by leaps and bounds. Freeman (2016) acknowledged, "the glories of social media [for education] are exciting to use and hold immense potential for a world of good things. Yet although its immediate effects [on social and emotional development] are still difficult to be sure about, its long-terms effects are entirely unknown" (p. 170). If harnessed effectively, however, by knowledgeable educators, social media could be a powerful force for learning.

For Discussion: Michael (from the case study presented earlier)

1. Which modality—Flipped Classroom, Digital Storytelling, or Social Media—do you think will best help Michael? Why?
2. What factors should Mrs. Soliz consider before using any of the three modalities to address Michael's social-emotional needs?
3. How could Mrs. Soliz utilize Social-Emotional Learning and identity development in each of the three modalities to support Michael's social-emotional development? What are some pitfalls that she might have to consider?
4. Compare and contrast each modality in terms of providing Michael with ways of expressing his thoughts and feelings through his classwork.
5. What are the challenges to using technology to support the social-emotional needs of students, particularly those in elementary grade levels?

Summary

Educational psychology forms the bedrock for the teaching and learning that occurs every day in our classrooms. In this chapter, we have discussed in-depth the ways in which flipped classrooms, digital storytelling, and social media can play a role in shaping the cognitive, behavioral, and social-emotional development of students in our classrooms, who, in turn, are likely to have more positive results academically. Through opportunities for collaborative learning, problem-solving, and critical and creative thinking, these learning strategies allow students to connect with the curriculum while offering the chance for increased engagement, motivation, self-concept, and achievement.

Good teaching is good teaching, and technology does not replace the time, effort, and energy it takes to get to know students and to personalize the learning experience. However, these technology-focused strategies and learning tools can be used to replace, transform, or amplify the traditional curriculum and can be used independently or collectively. Whether teachers use all or just some of these strategies, it is important to stress the value of professional development and training and the careful planning that is required for successful technology implementation.

In this chapter, we introduced three potential tools that can be used to address students' needs in and out of the classroom along with a number of resources. As with any tool or resource, there are times and places in which it is appropriate. We cannot tell you, as a teacher, what technology to use, when to use it, and whether a particular strategy will work best with your particular students. As stated at the beginning of this chapter, in educational psychology there is no magic bullet, but selecting and using technology that fits your classroom and learners should both enhance and transform the classroom experience in positive ways for students and teachers. We will not tell you to "do this, not that." Instead, we have given you principles and guidance to use in making good decisions as to how to use certain types of technology to best support the needs of your students. We trust that you, the teacher, will use your knowledge and professional judgment to determine the age and developmentally appropriate technology-based strategies to address the critical needs of your students.

In other chapters, using technology simply for the sake of using technology has been discouraged. In supporting that statement, we would always ask, "Why use this technology?"—and ask you to consider the answer carefully. An intentional teacher always considers the far-reaching effects of any instructional choice. Knowing the psychology behind one's classroom choices is an important part of selecting the technology that will benefit all learners.

References

Abeysekera, L., & Dawson, P. (2015). Motivation and cognitive load in the flipped classroom: Definition, rationale and a call for research. *Higher Education Research & Development, 34*(1), 1–14.

Allaire, F. S. (2014). *A multiple-case study on the navigation of personal, cultural, and professional identities of native Hawaiian members of Hawaii's science, technology, engineering, and math community* (Unpublished doctoral dissertation), University of Hawaii at Mānoa, Honolulu, HI.

Baillargeon, R. (2002). The acquisition of physical knowledge in infancy: A summary of eight lessons. In U. Goswami (Ed.), *Blackwell handbook of childhood cognitive development* (pp. 47–83). Malden, MA: Blackwell.

Barrett, H. (2006). Researching and evaluating digital storytelling as a deep learning tool. *Technology and Teacher Education Annual, 1*, 647.

Bereiter, C., & Scardamalia, M. (1989). Intentional learning as a goal of instruction. In L. B. Resnick (Ed.), *Knowing, learning, and instruction: Essays in honor of Robert Glaser* (pp. 361–392). Hillsdale, CA: Lawrence Erlbaum.

Besnoy, K. D. (2017, May). Virtual schools and gifted students. *Teaching for High Potential*, 11–13.

Bishop, J. L., & Verleger, M. A. (2013, June). The flipped classroom: A survey of the research. In Proceedings of the ASEE National Conference (Vol. 30, No. 9; pp. 1–18). American Society of Engineering Association, Atlanta, GA.

Blad, E. (2017). Scientists to schools: Social, emotional, development crucial for learning. Retrieved from www.blogs.edweek.org/edweek/rulesforengagement/2017/09/scientists_to_schools_social_emotional_development_crucial_for_learning.html

Bull, G., Thompson, A., Searson, M., Garofalo, J., Park, J., Young, C., & Lee, J. (2008). Connecting informal and formal learning: Experiences in the age of participatory media. *Contemporary Issues in Technology and Teacher Education, 8*(2), 100–107.

Butt, A. (2014). Student views on the use of a flipped classroom approach: Evidence from Australia. *Business Education and Accreditation, 6(1)*, 33–43.

Calao L.A., Moreno-León J., Correa H.E., Robles G. (2015) Developing mathematical thinking with Scratch. In G. Conole, T. Klobučar, C. Rensing, J. Konert, & E. Lavoué (Eds.) *Design for teaching and learning in a networked world: Lecture notes in computer science* (pp. 17–27). Toledo, Spain: Springer

Center for Digital Storytelling. (2005). Center for Digital Storytelling Website. Retrieved from www.youtube.com/watch?v=NipDAd3_7Do

Common Sense Media. (2015). *The common sense census: Media use by tweens and teens.* San Francisco, CA: Author.

Craft, A. (2012). Childhood in a digital age: Creative challenges for educational futures. *London Review of Education, 10*, 173–190.

Crain, W. (2010). *Theories of cognitive development: Concepts and applications* (6th ed.). New York, NY: Routledge.

Cramond, B. (1994). Attention deficit hyperactivity disorder and creativity—What is the connection? *Journal of Creative Behavior, 28*, 193–210.

Crews, T., & Butterfield, J. B. (2014). Data for flipped classroom design: Using student feedback to identify the best components from online and face-to-face classes. *Higher Education Studies, 4*(3), 38.

Cyberbullying Research Center. (2016). Cyberbullying data. Retrieved from www.cyberbullying.org/2016-cyberbullying-data

Davis, A. (2004a). Co-authoring identity: Digital storytelling in an urban middle school. *THEN: Technology, Humanities, Education, and Narrative, 1*(1), 1.

Davis, G. A. (2004b). *Creativity is forever* (5th ed.). Dubuque, IA: Kendall Hunt.

Deci, E. L., & Ryan, R. M. (2008). Self-determination theory: A macrotheory of human motivation, development, and health. *Canadian Psychology, 49*, 182–185.

Deschryver, M. D., & Yadav, A. (2015). Creative and computational thinking in the context of new literacies: Working with teachers to scaffold complex technology-mediated approaches to teaching and learning. *Journal of Technology and Teacher Education, 23*, 411–431.

Di Blas N., Garzotto F., Paolini P., Sabiescu A. (2009). Digital storytelling as a whole-class learning activity: Lessons from a three-years project. In I. A. Iurgel, N. Zagalo, P. Petta, (Eds.), *Interactive storytelling. ICIDS 2009. Lecture notes in computer science, 5915*. Berlin, Germany: Springer.

Durak, J. A., Weissberg, R. P., Dymnicki, A. B., Taylor, R. D., & Schellinger, K. B. (2011). The impact of enhancing students' social and emotional learning: A meta-analysis of school based universal interventions. *Child Development, 82,* 405–432.

Epstein, A. S. (2009, January/February). Think before you (inter)act: What it means to be an intentional teacher. *Exchange,* 46–49.

Feldman, R. S. (2012). *Understanding psychology.* New York, NY: McGraw-Hill.

Fewkes, A. M., & McCabe, M. (2012). Facebook: Learning tool or distraction? *Journal of Digital Learning in Teacher Education, 28*(3), 92–98.

Freeman, J. (2016). Possible effects of electronic social media on gifted and talented children's intelligence and emotional development. *Gifted Education International, 32*(2), 165–172.

Friesen, N., & Lowe, S. (2011). The questionable promise of social media for education: Connective learning and the commercial imperative. *Journal of Computer Assisted Learning, 28*(3), 183–194.

Fugate, C. M., Zentall, S. S., & Gentry, M. (2013). Creativity and working memory in gifted students with and without characteristics of Attention Deficit Hyperactive Disorder: Lifting the mask. *Gifted Child Quarterly, 57,* 234–246.

Grinder, R. E. (1989). Educational psychology: The master science. In M. C. Wittrock & F. Farley (Eds.), *The future of educational psychology* (pp. 3–18). Hillsdale, NJ: Lawrence Erlbaum Associates.

Hidi, S., & Renninger, K. A. (2006). The four-phase model of interest development. *Educational Psychologist, 41,* 111–127.

Hughes, J. (2005). The role of teacher knowledge and learning experiences in forming technology-integrated pedagogy. *Journal of Technology and Teacher Education, 13,* 277–302.

Hui, A. N. N., & Lau, S. (2010). Formulation of policy and strategy in developing creativity in education in four Asian Chinese societies: A policy analysis. *The Journal of Creative Behavior, 44,* 215–235.

Hung, C. M., Hwang, G. J., & Huang, I. (2012). A project-based digital storytelling approach for improving students' learning motivation, problem-solving competence and learning achievement. *Educational Technology & Society, 15,* 368–379.

Iaosanurak, C., Chanchalor, S., & Murphy, E. (2016). Social and emotional learning around technology in a cross-cultural, elementary classroom. *Education and Information Technologies, 21,* 1639–1662.

Jensen, J. L., Kummer, T. A., & Godoy, P. D. M. (2015). Improvements from a flipped classroom may simply be the fruits of active learning. *CBE-Life Sciences Education, 14*(1).

Jenkins, A. (2017). How school districts are leveraging Twitter to become rock stars. *eSchool News.* Retrieved from www.eschoolnews.com/2017/03/30/school-districts-twitter-rockstars

Junco, R., Elavsky, C. M., & Heiberger, G. (2013). Putting Twitter to the test: Assessing outcomes for student collaboration, engagement and success. *British Journal of Educational Technology, 44*(2), 273–287.

Junco, R., Heiberger, G., & Loken, E. (2010). The effect of Twitter on college student engagement and grades. *Journal of Computer Assisted Learning, 27,* 1–14.

Kajder, S. B. (2004). Enter here: Personal narrative and digital storytelling. *English Journal, 93*(3), 64–68.

Kapuler, D. (2013). 50 sites and apps for digital storytelling. Retrieved from www.techlearning.com/default .aspx?tabid=100&entryid=5656

Kerka, S. (2000). Incidental learning. *Trends and Issues, 18,* 2–4.

Kim, M. K., Kim, S. M., Khera, O., & Getman, J. (2014). The experience of three flipped classrooms in an urban university: An exploration of design principles. *The Internet and Higher Education, 22,* 37–50.

Kuhn, D. (2006). Do cognitive changes accompany developments in the adolescent brain? *Perspectives in Psychological Science, 1,* 59–67.

Leu, D. J., Jr., Kinzer, C. K., Coiro, J., Castek, J. & Henry, L. A. (2013). New literacies: A dual-level theory of the changing nature of literacy, instruction, and assessment. In R.B. Ruddell & D. Alvermann (Eds.), *Theoretical models and processes of reading* (6th ed.). Newark, DE: IRA

Malita, L., & Martin, C. (2010). Digital storytelling as web passport to success in the 21st century. *Procedia-Social and Behavioral Sciences, 2*(2), 3060–3064.

McCarthy, J. (2010). Blended learning environments: Using social networking sites to enhance the first-year experience. *Australasian Journal of Educational Technology, 26*(6), 729–740.

McLeod, S. (2007, updated 2016). Maslow's hierarchy of needs. Retrieved from www.simplypsychology.org/maslow.html

McLoughlin, C., & Lee, M. J. (2010). Personalized and self regulated learning in the Web 2.0 era: International exemplars of innovative pedagogy using social software. *Australasian Journal of Educational Technology, 26*(1), 28–43.

Milman, N. B. (2012). The flipped classroom strategy: What is it and how can it best be used? *Distance Learning, 9*(3), 85.

Mishra, P., & Yadav, A. (2013). Of art and algorithm: Rethinking technology & creativity in the 21st century. *TechTrends, 57*(3), 10–14.

Muñoz, C. L., & Towner, T. (2011). Back to the "wall": How to use Facebook in the college classroom. *First Monday, 16*(12). Retrieved from www.firstmonday.org/article/view/3513/3116.

National Research Council. (2000). *Eager to learn: Educating our preschoolers.* Washington, DC: National Academy Press.

Nielsen Company. (2012). *State of the Media: The Social Media Report 2012.* New York. Retrieved from www.nielsen.com/us/en/insights/reports/2012/state-of-the-media-the-social-media-report-2012.html

Nielsen Company. (2016). Social studies: A look at the social landscape. New York. Retrieved from www.nielsen.com/us/en/insights/reports/2017/2016-nielsen-social-media-report.html

Nussbaum, E. (2007). Say everything: Kids, the Internet, and the end of privacy. *New York Magazine.* Retrieved from www.nymag.com/news/features/27341/.

Payton, J. W., Wardlaw, D. M., Graczyk, P. A., Bloodworth, M. R., Tompsett, C. J., & Weissberg, R. P. (2000). Social and emotional learning: A framework for promoting mental health and reducing risk behavior in children and youth. *Journal of School Health, 70,* 179–185.

Pew Research Center. (2016). Pew Internet Initiative: Social Media Fact Sheet. Retrieved from www.pewinternet.org/fact-sheet/social-media/

Plucker, J. A., Beghetto, R. A., & Dow, G. T. (2004). Why isn't creativity more important to educational psychologists? Potentials, pitfalls, and future directions in creativity research. *Educational Psychologist, 59,* 83–96.

Price, E., Wardman, J., Bruce, T., & Millward, P. (2016). The juggling act: A phenomenological study of gifted and talented girls' experiences with Facebook. *Roeper Review, 38,* 162–174.

Ralph, M., & Ralph, L. (2013). Weapons of mass instruction: The creative use of social media in improving pedagogy. *Issues in Informing Science and Information Technology, 10,* 449–460.

Ravenscroft, A., Warburton, S., Hatzipanagos, S., & Conole, G. (2012). Designing and evaluating social media for learning: Shaping social networking into social learning? *Journal of Computer Assisted Learning, 28*(3), 177–182.

Rideout, V. J., Foehr, U. G., & Roberts, D. F. (2010). *Generation M [superscript 2]: Media in the lives of 8-to 18-Year-Olds.* Menlo Park, CA: Henry J. Kaiser Family Foundation.

Robin, B. R. (2008). Digital storytelling: A powerful technology tool for the 21st century classroom. *Theory into Practice, 47,* 220–228.

Russ, S. W. (1998). Play, creativity, and adaptive functioning: Implications for play interventions. *Journal of Clinical Child Psychology, 27,* 469–480.

Sadik, A. (2008). Digital storytelling: A meaningful technology-integrated approach for engaged student learning. *Educational technology research and development, 56,* 487–506.

Sawyer, K. (2011). *Structure and improvisation in creative teaching.* New York, NY: Cambridge University Press.

Slavin, R. E. (2018). *Educational psychology: Theory and practice* (12th ed.). Boston, MA: Pearson.

Sternberg, R. J. (1999). *Handbook of creativity.* Cambridge, England: Cambridge University Press.

Strayer, J. F. (2012). How learning in an inverted classroom influences cooperation, innovation and task orientation. *Learning Environments Research, 15*(2), 171–193.

Talbert, R. (2016). How much research has been done on flipped learning? Retrieved from www.rtalbert.org/blog/2016/how-much-research

Taylor, L. (2005). *Introducing cognitive development.* New York, NY: Psychology Press.

Tess, P. A. (2013). The role of social media in higher education classes (real and virtual)–A literature review. *Computers in Human Behavior, 29,* A60–A68.

The Flipped Learning Network. (2014). *Speak Up 2014 National Research Project Findings.* Retrieved from www.flippedlearning.org/wp-content/uploads/2016/07/Speak-Up-FLN-2014-Survey-Results-FINAL.pdf

The Flipped Learning Network. (2017). Definition of flipped learning. Retrieved from www.flippedlearning.org/definition-of-flipped-learning/

Tierney, P., Farmer, S. M., & Graen, G. B. (1999). An examination of leadership and employee creativity: The relevance of traits and relationships. *Personnel Psychology, 52,* 591–620.

Torrance, E. P. (1972). Career patterns and peak creative achievements of creative high school students 12 years later. *Gifted Child Quarterly, 16,* 75–88.

Torrance, E. P. (1981). Predicting the creativity of elementary school children (1958–1980)—and the teacher who "made a difference". *Gifted Child Quarterly, 25,* 55–62.

Towner, T. L., & Muñoz, C. (2011). Facebook and education: a classroom connection? In C. Wankel (Ed.), *Educating educators with social media* (pp. 33–57). Bingley, UK: Emerald Group Publishing Limited.

Wang, H. (2014). Enabling technologies for incidental learning on the Web. In T. Bastiaens (Ed.), *Proceedings of E-Learn: World Conference on E-Learning in Corporate, Government, Healthcare, and Higher Education 2014* (pp. 1997–2002). Chesapeake, VA: Association for the Advancement of Computing in Education (AACE).

Wigfield, A., & Eccles, J. S. (2000). Expectancy-value theory of achievement motivation. *Contemporary Educational Psychology, 25,* 68–81.

Wing, J. M. (2006). Computational thinking. *Communications of the ACM, 49*(3), 33–35.

Yadav, A., Hong, H. & Stephenson, C. (2016). Computational thinking for all: Pedagogical approaches to embedding 21st Century problem solving in K-12 classrooms. *TechTrends: Linking Research and Practice to Improve Learning, 60,* 565–568.

Yadav, A., Mayfield, C., Zhou, N., Hambrusch, S., & Korb, T. (2014). Computational thinking in elementary and secondary teacher education. *ACM Transactions on Computing Education, 14*(1), 1–16.

Yang, Y. C., & Wu, W. I. (2012). Digital storytelling for enhancing student academic achievement, critical thinking, and learning motivation: A year-long experimental study. *Computers & Education, 59,* 339–352.

Chapter 17

From Culturally Responsive Teaching to Digital Citizenship Education

Irene Chen, *University of Houston - Downtown*

Crystal Belle, *University of Rutgers*

Janice L. Nath, *Professor Emeritus, University of Houston - Downtown*

Meet Ms. Turner

Monkey Business Images / Shutterstock.com

My teaching career began in 2006 in what was considered to be the poorest district in Brooklyn at the time: East New York. It was determined to be "poor" based on factors like socioeconomic status (SES), housing quality, access to healthcare, and how unattractive the school buildings were. As a Brooklyn native who had been geographically removed for four years and due to a private education at a liberal arts institution in New England, my lens of Brooklyn had changed. Although I was not from this specific section of Brooklyn, I felt a particular ownership of the entire borough, as if somehow every perception and stereotype of what Brooklyn was somehow connected to my identity. I soon learned that these naïve beliefs were dangerous, which was revealed to me upon meeting my students on that warm September of my first day.

I entered the building the week before school started in late August to set up my classroom, which according to all of the established teachers whom I knew, was a standard practice. Upon seeing my classroom, I became filled with both excitement and apprehension. I was excited because the room was massive, with high contoured ceilings—remnants of what appeared to be Victorian architecture in the midst of educational stratification. I was apprehensive because the only technology visible was a dated Dell desktop computer in the corner of the room on a dilapidated desk that resembled the computers I had back in high school 10 years beforehand. Suddenly, I realized that my experiences as a former Brooklyn student and those of my new students were already different in nature. The desks were old, sturdy, and made of iron. The chalkboard was green and dusty, and the bulletin boards were numerous, surrounding the room like Big Brother.

Two of the most important questions I asked myself at that time was, "How could I engage my students with technology when there seemed to be so very few technological resources," and "How would I make this classroom a rich experience for the multicultural group that I knew would be walking through my doors in a few short days?" A few years have passed since my first day of teaching. Students who walk in to my classroom now are among the first generations of Digital Natives—those who grew up with the Internet and use all sorts of media daily. When they participate on social media, they are no longer simply students from Brooklyn—they can become a part of the world conversation. I then ask myself this new question, "How do I, as a culturally responsive teacher, better educate them to become good Digital Citizens?"

Introduction

In addition to academic achievement, educators are charged with both preparing students to be successful in life and to become productive members of society; however, with a strong focus on standardized test scores in today's schools, it is easy for schools to overlook differences in students that would address these two areas as teachers feel the pressure of simply getting through the required curriculum. Understanding and addressing learners' cultures, however, can make a difference in instructional success and can prepare *all* students for a future of working with many peoples who may be "different from them." Differences cannot only include those who are of another color and/or come from a different country and, perhaps, speak a different language or speak English with a distinctly different accent, but they may also include those who are from dissimilar income levels, hold different religious beliefs, are of different genders or sexual orientations, and/or may be differently abled. Belonging to one or more of these groups brings with it a culture that may be very different from the school culture in which they are to be educated and/or from the teacher who will educate them. Yet, each of these groups may come with its own culture, or set of behaviors and beliefs. Nearly all books and articles about multiculturalism show that the populations of classrooms are changing dramatically, so a teacher can assume that regardless of the culture(s) which he or she claims, the classroom will contain students who are different.

Each teacher who steps into a classroom will have his or her own worldview which is dependent upon the life experiences from which he or she came—along with the cultural norms from those experiences. However, the "intentional teacher" recognizes that his or her "lens of the world" can be very similar *or* can be quite different from that of his/her students who have come from different communities, and, to reach all learners, he or she may be required to select strategies based on students' best chances of achievement (rather than the teacher's preferences in ways of teaching). Technology may offer excellent choices in helping diverse students to achieve their full potential and to ensure that *all* students gain tolerance and cultural understanding of diverse peoples and their backgrounds.

Use of the Internet grew rapidly in the West from the mid-1990s, and from the late 1990s onward, has spread into the developing world (Stokes & Wilson, 2006). Ever since, digital technologies have become used to some aspect by people in almost every area of the globe (see Figure 17.1). Some of those young users may become a part of our classrooms as their parents immigrate to the United States, but others may be culturally diverse in other ways.

In human history, the first generation of social media users has become adults. The Internet also has been a key factor in driving globalization. The Information Age has brought a number of positive world values, such as support for democracy, tolerance of foreigners and ethnic minorities, understanding of the needs of those with disabilities, and gender equity. It has opened up the world to the role of religion, the impact of globalization, and attitudes toward the environment, work, family, politics, identity, diversity, and subjective well-being. Teaching technology skills is not the only area needed for success in students' futures. Digital Citizenship, however, is important not only in the United States but all around the world. Using technology to teach about multiculturalism touches on the idea of global Digital Citizenship and respect for Digital Equity in a world that increasingly operates electronically. Furthermore, social media experts like Collier (www.twitter.com/annecollier) suggest that we should drop the word "digital" from the phrase "Digital Citizenship" in terms of teaching values through technology because we are simply teaching *citizenship* to students with the knowledge and skills that students need to navigate the world today.

Elements for integrating technology in culturally diverse classrooms have been discussed in the past (Chisholm, 1998); these include currently relevant issues such as cultural awareness, cultural relevance, a culturally supportive environment, equitable access, instructional flexibility, and instructional integration.

Figure 17.1 Digital technologies have come to be used by people throughout the world. As parents immigrate to the United States, some of these young users will become part of our classrooms.

CECIL BO DZWOWA / Shutterstock.com

These elements are not exhaustive of good instructional practices for technology use with diverse learners. Instead, they focus on key multicultural concepts that are supported by the literature on effective multicultural teaching. They also highlight the complexity of teaching in that they emphasize the need to orchestrate a variety of elements in the multicultural classroom and, indeed, are in common with good educational practice. (p. 251)

The purpose of this chapter will be: (1) to discuss technology as a resource for teacher and student understanding; (2) to consider ways in which technology may better reach the needs of learners in a multicultural classroom; (3) to help learners and teachers come to "know" about others who are not like them and, with this understanding, decrease the misunderstandings that often occur in schools, the workplace, and in their future lives; (4) to elaborate on issues relevant to Digital Citizenship; and (5) to ensure students and teachers understand the strengths, weaknesses, opportunities, threats (SWOT) faced by Digital Citizens. Multiculturalism aims not simply for knowledge of the differences of students but for celebrating those differences *and* similarities, and technology can often work in many ways toward that target.

Cultural Proficiency

As children develop, they are exposed to both the outward, obvious "way things are" or how people around them establish and maintain norms (e.g., what is normal for their group) and the "hidden norms" that are a part of the groups to which they belong. Everyone belongs to a number of groups—each with its own culture and norms. For example, one may belong to a church group and, when with them, act a bit differently than one does with a social group of friends who get together on Saturday nights, and one may act differently still when sent on a business trip for work. These differences may be large or small, but great differences may exist between groups from different parts of the country, different parts of the world, different family backgrounds and religions, and so forth. However, if a person can operate well in many diverse groups, he or she is said to be multiculturally proficient. Humans tend to adopt behaviors and beliefs attached to their own groups, which may or may not be understood or accepted by another group. These behaviors may sometimes be viewed in a negative way and can cause feelings and actions that do not deal with the value of the individual person but rather the associated behavior

Ms. Turner's Reflection

I have just gotten a new student, Munju, whose parents are from India. My new student was a high achiever, but I needed to talk to her parents about the manner in which Munju always interrupted much of what I was telling the class. It was rapidly becoming annoying all during the day, and I had tried to work with Munju on this issue. When Munju's parents came in, I greeted them and began to speak to them about how happy I was with Munju's achievement so far. "But why are we here, then?" interrupted Mrs. Gupta. "Well, I wanted . . ." I began. "Well, if she is doing so well, why have you called us?" "I thought that I would . . ." I continued. "But is she getting enough work? I'm not sure she is bringing home enough work," said Mr. Gupta. "I think she is, but . . ." I began again. At that point, I became flustered; they were not letting me get a word in edgewise—and I also realized that Munju elicited the very same feelings in me that her parents were doing right now. I thought that they were being rude and aggressive. In an instant, however, I remembered my multicultural training experienced during my education courses: when a teacher begins to feel negatively about a child, he or she should question whether there might be clashing norms first. In this reflection, I realized that my conversational norms were different from this family's. I immediately began to do some research on the Internet about "Wait or Interrupt" cultural conversational styles, and I instantly found that different cultures around the world had different norms for each style. As I read the number of articles available, I became aware of multiple issues on the culture of my student and her parents, which gave me considerable insight. Rather than just letting my feelings dictate my behavior toward this learner and her family, I began to see that they intended no disrespect, but their cultural conversation norms were simply different from mine.

of the culture. Motivation theory tells us that belonging is a powerful force, so that when one feels that he or she does not and cannot belong, there is often little motivation to go forth. The importance of this to schools and to teacher education should be obvious—both in helping learners become accepting and accepted and to help them learn to work with others throughout their lives in a society that is becoming more and more diverse with time.

The Internet is often an educator's best resource for issues related to cultural norms. There are few cultures in the world that have not been researched for their norms so that others can gain an understanding about differences. In the past, one could go to a bookstore to purchase a travel book on what to expect or how to act with people when visiting their country or a business guide to interacting with others from a particular place, but now this type of information is also instantly available in many different forms electronically. Not only can teachers gain knowledge about students from other lands but also from different social levels, different religions, culturally different learning styles, and so forth. The multicultural teacher is not just able to know about "Asian" culture, for instance, but about the nuances and differences in norms of students coming from Japan, China, Korea, Malaysia, Vietnam, Thailand, Indonesia, and so forth—all of whom are considered Asian—but different from each other. The same is true of those in the wide range of different Hispanic/Latino countries, Middle Eastern countries, areas of Africa, and other cultures. Knowing what might offend students (such as placing a hand on a child's shoulder or head in some cultures, for example) or just understanding and being able to defuse examples such as we saw with Ms. Turner with Munju can make a difference in the way a teacher/student relationship develops and learning occurs in a positive environment. Thanks to technology, there is no reason for a teacher not to know and reflect upon differences or discover how to make connections with diverse learners and their parents.

A teacher may use a search engine to type in "cultural differences in ___" (include almost any country or other cultural difference in the world from Myanmar to Samoa to Nigeria) to receive a long listing of articles or lists that will help a teacher with understanding her students and their parents. YouTube videos give very good illustrations (www.youtube.com/watch?v=haohj1sVnyk) and often with an age group to which students can relate. With technology, teachers no longer simply tell students about people who are different. There is a wealth of examples that show students about each other's cultures and body language (such as demonstrating the Indian head bobble [www.youtube.com/watch?v=tRwzcnOdNFc]) to common cultural differences as seen by Korean teens (www.youtube.com/watch?v=M68q_7YQVCc). Teachers should always screen any videos they plan to show or place in technology centers for students to watch for information and/or assignments for issues that would be inappropriate, particularly for specific age groups. Of course, *knowing* cultural differences is only a beginning.

Each year, Americans observe National Hispanic Heritage Month from September 15 to October 15 by celebrating the cultures of American citizens whose ancestors came from Spain, the Caribbean, and Central and South America.

Ms. Turner was assigned to coordinate the Hispanic Heritage Month, which was occurring for the first time in her school. After two weeks of promoting the integration of multicultural education topic in curriculum, some teachers on her campus agreed to use one class period to "celebrate" while other teachers hesitated to integrate multicultural education.

"We don't need multicultural education here; most of our students are Black," one student commented.

"We shouldn't talk about racism in school because it has nothing to do with learning. Besides, it'll just make everybody feel bad," one school PTO member said.

"I don't see colors. All my students are the same to me," a teacher added.

"I want to include multicultural education in my curriculum, but there's just no time for it," yet another teacher added.

"Let's not focus on negative things. Can't we all just get along?" a student asked.

Seeing the hesitation to incorporate the celebration of cultures, Ms. Turner thought that it was important for the younger generation to deliberate answers for the critiques they could face when practicing cultural awareness behaviors. She created Voki avatars to ask a number of common challenging questions about integrating multicultural education in to the curriculum, and, as an exercise, had students answer through the Voki avatars that they created in response to the critiques. Students had a chance to role-play as community members, teachers, and students through the avatar characters of their choices. Click to see if the teacher avatar explains the challenge of integrating multicultural education into the curriculum and a parent avatar responds that, with globalization of the business world, multicultural education is needed.

A teacher's statement (acted by a student-created avatar):
"I want to include multicultural education in my curriculum, but there's just no time for it."
Try out this Website to see an avatar: www.tinyurl.com/l2php9s

A parent's response (acted by a student-created avatar):
"I own my own business with customers from Asia. And I expect my daughter to become a successful business woman with customers from all over the world. She will need to get her multicultural education from school–not just math, English, history and government."
Try out this Website to see an avatar: www.tinyurl.com/l87xxqy

Mrs. Turner

I had to think hard about what they said, but I wanted to come back to the idea of understanding others. We don't have to take on the norms of those who are different from us, but understanding their norms and behaviors that are cultural (and what others value) helps us to know where others are coming from.

It makes me such a better teacher! For example, we do have some Hispanic girls in our school, and now I understand how excited they are about their family celebrating certain holidays and milestones such as girls' fifteenth birthday (Quinceañera).

Michael Zysman / Shutterstock.com

mark stephens photography / shutterstock.com

Technology as a Tool for Reflection

As noted, technology is an excellent tool in teacher reflection on multicultural behaviors—in a variety of ways. The author of *How to Teach Students Who Don't Look Like You* (Davis, 2006) suggests:

> Do some reflection. If 20% of your students are into hip-hop and you can't stand it, how might that play out in your class? If you find some students' cultural norms, behaviors, or hidden rules repugnant, how might that be reflected in our body language as you interact with them? (p. 91)

Recording oneself teaching using technology is a quick and straightforward way to determine if a teacher is using negative body language or biased oral language that would indicate a difference in interactions between oneself and diverse students. Videos can show a teacher's differences in, for instance, the space he/she keeps from a student, facial expressions, word choices, which learners are called upon and for what level of questions, and so forth that could demonstrate that a teacher was not treating diverse students in the same way as he/she does with those with whom he/she may share a culture. This said, treating all students as *individuals* within their cultures is also an aim in good instruction. Even though we might say that the majority of any group may act in certain ways or have certain values and norms, the student is still an individual. In fact, a teacher should be sensitive to many different kinds of interactions with diverse students; however, these differences should not result in unequal or negative treatment that would affect achievement.

Ms. Turner's Reflection

I was thinking about a few of my other students who were from cultures different than me. I know, for example, that my Greek student who "got into my personal space" didn't bother me because I understood this is "normal" for many Greeks, and then some of my students from Mexico and Asia would not look me in the eyes. At first, I didn't understand that these were commonplace norms in their cultures, but now I clearly accept that not looking into an adult's eyes is a sign of respect in these cultures rather than of "shiftiness or not telling the truth" for them. Had it not been for my videotapes, I might not have "heard myself" raising my voice a bit and telling them to "look at me when I'm talking to you." Using videotaping can help to uncover negativity toward students, particularly those "who are different."

Not everything may come to light about a culture and/or various human norms in one's research, but major issues found on the Internet can help with considerable understanding. For students coming from different countries, there is a continuum about how close they are to American culture and how much experience they have with current technology. They may have been born here but their parents stay close to their community, or they may have just arrived and have little concept of the life or language here. Their parents may be of higher income or status in a company or a business in which there are many advantages (including technology) at home, or they may be coming from a refugee- or poverty-stricken area with little technology background. It is always a consideration for the teacher to know more about the culture of the student *and* what his or her technological background is and to know what could be currently available at home. The Digital Divide tells us that lower income families may not have computers or other technology at home and may not have had it as a part of growing up for homework assignments and so forth. This could cause students to be disadvantaged in school assignments without the teacher realizing it. The Digital Citizenship SWOT section further on in this chapter will provide more about the Digital Divide and its impact.

Technology offers excellent opportunities to make connections as well. Posters hung in classrooms with women astronauts or African-American poets in the Digital Age have moved into live interviews about their professions and/or instant access to their work on the Internet. Typing in, for example, "famous South American scientists" brings up numerous examples to connect with students. Here are some diverse examples for those noted in their fields:

Woman astronaut Dr. Mae Jemison:

www.youtube.com/watch?v=Fv4TditrXt8

Nobel Laureate Derek Walcott on his life and work:

www.youtube.com/watch?v=d_6mgbRSUzo

Time Magazine Person of the Year, 1996, Dr. David Ho on AIDS research:

www.youtube.com/watch?v=HCt-QeGj0Q8

Egyptian-American news anchor Hoda Kotb of the Today's Show on heritage:

www.youtube.com/watch?v=plVNKOc6QGE

Technology also offers students books and movies that delve into successes that have been hard won (e.g., *Hidden Figures: The Story of the African-American Women Who Helped Win the Space Race* by Margot Lee Shetterly).

In addition, almost any type of music and any song can be downloaded from the Internet, and music is an effective way to use connections to make a student feel at home and/or to show the universality of music. Playingforchange.com (with links to many songs) has a number of selections that are a mix of musicians from all over the world who are singing and playing the same well-known song; the music is mixed to create a single recording. For example, the song "Stand by Me" is sung by artists in America (including a Native American tribe), the Netherlands, France, Brazil, Italy, Russia, Venezuela, Spain, and South Africa. "What a Wonderful World" is a mix of children and adults from France, Uganda, and the United States. "Guantanamera" and "La Bamba" offer a mix of singers from all over Mexico, Cuba, and Central and South America. These productions emphasize the point of bringing all people together through a common love of music.

Technology can offer a warm welcome to a student and parents from another country or those coming from poverty without backgrounds of schooling. One school district near a large urban area uses technology to film "the first day of school" from the perspective/eyes of an elementary student arriving at the curb of the school, walking to the office, getting his/her room assignment, going down the hall and finding his/her grade-level area and teacher(s) for the year at the door, and so forth. The way to the cafeteria (along with how to take a tray and pay), the locations of the restrooms, the route to the gym and music rooms are all filmed. Some schools include shots of documents and downloads to be filled out and other school-related information. This technology allows students and their parents to look at the videos at home several times to feel as if they already know the school very well. Even if a school does not offer this, a teacher can easily construct his/her own welcome message (even using the digital camera on his or her phone). This could benefit all children new to a school. Here is an example:

Must-Have Videos for the Start of the School Year:

www.animoto.com/blog/education/videos-start-school-year/

Another area of diversity includes students who are differently abled. Technology can also be most effective for these learners. Being a student with special needs in today's classroom is, in many ways, very different than in the past. If a student's individual education plan requires that special technology be provided, then a teacher is required to know and use the equipment with the student. Often, a special education aide can be on the scene—but that is not always the case. Young children can also have quite a bit of curiosity about devices that belong to their peers with special needs, and technology can often provide guidance for everyone around the devise. One idea for inclusion is having students design projects and equipment (www.youtube.com/watch?v=jJ8uZT6LyS8). Schools may help to bring devices to their peers in group projects (www.youtube.com/watch?v=m3Pb9F7sbNY). See many more ideas for using technology for students with special needs in Chapter 6.

Making a Case for Technology in Urban Schools or Low SES Rural Districts

Ms. Turner's Reflection

One of the most important questions I had at the time I was entering my new school years ago was: how could I engage my students with technology when there were so few technological resources? The principal mentioned smartboards, but why was this not the case in my classroom? Where were the laptop carts I had heard about? As these questions floated through my mind, I continued to set up my classroom, which meant sweeping, dusting, and making the bulletin boards look administrator-friendly.

Upon meeting my students, it was apparent that not having access to adequate technology was going to be a problem. As eighth graders, they had become accustomed to the school culture at this particular school which enforced "drill-and-kill", an overwhelming focus on test preparation skills with little focus on who these students were, much less what they could contribute to the classroom for their own learning development. I was given a scripted curriculum that only included using textbooks focused on the standardized English Language Arts exam in New York State at the time. How could I teach in an English classroom while completely ignoring who the students were—culturally, socially, and emotionally—due to the demands of testing, and how could I prepare them for the world of the future with technology?

Most of my students were Black and Latino and lived in the surrounding community. From what I witnessed as they walked through the hallways and in the lunchroom, they had their own ideas about life, love, and the community. Only a few of them had computers in their homes (although many had personal phones); thus, school was one of the few places where they should have been able to access technology. Due to a lack of resources, I made use of overhead projectors, music (my personal collection), and borrowing one of the four smartboards in the school at least once or twice per week. However, borrowing this equipment also entailed a level of bureaucracy and stress. Yet still, during these lessons, students were much more engaged and centered, and it always pained me to realize that I could not provide these resources on a daily basis at this school. As a result, I felt like I was shortchanging my students due to a school culture that was shortchanging all of us—students, families, and teachers.

It is no secret that despite a plethora of government-funded programs and initiatives, students in urban school districts continue to be taught in classrooms that lack adequate technology for academic and social emotional learning (SEL) success. This can also occur in poorer rural districts. SEL includes "self-awareness, self-management, relationship skills, social awareness, and responsible decision-making" (Sink, 2015). Culturally responsive teaching focuses on "a pedagogy that empowers students intellectually, socially, emotionally, and politically by using cultural referents to impart knowledge, skills, and attitudes" (Ladson-Billings, 1994) and should include the SEL skills as it integrates student identities with academic achievement.

Ms. Turner's Reflection

I was surprised by the high percentage of my urban students who were on the school's free lunch program. After some quick online research, I found that urban children were more than twice as likely to be living in poverty than those in suburban locations (30% compared with 13%), while 22% of rural children were poor in 1990 (Lippman, Burns, & McArthur, 1996).

The situation remains the same twenty years later. Here are some highlights from the 2015 national data published by U.S. Bureau of the Census (www.census.gov/library/publications/2016/demo/p60-256.html):

- The official national poverty rate was 13.5%.
- For non-Hispanic Whites the poverty rate was 9.1%.
- The poverty rate for Blacks was 24.1%.
- The poverty rate for Hispanics was 21.4% in 2015.
- For Asians, the poverty rate was 11.4%.
- For children under age 18, 19.7% were in poverty.
- Among those who lived in principal cities, the 2015 poverty rate was 16.8%.

I wanted to have students go through an activity that served to empower them socially and emotionally by using cultural referents about classism and poverty. I asked students to complete the following scavenger hunt activity by watching an animation "Poverty in the Classroom" (www.youtube.com/watch?v=y2r55tAOXAc) and exploring an external resource (www.michigan.gov/documents/mde/Understanding_and_Working_with_Students_and_Adults_from_Poverty_360998_7.pdf) to enlighten them on the topics of classism and poverty.

I then asked students to check on their understanding and to make connections to their social classes:

1. What are "generational poverty" and "situational poverty?"
2. How does poverty affect academic achievement?
3. What is your personal experience on the impact of social classes on your education?
4. What is your personal experience on the impact of poverty on your education?

I think making the connection from statistic numbers with concepts such as "generational poverty" and "situational poverty" with their personal experiences enlightened students on the unequal playing field that they, peers, or those in other areas must challenge for eventual success in education. I then had them, in groups, tell what jobs they might want to do in the future and research on the computer skills needed in that job.

Many in education have felt that in this generation, technical skills or the lack of them will greatly affect this group (Vass Gal, 2015). There was not one job brainstormed by the class that didn't require some computer skills. Hopefully, with this awareness, students would have a good rationale for learning the needed knowledge and skills for success.

Similarly, access to technology in the classroom is directly linked to social justice teaching and learning practices that mirror culturally responsive teaching practices. Yet still, having access to technology does not automatically mean that students are learning. It has been noted that "a fundamental issue around the interaction between technology and education is the conditions under which technology can be used effectively in classrooms to improve student learning" (Zhao, Pugh, Sheldon, & Byers, 2002, page 483).

Therefore, how do we ensure student learning, particularly in urban classrooms?

Ms. Turner's Reflection

Here is an online activity that I used to incorporate SEL.

This "Privilege Walk" activity (www.buzzfeed.com/dayshavedewi/what-is-privilege#.vlrp32wxz) was intended to help students understand the effects of social privilege. In the online video, a list of 35 social privilege or disadvantage statements was read to 10 people. The 10 were lined up in front of the classroom and then took a step forward or a step back based on how s/he identified with the statement.

Out of the 35 statements, I asked students to pay special attention to statements such as the following:

If the primary language spoken in your household growing up was not English, take one step back.
If you feel comfortable being emotionally expressive/open, take one step forward.
If you have ever been the only person of your race/gender/SES/sexual orientation in a classroom or workplace setting, please take one step back.

Once students have watched the video, I asked the following thinking questions:

- After watching the entire video, with one step forward or one step back, where do you stand when compared with others?

And

- When you see some groups have more privilege (i.e., the "have" groups) than other groups (i.e., the "have not" groups), how far are you, as a world citizen, willing to go to advocate for the "have not" groups?

In the summary essays, Student A wrote, "This is incredibly eye-opening, and somewhat depressing. I didn't count, but I assume I ended up somewhere in the middle. It's so sad that privilege is such a definite part of our society."

Student B wrote, "I ended up 9 steps in front of Start. I like the idea behind this. It really gives people something to think about and goes to show that there are struggles and challenges that people deal with that make everyday life more difficult."

Student C wrote, "There are a lot of questions that have gray areas, where maybe the person was to step forward or back, but it doesn't really have anything to do with their privilege."

Ms. Turner was glad to see that Student C "questioned" the questions.

In my next lessons, I wanted to have them use technology to research a person who has currently become successful such as Frank Rubio who has been selected for a new team of astronauts and who has family roots in El Salvador (www.wearemitu.com/things-that-matter/army-pilot-and-surgeon-from-miami-becomes-first-salvadorian-american-astronaut-in-nasa-history).

To be clear, because the term "urban classroom" typically alludes to negative connotations, the term "urban classroom" used here refers to a classroom that is located in an area that includes a high concentration of minority students within cities with large percentages of underserved populations in housing, healthcare, and quality food choices. It is important to have a holistic understanding of urban classrooms and what students must navigate on a daily basis—inside and outside of schools. According to Milner, Murray, Farinde, and Delale-O'Connor (2015), this kind of classroom would be categorized as "urban intensive" which refers to "schools that are concentrated in large, metropolitan cities across the U.S., such as New York, Chicago, Los Angeles, and Atlanta. These cities have populations in excess of 1,000,000 people, tend to be densely populated, and, sometimes, are expected to service a large number of students with limited resources" (Milner et al., 2015). As such, urban education, culturally responsive teaching, and social justice are intersectional factors that impact how students receive, produce, and question knowledge. It is in these schools in particular where teachers must know how to make connections between the technology and diverse learners to motivate them to succeed.

A teacher's level of technological competence is important as well in diverse classrooms. There is an assumption that in the twenty-first century, everyone has a general concept of how to use technology. Although part of that is true, using technology effectively as a teaching tool is a completely different skill. Since teachers draw on their own beliefs and knowledge during instruction, how can they connect some of their beliefs to see technology as a tool that can improve cultural responsiveness and social justice curriculum? Additionally, when faced with a lack of technological resources, how does a teacher proceed? Teachers must often make the best of the resources that are available, but many may feel that other schools or districts which are located in more affluent areas offer teachers more. If all teachers are forced to abandon certain schools due to a lack of resources, how will those school districts and students get better? A teacher of diverse students (be it racially, socioeconomically, challenged, gender identity, or other diversities) needs to prepare to go forward in obtaining and connecting technology to his or her students.

What Does Digital Citizenship Entail?

Living in the Information Age, everything that everyone does "counts." Not only do teacher candidates have to behave as good Digital Citizens, but, as future educators, they also have the responsibility to prepare future students to be good Digital Citizens for this global village (see Figure 17.2). Everyone is expected to know how to act when he or she is online and how to thrive in the increasingly global economy. Teachers have the responsibility to prepare future generations to become Digital Citizens who are active, well-informed, and are expert researchers and powerful communicators.

Because of the origin of the Internet and many other factors, English has been the most prevalent language on the Web and is a means of exchanging information between peoples of different nationalities (Moschovitis, 1999). According to *Internet World Stats* (2017a), after English (25.5%), the most popular languages on the Web are Chinese (20.4%), Spanish (7.9%), and Arabic (4.6%). Also, *Internet World Stat* (2017b) tells us that by region, 50.2% of the world's Internet users are based in Asia, 17.1% in Europe, 10.3% in Latin America and the Caribbean together, 9.3% in Africa, 8.6% in North America, 3.8% in the Middle East, and 1% in Australia/Oceania.

Figure 17.2 A concept word cloud that contains key words related to Digital Citizenship.

Ms. Turner's Reflection

I had a couple of recent refugee students join my class in the middle of the semester. While observing how these new students integrated into the urban school, I realized that the students, even though they were new immigrants to this country, had a pretty common understanding of current world issues such as the escalating refugee crises, global warming, Zika virus spreading across certain parts of the world, or even American consumer issues such as a customer being dragged off a flight from Chicago, or entertainment news such as the birth of children, weddings, and divorces of major Western entertainers, and many more. My students said that they did not get the information from TV or radio, which is the way most of the older generation receive news. Instead, news items like these just popped up on their social media pages through their peers and media companies.

I believe that the Internet is the key factor in disseminating the current globalized culture, so there are so many similarities among the younger generation, despite the fact that my students came from very different home cultures.

I think that all educators need to consider the new information context: students now live in a fully globalized world in which more people than ever are connected via the Web. In this new context, positive world values, such as **showing respect to others**, for instance, or **caring for the environment**, and **showing tolerance and understanding to those less fortunate** have become the norms.

I decided to lead by example. If I want my students to show solidarity, I have to be supportive. If I want my students to show empathy, then I have to demonstrate empathy, too.

I created some scenarios in which students would feel outside of their comfort zones and were confronted with situations that reinforced positive world values. Doing so allowed students to become familiar with examining different points of view.

I also integrated external resources, including films, short film, documentaries, news, and numerous other study resources that allowed students to explore situations that might otherwise be impossible in brick-and-mortar classrooms.

In this rapidly changing world, the values that students need to develop are also changing. I see that the education system desperately needs *citizenship* back in the curriculum—a new Digital Citizenship education, to be more specific. My urban classroom is the right place to start teaching about being Digital Citizens.

Fortunately, almost any Web content across the globe can be accessed on the Internet, and, if the person does not speak any of the major languages, the Web content can often be communicated through translation services such as Google Translate. In addition to the spread of the English-speaking culture throughout the world, smaller countries are now able to export cultures and news through English translation. When a Texas school administrator, for example, asks a question through a professional online forum, his questions can be answered by school administrators from Arizona. By the same token, when a Texas teacher publishes a WebQuest online, teachers across state lines (or even international boundaries) can download and use it in their classrooms. When a student in California posts a photograph through social media, such as Instagram, his cousins and friends in Mexico, and even strangers from another corner of the world, receive a notice in just a few seconds and can start to make comments. The current globalized culture shows that from a technological standpoint, there is a two-way flow of information and culture across the globe from region to region. With anyone having access to obtaining a world of information and participating in worldwide conversations, the Internet has made pop culture transmission and the cross-fertilization of pop culture from around the world a commonplace occurrence.

The role of Digital Citizen starts as soon as one clicks on the Internet. Digital Citizenship, sometimes called "digital wellness" or "digital ethics", is important not only in the United States but all around the world. Digital Citizens are those who have a fundamental sense of media literacy and the ability to self-check news and get the facts. According to DigitalCitizenship.org (Ripple, 2017, para 1), "**Digital Citizenship** is the norms of appropriate, responsible technology use." It is a concept that helps teachers and parents understand what students should know and should be competent with for a worldwide society full of technology.

Here are additional resources with videos and other information for Digital Citizenship that have a fundamental sense of media literacy and the ability to self-check news and get the facts:

Super Digital Citizen

www.commonsensemedia.org/videos/super-digital-citizen

What Your Students Really Need to Know About Digital Citizenship

www.edutopia.org/blog/digital-citizenship-need-to-know-vicki-davis

Digital Citizenship: Making the Online World a Better Place Starts with You

www.brainpop.com/technology/digitalcitizenship/

The SWOT (Strengths, Weaknesses, Opportunities, and Threats) Faced by Digital Citizens

Too often, we are seeing students (as well as adults, including teachers) misusing and abusing technology. Because so many events are recorded on social networks for instant communication, trust and norms are becoming of great importance for worldwide technology users. The Internet is all about speed and people, and this can be both a strength and a threat. The following section discusses the SWOT faced by Digital Citizens through digital age phenomena, such as online collaboration, the power-of-people, citizen journalism, crowdsourcing, flash mobs, online criminal activities, fake news, and the Digital Divide (see Figure 17.3 and Figure 17.4).

Figure 17.3 SWOT (strengths, weaknesses, opportunities, threats).

The "Power-of-People" and Online Collaboration

The number of Web users and the "power-of-people" present many opportunities, and online collaboration proves to be a strength of the digital age. When talking about online collaboration, one cannot help but think of Wikipedia as the best example of online collaboration. The creator of the Wikipedia, Jimmy Wales (2016, para. 1), noted that on 13 November 2015, a terrorist attack on Paris seized the world's attention. Almost immediately, someone in London wrote a Wikipedia article outlining a few facts of the incident, and within two hours, the article had been edited hundreds of times, with references to 10 different sources. Wales continued to write, "The most exceptional thing is that it is a collaboration, built by volunteer contributors from every walk of life" (para. 5). Without online collaboration, many large projects will not be possible. In addition to general purpose projects that are completed through online collaboration, there are also academic social networks which connect educators, students, and researchers of common interests.

ResearchGate, Academia.edu, and Mendeley, which are gaining popularity among researchers and graduate students, are essentially a scholarly version of Facebook

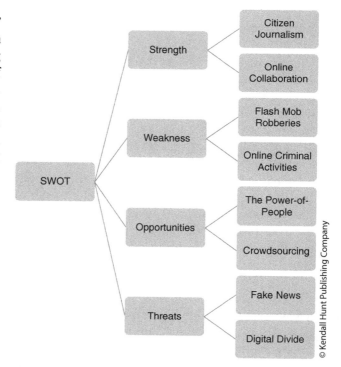

Figure 17.4 Digital Citizenship SWOT.

or LinkedIn but are academic social networks that ask members to create profiles, share papers, track views and downloads, and discuss research. Some scientists collaborate and exchange results data with other scientists whom they have never met in different countries and continents. Here is a list of some academic social networks example to benefit K–12 teachers:

English Teache.r Ning

www.englishcompanion.ning.com/

Book Discussion Forum

www.bookspot.com/discussion/

ePALS Classroom Exchange

www.eduscapes.com/tap/topic14.htm

Citizen Journalism

Today's social networking and other Websites are widely used by individuals, organizations, and businesses to encourage posts to reach to a larger population than ever before. The term "citizen journalism" is based on public citizens playing an active role in the process of collecting, reporting, analyzing, and disseminating news and information (Bowman & Willis, 2003). More well-known examples of citizen journalism reporting from major world events are the 2010 Arab Spring, the 2016 Nice terrorist attacks, and the Florida school shootings in 2018.

Technology, such as livestreaming videos and media-sharing Websites, in addition to the increasing prevalence of cell phones, has made citizen journalism more accessible to people worldwide (see Figure 17.5 and Figure 17.6). Bloggers can be in more places than professional journalists, reporting on breaking events from an eye-witness perspective. U. S. soldiers' blogging during the Iraq War demonstrated what citizen journalism can achieve. Large numbers of drones with cameras were sent out to gather aerial images of rainforests to develop geo-referenced maps in order to support the efforts in protecting the forest and indigenous communities, thus promoting environmental and social justice. Protesters streamed live on Facebook with their smartphones while marching. These examples are what Rosen (2008) proposed as: "When the people formerly known as the audience employ the press tools they have in their possession to inform one another, *that's* citizen journalism" (para. 1) Citizen journalism can reinforce positive world values such as support for democracy, tolerance of foreigners and

Figure 17.5   With many events recorded on social networks for instant communication, trust and norms are becoming of great importance for worldwide technology users.

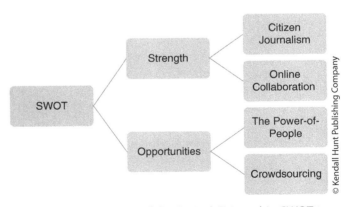

Figure 17.6   A subset of the Digital Citizenship SWOT to show its strength and opportunities.

ethnic minorities, understanding of the needs of those with disabilities, gender equity, and so forth.

Most educators feel a sense of responsibility to talk with students about what is going on in society and the world. Teaching about current social events through a social justice lens has enormous benefits for students to discover and analyze the world around them. Projects such as "young and homeless in the city" described below that are of an interdisciplinary nature can help students make important connections between a variety of school subjects, including technology. These projects empower students to make change through awareness, advocacy, activism, and aid. They are collaborative activities that develop critical thinking, writing, and media literacy skills. The interdisciplinary nature of these types of projects helps students make important connections between history, culture, economics, and technology.

Ms. Turner's Reflection

One of the best ways to develop students' cultural literacy was through social justice projects with activities that develop a mind-set of concern for community. Previously, many students were unaware of the rights they have when exposing injustice. I explained that, thanks to smartphones, social media accounts, and inexpensive video cameras, ordinary people are finding themselves in a new role—that of a citizen journalist.

For one class project, I had students generate a list of concerns through a social justice lens and pick one of these as the focus of their project. The class decided to settle on the topic of "young and homeless in the city" after Pat displayed the photographs taken from his phone that showed a young homeless person in the city.

I brought to the center of the discussion the specific aspect that homelessness raised, and I continued to have the class research homelessness. As students, they explored the stigma and stereotypes of many of the homeless people in the city. One class began to focus on children who were homeless and what their school district did to make sure they still attended school. Another examined a nearby university's collaborative project in a preschool, especially for children of homeless parents.

I took advantage of students' interest in technology by integrating smartphone photos/videos, student blogs, social media platforms, and by following specific hashtags and infographics. Students worked in teams on this project and were encouraged to get involved in larger efforts on issues that were important to them.

I engaged students in reading about and listening to the opinions of others, including those of columnists and subject matter experts—oftentimes through video conferences or social media—so that they could sharpen their points of views and articulate those positions *with evidence*.

When the stories were complete, they were picked up by mainstream media and shared directly with the community. The students felt very proud that they were able to be involved in a meaningful issue.

I really thought this lesson offered opportunities for students to ask questions, dig deeper, and explore the many facts of the homeless issue and how they felt about an important social issue. Students could also build and practice their social and emotional skills. Society is often concerned about young people who "use technology too much" and therefore become anesthetized to human emotion, but this was one way to "make it real". I wanted to impress upon them that without the facts and support, there was no power. However, technology allows them the resources to become "experts" on the subjects.

Crowdsourcing

A benefit of the Internet that can bring opportunities to users is referred to as "**crowdsourcing**." In the Internet Age, the term "crowdsourcing" offers an alternative for problem-solving. Students already know that reading customer ratings online is a way to tap into the collective wisdom of customers. Crowdsourcing also extends to the fields of science and education. For instance, science teachers can use SciStarter (www.scistarter.com), a Website that matches scientific projects with volunteers to solicit and screen science fair coaches and judges for schools, rather than counting only on parent volunteers.

A variety of crowdsourcing is crowdfunding. With tightened budgets, educators are increasingly turning to crowdfunding, a variety of crowdsourcing activities as the twenty-first-century method of fundraising for a wide variety of projects. Many educators have experiences with ClassWish and similar crowdfunding platforms, including Indiegogo, StartSomeGood, and DonorsChoose. Websites such as Crowd101 and the crowdfunding section of ConsumerAffairs compare platforms and offer tips on choosing the right one to meet teachers' needs to bridge the Digital Divide gap.

Ms. Turner's Reflection

The school where I teach has a Bring Your Own Device, or BYOD, policy to allow students to bring their own digital devices to school. However, I felt the need to purchase a classroom set of tablets for students. I had requested for the past two years that the school and PTA purchase digital devices for his class without success.

The teachers with whom I had consulted suggested that I start with a number of crowdfunding sites, since the school was unlikely to provide resources out of the already tight budget. Teachers who had conducted crowdsourcing before suggested that I pay attention to the fees section of crowdsourcing sites, which varied among crowdfunding platforms, as they could be significant in relevance to the donation. Teachers also reminded me to be aware of and follow school guidelines on fundraising.

After much consideration, I was considering "out-of-the-box" Websites which required a monthly subscription fee. I came up with these steps for planning and managing a crowdfunding campaign for the project:

- ❏ Step 1: Assemble a small workgroup
- ❏ Step 2: Identify the project's needs and timeline
- ❏ Step 3: Evaluate alternatives and finalize on a crowdfunding platform which was safe, flexible, and transparent
- ❏ Step 4: Write a project description and create a project video to tell the story to the public. Since donors like knowing exactly how their money will be used, select concrete and interesting outcomes that would engage potential contributors.
- ❏ Step 5: Kick off the project
- ❏ Step 6: Broadcast the project internally through parents and community networks
- ❏ Step 7: Market the project externally through channels such as local media, social media, newsletters, blogs, and email lists
- ❏ Step 8: Monitor the crowdfunding account
- ❏ Step 9: Debrief the campaign to the school, parents, and networks

---

Ms. Turner felt the need to provide classroom technology equipment for students who could not afford them to bridge the Digital Divide. Teachers who conduct crowdfunding are encouraged to take advantage of the teachable moments to offer students leadership opportunities, including project management, money management skills, marketing, communications, and creativity. The crowdfunding workgroup experiences also inspired students' entrepreneurial thinking and showcased the benefit of planning for long-term goals. More importantly, teachers can connect crowdfunding to initiatives that address poverty and inequities in technology access (Provini, 2014).

As citizen journalism is considered a strength of Digital Citizenship, it also ushers in weaknesses and threats (see Figure 17.7). Among the weakness and

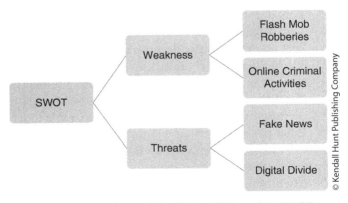

Figure 17.7   A subset of the Digital Citizenship SWOT to show its weakness and threats.

threats are **fake news, Digital Divide, online criminal activities**, and **flash mobs**. As with any trend, online collaboration such as citizen journalism has negatives as well as positives. On the one hand, it introduces more creative solutions. On the other hand, it can lower standards and lead to sloppiness.

Fake News

Critics of the citizen-journalism phenomenon, including professional journalists, claim that citizen journalism is unregulated, too subjective, amateur, and haphazard in quality and coverage. In the past, journalists typically use multiple expert sources to report information that needs to be reported, and they are typically supervised by editors and supported by fact checkers. Today's media authors and bloggers, in general, write from an individual perspective on issues about which they feel strongly–sometimes without double-checking their information. The rush to outdo competitors has always been a part of journalism, but the Internet has made it more intense. A risk for writing posts on social networking Websites is that these posts occasionally lead to unexpected reactions that can lead to controversial behaviors, including backlashes, public mockery, hate speeches, and even death threats.

A well-known 2008 incident involving a CNN iReport (www.ireport.com) sheds light on the concern of **fake news.** iReport described itself as "Unedited. Unfiltered. News." In October 2008, a poster reported that Apple cofounder Steve Jobs had suffered a severe heart attack. Apple's stock was hit by Web rumors. The report was false. The U. S. Securities and Exchange Commission then launched an investigation to determine whether the posting was intended to depress the company's stock price. In another fake news incident, during the 2016 presidential election, a Website made to look like a real news organization posted a headline that claimed a religious leader endorsed a certain presidential candidate. The stories went viral, and some people believed them. In both incidents, fake news stories led to real-life consequences. These types of stories can have a severe effect on individuals and groups who are the target.

Ms. Turner's Reflection

I was bothered by recent fake news and flash mob robberies and wanted to make sure my students had the skills to tell valid social media communications from negative communications. I believed that teachers could help students understand the ramifications of creating and believing messages that were harmful or not true, especially when used as a method to incite different diverse groups against each other. Also, in the wake of many terrorist activities, I wanted them to understand the dangers of radicalization by various groups via technology who were, in turn, convinced to hurt others.

I first trained my students by using the process that professional fact checkers used for the claims with which they dealt. Then I told students to first isolate a claim that has something that can be objectively verified by double-checking the best primary sources on the specific topic. Students were then find whether the sources match or reject the claim being made.

Seeing students referencing questionable sources, misleading, satirical, and fake sites, I directed them to the online quick guide titled "False, Misleading, Clickbait-y, and/or Satirical News Sources" (www.docs.google .com/document/d/10eA5-mCZLSS4MQY5QGb5ewC3VAL6pLkT53V_81ZyitM/edit) as their pocket guide.

I also shared the following guidelines that good Digital Citizens use when reading news articles online:
Pay attention to the domain and URL

Verify when the site looks professional and has semi-recognizable logos. Sites with such endings like .com. co may not be legitimate news sources despite their similar appearances to the established news organizations
Read the "About Us" section

Legitimate sites will have a considerable amount of information about the news outlet,
Look at the quotes in a story and look at who said them

Legitimate publications have multiple sources in each story who are professionals and have expertise in the fields they talk about.
Check the comments

If a number of reader comments accuse the article for being fake or misleading, it probably is.

The above steps are just a starting point in determining what type of news an article is. These are ways for everyone to do a bit of fact checking themselves. If more Digital Citizens follow these steps, they will be helping others by not increasing the circulation of these stories. In the end, it depends on everyone being a responsible consumer of news. A society which makes decisions on facts will be a more just society overall.

The following case story describes a technique called "reverse image searches" used by many professional fact checkers.

Ms. Turner's Reflection

After being given guidelines for reading news articles, a number of students were still having a difficult time judging the credibility of online news and distinguishing real news from fake news, slander, stock manipulation, advertisements, and what not. More specifically, I saw the problem of false reports concealed as news shared widely on social media during the 2016 election on both sides of the aisle. I felt the need to teach students to distinguish real news from fake because I thought that fake news posed a direct threat to our democracy in that we can build beliefs and actions on falsehoods.

I integrated a technique called "reverse image searches" that many professional fact checkers conduct by asking each student to investigate a news article that looked suspicious to them. They were to conduct detective work and reverse search for the images on those suspicious articles by right-clicking on the images and searching them through Google. For instance, I found that through the Firebox browser, by right-clicking an image, followed by "View Image Info", then "Media", a list of webpages where this image was used on the Internet can be seen.

If the images had appeared on many stories about many different topics, there was a good chance that they were not images of what the news articles said they were on the news stories. If people who wrote these fake news stories did not even leave their homes or interview someone for the stories, it was unlikely that they took their own photographs.

To verify the validity of news, I also reminded students to resort to unbiased organizations such as FactCheck.org which is sponsored by the Annenberg Public Policy Center and the Fact Checking homepage via American Press Institute. Students could refer to the International Fact Checking Network for checking international fake news.

I believe that students should learn this reasoning technique to assess the news they read online because their job as Digital Citizens requires more than just being informed. They had also learned the secrets to digging up the truth, keeping it organized, and making crucial connections. I also reminded them to be vigilant about verifying information before posting it on social media to avoid being a "troll" who, in Internet slang, sows discord on the Internet.

In addition, I persuaded teachers in other schools to suggest new curriculum standards for all academic subjects that include strategies for identifying false stories.

Flash Mob Robberies and Other Online Criminal Activities

As notified by electronic communication, **flash mobs** message people to gather in a crowd very rapidly and at a designated locale for a particular purpose (demonstration, songs/dances, and so forth). In viewing flash mob activities on one's search engine, one can view positive usage of flash mob for thanks and recognition (Massive Mob Overwhelms School's Favorite Police Officer (www.youtube.com/watch?v=T1uAp69IJnk) or entertainment/dance (www.youtube.com/watch?v=ZMG2vNVq0ww)–or for more sinister purposes such as robbery (www.youtube.com/watch?v=WUdWgeu59RE), where the messages go out regarding where and when to meet to overwhelm a target. These events, when used for positive purposes, however, can encourage strong emotions among all participants and watchers (www.youtube.com/watch?v=fj6r3-sQr58). These positive uses of electronic communication can be taught as a way to look at people all over the world gathering for the purpose of a pleasurable experience for others (see Figure 17.8).

Figure 17.8 Youth dance flash mob in a shopping center.

Figure 17.9 "Flash mob robberies" are robberies and assaults perpetrated suddenly by groups of teenage youth for the purpose of criminal acts.

On the other hand, the term "flash mob robberies" has been used to describe a number of robberies and assaults perpetrated suddenly by groups of teenage youth (see Figure 17.9). In the cases of flash mob robberies for the purpose of criminal acts, messages on cells and computers can be traced, and most group members can be easily identified for prosecution.

Refer to Chapter 10 for a discussion on other online criminal activities, including cyber hacking, ransomware, online cheating, and other types of frauds that take place in the cyberspace.

Digital Divide

As discussed, there are currently very few jobs that do not require some computer literacy. The power of technology, as Molnar pointed out in his article "The Next Great Crisis in American Education: Computer Literacy," is a two-edged sword (Molnar, 1978). While information literacy presents opportunities for empowering teachers and students, it also further divides people. A **Digital Divide**, a threat to Digital Citizenship, is an inequality with regard to access to, use of, or impact of information and communication technologies (*Falling through the Net: Defining the Digital Divide*, 1999). The divide within countries may refer to inequalities between individuals, households, businesses, or geographic areas, usually at different socioeconomic levels or other demographic categories (Rawson, 2016). When students are not technologically literate, their equal opportunities for higher education and better jobs are compromised (see Figure 17.10 and Figure 17.11).

In 2011, Ms. Estella Mims Pyfrom, a former teacher, saw that the sluggish economy forced many families to prioritize their money and use it for more pressing needs, such as food and rent. She feared that many of these students would get left behind without a computer at home or reliable transportation to get to a computer. To deal with the problem, Ms. Pyfrom bought a bus, filled it with computers, and brought technology and tutorial helps to the neighborhoods.

"The Digital Divide is absolutely real. And it didn't just become a reality. It's been there for years, and it's getting bigger and more important" (Berger, 2013, para. 9).

"If people don't have some knowledge of technology, they're going to be limited," said Ms. Pyfrom (Berger, 2013, para. 7). "It's absolutely essential that they get involved technologically."

For more information about Ms. Pyfrom's brilliant bus idea, refer to www.estellasbrilliantbus.org/our-ceo.

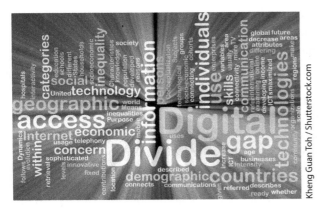

Figure 17.10 The concept word cloud illustrating the concept of Digital Divide.

Figure 17.11 Members of the "have-not" group do not have the information technology capacity needed for civic and cultural participation, employment, lifelong learning, and access to essential services.

Virtual societies are here to stay; more and more, they are becoming a part of our daily lives. Teachers can no longer ignore the fact that individuals socialize and conduct a great portion of their lives in the virtual communities of the Internet for entertainment, for making connections, in productivity, and many other social issues. Using technology to teach about multiculturalism touches on the responsibility for Digital Equity. **Digital Equity**, a concept related to social justice, seeks to ensure that *all* citizens have the information technology capacity needed for civic and cultural participation, employment, lifelong learning, and access to essential services (see Figure 17.12). Accessibility of online information is vital. For example, people who are deaf need captions on videos. People who are blind need screen reader accessibility. A number of factors greatly impact technology use in teacher education programs worldwide along socioeconomic, ethnic, cultural, disability, and gender

Figure 17.12 Teachers work toward Digital Equity to make sure their students do not fall into "have not" group in terms of technology skills and access.

gaps. The question was asked earlier about how teachers can work toward Digital Equity for their students to make sure they fall in the "have" rather than the "have not" group in terms of technology skills and access.

Technology-Based Solutions for Culturally Responsive Teachers

Let us return to the notion of culturally responsive teaching. Here are five technology-based solutions for culturally responsive teachers.

1. *Use technology in ways that are both engaging and intellectually stimulating.*
   Using technology in the classroom is not only about having laptop carts, electronic whiteboards, and playing videos for student engagement; rather, it is a pedagogical tool that must be implemented in a way that is engaging and critical on a daily basis. Having students use technology should not be considered a consolation prize but more so an integral learning skill that they will need for career or college readiness, everyday life, and social connections. One pedagogical example of how technology can be used to develop a culturally responsive classroom is by having students create WordPress blogs in English class as a way to write about the intersections among their communities and the literature read in the

classroom. As a result, students use technology to make connections to themselves and to literature, which is at the heart of culturally responsive teaching and learning practices.

2. *Refrain from using technology as props in Title I schools, with the belief that "certain students" are not capable of using technology wisely.*

There is a disparaging belief by some that students cannot handle using technology in a "smart" way, particularly those in urban schools. What typically happens is that technology is used as a prop as opposed to a structured curricular resource. For example, many teachers will use PowerPoint presentations for their lessons that are basically notes without any attractive visuals such as photos, embedded videos, and student online activities such as interactive Websites that encourage students to use their smartphones. Some of these teacher behaviors are tied to traditional conceptions of classrooms as top-down hierarchies that are teacher-centered and less student-focused. This not only leads to student disengagement, but it is also a rather oppressive classroom space that operates through a "banking model" (Freire, 1970). The banking model is when teachers "fill" students top down with their understanding of knowledge without offering students the space to be critical or social with their peers in the classroom. Therefore, using technology as a prop can be tied to a "banking model" of education because it positions students as passive objects as opposed to active learners.

For more information about the banking model, review the following resource:

Freire's Banking Concept of Education

www.youtube.com/watch?v=QoxHpNYFg5E

3. *Teacher's technological competency matters.*

Although it is clear that some school districts need access to more technological resources, there is insight into how to operate in a technologically inclined way when resources are scarce. Teachers in schools where technology is not always easily accessible need professional development about how to use the resources they do have to foster the development of the twenty-first-century classroom. Additionally, teachers need professional development to learn how to acquire resources through philanthropic educational sites such as www.donorschoose.org and educational grants from the Department of Education as a means of building twenty-first-century classrooms. Many teachers acquire outside grants in urban or technologically disadvantaged schools as a means of enhancing the teaching and learning experience for themselves and their students. For example, in school districts that may not be able to support upper-level courses, such as trigonometry or certain foreign languages, students have distance options to make their education more equal—*if* the technology is available to them. Numerous districts have grant writers who will try to gain funds for schools, but teachers may have to initiate the call for these types of grants. Small grants can also be written by teachers to obtain local funds from business and organizations such as the Junior League. Online professional development can often also be obtained through publishing companies, universities, and so forth. Teachers may also ask for funds to attend conferences where technology in the classroom is a focus or visit schools which are designed around technology such as High Tech High in San Diego (www.hightechhigh.org); (also see a large number of student projects on their Website, many of which investigate local and global issues).

4. *Allow students to have free computer time that is structured in nature.*

Part of enhancing students' computer literacy is allowing them to explore using the computer in a way that does not always mean working on a specific assignment for class. For example, a teacher can have students pose questions about a particular unit that is being taught in the classroom and ask them to come up with some resources on the Internet that help answer their essential questions. Such an activity fosters critical thinking and student engagement in a way that helps create trust and intellectual development in the classroom.

5. *Lay the groundwork for policy and best practice now on how to minimize potential harm as the first generation of social media users become adults.*

Social media that are supposed to help young people connect with each other may actually be fueling many negative issues. Fake news, flash mob robberies, sexting, and other dangers to Digital Equity can be threats to modern society and democracy. Stopping the spread of the negatives, such as psychological pressures to act in negative ways, bullying and so forth, is not just the responsibility of the social media platforms used to spread it. Digital Citizens who consume news, for example, also need to find ways to determine truth from fiction. Digital teachers who are culturally responsive should educate learners about how to cope with all traits of social media—good and bad—to prepare them for an increasingly digitized multicultural world.

Summary

Although the term "culturally responsive teaching" has been used as a buzzword in education for the past twenty years, how does one know that he or she is a culturally responsive teacher? Furthermore, how does a culturally responsive classroom directly link to the social justice practice of equal opportunity for *all* learners, particularly in this rapidly changing electronic world? First and foremost, a teacher must be able to *see* students beyond their test scores and into their identities, whether that be related to ethnicity, gender, ability, sexual orientation, and so forth. Part of being a culturally responsive educator is being able to identify the whole child: emotions, respective communities, socioeconomic factors, and their personal and academic interests. Without this cultural competence of students, a teacher's use of technology will not matter as much because it will be employed as a prop as opposed to an extension of a student's cultural and academic values. A teacher must commit to finding strategic ways of ensuring access to technology. Truthfully speaking, teaching in many different situations throughout the United States sometimes means that one does not have all the resources needed; however, that does not mean teachers should not give students every opportunity that can be devised in their classrooms. It does mean that teachers learn how to find the necessary resources for students either through grants or working with the school administration to acquire the necessary technological resources.

A culturally responsive educator is one who understands that to teach with empathy and caring means that he or she *sees* students who are individuals but who may come with many cultural traits, and a teacher can use this knowledge to make a difference in how students learn. Because many school districts are culturally and racially similar, there is often a misconception that students within them are "the same." As frequently noted, diversity is continuing to grow in schools across the country, and teachers do not always recognize that each student, though part of various cultures, has his or her own respective identity that must be honored in the classroom through curriculum that is both technologically and culturally inclined.

References

Berger, D. (2013, November, 1). 'Brilliant Bus' shrinking digital divide. Retrieved from www.edition.cnn.com/2013/04/04/us/cnnheroes-pyfrom-brilliant-bus

Bowman, S., & Willis, C. (2003). We media. Retrieved from www.hypergene.net/wemedia/weblog.php?id=P36

Chisholm, I. M. (1998). Six elements for technology integration in multicultural classrooms. *Journal of Information Technology for Teacher Education, 7*(2), 247–268.

Davis, B. (2006). *How to teach students who don't look like you.* Thousand Oaks, CA: Corwin Press.

Davis, W. (2016). Fake or real? How to self-check: The news and get the facts. Retrieved from www.npr.org/sections/alltechconsidered/2016/12/05/503581220/fake-or-real-how-to-self-check-the-news-and-get-the-facts

Freire, P. (1970). *Pedagogy of the oppressed.* New York, NY: Bloomsbury.

Internet World Stats. (2017a). World Internet users by language. Retrieved from www.internetworldstats.com/stats7.htm

Internet World Stats. (2017b). World Internet usage and population statistics. Retrieved from www.internetworldstats.com/stats.htm

Ladson-Billings, G. (1994). *The dreamkeepers: Successful teaching for African-American students.* San Francisco, CA: Jossey-Bass, pp. 17–18.

Lippman, L., Burns, S., & McArthur, E. (1996). *Urban schools: The challenge of location and poverty: Executive summary.* Washington, DC: U.S. Dept. of Education, Office of Educational Research and Improvement, National Center for Education Statistics.

Milner, H. R., Murray, I. E., Farinde, A. A., & Delale-O'Connor, L. (2015). Outside of school matters: What we need to know in urban environments. *Equity and Excellence in Education, 48*(4), 529–548.

Molnar, A. (1978). The next great crisis in American education: Computer literacy. *AEDS Journal, 12*(1), 11–12.

Moschovitis, C. P. (1999). *History of the Internet: A chronology, 1843 to the present.* Santa Barbara, CA: ABC-CLIO.

National Telecommunications and Information Administration. (1999). *Falling through the net: Defining the digital divide.* Washington, D.C.: U.S. Dept. of Commerce, National Telecommunications and Information Administration.

Provini, C. (2014). Raise money with crowdfunding: Top 9 tips for schools. Retrieved from www.educationworld .com/a_admin/crowdfunding-fundraising-schools-tips-best-practices.shtml

Rawson, G. (2016). Bridging the Digital Divide bit by bit. *Capitol Ideas, 59*(3), 38.

Ribble, M. (2017). DigitalCitizenship. Retrieved from www.digitalcitizenship.net

Rosen, J., (2008). A most useful definition of citizen journalism. *PressThink.* Retrieved from www.archive.pressthink .org/2008/07/14/a_most_useful_d.html

Sink, C. (2015). Social emotional learning. Retrieved from www.wa-schoolcounselor.org/Files/Bermanwsca2016%20 elementarycounselors.pdf

Stokes, D., & Wilson, N. (2006). *Small business management and entrepreneurship.* London: Thomson Learning, p. 107

Vass Gal, A. (2015). *Generational poverty: An economic look at the culture of the poor.* Wilmington, Delaware: Vernon Press.

Wales, J. (2016, January 15). Wikipedia's strength is in collaboration – as we've proved over 15 years. *The Guardian.* Retrieved from: www.theguardian.com/commentisfree/2016/jan/15/wikipedia-israel-palestine-15-years-encyclopedia

Zhao, Y., Pugh, K., Sheldon, S., & Byers, J. L. (2002). Conditions for classroom technology innovations. *Teachers College Record, 104*(3), 482–515.

9 781524 949136